ISBN 978-1-330-98821-3
PIBN 10130280

This book is a reproduction of an important historical work. Forgotten Books uses
state-of-the-art technology to digitally reconstruct the work, preserving the original format
whilst repairing imperfections present in the aged copy. In rare cases, an imperfection in
the original, such as a blemish or missing page, may be replicated in our edition. We do,
however, repair the vast majority of imperfections successfully; any imperfections that
remain are intentionally left to preserve the state of such historical works.

1 MONTH OF
FREE
READING

at

www.ForgottenBooks.com

By purchasing this book you are eligible for one month membership to ForgottenBooks.com, giving you unlimited access to our entire collection of over 1,000,000 titles via our web site and mobile apps.

To claim your free month visit:

www.forgottenbooks.com/free130280

English
Français
Deutsche
Italiano
Español
Português

www.forgottenbooks.com

Mythology Photography **Fiction**
Fishing Christianity **Art** Cooking
Essays Buddhism Freemasonry
Medicine **Biology** Music **Ancient
Egypt** Evolution Carpentry Physics
Dance Geology **Mathematics** Fitness
Shakespeare **Folklore** Yoga Marketing
Confidence Immortality Biographies
Poetry **Psychology** Witchcraft
Electronics Chemistry History **Law**
Accounting **Philosophy** Anthropology
Alchemy Drama Quantum Mechanics
Atheism Sexual Health **Ancient History**
Entrepreneurship Languages Sport
Paleontology Needlework Islam
Metaphysics Investment Archaeology
Parenting Statistics Criminology
Motivational

DEATH

BY

WRONGFUL ACT

A TREATISE ON THE LAW PECULIAR
TO ACTIONS FOR INJURIES
RESULTING IN DEATH

INCLUDING

THE TEXT OF THE STATUTES AND AN ANALYTICAL
TABLE OF THEIR PROVISIONS

SECOND EDITION

BY

FRANCIS B. TIFFANY

KANSAS CITY, MO.
VERNON LAW BOOK COMPANY
1913

PREFACE TO SECOND EDITION

IN THE nineteen years that have elapsed since the publication of the first edition of this book many changes in the statutes have been made and many decisions upon questions that were then unsettled have been rendered. For this reason it has been necessary to revise the book and to rewrite parts of it. The author has endeavored to cite all the subsequent American cases, and the more important English cases, which relate to the matters dealt with.

The statutes of the various states which create causes of action for injuries resulting in death are characterized by a lack of uniformity, in substance as well as in form, which is all the more striking when it is remembered that a fairly good model of legislation was furnished by Lord Campbell's act. The statutes of a majority of the states do, indeed, while differing among themselves on many points, follow the broad lines of the English act, conferring a right of action in favor of the decedent's family or of other designated beneficiaries for the recovery of the damages which have resulted to them from the death. In many states, however, the action given is for the recovery of the damages which result, not to certain beneficiaries, but to the estate of the person killed; while in other states the statute takes the form of a survival act; and many states have a survival act, as well as a death act, the existence of both presenting questions which are differently answered in different states. In some states, again, punitive damages may be recovered; and in one the damages are assessed with reference to the degree of culpability of the defendant. The list of statutory peculiarities, which have required judicial interpretation and multiplied litigation, might be extended indefinitely. Moreover, in addition to other differences, the statutes differ in respect to the limit of recovery, some fixing one limit, some another, and some no limit.   To the wife and children of a man killed in a railway accident on a journey from San Francisco to New York it would be a matter of grave concern, affecting vitally the extent of their redress, in which one of the dozen or more states on the line of travel the accident occurred.

The conflicting and often crude legislation of the forty-eight states upon this important subject presents a forcible argument in favor of a uniform act.   The diversity cannot be justified, or explained, by the existence of diverse local needs and conditions; it arose from the fact that by reason of the failure of the courts to entertain jurisdiction over death actions the matter came to be dealt with by forty-eight independent legislative bodies.   Some measure of uniformity has been brought about by the recent federal employers' liability act relating to common carriers engaged in interstate commerce, but the field of federal legislation is comparatively small.   The drafting of a uniform death act might well be undertaken by the Commissioners on Uniform State Laws.

St. Paul, Minnesota, November 1, 1912.   F. B. T.

PREFACE TO FIRST EDITION

THE purpose of this book is to treat of those questions of law which are peculiar to the various statutory civil actions maintainable when the death of a person has been caused by the wrongful act or negligence of another. The statutes by which a right of action in such case has been created are to a great extent modeled upon the English statute known as "Lord Campbell's Act," which was enacted in 1846. Lord Campbell's act provides that, "whensoever the death of a person shall be caused by the wrongful act, neglect, or default of another, and the act, neglect, or default is such as would, if death had not ensued, have entitled the party injured to maintain an action and recover damages in respect thereof, then, and in every such case, the person who would have been liable if death had not ensued shall be liable to an action for damages notwithstanding the death of the person injured." The American acts, with some exceptions, have followed the language of the parent act in providing that the action may be maintained whenever death is caused by "wrongful act, neglect, or default." For the sake of brevity, the book has been entitled "Death by Wrongful Act," though "Death by Wrongful Act or Negligence" would more accurately describe it. This subject, although it has been briefly considered in several text-books, has never been treated with any degree of fullness.

These acts in effect provide that the statutory action may be maintained for the benefit of the persons whom they designate, whenever the wrongful act, neglect, or default is such that if it had resulted merely in bodily injury, without causing death, the person injured might have maintained an action. It is obvious, therefore, that in the statutory action the same

questions in respect to the wrongfulness of the act or the
negligence of the defendant must arise that would arise in
an action for personal injury founded upon the same wrongful act, neglect, or default.   These questions are sufficiently
treated in books upon torts, upon personal injuries, and especially upon negligence.   It is not the purpose of this book
to consider the rules and principles of law upon which the
answers to questions of this character depend.   Its purpose
is simply to treat of those questions which are peculiar to the
various statutory actions.   In other words, it is, as a rule, assumed that the death was caused under such circumstances
that, if death had not ensued, an action might have been maintained by the person injured.

Although most of the acts have been to a great extent modeled upon Lord Campbell's act, and consequently can be considered together, some of the acts are peculiar in whole and
many in part; and all these, so far as they are peculiar, require separate treatment.   Again, some states, while they
have passed acts similar to Lord Campbell's act, have enacted
additional provisions granting a right of action when death
is caused under particular circumstances; for example, when
it is caused by certain kinds of negligence on the part of common carriers, or when the person killed is a minor and leaves
a surviving parent.   Peculiar provisions of this sort also require separate treatment.   It is the plan of the book to consider the peculiarities of the various statutes separately before
proceeding to a discussion of the principles common to those
of the general type of Lord Campbell's act.   The writer has
endeavored to cite all the cases that have arisen in the United
States and in England under these acts, so far as the decisions relate to matters peculiar to the statutory actions, whether the cases turn upon the special features of particular acts
or are of more general applicability.   The Canadian cases
have also been freely cited.   References have been given, in
all cases concurrently reported, to the National Reporter System, as well as to the official reports.   Whenever it seemed

to the writer that a statement of the facts of the case would be of value, such a statement has been given in the text or in the notes.

In determining the effect of a decision, it is of course necessary to have in mind the provisions of the statute under which the action was brought. For this reason the various enactments * * * have been printed in full in the appendix. An analytical table of these statutes has also been prepared. It is believed that the analytical table will be found of convenience (1) as a ready means of ascertaining the provisions of a particular statute upon a given point, and (2) as a means of ascertaining what statutes have provisions of a similar nature to the statute which may be under consideration. It is believed that the table will be found of especial value in the newer states and territories whose statutes have not yet been construed by the courts. For example, an examination of the table would inform a person wishing to arrive at a proper construction of the many peculiar provisions of the act of New Mexico, which has received little or no construction, or of the act of Colorado, which has received comparatively little, that these acts are nearly identical with that of Missouri, which has been fully construed by the courts of that state, and which is discussed in the text and notes. The table may also be useful to persons interested in legislation upon this subject.   F. B. T.

St. Paul, March 1, 1893.

TABLE OF CONTENTS

CHAPTER I

THE COMMON LAW

Section
1. No action for death at common law.
2. Higgins v. Butcher.
3. Baker v. Bolton.
4. Lord Campbell's act.
5. Osborn v. Gillett.
6. Early American cases.
7. Carey v. Berkshire R. Co.
8. Eden v. Lexington & F. R. Co.
9. James v. Christy.
10. Shields v. Yonge.
11. Later American cases.
12. Reason for the rule.
13. Merger.
14. Forfeiture.
15. Actio personalis moritur cum persona.
16. Public policy.
17. Limitation of the rule.
18. Right of action where death is caused by breach of contract.

CHAPTER II

THE STATUTES

CHAPTER III

THE STATUTES (WHEN ACTION LIES)

CHAPTER IV

THE WRONGFUL ACT, NEGLECT, OR DEFAULT

CHAPTER V

THE BENEFICIARIES

CHAPTER VI

PARTIES

CHAPTER VII

STATUTES OF LIMITATION.

CHAPTER VIII

MATTERS OF DEFENSE

CHAPTER IX

DAMAGES—THE STATUTES

CHAPTER X

DAMAGES

CHAPTER XI

PLEADING AND PRACTICE

CHAPTER XII

EVIDENCE

CHAPTER XIII

JURISDICTION OF STATE COURTS—CONFLICT OF LAWS

CHAPTER XIV

JURISDICTION OF FEDERAL COURTS AND IN ADMIRALTY

ANALYTICAL TABLE

SHOWING IN COMPARATIVE FORM THE LEADING PROVI-
SIONS OF THE STATUTES NOW IN FORCE GOVERN-
ING ACTIONS FOR PERSONAL INJURIES
RESULTING IN DEATH

NOTE. Many of the statutes provide that the action may be maintained, although the death shall have been caused under such circumstances as
amount in law to felony. (See § 79.) These provisions have not been included in this table. The language of the provisions included has been
followed so far as is consistent with brevity, but for the exact phraseology
the reader is referred to the Appendix.

TIFF.DEATH W.A.(2D ED.)   (xix)

State and Statute	When Action Lies	Who may Sue	For Whose Benefit
ENGLAND 9 and 10 Vict. c. 93. 27 and 28 Vict. c. 95; 8 Edw. 7, c. 7.	Whenever death is caused by wrongful act, neglect, or default, such as would, if death had not ensued, have entitled party injured to maintain action. Not more than one action lies for same subject-matter.	Executor or administrator. If no executor or administrator, or if no action is brought in his name within six calendar months, action may be brought by all or any of persons for whose benefit action lies.	Wife, husband, parent, (which includes grandparent and stepparent,) and child, (which includes grandchild and stepchild.)
ALABAMA Code 1907, §§ 2484, 2485.	When death of minor child is caused by wrongful act or omission or negligence.	Father, or, in case of his death, or desertion of his family, or of his imprisonment for a term of two years, under conviction for crime, or of his confinement in insane asylum, or if he has been declared of unsound mind, mother, or, if they decline to bring the action or fail to do so within 6 months from the death of the minor, personal representative. But suit by any one of them is a bar to another action under section 2485 or section 2486.	
Code, § 2486 (as amend. Gen. Laws 1911, No. 455).	When death is caused by wrongful act, omission, or negligence, if the testator or intestate could have maintain an action if it had not caused death.	Personal representative.	
Code, §§ 3910, 3912 (as amend. Gen. Laws 1911, Nos. 456, 454).	Master or employer is liable for death of servant or employé in certain cases enumerated in section 3910 (Employers' Liability Act.)	do.	

How Distributed	Measure of Damages	When to be Commenced	Remarks
After deducting costs not recovered from defendant, among parties for whose benefit action is brought, in such shares as jury by verdict shall find.	Jury may give such damages as they may think proportioned to injury resulting from death to parties, respectively, for whose benefit action is brought. There shall not be taken into account any sum paid or payable on death under contract of assurance or insurance.	Within 12 calendar months after death.	Plaintiff must, together with declaration, deliver to defendant full particulars of persons for whom action is brought, and of nature of claim in respect to damages sought to be recovered. Defendant may pay money into court, and, if an issue is taken as to its sufficiency, and jury shall think it sufficient, defendant shall be entitled to verdict on that issue.
	Such damages as jury may assess.		
Damages are not subject to payment of debts or liabilities of testator or intestate, but must be distributed according to statute of distributions.	do.	Within two years after death.	Action maintainable in a court of competent jurisdiction within State of Alabama and not elsewhere. Action shall not abate by death of defendant.

State and Statute	When Action Lies	Who may Sue	For Whose Benefit
ALASKA Code Civ. Proc. § 353.	When death of a person is caused by wrongful act or omission, if decedent might have maintained action, had he lived.	Personal representatives.	Exclusive benefit of decedent's husband or wife and children when he or she leaves husband, wife or children surviving.
ARIZONA Rev. St. 1901, §§ 2764, 2765, and section 2766 (as amend. Laws 1909, c. 16).	Whenever death is caused by wrongful act or default, such as would, if death had not ensued, have entitled party injured to maintain action.	Personal representative. Father, or in case of his death or desertion of his family, mother, for a child. Guardian, for ward.	
ARKANSAS Kirby's Dig. 1904, §§ 6289, 6290.	Whenever death is caused by wrongful act, neglect, or default, such as would, if death had not ensued, have entitled party injured to maintain an action.	Personal representatives, and, if none, heirs at law.	Exclusive benefit of widow and next of kin.
§ 6285.	For wrongs done to person of another action may be brought after his death, against wrongdoer.	Executor or administrator.	
§ 6287.	When adult be killed by railroad trains running in state.	Husband, for damages to wife.	
§ 6288.	When a wife be killed in state by wrongful act, neglect or default.	Husband.	Husband.
CALIFORNIA Code Civil Proc. §§ 335, 340, 376, 377.	When death is caused by wrongful act or neglect.	Heirs or personal representatives. Father, or, in case of his death or desertion of his family, mother, for a minor child. Guardian for ward.	

How Distributed	Measure of Damages	When to be Commenced	Remarks
As if unbequeathed assets left in hands of plaintiff, after payment of debts and expenses of administration; and when no husband, wife or children. amount recovered shall be administered as other personal property; but plaintiff may deduct expenses of action, etc.	Damages shall not exceed $10,000.	Within two years after death.	
To parties and in proportions provided by law in relation to personal estate left by persons dying intestate. Amount recovered not subject to debts and liabilities of deceased.	Jury shall give such damages as they shall deem fair and just.	Within one year after death.	If defendant pending suit, his ex utor or administra may be made pa and suit be prosec ed to judgment; judgment in favor plaintiff shall be p in due course of ministration.
In proportion provided by law in relation to distribution of personal property of intestates.	Jury may give such damages as they shall deem fair and just compensation, with reference to pecuniary injuries resulting from such death to wife and next of kin.	Within two years after death.	
			After death wrongdoer, action n be brought against executor or admir trator.
	Damages for services and companionship, in amount jury may consider he is entitled to.	Within two years from time cause of action occurs.	
	Such damages may be given as, under all circumstances of case, may be just.	Within one year.	

tate and Statute	When Action Lies	Who may Sue	For Whose Benefit
COLORADO r. St. 1908, §§ 2056-)59.	Whenever any person shall die from any injury occasioned by negligence, unskillfulness, or criminal intent of any officer, agent, servant, or employé, while running, conducting, or managing any locomotive, car, or train of cars, or of any driver of any coach or other public conveyance, and when any passenger shall die from any injury occasioned by any defect or insufficiency in any railroad or part thereof, or in any locomotive or car, stage-coach, or other public conveyance, employer or owner shall be liable. Defendant may show in defense that defect or insufficiency was not negligent. Whenever death is caused by wrongful act, neglect, or default, such as would, if death had not ensued, have entitled party injured to maintain action.	Husband or wife; and, if no husband or wife, or if he or she fails to sue within one year after death, heirs; and, if deceased was a minor or unmarried, father or mother, who may join, or survivor. do.	If action be brought by husband or wife, judgment shall be owned by such persons as are heirs at law of deceased, and be divided as real estate according to statute of descents and distributions.
e Civil Proc. § 9.	Father, or, in case of his death or desertion of his family, mother, may maintain action for death of child, and guardian for death of ward.		
. Laws 1911, c. 3.	Employer is liable for death of agent, servant or employé in cases mentioned in section 1.	(1) Husband or wife; or, if no husband or (2) wife, or if he or she fails to sue within one year after death, children or their descendants; or (3) if deceased was a minor or unmarried, without issue, father or mother or both jointly; or (4) if no such person entitled to sue, such other next of kin as may be dependent on deceased for support.	Any person entitled to sue and others so entitled.

How Distributed	Measure of Damages	When to be Commenced	Remarks
	Defendant shall forfeit not exceeding $5,000, and not less than $3,000.	Within two years from commission of negligence.	
	Jury may give such damages as they may deem fair and just, not exceeding $5,000, with reference to necessary injury resulting from such death, to surviving parties who may be entitled to sue, having regard to mitigating or aggravating circumstances.	do.	
	Jury may give such damages as they deem fair and just not exceeding $5,000, with reference to necessary injury resulting from such death, to party or parties who may be entitled to sue.	Within two years from death.	Verdict and judgment shall specify amount of damages awarded to each. If actions separately brought, they shall be consolidated.

State and Statute	When Action Lies	Who may Sue	For Whose Benefit
CONNECTICUT Pub. Acts 1903, c. 193. Rev. Gen. St, 1902, §§ 399, 1119, 1130, 1136.	No cause or right of action shall be lost or destroyed by death of any person, but shall survive in favor of or against executor or administrator of deceased.	Executor or administrator.	
DELAWARE Laws 1866, vol. 13, c. 31, §§ 1, 2 (as amend. Laws 1901-03, c. 210).	Whenever death shall be occasioned by unlawful violence or negligence, and no suit is brought by party injured.	Widow or widower, or, if no widow or widower, personal representatives.	
DIST. OF COLUMBIA Act Feb. 17, 1885, c. 126, 23 St. 307.	Whenever death is caused by wrongful act, neglect, or default, such as would, if death had not ensued, have entitled the person injured, or, if person injured be a married woman, have entitled her husband, either separately or joining with wife, to maintain an action, provided person injured has not recovered damages.	Personal representative.	Family.
FLORIDA Gen. St. 1906, §§ 3145-3147, 1725.	Whenever death is caused by wrongful act, negligence, carelessness, or default such as would, if death had not ensued, have entitled party injured to maintain action. Whenever death of minor child is caused by wrongful act, negligence, carelessness or default of private association of persons, or of officer, agent or employé, or of corporation, or of officer, agent, or employé of corporation acting in capacity as such.	Widow or husband; if there is neither surviving deceased, minor children; if neither husband, widow, nor minor child, any persons dependent on deceased for support; if neither of the above, executor or administrator. Action in behalf of a person under 21 years of age shall be brought in name of next friend. Father, or, if not living, mother, as legal representative.	

How Distributed	Measure of Damages	When to be Commenced	Remarks
After deducting costs and expenses of suit, half to husband or widow, and half to lineal descendants, per stirpes; but if no descendants, whole to husband or widow, and if no husband or widow, to heirs, according to law regulating distribution of intestate personal estate.	In all actions surviving or to be brought by executor or administrator for injuries resulting in death, whether instantaneous or otherwise, executor or administrator may recover from party legally in fault for such injuries just damages, not exceeding $10,000.	Within one year from neglect. Action against corporation within one year from decease.	Notice of inj must be given in c tain cases. No civil action sh abate by death of party, but may be c tinued by or agai executor or admin trator.
	Damages for the death and loss thus occasioned.		No action to reco damages for inju to the person by ne gence or default sh abate by reason death of plaintiff, personal represen tives of deceased n be substituted.
According to provisions of statute of distributions, free from debts and liabilities of deceased.	Damages for the death, which shall be assessed with reference to injury resulting from act, neglect, or default causing death, to widow and next of kin, not exceeding $10,000.	Within one year after death.	
	Jury shall give such damages as party or parties entitled to sue may have sustained by reason of death. Not only for loss of service, but in addition such sum for mental pain and suffering of parent or parents as jury may assess.	Within one year. do.	

State and Statute	When Action Lies	Who may Sue	For Whose Benefit
GEORGIA Code 1910, §§ 4421, 4424-4426, 4460-4462.	In case of homicide of husband, wife, parent, or child upon whom parent is dependent for support, unless child leave wife, husband, or child. "Homicide" includes all cases where death results from crime or from criminal or other negligence.	Widow, or, if no widow, children, for homicide of husband or parent, and, if suit be brought by widow or children, and former or one of latter dies, action survives in first case to children, and in latter case to surviving children. Husband for homicide of wife, and, if she leave children, husband and children jointly, with right of survivorship in action. Mother, or, if no mother, father, for homicide of child upon whom she or he is dependent, or who contributes to his or her support, unless child leave wife, husband, or child.	
IDAHO Rev. Codes 1908, §§ 4099, 4100, 4050, 4055.	When death is caused by wrongful act or neglect.	Heirs or personal representatives, for a person not minor. Father, or, in case of his death or desertion of his family, mother, for a minor child. Guardian, for ward.	

How Distributed	Measure of Damages	When to be Commenced	Remarks
Widow shall hold amount recovered as personal property descending to her and children from the deceased. No recovery shall be subject to debts of deceased husband or parent.	Full value of life, as shown by evidence, without any deduction for necessary or other personal expenses of deceased had he lived.		Cause of action not abate by death either party; on de of plaintiff, if no ri of survivorship in other person, surv to personal represe ative.
	Such damages may be given as, under all circumstances of case, may be just.	Within two years.	

ate and Statute	When Action Lies	Who may Sue	For Whose Benefit
ILLINOIS rd's Rev. St. 1911, 70, §§ 1, 2.	Whenever death is caused by wrongful act, neglect, or default, such as would, if death had not ensued, have entitled party injured to maintain action.	Personal representatives.	Exclusive benefit of widow and next of kin.
3, § 29(c).	In case of loss of life by reason of willful violation of this act, (Miners' Act,) or willful failure to comply with any of its provisions.	Personal representatives.	Exclusive benefit of widow and next of kin and to any other persons who were dependent for support on deceased.
, § 122.	Actions to recover damages for injury to person survive.		
3, § 126 et seq.	Employer's Liability Act. Employer may elect to provide and pay compensation according to provisions of act, and thereby relieve himself from liability for damages except as provided. If employer elect not to provide and pay compensation to employé who has elected to accept provisions of act, employer shall not escape liability for certain causes. No compensation, other than provided is available to employé who accepts provisions or to any one dependent on him or responsible for his estate, with certain exceptions.		

How Distributed	Measure of Damages	When to be Commenced	Remarks
In proportion provided by law in relation to distribution of personal property left by persons dying intestate.	Jury may give such damages as they shall deem a fair and just compensation, with reference to pecuniary injuries resulting from such death to wife and next of kin, not exceeding $10,000.	Within one year after death.	No 'action shall be brought or prosecuted in this state to recover damages for a death occurring outside of this state.
To the widow and next of kin in the proportion provided by law in relation to the distribution of personal property left by persons dying intestate.	Damages for the injuries sustained by reason of such loss of life, not to exceed $10,000.	do.	If and when there shall be in force in this state a statute or statutes for compensation of workmen for all injuries received in course of employment, provisions thereof shall apply in lieu of right of action for damages provided in this act. (See Employers' Liability Act. infra.)
	Compensation as provided.		

ate and Statute	When Action Lies	Who may Sue	For Whose Benefit
INDIANA ns' Ann. St. 1908, 285.	When death of one is caused by wrongful act or omission of another, if former might have maintained action had he lived.	Personal representatives.	Exclusive benefit of widow or widower and children, if any, or next of kin.
37.	Father, or, in case of his death, or desertion of his family, or imprisonment, mother, may maintain action for death of child; and a guardian for death of ward.		
97.	In case of loss of life by reason of violation of act (Miners' Act) or willful failure to comply with any of its provisions.	(1) Widow, if any; (2) if no widow, children or adopted children jointly; (3) if neither foregoing classes, parents jointly, or parent; (4) or any persons jointly who were dependent for support on deceased.	
; 1911, c. 88.	Employer is liable for death of employé in certain cases.	Personal representative.	Surviving widow or husband and children; and if none, parents; and if none, next of kin dependent on deceased.
IOWA ; 1897, §§ 3443- 45, 3313, 3447.	All causes of action survive, and may be brought, notwithstanding death of person entitled or liable to same.	Legal representatives, or successors in interest of deceased.	
1.	Father, or, in case of his death or imprisonment, or desertion of his family, mother, may prosecute, as plaintiff, action for expenses and actual loss of service resulting from death of a minor child.		
KANSAS St. 1909, §§ 6014, 5.	When death of one is caused by wrongful act or omission of another, if former might have maintained action had he lived.	Personal representatives. Where deceased was a nonresident, or no personal representative has been appointed, widow, and if no widow, next of kin.	Exclusive benefit of widow and children, if any, or next of kin.
2.	Actions for injury to person survive.		

How Distributed	Measure of Damages	When to be Commenced	Remarks
In same manner as personal property of deceased.	Cannot exceed $10,000.	Within two years.	
	Damages for injury sustained by reason of such loss of life.		
	Damages shall be commensurate with injuries sustained, not to exceed $10,000.	Within two years from date cause of action accrued.	In case death re from injury, a survives.
When wrongful act produces death, damages shall be disposed of as personal property, belonging to estate of deceased, except that, if deceased leaves husband, wife, child, or parent, it shall not be liable for payment of debts.		Within two years. The action shall be deemed a continuing one, and to have accrued to representative or successor at same time it did to deceased, if he had survived.	May be brought or continued aga legal representa or successors in i est of deceased.

e and Statute	When Action Lies	Who may Sue	For Whose Benefit
KENTUCKY § 241; St. § 6.	Whenever death results from injury inflicted by negligence or wrongful act.	Personal representative.	Amount recovered, less funeral expenses and costs of administration and of recovery, etc., shall be for benefit of and go to kindred in following order; (1) If widow or husband and no children or their descendants, whole to widow or husband; (2) if either widow and children or husband and children, one-half to widow or husband and one-half to children; (3) if child or children, but no widow or husband, whole to child or children. If no widow, husband or child, recovery shall pass to mother or father, one moiety to each if both living; if mother dead and father living, whole to father; if father dead and mother living, whole to mother; if both father and mother dead, whole shall become part of personal estate of deceased, and after payment of debts remainder shall pass to kindred more remote than above named, as directed by general law on descent and distribution.
	Where person is killed by the careless, wanton, or malicious use of firearms, etc., not in self-defense, action lies against person committing killing and all others aiding or promoting.	Widow and minor child, or either or both.	
	Where person is killed in duel, action lies against principal, seconds, and all others aiding or promoting the duel, for reparation of injury.	Widow and minor child, or either.	
	No right of action for personal injury shall cease or die with person injuring or injured, except actions for assault, etc.		

How Distributed	Measure of Damages	When to be Commenced	Remarks
	Damages may be recovered from person or persons, company or companies, corporation or corporations, their agents or servants, causing same; and when act is wilful or negligence gross, punitive damages may be recovered.		

tate and Statute	When Action Lies	Who may Sue	For Whose Benefit
LOUISIANA v. Civ. Code, 1909, rt. 2315.	Every act of man that causes damage to another obliges him by whose fault it happened to repair it. The right of this action survives, in case of death.	Right of action survives in favor of children or widow or either; and, in default of these, surviving father and mother or either; and in default of the above, surviving brothers and sisters or either for one year from death. If deceased leave widow and minor children, right of action accrues to both. Right of action accrues to major children only where no surviving widow or minor child or children.	
MAINE 7. St. 1903, c. 89, 8, 9, 10.	Whenever death is caused by wrongful act, neglect, or default, such as would, if death had not ensued, have entitled party injured to maintain action.	Personal representatives.	Exclusive benefit of widow, if no children, and of children, if no widow; if both, then of her and them equally; if neither, of heirs.
!3, § 76.	If life of any person is lost through any defect in any highway, etc., action lies against county or town, if it had notice of defect, etc.	Executors or administrators.	Estate of deceased.
9, § 8.	Actions for assault and battery, trespass and trespass on the case survive.		
MARYLAND i. Code Pub. Civ. ws 1911, art. 67, 1-4.	Whenever death is caused by wrongful act, neglect, or default, such as would, if death had not ensued, have entitled party injured to maintain action. Not more than one action lies in respect to the same subject-matter.	The state, for use of the person entitled to damages.	Wife, husband, parent, and child.
93, § 104.	Executor or administrator may prosecute any personal action decedent might have prosecuted excepting for slander.		

How Distributed	Measure of Damages	When to be Commenced	Remarks
	Survivors may also recover damages sustained by death of parent or child or husband or wife or brothers or sisters.	Within one year after death.	
	Jury may give such damages as they shall deem fair and just compensation, not exceeding $5,000, with reference to pecuniary injuries resulting from such death to persons for whose benefit action is brought. Such sum as jury may deem reasonable as damages.	Within two years after death.	
After deducting costs not recovered from defendant, among parties for whom the action is brought, in such shares as jury by verdict shall find.	Jury may give such damages as they may think proportioned to injury resulting from such death to parties, respectively, for whom and for whose benefit the action is brought.	Within twelve calendar months after death.	Equitable plain must deliver to fendant full partilars of persons whom and on who behalf action brought, and of nate of claim.

State and Statute	When Action Lies	Who may Sue	For Whose Benefit
MASSACHUSETTS Rev. Laws 1902, c. 171, § 1.	Actions for tort for assault, battery, imprisonment or other damage to the person, survive.		
chapter 171, § 2 (as amend. Acts 1907, c. 375).	If a person or corporation by his or its negligence or by negligence of his or its agents or servants while engaged in his or its business causes death of person who is in exercise of due care and not in his or its employment or service.	Executor or administrator.	
Acts 1906, c. 463, pt. 1, § 63 (as amend. Acts 1907, c. 392).	If corporation which operates railroad or street railway by reason of its negligence or by reason of an unfitness or gross negligence of its agents or servants while engaged in its business, causes death of passenger, or of person who is in exercise of due care and who is not a passenger or in its employ. Corporation which operates railroad shall not be liable for death of person while walking or being on railroad contrary to law or reasonable rules and regulations. If employé of railroad corporation, being in exercise of due care, is killed under such circumstances as would have entitled him to maintain action if death had not resulted, corporation is liable as if he had not been an employé.	Commonwealth by indictment; or executor or administrator, in action of tort; but no executor or administrator shall, for same cause, avail himself of both remedies.	
Acts 1906, c. 463, pt. 2, § 245.	If life of a person is lost by collision with engines or cars of railroad corporation at crossing such as described in section 147, and corporation neglected to give signals required by said section, and such neglect contributed to injury, unless it is shown that in addition to mere want of ordinary care, person injured or person having charge of his person was guilty of gross or willful negligence, or was acting in violation of law, and that such negligence or act contributed to injury.	Executor or administrator, in action of tort.	

How Distributed	Measure of Damages	When to be Commenced	Remarks
One-half to use of widow and one-half to use of children; or, if no children, whole to use of widow; or, if no widow, whole to use of next of kin.	Damages, not less than $500 nor more than $10,000, to be assessed with reference to degree of culpability of defendant or that of his or its agents or servants.	Within two years after injury which caused death.	
To executor or administrator, one-half to use of widow and one-half to use of children; or, if no children, whole to use of widow; or, if no widow, whole to use of next of kin.	Fine, not less than $500 nor more than $5,000; or (in action of executor or administrator) damages not less than $500 nor more than $5,000, assessed with reference to degree of culpability of corporation, its servants or agents.	One year after injury causing death.	

State and Statute	When Action Lies	Who may Sue	For Whose Benefit
MASSACHUSETTS —Cont'd Rev. Laws 1902, c. 70, § 6.	If proprietor of steamboat or stage coach or common carrier of passengers, except railroad corporation or street railway company, by reason of his or its negligence, or by reason of unfitness or gross negligence or carelessness of his or its servants or agents, causes death of passenger.	Executor or administrator, in action of tort.	
Rev. Laws 1902, c. 51, § 17.	If life of a person is lost by defect, etc., of highway, etc., county, city, town, or person obliged to repair same is liable, provided defendant had reasonable notice of defect.	do.	
Acts 1909, c. 514, §§ 127-132.	If personal injury (caused to employé as result of negligence of employer or of person for whose negligence employer is liable by employer's liability act) results in death of employé, legal representatives shall have same right to compensation and of action as if he had not been an employé.	Personal representatives.	
	If such death is not instantaneous or is preceded by conscious suffering, and if there is any person who would have been entitled to bring action had employé been instantly killed and died without conscious suffering, legal representatives may in action for personal injury recover damages for death in addition to those for injury, and also damages for conscious suffering.	Personal representatives.	
	If such employé is instantly killed or dies without conscious suffering.	Widow, or if none, next of kin, who were dependent on deceased's wages for support.	

How Distributed	Measure of Damages	When to be Commenced	Remarks
To executor or administrator, one-half to use of widow and one-half to use of children; or, if no children, whole to use of widow; or, if no widow, whole to use of next of kin.	Damages, not less than $500 nor more than $5,000, assessed with reference to degree of culpability of proprietor or common carrier, his or its servants or agents.	One year after injury causing death.	
do.	Not exceeding $1,000, to be assessed with reference to degree of culpability of defendant.	do.	
	Damages for personal injury in action in which no damages for death are awarded, shall not exceed $4,000.	Within one year of the accident which causes the injury or death.	Notice of inju must be given.
	If damages are awarded, they shall be assessed with reference to degree of culpability of employer or of person for whose negligence employer is liable. If damages for death are awarded, they shall not exceed $5,000 for both injury and death, and shall be apportioned by jury between legal representatives and persons who would have been entitled to bring action for death if instantaneous and without conscious suffering.	do.	do.
	If damages for death are awarded, they shall be assessed, as last above set forth. Amount of damages shall not be less than $500 nor more than $5,000.	do.	do.

State and Statute	When Action Lies	Who may Sue	For Whose Benefit
MICHIGAN Comp. Laws 1897, §§ 10427, 10428. See, also, §§ 6308, 6309, 6389, 6390.	Whenever death is caused by wrongful act, neglect, or default, such as would, if death had not ensued, have entitled party injured to maintain action.	Personal representatives.	
Comp. Laws 1897, § 10,117a. Pub. Acts 1905, p. 120, No. 89.	Actions for assault and battery and negligent injury to persons survive.	Executor or administrator.	
MINNESOTA Rev. Laws 1905, § 4502, and section 4503 (as amend. Laws 1911, c. 281.)	When death is caused by wrongful act or omission, if decedent might have maintained action had he lived.	Personal representative.	Exclusive benefit of surviving spouse and next of kin.
MISSISSIPPI Code 1906, § 721 (as amend. Laws 1908, c. 167).	Whenever death is caused by wrongful or negligent act or omission, or by such unsafe machinery, way or appliances, as would, if death had not ensued, have entitled party injured to maintain action, and decedent shall have left any of beneficiaries named. Fact that death was instantaneous shall not defeat recovery. Applies to all personal injuries of servants or employés received in service or business of master or employer.	Widow, for husband; husband, for wife; parent, for child; child, for parent; brother, for brother or sister; sister, for sister or brother. All parties interested may join, and there shall be but one suit. If no husband, wife, children, father, mother, sister or brother, executor may sue.	

How Distributed	Measure of Damages	When to be Commenced	Remarks
To persons and in proportions provided by law in relation to distribution of personal property left by persons dying intestate.	Jury may give such damages as they shall deem fair and just, with reference to pecuniary injury resulting from such death, to those persons who may be entitled to such damages.		
Not subject to claims of creditors, but shall otherwise be distributed to persons and in proportions provided by law in relation to distribution of personal property left by persons dying intestate.	In actions for negligent injury to persons, measure of damages shall be such sum as court or jury shall deem fair and just with reference to pecuniary injury resulting from death to persons who may be entitled to such damages under law providing for distribution of personal property left by persons dying intestate.		
To surviving spouse and next of kin, in same proportion as personal property of persons dying intestate; any demand for support of decedent and funeral expenses allowed by probate court to be first deducted.	Cannot exceed $7,500.	Within two years after act or omission.	A cause of action ari out of an injury to the son dies with the perso either party, except as vided in § 4503. Action for personal jury commenced by d dent may be continued representative for be of same persons and re ery of same damages a commenced by represe tive.
Damages are not subject to debts or liabilities of deceased, and shall be distributed: If married man, to wife and children, and if no children, to wife; if married woman, to husband and children, and if no children, to husband; if unmarried, to children; if unmarried and no children, to father, mother, brothers and sisters. If none of the above, to legal representatives, subject to debts and general distribution. Illegitimate child of mother	Such damages as jury may determine to be just, taking into consideration all damages of every kind to decedent and to all parties interested.		Representatives of son whose act or omis caused death are lia Determination of suit s not bar another action less determined on me

State and Statute	When Action Lies	Who may Sue	For Whose Benefit
MISSOURI Rev. St. 1909, §§ 5425-5427, 5429.	Whenever any person, including an employé whose death is caused by negligence of coemployé, shall die from any injury occasioned by negligence, unskillfulness, or criminal intent of any officer, agent, servant, or employé while running, conducting, or managing any locomotive, car, or train of cars, or of any street, electric or terminal car or train of cars, or of any master, pilot, engineer, agent, or employé, while running, conducting, or managing any steamboat, or any machinery thereof, or of any driver of any stagecoach, automobile, motor car or other public conveyance; and when any passenger shall die from any injury occasioned by any defect or insufficiency in any railroad, whether steam, street, electric or terminal, or any part thereof, or in any locomotive, car, street car, electric car or terminal car, steamboat, or the machinery thereof, or in any stagecoach, automobile, motor car, or other public conveyance, employer or owner shall be liable. Defendant may show in defense that defect or insufficiency was not negligent, etc.	Husband or wife, or, if no husband or wife, or if he or she fails to sue within six months after death, minor children, whether natural born or adopted; and if deceased was minor and unmarried, whether natural born or adopted, father and mother, who may join, or survivor; and if there be no husband, wife, or minor child, or if deceased be unmarried minor and there be no father or mother, administrator or executor may sue, and recovery shall be distributed according to laws of descent.	
	Whenever death is caused by wrongful act, neglect, or default, such as would, if death had not ensued, have entitled the party injured to maintain action.	do.	
§ 8471.	In case of loss of life by willful violation of this article, (Miners' Act,) or willful failure to comply with any of its provisions.	Widow, lineal heirs or adopted children, or any persons who were dependent on deceased for support.	

How Distributed	Measure of Damages	When to be Commenced	Remarks
	Defendant shall forfeit and pay as penalty not less than $2,000 and not exceeding $10,000, in discretion of jury.	Within one year after cause of action shall accrue, subject to exceptions.	
	Jury may give such damages, not exceeding $10,000, as they may deem fair and just, with reference to necessary injury resulting from such death to surviving parties who may be entitled to sue, and also having regard to mitigating or aggravating circumstances.	do.	
	Direct damages sustained by reason of such loss of life, not exceeding $10,000.	Within one year after cause of action shall have accrued.	

State and Statute	When Action Lies	Who may Sue	For Whose Benefit
MONTANA Rev. Codes 1907, §§ 6485, 6486.	Where death is caused by wrongful act or neglect.	If decedent be not minor, heirs or personal representatives. Father, or, in case of his death or desertion of his family, mother, may maintain action for death of minor child, and guardian for death of ward.	
§§ 5248-5250.	In case of death of employé of company, corporation or individual operating mine, smelter or mill for refining ores, in consequence of injury or damages sustained, without contributory negligence, when caused by negligence of superintendent, foreman, shift boss, hoisting or other engineer, or craneman, action survives.	Heirs or personal representatives.	
§§ 5251, 5252.	In case of death of employé of person or corporation operating railway or railroad from injury or damage sustained in consequence of neglect or by mismanagement or of willful wrongs, whether of commission, or omission, of another employé, connected with use or operation of railway or railroad, etc., right of action survives.	do.	
NEBRASKA Cobbey's Ann. St. 1911, §§ 5199, 5200.	Whenever death is caused by wrongful act, neglect, or default, such as would, if death had not ensued, have entitled party injured to maintain action.	Personal representatives.	Exclusive benefit of widow or widower and next of kin.

How Distributed	Measure of Damages	When to be Commenced	Remarks
	Such damages may be given as, under all circumstances of case, may be just. do.		
In proportion provided by law in relation to distribution of personal property left by persons dying intestate.	Jury may give such damages as they shall deem a fair and just compensation, with reference to pecuniary injuries resulting from such death to widow or widower and next of kin.	Within two years after death.	

State and Statute	When Action Lies	Who may Sue	For Whose Benefit
NEVADA Rev. Laws 1912, §§ 5647, 5648.	Whenever death is caused by wrongful act, neglect, or default, such as would, if death had not ensued, have entitled party injured to maintain action.	Personal representatives.	
§ 4996.	Father, or in case of his death or desertion of his family, mother, may maintain action, for death of minor child; and guardian, for death of ward, if of lawful age; when death is caused by wrongful act or neglect.		Action by guardian for benefit of heirs of ward.
§ 4997.	When death of a person not a minor is caused by wrongful act or neglect.	Heirs or personal representatives.	Benefit of heirs.

How Distributed	Measure of Damages	When to be Commenced	Remarks
If there be surviving husband or wife, and no child, to such husband or wife; if there be surviving husband or wife, and a child, or children, or grandchildren, then equally to each, the grand child or children taking by right of representation; if there be no husband or wife, but a child or children, or grand child or children, then to such child or children and grand child or children by right of representation; if there be no child or grandchild, then to surviving father or mother; if no father or mother, then to surviving brother or sister, or brothers or sisters; if there be none of kindred above named, then in manner authorized by law for disposition of personal property of deceased persons. Not liable for any debt of deceased, if he or she left husband, wife, child, father, mother, brother, sister, or child of deceased child.	Jury may give such damages pecuniary and exemplary, as they shall deem fair and just, and may take into consideration pecuniary injury resulting from such death to kindred named.		
	Such damages as under all the circumstances of the case may be just.		
	do.		

State and Statute	When Action Lies	Who may Sue	For Whose Benefit
NEVADA—Cont'd §§ 5649-5652.	Every common carrier engaged in trade or commerce in state and every mine or millowner and operator actually engaged in mining, or in milling or reduction of ores is liable in case of death of employé for all damages which may result from negligence of its officers, agents or employés, or by reason of defect or insufficiency due to their negligence in its cars, engines, appliances, machinery, track, roadbed, ways or works, or to their negligent handling or storing of explosives.	Personal representative.	Benefit of widow and children, if any, and, if none, then of next of kin.
NEW HAMPSHIRE Pub. St. 1901, c. 191, §§ 8-14.	Actions of tort for physical injuries to the person, and the causes of action therefor, survive.	Administrator.	
NEW JERSEY Comp. St. 1909-1910, p. 1907 et seq., §§ 7-9.	Whenever death is caused by wrongful act, neglect, or default, such as would, if death had not ensued, have entitled party injured to maintain action.	Personal representatives.	Exclusive benefit of widow and next of kin.

How Distributed	Measure of Damages	When to be Commenced	Remarks
			Contributory ne gence does not bar covery where s and negligence of ployer, etc., gross comparison. Cont of insurance or demnity, etc., does bar recovery.
Damages, less expenses of recovery, shall be distributed (1) to widow or widower one half, and to children one half, in equal shares; (2) if no child, to widow or widower; (3) if no child, widow, or widower, to heirs at law, according to laws of distribution; (4) if child and children, and no widow or widower, to children in equal shares.	Shall not exceed $7,-000. If death was caused by injury complained of, mental and physical pain suffered by deceased in consequence of injury, reasonable expenses occasioned to his estate by injury, probable duration of his life but for injury, and his capacity to earn money, may be considered as elements of damage, in connection with other elements allowed by law.	If not barred by statute of limitations, within two years after death.	All actions causes of action in vor of or against ceased person, ex for penalties and feitures, survive, may be prosecute defended by adm trator.
To widow and next of kin in proportions provided by law in relation to distribution of personal property left by persons dying intestate; but if a widow and no children or descendants of children, widow is entitled to whole damages she sustains.	Jury may give such damages as they shall deem fair and just, with reference to pecuniary injury resulting from such death to wife and next of kin.	Within 24 calendar months after death.	On request, plai must deliver part lar account of na of claim.

State and Statute	When Action Lies	Who may Sue	For Whose Benefit
NEW MEXICO Comp. Laws 1897, §§ 3213-3215.	Whenever any person shall die from any injury occasioned by negligence, unskillfulness, or criminal intent of any officer, agent, servant, or employé, while running, conducting, or managing any locomotive, car, or train of cars, or of any driver of any stagecoach or other public conveyance, and when any passenger shall die from any injury occasioned by any defect or insufficiency in any railroad or part thereof, or in any locomotive or car, stagecoach, or other public conveyance, employer or owner shall be liable. Defendant may show in defense that defect or insufficiency was not negligent. Whenever death is caused by wrongful act, neglect, or default, such as would, if death had not ensued, have entitled party injured to maintain action.	Husband or wife; if no husband or wife, or if he or she fails to sue within six months after death, minor children; and if deceased was minor and unmarried, father and mother, who may join, or survivor. Personal representatives.	
§§ 3216, 3218.	Whenever death of employé of corporation operating railway is caused under circumstances from which cause of action would have accrued under sections 3216, 3217, if death had not ensued.	do.	

How Distributed	Measure of Damages	When to be Commenced	Remarks
	Defendant shall forfeit $5,000.		
To surviving husband or wife, if no child; if there be surviving husband or wife and child or children or grandchildren, then equally to each, grandchildren by right of representation; if there be no husband or wife, but children or grandchildren, then to children and grandchildren by right of representation; if there be no child or grandchild, then to surviving brothers or sisters. If there are any of the kindred above named, the proceeds are not liable for debts of deceased. In default of any such kindred, proceeds shall be disposed of in manner of personal property of deceased persons.	Jury may give such damages, compensatory and exemplary, as they shall deem fair and just, taking into consideration pecuniary injuries resulting from such death to surviving parties entitled to judgment, or any interest therein, and also having regard to mitigating or aggravating circumstances.		
do.	do.		

State and Statute	When Action Lies	Who may Sue	For Whose Benefit
NEW YORK Code .Civil Proc.1909, § 1902, and section 1903 (as amend. Laws 1911, c. 122) and sections 1904, 1905, 1870.	Action may be maintained for wrongful act, neglect, or default by which death of decedent, who has left husband, wife, or next of kin, was caused, against person who, or corporation which, would have been liable to action in favor of decedent, if death had not ensued.	Executor or administrator. When husband, wife or next of kin do not participate in estate, under will appointing executor, other than such husband, wife or next of kin, who refuses to bring action, husband, wife or next of kin may have administrator appointed to prosecute action for their benefit.	Exclusive benefit of husband or wife and next of kin; but if decedent left wife or husband, and no children, damages are for sole benefit of such wife or husband.
NORTH CAROLINA Revisal 1905, §§ 59, 60.	Whenever death is caused by wrongful act, neglect, or default, such as would, if injured party had lived, have entitled him t action.	Executor, administrator, or collector.	
NORTH DAKOTA Rev. Codes 1905, §§ 7686-7691.	Whenever death is caused by wrongful act, neglect or default, such as would. if death had not ensued have entitled party injured to maintain action.	Following persons in order named: (1) husband or wife ; (2) children; (3) personal representative. If person entitled to bring action refuses or neglects to do so for 30 days after demand of person next in order, such person may bring action.	Exclusive benefit of heirs at law.

How Distributed	Measure of Damages	When to be Commenced	Remarks
As if unbequeathed assets, left in hands of plaintiff after payment of debts and expenses of administration; but plaintiff may deduct reasonable expenses of action, reasonable funeral expenses, and commissions.	Damages may be such sum as jury, court, or referee deems to be a fair and just compensation for pecuniary injuries resulting from decedent's death to persons for whose benefit action is brought. Amount recovered shall draw interest from time of death, which interest shall be added to verdict, and inserted in entry of judgment.	Within two years after death.	
Not liable as assets for debts or legacies, but shall be disposed of as provided for distribution of personal property in case of intestacy.	Plaintiff may recover such damages as are a fair and just compensation for pecuniary injury resulting from death.	Within one year after death.	Defendant's ex tors, administra collectors or suc sors are liable.
Not liable for debts of decedent, but shall inure to exclusive benefit of heirs at law in such shares as trial judge shall fix in order for judgment.	Jury shall give such damages as they shall think proportionate to injury resulting from death to persons entitled to recovery.		Action does abate by death o ther party. If p tiff dies, person in order shall be r plaintiff. Person entitled bring action may c promise.

State and Statute	When Action Lies	Who may Sue	For Whose Benefit
OHIO Gen. Code 1912, §§ 10770, 10772, 10773, 10773-1.	When death is caused by wrongful act, neglect, or default, such as would, if death had not ensued, have entitled party injured to maintain action. When death is caused by wrongful act, neglect or default in another state, country or territory, which by statute gives right to maintain action and recover damages in respect thereof, such right of action may be enforced in this state in all cases where such state, territory or country allows enforcement in its courts of statute of this state of like character; but damages shall not exceed amount limited by this state; and foreign limitation shall govern time for commencement of action.	Personal representative.	Exclusive benefit of wife, or husband and children, or, if neither, of parents and next of kin.
Gen. Code 1912, § 11235.	Actions for injury to person survive.		
§§ 6242-6245(3).	Employer's Liability Act		
OKLAHOMA Comp. Laws 1909, §§ 5945, 5946.	When death is caused by wrongful act or omission, if person injured might have maintained action had he lived... See Const. art. 9, § 36.	Personal representatives. When decedent's residence is or at death was in another state or territory, or when, decedent being a resident, no personal representative is appointed, action may be brought by widow, or, if no widow, by next of kin.	Exclusive benefit of widow and children, if any, or next of kin.
§ 59483.	Actions for injury to person survive, and may be brought notwithstanding death of person entitled or liable to same.		

How Distributed	Measure of Damages	When to be Commenced	Remarks
Among beneficiaries, unless adjusted between themselves, by court making appointment, administrator, in such manner as shall be fair and equitable, having reference to their age and condition and laws of descent and distribution of personal estates left by persons dying intestate.	Where action is for benefit of children, widow, widower, mother, father, brother or sister, jury may give such damages, not exceeding $10,000, and where for benefit of widow and one or more minor children, jury may give such damages, not exceeding $12,000, as they may think proportioned to pecuniary injury resulting from death to persons, respectively, for whose benefit action is brought.	Within two years after death; except as provided in section 10773-1.	Action lies agai executor or admi trator of person whose wrongful neglect or defa death was caused. Personal represe ative, if appointed state, with consent court making appoi ment, may settle w defendant.
In same manner as personal property of the deceased.	Cannot exceed $10,000. See Const. art. 23, § 7.	Within two years.	

State and Statute	When Action Lies	Who may Sue	For Whose Benefit
OREGON Lord's Oregon Laws 1910, §§ 378-380.	When death is caused by wrongful act or omission, if person injured might have maintained action had he lived.	Personal representatives.	
§ 34.	Father, or, in case of death or desertion of his family, mother, may maintain action for death of child; and guardian for death of ward.		
p. XXXVI.	If there be loss of life by reason of defects or failures or violations of provisions of Employer's Liability Act by owner, contractor, subcontractor, or any person liable thereunder.	Widow, lineal heirs or adopted children, or husband, mother, or father.	
PENNSYLVANIA Pepper & Lewis' Dig. p. 5331, §§ 1, 2, and section 3 (as amend. Laws 1911, p. 678) and section 4. See, also, §§ 5-9.	Whenever death shall be occasioned by unlawful violence or negligence, and no suit for damages be brought by party injured. See Const. art. 3, § 21.	Husband, widow, children, or parents. They may recover whether citizens or residents of the commonwealth or otherwise.	Husband, widow, children, or parents, and no other relatives.
Pepper & Lewis' Dig. p. 5131, § 265.	In case of loss of life by violation of act, (Miners' Act,) or willful failure to comply with its provisions.	Widow and lineal heirs.	
RHODE ISLAND Gen. Laws 1909, c. 283, §§ 14, 15.	Wherever death is caused by wrongful act, neglect or default, such as would, if death had not ensued, have entitled party injured to maintain action.	Executor or administrator, whether appointed or qualified within or without state. If no executor or administrator, or if, being one, no action is brought in his name within 6 months, one action may be brought by beneficiaries, etc.	
§§ 7-9.	Causes of action for trespass on case for damages to person survive; and may be originally brought and prosecuted by and against executors and administrators; and if brought or prosecuted against any person may be prosecuted or defended by his executor or administrator.		

How Distributed	Measure of Damages	When to be Commenced	Remarks
Shall be administered as other personal property of the deceased.	Shall not exceed $7,500.	Within two years after death.	
	Without limit as to amount of damages which may be awarded.		
In proportion persons entitled would take personal estate of deceased in case of intestacy, without liability to creditors.	Damages for the death. See Const. art. 3, § 21. Direct damages for the injury sustained by the loss of life.	Within one year after death.	Declaration st state who are part entitled. No action to reco damages for inju to person by ne gence or default sl abate by death plaintiff.
One-half to husband or widow, and one-half to children; and if no children, whole to husband or widow; and if no husband or widow, to next of kin, in proportion provided by law in relation to distribution of personal property left by persons dying intestate.	Damages. Damage actually sustained, without vindictive or exemplary damages, or damages for outrage to feelings of injured party.	Within two years after death.	

State and Statute	When Action Lies	Who may Sue	For Whose Benefit
SOUTH CAROLINA Civ. Code 1902, §§ 2851, 2852, and section 2853 (as amend. Laws 1903, No. 60), and section 2854.	Whenever death is caused by wrongful act, neglect, or default, such as would, if death had not ensued, have entitled party injured to maintain action. No action lies in case there has been final judgment before his death in action by him for the injury.	Executor or administrator.	Benefit of wife or husband and child, or children; and if no wife, or husband, or child or children, benefit of parent or parents; and if none such, benefit of heirs at law or distributees dependent on decedent for support.
SOUTH DAKOTA Comp. Laws 1910, p. 444a, c. 301, §§ 1, 2.	Whenever death is caused by wrongful act, neglect or default, such as would, if death had not ensued, have entitled party injured to maintain action. Whenever death of citizen of state has been caused by wrongful act, neglect or default in another state, territory or country, which by statute gives right to maintain action and recover damages in respect thereof, such right of action may be enforced in state within time prescribed by such statute.	Personal representatives.	Exclusive benefit of wife or husband and children; or if there be neither, of parents and next of kin.
TENNESSEE Code 1896, §§ 4025-4029; Acts 1897, c. 86; Acts 1903, c. 317.	The right of action which a person who dies from injuries received from another, or whose death is caused by wrongful act, omission, or killing by another, would have had in case death had not ensued, shall not abate by his death, but shall pass to widow, and in case there is no widow, to children or personal representative, for benefit of widow or next of kin, free from claims of creditors.	Personal representative; but, if he declines, widow and children may, without his consent, use his name, on giving bond. Also widow in her own name, or, if no widow, children. Suit for death of wife may be brought in name of husband for benefit of himself and wife's children, or in name of her administrator. If deceased had commenced action, it shall proceed without revivor.	Widow, and, in case there is no widow, children, or personal representative, for benefit of widow or next of kin.

How Distributed	Measure of Damages	When to be Commenced	Remarks
Among beneficiaries in such shares as if deceased had died intestate and amount recovered were personal assets.	Jury may give such damages, including exemplary damages, where wrongful act, neglect or default was result of recklessness, willfulness or malice, as they may think proportioned to injury resulting from death to parties, respectively, for whom action is brought.	Within 6 years from death.	Executor or administrator is liable costs of action out estate, if any.
Among beneficiaries, unless adjusted between themselves, by court making appointment, in such manner as shall be fair and equitable, having reference to their age and condition and laws of descent and distribution of personal estate left by persons dying intestate.	Jury may give such damages, not exceeding $10,000, as they think proportionate to pecuniary injury resulting from death to persons respectively for whose benefit action is brought.	Within three years after death.	Action may maintained against executor or administrator of person who wrongful act, neg. or default caus death. Personal representative, if appointed state, with consent court making appointment, may settle with defendant.
To widow and next of kin, free from claims of creditors, as personal property. For death of wife, to husband and children equally, husband taking a child's share, and descendants of deceased child taking such child's part; and if no children or descendants, exclusively to husband. If husband die after cause accrued and before recovery collected, his share goes to his next of kin	Party suing shall have right to recover for mental and physical suffering, loss of time, and necessary expenses resulting to deceased from personal injuries, and also damages resulting to parties for whose benefit right of action survives from death.		Pending suit do not abate because death of beneficiar and shall be proceed with for benefit their heirs at law.

State and Statute	When Action Lies	Who may Sue	For Whose Benefit
TEXAS Rev. St. 1895, art. 3017-3027, 3353.	(1) When death is caused by negligence or carelessness of proprietor, owner, charterer, or hirer of any railroad, steamboat, stagecoach, or other vehicle for conveyance of goods or passengers, or by unfitness, negligence or carelessness of their servants or agents; or when death is caused by negligence or carelessness of receiver or other person in charge or control of railroad, their servants or agents, and liability of receivers extends to death caused by bad or unsafe condition of railroad or machinery or other reason by which action might be brought for injuries if railroad were operated by company. (2) When death is caused by wrongful act, negligence, unskillfulness, or default of another. Wrongful act, negligence, carelessness, unskillfulness, or default must be such as would, if death had not ensued, have entitled party injured to maintain action.	All parties entitled to action, or any one or more of them, for benefit of all. If they fail to sue within three months after death, executor or administrator must sue, unless requested by all parties entitled not to do so.	Exclusive benefit of surviving husband, wife, children, and parents.
UTAH Comp. Laws 1907, §§ 2911, 2912, 2873, 2878.	When death is caused by wrongful act or neglect.	Father, or, in case of his death or desertion of his family, mother, for minor child. Guardian, for ward of lawful age. Heirs or personal representatives for benefit of heirs, for person not a minor.	
VERMONT P. S. 1906, §§ 2835, 2839, 2840.	When death is caused by wrongful act, neglect, or default, such as would, if death had not ensued, have entitled party injured to maintain action.	Personal representative.	Wife and next of kin.

How Distributed	Measure of Damages	When to be Commenced	Remarks
Among persons entitled to benefit of action, or such of them as shall then be alive, in such shares as jury shall find by verdict. Not liable for debts of deceased.	Jury may give such damages as they may think proportioned to injury resulting from death. When death is caused by willful act or omission, or gross negligence of defendant, exemplary, as well as actual, damages may be recovered.	Within one year after death.	Action does no abate by death of ei ther party, if any per son entitled to benef survives, etc.
	Such damages may be given as, under all circumstances of case, may be just. See Const. art. 16, § 5.	Within two years.	
In same proportions as in distribution of personal estate of persons dying intestate.	Court or jury may give such damages as are just, with reference to pecuniary injury resulting from such death to wife and next of kin.	Within two years from decease.	If, during pendenc of action for recover of damages for bodil hurt or injury, eithe party dies, action su vives.

State and Statute	When Action Lies	Who may Sue	For Whose Benefit
VIRGINIA Code 1904, §§ 2902-2906.	Whenever death is caused by wrongful act, neglect, or default of any person or corporation, or of any ship or vessel, such as would, if death had not ensued, have entitled person injured to maintain an action, or to proceed in rem against ship or vessel, or in personam against owners or those having control of her.	Personal representative.	
WASHINGTON Rem. & Bal. Code 1909, §§ 183, 184, 194.	When man is killed in a duel, action lies against persons killing him, and seconds, aiders, and abettors.	Widow, or widow and her children, or children if no widow.	
	When death is caused by wrongful act or neglect of another.	Heirs or personal representatives. If deceased left no widow or issue, parents, sisters or minor brothers dependent on deceased for support who are residents within United States at death may sue.	
	When death is caused by injury received in falling through opening or defective place in sidewalk, street, alley, square, or wharf, action lies against person whose duty it was to keep in repair.	do.	
		Father, or, in case of his death or desertion of his family, mother, may maintain action for death of child, and guardian for death of ward.	

How Distributed	Measure of Damages	When to be Commenced	Remarks
After payment of costs and reasonable attorney's fees, to wife, husband, and child, or, if there be no wife, husband or child, to parents, brothers and sisters, in such proportion as jury may have directed, or, if they have not directed, according to statute of distributions, free from debts and liabilities of deceased; and if no wife, husband, child, parent, brother, or sister, the amount shall be assets to be disposed of according to law; but if widowed mother and widow, and no children, between mother and widow in such proportions as jury direct.	Jury may award such damages as to it may seem fair and just, not exceeding $10,000, and may direct in what proportion they shall be distributed to wife, husband, or child; or, if no wife, husband or child, to parents, brothers and sisters; but if widowed mother and widow, and no children, amount recovered shall be divided between mother and widow in such proportions as jury may direct.	Within 12 months after death, subject to exceptions.	Right of action d not determine, nor action, when broug abate, by death of fendant, or by disso tion of defendant c poration. An action by pa injured, in case of death, may be revi in name of perso representative. Personal represe ative may compron any claim, with c sent of persons e tled, or, if they incapable, with proval of a judge court.
	Jury may give such damages, as, under all circumstances of case, may seem just. do.		

State and Statute	When Action Lies	Who may Sue	For Whose Benefit
WASHINGTON—Cont'd	No action for personal injury to any person occasioning his death abates or determines by such death, if he have wife or child living, or, leaving no wife or issue, have dependent on him for support and resident within United States at death parents, sisters or minor brothers; but such action may be prosecuted, or commenced and prosecuted.		In favor of wife or of wife and children; or, if no wife, of child or children; or, if no wife or child or children, of parents, sisters or minor brothers, dependent on deceased for support and resident in United States at death.
WEST VIRGINIA Code 1906, §§ 3488, 3489.	Whenever death is caused by wrongful act, neglect, or default, such as would, if death had not ensued, have entitled party injured to maintain action.	Personal representative.	
WISCONSIN St. 1898, § 4255, and section 4256 (as amend. Laws 1911, c. 226), and sections 4219, 4224.	Whenever death is caused by wrongful act, neglect, or default, such as would, if death had not ensued, have entitled party injured to maintain action.	Personal representative.	
§ 4253 (as amend. Laws 1907, c. 353).	Actions for assault and battery, false imprisonment, and other damages to person survive.		
WYOMING Comp. St. 1910, §§ 4291, 4292.	Whenever death is caused by wrongful act, neglect, or default, such as would, if death had not ensued, have entitled party injured to maintain action.	Personal representative.	

To parties and in proportions provided by law in relation to distribution of personal estate left by persons dying intestate. Not subject to debts and liabilities of deceased.	Jury may give such damages as they shall deem fair and just, not exceeding $10,000.	Within two years after death.	
To husband or widow, if such relative survive deceased; if no husband or widow survive, to lineal descendants of deceased, and to his lineal ancestors in default of such descendants; but if no husband, or widow, or lineal descendant, or ancestor survive, to brothers and sisters. Nonresident alien surviving relatives are entitled to benefits.	Jury may give such damages, not exceeding $10,000, as they may deem fair and just, in reference to pecuniary injury resulting from such death, to relatives specified.	Within two years after cause of action accrued.	
To parties and in proportions provided by law in relation to distribution of personal estates left by persons dying intestate. Not subject to debts and liabilities of deceased.	Jury may give such damages as they shall deem fair and just.	Within two years after death.	

State and Statute	When Action Lies	Who may Sue	For Whose Benefit
UNITED STATES Act June 11, 1906, c. 3073, 34 Stat. 232 (U. S. Comp. St. Supp. 1911, p. 1316).	Every common carrier engaged in trade or commerce in District of Columbia, or in any territory of United States, or between any territory and another, or between any territory or territories and state or states or District of Columbia, or with foreign nations, or between state or states and foreign nations, is liable, in case of death of any of its employés, for all damages which may result from negligence of any of its officers, agents, or employés, or by reason of any defect or insufficiency due to its negligence in its cars, engines, appliances, machinery, tract, roadbed, ways or works. Contributory negligence of employé does not bar recovery where slight and that of employer gross in comparison (see "Measure of Damages").	Personal representatives.	Widow and children, if any; if none, parents; if none, next of kin dependent on employé.
Act April 22, 1908, c. 149, 35 Stat. 65 (as amend. Act April 5, 1910, c. 143, 36 Stat. 291 [U. S. Comp. St. Supp. 1911, p. 1324]).	Every common carrier (including receiver or receivers or other persons or corporations charged with duty of management and operation of business of common carrier) by railroad while engaged in commerce between any of states or territories, or between District of Columbia or any of states or territories and any foreign nation or nations, is liable in damages to any person suffering injury while employed by such carrier in such commerce and every common carrier by railroad in the territories, District of Columbia, Panama Canal Zone, or other possessions of the United States is liable to any person suffering injury while employed by such carrier in any of said jurisdictions, or in case of death of such employé to personal representative, for such injury or death resulting in whole or part from negligence of	Personal representative.	Widow or husband and children; if none, parents; if none, next of kin dependent on employé.

(Continued on p. lxx.)

How Distributed	Measure of Damages	When to be Commenced	Remarks
	All damages which may result. Contributory negligence of employé does not bar recovery where slight and that of employer gross in comparison, but damages shall be diminished by jury in proportion to amount of negligence attributable to employé. Questions of negligence and contributory negligence are for jury.	Within one year from time cause of action accrued.	No contract of employment, insurance, relief, benefit or indemnity for injury or death entered into by or on behalf of employé, nor acceptance of same by person entitled, is bar or defense. Defendant may set off any sum contributed by defendant towards such insurance, relief, benefit, or indemnity paid to injured employé or to personal representative.
	Damages resulting. Contributory negligence of employé does not bar recovery, but damages shall be diminished by jury in proportion to amount of negligence attributable to employé. Employé shall not be held guilty of contributory negligence, or to have assumed risks of employment, where violation by carrier of any statute for safety of employés contributed.	Within two years from day cause of action accrued.	Contract, rule, regulation, or device to exempt carrier is void. Defendant may set off any sum contributed or paid to any insurance, relief, benefit or indemnity paid to injured employé or person entitled.

ate and Statute	When Action Lies	Who may Sue	For Whose Benefit
ITED STATES— Cont'd	any of its officers, agents or employés, or by réason of any defect or insufficiency in its cars, engines, appliances, machinery, track, roadbed, works, boats, wharves, or other equipment. Contributory negligence of employé does not bar recovery (see "Measure of Damages").		
	Right of action to person suffering injury survives, but there shall be only one recovery for same injury.	Personal representative.	Widow or husband and children; if none, parents; if none, next of kin dependent on employé.

How Distributed	Measure of Damages	When to be Commenced	Remarks

DEATH BY WRONGFUL ACT

SECOND EDITION

CHAPTER I

THE COMMON LAW

§ 1.   No action for death at common law

At common law the right of action for an injury to the person abates upon the death of the party injured, the case falling within the familiar rule, "actio personalis moritur

TIFF.DEATH W.A.(2D ED.)—1

cum persona." Hence, where death results, whether instantaneously or not, from such an injury, no action can be
maintained by the personal representative of the party injured to recover damages suffered by the decedent.

In cases of injury to the person, however, in addition to
the right of action of the party receiving the physical injury, causes of action may accrue to persons who stand to
him or her in the relation of master, parent, or husband for
the recovery of damages for loss of service or society. To
these persons the rule of "actio personalis moritur cum persona" has no application. It might naturally be supposed,
therefore, that damages could be recovered by persons of
this description, not only for the loss of service or society
before the death, but also for the permanent loss of service
or society, caused by the death. It might perhaps be supposed that the law would even grant a remedy, as is done
by the Scotch law,[1] to the children and to other members of

---

[1] Weems v. Mathieson, 4 Macq. H. L. C. 215; Patterson v. Wallace,
1 Macq. H. L. C. 748; Cadell v. Black, 5 Paton, 567; Clark v. Coal
Co., [1891] App. Cas. 412. It is said in The Harrisburg, 119 U. S.
199, 7 Sup. Ct. 140, 30 L. Ed. 358, that such also is the law of
France, citing 28 Merlin Repertoire, 442, verbo "Reparation Civile,"
§ iv; Rolland v. Gosse, 19 Sirey (Cour de Cassation) 269. That such
was the civil law was denied in Hubgh v. New Orleans & C. R. Co.,
6 La. Ann. 495, and Hermann v. New Orleans & C. R. Co., 11 La.
Ann. 5. See Ravary v. Grand Trunk Ry. Co., 6 Low. Can. Jur. 49,
and Canadian Pac. Ry. Co. v. Robinson, 14 Can. Sup. Ct. 105, as
to the existence of such a right of action under the civil law as ad.
ministered in Lower Canada irrespective of statute. For the provisions of the various codes of continental Europe giving a right of
action for death, see 22 Harv. Law Rev. 408. In 1860 the supreme
court of the kingdom of Hawaii rejected the English common-law
rule, and sustained the right of a widow to sue for the wrongful
death of her husband. Kake v. Horton, 2 Hawaii, 209. The rule
so adopted is still in force as part of the common law of the ter.
ritory. The Schooner Robert Lewers Co. v. Kekauoha, 114 Fed. 849,
52 C. C. A. 483.

the family of the deceased who might have suffered injury by his death, irrespective of any technical loss of service or of society; but to both classes alike the common law denies a remedy. The law has not become established, indeed, without vigorous dissent upon the part of able judges, but the common-law rule may now be broadly stated to be that no civil action can be maintained against a person for causing the death of a human being.

§ 2. Higgins v. Butcher

The earliest case is Higgins v. Butcher,[2] which arose in the king's bench in 1606. The plaintiff declared that the defendant assaulted and beat his wife, of which she died, to his damage. It was objected "that the declaration was not good, because it was brought by the plaintiff for beating his wife; and that, being a personal tort to the wife, is now dead with the wife; and if the wife had been alive, he could not without his wife have this action, for damages shall be given to the wife for the tort offered to the body of his wife. Quod fuit concessum. And by Tanfield, J., if a man beats the servant of J. S., so that he dies of the battery, the master shall not have an action against the other for the battery and loss of service, because, the servant dying of the extremity of the battery, it is now become an offense to the crown, being converted into felony, and that drowns the particular offense and private wrong offered to the master before, and his action is thereby lost. Quod Fenner and Yelverton, concesserunt." The declaration seems to have been for the damage to the wife, and not for loss of services, so that all that the case actually decided is that, where a wrong is done to a person who dies, the action dies. In a

---

[2] Yelverton, 89.

report of the case in Rolle's Abridgment,[3] it is said: "If one beat my servant so that I lose his service for some months, and the servant then dies, still I shall have an action of trespass against the trespasser, for this was a distinct trespass to me." The case is usually cited as deciding that, in case of an injury resulting in death, the right of action is merged in the felony.

§ 3. Baker v. Bolton

The question was not again raised in England until 1808, in Baker v. Bolton,[4] which, although only at nisi prius, is the leading case upon the subject. This was an action against the defendants as proprietors of a stagecoach on which the plaintiff's wife was traveling when it was overturned, whereby she was so severely hurt that she died within a month. The declaration, besides other special damage, states that, "by means of the premises, the plaintiff had wholly lost and been deprived of the comfort, fellowship, and assistance of his said wife, and had from thence hitherto

[3] 2 Rolle's Abridgment, 575, placita 2 and 3. So in another report of the case (Noy, 18), Tanfield, J., is made to say "that it will not lie, as the case is, because the wife is dead, and that she ought to have joined in the action; but otherwise of a servant." In Smith v. Sykes, Freem. 224, it was held that if A. beat the wife of B., so that she dies, B. can have no action on the case for that, because it is criminal, and of a higher nature. And it was urged that if a man beat a feme covert, the husband could have no action per quod consortium amisit, but that the husband and wife ought to join in the action, and, if the husband dies, it shall survive to the wife; but the action shall not survive to the husband, if the wife dies. Curia advisare vult. The reporter adds: "Mes semble a moy: q'le action per quod consortium amisit gist bien per 2 Roll. 556; 2 Roll. Rep. 51."

[4] 1 Campb. 493.

suffered and undergone great grief, vexation, and anguish of mind." It appeared that the plaintiff was much attached to his wife, and that, being a publican, she had been of great use to him in conducting his business. Lord Ellen-borough told the jury that they could only take into consideration the loss of the wife's society to the plaintiff, and his distress of mind on her account, from the time of the accident till the moment of her dissolution. He then laid down his famous proposition that, "in a civil court, the death of a human being could not be complained of as an injury." In support of this, he cited no authority, and stated no reason. Nevertheless, his statement of the law has been accepted in nearly all subsequent cases as final.

§ 4. Lord Campbell's act

Such were the decisions in England when, in 1846, the statute commonly known as "Lord Campbell's Act"[5] was enacted—an act which has served as the model for similar acts in most of the states in this country. Lord Campbell's act is entitled "An act for compensating the families of persons killed by accidents." It gave an action to the family

---

[5] 9 & 10 Vict. c. 93. Probably the earliest statute giving a remedy for death caused by negligence was enacted in Massachusetts in 1648: "The court considering the great danger that persons, horses, teames, are exposed to by reasons of defective bridges, & country highways in this jurisdiction, Doth Order & declare: That if any person, at any time loose his life, in passing any such bridge or highway, after due warning given unto of any of the Select men of the towne in which such defect is, in writing under the hand of two witnesses or upon presentment to the shire Court, of such defective wayes or bridges, that then the county or towne which ought to secure such wayes or bridges, shall pay a fine of one hundred pounds, to the parents, husband, wife or children or next of kin, to the partie deceased." Colonial Laws of Massachusetts (reprinted from the edition of 1660) Boston, 1889, p. 126.

for the recovery of damages resulting from death, irrespective of any technical loss of service or of society, thereby introducing into the law an entirely new principle of recovery. It left the existing action for loss of service or of society untouched. Nevertheless, the preamble of the act broadly recites: "Whereas *no action* at law is now maintainable against a person who by his wrongful act, neglect, or default, may have caused the death of any person." As the preamble was doubtless intended to be declaratory of the law, it has generally been taken to be a parliamentary recognition of Lord Ellenborough's rule, though the force of the argument was denied by Bramwell, B., in the case of Osborn v. Gillett,[6] in which an effort was made, in 1873, to overrule Baker v. Bolton.

§ 5. Osborn v. Gillett

The declaration in Osborn v. Gillett stated that the defendant, by his servant, negligently drove a wagon and horses against the plaintiff's daughter and servant, whereby she was injured, and by reason thereof afterwards died; whereby the plaintiff lost her service, and incurred the expenses of burial. The defendant pleaded that she was killed on the spot, so that the plaintiff sustained no damages which entitled him to sue; and also that the acts of the defendant amounted to a felonious act by his servant, and that the servant had not been tried, convicted, or acquitted of, nor in any manner prosecuted for, the offense. The court (Kelly, C. B., Pigott, B., and Bramwell, B.) unanimously held the latter plea bad; but a majority of the court held the former plea good, Bramwell, B., dissenting. Pig-

[6] L. R. 8 Ex. 88; 42 L. J. Ex. 53; 28 L. T. (N. S.) 197; 21 Wkly. R. 409. See Jackson v. Watson, [1909] 2 K. B. 193, C. A.

ott, B., said: "It may seem a shadowy distinction to hold
that, when the service is simply interrupted by accident resulting from negligence, the master may recover damages,
while in case of its being determined altogether by the servant's death, from the same cause, no action can be sustained.
Still I am of opinion that the law has been so understood
up to the present time; and, if it is to be changed, it rests
with the legislature, and not with the courts, to make the
change. It is admitted that no case can be found in the
books where such an action as the present has been maintained, although similar facts must have been a matter of
very frequent occurrence. This alone is strong to show
that the general understanding has been to the effect laid
down by Lord Ellenborough in Baker v. Bolton. That
was, no doubt, a nisi prius decision; but it does not appear
that it has ever been questioned." He also relies on the
preamble to Lord Campbell's act. As to the plea that the
act amounted to a felony, he observed that "it only affords
a defense, *if at all*, when the action is brought against the
supposed criminal, and before prosecution."

The dissenting opinion of Bramwell, B., is a strong pres-
entation of the case against the existence of any rule for-
bidding the maintenance of an action for loss of service resulting from death. In conclusion he says: "It seems to
me that the principle the plaintiff relies on is broad, plain,
and clear, viz., that he sustained a damage from a wrongful
action for which the defendant is responsible; that the defendant, to establish an anomalous exception to the rule, for
which exception he can give no reason, should show a clear
and binding authority, either by express decision, or a long
course of uniform opinion, deliberately formed and expressed by English lawyers or experts in the English law. I find
neither. With the exception of a short note of the case of

(7)

Baker v. Bolton, there is no semblance of an authority on this side of the Atlantic, and the cases from the other side [7] are merely founded on that one, and some vague notion of a merger in a felony."

§ 6. Early American cases

The earliest American cases were not in accord with Baker v. Bolton. Cross v. Guthery,[8] in the supreme court of Connecticut (1794), was an action on the case against a surgeon for unskillfully performing an operation on the plaintiff's wife, as the result of which she died, whereby the plaintiff had been put to cost and expense, and had been deprived of her service, company, and consortship. After a verdict in favor of the plaintiff for £40, the defendant moved in arrest of judgment that the declaration was insufficient, on the ground that the offense charged appeared to be a felony, and by the laws of England the private injury was merged in the public offense. But the court held the declaration sufficient, saying that the rule urged was applicable in England only to capital crimes, where, from necessity, the offender must go unpunished, or the injured individual go unredressed.

In Ford v. Monroe,[9] in the supreme court of New York (1838), the declaration charged that, by the negligence of a servant of the defendant, an infant son of the plaintiff, of about 10 years, was run over and killed. The plaintiff al-

---

[7] The American cases referred to in his opinion are Carey v. Berkshire R. Co., Skinner v. Housatonic R. Corporation, infra, § 7, and Eden v. Lexington & F. R. Co., infra, § 8. The principal case was followed in Clarke v. London General Omnibus Co., [1906] 2 K. B. 648.

[8] 2 Root, 90, 1 Am. Dec. 61.   [9] 20 Wend. 210.

leged, by way of special damage, that in consequence of
the occurrence, his wife became sick, and that he was deprived of her society, and subjected to expense in attendance upon her; and also alleged the loss of service of the
child for a period of 10 years and upwards. The judge
charged the jury that the plaintiff would be entitled to recover for the value of the child's services until he became
21 years of age, and also the damages occasioned by his
wife's sickness. The main ground urged upon an application for a new trial, which was denied, was the failure of
proof that the servant was acting within the scope of his
authority. On the question of damages the court observed
that they were clearly proved to have been the direct consequence of the act complained of.

Both Cross v. Guthery and Ford v. Monroe, so far as
they are authorities that an action may be maintained for
loss of service caused by death, have been overruled.[10]
They are of interest, however, as showing that, at the time
they were decided, Lord Ellenborough's rule was not universally recognized in this country. This is shown, also,
by the dictum of Ware, J., in Plummer v. Webb,[11] which
arose in the United States district court for Maine, in 1825.
He was of opinion that a libel might be maintained by the
father for the consequential damages resulting from the
assault and battery of a minor child, on the high seas, per
quod servitium amisit, notwithstanding the death of the
child in consequence of the battery. The case was in admiralty, but he did not rest his opinion upon any difference
of the admiralty rule from that of the common law.

---

10 Infra, § 11.

11 1 Ware, 69, Fed. Cas. No. 11,234. See, also, Cutting v. Seabury,
1 Spr. 522, Fed. Cas. No. 3,521.

§ 7. Carey v. Berkshire R. Co.

The earliest discussion of the question in the United States, except the remarks of Ware, J., which were unnecessary to the decision, occurred in the cases of Carey v. Berkshire R. Co. and Skinner v. Housatonic R. Corp., which were considered together by the supreme court of Massachusetts, in 1848.[12] The first of these cases was an action on the case to recover damages for the loss of life of the plaintiff's husband, in consequence of the negligence of the defendant's servants. The second was an action on the case brought by the plaintiff for the loss of service of his son, aged 11 years, who was killed by the cars of the defendant. The court, in its opinion, by Metcalf, J., says that these cases raise a new question in our jurisprudence. Referring to the case of Higgins v. Butcher,[13] the court says that, whatever may be the meaning of the maxim that a trespass is merged in a felony, it has no application to the cases under consideration, in neither of which was the killing felonious. "If these actions, or either of them, can be maintained," the court says, "it must be upon some established principle of the common law; and we might expect to find that principle applied in some adjudged case in the English books, as occasions for its application must have arisen in very many instances. At least, we might expect to find the principle stated in some elementary treatise of approved authority. None such was cited by counsel, and we cannot find any. This is very strong evidence, though not conclusive, that such actions cannot be supported. But it is not necessary to rely entirely on this neg-

---

[12] 1 Cush. 475, 48 Am. Dec. 616. See, Palfrey v. Portland, S. & P. R. Co., 4 Allen (Mass.) 55.

[13] Supra, § 2.

(10)

ative evidence, for we find it adjudged in Baker v. Bolton and others that the death of a human being is not the ground of an action for damages. * * * Such, then, we cannot doubt, is the doctrine of the common law; and it is decisive against the maintenance of these actions." The court dismisses Ford v. Monroe [14] as a case in which the question under discussion was not raised. It was commented on as strange, by Bramwell, B., in Osborn v. Gillett,[15] that these two cases "are supposed to present a single question only for the court, while it is obvious that the case of master and servant raises a different question from that of husband and wife."

§ 8.   Eden v. Lexington & F. R. Co.

In Eden v. Lexington & F. R. Co.,[16] in 1853, the court of appeals of Kentucky held that a husband could not maintain an action for the injury sustained by him in consequence of the death of his wife, caused by the negligence of the defendant's servants. The court denied the existence in Kentucky of the common-law rule suspending the civil remedy in cases involving felony until after the conviction or acquittal of the felon, but declared that, "for injuries to life, the civil remedy is considered as being entirely merged in the civil offense." "This," the court incorrectly says, "was said to be the established common-law doctrine in the case of Baker v. Bolton."

[14] 20 Wend. 210.   [15] Supra, § 5.

[16] 14 B. Mon. 204.   See Louisville & N. R. Co. v. McElwain, 98 Ky. 700, 34 S. W. 236, 18 Ky. Law Rep. 379, 34 L. R. A. 788, 56 Am. St. Rep. 385.

§ 9. James v. Christy

In James v. Christy,[17] in the supreme court of Missouri, in 1853, it was assumed that an action could be maintained by the father to recover for the loss of the services of his minor son, who had been killed by the negligence of the defendant, a common carrier. After beginning suit the plaintiff died, and the point of the decision was that the action survived, under the Missouri statute governing the survival of actions. The court observed: "The statute extends to all cases where personal property is lessened. Here the father was entirely deprived of all property in his son's services." The case is cited without disapproval in a later Missouri decision.[18]

§ 10. Shields v. Yonge

In Shields v. Yonge,[19] in 1854, the supreme court of Georgia refused to follow Baker v. Bolton, and held that a suit could be maintained by a father for the death of a minor son, caused by the defendant's negligence, to recover damages for the loss of his service until the age of 21. Benning, J., in delivering the opinion of the court, takes the position that the supposed rule that in a civil court the death of a human being cannot be complained of as an injury is in reality no rule of law at all, but a mere statement of the practical working of the old law of forfeiture, taken in connection with the rule that, in cases where the wrong complained of amounted to a felony, the remedy was sus-

[17] 18 Mo. 162.
[18] Stanley v. Bircher's Ex'r, 78 Mo. 245.
[19] 15 Ga. 349, 60 Am. Dec. 698.

(12)

pended until after conviction. Because in former times, he argues, all homicides were felonies, and all felonies were punished by forfeiture of goods, if not of life, nothing remained after conviction out of which to satisfy a judgment in a civil action. Hence, he argues, arose the erroneous notion that in cases of homicide the private injury was merged in the public wrong, which he assumes to be equivalent to the rule declared by Lord Ellenborough. Shields v. Yonge has been approved by the same court.[20]

§ 11. Later American cases

The question under discussion has been repeatedly before the courts, and the cases, with the exception of those which have been above referred to, and of Sullivan v. Union Pac. R. Co.,[21] which will be referred to presently, have been unanimous in yielding to the authority of Baker v. Bolton. The rule has been applied equally in actions brought by the husband for the death of the wife;[22] by the wife for the death of the husband;[23] by the parent for the death

[20] Chick v. Southwestern R. Co., 57 Ga. 357; McDowell v. Georgia R. Co., 60 Ga. 320. See chapter III, note 19.

[21] Sullivan v. Union Pac. R. Co., 3 Dill. 334, Fed. Cas. No. 13,599.

[22] Worley v. Cincinnati, H. & D. R. Co., 1 Handy (Ohio) 481; Hyatt v. Adams, 16 Mich. 180; Green v. Hudson River R. Co., *41 N. Y. 294, 2 Abb. Dec. 277 (affirming 28 Barb. 9, 16 How. Prac. 230); Lucas v. New York Cent. R. Co., 21 Barb. (N. Y.) 245; Grosso v. Delaware, L. & W. R. Co., 50 N. J. Law, 317, 13 Atl. 233; Myers v. Holborn, 58 N. J. Law, 193, 33 Atl. 389, 30 L. R. A. 345, 55 Am. St. Rep. 606; Duncan v. St. Luke's Hospital, 113 App. Div. 68, 98 N. Y. Supp. 867.

[23] Lyons v. Woodward, 49 Me. 29; Wyatt v. Williams, 43 N. H. 102; Pulom v. Jacob Dold Packing Co. (C. C.) 182 Fed. 356; Earnest v. St. Louis, M. & S. E. R. Co., 87 Ark. 65, 112 S. W. 141; Major v. Burlington, C. R. & N. Ry. Co., 115 Iowa, 309, 88 N. W. 815.

of a minor child;[24] by the widow suing in her own right, and as tutrix of her minor children;[25] by the executor or administrator suing in his representative capacity;[26] and by an insurance company suing to recover damages by rea-

---

[24] Nickerson v. Harriman, 38 Me. 277; Kramer v. San Francisco Market St. R. Co., 25 Cal. 434; Covington St. Ry. Co. v. Packer, 9 Bush (Ky.) 455, 15 Am. Rep. 725; Little Rock & Ft. S. Ry. Co. v. Barker, 33 Ark. 350, 34 Am. Rep. 44; Davis v. St. Louis, I. M. & S. Ry. Co., 53 Ark. 117, 13 S. W. 801, 7 L. R. A. 283; Edgar v. Castello, 14 S. C. 20, 37 Am. Rep. 714; Natchez, J. & C. R. Co. v. Cook, 63 Miss. 38; Scheffler v. Minneapolis & St. L. Ry. Co., 32 Minn. 125, 19 N. W. 656; Sherman v. Johnson, 58 Vt. 40, 2 Atl. 707; Thomas v. Union Pac. R. Co., 1 Utah, 232; Sullivan v. Union Pac. R. Co. (C. C.) 2 Fed. 447, 1 McCrary, 301. See, also, White v. Ward, 157 Ala. 345, 47 South. 166, 18 L. R. A. (N. S.) 568; Jackson v. Pittsburg, C., C. & St. L. Ry. Co., 140 Ind. 241, 39 N. E. 663, 49 Am. St. Rep. 192; City of Eureka v. Merrifield, 53 Kan. 794, 37 Pac. 113; Gregory v. Illinois Cent. R. Co., 80 S. W. 795, 26 Ky. Law Rep. 76; Ohnmacht v. Mt. Morris Electric Light Co., 66 App. Div. 482, 73 N. Y. Supp. 296; Harshman v. Northern Pac. Ry. Co., 14 N. D. 69, 103 N. W. 412; Gulf, C. & S. F. Ry. Co. v. Beall, 91 Tex. 310, 42 S. W. 1054, 41 L. R. A. 807, 66 Am. St. Rep. 892. No action lies in favor of parents to recover damages resulting from prevention of performance of contract by adult son to support them, due to his death through defendant's negligence. Brink v. Wabash R. Co., 160 Mo. 87, 60 S. W. 1058, 53 L. R. A. 811, 83 Am. St. Rep. 459.

[25] Hubgh v. New Orleans & C. R. Co., 6 La. Ann. 495; Hermann v. New Orleans & C. R. Co., 11 La. Ann. 5.

[26] Kearney v. Boston & W. R. Corp., 9 Cush. (Mass.) 108; Whitford v. Panama R. Co., 23 N. Y. 465; Crowley v. Panama R. Co., 30 Barb. (N. Y.) 99; Beach v. Bay State Steamboat Co., 30 Barb. (N. Y.) 433. These cases, however, are really rather illustrations of the rule of actio personalis, as was pointed out by Denio, J., in Whitford v. Panama R. Co. See § 195. See, also, Wabash R. Co. v. Hassett, 170 Ind. 370, 83 N. E. 705; Murphy v. Willow Springs Brewing Co., 81 Neb. 223, 115 N. W. 761; Bretthauer v. Jacobson, 79 N. J. Law, 223, 75 Atl. 560; Stevenson v. W. M. Ritter Lumber Co., 108 Va. 575, 62 S. E. 351, 18 L. R. A. (N. S.) 316; Brown v. Chicago & N. W. Ry. Co., 102 Wis. 137, 77 N. W. 748, 78 N. W. 771, 44 L. R. A. 579.

son of having been forced to pay an insurance policy on
the life of a person killed by the defendant.[27]   In Connecticut Mut. Life Ins. Co. v. New York & N. H. R. Co.,[28]
which was a case of the last description, the supreme court
of Connecticut gave its adherence to the rule, without even
referring to Cross v. Guthery.   In Green v. Hudson River
R. Co.,[29] the New York court of appeals overruled Ford
v. Monroe.   In Sullivan v. Union Pac. R. Co.,[30] mentioned
above as in conflict with the current of the decisions, which
arose in the United States circuit court for Nebraska, in
1874, it was held that an action was maintainable by a father, whose son had been killed by the defendant's negligence, to recover damages for the loss of service until the
son's majority; and Dillon, J., delivered an able opinion in
support of the position of the court.   But since that case
the question has been before the supreme court of the
United States in Mobile Life Ins. Co. v. Brame,[31] a case
similar in its facts to Connecticut Mut. Life Ins. Co. v. New

[27] Connecticut Mut. Life Ins. Co. v. New York & N. H. R. Co., 25
Conn. 265, 65 Am. Dec. 571; Mobile Life Ins. Co. v. Brame, 95 U.
S. 756, 24 L. Ed. 580.

[28] 25 Conn. 265, 65 Am. Dec. 571.

[29] *41 N. Y. 294, 2 Abb. Dec. 277, affirming s. c. 28 Barb. 9, 16
How. Prac. 230.   Views in accordance with the decision of this case
had been expressed by judges of the court, although the point had
never been formerly decided.   See, Pack v. Mayor, etc., of City of
New York, 3 N. Y. 493; Oldfield v. New York & H. R. R. Co., 14
N. Y. 310; Whitford v. Panama R. Co., 23 N. Y. 475.   A dictum op-
posed to the decision had been expressed in Lynch v. Davis, 12
How. Prac. 323.   But see McGovern v. New York Cent. & H. R. R.
Co., 67 N. Y. 417, in which Andrews, J., refers to Ford v. Monroe
as if it were good law.

[30] 3 Dill. 334, Fed. Cas. No. 13,599.   In Cutting v. Seabury, 1 Spr.
522, Fed. Cas. No. 3,521 (1860), Sprague, J., denied that it could be
considered as settled law that no action could be maintained for
damages occurring from the death of a human being.

[31] 95 U. S. 756, 24 L. Ed. 580.

York & N. H. R. Co. The court held that the action could not be maintained, and Hunt, J., who delivered the opinion, says: "The authorities are so numerous and so uniform to the proposition that by the common law no civil action lies for an injury which results in death, that it is impossible to speak of it as a proposition open to question." This statement of the law was approved by the same court in The Harrisburg,[32] which held that the same rule was applicable in this respect in courts of admiralty as at common law.

§ 12. Reason for the rule

No satisfactory reason for the rule has ever been suggested, though attempts have been made to base it upon the merger of the civil remedy in the felony, upon the law of forfeiture, upon the maxim "actio personalis moritur cum persona," and upon public policy.

§ 13. Merger

Blackburn, J., says [33] that the dictum of Tanfield, J., in Higgins v. Butcher, is the earliest authority we can find for the notion that the civil remedy was merged in the felony. Whether the doctrine of an absolute merger ever existed has been doubted.[34] In recent times it has been held in England that the merger is only temporary, and that it amounts only to a suspension of the civil remedy until the wrongdoer has been prosecuted.[35] Thus, the fact that the

[32] 119 U. S. 199, 7 Sup. Ct. 140, 30 L. Ed. 358. See § 204.
[33] Wells v. Abrahams, L. R. 7 Q. B. 554.
[34] Wells v. Abrahams, supra.
[35] Lutterell v. Reynell, 1 Mod. 282; Crosby v. Leng, 12 East, 409; Wells v. Abrahams, supra; Osborn v. Gillett, 8 Exch. 88, 42 L. J. Exch. 53; 28 L. T. (N. S.) 197, 21 Wkly. R. 409.

thief had not been prosecuted was held no defense in an action of trover against the innocent purchaser of stolen goods;[36] and where the wrong complained of was committed, not by the defendant, but by his servant, the failure to prosecute was no defense.[37]

It has been recently questioned,[38] moreover, whether the doctrine of merger existed even to this limited extent, and it has been held that, although the evidence shows that the wrong complained of amounts to a felony, this is no ground for a nonsuit. In the United States the doctrine of the suspension of the civil remedy has been held by some courts, but has more frequently been denied.[39] Be the rule of the common law what it may, it can obviously furnish no reason for Lord Ellenborough's rule; for in Baker v. Bolton it was not suggested that the killing was felonious, and Lord Ellenborough did not confine the rule to cases of felony. That merger was a ground for the rule was denied in Osborn v. Gillett, and the notion has been universally repudiated in this country.[40]

§ 14. Forfeiture

It was suggested in Shields v. Yonge, as has been pointed out,[41] that the explanation of the supposed existence, if not the reason, of the rule was to be found in the law of the forfeiture of the goods and life of the felon upon conviction, taken in connection with the suspension of the

---

[36] White v. Spettigue, 13 M. & W. 603.

[37] Osborn v. Gillett, supra.

[38] Wells v. Abrahams, supra.

[39] 2 Bishop, Criminal Law (7th Ed.) § 270 et seq.

[40] Carey v. Berkshire R. Co., 1 Cush. (Mass.) 475, 48 Am. Dec. 616; Hyatt v. Adams, 16 Mich. 180.

[41] Supra, § 10.

civil remedy until after prosecution. But this explanation is open to the objection that forfeiture and suspension of the civil remedy were not confined to homicide, but accompanied other felonies, in respect to which it is not pretended that a complete merger took place, so that the argument proves too much.[42]

§ 15. Actio personalis moritur cum persona

This maxim simply means that the right of action dies with the person who was a party to the action, and therefore does not meet the case of the master, parent, or husband. This argument was disposed of by Hunt, J., in Green v. Hudson River R. Co.,[48] which was an action by the husband for the killing of his wife. "That principle, in my judgment," he says, "does not touch the present class of cases. In its legal aspect, the injury here complained of was done to the plaintiff, and not to his deceased wife. The claim is for compensation for injury to his rights, and not to hers. Should her executors bring their action to recover damages for the pain and anguish suffered by her for the cause alleged, the principle of actio personalis would find its proper application. It is not applicable to the action of the present plaintiff, in which the party alleged to be injured, and the party inflicting the injury, are still in existence."

[42] Hyatt v. Adams, 16 Mich. 180; Grosso v. Delaware, L. & W. R. Co., 50 N. J. Law, 317, 13 Atl. 233.

[48] *41 N. Y. 294, 2 Abb. Dec. 277. See, also, opinion of Bramwell, B., in Osborn v. Gillett, and of Benning, J., in Shields v. Yonge, supra, § 10.

§ 16. Public policy

This term may be used to express various vague reasons which different judges have urged in support of the rule. For example, Christiancy, J.,[44] says that "the reason of the rule is to be found in that natural and almost universal repugnance among enlightened nations to setting a price upon human life." And Storrs, J.:[45] "It is manifestly not one reason but many, which lie at the basis of the common-law rule. Considerations of the most varied and grave character would present themselves to the minds of any court, even though the matter should be presented to them as an original question, to dissuade them from entertaining any action, sounding in damages, and seeking a recovery on account of the destruction of life. * * * If a suit should be brought to recover for the mental suffering, loss of society, comfort, support, and protection resulting from the death of another person, we should see at once, so intertwined is the web of human affection, interest, and relationship, that the author of his death, however slight or accidental his default, would be responsible in numberless actions brought on behalf of wives, children, friends, brothers, sisters, and dependents of all degrees, to say nothing, for the present, of creditors; and, for an injury of such incalculable extent, writers on jurisprudence, perhaps without strict accuracy, have assigned the awful magnitude of the wrong as the reason why neither court nor jury have ever been trusted by the law with the function of estimating it."

[44] Hyatt v. Adams, 16 Mich. 180.
[45] Connecticut Mut. Life Ins. Co. v. New York & N. H. R. Co., 25 Conn. 265, 65 Am. Dec. 571.

However strange it may be that the common law, which provides a remedy for the seduction of a daughter based upon what is in most cases the legal fiction of a loss of service, should have denied a remedy for a permanent loss of service caused by death, an examination of the cases leads to no more satisfactory conclusion than that reached by Leonard, J., in Green v. Hudson River R. Co.:[46] "It is of no practical utility to search for the reason of the rule. It remains somewhat obscure."

§ 17.   Limitation of the rule

The scope of the rule being that no action can be maintained for causing death, the rule does not preclude an action to recover damages for loss of the service of the injured party during the period between the injury and the death, although the death resulted directly from the injury. Thus, in Baker v. Bolton, Lord Ellenborough told the jury that they could take into consideration the loss of the wife's society, and the distress of mind the plaintiff had suffered on her account, from the time of the accident until the moment of her dissolution; and this distinction has been followed.[47]

---

[46] *41 N. Y. 294, 2 Abb. Dec. 277. But see article by R. C. McMurtrie, 16 Am. Law Rev. p. 128; Death as a Civil Cause of Action, by Gustavus Hay, Jr., 7 Harv. Law Rev. 170.

[47] Hyatt v. Adams, 16 Mich. 180; Nickerson v. Harriman, 38 Me. 277; Philippi v. Wolff, 14 Abb. Prac. N. S. (N. Y.) 196; Covington St. Ry. Co. v. Packer, 9 Bush (Ky.) 455, 15 Am. Rep. 725; Natchez, J. & C. R. Co. v. Cook, 63 Miss. 38; Davis v. St. Louis, I. M. & S. Ry. Co., 53 Ark. 117, 13 S. W. 801, 7 L. R. A. 283; Mowry v. Chaney, 43 Iowa, 609. An action by a father for loss of services of a minor child and for burial expenses cannot be sustained, where the minor's death was instantaneous. Bligh v. Biddeford & S. R. Co., 94 Me. 499, 48 Atl. 112.

§ 18. Right of action where death is caused by breach of contract

It has been held in England that, where death is caused by the breach of a carrier's implied contract for safe carriage, the executor or administrator, although he could not sue in tort, may sue in contract, and recover damages suffered by the decedent's estate. The first authority to this effect is a dictum in Knights v. Quarles [48] (1820), which was cited with approval in Alton v. Midland Ry. Co. [49] In Potter v. Metropolitan District Ry. Co. [50] it was held that the right of a husband to sue for loss in respect to injuries suffered by his wife, who had been injured while a passenger, by the defendant's negligence, being founded on a breach of contract, survived to his administratrix. In Bradshaw v. Lancashire & Y. Ry. Co. [51] (1875), where a passenger on a train was injured, and, after an interval, died in consequence, it was held that his executrix might, in an action for breach of contract, recover the damages to his personal estate arising in his lifetime from medical expenses, and loss occasioned by his inability to attend to business. Grove, J., remarks that up to Potter v. Metropolitan District Ry. Co. no action of this kind appears ever to have been brought, but that the case is indistinguishable, and that they are bound by it. Bradshaw v. Lancashire & Y. Ry. Co. was followed in Leggott v. Great Northern Ry. Co. [52] (1876), in which the queen's bench held on demurrer

[48] 2 Brod & B. 102.   [49] 19 C. B. (N. S.) 213.
[50] 30 L. T. (N. S.) 765.
[51] L. R. 10 C. P. 189; 44 L. J. C. P. 148.
[52] 1 Q. B. D. 599; 45 L. J. Q. B. 557; 35 L. T. (N. S.) 334; 24 Wkly. R. 784. Where a boiler sold by defendant to decedent exploded, injuring his goods and killing him, held, that a judgment

that a prior recovery by the plaintiff as administratrix under Lord Campbell's act was no bar to an action by her as
administratrix to recover damages to his personal estate
by his inability to attend to his business from the time of
the accident until his death, as the plaintiff sued in a different right in each case. The court (Mellor and Quain, JJ.),
however, while yielding to Bradshaw v. Lancashire & Y.
Ry. Co. as binding upon them, questioned its correctness.
In the recent case of Jackson v. Watson & Sons,[53] which
was an action for breach of a warranty that tinned salmon
sold by the defendants to the plaintiff was fit for consump-
tion as human food, the plaintiff claimed damages on the
ground, among other grounds, that his wife, having par-
taken of the salmon, had died in consequence, and that, she
having performed services for him in his household, he was
under the necessity of hiring some one else to perform such
services. The jury having found for the plaintiff and
awarded £200. in respect of such damages, it was held that,
the death not forming an essential part of the cause of action, but only an element in ascertaining the damages
arising therefrom, there was no rule of law which prevented their recovery. "On the whole," said Vaughan Williams, L. J., "I have come to the conclusion that this exception from the general principle on which damages are
based [i. e., the 'anomalous exception' dealt with by Bramwell, B., in his dissenting opinion in Osborn v. Gillett][54]

---

recovered by his administratrix under Lord Campbell's act was no
bar to a subsequent action by the administratrix to recover damages
from the same cause to his personal property. Barnett v. Lucas, 6
I. R. C. L. 247 (affirming s. c. 5 I. R. C. L. 140). See Pulling v. Great
Eastern Ry. Co., 9 Q. B. D. 110.

[53] [1909] 2 K. B. 193, C. A. See, also, Frost v. Aylesbury Dairy
Co., [1905] 1 K. B. 608, C. A.

[54] Ante, § 5.

only applies to cases where the cause of action is the wrong which caused the death, and does not apply to cases where there is a cause of action independently of such wrong."

The right of the personal representative to maintain an action for a breach of the contract of carriage, resulting in the death of his intestate, was sustained without discussion by Blatchford, J., in The City of Brussels,[55] and in Kentucky in Winnegar's Adm'r v. Central Pass. Ry. Co.[56] In New Hampshire it has been held that an action founded upon contract cannot be maintained against the personal representative of a deceased surgeon to recover damages arising from his unskillful treatment of the plaintiff, the court declaring that, when the breach of contract results in an injury purely personal, an exception arises to the general rule that actions ex contractu survive.[57] So in New York, where the plaintiff placed his insane wife as a patient in the hospital of the defendant, which contracted to keep a constant and careful guard over her, but negligently failed to do so, and in the absence of an attendant she jumped from a window and was killed, and the plaintiff brought action to recover damages for loss of her society and services resulting from the death, by reason of the

[55] 6 Ben. 370, Fed. Cas. No. 2,745.

[56] 85 Ky. 547, 4 S. W. 237.

[57] Vittum v. Gilman, 48 N. H. 416; Jenkins v. French, 58 N. H. 532. In Cregin v. Brooklyn Crosstown R. Co., 75 N. Y. 192, 31 Am. Rep. 459, the plaintiff sued the defendant, who was a carrier of passengers, for the loss of services of his wife, and for expenses paid in consequence of injuries to her person while she was a passenger. The court said that the action was grounded on tort, and that at common law it would have abated on the death of the plaintiff, although they held that the action survived under the New York statute preserving from abatement wrongs done to the property, rights, or the interest of another. S. C. 83 N. Y. 595, 38 Am. Rep. 474. See, also, Crowley v. Panama R. Co., 30 Barb. 99; Hyde v. St. L. & P. Ry. Co., 61 Iowa, 441, 16 N. W. 351, 47 Am. Rep. 820.

defendant's breach of contract, it was held that the action for such breach was ex delicto, and not ex contractu, and that since the cause of action did not fall within the statute, and no action for death lay at common law, no cause of action was stated. The complaint alleged that the death was the direct result of the negligence and careless omission of the defendant to keep a constant, careful, and continuous guard, and that as a direct result of its negligent omission so to do the plaintiff lost his wife. "This," said the court, "is to allege 'a wrongful act, neglect, or default by which the decedent's death was caused,' within the precise language of the statute. And the statute seems to give the cause of action, and to fix its limitations. There seems to be no difference between the negligent breach of this contract, as alleged, and the negligent breach of the contract of a common carrier to safely transport the passenger. In each case there is a contract, and in each case there is a tort. But the action for such a breach is ex delicto, and not ex contractu. * * * The learned counsel for the appellant, with great frankness, stated upon the argument that he desired no decision upon a technical point, that he might be entitled to nominal damages, or to a recovery of the consideration paid, but contended for the broad proposition that for the alleged breach of this contract causing his wife's death, plaintiff was entitled to recover for the value of her society and services. But the contract was to keep a constant watch and guard. It was not to prevent the unfortunate patient from committing suicide. Nor could it fairly be held to be within the reasonable intendment of this contract that the hospital agreed to pay to the husband the value of his wife's life to him in case she did commit suicide. There has been no case cited to us, nor have we been able to find one, which allows a recovery upon such a

(24)

complaint or such a state of facts. Nor can we see any reason why there should be any difference in the rule where the tortious act which caused death is alleged to be a breach of an express contract than where it is alleged to be a breach of an implied contract, or where no contractual relation at all existed. It is settled by innumerable cases that the right to recover for the death of a human being is a right solely given by statute, and, as the plaintiff comes not within the statute, the judgment should be affirmed, with costs." [58]

[58] Duncan v. St. Luke's Hospital, 113 App. Div. 68, 98 N. Y. Supp. 867, affirmed 192 N. Y. 580, 85 N. E. 1109. Breach of agreement by landlord to repair, resulting in tenant's death, will not furnish basis for action of tort within a statute giving a right of action for death due to wrongful act, but the remedy is an action for damages for breach of contract. Glenn v. Hill, 210 Mo. 291, 109 S. W. 27, 16 L. R. A. (N. S.) 699. Action against carrier for causing death of person transported on private car, in which complaint does not set up written contract entered into between the carrier and the owner of car, sounds in tort. Cleveland, C., C. & St. L. Ry. Co. v. Henry (Ind. App.) 80 N. E. 636, rehearing denied 81 N. E. 592.

CHAPTER II

THE STATUTES

§ 19. Lord Campbell's act

Lord Campbell's act was passed in 1846, and beginning with New York, whose act was passed in 1847, all the states and territories of the United States have followed the example of England, and have granted a remedy to the families of persons killed by wrongful act, neglect, or default. Similar statutes have also been enacted in Canada.

§ 20. Scope of Lord Campbell's act

The scope of Lord Campbell's act is indicated by its title, viz.: "An act for compensating the families of persons

(26)

killed by accidents." The preamble recites: "Whereas, no action at law is now maintainable against a person who, by his wrongful act, neglect, or default, may have caused the death of another person, and it is often expedient and right that the wrongdoer in such case should be answerable in damages for the injury so caused by him." The title and preamble together show the intention of the framers of the act, namely, to make an exception to the common-law rule, by creating a new right of action in favor of the family of the deceased.

§ 21. Provisions of the act

The act provides as follows: (1) That whensoever the death of a person shall be caused by wrongful act, neglect, or default, such as would, if death had not ensued, have entitled the party injured to maintain an action and recover damages in respect thereof, then the person who would have been liable if death had not ensued shall be liable to an action for damages, notwithstanding the death of the person injured; and (2) although the death shall have been caused under such circumstances as amount in law to felony; (3) that the action shall be for the benefit of the wife, husband, parent (which includes grandparent and stepparent), and child (which includes grandchild and stepchild); (4) that the action shall be brought by and in the name of the executor or administrator; (5) that the jury may give such damages as they may think proportioned to the injury resulting from such death to the parties, respectively, for whom and for whose benefit such action shall be brought; (6) that the amount so recovered, after deducting costs not recovered from the defendant, shall be divided among the before-mentioned parties in such shares as the

jury by their verdict shall find and direct; (7) that not ·
more than one action shall lie for and in respect of the same
subject-matter; (8) that every such action shall be commenced within 12 calendar months after the death; (9) that
the plaintiff shall be required, together with the declaration,
to deliver to the defendant or his attorney a full particular
of the person or persons, for whom and on whose behalf
such action shall be brought, and of the nature of the
claim in respect of the damages sought to be recovered.

In 1864 the act was amended as follows: (1) That if
there shall be no executor or administrator, or if, there
being such executor or administrator, no action shall within six calendar months after the death have been brought
by the executor or administrator, then such action may be
brought by all or any of the persons for whose benefit such
action would have been brought, if brought by the executor
or administrator; and (2) that the defendant may pay a
sum of money into court as compensation to all persons
entitled, without specifying the shares into which it is to be
divided by the jury, and if such sum is not accepted, and
an issue is made as to its sufficiency, and the jury shall
think it sufficient, the defendant shall be entitled to the verdict upon that issue.

In 1908 the act was again amended by providing that in
assessing damages there shall not be taken into account any
sum paid or payable on the death of the deceased under
any contract of assurance or insurance.

§ 22. Distinguishing features of action

The distinguishing features of the new action are three
in number: (1) That it may be maintained whenever
death is caused by wrongful act, neglect, or default, such as

(28)

would, if death had not ensued, have entitled the party injured to maintain an action; (2) that it is for the exclusive benefit of certain designated members of the family of the deceased; and (3) that the damages recoverable are such as result to the beneficiaries from the death.

§ 23. The act creates a new cause of action

It is manifest that the act did not repeal, or create an exception to, the rule of "actio personalis moritur cum persona," by providing for the survival of the action which the party injured might have maintained; for, though the action can be maintained only when the death is caused under such circumstances as would have entitled the party injured to maintain an action, it is not maintainable for the recovery of the damages resulting from the personal injury to him, and hence, by survival, to his estate; but is maintainable only for the recovery of damages for the pecuniary loss resulting from the death to the surviving members of his family. As Coleridge, J., said in one of the first cases [1] that arose under the act: "This act does not transfer this right of action to his representative, but gives to his representative a totally new right of action, on different principles." It must be admitted that expressions occur in some of the opinions to the effect that the statute gives a substituted, and not a new, right of action; [2] but, having regard to the provisions of the act in respect to the persons who are entitled to the benefit of the action and the meas-

[1] Blake v. Midland Ry. Co., 18 Q. B. 93, 21 L. J. Q. B. 233, 16 Jur. 562.

[2] St. Louis, I. M. & S. R. Co. v. McNamare, 91 Ark. 515, 122 S. W. 102 (Missouri statute); Bellamy v. Whitsell, 123 Mo. App. 610, 100 S. W. 514; Louisville Ry. Co. v. Raymond's Adm'r, 135 Ky. 738, 123 S. W. 281, 27 L. R. A. (N. S.) 176. See § 124.

ure of damages, such a position is entirely untenable.[3] Said
Lord Blackburn, in Seward v. The Vera Cruz:[4] "A totally
new action is given against the person who would have
been responsible to the deceased if the deceased had lived
—an action which * * * is new in its species, new in its
quality, new in its principle, in every way new, and which
can only be brought if there is any person answering the
description of the widow, parent, or child, who, under such
circumstances, suffers pecuniary loss."

§ 24. Statutes similar to Lord Campbell's act

The states and territories, including the District of Columbia, which have to-day upon their statute books acts
substantially similar to Lord Campbell's act are the following: Alabama, Arkansas, California, Colorado, Delaware,
District of Columbia, Florida, Idaho, Illinois, Indiana, Kansas, Louisiana, Maine, Maryland, Michigan, Minnesota, Mississippi, Missouri, Montana, Nebraska, Nevada, New Jersey,
New Mexico, New York, North Dakota, Ohio, Pennsylvania, Rhode Island, South Carolina, South Dakota, Texas,
Utah, Vermont, Wisconsin, and Wyoming.

[3] Leggott v. Great Northern Ry. Co., 1 Q. B. D. 599; Whitford v.
Panama R. Co., 23 N. Y. 465; Littlewood v. Mayor, etc., of City of
New York, 89 N. Y. 24, 42 Am. Rep. 271; Russell v. Sunbury, 37
Ohio St. 372, 41 Am. Rep. 523; Hamilton v. Jones, 125 Ind. 176, 25
N. E. 192; Hulbert v. City of Topeka (C. C.) 34 Fed. 510; Mason v.
Union Pac. Ry. Co., 7 Utah, 77, 24 Pac. 796. See, also, Robinson v.
Railway Co. [1892] App. Cas. 481; Matz v. Chicago & A. R. Co. (C.
C.) 85 Fed. 180; Kennedy v. Davis, 171 Ala. 609, 55 South. 104;
Perry v. Philadelphia, B. & W. R. Co. (Del.) 77 Atl. 725; Anderson
v. Wetter, 103 Me. 257, 69 Atl. 105, 15 L. R. A. (N. S.) 1003; Osteen
v. Southern Ry., Carolina Division, 76 S. C. 368, 57 S. E. 196; Beavers' Adm'x v. Putnam's Curator, 110 Va. 713, 67 S. E. 353; Quinn
v. Chicago, M. & St. P. Ry. Co., 141 Wis. 497, 124 N. W. 653.
[4] 10 App. Cas. 59.

(30)

These various statutes differ greatly in the language in which they are expressed, both from the English act and from each other, even in respect to the three features which have been called the "distinguishing features" of the action created by Lord Campbell's act. For example, in some statutes it is not expressly provided that the act, neglect, or default must be such as would have entitled the party injured to maintain an action; in others it is not expressly provided that the action is for the benefit of particular members of the family; and in others it is not expressly provided that the damages recoverable are such as result from the death. It is believed, however, that in all these statutes there is, in effect, no substantial difference in these respects. On the other hand, in matters which are not distinguishing features of the action created by Lord Campbell's act, these statutes differ greatly from that act, and from each other. These differences are mainly in respect (1) to the particular members of the family for whose benefit action may be brought; (2) the persons in whose names it may be brought; (3) the time within which it may be brought; (4) the manner of distribution; and (5) in respect to practice. They differ also materially in their provisions concerning (6) the measure of damages; some fixing one amount, some another, and some none at all, as the limit of recovery; and a few providing for the recovery, also, of exemplary or punitive damages, or containing other peculiar provisions.

§ 25. Statutes giving damages resulting from the death to the estate

Alaska, Arizona, Iowa, Kentucky, Oregon, and Washington have not been included with the states having statutes similar to Lord Campbell's act, for the reason that the acts

(31)

of these states, as construed by the courts, provide for a recovery, not for the benefit of the family, but for the benefit of the estate. Moreover, in Iowa the statute in terms provides that the right of action of the party injured shall survive.

North Carolina, Virginia, and West Virginia have not been included, for the reason that in these states it is held, for different reasons, that the action is maintainable notwithstanding that there may be in existence no one of the relatives for whose benefit the action is primarily given.

In their other features, however, the statutes of these states substantially resemble those of the states included in the preceding group.

§ 26. Statutes providing for survival of right of action of party injured

Connecticut, Iowa, New Hampshire, and Tennessee, instead of in terms creating a new right of action, provide that the right of action of the party injured shall survive. In different ways, however, the statutes of these states provide for the recovery of damages resulting from the death, and indirectly accomplish nearly the same result as do those statutes which expressly create a new cause of action.

In many states in which statutes similar to Lord Campbell's act exist, it is now also enacted that actions for injuries to the person shall survive.

§ 27. Georgia

In Georgia the measure of damages is arbitrarily fixed at the full value of the life, without deducting the expenses of the deceased had he lived.

§ 28. Statutes granting remedy by indictment

Remedy by indictment also exists, with other remedies, in Massachusetts, and formerly existed in Maine and in New Hampshire.

§ 29. Massachusetts

In Massachusetts, besides the remedy by indictment, various actions may be maintained, in different cases, by the executor or administrator, for the benefit of the widow or children or heirs. The provisions of the Massachusetts statutes are various and complicated, and are in most respects totally unlike those of the other states. They require separate consideration.

§ 30. Statutes granting additional remedies

Many of the states and territories provide for still other actions which may be maintained in certain cases for causing death. Thus, in Alabama, California, Colorado, Florida, Idaho, Indiana, Iowa, Montana, Oregon, Utah, and Washington, a special action may be maintained by the parent for the death of a child. In Colorado, Missouri, and New Mexico, if the death is caused by the negligence of a railroad company or common carrier, under certain circumstances, the defendant is liable to a forfeiture, to be recovered in a civil action. In Kentucky and Washington, an action is given where a person is killed in a duel; and in Kentucky another action is given where a person is killed by the careless use of firearms. In Illinois, Missouri, and Pennsylvania, an action may be maintained, in case of loss of life, by reason of willful failure to comply with the provisions of acts regulating the operation of mines. These various provisions will be considered in their proper connection. All the statutes in force in the United States, together with those of England, are contained in the appendix.

§ 31. Constitutionality of statutes

In some states the right of action for death is secured or regulated by constitutional provisions. In New York [5] and Utah it is provided that the right of action to recover damages for injuries resulting in death shall never be abrogated, and the amount recoverable shall not be subject to any statutory limitations. Provisions somewhat similar, varying in some particulars, are found in the constitutions of Arkansas, Kentucky, Oklahoma, Pennsylvania, Texas and Wyoming. In Mississippi and Oklahoma the constitutions make certain changes in the common law of master and servant with reference to actions for personal injuries and for death. In most states, however, the constitutions are silent upon the subject, and the constitutionality of the various acts which give a remedy in case of death has rarely

[5] Const. 1895, art. 1, § 18, which provides that "the right of action now existing to recover damages for injuries resulting in death shall never be abrogated, and the amount recoverable shall never be subject to any statutory limitation" does not authorize recovery of any except actual damages in excess of the limit which theretofore prevailed. Medinger v. Brooklyn Heights R. Co., 6 App. Div. 42, 39 N. Y. Supp. 613. The death, and not the injury from which the death resulted, is the cause of action, and, where the death occurred after the constitution of 1895 had removed the limitation on the amount recoverable, an action to recover damages therefor is within the constitutional provision, though the injury from which death resulted was sustained before it went into effect. Smith v. Metropolitan St. Ry. Co., 15 Misc. Rep. 158, 35 N. Y. Supp. 1062. "The right of action now existing" was originally conferred by statute, and has been continued by Code Civ. Proc. § 1902. Held, that the require-

been questioned.[6] Such an act does not impair the obligation of the contract entered into between the state and a previously chartered corporation, the act imposing no new duties, and simply giving a new remedy for the breach of an acknowledged obligation.[7] Even when the act is made to apply exclusively to railroad corporations, it is not open to exception on that account.[8] This objection was considered by the court in passing upon the constitutionality of the former New Hampshire act, which gave a remedy by indictment, but solely against the proprietors of railroads. "This law," says Bell, J., "applies to a class, well defined, of common carriers, distinguished by the circumstance that they use, in their business, steam locomotives, * * * and attended with risks peculiar to themselves, and far exceeding those of other carriers. The same reason for this provision does not apply to any other class of persons, and

ment of Laws 1902, c. 600, p. 1748, that notice of the injury to an employé shall be given to the employer before suit, did not take away the right of action or abrogate it, and the act was not unconstitutional. Judgment, 80 App. Div. 541, 80 N. Y. Supp. 705, affirmed on rehearing. Gmaehle v. Rosenberg, 83 App. Div. 339, 82 N. Y. Supp. 366. Const. 1895, art. 1, § 18, is prospective only, and does not affect the amount of damages recoverable for a death occurring before adoption of the constitution, which amount was then limited to $5,000. O'Reilly v. Utah, N. & C. Stage Co., 87 Hun, 406, 34 N. Y. Supp. 358. But see, Isola v. Weber, 13 Misc. Rep. 97, 34 N. Y. Supp. 77.

[6] See James v. Emmet Mining Co., 55 Mich. 335, 21 N. W. 361.

[7] Boston, C. & M. R. Co. v. State, 32 N. H. 215; Southwestern R. Co. v. Paulk, 24 Ga. 356; Board of Internal Improvement of Shelby County v. Scearce, 2 Duv. (Ky.) 576. See Georgia R. & Banking Co. v. Oaks, 52 Ga. 410.

[8] Boston, C. & M. R. Co. v. State, supra. But under Const. Ala. art. 14, § 12, providing that "all corporations shall have the right to sue, and shall be subject to be sued, in all courts, in like cases as natural persons," etc., section 2899 of the Code of 1876, which gave an action exclusively against incorporated companies and private associations, was held unconstitutional. Smith v. Louisville & N. R. Co., 75 Ala. 449.

(35)

we think the law is free from just exception on this account." [9]   And a Kentucky case has held that a provision which gave a right of action to the representatives of one who should lose his life through the negligence of the operators of a railroad was not in violation of the fourteenth amendment to the constitution of the United States, which declares that no state shall deny to any person within its jurisdiction the equal protection of the laws, and also was not in violation of the provisions of the state bill of rights which guarantees equal rights to all persons under the law, and the impartial administration of justice.[10]   It has also been held in Missouri that a provision which authorizes the recovery of the fixed sum of $5,000 in case of death occasioned by the negligence of certain classes of carriers was not in violation of the same provision of the fourteenth amendment, in authorizing a judgment against such defendant as one of a special class.   The same provision of the Missouri statute was held not to be in violation of the seventh amendment to the constitution of the United States, as arbitrarily liquidating damages without a trial by jury as to the amount.[11]

In Kentucky the act entitled "An act for the redress of injuries arising from the neglect or misconduct of railroad companies or others," which gave a right of action for death against railroad companies in case of negligence, and against all persons in case of willful neglect, was held not to be in conflict with an article of the constitution that no law shall relate to more than one subject, which shall be expressed in the title.[12]

[9] Boston, C. & M. R. Co. v. State, supra.

[10] Schoolcraft's Adm'r v. Louisville & N. R. Co., 92 Ky. 233, 17 S. W. 567, 14 L. R. A. 579.

[11] Carroll v. Missouri Pac. Ry. Co., 88 Mo. 239, 57 Am. Rep. 382.

[12] Chiles v. Drake, 2 Metc. (Ky.) 146, 74 Am. Dec. 406.

Such statutes, although they apply to persons engaged in interstate commerce, and to marine torts occurring upon the navigable waters of the United States, within the limits of the states by which they are enacted, do not constitute an encroachment upon the commercial power of congress.[13]

§ 31—1. Amendment or Repeal of Statutes

Where a right of action has accrued under a statute giving a remedy in case of death, a constitutional provision against retroactive legislation has been held to operate to preserve the right, notwithstanding the repeal of the statute,[14] as well as to exclude the persons entitled to such a right of action from the benefit of an amendment authorizing the recovery of damages additional to those previously allowed.[15] If a cause of action has accrued, it is not affected by a subsequent change in the law.[16] It seems, how-

[13] Sherlock v. Alling, 93 U. S. 99, 23 L. Ed. 819. See § 199.

[14] Denver, S. P. & P. Ry. Co. v. Woodward, 4 Colo. 162; Lundin v. Kansas Pac. Ry. Co., 4 Colo. 433.

[15] Chicago, St. L. & N. O. R. Co. v. Pounds, 11 Lea (Tenn.) 130.

[16] An amendment, declaring who can recover, does not apply to a cause of action arising before the amendment was adopted. Nohrden v. Northeastern R. Co., 54 S. C. 492, 32 S. E. 524. Pub. Acts 1905, p. 120, No. 89, providing that in all actions for negligent injury to persons "hereafter" prosecuted by the executor or administrator, under the statute declaring that such action shall survive, the measure of damages shall be fair and just compensation for the pecuniary injury, etc., applies only to actions begun after the act took effect. Davis v. Michigan Cent. R. Co., 147 Mich. 479, 111 N. W. 76. See, also, Little v. Bousfield & Co., 154 Mich. 369, 117 N. W. 903; Norblad v. Minneapolis, St. P. & S. S. M. Ry. Co., 156 Mich. 697, 118 N. W. 595. The repeal, pending an action brought under the survival act (Pub. Acts 1905, p. 120, No. 89), did not affect pending actions, and hence did not authorize plaintiff to recover damages under the law as it

ever, that the right of action, although it does not come into existence until the death of the person injured, is to be determined by the law in force at the time of the injury. Thus in Wisconsin it was held that an amendment adding collateral relatives to the classes of persons for whose benefit action might be brought did not give such persons a right of action for death from an injury occurring before the amendment went into effect. "All rights of action for the death of a person," said the court, "must depend upon the status as regards the law at the time of the injury, for it is then that the remedial right, as against the wrongdoer, must exist and its violation commence, in contemplation of the statute, in order that the final event terminating the possibility of pecuniary benefits accruing to the statutory beneficiary by a continuance of the life may constitute a remedial wrong." [17] On the other hand, under a survival statute, in New Hampshire, it was held that the right of the administrator to prosecute an action for personal injuries suffered by the intestate is to be determined by the statute in force at his death.[18]

---

existed before the enactment of the statute. Walker v. Lansing & Suburban Traction Co., 156 Mich. 514, 121 N. W. 271. The amendment of 1903 (Laws 1903, p. 217), providing that "no action shall be brought or prosecuted in this state to recover damages for a death occurring outside of this state," is not retrospective in its operation. Brennan v. Electrical Installation Co., 120 Ill. App. 461.

[17] Quinn v. Chicago, M. & St. P. Ry. Co., 141 Wis. 497, 124 N. W. 653. See, also, Henderson v. Terminal R. Ass'n of St. Louis, 154 Mo. App. 174, 133 S. W. 151.

[18] Piper v. Boston & M. R., 75 N. H. 435, 75 Atl. 1041.

(38)

§ 32.   Liberal or strict construction of statutes

The cases contain many conflicting dicta as to whether these statutes are to be liberally or strictly construed. On the one hand, it is said that they are remedial, and should consequently receive a liberal construction;[19] and, on the other hand, it is said that they are in derogation of the common law, and should consequently receive a strict construction.[20] In Kentucky it has been said that the first section of the former act, being entirely remedial, should be construed liberally; but that the third section, which allowed punitive damages, was chiefly penal, and should be interpreted more strictly.[21]

[19] Merkle v. Bennington Tp., 58 Mich. 156, 24 N. W. 776, 55 Am. Rep. 666; Haggerty v. Central R. Co., 31 N. J. Law, 349; Bolinger v. St. Paul & D. R. Co., 36 Minn. 418, 31 N. W. 856, 1 Am. St. Rep. 680; Wabash, St. L. & P. Ry. Co. v. Shacklett, 10 Ill. App. 404; Hayes v. Williams, 17 Colo. 465, 30 Pac. 352; Beach v. Bay State Co., 6 Abb. Prac. (N. Y.) 415, 16 How. Prac. 1, 27 Barb. 248; Soule v. New York & N. H. R. Co., 24 Conn. 575; Lamphear v. Buckingham, 33 Conn. 237. See, also, Hunt v. Conner, 26 Ind. App. 41, 59 N. E. 50 (but see L. T. Dickason Coal Co. v. Liddil [Ind. App.] 94 N. E. 411); Farmers' & Mechanics' Nat. Bank v. Hanks (Tex.) 137 S. W. 1120, reversing judgment (Civ. App.) 128 S. W. 147.

[20] Pittsburgh, C. & St. L. Ry. Co. v. Hine, 25 Ohio St. 629; Hamilton v. Jones, 125 Ind. 176, 25 N. E. 192 (see Burns v. Grand Rapids & I. R. Co., 113 Ind. 169, 15 N. E. 230); Jackson v. St. Louis, I. M. & S. Ry. Co., 87 Mo. 422, 56 Am. Rep. 460; Daly v. Stoddard, 66 Ga. 145 (statute giving a right of action for homicide). See Eustace v. Jahns, 38 Cal. 3. See, also, Bowen v. Illinois Cent. R. Co., 136 Fed. 306, 69 C. C. A. 444, 70 L. R. A. 915; Smith v. Louisville & N. R. Co., 75 Ala. 449; Chicago Bridge & Iron Co. v. La Mantia, 112 Ill. App. 43; Vaughan v. Dalton-Lard Lumber Co., 119 La. 61, 43 South. 926; Clark v. Kansas City, St. L. & C. R. Co., 219 Mo. 524, 118 S. W. 40 (cf. Boyd v. Missouri Pac. Ry. Co., 236 Mo. 54, 139 S. W. 561).

[21] Board of Internal Improvement of Shelby County v. Scearce, 2 Duv. (Ky.) 576.

§ 33. Analytical table

The analytical table of the statutes has been prepared as a ready means of ascertaining what states have statutory provisions upon a given subject similar to those which may be under consideration, and thereby as a guide to the decisions in which such provisions may have been construed.[22]

[22] See preface.

(40)

CHAPTER III

THE STATUTES (WHEN ACTION LIES)

§ 34. Peculiar provisions

Many of the statutes in force in the United States contain peculiar provisions which cannot conveniently be considered in the general treatment of the subjects to which they relate. So far as these peculiar provisions relate to the circumstances under which an action can be maintained, they will be considered in the present chapter. The statutes of some of the newer states and of the territories have not yet been construed by the courts, and so far as this is the case no discussion of these statutes will be attempted, and the reader is referred to the analytical table and to the appendix for information.

§ 35. Alabama

Code 1907, § 2486,[1] gives to the personal representative a right of action for wrongful act, omission, or negligence,

---

[1] A personal representative may maintain action for death of servant, caused by negligence of master. Mobile, J. & K. C. R. Co. v. Bromberg, 141 Ala. 258, 37 South. 395. The personal representative

(42)

whereby the death of the testator or intestate was caused, if the testator or intestate might have maintained an action. The employés' act (sections 3910–3913) enlarges the liability of employer to employé in certain cases, and provides that an action may be maintained under it both by the party injured and by his personal representative if the injury results in death. In addition to the right of action given by these sections to the personal representative, a right of action is by section 2485 given to the father or mother, and, under some circumstances, to the personal representative when the death of a minor child is caused by wrongful act, omission, or negligence. The right of action under section 2485 is not restricted in express terms to cases where the party injured could have maintained an action, and it has been held [2] that no such limitation will be

---

being given right, by Code 1907, §§ 2486, 3912, to sue only for acts and omissions causing death of intestate, and not for those merely causing pain and suffering, counts of an administrator's complaint, merely averring that certain acts or omissions aggravated or intensified decedent's pain and suffering, are demurrable; such cause of action not surviving, and a suit for such matters not being maintainable by the administrator. Whitmore v. Alabama Consol. Coal & Iron Co., 164 Ala. 125, 51 South. 397, 137 Am. St. Rep. 31. See Buckalew v. Tennessee Coal, I. & R. Co., 112 Ala. 146, 20 South. 606. Negligence may result from omission respecting duty. An "act" or "wrongful act" denotes affirmative action or performance, and an expression of will or purpose as distinguished from "omission" or "wrongful omission," which denotes a negative and inaction. Randle v. Birmingham Ry., Light & Power Co., 169 Ala. 314, 53 South. 918.

[2] Williams v. South & N. A. R. Co., 91 Ala. 635, 9 South. 77. The fact that a minor's death was caused by his fellow servant is a defense in an action against his employer under this section. Harris v. McNamara, 97 Ala. 181, 12 South. 103. In an action by a father, contributory negligence on his part precludes a recovery, unless it is overcome by more than simple negligence of defendant. Alabama G. S. R. Co. v. Dobbs, 101 Ala. 219, 12 South. 770.

implied, and declares that the father can recover in all
cases where at common law he might have recovered if the
injury had not resulted in death. The case turned upon the
question whether the father consented to the employment
of the minor, the court holding that, if the father did consent, he would be barred by the minor's contributory negligence, but that, if he did not consent, the negligence of
the child would not be imputed to the father. The action
given by the employés' act exists only in favor of the personal representative, and its provisions do not inure to the
benefit of the parent in a suit under section 2485.[3] This
action, as well as that given by section 2486, may be maintained in a court of competent jurisdiction within the state
of Alabama and not elsewhere.

[3] Lovell v. De Bardelaben, C. & I. Co., 90 Ala. 13, 7 South. 756.
See Grimsley v. Hankins (D. C.) 46 Fed. 400. An action under the
employers' act is not governed by the two-year limitation of section
2486, but by the one-year limitation applicable to "actions for injury
to the person or right of another, not arising from contract." O'Kief
v. Memphis & C. R. Co., 99 Ala. 524, 12 South. 454; Louisville & N.
R. Co. v. Chamblee, 171 Ala. 188, 54 South. 681. As no one is authorized to sue under the employers' liability act for injuries resulting in death except the personal representative of deceased (Code,
§ 2591), a suit by a mother for the death of her son is no bar to a
suit by the personal representative on the same cause of action.
Tennessee Coal, I. & R. Co. v. Herndon, 100 Ala. 451, 14 South. 287.
An action by the administrator against the employer of the intestate,
in the absence of imputation of negligence or other wrong to any
fellow servant of intestate, is not brought under the employers' act,
but is to be regarded as brought under section 2486. Northern Alabama Ry. Co. v. Mansell, 138 Ala. 548, 36 South. 459. The right of
the personal representative of an employé to recover for injuries resulting in death in an action against the employer under the homicide act must be determined by the common-law rules, and not by
the employers' liability act. Louisville & N. R. Co. v. Chamblee, 171
Ala. 188, 54 South. 681. Section 3912, providing that the damages
shall be distributed according to the statute of distributions, continues the cause of action which the injured servant had, and does

§ 35—1.   Alaska [4]

§ 35—2   Arizona [5]

§ 35—3.   Arkansas

The constitution (article 5, § 31) provides that no act shall limit the amount to be recovered for injuries resulting in death, or for injuries to persons, and in case of death from such injuries the right of action shall survive, and the general assembly shall prescribe for whose benefit such action shall be prosecuted. Kirby's Dig. § 6285, provides that an action for a wrong done to the person after the death of the person injured may be brought by his executor or administrator. Sections 6289, 6290, provide for an action for death to be brought by the personal representative of deceased, and, if there be none, by the heirs at law, substantially like the action provided for by Lord Campbell's act. It follows that the personal representative of one whose death is caused by wrongful act, neglect, or default may maintain two actions, one under section 6285 for the benefit of the estate, and the other under sections 6289, 6290, for the benefit of the widow and next of kin.[6]

---

not create an entirely new right of action. Williams v. Alabama Great Southern R. Co., 158 Ala. 396, 48 South. 485, 17 Ann. Cas. 516.

[4] See § 81.

[5] See § 81.

[6] Davis v. St. Louis, I. M. & S. Ry. Co., 53 Ark. 117, 13 S. W. 801, 7 L. R. A. 283; St. Louis, I. M. & S. Ry. Co. v. Sweet, 63 Ark. 563, 40 S. W. 463; St. Louis, I. M. & S. Ry. Co. v. Corman, 92 Ark. 102, 122 S. W. 116; Murphy v. St. Louis, I. M. & S. R. Co., 92 Ark. 159, 122 S. W. 636. See Kansas & T. Coal Co. v. Gabsky, 70 Ark. 434, 66 S. W. 915, 72 S. W. 572.

Section 6288 gives the husband the right to maintain an action for the death of his wife.[7]

§ 36. Colorado

The provisions of Rev. St. 1908, §§ 2056–2059, are in most respects like those which have existed in Missouri.[8] There is also an employers' liability act, under which an action for death is maintainable.[9]

§ 37. Connecticut [10]

§ 38. Georgia

Code 1910, § 4424 (Code 1882, § 2971,[11] as amended by Laws 1887, p. 43) [12] provides that a widow, or, if no widow, a child or children, may recover for the homicide of the husband or parent; [13] that the husband may recover for the homicide of his wife; and that, if she leaves child or children surviving, the husband and children shall sue joint-

---

[7] See, also, Kirby's Dig. 1904, § 6287.

[8] See § 45, post.

[9] Sess. Laws 1911, c. 113.

[10] See § 132.

[11] Section 2971 was based on Act Feb. 23, 1850 (Cobb's Digest, p. 476), and Acts 1855–56, p. 155, which were section 2971 in Code 1873, as modified by Act Dec. 16, 1878. See Mott v. Central R. R., 70 Ga. 680, 48 Am. Rep. 595.

[12] The amendatory act is not unconstitutional, as containing more than one subject-matter, or in usurping a judicial function (by defining "full value of the life"), or as a special act. Clay v. Central R. & B. Co., 84 Ga. 345, 10 S. E. 967.

[13] A child has no right of action for the homicide of its stepfather. Marshall v. Macon Sash Door & Lumber Co., 103 Ga. 725, 30 S. E. 571, 41 L. R. A. 211, 68 Am. St. Rep. 140.

ly,[14] with the right of survivorship in the action; and that a mother, or, if no mother, a father,[15] may recover for the homicide of a child, minor or sui juris, upon whom he or she is dependent, or who contributes to his or her support, unless said child leave a wife, husband, or child. The amendment enacts that the word "homicide" "shall be held to include all cases where the death of a human being results from a crime, or from criminal or other negligence."

Before the amendment, this section provided simply that "a widow, or, if no widow, a child or children, may recover for the homicide of a husband or parent." It was held, therefore, before the amendment, that no action could be maintained for the homicide of a wife [16] or child,[17] though, in accordance with Shields v. Yonge,[18] a common-law action was maintainable by a parent, based upon the loss of service of a child whose death had been caused by the defendant.[19] A recovery could be had by a minor child for

[14] Children, though adults, are necessary parties. Roberts v. Central of Georgia R. Co. (C. C.) 124 Fed. 471.

[15] A father has no right of action if the mother was in life at the time of the homicide, and if she died without bringing action, no right survived to him. Frazier v. Georgia R. & B. Co., 96 Ga. 785, 22 S. E. 936.

[16] Georgia R. & B. Co. v. Wynn, 42 Ga. 331; Womack v. Central R. & B. Co., 80 Ga. 132, 5 S. E. 63.

[17] Bell v. Wooten, 53 Ga. 684; Allen v. Atlanta Street R. Co., 54 Ga. 503; Bell v. Central R. R., 73 Ga. 520; Smith v. East & West R. Co., 84 Ga. 183, 10 S. E. 602; Perry v. Georgia R. & B. Co., 85 Ga. 193, 11 S. E. 605.

[18] 15 Ga. 349, 60 Am. Dec. 698; ante, § 10.

[19] In Bell v. Wooten, 53 Ga. 684, a father sued defendant for negligently amputating the leg of his son, whereby he died, and a demurrer to the declaration was sustained on the ground that no action lay for the homicide of a child. Warner, C. J., observed that it was not alleged that the son was a minor, or that the father was entitled to his services as such minor, and that consequently the case was not within Shields v. Yonge. In Allen v. Atlanta St. R. Co., 54

the homicide of a mother,[20] but not by an adult child of one who left no widow,[21] nor by a minor child if the father was still alive.[22] Under the amendment, a mother

Ga. 503, the declaration alleged that the child was two years old, and would have become, at an early age, of great value to the plaintiff, to wit, the sum of $3,000 for services to be rendered by the child until his majority. A demurrer was sustained, the court distinguishing the case from Shields v. Yonge on the ground that the child was not old enough to render service. In Chick v. Southwestern R. Co., 57 Ga. 357, the declaration claimed damages for the loss of service of a minor son who died four days after the injury, and alleged the value of the services. It was held that the action was not under section 2971, for the homicide, but was for loss of service; that the right to recover was authorized by Shields v. Yonge; but that the declaration, failing to allege that the plaintiff had complied with section 2970 in respect to prosecuting for a felony, was bad on demurrer. In McDowell v. Georgia R. Co., 60 Ga. 320, it was held that a father might recover damages for the loss of services of his minor daughter, to the time of her majority, sustained by reason of her killing. Followed in Augusta Factory v. Davis, 87 Ga. 648, 13 S. E. 577. See, also, Augusta Ry. Co. v. Glover, 92 Ga. 132, 18 S. E. 406; Atlanta & C. Air Line Ry. Co. v. Gravitt, 93 Ga. 369, 20 S. E. 550, 26 L. R. A. 553, 44 Am. St. Rep. 145. In Bell v. Central R. R., 73 Ga. 520, the declaration, in an action by the father, merely alleged killing by negligence, and it was held that there was no foundation for an amendment setting up loss of service, the court observing that the amendment would have made a good cause of action, but that without it no cause of action was set out. Referring to section 2960, which provides that "every person may recover for the torts committed to himself, or his wife, or his child, or his ward, or his servant," Blandford, J., says that this is but declaratory

[20] Atlanta & W. P. R. Co. v. Venable, 65 Ga. 55; s. c. 67 Ga. 697. "Parent" is held to include either parent on whom the duty of supporting the child was cast by law.

[21] Mott v. Central R. R., 70 Ga. 680, 48 Am. Rep. 595. Under Civ. Code 1895, § 3828, the right of action for the death of a father is, where there is no widow, vested in the minor children of the deceased, and an adult child has no right to institute such suit. Western & A. R. Co. v. Harris, 128 Ga. 394, 57 S. E. 722. See, also, Coleman v. Hyer, 113 Ga. 420, 38 S. E. 962.

[22] Scott v. Central R. R., 77 Ga. 450; Snell v. Smith, 78 Ga. 355.

cannot recover for the homicide of a child who contributed to her support, unless she was dependent upon him,[23] but it is not necessary that she be wholly dependent upon him.[24] Where a widow recovers for the negligent killing

of the common law, and that it must be averred that such torts resulted in loss of service. Smith v. East & West R. Co., 84 Ga. 183, 10 S. E. 602, is to the same effect as Bell v. Central R. R., the court distinguishing the case from East Tennessee, V. & G. R. R. v. Maloy, 77 Ga. 237, 2 S. E. 941, in which the loss of service and the mother's right to the same were alleged, and it was held that the action was maintainable. And in Perry v. Georgia R. & B. Co., 85 Ga. 193, 11 S. E. 605, it was held that, under the law of Georgia in 1886, the parent's only right of action for the negligent killing of a minor child was for the loss of service; and that a declaration which failed to allege loss of service was fatally defective. It seems that the rule of Shields v. Yonge would not be applied in actions by a husband for the loss of his wife's services, except during the interval between the injury and her death. Womack v. Central R. & B. Co., 80 Ga. 132, 5 S. E. 63. And see Georgia, R. & B. Co. v. Wynn, 42 Ga. 331. A mother has a right of action for causing the death of her son, when the father has abandoned his family and all custody and control of the minor. Amos v. Atlanta Ry. Co., 104 Ga. 809, 31 S. E. 42.

23 Clay v. Central R. & B. Co., 84 Ga. 345, 10 S. E. 967. Blandford, J.: "We read the little word 'or' as 'and,' by which we think we have correctly construed the intent of the legislature." See, also, Smith v. Hatcher, 102 Ga. 158, 29 S. E. 162; Augusta Southern R. Co. v. McDade, 105 Ga. 134, 31 S. E. 420; Georgia R. & Banking Co. v. Spinks, 111 Ga. 571, 36 S. E. 855; Trammell v. Southern R. Co., 182 Fed. 789, 105 C. C. A. 221. Cf. Western Union Tel. Co. v. Harris, 6 Ga. App. 260, 64 S. E. 1123. Plaintiff had lost his right to sue for the value of the child's services by voluntarily releasing his parental control and by failing to provide for its maintenance. Southern R. Co. v. Flemister, 120 Ga. 524, 48 S. E. 160.

24 Plaintiff was dependent on her son, on her husband, and on her own labor for support. Her son contributed. Held, that the judge erred in ordering a nonsuit. Daniels v. Savannah, F. & W. Ry. Co., 86 Ga. 236, 12 S. E. 365; Richmond & D. R. Co. v. Johnston, 89 Ga. 560, 15 S. E. 908. Where the declaration fails to allege that plaintiff was dependent, it may be amended. Ellison v. Georgia R. Co., 87 Ga. 691, 13 S. E. 809. See, also, Middle Georgia & A. Ry. Co.

of her husband, his children who were adults at the time
of his death are not entitled to share in the judgment;[25]
but a minor child is entitled to a distributive share, which
may be recovered from the widow, by a legal representative.[26]

This section, before the amendment, contained no definition of "homicide." It was then held that, to authorize
a recovery, it must be made to appear that the homicide
amounted to a crime,[27] although an exception existed in ac-

---

v. Barnett, 104 Ga. 582, 30 S. E. 771; Central of Georgia Ry: Co.
v. Henson, 121 Ga. 462, 49 S. E. 278; Savannah Electric Co. v. Bell,
124 Ga. 663, 53 S: E. 109; Seaboard Air Line Ry. Co. v. Witt, 4 Ga.
App. 149, 60 S. E. 1012; Atlantic Coast Line R. Co. v. McDonald, 135
Ga. 635, 70 S. E. 249; Georgia Ry. & Electric Co. v. Bailey, 9 Ga.
App. 106, 70 S. E. 607. A parent has a right of action for the death
of a minor son, although at the time of his death he was serving a
term in the chain gang, for the violation of a penal law. Amos
v. Atlanta Ry. Co., 104 Ga. 809, 31 S. E. 42. Whether a particular
child 4½ years of age was capable of rendering any valuable service to its father should be left to a jury to determine, in the light
of the evidence. Crawford v. Southern Ry. Co., 106 Ga. 870, 33 S.
E. 826.

25 Coleman v. Hyer, 113 Ga. 420, 38 S. E. 962.

26 Griffith v. Griffith, 128 Ga. 371, 57 S. E. 698.

27 For the unlawful, willful homicide of a husband, whether it be
murder or only voluntary manslaughter, his widow may recover.
Weekes v. Cottingham, 58 Ga. 559. The declaration alleged that the
defendant employed a careless and negligent superintendent to manage a derrick, and careless, incompetent, and negligent laborers,
whereby the plaintiff's husband fell, by want of their care and diligence. Held, that these facts did not amount to criminal negligence.
and did not constitute a cause of action. McDonald v. Eagle & P.
Manuf'g Co., 67 Ga. 761; s. c. 68 Ga. 839. The declaration alleged
that defendants erected and rented a building having a platform as
the only means whereon to move furniture therein, and that the deceased, while endeavoring to move an iron safe into the building, at
the request of certain of defendants' tenants, was killed by the platform giving way, resulting from its defective construction. Held
demurrable, for not showing criminal negligence, as defendants' act

(50)

tions against railroad companies, and such actions were maintainable although the negligence was not criminal.[28] It would seem that the amendment is broad enough to cover all cases of negligence for which a recovery can be had for wrongful death under the statutes of other states.

Section 4421 provides that an action of tort for the recovery of damages for homicide or injury to the person shall not abate by the death of either party; but the cause of action, in case of the death of plaintiff, shall, in the event there is no right of survivorship in any other person, survive to the personal representative of the plaintiff.[29]

§ 38—1. Illinois

Hurd's Rev. St. 1911, c. 70, §§ 1, 2, gives a right of action for death substantially on the lines of Lord Campbell's act.[30] Under chapter 48, § 126 et seq., any employer may elect to provide and pay compensation for injuries sustained

or negligence was not murder, manslaughter, or "involuntary manslaughter." Daly v. Stoddard, 66 Ga. 145; Rankin v. Merchants' & M. T. Co., 73 Ga. 229, 54 Am. Rep. 874; Bain v. Athens F. & M. Works, 75 Ga. 718; Allen v. Augusta Factory, 82 Ga. 76, 8 S. E. 68; Augusta Factory v. Hill, 83 Ga. 709, 10 S. E. 450.

[28] Central R. R. v. Roach, 70 Ga. 434. The reason for this distinction is not clear. In McDonald v. Eagle & P. Manuf'g Co., the court had said that "the liability of railroad companies rests on other grounds."

[29] Where a woman died after suit to recover damages for pain and suffering from personal injuries, her administrator was properly made a party, and the case should not have been nonsuited on the ground that there was a right of survivorship in her husband, under section 4424, authorizing an action by him to recover for the wrongful death of his wife; the only recovery sought being for the pain and suffering of the wife. Stephens v. Columbus R. Co., 134 Ga. 818, 68 S. E. 551.

[30] See, also, § 59.

by an employé, arising out of and in the course of the employment and resulting in death, according to the provisions thereof, and thereby relieve himself from any liability for the recovery of damages, except as therein provided; while if the employer does not so elect, he is liable for such injuries sustained by the employé, and the common law of master and servant is enlarged in favor of the employé. Hurd's Rev. St. 1911, c. 3, § 122, provides that, in addition to the actions which survive at common law, actions to recover damages for injury to the person shall survive. It is held that this enactment is applicable only to cases where death results from some other cause than the injury, and that, if death results from the injury, the only right of action is for the death.[31]

§ 39.   Indiana

Burns' Ann. St. 1908, § 267 (Rev. St. 1881, § 266),[32] provides that a father, or in case of his death, or desertion of

---

[31] Post, § 126.

[32] This section is substantially a re-enactment of Civil Code 1852, § 784 (2 Rev. St. 1876, p. 309), the only material change being that under the former the damages could not exceed $5,000. Stewart v. Terre Haute & I. R. Co., 103 Ind. 44, 2 N. E. 208. Civil Code 1852, § 784, repealed by implication 1 Rev. St. 1852, p. 426, § 3, which gave the action to the wife, etc., of a person killed by the negligence of the officers of a railroad, etc. Peru & I. R. Co. v. Bradshaw, 6 Ind. 146; Madison & I. R. Co. v. Bacon, 6 Ind. 205; Indianapolis & C. R. Co. v. Davis, 10 Ind. 398. This section confers no right upon one who marries the mother of a bastard child and who receives the child as a member of the family to sue for the child's death. Thornburg v. American Strawboard Co., 141 Ind. 443, 40 N. E. 1062, 50 Am. St. Rep. 334. A father may not maintain an action for the death of his bastard child. McDonald v. Pittsburgh, C., C. & St. L. Ry. Co., 144 Ind. 459, 43 N. E. 447, 32 L. R. A. 309, 55 Am. St. Rep. 185. See Louisville, E. & St. L. Consol. R. Co. v. Lohges, 6 Ind. App. 288, 33 N. E. 449.

his family, or imprisonment, the mother, may maintain an action for the injury or death of a child, and a guardian for the injury or death of his ward. Section 285 (Rev. St. 1881, § 284, as amended), provides that, when the death of any one is caused by wrongful act or omission, the personal representative may maintain an action, for the benefit of the widow or widower and children, if any, or next of kin, if the party injured, had he lived, might have maintained an action.[33]

It was formerly held that these sections must be construed together, and that while the former applied to infants, and the latter to adults, the father or mother in the one case, as the personal representative in the other, could sue only in a representative capacity.[34] But this construc-

---

[33] An administrator is a "personal representative," though deceased died without assets and right of action inures to the benefit of the widow and children. Toledo, St. L. & K. C. R. Co. v. Reeves, 8 Ind. App. 667, 35 N. E. 199. This section recognizes two classes of beneficiaries, the widow or widower and children and next of kin; and, if there are persons of the first class entitled to damages, they will take exclusively, and grandchildren are not "children," but come within the second class, and may take as beneficiaries if there are none of the first class, nor are minor children "next of kin," though they are in fact decedent's next of kin   Pittsburg, C., C. & St. L. Ry. Co. v. Reed, 44 Ind. App. 635, 88 N. E. 1080. See Baltimore & O. R. Co. v. Ray, 36 Ind. App. 430, 73 N. E. 942. The section creates two distinct classes, and the first, composed of the widow or widower and children, take to the exclusion of the next of kin; so where decedent left a widow, but no children, and a mother dependent on him, the mother was not entitled to share. Leyhan v. Leyhan, 47 Ind. App. 280, 94 N. E. 337. "Next of kin" include a person entitled to inherit personal property of decedent, and the mother of an illegitimate child and his half-brothers are included. L. T. Dickason Coal Co. v. Liddil (Ind. App.) 94 N. E. 411.

[34] An action for causing the death of a child cannot be brought by the administrator. Pittsburgh, F. W. & C. Ry. Co. v. Vining's Adm'r, 27 Ind. 513, 92 Am. Dec. 269. The court said that the sections must be construed together; that, if there were neither father,

(53)

tion was repudiated in Mayhew v. Burns.[35] In that case
the father sued to recover damages for the loss of the services and society of his child from the time of his death
until he should have attained his majority, and it was held
that the action could be maintained. The court said: "The
reasonable and natural interpretation of the language employed in the first section is to give the parent who sustains injury by the death of his child a remedy for such
injury in his own right, while the latter gives to the widow
or next of kin, through the personal representative, a right
to recover for any injury which they may have sustained
by reason of the death of an adult, or one emancipated

mother, nor guardian, the administrator would be the proper plaintiff; and that in either case the limitation of the action, the amount
of recovery, and the distribution would be governed by section 784.
In Cincinnati, H. & D. R. Co. v. Chester, 57 Ind. 297, it was held
that an action by the father to recover damages for the death of
a minor child could not be joined with an action by him to recover
for personal injuries received by himself, and caused by the same
wrongful act, since, in the first action, he sued in a representative
capacity. In Gann v. Worman, 69 Ind. 458, it was held that by the
construction of the two sections, when taken together, the father
could not maintain the action in his own right, but only as the representative of his child's right. It was said in that case that "there
is no statute in this state giving the father the right of action for
the lost services of his child after the child's death."

[35] 103 Ind. 328, 2 N. E. 793, approved in Ft. Wayne, C. & L. R. Co.
v. Beyerle, 110 Ind. 100, 11 N. E. 6. In the latter case it was held
that there could be no recovery against the defendant for causing
the son's death, he having been guilty of contributory negligence;
but that the defendant, having knowingly employed the infant without the father's consent, was liable by the common law for the value
of the son's services up to the time of his death. In Louisville, N.
A. & C. Ry. Co. v. Goodykoontz, 119 Ind. 111, 21 N. E. 472, 12 Am.
St. Rep. 371, Mitchell, J., said: "Section 284 [285] * * * is entirely disconnected from section 266 [267], and exerts no sort of influence upon the construction of or right conferred under the latter
section."

(54)

from parental service,[36] and in whose life they may have had a pecuniary interest. * * * In our view, both the common-law and statutory damages may be recovered under that section,[37] * * * and, when recovered, they belong to the parent in his own right, and are not distribu_ table under section 285 (284). During the continuance of the relation of parent and child, the right of action is in the parent entitled to its service. This relation presumptively continues during the minority of the child. If the relation does not exist, then the action is to be brought by the per- sonal representative, regardless of the age of the person whose death has been caused, provided there are persons sustaining such relation to it as that they may be supposed to have sustained pecuniary injury on account of its death. If the relation of parent and child continues after majority, the parent receiving the support or service may, neverthe- less, maintain the action." The right of action of the guardian under section 267 is limited to the recovery of damages to reimburse the personal estate of the ward for any actual loss.[38]

An employers' liability act was enacted in 1911.[39]

---

[36] Unless a minor has been emancipated, the father cannot, instead of suing under section 267, sue as administrator under section 285. Berry v. Louisville, E. & St. L. R. Co., 128 Ind. 182, 28 N. E. 182.

[37] The measure of damages under section 267 is the value of the child's services from the time of the injury until majority, taken in connection with his prospects in life, less· his support and mainte- nance. To this may be added in proper cases the expense of care, attendance, funeral expenses, and medical services. Pennsylvania Co. v. Lilly, 73 Ind. 252. See Baltimore & O. S. W. R. Co. v. Brad- ford, 20 Ind. App. 348, 49 N. E. 388, 67 Am. St. Rep. 252.

[38] Where a minor is instantly killed, and has a mother living, and it does not appear that the guardian paid from the ward's estate

---

[39] Acts 1911, c. 88. For miners' act, see § 59, post. See Pitts- burgh, C., C. & St. L. Ry. Co. v. Hosea, 152 Ind. 412, 53 N. E. 419.

§ 40. Iowa

Code 1897, § 3443, provides that all causes of action shall survive, and may be brought notwithstanding the death of the person entitled to the same; section 3444 provides that the right of civil remedy is not merged in the public offense; section 3445 provides that the action contemplated in the last two sections may be brought or continued by the legal representative of the deceased, and shall be deemed a continuing one, and to have accrued to the representative at the same time it did to the deceased if he had survived; and section 3313 provides that, when a wrongful act produces death, the damages shall be disposed of as personal property belonging to the estate, except that, if the deceased leaves a husband, wife, child, or parent, it shall not be liable for the payment of debts. It is held that the effect of these provisions is to give the representative an action for death for the benefit of the estate.[40] Section 3471 provides that "a father, or in case of

for the funeral expenses, no suit lies by the guardian under section 267. Louisville, N. A. & C. Ry. Co. v. Goodykoontz, 119 Ind. 111, 21 N. E. 472, 12 Am. St. Rep. 371.

[40] Conners v. Burlington, C. R. & N. Ry. Co., 71 Iowa, 490, 32 N. W. 465, 60 Am. Rep. 814; Worden v. Humeston & S. R. Co., 72 Iowa, 201, 33 N. W. 629. In Conners v. Burlington, C. R. & N. Ry. Co., Reed, J., observed: "For many years before the enactment of the present Code, a statute was in force in this state which provided, in express terms, that, 'when a wrongful act produces death, the perpetrator is civilly liable for the injury.' Revision 1860, § 4111; Code 1851, § 2501. When the present Code was enacted, the section in which the provision was contained was repealed, and the sections quoted above were enacted in lieu thereof. As appears, the language of this provision is not contained in any of them. But we think the effect of these provisions is the same as though that express language had been retained." The court goes on to say that the common-law rule that in a civil court the death of a human being could

his death or imprisonment, or desertion of his family, the mother, may as plaintiff maintain an action for the expenses and loss of service resulting from the injury or death of a minor child." For the death of a minor two actions may be maintained—one, under section 3445, to recover damages to his estate accruing after the infant should have attained his majority; and one by the father or mother, under section 3471, to recover damages for the loss of his services until his majority.[41]

§ 40—1. Kansas

The statutes confer a right of action for death, substantially like that created by Lord Campbell's act, and also enact that, in addition to the causes of action which survive at common law, causes of action for an injury to the person shall also survive, and that the action may be brought notwithstanding the death of the person entitled

not be complained of as an injury was founded (1) on the merger of the civil remedy in the public offense; and (2) on the rule of actio personalis. Both of these rules, the court holds, are abrogated by the statute. Sections 3443, 3444, construed in connection with section 3445, confer the right to sue for the wrongful killing of a person exclusively upon the personal representative, and hence do not create any cause of action in favor of the wife or children of the deceased, though they may share in the damages recovered, freed from any claim of creditors, as provided in section 3313. Major v. Burlington, C. R. & N. Ry. Co., 115 Iowa, 309, 88 N. W. 815. The widow of a testator, whose death was instantaneous and caused by the wrongful act of another, is entitled to receive, as sole beneficiary of testator's will, moneys collected by her as executrix as damages for testator's wrongful death, to the exclusion of testator's children. In re Cook's Estate, 126 Iowa, 158, 101 N. W. 747.

[41] Walters v. Chicago, R. I. & P. R. Co., 36 Iowa, 458; Lawrence v. Birney, 40 Iowa, 377; Walters v. Chicago, R. I. & P. R. Co., 41 Iowa, 71; Benton v. Chicago, R. I. & P. R. Co., 55 Iowa, 496, 8 N. W. 330; Morris v. Chicago, M. & St. P. Ry. Co. (C. C.) 26 Fed. 22.

or liable to the same.[42] It is held that the survival act is applicable only to cases where death results from some other cause than the injury, so that if death results from the injury the only right of action is for the death.[43]

§ 41. Kentucky

(a) General death act

Const. § 241,[44] adopted in 1891, provides: "Whenever the death of a person shall result from an injury inflicted by negligence or wrongful act, then, in every such case, damages may be recovered for such death, from the corporations and persons so causing the same. Until otherwise provided by law, the action to recover such damages shall in all cases be prosecuted by the personal representative of the deceased person. The general assembly may provide how the recovery shall go and to whom belong; and until such provision is made the same shall form part of the personal estate of the deceased person." [45] Under this provision the legislature passed an act, now St. 1909, § 6, as follows: "Whenever the death of a person shall result from an injury inflicted by negligence or wrongful act, then in

[42] See Appendix.   [43] Post, § 126·

[44] Const. § 54, provides that the general assembly shall have no power to limit the amount to be recovered for injuries resulting in death, or for injuries.

[45] As to the reason for adopting this provision, see Passamaneck v. Louisville Ry. Co., 98 Ky. 195, 32 S. W. 620, 17 Ky. Law Rep. 763. As to the effect of this provision before the enactment of legislation, see Thomas' Adm'r v. Royster, 98 Ky. 206, 32 S. W. 613, 17 Ky. Law Rep. 783; Lexington & Carter County Min. Co. v. Huffman's Adm'r, 32 S. W. 611, 17 Ky. Law Rep. 775; East Tennessee Tel. Co. v. Simms' Adm'r, 99 Ky. 404, 36 S. W. 171, 18 Ky. Law Rep. 761.

every such case, damages may be recovered for such death from the persons or person, company or companies, corporation or corporations, their agents or servants causing the same,[46] and when the act is willful or the negligence is gross, punitive damages may be recovered, and the action to recover such damages shall be prosecuted by the personal representative of the deceased. The amount recovered, less funeral expenses and the costs of administration, and such costs about the recovery, including attorney's fees as are not included in the recovery from the defendant, shall be for the benefit of and go to the kindred of the deceased in the following order, viz.: (1) If the deceased leaves a widow or husband, and no children or their descendants, then the whole to such widow or husband. (2) If the deceased leaves either a widow and children or a husband and children, then one-half to such widow or husband and the other one-half to the children of the deceased. (3) If the deceased leaves a child or children, but no widow or husband, then the whole to such child or children. If the deceased leaves no widow, husband or child, then such recovery shall pass to the mother and father of deceased, one moiety each, if both be living; if the mother be dead and the father be living, the

---

[46] A corporation and its servant may be sued jointly for a death resulting from the negligence of the servant. Cincinnati, N. O. & T. P. Ry. Co. v. Cook's Adm'r, 113 Ky. 161, 67 S. W. 383, 23 Ky. Law Rep. 2410. See, also, Winston's Adm'r v. Illinois Cent. R. Co., 111 Ky. 954, 65 S. W. 13, 23 Ky. Law Rep. 1283, 55 L. R. A. 603. This section did not confer a right of action against a municipal corporation for the death of a person occurring as the result of an act done in the performance of a governmental function in removing and caring for such person, who was suffering from smallpox, at the pesthouse. Twyman's Adm'r v. Board of Councilmen of Frankfort, 117 Ky. 518, 78 S. W. 446, 25 Ky. Law Rep. 1620, 64 L. R. A. 572, 4 Ann. Cas. 622.

whole thereof shall pass to the father; and if the father
be dead and the mother living, the whole thereof shall go
to the mother; and if both father and mother be dead,
then the whole of the recovery shall become a part of the
personal estate of the deceased; and after the payment of
his debts, the remainder, if any, shall pass to his kindred
more remote than those above named, as is directed by the
general law on descent and distribution."

Before this constitutional provision was adopted, the
words "wrongful act" had no place in the statutes relating
to actions for death,[47] which were unlike those to be
found in any other state. The adoption of the constitutional provision did not have the effect of repealing the
prior legislation,[48] but the above enactment did repeal Gen.
St. 1888, c. 57, § 3, which gave a remedy for the loss or
destruction of life by "willful neglect" and authorized the
recovery of punitive damages therefor,[49] and no right of
action for "willful neglect" now exists. Under Gen. St.
1888, c. 57, § 3, the contributory negligence of the dece-

[47] Clark's Adm'x v. Louisville & N. R. Co., 101 Ky. 34, 39 S. W. 840,
18 Ky. Law Rep. 1082, 36 L. R. A. 123. Section 6 is remedial, and
should be liberally construed to effect its object, and is applicable
to an injury inflicted by an overt act as well as to those resulting
from the neglect of a legal duty. Randolph's Adm'r v. Snyder, 139
Ky. 159, 129 S. W. 562. One who unlawfully sold intoxicants to decedent, drinking of which caused his death, is not liable as for
wrongful death, under section 6, unless the sale was made to injure
decedent or with knowledge that he intended to drink to such extent
as to produce injury or death, or unless the seller had reasonable
grounds to believe that decedent could not be safely trusted with the
liquor. Britton's Adm'r v. Samuels, 143 Ky. 129, 136 S. W. 143, 34
L. R. A. (N. S.) 1036.

[48] Wright v. Woods' Adm'r, 96 Ky. 56, 27 S. W. 979, 16 Ky. Law
Rep. 337.

[49] Clark's Adm'x v. Louisville & N. R. Co., supra.

dent was not available as a defense,[50] but it is a defense under St. 1909, § 6, even if the death results from gross negligence.[51] There may be, of course, a recovery where death is caused by ordinary negligence.[52] There can be no recovery against a master for the death of a servant caused by the negligence of a fellow servant, even if the negligence be gross;[53] but if the negligence be that of a superior servant there may be a recovery, even if the negligence be ordinary.[54]

[50] See Eskridge's Ex'rs v. Cincinnati, N. O. & T. P. Ry. Co., 89 Ky. 367, 12 S. W. 580, 11 Ky. Law Rep. 557; Union Warehouse Co. v. Prewitt's Adm'r, 50 S. W. 964, 21 Ky. Law Rep. 67.

[51] Clark's Adm'x v. Louisville & N. R. Co., 101 Ky. 34, 39 S. W. 840, 18 Ky. Law Rep. 1082, 36 L. R. A. 123; Smith's Adm'r v. National Coal & Iron Co., 135 Ky. 671, 117 S. W. 280. Contributory negligence is a good defense, if it be of such a character that death would not have occurred except for it. Cincinnati, N. O. & T. P. Ry. Co. v. Lovell's Adm'r, 141 Ky. 249, 132 S. W. 569, 142 Ky. 1, 133 S. W. 788. Const. § 241, does not deny the right to rely on contributory negligence as a defense. Passamaneck v. Louisville Ry. Co., 98 Ky. 195, 32 S. W. 620, 17 Ky. Law Rep. 763. See, also, Singleton v. Felton, 101 Fed. 526, 42 C. C. A. 57; Illinois Cent. R. Co. v. O'Neill, 177 Fed. 328, 100 C. C. A. 658.

[52] Southern Ry. Co. in Kentucky v. Otis' Adm'r, 78 S. W. 480, 25 Ky. Law Rep. 1686; Cincinnati, N. O. & T. P. Ry. Co. v. Evans' Adm'r, 129 Ky. 152, 110 S. W. 844, 33 Ky. Law Rep. 596; Louisville & N. R. Co. v. Stewart's Adm'x, 131 Ky. 665, 115 S. W. 775. See, also, Lexington & Carter County Min. Co. v. Stephens' Adm'r, 104 Ky. 502, 47 S. W. 321; Cincinnati, N. O. & T. P. Ry. Co. v. Yocum's Adm'r, 137 Ky. 117, 123 S. W. 247.

[53] Edmonson v. Kentucky Cent. Ry. Co., 105 Ky. 479, 49 S. W. 200, 448, 20 Ky. Law Rep. 1296; Linck's Adm'r v. Louisville & N. R. Co., 107 Ky. 370, 54 S. W. 184, 21 Ky. Law Rep. 1097; Illinois Cent. R. Co. v. Josey's Adm'x, 110 Ky. 342, 61 S. W. 703, 22 Ky. Law Rep. 1795, 54 L. R. A. 78. See Lewis' Adm'r v. Taylor Coal Co., 112 Ky. 845, 66 S. W. 1044, 57 L. R. A. 447, 23 Ky. Law Rep. 2218; Casey's Adm'r v. Louisville & N. R. Co., 84 Ky. 79.

[54] Cincinnati, N. O. & T. P. Ry. Co. v. Cook's Adm'r, 113 Ky. 161, 67 S. W. 383.

St. 1909, § 6, provides that punitive damages may be recovered when the act is willful or the negligence is gross; but even prior to the enactment of this section it was held that in an action arising under the constitutional provision punitive damages were recoverable for death by gross negligence.[55] Under the present act there may be a recovery of compensatory damages if there was ordinary negligence, and of punitive damages if there was gross negligence.[56] The measure of compensatory damages is such sum as would fairly compensate the estate of the deceased for the destruction of his power to earn money.[57] The ques-

---

[55] Louisville & N. R. Co. v. Kelly's Adm'x, 100 Ky. 421, 38 S. W. 852, 19 Ky. Law Rep. 69; Owensboro & N. Ry. Co. v. Barclay's Adm'r, 102 Ky. 16, 43 S. W. 177, 19 Ky. Law Rep. 997. See, also, Louisville & N. R. Co. v. Ward's Adm'r, 44 S. W. 1112, 19 Ky. Law Rep. 1900.

[56] Cincinnati, N. O. & T. P. Ry. Co. v. Cook's Adm'r, 113 Ky. 161, 67 S. W. 383, 23 Ky. Law Rep. 2410. Where a railroad was guilty of gross negligence in running a defectively equipped train over an unsafe track at a high rate of speed, it was proper to submit to the jury the question of punitive damages. Illinois Cent. R. Co. v. Sheegog's Adm'r, 126 Ky. 252, 103 S. W. 323, 31 Ky. Law Rep. 691. See, also, Louisville & N. R. Co. v. King's Adm'r, 131 Ky. 347, 115 S. W. 196.

[57] Chesapeake & O. Ry. Co. v. Lang's Adm'r, 100 Ky. 221, 38 S. W. 503, 19 Ky. Law Rep. 65; Louisville & N. R. Co. v. Kelly's Adm'x, 100 Ky. 421, 38 S. W. 852, 19 Ky. Law Rep. 69; Louisville & N. R. Co. v. Ward's Adm'r, 44 S. W. 1112, 19 Ky. Law Rep. 1900; Louisville & N. R. Co. v. Milet's Adm'r, 46 S. W. 498, 20 Ky. Law Rep. 532; Chesapeake & O. Ry. Co. v. Dixon's Adm'x, 104 Ky. 608, 47 S. W. 615, 20 Ky. Law Rep. 792; Id., 50 S. W. 252, 20 Ky. Law Rep. 1883; Louisville & N. R. Co. v. Clark's Adm'r, 105 Ky. 571, 49 S. W. 323, 20 Ky. Law Rep. 1375; Southern Ry. Co. v. Barr's Adm'x, 55 S. W. 900, 21 Ky. Law Rep. 1615; Louisville & N. R. Co. v. Tucker's Adm'r, 65 S. W. 453, 23 Ky. Law Rep. 1929; Louisville & N. R. Co. v. Sullivan's Adm'x, 76 S. W. 525, 25 Ky. Law Rep. 854; Louisville & N. R. Co. v. Lucas' Adm'r, 98 S. W. 308, 30 Ky. Law Rep. 359; Id., 99 S. W. 959, 30 Ky. Law Rep. 539; Big Hill Coal Co. v. Abney's Adm'r, 125 Ky. 355, 101 S. W. 394; Paducah City Ry. v.

tion is: What was the value of the deceased's life to his estate? And whether he left a wife or children or other persons dependent on him has no bearing upon the question.[58] Nothing is to be allowed for the pain and suffering

Alexander's Adm'r, 104 S. W. 375, 31 Ky. Law Rep. 1043; Louisville & N. R. Co. v. Simrall's Adm'r, 127 Ky. 55, 104 S. W. 1011, 31 Ky. Law Rep. 1269; Id., 104 S. W. 1199, 32 Ky. Law Rep. 240; Louisville & N. R. Co. v. Stewart's Adm'x, 131 Ky. 665, 115 S. W. 775. An instruction to fix the damages at a fair equivalent "for the power of deceased to earn money, lost by the destruction of his life," is sufficient, without a direction to consider the cost of living, earning capacity, and probable duration of life, to which undue attention should not be called by special reference to them. Chesapeake & O. Ry. Co. v. Lang's Adm'r, 100 Ky. 221, 40 S. W. 451, 41 S. W. 271, 19 Ky. Law Rep. 65. An instruction authorizing a verdict for such sum as will fairly compensate the estate of the decedent for the destruction of his power to earn money is proper, this being sufficient to authorize the jury to consider the cost of living without a direction to that effect, which would not be proper. Louisville & N. R. Co. v. Kelly's Adm'x, 100 Ky. 421, 40 S. W. 452, 19 Ky. Law Rep. 69. An instruction that, upon finding for plaintiff, the jury should find such damages as would reasonably compensate decedent's estate for the destruction of his power to earn money, "and the jury may consider the age of decedent and his reasonable expectancy of life," was erroneous for containing the words quoted, as authorizing an inference that the jury should base their finding upon such facts, when they should be left to fix a reasonable compensation to decedent's estate for the destruction of his earning power, according to all the evidence. Louisville & N. R. Co. v. Hays' Adm'r, 128 S. W. 289. In estimating compensatory damages the jury may receive evidence concerning the habits, character, physical condition, earning capacity, and probable duration of life of deceased. Cincinnati, N. O. & T. P. Ry. Co. v. Lovell's Adm'r, 141 Ky. 249, 132 S. W. 569; Id., 142 Ky. 1, 133 S. W. 788. An instruction authorizing the jury to find such a sum in damages as they might believe from the evidence would reasonably compensate the estate of decedent, for the destruction of his power to earn money, not exceeding the amount claimed in the petition, was proper. Cincinnati, N. O. & T. P. Ry. Co. v. Lovell's Adm'r, supra.

[58] Louisville & N. R. Co. v. Eakins' Adm'r, 103 Ky. 465, 45 S. W. 529, 46 S. W. 496, 47 S. W. 872, 20 Ky. Law Rep. 736. See, also,

of the decedent [59] or of the survivors.[60] In an action for
the death of a child, since the damages are given for destruction of the power of the decedent to earn money, and
are to compensate the estate of the child, and not, as is
generally the case under most statutes, to compensate the
parent, it seems that the calculation is to be based upon
the child's expectancy of life.[61] The application of the rule

Louisville & N. R. Co. v. Taafe's Adm'r, 106 Ky. 535, 50 S. W. 850,
21 Ky. Law Rep. 64. It was error to permit plaintiff to prove that
intestate left a wife and children, and that her income was not sufficient to support her. Southern Ry. Co. in Kentucky v. Evans'
Adm'r, 63 S. W. 445, 23 Ky. Law Rep. 568. In case of an infant,
the value of his earning power during minority is not to be taken
into account; nor is the expense of his maintenance and education
during that time to be deducted, though the administrator suing is
a parent, and one of the beneficiaries. Linss v. Chesapeake & O. Ry.
Co. (C. C.) 91 F. 964.

[59] Louisville & N. R. Co. v. Sander's Adm'r, 44 S. W. 644, 19 Ky.
Law Rep. 1941; Chesapeake & O. R. Co. v. Banks' Adm'r, 142 Ky.
746, 135 S. W. 285.

[60] Louisville & N. R. Co. v. Creighton, 106 Ky. 42, 50 S. W. 227,
20 Ky. Law Rep. 1691. See, also, Louisville & N. R. Co. v. Schu-
maker's Adm'x, 112 Ky. 431, 53 S. W. 12, 21 Ky. Law Rep. 803.

[61] "It is claimed that the verdict was excessive, that the earning
capacity of a girl of 9 years old is not so susceptible of proof that
its value after she might become 21 can be measured, which is to
say that, for negligently killing female children there is only a nominal liability. A girl 9 years old has an expectation of living 39
years longer. Her expectancy is hers, not her father's, though her
services until she is 21 may belong to him. But the jury do not
award compensation for her labor. It is for the destruction of her
power to earn money, a power which is hers alone, and, while it may
be difficult to prove, is nevertheless of certain and substantial value.
We cannot say, and who could, that $6,000 was too great a value,
or even enough. , Certain it is, it does not strike us as being so excessive as to indicate passion or prejudice on the part of the jury,
or excessive at all." Louisville & N. R. Co. v. Kimble's Adm'x, 140
Ky. 759, 131 S. W. 790. $10,500 for a child under 4 years of age
held excessive. Louisville & N. R. Co. v. Creighton, 106 Ky. 42, 50
S. W. 227, 20 Ky. Law Rep. 1691. $15,000 for a girl of 14 years is

with reference to the amount of the verdict is illustrated in the cases in the subjoined note.[62]

Under St. 1909, § 6, the action is to be prosecuted by the personal representative of the deceased.[63]

so excessive as to indicate passion or prejudice. Board of Internal Improvement for Lincoln County v. Moore's Adm'r, 66 S. W. 417, 23 Ky. Law Rep. 1885. For a boy of 9 years, $18,000 was palpably excessive. Illinois Cent. R. Co. v. Watson's Adm'r, 117 Ky. 374, 78 S. W. 175, 25 Ky. Law Rep. 1360.

[62] Chesapeake & O. Ry. Co. v. Judd's Adm'x, 106 Ky. 364, 50 S. W. 539, 20 Ky. Law Rep. 1978; Union Warehouse Co. v. Prewitt's Adm'r, 50 S. W. 964, 21 Ky. Law Rep. 67; Louisville & N. R. Co. v. Scott's Adm'r, 108 Ky. 392, 56 S. W. 674, 22 Ky. Law Rep. 30, 50 L. R. A. 381; Chesapeake & O. Ry. Co. v. Dupee's Adm'r, 67 S. W. 15, 23 Ky. Law Rep. 2349; Louisville & N. R. Co. v. Mulfinger's Adm'x, 80 S. W. 499, 26 Ky. Law Rep. 3; Louisville Water Co. v. Phillips' Adm'r, 139 Ky. 614, 89 S. W. 700, 28 Ky. Law Rep. 557; Gould Const. Co. v. Childers' Adm'r, 129 Ky. 536, 112 S. W. 622, 33 Ky. Law Rep. 1069, 130 Am. St. Rep. 473. $10,000 was not excessive for the death of a prosperous farmer about 60 years old, with an income of about $1,500 a year from his business. Louisville & N. R. Co. v. Ueltschi's Ex'rs, 97 S. W. 14, 29 Ky. Law Rep. 1136. $15,000 for the death of a healthy young locomotive engineer earning $125 a month will not be disturbed as excessive; one former jury having awarded $15,000, and another $17,000. Southern Ry. Co. in Kentucky v. Scanlon's Adm'r, 105 S. W. 152, 32 Ky. Law Rep. 38. $12,500 for death of a railroad brakeman held not so large as to show it to have been the result of caprice, passion, or prejudice of the jury. Cox's Adm'r v. Louisville & A. R. Co., 137 Ky. 388, 125 S. W. 1056. For the death of a railroad yard foreman, 27 years of age, strong and vigorous, of good character and habits, who had already been promoted in the service of the railroad, a verdict for $15,000 was not excessive. Cincinnati, N. O. & T. P. Ry. Co. v. Lovell's Adm'r, 141 Ky. 249, 132 S. W. 569, rehearing denied 142 Ky. 1, 133 S. W. 788. $3,500 for the death of a brakeman 25 years old, in good health, earning $960 a year, with a life expectancy of 32 years, is not flagrantly inadequate. Stewart's Adm'x v. Louisville & N. R. Co., 136 Ky. 717, 125 S. W. 154.

[63] Harris v. Kentucky Timber & Lumber Co., 43 S. W. 462, 45 S. W. 94, 19 Ky. Law Rep. 1731; Randolph's Adm'r v. Snyder, 139 Ky. 159, 129 S. W. 562. But see Carden v. Louisville & N. R. Co., 37

Although the measure of damages is based on compensation to the estate of the deceased for the destruction of his power to earn money, the amount recovered, less funeral expenses and the cost of recovering and administering the particular fund, is to be distributed among the kindred named in the order provided, and only in default of such kindred are creditors of the estate entitled to participate in the fund.[64]

(b) Killing by deadly weapon—In duel

St. 1909, § 4, provides: "The widow and minor child or either or any of them,[65] of a person killed by the careless,

S. W. 839. The legislature is empowered to direct what persons may bring actions for negligent or wrongful death. City of Louisville v. Hart's Adm'r, 143 Ky. 171, 136 S. W. 212, 35 L. R. A. (N. S.) 207. Where an administrator and one responsible for the death conspire together to prevent a suit for the death, the widow and children of decedent may sue, though Const. § 241, St. 1903, § 6, and Civ. Code Prac. § 21, provide that an action for wrongful death shall be prosecuted by the personal representative for the benefit of the widow and children of the decedent, and though St. 1903, § 3882, authorizes the administrator to settle any claim for damages for a wrongful death; Civ. Code Prac. § 24, providing that, if the consent of one who should be joined as plaintiff cannot be obtained, he may be made defendant. McLemore v. Sebree Coal & Min. Co., 121 Ky. 53, 88 S. W. 1062, 28 Ky. Law Rep. 25. The right may be enforced by the appointment of an administrator and suit by him, though decedent was an alien and had no property and no relatives living in this country. Trotta's Adm'r v. Johnson, Briggs & Pitts, 121 Ky. 827, 90 S. W. 540, 28 Ky. Law Rep. 851, 12 Ann. Cas. 222.

[64] O'Malley's Adm'r v. McLean, 113 Ky. 1, 67 S. W. 11, 23 Ky. Law Rep. 2258. Cf. Berg v. Berg's Adm'r, 105 Ky. 80, 48 S. W. 432, 20 Ky. Law Rep. 1083.

[65] Const. § 241, which provides that, when death results from negligence or "wrongful act," the action for damages shall be prosecuted by the personal representative, does not apply to this section which gives a right of action for damages to "the widow or minor child of a person killed by the wanton or malicious use of firearms," since

wanton or malicious use of firearms, or by any weapon popularly known as colt's, brass knuckles, or slung shot, or other deadly weapon,[66] or sand bag or any imitation or substitute therefor, not in self-defense,[67] may have an action against the person or persons who committed the killing, and all others aiding or promoting the killing, or any one or more of them,[68] and in such action the jury may give vindictive damages."

St. 1909, § 5, confers a right of action in favor of the widow and minor child of a person killed in a duel, against the surviving principal, and the seconds, etc., and provides for vindictive damages.

---

the words "wrongful act" were intended only to denote acts from which negligence could arise. McClure v. Alexander, 24 S. W. 619, 15 Ky. Law Rep. 732. See, also, Spring's Adm'r v. Glenn, 12 Bush, 172; Morgan v. Thompson, 82 Ky. 383. The administrator of one whose death was caused by the wrongful use of firearms has a right of action therefor; deceased not being survived by widow or child, and the words "wrongful act" as used in the Constitution and St. 1903, § 6, embracing every injury that might be committed against the person, whether negligently done or not. Howard's Adm'r v. Hunter, 104 S. W. 723, 31 Ky. Law Rep. 1092 (overruling McClure v. Alexander, supra). A father cannot maintain the action. Harris v. Kentucky Timber & Lumber Co., 43 S. W. 462, 45 S. W. 94, 19 Ky. Law Rep. 1731. Where a widow sues alone, the minor children have the right to be made parties plaintiff. Martin v. Smith, 110 S. W. 413, 33 Ky. Law Rep. 582. The action survives under St. 1909, § 10. Morehead's Adm'x v. Bitner, 106 Ky. 523, 50 S. W. 857, 20 Ky. Law Rep. 1986.

66 This section embraces a killing with a weapon either in itself deadly, or deadly as used, and therefore embraces a killing with a bar of iron. Morehead's Adm'x v. Bittner, 106 Ky. 523, 50 S. W. 857, 20 Ky. Law Rep. 1986.

67 The declaration must allege that the killing was not in self-defense. Becker v. Crow, 7 Bush, 198. Cf. Young v. Young, 141 Ky. 76, 132 S. W. 155.

68 Joinder of defendants: Bolton v. Ayers, 110 S. W. 385, 33 Ky. Law Rep. 591.

Survival act

St. 1909, § 10, provides that "no right of action for personal injury * * * shall cease or die with the person injuring or the person injured, except actions for assault; * * * but for an injury other than those excepted, an action may be brought or revived by the personal representative. * * *" Under this section a personal representative may maintain an action for the recovery of damages for the pain and suffering of the decedent;[69] but no such action lies if the death was instantaneous.[70] The two causes of action cannot be united, and the plaintiff must elect which he will prosecute.[71]

[69] Quinn's Adm'r v. Newport News & M. V. Co., 22 S. W. 223, 15 Ky. Law Rep. 74; Randolph's Adm'r v. Snyder, 139 Ky. 159, 129 S. W. 562. An action to recover damages for pain endured by a child from the time of an injury until his death survives to the personal representatives, and does not belong to his parents as such, so that an attempted compromise of the right of action by the parents prior to the death, and before they had even a beneficial interest in any recovery which might be obtained in the action, was void, and did not preclude the maintenance of the action by the administrator after the child's death. Meyer's Adm'r v. Zoll, 119 Ky. 480, 84 S. W. 543, 27 Ky. Law Rep. 167. If the administrator sues for the injury within a year after the infliction thereof, as provided by St. 1903, § 2516, he may recover for intestate's mental and physical suffering, to the time of intestate's death. Louisville & N. R. Co. v. Simrall's Adm'r, 104 S. W. 1011, 31 Ky. Law Rep. 1269; Id., 104 S. W. 1199, 32 Ky. Law Rep. 240. The action cannot be maintained by the personal representative. Spring's Adm'r v. Glenn, 12 Bush, 172; Morgan v. Thompson, 82 Ky. 383. See O'Donoghue v. Akin, 2 Duv. 478.

[70] Louisville & P. Canal Co. v. Murphy, 9 Bush, 522; Hansford's Adm'x v. Payne, 11 Bush, 380; Newport News & M. V. R. Co. v. Dentzel's Adm'r, 91 Ky. 42, 14 S. W. 958, 12 Ky. Law Rep. 626. Shooting and wounding another, although unintentionally, is an assault and battery, and an action therefor does not survive. Anderson v. Arnold's Ex'r, 79 Ky. 370.

[71] Hackett v. Louisville, St. L. & T. P. Ry. Co., 95 Ky. 236, 24 S. W.

§ 42. Louisiana

Rev. Civ. Code 1909, § 2315, reads: "Every act whatever of man that causes damage to another, obliges him by whose fault it happened to repair it; the right of this action shall survive in case of death in favor of the children or widow of the deceased or either of them, and in default of these in favor of the surviving father and mother or either of them, and in default of any of the above persons, then in favor of the surviving brothers and sisters or either of them for the space of one year from the death; provided, that should the deceased leave a widow together with minor children, the right of action shall accrue to both the widow and minor children; provided further, that the right of action shall accrue to the ,major children only in those cases where there is no surviving widow or minor child or children. The survivors above mentioned may also recover the damages sustained by them by the death of the parent or child or husband or wife or brothers or sisters, as the case may be." Originally this section merely contained the provision that every act whatever of man that causes damage to another obliges him by whose fault it happened to repair it, and no action was maintainable to recover damages for injuries resulting in death.[72] In 1855 the section was amended by adding that "the right of this action shall survive in case of death in favor of the minor children and widow of the deceased or either of them, and, in default of these, in favor of the surviving father or mother or either of

871, 15 Ky. Law Rep. 612; Louisville Ry. Co. v. Will's Adm'x, 66 S. W. 628, 23 Ky. Law Rep. 1961; Bowling Green Gaslight Co. v. Dean's Ex'x, 142 Ky. 678, 134 S. W. 1115. See Conner's Adm'x v. Paul, 12 Bush, 147.

72 Hubgh v. New Orleans & C. R. Co., 6 La. Ann. 495; Hermann v. New Orleans & C. R. Co., 11 La. Ann. 5.

them, for the space of one year from the death." [73]   This amendment simply gave the right to maintain an action for the same damages which the party injured might have recovered. [74]   In 1884 the section was again amended by adding that "the survivors above mentioned may also recover the damage sustained by the death of the parent or child, or husband or wife, as the case may be." [75]   This amendment gave a new right of action, viz., for damages resulting from the death. [76]   The section has been since further amended, and now reads as above set forth. [77]

[73] Acts La. 1855, p. 270.

[74] Earhart v. New Orleans & C. R. Co., 17 La. Ann. 243; Frank v. New Orleans & C. R. Co., 20 La. Ann. 27; Vredenburg v. Behan, 33 La. Ann. 627; Van. Amburg v. Vicksburg, S. & P. R. Co., 37 La. Ann. 651, 55 Am. Rep. 517; McCubbin v. Hastings, 27 La. Ann. 713. The right of action did not survive in favor of the husband, but in case of the death of a minor married daughter the parents might sue. Walton v. Booth, 34 La. Ann. 913. The right did not survive the widow in favor of the children of age, and, though it survived to the children not of age upon their coming of age their right abated. Huberwald v. Orleans R. Co., 50 La. Ann. 477, 23 South. 474.

[75] Acts La. 1884, p. 94.

[76] Myhan v. Louisiana Electric Light & Power Co., 41 La. Ann. 964, 6 South. 799, 7 L. R. A. 172, 17 Am. St. Rep. 436; McFee v. Vicksburg, S. & P. R. Co., 42 La. Ann. 790, 7 South. 720. See, also, Robertson v. Town of Jennings, 128 La. 795, 55 South. 375. Under Acts 1884, No. 71, two causes of action arose when deceased left a widow and minor children—one to recover the damages the father might have recovered if he had survived, and the other founded on his death; the first surviving in favor of the widow or minor children. When the widow sued alone, a judgment in her favor exhausted the first cause of action, leaving to the minors only a right

[77] Under Act No. 120 of 1908, by which brothers and sisters, in default of child, widow, or parent, succeed to the right of action which person who dies from injury had, at moment of his death, and giving brothers and sisters also right of action, for damages sustained by the death, they may recover damages for moral or mental, as well as the material, injury resulting from the death. Underwood v. Gulf Refining Co. of Louisiana, 128 La. 968, 55 South. 641.

§ 43. Maine

Formerly the statute provided that any railroad corporation by whose negligence the life of any person, in the exercise of due care, was lost, should forfeit not more than $5,000, nor less than $500, to be recovered by indictment,

of action for the death of their father. Eichorn v. New Orleans & C. R., Light & Power Co., 112 La. 236, 36 South. 335, 104 Am. St. Rep. 437. Contributory negligence of parents was a defense in the latter action, but not in the former. Westerfield v. Levis, 43 La. Ann. 63, 9 South. 52. The statute includes acts of omission as well as of commission, and applies when death results from negligence for which the master is responsible. American Sugar Refining Co. v. Johnson, 60 Fed. 503, 9 C. C. A. 110; Same v. Tatum, 60 Fed. 514, 9 C. C. A. 121. An action for the death of a husband and father may be brought by the widow individually and as tutrix of her minor children. Curley v. Illinois Cent. R. Co., 40 La. Ann. 810, 6 South. 103; Clairain v. Western Union Tel. Co., 40 La. Ann. 178, 3 South. 625. Minors have a cause of action for the personal injury which resulted in the death of their mother. The right of action of the mother is made to survive in the name of her children. Delisle v. Bourriague, 105 La. 77, 29 South. 731, 54 L. R. A. 420. See, also, Chivers v. Roger, 50 La. Ann. 57, 23 South. 100. Under Acts 1884, No. 71, giving the right of action to recover for the death of a minor to the father and mother, or "either of them," where the wife had before the death of the child obtained a divorce from her husband, and had the care of the minor children, she could bring the action without his authority or consent. Wilson v. Banner Lumber Co., 108 La. 590, 32 South. 460. Minor grandchildren cannot recover damages for personal injuries to their grandfather, resulting in death. Walker v. Vicksburg, S. & P. R. Co., 110 La. 718, 34 South. 749. The right granted to the surviving father or mother to recover damages for the death of their son, is a right granted to the actual father or mother, and not to an adopting parent. Mount v. Tremont Lumber Co., 121 La. 64, 46 South. 103, 126 Am. St. Rep. 312, 15 Ann. Cas. 148. In an action by minors for death of their father, the fact that one became of age after bringing the suit, but before judgment, did not cut her off from the benefit of the statute during her minority. Eichorn v. New Orleans & C. R., Light & Power Co,. 114 La. 712, 38 South. 526, 3 Ann. Cas. 98. The widow and minor

(71)

to the use of persons specified, the remedy by indictment being applicable to only a small class of persons.[78] An indictment could be maintained only when death was instantaneous, and in other cases an action was maintainable for the recovery of such damages as the party injured might have recovered had he lived under the survival act, now Rev. St. 1903, c. 89, § 8.[79] In 1891, the legislature passed a death act (St. 1891, c. 124, Rev. St. 1903, c. 89, §§ 9, 10), substantially on the lines of Lord Campbell's act, which by implication repealed the remedy by indictment.[80] The construction given to the statute providing a remedy by in-

children by a second marriage could exercise the right of action conferred by Acts 1884, No. 71, without joining as plaintiffs decedent's minor children by a previous marriage. Robideaux v. Hebert, 118 La. 1089, 43 South. 887, 12 L. R. A. (N. S.) 632. Both the father and the mother have each cause of action for the death of their son. Le Blanc v. United Irrigation & Rice Milling Co., 129 La. 196, 55 South. 761. Assuming that desertion, without lawful excuse, on the part of a wife, is sufficient to deprive her as widow of the right to sue for the death of her husband, such desertion is not shown by the fact that she lived separate from him during a divorce suit by him. Williams v. Nona Mills Co., 128 La. 811, 55 South. 414.

[78] Rev. St. 1883, c. 51, §§ 68, 69. See State v. Grand Trunk Ry. Co. of Canada, 60 Me. 145; State v. Maine Cent. R. Co., 76 Me. 357, 49 Am. Rep. 622; State v. Maine Cent. R. Co., 77 Me. 538, 1 Atl. 673.

[79] State v. Maine Cent. R. Co., 60 Me. 490; State v. Grand Trunk Ry., 61 Me. 114, 14 Am. Rep. 552. Walton, J., says, in State v. Maine Cent. R. Co., that, if the party injured does not die immediately, a right of action accrues to him which survives, and that no other remedy is needed; but that, if he does die immediately, no right of action accrues to him, and consequently none survives. "The remedy by indictment was intended to apply to the latter class of cases alone. To hold otherwise would involve the legislature in the absurdity of creating two independent, and, to some extent, conflicting, remedies, for one and the same injury." An action upon the statute against a town for a personal injury, caused by a defect in a highway, may be prosecuted under the survival statute. Hooper v. Inhabitants of Gorham, 45 Me. 209.

[80] State v. Maine Cent. R. Co., 90 Me. 267, 38 Atl. 158.

dictment was adhered to, however, in so far that it is held that the death act is limited to cases where the person injured died immediately, upon the ground that the legislature must have intended by this act to extend the means of redress to a class of cases where none existed before, and not to give two actions for a single injury, one for the benefit of the decedent's estate, and another for the benefit of the widow and children or next of kin.[81]

§ 44. Massachusetts

The provisions of the Massachusetts statutes are various and complicated, and in most respects are unlike those of the other states. The earlier acts provided remedies in certain cases where death was caused by the negligence of certain classes of corporations and common carriers, as well as by the negligence of counties, towns, and persons in failing to maintain or repair highways, bridges, and the like, and later acts provided a remedy where death was caused by the negligence of employers in certain cases. It was not until 1897 that a remedy was provided against all

---

[81] Sawyer v. Perry, 88 Me. 42, 33 Atl. 660. An immediate death is not necessarily an instantaneous death. Id. See, also, Anderson v. Wetter, 103 Me. 257, 69 Atl. 105, 15 L. R. A. (N. S.) 1003. Pub. Laws 1891, c. 124, affords a right of action for injuries causing death where an employé is instantly killed or dies without conscious suffering. Conley v. Portland Gaslight Co., 96 Me. 281, 52 A. 656. Rev. St. 1903, c. 89, § 9, is designed to cover cases of immediate death, which includes both instantaneous death and death preceded by total unconsciousness following immediately upon the accident, irrespective of the duration of such unconsciousness. Perkins v. Oxford Paper Co., 104 Me. 109, 71 A. 476. See § 74, post. It is not necessary that the declaration should contain an averment of such immediate death, but it is sufficient if it necessarily appears that the death was immediate. Carrigan v. Stillwell, 97 Me. 247, 54 A. 389, 61 L. R. A. 163.

persons and corporations, other than employers,[82] although at a comparatively early day it was provided that actions of tort for damage to the person should survive. The earlier enactments, which coexist with the general death act, will be first considered.

1. SURVIVAL ACT

"In addition to the actions which survive by the common law, the following shall also survive: Actions * * * of tort for assault, battery and imprisonment or other damage to the person," etc.[83] An executor or administrator may maintain an action upon the cause of action which accrued to the party injured for the recovery of the same damages which he might have recovered had he lived;[84] but this action cannot be maintained if the death was instantaneous.[85] In the absence of evidence of conscious suffering, or of loss incurred before the death by means of the injury, the damages are only nominal.[86]

[82] See Hudson v. Lynn & B. R. Co., 185 Mass. 510, 71 N. E. 66.

[83] Rev. Laws 1902, c. 171, § 1. See Pub. St. 1882, c. 165, § 1.

[84] Demond v. City of Boston, 7 Gray, 544; Norton v. Sewall, 106 Mass. 143, 8 Am. Rep. 298.

[85] See § 74, post.

[86] Kennedy v. Standard Sugar Refinery, 125 Mass. 90, 28 Am. Rep. 214; Tully v. Fitchburg R. Co., 134 Mass. 499; Mulchahey v. Washburn Car Wheel Co., 145 Mass. 281, 14 N. E. 106, 1 Am. St. Rep. 458

2. REMEDIES AGAINST CERTAIN CORPORATIONS, CARRIERS, MU-
NICIPALITIES, ETC.

(a) Indictment

The statute [87] provides that an indictment may be maintained against a corporation which operates [88] a railroad or

[87] St. 1906, c. 463, pt. 1, § 63 (as amended St. 1907, c. 392); part
2, § 245. See Pub. St. 1882, c. 112, §§ 212, 213. The first statute upon
this subject was St. 1840, c. 80, which provided: "If the life of any
person, being a passenger, shall be lost by reason of the negligence
or carelessness of the proprietor or proprietors of any railroad,
steamboat, stage coach, or of common carriers of passengers, or by
the unfitness or gross negligence or carelessness of their servants
or agents, in this commonwealth, such proprietor or proprietors, and
common carriers, shall be liable to a fine not exceeding $5,000, nor
less than $500, to be recovered by indictment, to the use of the exec-
utor or administrator of the deceased person, for benefit of his
widow and heirs; one moiety thereof to go to the widow, and the
other to the children of the deceased; but, if there shall be no children the whole to the widow, and, if no widow, to heirs according
to the law regulating the distribution of intestate personal estate
among heirs." The difference between this statute and Lord Campbell's act was pointed out in Carey v. Berkshire R., 1 Cush. 475, 48
Am. Dec. 616, in which case the court said: "These statutes are
framed on different principles, and for different ends. The English
statute gives damages, as such, and proportioned to the injury, to
the husband or wife, parents and children, of any person whose
death is caused by the wrongful act, neglect, or default of another

[88] The statute applies to a case where such a corporation is using
a railroad track reasonably incident to the business in which the
corporation is lawfully engaged, although the track is not within
the chartered limits of the corporation, or of a road then under its
control, but is a private track which it is using by the mere suffer-
ance and license of its owner. Commonwealth v. Boston & L. R.
Corp., 126 Mass. 61. Also to a case where death is caused through
the negligence of a railroad corporation in unloading coal from a
vessel into its cars. Daley v. Boston & A. R. Co., 147 Mass. 101, 16
N. E. 690.

(75)

street railway for the recovery of a fine of not less than
$500, nor more than $5,000, to be paid to the executor or
administrator [89] one-half to the use of the widow and one-
half to the use of the children, or, if there are no children,
the whole to the use of the widow, or, if there is no widow,

person, adopting, to this extent, the principle on which it has been
attempted to support the present actions. Our statute is confined
to the death of passengers carried by certain enumerated modes of
conveyance. A limited penalty is imposed as a punishment of carelessness in common carriers; and as this penalty is to be recovered
by indictment, it is doubtless to be greater or smaller, within the
prescribed maximum and minimum, according to the degree of blame
which attaches to the defendants, and not according to the loss sustained by the widow and heirs of the deceased. The penalty, when
thus recovered, is conferred on the widow and heirs, not as damages
for their loss, but as a gratuity from the commonwealth." "The system of imposing a punishment for wrongfully causing death, in place
of giving to the family of the deceased an action for compensation,
has been adhered to and extended since the decision in Carey v. Berkshire Railroad, when it applied only to travelers on defective highways
and to passengers of common carriers." Hudson v. Lynn & B. R. Co.,
185 Mass. 510, 71 N. E. 66. The civil remedy was subsequently added,
but the recovery in such case was in substance "a penalty given to
the widow and children and next of kin, instead of to the Commonwealth." Doyle v. Fitchburg R. Co., 162 Mass. 66, 37 N. E. 770, 25
L. R. A. 157, 44 Am. St. Rep. 335. "The action which is given to
the administrator is merely a substitute for the indictment also
provided for, and it is expressly enacted that the damages shall be
assessed with reference to the culpability of the corporation, or
its servants or agents.'" Littlejohn v. Fitchburg R. Co., 148 Mass.
478, 20 N. E. 103, 2 L. R. A. 502. For the history of the various enactments, see Commonwealth v. Boston & L. R. Corp., 134 Mass. 211;
Hudson v. Lynn & B. R. Co., 185 Mass. 510, 71 N. E. 66.

[89] The indictment must allege that administration has been taken
out in Massachusetts. If it alleges appointment by the laws of Maine,
without alleging ancillary administration in Massachusetts, it is fatally defective. Commonwealth v. Sanford, 12 Gray, 174. But an
indictment describing the deceased as of Boston, etc., and alleging
that A. B., of said Boston, has been appointed administrator, sufficiently shows that administration was taken out in the state.
Commonwealth v. East Boston Ferry Co., 13 Allen, 589.

the whole to the use of the next of kin,[90] in the following cases: (1) If by reason of the negligence of the corporation,[91] or of the unfitness or gross negligence of its servants or agents [92] while engaged in its business, it causes

[90] An indictment cannot be maintained unless the deceased left widow or children, or next of kin. It must aver that he left widow or heirs, or both, as the case may be. Commonwealth v. Eastern R. Co., 5 Gray, 473; Commonwealth v. Boston & A. R. Co., 121 Mass. 36. But it need not set out their names, if it aver that they are unknown. Commonwealth v. Boston & W. R. Corp., 11 Cush. 512.

[91] An indictment alleged the neglect of the corporation to reduce the speed of train, and to give the proper signals. Held, that the negligence alleged was that of the servants of the corporation, and not of the corporation itself, and that the indictment was insufficient. Commonwealth v. Boston & M. R. R., 133 Mass. 383. What was said inconsistent with this in Commonwealth v. Fitchburg R. Co., 120 Mass. 372, was not necessary to the decision. A corporation operating a leased railroad was not responsible for the defective condition of the road unless it had, or by the exercise of due care might have had, notice of the same. "The present action is statutory and penal in its character. * * * The action which is given to the administrator is merely a substitute for the indictment." Per Holmes, J., Littlejohn v. Fitchburg R. Co., 148 Mass. 478, 20 N. E. 103, 2 L. R. A. 502. A memorandum on a season ticket that the corporation assumes no liability for any personal injury held no defense to an indictment. Commonwealth v. Vermont & M. R. Co., 108 Mass. 7, 11 Am. Rep. 301. A railroad company, delivering to the mills of an owner defective cars loaded with coal for unloading by the owner, may be liable at common law and under St. 1906, c. 463, pt. 1, § 63, concurrently with the owner for their joint negligence, causing the death of an employé of the owner while unloading cars; and where the proximate cause of the death was a defective car, the railroad or the owner or both could be sued. D'Almeida v. Boston & M. R. R., 209 Mass. 81, 95 N. E. 398.

[92] An allegation that by reason of the unfitness, gross negligence, and carelessness of A., the servant of defendant corporation and engaged in its business, the life of a passenger was lost, is sufficient. Commonwealth v. Brockton St. R. Co., 143 Mass. 501, 10 N. E. 506. Plaintiff must show that the death was caused either by the negligence of the company, or the unfitness or gross negligence of its servants. Caswell v. Boston Elevated R. Co., 190 Mass. 527, 77 N. E. 380.

the death [93] of a passenger; [94] (2) or of a person who is
in the exercise of due care, [95] and not a passenger or in the
employ of such corporation; (3) or if the life of a person

An action cannot be maintained upon proof of negligence of the defendant's servants, without proof that the negligence was gross.
Hicks v. New York, N. H. & H. R. Co., 164 Mass. 424, 41 N. E. 721,
49 Am. St. Rep. 471. "Gross negligence," means something more
than a want of ordinary care. Galbraith v. West End St. Ry. Co.,
165 Mass. 572, 43 N. E. 501. While "gross negligence" does not include wanton or willful misconduct which would warrant criminal
prosecution or a suit for damages by a trespasser or one guilty of
negligence on his own part, yet it is something more than mere ordinary negligence. Lanci v. Boston Elevated R. Co., 197 Mass. 32, 83
N. E. 1. "Gross negligence" is not the same as a wanton act, which
dispenses with proof by plaintiff of freedom from contributory negligence, but, where the degree of care due is the highest, means a
gross failure to exercise that degree of care; and, where the duty
owed is ordinary care, gross negligence is a materially greater degree of negligence than lack of ordinary care, and is also a failure
to exercise a slight degree of care. Dimauro v. Linwood St. R. Co.,
200 Mass. 147, 85 N. E. 894. See, also, Gordon v. West End St. Ry.
Co., 175 Mass. 181, 55 N. E. 990; Moran v. Milford & U. St. R. Co.,
193 Mass. 52, 78 N. E. 736; Marshall v. Boston Elevated R. Co., 203
Mass. 40, 88 N. E. 1094; Gagnon v. Boston Elevated R. Co., 205
Mass. 483, 91 N. E. 875.

[93] It is immaterial that the death was not instantaneous. Commonwealth v. Metropolitan R. Co., 107 Mass. 236. The voluntary, willful
act of suicide of an insane person, whose insanity was caused by a
railroad accident, and who knows the purpose and physical effect of
his act, is a new cause, so that his death is not by reason of the
negligence of the railroad company, within Pub. St. 1882, c. 112, §
213, in such case giving a right of action therefor. Daniels v. New
York, N. H. & H. R. Co., 183 Mass. 393, 67 N. E. 424, 62 L. R. A.
751.

[94] A passenger left the train after the conductor had called the station and the car had almost stopped, and while crossing the track
to the station was killed by a locomotive on a parallel track, which
he might have seen. Held, that deceased had ceased to be a passenger
by leaving the train while it was in motion. Commonwealth v. Boston & M. R. Co., 129 Mass. 500, 37 Am. Rep. 382. A person who gets

[95] See note 95 on following page.

(78)

is lost by collision with the engines or cars of a railroad corporation at a crossing upon the level with the highway, and it appears that the corporation neglected to give the

upon a train after it has started does not become a passenger until he reaches a place of safety inside the car. Merrill v. Eastern R. R. Co., 139 Mass. 238, 1 N. E. 548, 52 Am. Rep. 705. The mere fact that one has not paid his fare or delivered up his ticket does not prove that he is not a passenger. If a passenger, he continues to be such while rightfully leaving the train and station. McKimble v. Boston & M. R. R., 139 Mass. 542, 2 N. E. 97; s. c., 141 Mass. 463, 5 N. E. 804. A person ceases to be a passenger when he has alighted from a train, taken a position upon the highway, and thence started to cross the track upon his way from the station. Allerton v. Boston & M. R. R., 146 Mass. 241, 15 N. E. 621. Defendant, in consideration of payment to it, and of an agreement to supply passengers on one of its trains with ice water, issued a season ticket to deceased, and permitted him to sell pop corn on all its trains. Held, that he was a passenger. Commonwealth v. Vermont & M. R. Co., 108 Mass. 7, 11 Am. Rep. 301. Children of such an age that they are carried free, if accompanied by adults, are passengers, though the accompanying adults are riding on free passes. Littlejohn v. Fitchburg R. Co., 148 Mass. 478, 20 N. E. 103, 2 L. R. A. 502. The statute being penal, it is no defense to an indictment or action for causing the death of a passenger that the deceased was not in the exercise of due care. Commonwealth v. Boston & L. R. Corp., 134 Mass. 211; McKimble v. Boston & M. R. R., 139 Mass. 542, 2 N. E. 97; s. c., 141 Mass. 463, 5 N. E. 804; Jones v. Boston & N. St. R. Co., 205 Mass. 108, 90 N. E. 1152. A person attempting to cross the tracks to a platform, in order to take an approaching train, was a passenger. Young v. New York, N. H. & H. R. Co., 171 Mass. 33, 50 N. E. 455, 41 L. R. A. 193. A passenger on a street car ceases to be such on failing to pay a second fare when due. Hudson v. Lynn & B. R. Co., 185 Mass. 510, 71 N. E. 66.

95 Where plaintiff's intestate was carried from defendant's street car in an unconscious condition, and laid by the side of the track, and afterwards run over by a car and killed, he was not in the exercise of due diligence. Hudson v. Lynn & B. R. Co., 185 Mass. 510, 71 N. E. 66. The administrator is bound to show that his intestate was in the exercise of due care, and that the accident happened through the negligence of the corporation or the unfitness or gross carelessness of its servants. Walsh v. Boston & M. R. R., 171 Mass. 52, 50 N. E. 453. An action cannot be maintained against a street railway

(79)

signals required by St. 1906, c. 463, pt. 1, § 63, and that such
neglect contributed to the death, unless it be shown that,
in addition to mere want of ordinary care, the person injured, or the person having charge of his person, was, at
the time of the collision, guilty of gross or willful negligence, or was acting in violation of the law, and that such
gross or willful negligence or unlawful act contributed
to the injury.[96]   In the first and second cases a railroad

corporation for causing the death of a child, who was injured by an
unfastened brake while playing with other children upon cars left
standing unguarded for several days on a public street of a city.
Gay v. Essex Electric St. Ry. Co., 159 Mass. 242, 34 N. E. 258. See,
also, Galbraith v. West End St. Ry. Co., 165 Mass. 572, 43 N. E. 501;
Slattery v. New York, N. H. & H. R. Co., 203 Mass. 453, 89 N. E.
622, 133 Am. St. Rep. 311; Haynes v. Boston Elevated R. Co., 204
Mass. 249, 90 N. E. 419. Where plaintiff's intestate was carried from
defendant's street car in an unconscious condition, and laid by the
side of the track, and afterwards run over by a car and killed, he
was not in the exercise of due diligence, within the meaning of St.
1886, p. 117, c. 140, authorizing the recovery of damages from a street
railway company for negligence causing the death of any person
not a passenger, being in the exercise of due diligence. Hudson v.
Lynn & B. R. Co., 185 Mass. 510, 71 N. E. 66.

   [96] St. 1906, c. 463, pt. 2, § 245. See Pub. St. c. 112, § 213, founded
on St. 1874, c. 372, § 164, and St. 1881, c. 199, §§ 2, 5, 6. St. 1874,
c. 372, § 164, was substantially a re-enactment of St. 1871, c. 352.
See Commonwealth v. Boston & M. R. R., 133 Mass. 383; Kelley v.
Boston & M. R. R., 135 Mass. 448. The civil remedy was added by
St. 1881, c. 199, §§ 2, 5, 6. In an action to recover for killing B.
at a highway crossing, there was evidence that there was a gate
which, when closed to indicate the approach of a train, crossed the
highway at the side of the railroad opposite to that from which B.,
approaching in a covered wagon, was about to cross; that the gate-
keeper began to close the gate, swung his lantern, and shouted to
B. to stop, but immediately afterwards shouted to hurry up; that
B. then started his horse, but before getting across the track was
struck by the locomotive, and that no bell or whistle was sounded
as required. Held, that the jury were warranted in finding for the
plaintiff. Bayley v. Eastern R. Co., 125 Mass. 62. The distance
across defendant's railway tracks, at a street crossing, was about 160

corporation is not liable for the death of a person while
walking or being upon its road contrary to law or its reasonable rules and regulations.[97] The indictment must be
prosecuted within one year from the time of the injury
causing the death.

feet. Plaintiff's evidence tended to show that on a dark morning
plaintiff's intestate had driven half-way across when the gates were
closed, and the gateman shouted to him to stop, whereupon he whip-
ped up his horse, and the gateman then shouted to him to "Come
on," at the same time opening the gate in front. Before reaching
the opposite side he was struck by an engine, and killed. Held that,
as a matter of law, deceased was not guilty of such gross or willful
negligence as would, under section 213, preclude recovery. Doyle v.
Boston & A. R. Co., 145 Mass. 386, 14 N. E. 461. If an indictment
alleges, as the only act of negligence, that the servants of the corporation ran a locomotive engine "rashly, and without watch, care,
or foresight, and with great, unusual, unreasonable, and improper
speed," evidence is inadmissible to show that the servants neglected
to ring the bell on the engine or to sound the whistle. Commonwealth v. Fitchburg R. Co., 126 Mass. 472. A declaration contained
two counts, the first alleging that plaintiff's intestate was a passenger, and claiming under Pub. St. 1882, c. 112, § 212; the second
claiming under the second part of the same section. Held, that the
pleadings did not state facts sufficient to bring the case within section 213, it being nowhere alleged that the accident occurred at a
highway crossing, or was caused by a collision with cars or engines.
Allerton v. Boston & M. R. R., 146 Mass. 241, 15 N. E. 621. An administrator was entitled to recover if he showed that the corporation neglected to give the required signals, and that such neglect
contributed to the death of his intestate, without showing that his
intestate exercised due care. Walsh v. Boston & M. R. R., 171 Mass.
52, 50 N. E. 453. The burden of proving gross negligence of decedent
is on the railroad. Slattery v. New York, N. H. & H. R. Co., 203
Mass. 453, 89 N. E. 622, 133 Am. St. Rep. 311. See, also, Livermore
v. Fitchburg R. Co., 163 Mass. 132, 39 N. E. 789; Phelps v. New
England R. Co., 172 Mass. 98, 51 N. E. 522; Durbin v. New York,
N. H. & H. R. Co., 194 Mass. 181, 80 N. E. 219.

97 An indictment need not negative that the deceased was on the
track contrary to law, etc. Commonwealth v. Fitchburg R. Co., 10
Allen, 189. Recovery cannot be had for death of a trespasser on the
track, unless willful or reckless misconduct of the engineer is shown.

(b) Civil action

An action for tort may also be maintained against such corporation by the executor or administrator for the recovery of damages, not less then $500, nor more than $5,000, which shall be assessed with reference to the degree of culpability of the defendant or its servants or agents, for the use of the persons above specified in the case of an indictment, when the life of the deceased was lost under the circumstances which authorize the maintenance of an indictment, and if an employé of a railroad corporation, being in the exercise of due care, is killed under such circumstances as would have entitled him to maintain an action for damages against such corporation if death had not resulted, the corporation shall be liable in the same manner and to the same extent as if the deceased had not been an employé; [98] but no executor or administrator shall, for the same cause, avail himself of more than one of the remedies given. [99]

The executor or administrator may also maintain a like action for tort (4) against the proprietor of a steamboat or

Durbin v. New York, N. H. & H. R. Co., 194 Mass. 181, 80 N. E. 219. In an action against a street railway for the death of a pedestrian struck by a car while deceased was walking along the track, the burden was on plaintiff to prove that deceased was in the exercise of due care. Adams v. Boston & N. St. R. Co., 191 Mass. 486, 78 N. E. 117.

[98] The corporation is not liable for the loss of life of an employé who is killed by the negligence of a coemployé. Dacey v. Old Colony R. Co., 153 Mass. 112, 26 N. E. 437.

[99] St. 1906, c. 463, pt. 1, § 63 (as amended St. 1907, c. 392); pt. 2, § 245. See Pub. St. c. 112, §§ 212, 213; St. 1886, c. 140. Before St. 1886, c. 140, the remedy against a street railway corporation was solely by indictment. Holland v. Lynn & B. R. Co., 144 Mass. 425, 11 N. E. 674.

stagecoach or a common carrier of passengers, except a railroad corporation or street railway company, if such proprietor or common carrier causes the death of a passenger by reason of his or its negligence or carelessness, or by reason of the unfitness or gross negligence or carelessness of his or its servants or agents, for the recovery of damages not less than $500, nor more than $5,000, which shall be assessed with reference to the degree of culpability of the proprietor or common carrier liable, or of his or its servants or agents, to the use of the persons above specified; [100] (5) if the life of a person is lost by reason of a defect or want of repair of, or want of a sufficient railing in or upon a way, causeway, or bridge, against the county, city, town, or person by law obliged to repair the same, provided the defendant had previous reasonable notice of the defect or want of repair or want of railing, for the recovery of damages, not exceeding $1,000, which shall be assessed with reference to the degree of culpability of the defendant,[101] for the use of the persons above specified. All such actions must be commenced within one year from the injury causing the death.[102]

---

[100] Rev. Laws 1902, c. 70, § 6.   See Pub. St. c. 73, § 6;   Commonwealth v. Coburn, 132 Mass. 555.

[101] Rev. Laws 1902, c. 51, § 17.   See Pub. St. c. 52, § 17.   The remedy was formerly by indictment.   Gen. St. c. 44, § 21.   Commonwealth v. Inhabitants of Wilmington, 105 Mass. 599.   Where a woman, four or five months pregnant, fell on a defective highway, and was delivered of a child, which survived but a few minutes, held, that the child was not a "person" within the statute.   Dietrich v. Inhabitants of Northampton, 138 Mass. 14, 52 Am. Rep. 242.   The right of action is independent of the administrator's right to sue for damages suffered by the intestate during his lifetime from the injury which caused his death, and both actions may proceed at the same time.   Bowes v. City of Boston, 155 Mass. 344, 29 N. E. 633, 15 L. R. A. 365;   Fegan v. Same, Id.

[102] As to notice of the injury to be given to the defendant.   Mit-

3. Employers' Liability Act

By the employers' liability act,[103] if personal injury is caused to an employé who is in the exercise of due care,[104] in the cases therein provided for, which results in death, the legal representatives have the same right of compensation and remedies against the employer as if the employé had not been an employé, etc.[105] By this act damages or compensation in lieu thereof may also be recovered for the death, as follows: (1) If such death is not instantaneous, or preceded by conscious suffering,[106] and there is any

chell v. Worcester, 129 Mass. 525; Taylor v. Inhabitants of Woburn, 130 Mass. 494; Nash v. Town of South Hadley, 145 Mass. 105, 13 N. E. 376.

[103] St. 1909, c. 514, §§ 127–132. See St. 1887, c. 270, as amended by St. 1888, c. 155, and St. 1892, c. 260. See Welch v. Grace, 167 Mass. 590, 46 N. E. 387; Oulighan v. Butler, 189 Mass. 287, 75 N. E. 726.

[104] Lothrop v. Fitchburg R. Co., 150 Mass. 423, 23 N. E. 227; Shea v. Boston & M. R. Co., 154 Mass. 31, 27 N. E. 672; McLean v. Chemical Paper Co., 165 Mass. 5, 42 N. E. 330; Tumalty v. New York, N. H. & H. R. Co., 170 Mass. 164, 49 N. E. 85; McCarty v. Clinton Gaslight Co., 193 Mass. 76, 78 N. E. 739.

[105] See Dacey v. Old Colony R. Co., 153 Mass. 112, 26 N. E. 437; Clark v. New York, P. & B. Co., 160 Mass. 39, 35 N. E. 104.

[106] A dump car going 10 or 12 miles an hour struck deceased on the back of the head, and bounced him against a stationary car. The blood gushed from his nose and mouth in streams. He was picked up apparently unconscious, and died within two hours. There was no testimony as to whether he regained consciousness, though the actual facts might have been shown. Held, that the evidence failed to prove that deceased died "without conscious suffering." Hodnett v. Boston & A. R. Co., 156 Mass. 86, 30 N. E. 224. Where decedent was struck by a car, and the evidence tended to show that his body was crushed, and a witness, who was near him at the time, testified that he was "stone dead" when the witness reached him, and that he took two or three steps after he was struck, and then fell, there was evidence that he died without conscious suffering.

one who would have been entitled to bring an action, had
the employé been killed instantly or died without conscious suffering, the legal representatives may, in the action under the act upon the cause of action of the party injured, recover damages for the death,[107] in addition to those
for the injury, and in the same action under a separate
count at common law may recover damages for conscious
suffering resulting from the same injury; (2) if the employé
is instantly killed, or dies without conscious suffering, the
widow, or, if no widow, the next of kin,[108] who, at the time
of his death, were dependent upon his wages for support,[109]

Mears v. Boston & M. R. R., 163 Mass. 150, 39 N. E. 997. Where
decedent, while descending from a car which was traveling about
4 miles an hour, fell and caught his foot in the car, and was carried for about 180 feet, and then instantly killed, defendant's death
could not be said to be without conscious suffering. Martin v. Boston & M. R. R., 175 Mass. 502, 56 N. E. 719.   See Willey v. Boston
Electric Light Co., 168 Mass. 40, 46 N. E. 395, 37 L. R. A. 723; Green
v. Smith, 169 Mass. 485, 48 N. E. 621; Knight v. Overman Wheel
Co., 174 Mass. 455, 54 N. E. 890.

[107] Before the amendment of St. 1892, c. 260, the legal representative could not recover for the death. Ramsdell v. New York & N.
E. R. Co., 151 Mass. 245, 23 N. E. 1103, 7 L. R. A. 154.   Under the employer's liability act (Rev. Laws, c. 106, §§ 72, 73) an action for causing the death of an employé after conscious suffering must be
brought by his legal representatives, while, for causing his instant
death, an action can be brought only by his widow, or, if he leaves
no widow, by his next of kin who were dependent on his wages for
support. Silva v. New England Brick Co., 185 Mass. 151, 69 N. E.
1054.

[108] An action may be maintained by a nonresident alien. Mulhall
v. Fallon, 176 Mass. 266, 57 N. E. 386, 54 L. R. A. 934, 79 Am. St.
Rep. 309; Vetaloro v. Perkins (C. C.) 101 Fed. 393.

[109] Only such of the next of kin as have been dependent need join.
Daly v. New Jersey S. & I. Co., 155 Mass. 1, 29 N. E. 507.   An invalid sister, unable to work regularly, or to earn enough to pay her
doctors' bills, who has received from her brother on an average
$30 to $35 a month for three or four years, and who in fact receives
from and in dependent on him for support, is within the statute.

(85)

may maintain an action for damages against the employer. If damages are awarded for the death, they shall be assessed with reference to the degree of culpability [110] of the employer or of the person for whose negligence the employer is liable. In an action for personal injury to the employé, in which no damages for his death are awarded, the damages shall not exceed $4,000. In an action for a personal injury to the employé, if damages for his death are also awarded, they shall not exceed $5,000 for both the injury and the death, and shall be apportioned by the jury between the legal representative of the employé and the persons who would have been entitled to bring an action for his death, if it had been instantaneous or without conscious suffering. In an action for the death of an employé who was instantly killed, or died without conscious suffering, the damages shall not be less than $500 nor more than $5,000. The action must be commenced within one year from the accident. No action can be maintained unless no-

Daly v. New Jersey S. & I. Co., 155 Mass. 1, 29 N. E. 507. Plaintiff testified that she was decedent's half-sister, and had two children; that he came to see her at times, and gave her money, and sent her money every other week or so to pay her rent; and that she had no other means of support but her earnings, and since his death she had to support herself. There was nothing to show what her earnings or expenses were, or that she was in fact dependent on him. Held, that the evidence failed to show that plaintiff was dependent on deceased for support. Hodnett v. Boston & A. R. Co., 156 Mass. 86, 30 N. E. 224. See Houlihan v. Connecticut R. R. Co., 164 Mass. 555, 42 N. E. 108; Mulhall v. Fallon, 176 Mass. 266, 57 N. E. 386, 54 L. R. A. 934, 79 Am. St. Rep. 309; Welch v. New York, N. H. & H. R. Co. 176 Mass. 393, 57 N. E. 668; Welch v. New York, N. H. & H. R. Co., 182 Mass. 84, 64 N. E. 695; Boyle v. Columbian Fire Proofing Co., 182 Mass. 93, 64 N. E. 726; Mehan v. Lowell Electric Light Corp., 192 Mass. 53, 78 N. E. 385; Morena v. Winston, 194 Mass. 378, 80 N. E. 473.

[110] Howard v. Fall River Iron Works Co., 203 Mass. 273, 89 N. E. 615.

tice in writing, signed by the person injured, or by some person in his behalf, of the time, place, and cause of the injury, be given to the employer within 60 days. A notice shall not be deemed invalid or insufficient solely by reason of any inaccuracy in stating the time, place, or cause, if it is shown that there was no intention to mislead, and that the party entitled to the notice was not in fact misled.[111] If from physical or mental incapacity it is impossible for the person injured to give the notice within the time provided,[112] he may give it within 10 days after the incapacity is removed; and in case of his death without having given the notice, and without having been for 10 days at any time of sufficient capacity to give the notice, his executor or administrator may give it within 60 days after his appointment.[113]

4. GENERAL DEATH ACT [114]

"If a person or corporation by his or its negligence, or by the negligence [115] of his or its agents or servants while

[111] A description of the injury is not necessary. Herlihy v. Little, 200 Mass. 284, 86 N. E. 294; Crane v. Same, Id.

[112] See Mitchell v. Worcester, 129 Mass. 525.

[113] In case of death without conscious suffering, it is not necessary to appoint an administrator to give the notice, but it may be given by the widow or her attorney. Gustafsen v. Washburn & Moen Mfg. Co., 153 Mass. 468, 27 N. E. 179. Cf. Nash v. Town of South Hadley, 145 Mass. 105, 13 N. E. 376; Taylor v. Inhabitants of Woburn, 130 Mass. 494. But notice given by the administrator within the required time after his appointment will support an action by the widow or next of kin. Daly v. New Jersey S. & I. Co., 155 Mass. 1, 29 N. E. 507; Jones v. Boston & A. R. Co., 157 Mass. 51, 31 N. E. 727; Dickerman v. Old Colony R. Co., 157 Mass. 52, 31 N. E. 728.

[114] Rev. Laws 1902, c. 171, § 2, as amended St. 1907, c. 375.

[115] Prior to the amendment of 1907, the section read "gross negligence of his or its servants or agents," etc. See Evensen v. Lexington & B. St. R. Co., 187 Mass. 77, 72 N. E. 355; Brennan v.

engaged in his or its business, causes the death of a person who is in the exercise of due care [116] and not in his or its employment or service, he or she shall be liable in damages in the sum of not less than $500 nor more than $10,-000 to be assessed with reference to the degree of his or its culpability or that of his or its agents or servants,[117] to be recovered in an action of tort, commenced within two years after the injury which caused the death, by the executor or administrator of the deceased, one-half thereof to the use of the widow and one-half to the use of the children of the deceased; or, if there are no children, the whole to the use of the widow; or, if there is no widow, the whole to the use of the next of kin." [118]

Standard Oil Co., 187 Mass. 376, 73 N. E. 472; Oulighan v. Butler, 189 Mass. 287, 75 N. E. 726; Pearlstein v. New York, N. H. & H. R. Co., 192 Mass. 20, 77 N. E. 1024; Manning v. Conway, 192 Mass. 122, 78 N. E. 401; Hamma v. Haverhill Gas Light Co., 203 Mass. 572, 89 N. E. 1043.

[116] Plaintiff has the burden of proving that decedent exercised due care; and where no positive testimony can be procured, proof of circumstances excluding any act of contributory negligence is sufficient. Hamma v. Haverhill Gas Light Co., 203 Mass. 572, 89 N. E. 1043. See, also, Manning v. Conway, 192 Mass. 122, 78 N. E. 401. In an action for the death of a child 4 years and 8 months old, it was incumbent on the plaintiff to show that there was no contributory negligence on the part of the deceased, or of those who had charge of him. Brennan v. Standard Oil Co., 187 Mass. 376, 73 N. E. 472.

[117] In an action for wrongful death it was proper for the court to charge that recovery could not be had for damages as in an action for personal injuries, but that the remedy provided was in the nature of a penalty, which was assessed according to the degree of defendant's culpability or that of its servants. Oulighan v. Butler, 189 Mass. 287, 75 N. E. 726.

[118] A declaration failing to allege that decedent left widow, children, or next of kin was demurrable. Oulighan v. Butler, 189 Mass. 287, 75 N. E. 726.

§ 44—1. Michigan

The statutes give a death act,[119] substantially like Lord Campbell's act enacted in 1848, and a survival act,[120] which provides that, "in addition to the actions which survive by the common law, the following shall also survive; that is to say: * * * actions of assault and battery, * * * for negligent injury to persons," etc. The provision for the survival of actions for assault and battery has been in force since 1838, and the addition of actions for negligent injuries to the person was made in 1885. A recovery cannot be had under both acts.[121] At one time the court inclined to the view that the survival act applied only where death results from other causes than the injury, and that the death act applied where death results from the injury, whether instantaneous or not;[122] but the view that has prevailed is that if the death which results from the injury is instantaneous the remedy is under the death act, while if the death is not instantaneous the remedy is under the survival act.[123] "This act [the death act] was designed to cover cases of instantaneous death, where there was no other remedy, and that it was not designed to give a double remedy in cases where assault and battery caused death, in which cases the survival act already furnished a com-

---

[119] Comp. Laws 1897, §§ 10,427, 10,428.

[120] Comp. Laws 1897, § 10,117.

[121] Sweetland v. Chicago & G. T. R. Co., 117 Mich. 329, 75 N. W. 1066, 43 L. R. A. 568; Dolson v. Lake Shore & M. S. R. Co., 128 Mich. 444, 87 N. W. 629.

[122] Sweetland v. Chicago & G. T. R. Co., 117 Mich. 329, 75 N. W. 1066, 43 L. R. A. 568.

[123] Dolson v. Lake Shore & M. S. R. Co., 128 Mich. 444, 87 N. W. 629; Jones v. McMillan, 129 Mich. 86, 88 N. W. 206; Storrie v. Grand Trunk Elevator Co., 134 Mich. 297, 96 N. W. 569.

plete remedy, giving to the next of kin all of the redress
which the deceased would have been entitled to, and not
making it dependent upon or limited to an amount of actual contribution to his or her support. It may be said
that this view left no redress to the widow and next of kin
for negligent homicides not instantaneous, because such
did not survive under section 7397, How. Ann. St., and
would not be covered by this construction of section 8313,
as originally passed. This is true, but it does not justify
our disregarding a plain condition upon which the right
of action was made to rest, viz., that the death prevents a
right of action accruing to the deceased. Subsequently this
omission was supplied by the insertion in the survival act
of the words 'for negligent injuries to the person.' So, as
the law now stands, the right of action is readily determinable. If the death be not instantaneous, the administrator recovers under the survival act the full measure of
damages for the benefit of the next of kin. If it be instantaneous, he recovers under the death act, for the same persons, a limited amount of damages, viz., for such pecuniary
injury only as they can be shown to have suffered." [124]
The line between deaths which are and are not instantaneous is not always easy to draw. Thus it was held that
where the decedent survived the injury for a moment,
whether in a conscious or unconscious condition, the action
was under the survival act, and not under the death act.
"We see no reason," said the court, "for splitting hairs as
to what is meant by instantaneous death, though we can'
appreciate the difference between a continuing injury resulting in drowning, or death by hanging, throwing from a
housetop, etc., and one where a person survives the wrongful act in an injured condition. There is no occasion for

[124] Dolson v. Lake Shore & M. S. R. Co., supra, per Hooker, J.

saying that one dies instantly because such survival is accompanied by a comatose condition, or unconsciousness, or insanity, or idiocy." [125] On the other hand, where the decedent was dead when taken from beneath the car which struck him, though he lived some 15 minutes after being struck, it was held that the death was "instantaneous," so as to constitute a cause of action under the death act. "Where there is a continuing injury, resulting in death within a few moments," said the court, "it is 'instantaneous' within the meaning of the statute." [126] And where the decedent was struck on the head by a trolley pole and survived from 10 to 30 minutes, it was ruled that it could not be said as matter of law that the survival act was not applicable.[127]

§ 44—2. Mississippi

The constitution of 1890 (section 193), after defining specified cases in which the servant does not assume the risk of negligence of fellow servants, or of defective machinery or appliances, declares that, where death ensues from an injury to an employé, the legal or personal representatives of the person injured shall have the same rights and remedies as are allowed by law to such representa-

[125] Oliver v. Houghton County St. R. Co., 134 Mich. 367, 96 N. W. 434, 104 Am. St. Rep. 607, 3 Ann. Cas. 53.

[126] West v. Detroit United Ry., 159 Mich. 269, 123 N. W. 1101.

[127] Ely v. Detroit United Ry., 162 Mich. 287, 127 N. W. 259. "This case does not fall within the principle of West v. Detroit United Ry.," said the court. "In that case the direct cause of death continued to operate directly upon the injured person until life was extinct. In the present case the direct cause of death did not operate continuously, but ceased with the first blow, and plaintiff survived the original injury from 10 minutes to perhaps half an hour. In our opinion, the facts disclosed by this record bring the case within the principle of Oliver v. Houghton County St. R. Co."

tives of other persons. This provision is self-executing, so that whatever enlargement or restriction is applied to the rights and remedies of persons not employés for injuries is also applicable proprio vigore to employés in the specified cases.[128]

The present death act was enacted in 1898, and is now section 721 of the Code of 1906.[129] This section provides that whenever death is caused by any such wrongful or negligent omission, or by such unsafe machinery, way, or appliances as would, if death had not ensued, have entitled the party injured to maintain an action and recover damages, and the deceased shall have left a widow or children, or both, or husband, father, mother, brother, or sister, the person or corporation, or both, that would have been liable, if death had not ensued, and the representatives of such person, shall be liable for damages notwithstanding the death, whether instantaneous or not; that the action may be brought in name of the widow for the death of her husband, and vice versa, of the parent for the death of a child, and vice versa, of a brother for the death of brother or of a sister, and vice versa,[130] and that all parties inter-

---

[128] Mobile, J. & K. C. R. Co. v. Hicks, 91 Miss. 273. 46 South. 360, 124 Am. St. Rep. 679.

[129] For the history of the statutes, see Mobile, J. & K. C. R. Co. v. Hicks, 91 Miss. 273, 46 South. 360, 124 Am. St. Rep. 679. See, also, Illinois Cent. R. Co. v. Pendergrass, 69 Miss. 425, 12 South. 954; Illinois Cent. R. Co. v. Hunter, 70 Miss. 471, 12 South. 482; Bussey v. Gulf & S. I. R. Co., 79 Miss. 597, 31 South. 212; Amos v. Mobile & O. R. Co., 63 Miss. 509; Vicksburg & M. R. Co. v. Phillips, 64 Miss. 693, 2 South. 537.

[130] An action for the death of a railroad employé, who leaves a widow and minor children, can only be brought by them. Mobile, J. & K. C. R. Co. v. Hicks, 91 Miss. 273, 46 South. 360, 124 Am. St. Rep. 679. See Bussey v. Gulf & S. I. R. Co., 79 Miss. 597, 31 South. 212. Cf. Yazoo & M. V. R. Co. v. Washington, 92 Miss. 129, 45 South. 614.

ested may join, and there shall be but one suit for the same death, which shall inure for the benefit of all parties concerned; [131] that the recovery shall be of such damages of every kind to the party or parties suing as the jury may deem to be just, taking into consideration all the damages of every kind to the decedent and all parties interested; that executors and administrators shall not sue except as below provided; that the action shall be commenced within one year after the death; [132] that the section shall apply to all personal injuries received in the business or services of the master or employer where they result in death; that the damages shall not be subject to the debts and liabilities of the deceased, and shall be distributed to the persons mentioned respectively in the manner specified; that if the deceased have none of the relatives specified, the damages shall go to the legal representatives, subject to the debts and general distribution, and the executor may recover such damages on the same terms as prescribed for the next of kin. The section was amended in 1908 by making it applicable to illegitimate

[131] Where a widow and children brought action for the death of the husband and father, a railroad employé, the widow could not maintain another action as administratrix to recover damages sustained by the husband himself. Mobile, J. & K. C. R. Co. v. Hicks, 91 Miss. 273, 46 South. 360, 124 Am. St. Rep. 679. It was not necessary for the widow to join her children in a suit for the husband's wrongful death. Foster v. Hicks, 93 Miss. 219, 46 South. 533. The children are in effect coplaintiffs in an execution on a judgment obtained by the widow, and the sheriff owes them the same duty as he owes the widow from the time he has notice of their interests. Kelly v. Howard, 98 Miss. 543, 54 South. 10.

[132] No action can be brought after the expiration of one year, in whomsoever the right of action may be. Pickens v. Illinois Cent. R. Co., 92 Miss. 210, 45 South. 868.

children on account of the death of the mother and to the mother on account of the death of an illegitimate child.[133]

§ 45. Missouri

In addition to the action for the recovery of such damages, not exceeding $10,000 ($5,000 prior to the amendment of 1907),[134] as the jury shall deem fair and just with reference to the necessary injury resulting·from the death, which is given by Rev. St. 1909, § 5426, whenever death is caused by wrongful act, neglect, or default such as would, if death had not ensued, have entitled the party injured to maintain an action, an action is by section 5425 given when death is caused by the negligence of railroad companies and certain other corporations, and individuals in certain cases, for the recovery of not less than $2,000 and not exceeding $10,000 by way of forfeiture. Section 5425 now provides that (1) whenever "any person," *including an employé of the corporation, individual, or individuals hereinafter referred to, whose death is caused by the negligence of a coemployé thereof,* shall die from any injury resulting or occasioned by the negligence, unskillfulness, or criminal intent [135] of any officer, agent, servant or employé [136] whilst

---

[133] Laws 1908, c. 167. Since Acts 1898, p. 82, giving a sister or brother a right of action for the wrongful or negligent death of a sister or brother, should be strictly construed as in derogation of the common law, it does not give a right of action to an illegitimate sister. Illinois Cent. R. Co. v. Johnson, 77 Miss. 727, 28 South. 753, 51 L. R. A. 837. See, also, Alabama & V. Ry. Co. v. Williams, 78 Miss. 209, 28 South. 853, 51 L. R. A. 836, 84 Am. St. Rep. 624.

[134] Laws 1907, p. 252.

[135] The negligence of a railway company may consist either in a violation of some duty imposed by the general municipal law of the land or some duty imposed by some more definite enactment.

---

[136] See note 136 on following page.

running, conducting, or managing any locomotive, car,[137] or train of cars, *or any street,*[138] *electric or terminal car or*

Kenney v. Hannibal & St. J. R. Co., 105 Mo. 270, 15 S. W. 983, 16 S. W. 837. The right of action includes death from negligence generally, whether consisting of negligence as defined by the common law, or arising from a failure to discharge a duty imposed by statute or municipal ordinance. McQuade v. St. Louis & Suburban Ry. Co., 200 Mo. 150, 98 S. W. 552. When the death of any person is caused by the failure of a railway company to comply with the statute relating to the giving of signals on the approach of trains to a public crossing, an action may be maintained for the forfeiture. Senn v. Southern Ry. Co., 135 Mo. 512, 36 S. W. 367. The section does not authorize an action for negligent death caused by the maintenance of an obstruction across a public highway. Crohn v. Kansas City Home Telephone Co., 131 Mo. App. 313, 109 S. W. 1068. A petition which charges both negligence and criminal acts is sustained by proof of either. O'Brien v. St. Louis Transit Co., 212 Mo. 59, 110 S. W. 705, 15 Ann. Cas. 86. A criminal intent, followed by criminal conduct resulting in death, must be shown. Garrett v. St. Louis Transit Co., 219 Mo. 65, 118 S. W. 68, 16 Ann. Cas. 678. That a passenger brought on the altercation in which he was shot and killed by the conductor in charge of defendant's street car will not preclude a recovery against the carrier, under Rev. St. 1899, § 2864, for the passenger's death. O'Brien v. St. Louis Transit Co., 212 Mo. 59, 110 S. W. 705, 15 Ann. Cas. 86. One suing a street railway company for the death of a person ejected from a car by the conductor thereof, and basing his right to recover on the ground that decedent was a passenger

---

[136] The negligence need not be that of the superior in charge. Rine v. Chicago & A. R. Co., 100 Mo. 228, 12 S. W. 640. A train dispatcher was an employé engaged in running trains, within the meaning of the statute. Rinard v. Omaha, K. C. & E. Ry. Co., 164 Mo. 270, 64 S. W. 124.

[137] A hand car is a car within Rev. St. 1909, § 5425. Boyd v. Missouri Pac. Ry. Co., 236 Mo. 54, 139 S. W. 561.

[138] The section applied to street railroads, irrespective of the amendment of 1905 (Laws 1905, p. 135). Higgins v. St. Louis & S. Ry. Co., 197 Mo. 300, 95 S. W. 863; McQuade v. St. Louis & S. Ry. Co., 200 Mo. 150, 98 S. W. 552; McKenzie v. United Rys. Co., 216 Mo. 1, 115 S. W. 13. Cf. Drolshagen v. Union Depot R. Co., 186 Mo. 258, 85 S. W. 344. See, also, Chicago, R. I. & P. Ry. Co. v. Stepp (C. C.) 151 Fed. 908.

train of cars, or of any master, pilot, engineer, agent or employé whilst running, conducting, or managing any steamboat,[139] or any of the machinery thereof, or of any driver of any stagecoach, *automobile, motor car* or other public conveyance whilst in charge of the same as a driver; and (2) when "any passenger"[140] shall die from any injury resulting from or occasioned by any defect or insufficiency in any railroad, *whether the same be a steam, street, electric or terminal railroad* or any part thereof, or in any steamboat, or the machinery thereof, or in any stagecoach, *automobile, motor car,* or other public conveyance, the corporation, individual or individuals in whose employ any such officer, agent, servant, employé, master, pilot, engineer or driver shall be or who owns, *operates, or conducts*[141]

and criminally assaulted by the conductor, must show, not only that decedent was assaulted and killed by the conductor, but that he was a passenger. Garrett v. St. Louis Transit Co., supra. It is as much the law since, as before, the amendment of Laws 1905, p. 136, fixing recovery for death at not less than $2,000 nor more than $10,000, that recovery cannot be had where the injury was not the result of unskillfulness, negligence, or criminal intent. Potter v. St. Louis & S. F. R. Co., 136 Mo. App. 125, 117 S. W. 593. See, also, Lynch v. Metropolitan St. Ry. Co., 112 Mo. 420, 20 S. W. 642; O'Brien v. St. Louis Transit Co., 185 Mo. 263, 84 S. W. 939, 105 Am. St. Rep. 592; McKenzie v. United Rys. Co. of St. Louis, 216 Mo. 1, 115 S. W. 13; Peters v. St. Louis & S. F. R. Co. 150 Mo. App. 721, 131 S. W. 917.

[139] A suit for death, based on the theory that defendant, a steamboat company, wrongfully landed deceased at an unsafe place, so that, after landing, he fell into the river, comes under this clause. Buddenberg v. Charles P. Chouteau Transp. Co., 108 Mo. 394, 18 S. W. 970.

[140] The petition should allege that deceased was a passenger, but the defect is waived if defendant, without objection, by his answer puts that question directly in issue. Wagner v. Missouri Pac. Ry. Co., 97 Mo. 512, 10 S. W. 486, 3 L. R. A. 156; Zuendt v. Same, 10 S. W. 491.

[141] No new right is given by the second clause of the section to

any such railroad, locomotive, car, etc., at the time of the injury, shall forfeit and pay *as a penalty*, for every such person, employé, or passenger so dying, the sum of not less than $2,000 and *not exceeding $10,000, in the discretion of the jury*, which may be sued for by the persons designated; but that the defendant may show as a defense that the defect or insufficiency was not negligent, and that the injury was not the result of unskillfulness, negligence, or criminal intent.[142] The section was amended in 1905 [143] by adding the provisions above printed in italics, and by changing the amount recoverable from $5,000 to a sum not less than $2,000 and not exceeding $10,000. The section as amended is not a' delegation to the jury of the legislative power of fixing penalties, so as to deprive one liable thereunder of his property without due process of law, in violation of the constitution.[144] The statute is remedial as well as penal.[145]

Under this section in its original form it was once held that "any person," as used in the first branch of the section, included fellow servants of a servant whose negli-

the representative of a deceased passenger against an "owner" of the road as contradistinguished from the corporation having charge of it. The term "owner" is therein used in the sense of "proprietor" or "operator" at the time of the accident. Proctor v. Hannibal & St. J. R. Co., 64 Mo. 112. The section gives no right of action against an employé of a carrier, but only against the carrier. Chicago, R. I. & P. Ry. Co. v. Stepp (C. C.) 151 Fed. 908.

[142] It seems that the act implies a prima facie case of negligence which the defendant may rebut. Schultz v. Pacific R. Co., 36 Mo. 13.

[143] Laws 1905, p. 135.

[144] Young v. St. Louis, I. M. & S. Ry. Co., 227 Mo. 307, 127 S. W 19.

[145] Boyd v. Missouri Pac. Ry. Co., 236 Mo. 54, 139 S. W. 561. See, also, Hennessy v. Bavarian Brewing Co., 145 Mo. 104, 46 S. W. 966, 41 L. R. A. 385, 68 Am. St. Rep. 554; Strottman v. St. Louis, I. M. & S. Ry. Co., 211 Mo. 227, 109 S. W. 769; Crohn v. Kansas City Home Telephone Co., 131 Mo. App. 313, 109 S. W. 1068.

gence caused the death.[146] But this construction was overruled, and the later cases hold that under this section, as
at common law, the master could not be held liable for injuries caused by the negligence of a fellow servant of the
party injured, unless the master was negligent in selecting
the servant or in retaining him after knowledge of his character.[147] The court said that "any person" did not include
fellow servants, and that the right conferred thereby was
analogous to that conferred by section 5426, and was not
an original right created on the death of the employé.[148]
But "any person" included an employé whose death was
caused by the negligence of a servant not a fellow servant.[149] On the other hand, "any passenger," as used in the

[146] Schultz v. Pacific R. Co., 36 Mo. 13; Connor v. Chicago, R. I.
& P. R. Co., 59 Mo. 285 (by a divided court).

[147] Proctor v. Hannibal & St. J. R. Co., 64 Mo. 112 (overruling
Schultz v. Pacific R. Co., supra). Proctor v. Hannibal & St. J. R. Co.
was approved in Elliott v. St. Louis & I. M. R. Co., 67 Mo. 272, but
Henry, J., erroneously stated the doctrine of that case to be that no
action could be maintained under that section by an employé. This
is pointed out in Miller v. Missouri Pac. Ry. Co., 109 Mo. 350, 19 S.
W. 58, 32 Am. St. Rep. 673. Prior to Act April 13, 1905 (Laws 1905,
p. 136), amending Rev. St. 1899, c. 17, § 2864, so as to authorize a
recovery for the death of an employé caused by a fellow servant's
negligence, there was no statute in force allowing a recovery for a
death so occasioned. Strottman v. St. Louis, I. M. & S. Ry. Co., 211
Mo. 227, 109 S. W. 769. See, also, McMurray v. St. Louis, I. M. &
S. Ry. Co., 225 Mo. 272, 125 S. W. 751.

[148] Proctor v. Hannibal & St. J. R. Co., supra. The petition embraced two counts, framed, respectively, on two sections, the first
charging that the killing was caused through the negligence, unskillfulness, and criminal intent of defendant's employés; the second that the death was owing directly to the negligence or default
of the company. Held, that the two counts contained but one subject-matter of complaint, although stated in different ways to meet
the evidence; that there could be but one verdict and one assessment; and that a general verdict was properly returned. Brownell
v. Pacific R. Co., 47 Mo. 240.

[149] Where a track hand was run over and killed by reason of the

second branch, does not include employés;[150] so that if an employé dies from an injury occasioned by any defect or insufficiency in the railroad, etc., the remedy is under section 5426, and not under section 5425.[151] Neither does "any passenger" include persons driving across the railroad; so that, if the death of such person is caused by a defective crossing or other defect or insufficiency in the railroad, his remedy is solely under section 5426, though, if his death is caused by the failure of the railroad company to ring the bell or sound the whistle, such failure entitles his representative to sue under the first branch of section 5425, the deceased in such case being a "person" whose death results from the negligence of the servants running the locomotive.[152]

negligence of the engineer and fireman of a locomotive, held, that the engineer and fireman were not fellow servants of the deceased, and that an action could be maintained for his death under Rev. St. 1889, § 4425. Sullivan v. Missouri Pac. Ry. Co., 97 Mo. 113, 10 S. W. 852, followed in Miller v. Missouri Pac. Ry. Co., 109 Mo. 350, 19 S. W. 58, 32 Am. St. Rep. 673; Parker v. Hannibal & St. J. R. Co., 109 Mo. 362, 19 S. W. 1119, 18 L. R. A. 802; Schlereth v. Missouri Pac. Ry. Co., 19 S. W. 1134 (the decision on this point in the same case, 96 Mo. 509, 10 S. W. 66, was erroneous). For the death of a postal clerk in a collision occasioned by negligence, the railroad company was liable under the first branch of section 4425. Magoffin v. Missouri Pac. Ry. Co., 102 Mo. 540, 15 S. W. 76, 22 Am. St. Rep. 798.

150 Where a brakeman not on duty was killed while riding in the baggage car contrary to the rules of the company, held, that he was not a "passenger" within section 4425, and that, if a passenger, his misconduct or negligence contributed to the death, and prevented a recovery. Higgins v. Hannibal & St. J. R. Co., 36 Mo. 418.

151 Holmes v. Hannibal & St. J. R. Co., 69 Mo. 536; Elliott v. St. Louis & I. M. R. Co., 67 Mo. 272; Flynn v. Kansas City, St. J. & C. B. R. Co., 78 Mo. 195, 47 Am. Rep. 99; Parsons v. Missouri Pac. Ry. Co., 94 Mo. 286, 6 S. W. 464.

152 In an action for the death of one killed while driving over a railroad crossing, the court instructed the jury that if they found for

The Colorado [153] and New Mexico [154] statutes are in most respects substantial copies of the Missouri statute. In Colorado it was held, following Missouri, that "any per-

the plaintiff (both causes of action having been set up in the petition), either on the ground of a failure to ring the bell or sound the whistle, or on the ground of a failure to construct and maintain a crossing as prescribed by the statute, or on both grounds, they should assess damages at $5,000. The verdict was for the plaintiff for $5,000. The record failed to show on what ground the finding was based. Held, that the judgment must be set aside; that the first ground came within the first branch of Rev. St. 1889, § 4425, but that the second ground (the deceased not being a passenger) did not come within the second branch of section 4425, but came within section 4426; and that, as the jury might have found on the second ground, the instruction, as to damages, was erroneous. Crumpley v. Hannibal & St. J. R. Co., 98 Mo. 34, 11 S. W. 244. In an action for negligently killing plaintiff's husband at a railroad crossing, it was error to direct a verdict for the plaintiff for $5,000, if the death resulted from failure to ring the bell or sound the whistle, or from failure to erect a signboard, because, while failure to ring the bell or sound the whistle brought the case within the first branch of Rev. St. 1889, '§ 4425, failure to erect a signboard (the deceased not being a passenger) brings the case within section 4426. King v. Missouri Pac. Ry. Co., 98 Mo. 235, 11 S. W. 563. Where the deceased was killed at a railroad crossing, held, proper to instruct the jury that, if the death resulted from the failure to light the headlight of the locomotive, they should find a verdict for the plaintiff for $5,000. Becke v. Missouri Pac. Ry. Co., 102 Mo. 544, 13 S. W. 1053, 9 L. R. A. 157. Where the deceased was using the railroad by license of defendant as a towpath, and was run over by defendant's cars owing to the negligence of defendant's employés managing the same, held, that an instruction that if the jury found for plaintiff it should be in the sum of $5,000 was correct. Le May v. Missouri Pac. Ry. Co., 105 Mo. 361, 16 S. W. 1049. Where a person is killed

---

[153] Rev. St. 1908, §§ 2056–2059. See Gen. St. 1883, §§ 1030–1033, the act of March 7, 1877, which repealed the act of February 8, 1872. Rev. St. 1908, § 2056, is Gen. St. 1883, § 1030, as amended by Laws 1907, p. 296, § 1, the last sentence being new. Gen. St. 1883, §§ 1030–1033 were sections 1508–1511, in Mills' Annotated Statutes, 1891. See § 36, ante.

[154] Comp. Laws 1897, §§ 3213–3215. See § 48, post.

son" did not include servants killed by the negligence of a fellow servant while acting in the common employment,[155] and the holding in New Mexico has been the same.[156]

§ 45—1. Montana [157]

Rev. Codes 1907, § 6486, provides for an action, to be maintained by the heirs or personal representatives of the decedent,[158] substantially like that given by Lord Campbell's act. Section 6485 provides that the father, or, in certain cases the mother, may maintain an action for the death of a minor child, and a guardian for the death of a ward. Sections 5251, 5252, provide that every person or corporation operating a railway or railroad shall be liable for all damages sustained by employés in consequence of

at a crossing by a train, and the negligence relied on is the maintenance by the company of obstructions along its right of way, it is error to charge that if the company was so negligent, and the death resulted therefrom, the verdict should be for $5,000. Rapp v. St. Joseph & I. R. Co., 106 Mo. 423, 17 S. W. 487. It has been uniformly ruled that where different acts of negligence are alleged and relied on, and some of them bring the case within the penalty clause of Rev. St. 1889, § 4425, and others bring the case within section 4426, it is error to instruct solely for the penalty. Culbertson v. Metropolitan St. Ry. Co., 140 Mo. 35, 36 S. W. 834.

[155] Atchison, T. & S. F. R. Co. v. Farrow, 6 Colo. 498.

[156] Lutz v. Atlantic & P. R. Co., 6 N. M. 496, 30 Pac. 912, 16 L. R. A. 819.

[157] See § 139—1.

[158] Under the statutes of Montana the property of a deceased intestate who leaves no issue or husband or wife goes to his father and mother in equal shares. Held, that the right of action for death was joint, and an action could not be maintained by the mother alone where the father was also living, even though at the time the question was presented by a plea in abatement the right of the father to bring an action was barred by limitation. Whelan v. Rio Grande Western Ry. Co. (C. C.) 111 Fed. 326. See Alder Co. v. Fleming, 159 Fed. 593, 86 C. C. A. 419.

(101)

the neglect, or mismanagement, or willful wrongs, whether of omission or commission, of other employés, when such neglect, mismanagement, or wrongs are in any manner connected with the use and operation of any railway or railroad about which they are employed, etc., and that, in case of death of any such employé in consequence of any injury or damage so sustained, the right of action shall survive, and may be prosecuted and maintained by his heirs or personal representatives. Sections 5248–5250 provide that every company, corporation, or individual operating any mine, smelter, or mill for the refining of ores shall be liable for any damages sustained by any employé, without contributing negligence on his part, when such damage is caused by the negligence of any superintendent, foreman, shiftboss, hoisting or other engineer, or craneman, etc., and that in case of the death of any such employé, in consequence of any injury or damage so sustained, the right of action shall survive, and may be prosecuted and maintained by its heirs or personal representatives.

The railroad act is a survival act, and not a death act, and no action can be prosecuted under it if the death was instantaneous.[159] So, also, the miners' act is a survival act, and the damages are for the injuries sustained by the decedent at the time of death, as distinguished from the damages suffered by him or his estate by reason of the death.[160]

[159] Dillon v. Great Northern Ry. Co., 38 Mont. 485, 100 Pac. 960.

[160] Johnson v. Butte & Superior Copper Co., 41 Mont. 158, 108 Pac. 1057; Beeler v. Butte & London Copper Development Co., 41 Mont. 465, 110 Pac. 528; post, § 139—1. Within the statute of limitations, the action is founded on actionable negligence, and not on a "liability created by statute." Beeler v. Butte & London Copper Development Co., supra.

§ 46. Nevada

Gen. St. 1885, §§ 3898, 3899, provide that whenever death is caused by wrongful act, etc., the personal representative may maintain an action for the benefit of the kindred named, but in default of such kindred, the proceeds to be disposed of as personal property; and that the jury "may give such damages, pecuniary and exemplary, as they shall deem fair and just, and may take into consideration the pecuniary injury resulting from such death to the kindred" named.

Under this statute there are two causes of action,—one for the injury to the deceased for the recovery of such damages, pecuniary and exemplary, as the jury shall deem fair and just, and one for the injury to the kindred for the pecuniary injury to them. Under the first cause of action the plaintiff need not allege or prove the existence of such kindred, but under the second he must do so.[161]

§ 47. New Hampshire

Pub. St. 1901, c. 191, § 8, provides that actions for tort for physical injuries to the person, and the causes of such actions, shall survive. Section 11 provides that the damages shall not exceed $7,000. Section 12 provides that, if death was caused by the injury, the mental and physical pain of the deceased, the expenses occasioned to his estate by the injury, the probable duration of his life but for the injury, and his capacity to earn money, may be considered as ele-

---

161 Roach v. Imperial Min. Co. (C. C.) 7 Sawy. 224, 7 Fed. 698. The decision rests on the peculiarity of the statute in allowing exemplary, as well as pecuniary, damages and a recovery in default of kindred.

ments of damage, in connection with other elements allowed by law.[162] Section 13 designates the persons among whom the damages shall be distributed. These provisions do not create a new right of action in the administrator, but keep alive a former right.[163]

Until 1879 the only remedy was by indictment, under a statute similar to those of Maine and Massachusetts.[164] This remedy was abolished in 1879, by an act which gave a right of action to the executor or administrator for injuries resulting in death.[165] In 1885 an additional act was passed, providing that all actions and causes of action should survive.[166] In 1887 the act of 1879 was repealed,

---

[162] Capacity to earn money means capacity to earn for the estate. An instruction should be given, in an action for the death of a child, that he would have been incapable of earning money for his estate during his minority. Carney v. Concord St. Ry., 72 N. H. 364, 57 Atl. 218. See, also, Warren v. Manchester St. Ry., 70 N. H. 352, 47 Atl. 735; Dillon v. Hudson Pelham S. Electric Ry. Co., 73 N. H. 367, 62 Atl. 93. Where deceased was killed in a collision, his administrator was entitled to recover for fright or mental suffering preceding the injury, though not for fright due to deceased's own acts in driving on the track. Yeaton v. Boston & M. R. R., 73 N. H. 285, 61 Atl. 522.

[163] Lyon v. Boston & M. R. Co. (C. C.) 107 Fed. 386. In an action for an injury by a locomotive explosion, causing the death of the locomotive engineer, it merely appeared that the explosion had occurred, and that decedent's body was found on the snow about 200 feet away, with life extinct and showing no signs of mangling, with blood escaping from the mouth, nose, and ears. Held, error to submit to the jury the issue of physical suffering as an element of damages. Hastings Lumber Co. v. Garland, 115 Fed. 15, 52 C. C. A. 609.

[164] Gen. Laws 1878, c. 282, § 14. See State v. Gilmore, 24 N. H. 461; State v. Boston & M. R. R., 58 N. H. 410.

[165] Laws 1879, c. 35, § 1. Under this act the right of action did not depend on whether the death was instantaneous. The damages were for the injury resulting in death, not for the injury to the surviving relatives. Clark v. City of Manchester, 62 N. H. 577; Corliss

[166] Laws 1885, c. 11.

and a remedy given similar to that now embodied in the provisions of Pub. St. 1901, c. 191, §§ 8–13.[167]

§ 48. New Mexico

The provisions of Comp. Laws 1897, §§ 3213–3215, are in most respects like those which have existed in Missouri.[168] There is also an employers' liability act applicable to railroad corporations, under which an action for the death of an employé may be maintained in the manner provided in section 3215.[169]

§ 49. North Carolina

Revisal 1905, §§ 59, 60,[170] provides that whenever death is caused by wrongful act, neglect, etc.,[171] the executor, administrator, or collector may maintain an action, and recover

v. Worcester, N. & C. R. Co,. 63 N. H. 404; Clark v. Manchester, 64 N. H. 471, 13 Atl. 867.

[167] Laws 1887, c. 71. This act did not repeal Laws 1885, c. 11. French v. Mascoma Flannel Co., 66 N. H. 90, 20 Atl. 363. This case gives the history of the New Hampshire legislation. Laws 1885, p. 223, c. 11, and Laws 1887, p. 454, c. 71, providing for the survival of actions of tort for personal injuries, were superseded by Pub. St. 1891, c. 191, §§ 8–13, on the same subject. Poff v. New England Telephone & Telegraph Co., 72 N. H. 164, 55 Atl. 891. See, also, Chaloux v. International Paper Co., 75 N. H. 281, 73 Atl. 301, 139 Am. St. Rep. 690; Piper v. Boston & M. R. R., 75 N. H. 435, 75 Atl. 1041.

[168] See ante, § 45.

[169] See Denver & R. G. R. Co. v. Warring, 37 Colo. 122, 86 Pac. 305.

[170] See Code 1883, §§ 1498–1500. For history of the legislation, see Killian v. Southern Ry. Co., 128 N. C. 261, 38 S. E. 873. See, also, Kesler v. Smith, 66 N. C. 154.

[171] A cause of action for personal injuries does not survive to the administrator in case of the death of the injured person as the result of such injuries, but abates with such death, and merges in the cause of action for the death, which then becomes the only available

such damages as are a fair and just compensation for the pecuniary injury resulting from the death, and that the amount recovered "is not liable to be applied as assets, in the payment of debts and legacies, but shall be disposed of as provided in this chapter for the distribution of personal property in case of intestacy." Section 153 provides that all sums of money which shall remain in the hands of the executor, administrator, or collector for five years after his qualification, unrecovered or unclaimed by suit, by creditors, next of kin, or others entitled thereto, shall be paid to the University of North Carolina. By reason of the latter provision it is held, anomalously, that the statute gives the action in any event, irrespective of the existence of next of kin.[172]

remedy. Bolick v. Southern Ry. Co., 138 N. C. 370, 50 S. E. 689. It is immaterial, for the purpose of establishing a cause of action for wrongful death, whether the act causing the death was wanton or cruel; it being sufficient that it was merely negligent. Western Union Telegraph Co. v. Catlett, 177 Fed. 71, 100 C. C. A. 489. Priv. Laws N. C. 1897, p. 83, c. 56, giving a remedy for death by wrongful act to any employé of a railroad company operated in the state is only an enlargement of the Lord Campbell act (Revisal 1905, §§ 59, 60), and must be construed with it. Dennis v. Atlantic Coast Line R. R., 70 S. C. 254, 49 S. E. 869, 106 Am. St. Rep. 746. See Ellerbe v. Carolina Cent. R. Co., 118 N. C. 1024, 24 S. E. 808. Under the provisions of the Code that every action must be prosecuted in the name of the real party in interest, a father may bring an action for damages resulting from the seduction of his infant daughter, the loss of her services, expenses of her illness, her death, and the consequent injury to his affections. Scarlett v. Norwood, 115 N. C. 284, 20 S. E. 459. Plaintiff, as administrator, was entitled to recover damages for the wrongful death of his wife, and was not prevented because as husband he was entitled to her earnings, so that she could accumulate nothing, and was valueless to her estate. Hunter v. Southern Ry. Co., 152 N. C. 682, 68 S. E. 237.

[172] Warner v. Western North Carolina R. Co., 94 N. C. 250.

§ 49—1. Ohio

Gen. Code 1912, §§ 10,770, 10,772, confer a right of action for death substantially similar to that created by Lord Campbell's act. Section 11,235 provides that, in addition to the causes which survive at common law, causes of action for injuries to the person shall survive, and that the action may be brought notwithstanding the death of the person entitled or liable thereto. The two actions are not in the same right, and a recovery and satisfaction in the one is not a bar to a recovery in the other.[173] There is also an employers' liability act.[174]

§ 50. Oklahoma

Const. art. 23, § 7, provides that the right of action to recover damages for injuries resulting in death shall never be abrogated, and the amount recoverable shall never be subject to any statutory limitation. By Const. art. 9, § 36, the common-law doctrine of the fellow servants, so far as it affects the liability of the master for injuries to his servant, resulting from the acts of other servants, is abrogated as to employés of railroad, street railway, or interurban railway companies, and persons, firms, or corporations engaged in mining, including receivers, and such employés shall have the same rights to recover for injuries suffered by them for the acts or omissions of other employés that a servant would have if such acts or omissions were those of the master in the performance of a nonassignable duty; and when death, whether instantaneous or not, results to an employé from any injury for which he could have re-

[173] Mahoning Valley Ry. Co. v. Van Alstine, 77 Ohio St. 395, 83 N. E. 601, 14 L. R. A. (N. S.) 893.
[174] Gen. Code 1912, §§ 6242 to 6245—3.

covered thereunder, his legal or personal representatives, surviving consort, or relatives, etc., shall have the same rights and remedies as if death had not been caused by the negligence of the master; and the legislature may extend to the employés of others the same rights and remedies. Comp. Laws 1909, § 5943, provides that, in addition to the causes of action which survive at common law, causes of action for "an injury to the person" shall survive, and the action may be brought, notwithstanding the death of the person entitled or liable to the same. Sections 5945, 5946, provide that, when death is caused by the wrongful act or omission of another, the personal representatives of the former may maintain an action, if the former might have maintained an action, for an injury from the same cause or omission; that the action must be commenced within two years, and that the damages cannot exceed $10,000, and inure to the exclusive benefit of the widow and children, if any, or next of kin, to be distributed in the same manner as personal property of the deceased; and that if the residence of the deceased was in another state or territory, or if, being a resident of the state, no personal representative is appointed, the action may be brought by the widow, or, if there be none, by the next of kin.[175]

§ 50a. Oregon

In addition to the action for death conferred by L. O. L., § 380,[176] an employers' liability act has recently been enacted.[177] This enactment does not abrogate section 380.[178]

---

[175] See St. Louis, I. M. & S. Ry. Co. v. Hesterly, 98 Ark. 240, 135 S. W. 874. Oklahoma Gas & Electric Co. v. Lukert, 16 Okl. 397, 84 Pac. 1076.

[176] See §§ 81, 144.

[177] Laws 1911, c. 3 (L. O. L. 1910, p. xxxvi).

[178] Staats v. Twohy Bros. Co. (Or.) 123 Pac. 909.

§ 51. Pennsylvania

The act of April 15, 1851, § 19,[179] provides that whenever death shall be occasioned by unlawful violence or negligence, and no suit for damages be brought by the party injured during his life, the widow, or, if no widow, the personal representatives, may maintain an action. The act of April 26, 1855, §§ 1, 2,[180] provides that the persons entitled to recover shall be the husband, widow, children, or par-

---

[179] Pepper & Lewis' Dig. pp. 5332, 5333, § 2.   An action for personal injuries having been commenced by the injured person, and after his death carried on by his mother, as his administratrix, under Act April 15, 1851, § 18, giving to a common-law action the quality of survivorship, damages cannot be recovered therein for his death under section 19, creating a new right of action, limited to cases where death is caused by violence or negligence, and no suit has been brought by the injured person in his lifetime. McCafferty v. Pennsylvania R. Co., 193 Pa. 339, 44 A. 435, 74 Am. St. Rep. 690. Under Act April 15, 1851, § 18, providing that no action to recover damages for personal injuries shall abate by the death of plaintiff, but his personal representatives may be substituted, and the action prosecuted to judgment, recovery for the death of plaintiff cannot be had in such action on the substitution of his personal representatives. Edwards v. Gimbel, 202 Pa. 30, 51 A. 357. Under Act April 15, 1851, § 19, action for decedent's death cannot be maintained, he having sued for damages for injury, and died pending the action. Edwards v. Gimbel, supra.

[180] Pepper & Lewis' Dig. pp. 5333–5336, § 3. The act of 1851 gives the right of action; the act of 1855 defines who may sue. North Pennsylvania R. Co. v. Robinson, 44 Pa. 175. See Conroy v. Pennsylvania R. Co., 1 Pittsb. R. 440. The section was amended in 1911, by adding the provision in respect to citizenship and residence of the plaintiffs. Act June 7, 1911 (P. L. 678). Act 1851 and Act 1855 being general laws, and not affecting corporations only, are not repealed by Const. art. 3, § 21, providing that "no act shall prescribe any limitation" for suits "against corporations" different from those fixed by general laws, and avoiding any such existing acts. Bachman v. Philadelphia & R. R. Co., 185 Pa. 95, 39 A. 834.

(109)

ents. The act of April 4, 1868, § 1,[181] limits the application of the act of 1851, by providing that when any person, not a passenger, shall sustain loss of life while lawfully engaged or employed on or about the roads, works, depots, and premises of a railroad company, or in or about any train or car therein or thereon, of which company such person is not an employé, the right of action and recovery shall be such only as would exist if such person were an employé.[182] Act June 10, 1907 (P. L. 523) §§ 1, 2, abolishes the fellow servant rule in certain cases.[183]

§ 52. Rhode Island

In addition to an action for death on the general lines of that of Lord Campbell's act, which is given by Gen. Laws 1909, c. 283, § 14,[184] it is provided by sections 7–9 that causes of action and actions of trespass and trespass on the case for damages to the person shall survive; that they may be originally brought and prosecuted by and against executors and administrators, and, if brought or prosecuted by or

[181] Pepper & Lewis' Dig. pp. 5337–5340, § 6. The acts of 1855 and 1868 are in pari materia, and both make a system. Pennsylvania R. Co. v. Keller, 67 Pa. 300. Section 6 is constitutional as a police regulation. Kirby v. Pennsylvania R. Co., 76 Pa. 506.

[182] No action can be maintained against a railroad company for the death of one employed by contractors to work on its railroad, and killed by the negligence of its servants. Fleming v. Pennsylvania R. Co., 134 Pa. 477, 19 Atl. 740.

[183] Pepper & Lewis' Dig. p. 5339, §§ 7, 8.

[184] For decisions under former statute, which by its terms was limited to death caused by "wrongful act," without expressly including neglect and default, see Chase v. American Steamboat Co., 10 R. I. 79; McCaughey v. Tripp, 12 R. I. 449; Cassidy v. Angell, 12 R. I. 447, 34 Am. Rep. 690; Bradbury v. Furlong, 13 R. I. 15, 43 Am. Rep. 1; Myette v. Gross, 18 R. I. 729, 30 Atl. 602. As to parties under former statute, see Goodwin v. Nickerson, 17 R. I. 478, 23 Atl. 13.

against any person in his lifetime, may be prosecuted or defended by his executor or administrator; and that the plaintiff may recover only the damages actually sustained, without vindictive or exemplary damages or damages to the feelings of the injured party.[185]

§ 53.   South Dakota

Comp. Laws 1910, p. 444a, c. 301, §§ 1–3,[186] provide for an action for death substantially on the lines of that given by Lord Campbell's act, and expressly provides that whenever the death of a citizen of the state is caused by wrongful act, neglect, or default in another state, territory, or country, in which a right to maintain an action in respect thereof is given by statute, such right of action may be enforced in the state within the time limited by the foreign statute.

[185] The right of action given by Rev. St. 1857, c. 176, §§ 16–21, to personal representatives, for the benefit of the widow and next of kin of one killed by wrongful act, is exclusive, and section 10, adding to the causes of action which survive that of "trespass on the case for damages to the person," gives the personal representative no additional right of action for injuries to the person which result in death.   Lubrano v. Atlantic Mills, 19 R. I. 129, 32 Atl. 205, 34 L. R. A. 797.   See, also, McLaughlin v. Hebron Mfg. Co. (C. C.) 171 Fed. 269.

[186] For decisions under former statutes, see Belding v. Black Hills & Ft. P. R. Co,. 3 S. D. 369, 53 N. W. 750; Lintz v. Holy Terror Min. Co., 13 S. D. 489, 83 N. W. 570; Bowen v. Illinois Cent. R. Co., 136 Fed. 306, 69 C. C. A. 444, 70 L. R. A. 915.

(111)

§ 54.   Tennessee [187]

§ 55.   Texas

Rev. St. 1895, art. 3017,[188] provides that an action for actual damages may be brought when the death of any person is caused (1) by the negligence or carelessness of the proprietor, owner, charterer, or hirer of any railroad, steamboat, stagecoach, or other vehicle for the conveyance of goods or passengers, or by the unfitness, negligence, or carelessness of their servants or agents; [189] (2) by the

---

[187] See § 107.

[188] See Sayles' Civ. St. 1888, art. 2899. The article is based on Act Feb. 2, 1860. The original act reads "unfitness, gross negligence, or carelessness of their servants," etc. This was amended by Act March 25, 1887, by omitting "gross." Before the amendment a defendant was not liable for the ordinary negligence, but only for the gross negligence, of his servants. Sabine & E. T. Ry. Co. v. Hanks, 73 Tex. 323, 11 S. W. 377; Id., 79 Tex. 642, 15 S. W. 476; Dallas City R. Co. v. Beeman, 74 Tex. 291, 11 S. W. 1102; Missouri Pac. Ry. Co. v. Brown, 75 Tex. 267, 12 S. W. 1117; Galveston, H. & S. A. Ry. Co. v. Kutac, 76 Tex. 473, 13 S. W. 327; San Antonio St. Ry. Co. v. Cailloutte, 79 Tex. 341, 15 S. W. 390; Galveston, H. & S. A. Ry. Co. v. Cook (Sup.) 16 S. W. 1038; Texas & P. Ry. Co. v. Hill, 71 Tex. 451, 9 S. W. 351. See Austin v. Cameron, 83 Tex. 351, 18 S. W. 437. The wrongful act, negligence, carelessness, unskillfulness, or default mentioned in the article must be such as would, if death had not ensued, have entitled the party injured to maintain an action. Rev. St. 1895, art. 3018.

[189] The first branch of article 3017 gave no action against an express company which, under contract, had a particular car, or a part of a car, in a train exclusively controlled by a railroad. Lipscomb v. Houston & T. C. Ry. Co., 95 Tex. 5, 64 S. W. 923, 55 L. R. A. 869, 93 Am. St. Rep. 804. See, also, Houston & T. C. Ry. Co. v. Wells Fargo & Co. (Civ. App.) 125 S. W. 971. Action lies for an intentional killing by an employé of a railroad, committed in guarding its property, because of a mistake resulting from want of due care. Lipscomb v. Houston & T. C. Ry. Co., supra. A railroad maintained

wrongful act, negligence, unskillfulness, or default of another.[190]   Article 3019 [191] provides that exemplary, as well as actual, damages may be recovered when the death is

a hospital for the care of employés, and a surgeon employed by the road hired an incompetent nurse to care for a servant afflicted with smallpox, and the nurse went on the public streets without disinfecting himself, and communicated the disease to plaintiff's intestate, from which he died. Held, that the railroad company was not liable for the death, as the negligence of the surgeon could not be regarded as the negligence of the road itself under subdivision 2, and the first subdivision was not applicable, since the maintenance of the hospital was not peculiar to the carrier's business, but merely col-

---

[190] Under the second branch of article 3017, an action may be brought against a private corporation. Fleming v. Texas Loan Agency, 87 Tex. 238, 27 S. W. 126, 26 L. R. A. 250. See, also, Burns v. Merchants' & Planters' Oil Co., 26 Tex. Civ. App. 223, 63 S. W. 1061; Citizens' Tel. Co. v. Thomas, 45 Tex. Civ. App. 20, 99 S. W. 879; Jacksonville Ice & Electric Co. v. Moses (Civ. App.) 134 S. W. 379. A locomotive engineer may be sued for negligently causing the death of one crossing the track in front of his train. Texas & P. Ry. Co. v. Tucker, 48 Tex. Civ. App. 115, 106 S. W. 764.

[191] Article 3019 is based on Const. art. 16, § 26. See appendix. The earlier constitutional provision (Const. 1869, art. 12, § 30) did not contain the words "gross neglect." See Houston & T. C. Ry. Co. v. Baker, 57 Tex. 419. Const. 1869 provided that the defendant should be responsible to the persons specified "separately and consecutively." The omission of these words in Const. 1876 indicates an intent to allow only one suit for the benefit of all persons jointly interested. Galveston, H. & S. A. R. Co. v. Le Gierse, 51 Tex. 189. The constitutional provisions did not repeal the earlier act, but gave the right to exemplary damages in the cases named in addition to compensatory damages. March v. Walker, 48 Tex. 372; Houston & T. C. Ry. Co. v. Moore, 49 Tex. 31, 30 Am. Rep. 98; Gohen v. Texas Pac. R. Co., 2 Woods, 346, Fed. Cas. No. 5,506. See Houston & T. C. R. Co. v. Bradley, 45 Tex. 171; March v. Walker, 48 Tex. 372. Where both actual and exemplary damages are sought, the allegations should be in the nature of two distinct counts. Galveston, H. & S. A. R. Co. v. Le Gierse. Where the evidence in such an action justifies the direction of a verdict for plaintiff it is not error to instruct as matter of law to award exemplary as well as actual damages. Morgan v. Barnhill, 118 F. 24, 55 C. C. A. 1.

caused by the willful act, omission, or gross negligence of the defendant.

Liability for the acts of servants and agents is confined to the persons enumerated in the first branch of article 3017, and other persons are liable only for their own acts.[192]

lateral thereto. Missouri, K. & T. Ry. Co. of Texas v. Freeman, 97 Tex. 394, 79 S. W. 9, 1 Ann. Cas. 481. See, also, Wm. Cameron & Co. v. McSween (Civ. App.) 137 S. W. 139. Conceding that the statute, giving an action against railroad companies for death caused by the unfitness, negligence, or carelessness of their servants, requires that the death be "negligently," as distinguished from "willfully," caused, it is not essential to liability that death should result from an act unintentionally done, and, if the servant negligently does an act with no purpose of inflicting injury, but it proximately causes death, the railroad is liable. Galveston, H. & S. A. Ry. Co. v. Currie, 100 Tex. 136, 96 S. W. 1073, 10 L. R. A. (N. S.) 367. Where one employed in a railroad roundhouse, while using compressed air in the line of his duty, in sport turned it on a subordinate, causing his death, the railroad was not liable. Galveston, H. & S. A. Ry. Co. v. Currie, supra. The first branch of article 3017, does not apply to tram railroads owned and operated by private individuals on their own premises for private purposes. Ott v. Johnson (Civ. App.) 101 S. W. 534. See, also, Halbert v. Texas Tie & Lumber Preserving Co. (Civ. App.) 107 S. W. 592. An electric company is liable for the negligence of its employés in leaving high voltage wires uninsulated. San Antonio Gas & Electric Co. v. Badders, 46 Tex. Civ. App. 559, 103 S. W. 229. Cf. Williams v. Northern Texas Traction Co. (Civ. App.) 107 S. W. 125. The first branch of article 3017 applies to carriers transporting persons or freight from some point of origin to some more or less distant point of destination, and not to an elevator in an office building used to transport persons visiting the building; the words "other vehicle" meaning a vehicle performing, substantially at least, the same office and serving the same necessities as a railroad, steamboat, or stage coach. Farmers' & Mechanics' Nat. Bank v. Hanks (Sup.) 137 S. W. 1120. See, also, Pulom v. Jacob Dold Packing Co. (C. C.) 182 Fed. 356.

[192] Hendrick v. Walton, 69 Tex. 192, 6 S. W. 749; Asher v. Cabell, 50 Fed. 818, 1 C. C. A. 693. See, also, Lipscomb v. Houston & T. C. Ry. Co., 95 Tex. 5, 64 S. W. 923, 55 L. R. A. 869, 93 Am. St. Rep. 804, 806; Cole v. Parker, 27 Tex. Civ. App. 563, 66 S. W. 135; Shippers' Compress & Warehouse Co. v. Davidson, 35 Tex. Civ. App. 558, 80 S. W. 1032.

Under article 3019 a corporation is liable in exemplary damages only for the willful act, omission, or gross negligence of persons representing it as corporate officers, not of mere servants or agents.[193]

Under article 3017, as it formerly existed, it was held that a receiver of a railroad company was not a "proprietor, own_er, charterer, or hirer," and hence was not liable thereunder.[194] The article was amended, and it is now provided, under the first branch, that an action may be brought when the death of any person is caused by the negligence or carelessness of the receivers or other persons in charge or control of "any railroad," their servants or agents, and that the liability of receivers shall extend to cases in which the death may be caused by reason of the bad or unsafe condition of the railroad or machinery or other reason or cause by which an action may be brought for damages on account of injuries, as if the railroad were being operated by the railroad company.[195]

[193] Houston & T. C. Ry. Co. v. Cowser, 57 Tex. 306. If the act of a servant, it must have been performed by the direction of the employer, or he must have ratified and adopted it. Mere retention of the servant after the act is not ratification. International & G. N. Ry. Co. v. McDonald, 75 Tex. 41, 12 S. W. 860; Winnt v. International & G. N. Ry. Co., 74 Tex. 32, 11 S. W. 907, 5 L. R. A. 172.

[194] Turner v. Cross, 83 Tex. 218, 18 S. W. 578, 15 L. R. A. 262; Yoakum v. Selph, 83 Tex. 607, 19 S. W. 145; Texas P. Ry. Co. v. Collins, 84 Tex. 121, 19 S. W. 365; Houston & T. C. Ry. Co. v. Roberts (Sup.) 19 S. W. 512. See, also, Texas P. Ry. Co. v. Collins, in Texas & P. Ry. Co. v. Geiger, 79 Tex. 13, 15 S. W. 214.

[195] The expression "any railroad" includes street railroads. Bammel v. Kirby, 19 Tex. Civ. App. 198, 47 S. W. 392. The word "railroad" in the part of the section creating the liability on receivers has the same import that it has in the first part of the section, so that the receivers of a lumber company owning a standard-gauge spur leading from a commercial railroad to its plant and timber, and used for the transportation of its products and supplies, were liable for the wrongful killing of a servant through the negligence of other

(115)

§ 56. Virginia

Code 1904, §§ 2902–2904, provide that whenever death is caused by wrongful act, neglect, etc., the personal representative may maintain an action; that the jury may award such damages as to it may seem fair and just, not exceeding $10,000, and may direct in what proportion they shall be distributed to the wife, husband, or child, or, if there be none, to the parents, brothers, and sisters; and that the amount recovered shall, after the payment of costs, etc., be distributed by the personal representative to the beneficiaries, in such proportion as the jury may have directed, or, if they have not directed, according to the statute of distributions, and shall be free from all debts and liabilities of the deceased; but that, if there be no wife, husband, child, parent, brother, or sister, the amount shall be assets in the hands of the personal representative, to be disposed of according to law.

By reason of the amount recovered being assets if there are none of the beneficiaries named, it is held that the existence of beneficiaries is not necessary to the maintenance of the action.[196]

servants operating the road. Receivers of Kirby Lumber Co. v. Owens, 56 Tex. Civ. App. 370, 120 S. W. 936.

[196] Baltimore & O. R. Co. v. Wightman's Adm'r, 70 Va. 431, 26 Am. Rep. 384. The point actually decided was that it is not necessary to aver in the declaration for whose benefit the suit is prosecuted. This case was followed in Matthews v. Warner's Adm'r, 70 Va. 570, 26 Am. Rep. 396; Baltimore & O. R. Co. v. Noell's Adm'r, 73 Va. 394; Harper v. Norfolk & W. R. Co. (C. C.) 36 Fed. 102. The existence, etc., of widow and children may be proved, however, for the ascertainment and apportionment of damages. Baltimore & O. R. Co. v. Sherman's Adm'x, 71 Va. 602. Cf. Richmond, F. & P. R. Co.. v. Martin's Adm'r, 102 Va. 201, 45 S. E. 894.

§ 57. Washington

Rem. & Bal. Code, § 183,[197] provides that the widow, or widow and her children, or child or children, if no widow, of a man killed in a duel, shall have a right of action against the person killing him, etc.; that, when the death of a person is caused by the wrongful act or neglect of another, his heirs or personal representatives may maintain an action for damages against the person causing the death; that, if the deceased leaves no widow or issue, his parents, sisters, or minor brothers, who may be dependent on him for support and who are residents within the United States at his death, may maintain the action; that when the death of a

[197] For the history of the statutes, see Atrops v. Costello, 8 Wash. 149, 35 Pac. 620; Noble v. City of Seattle, 19 Wash. 133, 52 Pac. 1013, 40 L. R. A. 822; Robinson v. Baltimore & S. Mining & Reduction Co., 26 Wash. 484, 67 Pac. 274. Laws 1869, p. 165, § 658, giving the personal representatives a right to maintain an action for wrongful death, and limiting the time to commence it to two years after the death, was repealed, including such limitation, by Ballinger's Ann. Codes & St. § 4828. Robinson v. Baltimore & S. Mining & Reduction Co., 26 Wash. 484, 67 Pac. 274. See, also, Graetz v. McKenzie, 3 Wash. 194, 28 Pac. 331; Northern Pac. R. Co. v. Ellison, 3 Wash. 225, 28 Pac. 333; Dahl v. Tibbals, 5 Wash. 259, 31 Pac. 868. Sections 183 and 194 should be taken separately, each to perform its distinct purpose. Swanson v. Pacific Shipping Co., 60 Wash. 87, 110 Pac. 795. "Heirs or personal representatives" include only widow and children. Noble v. City of Seattle, supra; Nesbitt v. Northern Pac. Ry. Co., 22 Wash. 698, 61 Pac. 141; Manning v. Tacoma Ry. & Power Co., 34 Wash. 406, 75 Pac. 994. Cf. Peterman v. Northern Pac. Ry. Co. (C. C.) 105 Fed. 335. While it is customary to prosecute an action for the death of a husband in the names of the widow and children, such an action may be prosecuted in the name of the personal representative, for the benefit of the widow and children. Archibald v. Lincoln County, 50 Wash. 55, 96 Pac. 831. The section contemplates one cause of action only, to be prosecuted in a single proceeding by the heirs or personal representatives of the deceased. Riggs v. Northern Pac. Ry. Co., 60 Wash. 292, 111 Pac. 162.

person is caused by an injury received in falling through a
defective place in the sidewalk, etc., his heirs or personal
representatives, or, if he leave none, his parents, sisters, or
minor brothers, who may be dependent on him for support and who are residents within the United States at his
death, may maintain an action against the person whose
duty it was to put the sidewalk, etc., in repair; and that in
every such action the jury may give such damages as under
all the circumstances of the case may be just. Section
184 [198] provides that a father, or in case of his death or desertion of his family the mother, may maintain an action for
the death of a child, and a guardian for the death of a ward.
Section 194 [199] provides that no action for a personal injury

---

[198] For death of a minor child two actions could be maintained,
one under section 183 for loss to the estate accruing after majority,
and one under section 184 for the loss of service accruing before.
Hedrick v. Ilwaco Ry. & Nav. Co., 4 Wash. 400, 30 Pac. 714. Section
183 does not authorize an action by a mother for death of her son,
who was more than 21 years of age. Nesbitt v. Northern Pac. Ry.
Co., 22 Wash. 698, 61 Pac. 141. Though the parents have been
divorced and custody of a son awarded to the father, yet, the father
having brought him to and left him with the mother, and then gone
away, and the son being thereafter supported by the mother, she can
sue for his death. Clark v. Northern Pac. Ry. Co., 29 Wash. 139,
69 Pac. 636, 59 L. R. A. 508. See Winfree v. Northern Pac. Ry. Co.,
173 Fed. 65, 97 C. C. A. 392.

[199] 2 Hill's Code, § 148, providing that no action for a personal
injury shall abate, nor shall such right of action determine, by reason of death "if he have a wife or child living, but such action may
be prosecuted" in favor of such wife or child, was not repealed by
section 138, giving such right of action to the "heirs or personal
representatives" of deceased. Noble v. City of Seattle, 19 Wash. 133,
52 Pac. 1013, 40 L. R. A. 822. Rem. & Bal. Code, §§ 183, 194, authorize an executor to maintain an action for the wrongful death of
his testator for the benefit of the surviving wife, and with her sanc-
tion. Copeland v. City of Seattle, 33 Wash. 415, 74 Pac. 582, 65 L.
R. A. 333. In order that the widow and children may recover in
the action brought by deceased for injuries, they must both allege and

to any person occasioning his death shall abate, nor such right of action determine, by reason of such death, if he have a wife or child living, or, leaving none, if he have dependent on him for support and resident within the United States at his death parents, sisters, or minor brothers, and that such action may be prosecuted or commenced in favor of the wife, or of the wife and children, or, if no wife, in favor of children, or, if no wife or children, of parents, sisters, and minor brothers, etc.

§ 58. West Virginia

Code 1906, §§ 3488, 3489, provide that whenever death is caused by wrongful act, neglect, etc., the personal representative may maintain an action; that the amount recovered shall be distributed to the parties and in the proportions provided by law in relation to the distribution of personal estate left by persons dying intestate; and that the jury may give such damages as they shall deem fair and just, not exceeding $10,000, and the amount recovered shall not be subject to any debts and liabilities of the deceased.

Although the statute declares that the amount recovered shall not be subject to the debts and liabilities of the de-

prove that the identical injuries for which deceased had sued, caused his death under section 194. Swanson v. Pacific Shipping Co., 60 Wash. 87, 110 Pac. 795. In a suit continued under section 194, providing that a deceased's widow may continue an action brought by him for injuries, she may recover such damages as he could have recovered; his death, therefore, not being an element of damage. Id. The action may be commenced within three years. Robinson v. Baltimore & S. Mining & Reduction Co., 26 Wash. 484, 67 Pac. 274. In an action for the wrongful death of plaintiff's adult son, evidence held not to show dependence within the meaning of the statute. Bortle v. Northern Pac. R. Co,. 60 Wash. 552, 111 Pac. 788, Ann. Cas. 1912B, 731. See, also, Dueber v. Northern Pac. R. Co. (C. C.) 100 Fed. 424.

ceased, it seems to be held that the existence of next of kin is not necessary to the maintenance of the action.[200]

§ 58—1. Wisconsin

The statutes confer a right of action for death, substantially like that created by Lord Campbell's act, and also enact that, in addition to the actions which survive at common law, actions for assault and battery, false imprisonment, or other damage to the person, shall survive. The right of action for death is not exclusive of the action under the survival act, and it seems that a recovery in the one action would not bar a recovery in the other.[201]

---

[200] It is not necessary to aver in the declaration that the decedent left wife, children, or other next of kin. Madden's Adm'r v. Chesapeake & O. Ry. Co., 28 W. Va. 610, 57 Am. Rep. 695. But the declaration is not demurrable because it names the widow and children. Searle v. Kanawha & O. Ry. Co., 32 W. Va. 370, 9 S. E. 248. Under an earlier act providing that the amount recovered should be for the exclusive benefit of the widow and next of kin, it was held that the declaration was defective for failure to allege that the decedent left widow or next of kin. Baltimore & O. R. Co. v. Gettle, 3 W. Va. 376.

[201] Brown v. Chicago & N. W. R. Co., 102 Wis. 137, 77 N. W. 748, 78 N. W. 771, 44 L. R. A. 579. See Lehmann v. Farwell, 95 Wis. 185, 70 N. W. 170, 37 L. R. A. 333, 60 Am. St. Rep. 111. The two causes of action may be joined. Nemecek v. Filer & Stowell Co., 126 Wis. 71, 105 N. W. 225. The right of action given for the benefit of the children of a deceased person under the death act constitutes no part of deceased's estate, and hence a final settlement of the estate does not operate as a bar to the children's right of action by a personal representative of deceased. Hubbard v. Chicago & N. W. Ry. Co., 104 Wis. 160, 80 N. W. 454, 76 Am. St. Rep. 855.

§ 59.   Miners' acts

In Illinois,[202] Indiana,[203] Missouri,[204] and Pennsylvania[205] there exist special acts for the protection of the life and safety of persons employed in coal mines. The Illinois act gives a right of action, in cases of loss of life by reason of willful violation of the act, or of willful failure to comply with its provisions, in favor of the widow and next of kin of the person so killed, and other persons dependent[206] upon him, for a recovery of damages for the injuries sustained by reason of such loss of life, not to exceed $10,000. The acts of Indiana, Missouri, and Pennsylvania are in their principal features the same. In order to render the defendant liable under the Illinois act, the failure must be willful,[207] and the safeguard omitted must have been such that it would have prevented the fatal result;[208] but, if it would have prevented such result, it is immaterial that the occasion for the safeguard arose from a purely accidental cause.[209] There can be no recovery unless the party injured could have maintained an action if death had not ensued.[210] The action is properly brought by the wid-

[202] Hurd's Rev. St. 1911, c. 93, § 29 (c).

[203] Burns' Ann. St. 1908, § 8597.

[204] Rev. St. 1909, § 8471.

[205] Pepper & Lewis' Dig. p. 5131, par. 265.

[206] Brothers or sisters have no cause of action unless they were dependent on deceased. Willis Coal & Mining Co. v. Grizzell, 198 Ill. 313, 65 N. E. 74.

[207] Hawley v. Dailey, 13 Ill. App. 391. See Athens Min. Co. v. Carnduff, 123 Ill. App. 178; Id., 221 Ill. 354, 77 N. E. 571.

[208] Coal Run Coal Co. v. Jones, 127 Ill. 379, 20 N. E. 89, affirming 8 N. E. 865.

[209] Wesley City Coal Co. v. Healer, 84 Ill. 126.

[210] Spiva v. Osage Coal & Mining Co., 88 Mo. 68; Silliman v. Marsden (Pa.) 9 Atl. 639; Cambria Iron Co. v. Shaffer (Pa.) 8 Atl. 204.

ow, not the personal representative;[211] and, as only one action is contemplated, evidence that the deceased left children, as well as a widow, is admissible.[212]

§ 59—1. Federal employers' liability acts

First act (1906)

Act June 11, 1906, c. 3073, 34 Stat. 232 (U. S. Comp. St. Supp. 1911, p. 1316), enacts that every common carrier engaged in trade or commerce in the District of Columbia, or in any territory, or between the several states, or between any territory and another, or between any territory or territories and any state or states, or the Distict of Colum-

---

[211] Litchfield Coal Co. v. Taylor, 81 Ill. 590: See Staunton Coal Co. v. Fischer, 119 Ill. App. 284; McCray v. Moweaqua Coal Mining & Mfg. Co., 149 Ill. App. 565; Hoover v. Empire Coal Co., 149 Ill. App. 258; Hougland v. Avery Coal & Mining Co., 152 Ill. App. 573, affirmed 246 Ill. 609, 93 N. E. 40. See, also, Boyd v. Brazil Block Coal Co. (Ind. App.) 50 N. E. 368; Boyd v. Brazil Block Coal Co., 25 Ind. App. 157, 57 N. E. 732; Maule Coal Co. of Princeton v. Partenheimer, 155 Ind. 100, 55 N. E. 751, 57 N. E. 710; L. T. Dickason Coal Co. v. Unverferth, 30 Ind. App. 546, 66 N. E. 759; Collins Coal Co. v. Hadley, 38 Ind. App. 637, 75 N. E. 832, 78 N. E. 353; Brown v. Sunday Creek Co. (C. C.) 165 Fed. 504 (Ohio statute). Rev. St. 1889, § 7074, as amended by Acts 1891, p. 182, providing that, in case of the death of an employé in a mine through the negligence of his employer, a right of action shall accrue to the widow of the person so killed, his lineal heirs or adopted children, etc, gives a separate right of action to the persons in the order named, and hence the widow may maintain an action without joining the children. Hamman v. Central Coal & Coke Co., 156 Mo. 232, 56 S. W. 1091. See, also, Poor v. Watson, 92 Mo. App. 89; Cole v. Mayne (C. C.) 122 Fed. 836.

[212] Beard v. Skeldon, 113 Ill. 584; Id., 13 Ill. App. 54; Consolidated Coal Co. v. Maehl, 130 Ill. 551, 22 N. E. 715. Judgment may not be awarded plaintiffs jointly, one of them not being entitled to sue. Willis Coal & Mining Co. v. Grizzell, 198 Ill. 313, 65 N. E. 74. See Hart v. Penwell Coal Mining Co., 146 Ill. App. 155.

bia, or with foreign nations, or between the District of Columbia and any state or states or foreign nations, shall be liable to any of its employés, or in case of his death to his personal representative, for the benefit of his widow and children, if any, and if none, then for his parents, and if none then for his next of kin, for all damages which may result from the negligence of any of its officers, agents, or employés, or by reason of any defect or insufficiency due to its negligence in its cars, engines, appliances, machinery, track, roadbed, ways, or works; that in actions so brought the contributory negligence of the employé shall not bar a recovery, where his contributory negligence was slight and that of the employer was gross in comparison, but the damages shall be diminished by the jury in proportion to the amount of negligence attributable to such employé, questions of negligence and contributory negligence being for the jury; that no contract of employment, and no insurance, relief benefit, or indemnity, or acceptance of the same by the person entitled, shall be a bar or defense, etc.; that no action shall be maintained unless commenced within one year from the time the cause of action accrued, etc.

In Employers' Liability Cases [213] it was held by the Supreme Court of the United States that while Congress may prescribe, as between an interstate carrier and such of its employés as are engaged in interstate commerce, that the carrier shall be liable for the death or injury of any such employé while so engaged which may result from the negligence of a fellow servant, a regulation of intrastate as well as of interstate commerce, and therefore one beyond the power of Congress to enact, is made by the provision that "every common carrier engaged in trade or commerce" in the District of Columbia or in the territories or between

[213] 207 U. S. 463, 28 Sup. Ct. 141, 52 L. Ed. 297.

the several states shall be liable for the death or injury
of "any of its employés" which may result from the negligence of "any of its officers, agents, or employés," and that
the invalidity of the provision as applied to intrastate commerce invalidates the provision as applied to interstate commerce. In El Paso & N. R. Co. v. Gutierrez,[214] it was held
that Congress had power to enact so much of the act as
provides that every common carrier engaged in trade or
commerce in any territory shall be liable for the death
or injury of any of its employés which so results; that
the invalidity, so far as interstate commerce is concerned,
of the act, does not invalidate such of its provisions as attempt to regulate commerce within the District of Columbia
and the territories; and that the act necessarily superseded
any otherwise applicable provisions of the New Mexico act
governing suits for death and personal injuries.

. Second act (1908)

Act April 22, 1908, c. 149, 35 Stat. 65 (U. S. Comp. St.
Supp. 1911, p. 1322),[215] enacts that every common carrier
by railroad, while engaged in commerce between any of the
states and territories or between the District of Columbia
and any of the states or territories, or between the District of Columbia or any of the states or territories and any
foreign nation or nations, shall be liable in damages [216] to
any person suffering injury while he is employed by such
carrier in such commerce, or, in case of the death of such

---

[214] 215 U. S. 87, 30 Sup. Ct. 21, 54 L. Ed. 106, affirming 102 Tex.
378, 117 S. W. 426. See, also, Hyde v. Southern R. Co., 31 App. D.
C. 466.

[215] As amended by Act April 5, 1910, c. 143, 36 Stat. 291 (U. S.
Comp. St. Supp. 1911, pp. 1324. 1325).

[216] An instruction permitting a recovery for the loss sustained by
decedent's children, consisting of their loss of care, attention, in.

(124)

employé, to his or her personal representative,[217] for the benefit of the surviving widow or husband, and children, and if none then of parents, and if none then of the next of kin dependent upon such employé, for such injury or death resulting in whole or in part from the negligence of any of the officers, agents, or employés of such carrier, or by reason of any defect or insufficiency due to the negligence in its cars, engines, appliances, machinery, track, roadbed, works, boats, wharves, or other equipment; that every common carrier by railroad in the territories, the District of Columbia, the Panama Canal Zone, or other possessions of the United States, shall be liable in damages to any person suffering injury while he is employed by such carrier in any of said jurisdictions, or in case of the death of such employé to his personal representative, for the benefit of the persons above specified, for such injury or death resulting as above specified; that in actions so brought the con-

struction, and training from their father's death, was not erroneous. Duke v. St. Louis & S. F. R. Co. (C. C.) 172 Fed. 684. The jury in estimating the damages to the surviving widow, who is the only beneficiary, may not allow damages for mental anguish as a result of her loss. Vreeland v. Michigan Cent. R. Co. (C. C.) 189 Fed. 495. That a wife was temporarily separated from her husband at the time he was killed while in defendant's employ did not affect her right to recover damages under the act for his wrongful death. Dunbar v. Charleston & W. C. Ry. Co. (C. C.) 186 Fed. 175.

[217] The widow and son of a deceased railway employé cannot sue in their own names, especially in Porto Rico. American Railroad Co. of Porto Rico v. Birch, 224 U. S. 547, 32 Sup. Ct. 603, 56 L. Ed. 879. The action must be brought by the executor or administrator, and cannot be maintained by the widow or beneficiary. Thompson v. Wabash R. Co. (C. C.) 184 Fed. 554. The next of kin have no right of action where there is no personal representative; "if none" referring to the beneficiaries. Fithian v. St. Louis & S. F. Ry. Co. (C. C.) 188 Fed. 842. See, also, Rich v. St. Louis & S. F. R. Co. (Mo. App.) 148 S. W. 1011; Gulf, C. & S. F. R. Co. v. McGinnis (Tex. Civ. App.) 147 S. W. 1188.

tributory negligence of the employé shall not bar a recovery, but the damages shall be diminished by the jury in proportion to the amount of negligence attributable to such employé; that no employé shall be held to have been guilty of contributory negligence, or to have assumed the risks of the employment, in any case where the violation by such carrier of any statute enacted for the safety of the employé contributed to the injury or death; that any contract, rule, regulation, or device whatsoever, the purpose and intent of which is to enable the carrier to exempt itself from liability created by the act, shall be to that extent void, etc.; that no action shall be maintained unless commenced within two years from the day the cause of action accrued; that an action may be brought in the circuit court of the United States, in the district of the residence of the defendant, or in which the cause of action arose, or in which the defendant shall be doing business; that the jurisdiction of the courts of the United States shall be concurrent with that of the state courts, and no case brought in a state court of competent jurisdiction shall be removed to any court of the United States;[218] that the term "common carrier" shall include receiver, etc.; that nothing in the act shall be held to limit the duty or liability of common carriers, or to impair the rights of their employés under any other act of Congress, etc.; and that any right of action given by the act to a person suffering injury shall survive to his or her personal representative, for the benefit of the persons above specified, but in such cases there shall be only one recovery for the same injury.[219]

[218] The provisions in respect to bringing action in the circuit court, jurisdiction, and removal were added by the amendment of 1910.

[219] The provision that the right of action of the person injured shall survive was added by the amendment of 1910. Before the

(126)

In Second Employers' Liability Cases,[220] the Supreme Court of the United States sustained the validity of the employers' liability act of April 22, 1908, against attack upon various grounds, and determined, among other questions, that Congress did not by the act exceed its powers to regulate the relations of interstate railway carriers and their employés engaged in interstate commerce, although the act abrogates the fellow servant rule, extends the carrier's liability in case of death, and restricts the defenses of contributory negligence and assumption of risk; that the power of

amendment the employé's right to sue for an injury did not survive death. Fulgham v. Midland Valley R. Co. (C. C.) 167 Fed. 660. See Walsh v. New York, N. H. & H. R. Co. (C. C.) 173 Fed. 494; Midland Valley R. Co. v. Le Moyne (Ark.) 148 S. W. 654.

[220] This case reversed Mondou v. New York, N. H. & H. R. Co., 82 Conn. 373, 73 Atl. 762 (which followed Hoxie v. New York, N. H. & H. R. Co., 82 Conn. 352, 73 Atl. 754, 17 Ann. Cas. 324), and affirmed judgments of the circuit courts for the districts of Minnesota and Massachusetts. The act supersedes all state statutes regulating the relations of railroad employers and employés engaged in interstate commerce. Fulgham v. Midland Valley R. Co. (C. C.) 167 Fed. 660. Cf. Thompson v. Wabash R. Co. (C. C.) 184 Fed. 554. A locomotive fireman was killed in New York while employed in an interstate trip, and his widow, as administratrix, brought suit under the federal act, and accepted defendant's offer of judgment, and judgment was entered and the sum paid. The intestate's father claimed one-half of the proceeds of judgment under the New York death act, which provides that the damages shall be distributed as unbequeathed assets. Held, that distribution was governed by the state act, and not by the federal act. The majority of the courts held that the power to regulate interstate commerce, so far as concerns employés of common carriers engaged in interstate commerce, ends with the death of the employé, and that the federal act, in so far as it attempts to distribute the fund, is unconstitutional. In re Taylor, 204 N. Y. 135, 97 N. E. 502. The cause of action having been created by the statute, which prescribes the distribution, it seems that the distribution must be made thereunder. See dissenting opinion of Hiscock, J. The case was decided before Second Employers' Liability Cases.

Congress under the commerce clause to regulate the liability of an interstate railway carrier for the death or injury of an employé engaged in interstate commerce, which may result from the negligence of a fellow servant, is not exceeded, although the act embraces instances where the causal negligence is that of an employé engaged in intrastate commerce; that the laws of the several states, in so far as they cover the field, were superseded by the act; that the enforcement of rights under the act cannot be regarded as impliedly restricted to the federal courts; and that jurisdiction of an action to enforce the rights arising under the act may not be declined by the courts of a state whose ordinary jurisdiction as prescribed by local laws is adequate to the occasion. Referring to the prior act, the court said: "The present act, unlike the one condemned in Employers' Liability Cases (Howard v. Illinois C. R. Co., 207 U. S. 463, 28 Sup. Ct. 141, 52 L. Ed. 297), deals only with the liability of a carrier engaged in interstate commerce for injuries sustained by its employés while engaged in such commerce. And this being so, it is not a valid objection that the act embraces instances where the causal negligence is that of an employé engaged in intrastate commerce; for such negligence, when operating injuriously upon an employé engaged in interstate commerce, has the same effect upon that commerce as if the negligent employé were also engaged therein."

(128)

CHAPTER IV

THE WRONGFUL ACT, NEGLECT, OR DEFAULT

§ 60. When action lies

In order that a cause of action under Lord Campbell's act and similar statutes shall exist, it is necessary that the following circumstances concur: (1) That the death shall have been caused by such wrongful act, neglect, or default of the defendant that an action might have been maintained therefor by the party injured if death had not ensued; (2) that there be in existence some one of the persons for whose benefit the action may be brought; (3) that there be in existence a proper party plaintiff—that is, that an executor or administrator shall have been appointed—unless the statute authorizes the action to be brought directly by the beneficiaries; (4) that the time within which the action must be brought has not elapsed; and, (5) according to some authorities, that the beneficiaries, or some one of them, shall have suffered pecuniary loss by reason of the death. Whether, if no pecuniary loss has been sustained, the action may be maintained for nominal damages, is a question upon which there is a conflict of authority, and which will be discussed later.

§ 61. The wrongful act, neglect, or default

Lord Campbell's act provides that whenever the death of any person is caused by wrongful act, neglect, or default, and the act, neglect, or default is such as would, if death had not ensued, have entitled the party injured to maintain an action and recover damages in respect thereof, then, and in every such case, the person who would have been liable if death had not ensued shall be liable notwithstanding the death.

This language has been followed in nearly all the American acts, except those which in terms provide for the survival of the action of the party injured, although some of the acts do not expressly provide that the act, neglect, or default must be such as would have entitled the party injured to maintain an action. Differences occur, however, in the description of the act or default. For example, the language used in Alabama is "wrongful act, omission, or negligence;" in Texas, "wrongful act, negligence, unskillfulness, or default;" in California, Idaho, Montana, Utah, and Washington "wrongful act or neglect;" in Arizona, "wrongful act or default;" in Delaware and Pennsylvania, "unlawful violence and negligence;" in Florida, "wrongful act, negligence, or carelessness;" in Indiana, Kansas, Minnesota, Oklahoma, Oregon, and Washington, "wrongful act or omission;" in Mississippi, "wrongful or negligent act or omission;" in Tennessee, "wrongful act, omission, or killing." In Georgia action lies in case of "homicide," which is made to include all cases where death results from a crime, or from criminal or other negligence.

§ 62. "Wrongful"

The word "wrongful" requires little comment. To be "wrongful," an act need not be intentional.[1] Whether an act is wrongful depends upon the duty or obligation which the defendant owed to the party injured. As was observed in a Minnesota case:[2] "In the case at bar, any act or omission violative of the obligations which the appellants as common carriers of passengers assumed towards the intestate would be a 'wrongful act or omission,' within the meaning of the statute. The word 'wrongful' in the statute is not used in the sense of 'willful' or 'malicious.'" So the Supreme Court of the United States: "The statute does

---

[1] Baker v. Bailey, 16 Barb. 54; McLean v. Burbank, 12 Minn. 530 (Gil. 438.) The words "wrongful" and "negligent" being synonymous, plaintiff, by asking to go to the jury on the question of the act being "wrongful," did not abandon the theory of negligence. Wells v. Sibley, 56 Hun, 644, 9 N. Y. Supp. 343.

[2] McLean v. Burbank, supra; State, to Use of Coughlan, v. Baltimore & O. R. Co., 24 Md. 84, 87 Am. Dec. 600; Baltimore & O. R. Co. v. State, to Use of Smith, 29 Md. 460; Evans v. Newland, 34 Ind. 112. The wrongfulness of an act is not determinable by the opinions of the parties to the action, but by the law applicable to the act and to the facts and circumstances which conditioned its performance. Rutherford v. Foster, 125 Fed. 187, 60 C. C. A. 129.

not provide that when one's life is taken by another the heirs of the former may recover damages, but only when it is wrongfully taken—that is, when it is taken in violation of the rights of the decedent; wrongful as against him. 'Neglect' stands in the same category with 'wrongful act.' It implies some omission of duty." [8]

§ 63.   Act or neglect must be such that party injured might have maintained action

An essential limitation upon the words "wrongful act, neglect, or default" is created by the provision that they must be such as would have entitled the party injured to maintain an action therefor.   This provision makes it a condition to the maintenance of the statutory action that an action might have been maintained by the party injured for the bodily injury.[4]   The condition has reference, of course, not to the loss or injury sustained by him, but to the circumstances under which the bodily injury arose, and to the nature of the wrongful act, neglect, or default; [5] and,

[8] Northern P. R. Co. v. Adams, 192 U. S. 440, 24 Sup. Ct. 408, 48 L. Ed. 513.

[4] Neilson v. Brown, 13 R. I. 651, 43 Am. Rep. 58; Martin v. Wallace, 40 Ga. 52; Wallace v. Cannon, 38 Ga. 199, 95 Am. Dec. 385; Malott v. Shimer, 153 Ind. 35, 54 N. E. 101, 74 Am. St. Rep. 278; Mahoning Valley Ry. Co. v. Van Alstine, 77 Ohio St. 395, 83 N. E. 601, 14 L. R. A. (N. S.) 893.   Where a mother was injured through the negligence of defendant so that she gave premature birth to a child, which died as a result of the premature delivery, since the child could not have maintained an action for injuries received while in his mother's womb, no action was maintainable for his death. Gorman v. Budlong, 23 R. I. 169, 49 Atl. 704, 55 L. R. A. 118, 91 Am. St. Rep. 629.

[5] Per Cockburn, C. J., in Pym v. Great Northern Ry. Co., 2 B. & S. 759.   The objection had been raised that no action could be maintained, inasmuch as action lay only in case the deceased could have

although this condition has not been expressed in California, Idaho, Kentucky, and Utah, no case has been found in which it has not been implied.[6]

A preliminary question arises, therefore, in every action for death, namely, was the act, neglect, or default complained of such that if it had simply caused bodily injury, without causing death, the party injured might have maintained an action?

§ 64. Intentional killing

Where the death results, not from mere negligence, but from intentional violence, the question whether the wrongful act was such that the party injured might have maintained an action if death had not ensued will of course depend upon whether the defendant had any excuse or justification.[7] This question, being the same as that which arises in actions for trespass to the person not resulting in death, requires no extended examination here. The law

recovered and he could have had no right of action in respect of a pecuniary loss arising only on his death.

[6] The condition is implied in the Pennsylvania act by the provision that the action may be maintained when no suit for damages be brought by the party injured.

[7] White v. Maxcy, 64 Mo. 552; Morgan v. Durfee, 69 Mo. 469, 33 Am. Rep. 508; Nichols v. Winfrey, 90 Mo. 403, 2 S. W. 305; Fraser v. Freeman, 56 Barb. (N. Y.) 234. See, also, Morgan v. Barnhill, 118 Fed. 24, 55 C. C. A. 1; Richards v. Burgin, 159 Ala. 282, 49 South. 294, 17 Ann. Cas. 898; Burnham v. Stone, 101 Cal. 164, 35 Pac. 627; Locher v. Kluga, 97 Ill. App. 518; McClurg v. Ingleheart (Ky.) 33 S. W. 80; Hollingsworth v. Warnock (Ky.) 47 S. W. 770; Johnson v. Williams' Adm'r, 111 Ky. 289, 63 S. W. 759, 54 L. R. A. 220, 98 Am. St. Rep. 416; Hollingsworth v. Warnock, 112 Ky. 96, 65 S. W. 163; Brinkman v. Gottenstroeter, 153 Mo. App. 351, 134 S. W. 584; Farmer v. Sellers, 89 S. C. 492, 72 S. E. 224; Garcia v. Sanders, 90 Tex. 103, 37 S. W. 314; Gray v. Phillips, 54 Tex. Civ. App. 148, 117 S. W. 870.

of self-defense is the same as in a criminal prosecution, with
the exception, it has been said, of the rule of evidence,
which in a criminal cause gives the defendant the benefit
of a reasonable doubt.[8] It has been held that the plea of
self-defense does not cause the burden to shift.[9] But the
better rule appears to be that the burden of proof is on
the plaintiff, as in other cases, to establish his case, and as
a part of it to show prima facie that the killing was wrongful, and that when he has done so the burden of proof is on
the defendant to show justification or excuse.[10] Contributory negligence on the part of the deceased, when the action is founded on intentional violence, is, of course, no de-

[8] March v. Walker, 48 Tex. 372. But the doctrine that he who
seeks and originates an affray resulting in homicide cannot avail
himself of the plea of self-defense is not applicable to a civil suit
for damages brought by a representative of the deceased. Besenecker v. Sale, 8 Mo. App. 211. In civil actions brought by the
administrator for death by wrongful act, plaintiff need not prove
his case beyond a reasonable doubt; the rule as to the weight and
sufficiency of the evidence being the same as if the action had been
brought by decedent, had he not died. Suell v. Derricott, 161 Ala.
259, 49 South. 895, 23 L. R. A. (N. S.) 996, 18 Ann. Cas. 636.

[9] Nichols v. Winfrey, 79 Mo. 544.

[10] Suell v. Derricott, 161 Ala. 259, 49 South. 895, 23 L. R. A. (N.
S.) 996, 18 Ann. Cas. 636; Brooks v. Haslam, 65 Cal. 421, 4 Pac. 399.
Where defendant admits the killing, but seeks to justify it on the
ground of defense of a servant, and where plaintiff's evidence shows
the shooting to have been without any justification, it is proper to
instruct that if defendant fired his pistol towards the deceased, and
shot and killed him, the burden is on defendant to show, by pre-
ponderating proof, justification for such shooting. Tucker v. State,
to Use of Johnson, 89 Md. 471, 43 Atl. 778, 44 Atl. 1004, 46 L. R. A.
181. A legal presumption arises from an assault and battery with
a deadly weapon that the act was wrongful, and when such act is
admitted or proved, and resulted in death, the burden is on defendant to show by a fair preponderance of the evidence facts and circumstances in justification or mitigation of it. Rutherford v. Foster, 125 Fed. 187, 60 C. C. A. 129.

fense.[11] And the same rule has been applied when the action is founded on wanton or willful negligence.[12] A judgment of acquittal, in a criminal prosecution for the homicide, is not a bar to a civil action for the wrongful death.[13]

§ 65. Death caused by negligence

Where the death results from negligence, the question whether the negligence was such that the party injured might have maintained an action will depend primarily upon the relation borne by the defendant to the party injured, as determining whether the neglect was in respect to any duty owed by the former to the latter. According to the circumstances of the particular case, the answer may depend upon the law of master and servant,[14] of passenger

[11] Gray v. McDonald, 104 Mo. 303, 16 S. W. 398; Kain v. Larkin, 56 Hun, 79, 9 N. Y. Supp. 89; Matthews v. Warner's Adm'r, 70 Va. 570, 26 Am. Rep. 396. Proof that the deceased commenced the fatal affray will not warrant an instruction that, if his fault contributed to the injury resulting in his death, no recovery can be had. Darling v. Williams, 35 Ohio St. 58. See, also, Suell v. Derricott, 161 Ala. 259, 49 South. 895, 23 L. R. A. (N. S.) 996, 18 Ann. Cas. 636; Tucker v. State, 89 Md. 471, 43 Atl. 778, 44 Atl. 1004, 46 L. R. A. 181. Where it appeared that deceased brought on the difficulty, and there was evidence that defendant's consciousness was impaired, if not destroyed, by the injuries inflicted by deceased, it was error to apply the doctrine that an unconscious or an insane man, while not liable for punitive damages for his torts, is liable for compensatory damages, since unconsciousness produced by deceased was an excuse for any injury inflicted on deceased. Jenkins v. Hankins, 98 Tenn. 545, 41 S. W. 1028.

[12] Louisville & N. R. Co. v. Markee, 103 Ala. 160, 15 South. 511, 49 Am. St. Rep. 21; Louisville & N. R. Co. v. Orr, 121 Ala. 489, 26 South. 35.

[13] Gray v. McDonald, 104 Mo. 303, 16 S. W. 398.

[14] See notes 23 and 24, infra.

and carrier,[15] of landlord and tenant,[16] of vendor and purchaser;[17] upon the law in respect to the liability of the owners of property of every description for injuries arising from its use;[18] upon the law of highways,[19] of municipal corporations[20]—in short, upon any one of the many branch-

15 Sheridan v. Brooklyn City & N. R. Co., 36 N. Y. 39, 93 Am. Dec. 490.

16 Moore v. Logan Iron & Steel Co. (Pa.) 7 Atl. 198; Albert v. State, 66 Md. 325, 7 Atl. 697, 59 Am. Rep. 159; State, to Use of Bashe, v. Boyce, 73 Md. 469, 21 Atl. 322.

17 The wife of G., being ill, expressed to her husband a desire for a harmless medicine. G. called at the drug store of D. for the desired medicine. D.'s agent, without informing himself by whom or for what it was intended, carelessly sold to G. a poisonous drug. G., supposing it to be what he had called for, gave it to his wife, who drank of it, in the belief that it was a harmless medicine, and instantly died. Held, that these facts constituted a cause of action against D., in favor of the administrator of the deceased wife. Davis v. Guarnieri, 45 Ohio St. 470, 15 N. E. 350, 4 Am. St. Rep. 548. In an action for negligently causing the death of plaintiffs' child, a complaint alleging that plaintiffs' agent, as customer of defendants, druggists, demanded quinine, but was by defendants' clerk given morphine instead, and, that relying on the representation of said clerk that the drug was quinine, plaintiffs administered the same to their daughter, from the effects of which she died, states a good cause of action. Brunswig v. White, 70 Tex. 504, 8 S. W. 85. See, also, Binford v. Johnston, 82 Ind. 426, 42 Am. Rep. 508.

18 Klix v. Nieman, 68 Wis. 271, 32 N. W. 223, 60 Am. Rep. 854; Simmons v. Everson, 124 N. Y. 319, 26 N. E. 911, 21 Am. St. Rep. 676; Trask v. Shotwell, 41 Minn. 66, 42 N. W. 699; O'Callaghan v. Bode, 84 Cal. 489, 24 Pac. 269; Sherman v. Anderson, 27 Kan. 333, 41 Am. Rep. 414; Callahan v. Warne, 40 Mo. 131; Casey v. Adams, 234 Ill. 350, 84 N. E. 933, 123 Am. St. Rep. 105, 17 L. R. A. (N. S.) 776.

19 Pennsylvania Tel. Co. v. Varnau (Pa.) 15 Atl. 624.

20 Kunz v. City of Troy, 104 N. Y. 344, 10 N. E. 442, 58 Am. Rep. 508; Koenig v. Town of Arcadia, 75 Wis. 62, 43 N. W. 734; Fisher v. City of Newbern, 140 N. C. 506, 53 S. E. 342, 111 Am. St. Rep. 857, 5 L. R. A. (N. S.) 542; Carty's Adm'r v. Village of Winooski, 78 Vt. 104, 62 Atl. 45, 2 L. R. A. (N. S.) 95, 6 Ann. Cas. 436; Hughes v. City of Auburn, 161 N. Y. 96, 55 N. E. 389, 46 L. R. A. 636.

es of the law that are commonly treated of in works upon negligence.[21]

[21] Defendant's dogs ran out and fought with a strange dog accompanying a passing wagon in which deceased was driving. The dogs got under the horses' feet and caused the horses to run away and to upset the wagon, thereby causing the death of deceased. Held that, upon proof of the vicious character of defendant's dogs and of his knowledge of it, an action was maintainable against him for wrongful death. Mann v. Weiand, *81 Pa. 243. Where the death was caused by the explosion of a blast in a thickly settled portion of a city, it is no defense that defendant used the highest degree of skill and care in exploding the blast. Munro v. Pacific Coast Dredging & Reclamation Co., 84 Cal. 515, 24 Pac. 303, 18 Am. St. Rep. 248. In an action by E.'s administratrix to recover for the drowning of E. by a collision with the defendant's steam tug, there was evidence that at the time of the accident E. and her husband, J., were crossing Buffalo river in a small scow which J. was sculling; that J. was blind but able-bodied, and familiar with the management of such boats; that the night was so light that the scow could be seen 100 feet distant, and there was a lighted lantern in it; that J. called out, but the tug did not slacken speed, and that the tug would not have collided if it had kept straight on without sheering towards the scow. There was no proof that the board of supervising inspectors had prescribed the manner of showing a light on the scow and similar craft. Held, that the evidence warranted a finding of negligence on the part of the defendant's employés. Harris v. Uebelhoer, 75 N. Y. 169. The court properly refused to instruct that if defendant's servant left the team beside the highway, and, while he was getting a drink of water at a well at a distance of only 10 or 12 feet away, the team ran away, causing decedent's death, that fact alone was not such negligence as would make defendant liable, as it ignored other facts, besides taking the question of negligence from the jury. Hudson v. Houser, 123 Ind. 309, 24 N. E. 243. Defendants, who were the board of health of a city, removed the deceased, who was ill with smallpox. Held that, if they failed to exercise the care which the circumstances demanded, they were liable in an action for wrongful death, though they acted under a city ordinance. Aaron v. Broiles, 64 Tex. 316, 53 Am. Rep. 764. Where plaintiff's deceased, while lawfully in a highway, was killed by a section of a tree hurled by a blast exploded by defendants on their land, plaintiff is entitled to recover without proof of negligence. Sullivan v. Dunham, 161 N. Y. 290, 55 N. E. 923, 47 L. R. A. 715, 76

A considerable proportion of all the actions for death turn simply upon the questions whether the party injured was guilty of contributory negligence,[22] whether he was a

Am. St. Rep. 274. Loss of life in rescuing another from peril gives no right of action against one guilty of no negligence, either as to the person saved or as to the rescuer. Jackson v. Standard Oil Co., 98 Ga. 749, 26 S. E. 60. The complaint in an action by an employé against a corporation alleged that the latter deducted a certain amount from his wages each month, under a contract by which such company was to provide competent medical treatment for the employé and family, and that, the employé's child being scalded, the company's physician was immediately notified, and requested to give the child necessary treatment, as provided by the contract, which the physician failed to do; the company also failing to require the physician to give the child attention. It was also alleged that plaintiff relied on the contract, and, by reason of being unable to procure treatment of other physicians, and the company's carelessness and negligence, the child died; there being, also, an averment of freedom from contributory negligence. Held to state a cause of action. American Tin Plate Co. v. Guy, 25 Ind. App. 588, 58 N. E. 738. A recovery cannot be had in the absence of proof of facts from which it can be inferred that in the doing of the thing which caused decedent's death, a duty rested on the defendant or his servants to use due care to provide for decedent's safety. Prosser v. West Jersey & Seashore R. Co., 72 N. J. Law, 342, 63 Atl. 494, affirmed 75 N. J. Law, 614, 68 Atl. 58.

[22] Tucker v. Chaplin, 2 Car. & K. 730; Thorogood v. Bryan, 8 C. B. 115, 18 L. J. C. P. 336; Dynen v. Leach, 26 L. J. Exch. 221; Senior v. Ward, 1 El. & El. 385, 28 L. J. Q. B. 139, 5 Jur. (N. S.) 172, 7 Wkly. R. 261; Witherley v. Regent's Canal Co., 12 C. B. (N. S.) 2, 3 Fost. & F. 61, 6 L. T. (N. S.) 255; Memphis & C. R. Co. v. Copeland, 61 Ala. 376; Holland v. Tennessee Coal, Iron & Railroad Co., 91 Ala. 444, 8 South. 524, 12 L. R. A. 232; Little Rock & F. S. Ry. Co. v. Cavenesse, 48 Ark. 106, 2 S. W. 505; Jackson v. Crilly, 16 Colo. 103, 26 Pac. 331; Chicago, B. & Q. R. Co. v. Triplett, 38 Ill. 482; Abend v. Terre Haute & I. R. Co., 111 Ill. 202, 53 Am. Rep. 616; Evansville & C. R. Co. v. Lowdermilk, 15 Ind. 120; Kansas Pac. Ry. Co. v. Salmon, 14 Kan. 512; Baltimore & O. R. Co. v. State, to Use of Miller, 29 Md. 252, 96 Am. Dec. 528; Northern Cent. Ry. Co. v. State, to Use of Burns, 54 Md. 113; Kelly v. Hendrie, 26 Mich. 255; Michigan Cent. R. Co. v. Campau, 35 Mich. 468; Harris v. Minneapolis & St. L. R. Co., 37 Minn. 47, 33 N. W. 12; Carney

fellow servant of the person actually causing the injury,[23] whether the injury was within the ordinary risks of the

v. Chicago, St. P., M. & O. Ry. Co., 46 Minn. 220, 48 N. W. 912; Fulmer v. Illinois Cent. R. Co., 68 Miss. 355, 8 South. 517; Devitt v. Pacific R. Co., 50 Mo. 302; Karle v. Kansas City, St. J. & C. B. R. Co., 55 Mo. 476; Telfer v. Northern R. Co., 30 N. J. Law, 188; Hamilton v. Delaware, L. & W. R. Co., 50 N. J. Law, 263, 13 Atl. 29; Willetts v. Buffalo & R. R. Co., 14 Barb. (N. Y.) 585; Lehman v. City of Brooklyn, 29 Barb. (N. Y.) 234; Button v. Hudson River R. Co., 18 N. Y. 248; Wilds v. Hudson River R. Co., 24 N. Y. 430; Wilds v. Hudson River R. Co., 29 N. Y. 315; Curran v. Warren Chemical & Mfg. Co., 36 N. Y. 153; San Antonio & A. P. Ry. Co. v. Wallace, 76 Tex. 636, 13 S. W. 565; Langhoff v. Milwaukee & P. du C. Ry. Co., 23 Wis. 43; Burhop v. City of Milwaukee, 21 Wis. 259; Baltimore & O. R. Co. v. Sherman's Adm'x, 71 Va. 602. See, also, Bunt v. Sierra Butte Gold Min. Co., 138 U. S. 483, 11 Sup. Ct. 464, 34 L. Ed. 1031, affirming 24 Fed. 847; Weisshaar v. Kimball S. S. Co., 128 Fed. 397, 63 C. C. A. 139, 65 L. R. A. 84; Mooney v. Carter, 152 Fed. 147, 81 C. C. A. 365; Payne v. Illinois Cent. R. Co., 155 Fed. 73, 83 C. C. A. 589; Atchison, T. & S. F. Ry. Co. v. Phillips, 176 Fed. 663, 100 C. C. A. 215; Birmingham Ry., Light & Power Co. v. Mosely, 164 Ala. 111, 51 South. 424; Weatherly v. Nashville, C. & St. L. Ry., 166 Ala. 575, 51 South. 959; Lemasters v. Southern Pac. Co., 131 Cal. 105, 63 Pac. 128; Harrington v. Los Angeles Ry. Co., 140 Cal. 514, 74 Pac. 15, 63 L. R. A. 238, 98 Am.

---

[23] Hutchinson v. York, N. C. & B. Ry. Co., 5 Exch. 343, 14 Jur. 837; Wigmore v. Jay, 5 Exch. 354, 19 L. J. Exch. 300; Smith v. Steele, L. R. 10 Q. B. 125, 44 L. J. Q. B. 60; Congrave v. Southern Pac. R. Co., 88 Cal. 360, 26 Pac. 175; Chicago & A. R. Co. v. Kelly, 127 Ill. 637, 21 N. E. 203; Id., 25 Ill. App. 17; Slattery's Adm'r v. Toledo & W. Ry. Co., 23 Ind. 81; Troughear v. Lower Vein Coal Co., 62 Iowa, 576, 17 N. W. 775; Kansas Pac. Ry. Co. v. Salmon, 11 Kan. 83; Fort Hill Stone Co. v. Orm's Adm'r, 84 Ky. 183; Connors v. Holden, 152 Mass. 598, 26 N. E. 137; Besel v. New York Cent. & H. R. R. Co., 70 N. Y. 171; Quinn v. Power, 87 N. Y. 535, 41 Am. Rep. 392; Butler v. Townsend, 126 N. Y. 105, 26 N. E. 1017; Kumler v. Junction R. Co., 33 Ohio St. 150; Shea v. Pennsylvania R. Co. (Pa.) 13 Atl. 193; Texas & N. O. R. Co. v. Berry, 67 Tex. 238, 5 S. W. 817; Baltimore & O. R. Co. v. Andrews, 50 Fed. 728, 1 C. C. A. 636, 17 L. R. A. 190; Petersen v. Sherry Lumber Co., 90 Wis. 83, 62 N. W. 948.

employment;[24] in all of which cases the same rule applies as if the action were brought by the party injured. It is obvious that if it were to be attempted to answer in detail

St. Rep. 85; Seaboard Air Line Ry. v. Shigg, 117 Ga. 454, 43 S. E. 706; Stollery v. Cicero & P. St. R. Co., 243 Ill. 290, 90 N. E. 709; Stack v. East St. Louis & S. R. Co., 245 Ill. 308, 92 N. E. 241, 137 Am. St. Rep. 318; Chicago & E. I. Ry. Co. v. Hedges, 118 Ind. 5, 20 N. E. 530; Cleveland, C., C. & St. L. Ry. Co. v. Miller, 149, Ind. 490, 49 N. E. 445; Cleveland, C., C. & St. L. Ry. Co. v. Henry (Ind. App.) 80 N. E. 636; Pittsburgh, C., C. & St. L. Ry. Co. v. Rogers, 45 Ind. App. 230, 87 N. E. 28; Warren's Adm'r v. Jeunesse (Ky.) 122 S. W. 862; McDonough v. Grand Trunk R. Co., 98 Me. 304, 56 Atl. 913; Tucker v. State, Use of Johnson, 89 Md. 471, 43 Atl. 778, 44 Atl. 1004, 46 L. R. A. 181; McClellan v. Ft. Wayne & B. I. Ry. Co., 105 Mich. 101, 62 N. W. 1025; McQuisten v. Detroit Citizens' St. R. Co., 150 Mich. 332, 113 N. W. 1118; Holwerson v. St. Louis & S. Ry. Co., 157 Mo. 216, 57 S. W. 770, 50 L. R. A. 850; Powell v. St. Louis & S. F. R. Co., 229 Mo. 246, 129 S. W. 963; Holmes v. Chicago, R. I. & P. R. Co., 73 Neb. 489, 103 N. W. 77; Baxter v. Auburn & S. Electric R. Co., 190 N. Y. 439, 83 N. E. 469; Lamb v. Union Ry. Co. of New York City, 195 N. Y. 260, 88 N. E. 371; Pegram v. Seaboard Air Line R. Co., 139 N. C. 303, 51 S. E. 975; Cameron v. Great Northern Ry. Co., 8 N. D. 618, 80 N. W. 885; Grant v. Philadelphia, B. & W. R. Co., 215 Pa. 265, 64 Atl. 463; Whaley v. Vidal (S. D.) 132 N. W. 248; Greenlaw v. Louisville & N. R. Co., 114 Tenn. 187, 86 S. W. 1072; Norfolk & W. R. Co. v. Carper, 88 Va. 556, 14 S. E. 328.

24 Dynen v. Leach, 26 L. J. Exch. 221; Coldrick v. Partridge, Jones & Co., Ltd., [1910] A. C. 77; Lord v. Pueblo Smelting & Refining Co., 12 Colo. 390, 21 Pac. 148; Drake v. Union Pac. R. Co., 2 Idaho (Hasb.) 487, 21 Pac. 560; Cincinnati, I., St. L. & C. Ry. Co. v. Lang, 118 Ind. 579, 21 N. E. 317; Kuhns v. Wisconsin, I. & N. Ry. Co., 70 Iowa, 561, 31 N. W. 868; Brown v. Chicago, R. I. & P. R. Co., 64 Iowa, 652, 21 N. W. 193; Carey v. Sellers, 41 La. Ann. 500, 6 South. 813; Baltimore & O. R. Co. v. State, to Use of Woodward, 41 Md. 268; Boyle v. New York & N. E. R. Co., 151 Mass. 102, 23 N. E. 827; Balle v. Detroit Leather Co., 73 Mich. 158, 41 N. W. 216; Devitt v. Pacific R. R., 50 Mo. 302; Elliott v. St. Louis & I. M. R. Co., 67 Mo. 272; Gleeson v. Excelsior Manuf'g Co., 94 Mo. 201, 7 S. W. 188; Gibson v. Erie Ry. Co., 63 N. Y. 449, 20 Am. Dec. 552; De Forest v. Jewett, 88 N. Y. 264; Titus v. Bradford, B. & K. R. Co., 136 Pa. 618, 20 Atl. 517, 20 Am. St. Rep. 944;

the question for what act, neglect, or default resulting in death an action may be maintained, it would be necessary to write a complete treatise upon the law relating to personal injuries. The answer to that question is outside the scope of this book.

It must be borne in mind that the law of master and servant, with respect to the rules governing contributory negligence, the fellow servant rule, the assumption of the risks of the employment, and kindred matters, has been changed by employers' liability acts in many states, and that these changes modify the law applicable to actions for death as well as to actions brought by the injured employé. No general discussion of the various employers' liability acts will be attempted, but many of them are referred to in the paragraphs which treat of the peculiar statutes of the various states.

§ 66.   Contributory negligence of deceased

As the contributory negligence of the party injured is in general a defense in an action by him, founded upon negligence, for the personal injury, it follows that his contributory negligence is to the same extent a defense in the statutory action.[25]

McGrath v. New York & N. E. R. Co., 14 R. I. 357; s. c., 15 R. I. 95, 22 Atl. 927; Southwest Imp. Co. v. Andrew, 86 Va. 270, 9 S. E. 1015; Carbine's Adm'r v. Bennington & R. R. Co., 61 Vt. 348, 17 Atl. 491; Davis' Adm'r v. Nuttallsburg, Coal & Coke Co., 34 W. Va. 500, 12 S. E. 539. See, also, Canadian Pac. R. Co. v. Elliott, 137 Fed. 904, 70 C. C. A. 242; Bonato v. Peabody Coal Co., 248 Ill. 422, 94 N. E. 69; Baltimore & P. R. Co. v. State, Use of Abbott, 75 Md. 152, 23 Atl. 310, 32 Am. St. Rep. 372; Cogdell v. Wilmington & W. R. Co., 124 N. C. 302, 32 S. E. 706.

25 Note 22, supra. The rule applies in an action by a parent for the death of a minor child, although the latter was employed by

The defense of the contributory negligence of the party injured applies not only under statutes which expressly provide that an action for death may be maintained whenever the party injured might have maintained an action, but also under statutes which do not contain this express provision; [26] and of course it applies under statutes which in terms provide for a survival of the original cause of action. [27] So, in jurisdictions where the rule of contributory negligence is modified by the rule of comparative negligence, the modification applies as much in actions by the party injured as in the statutory action. [28] In Kentucky, however, under a former statute, which provided for the recovery of damages where the life of any person was lost

the defendant without the parent's consent. Texas & P. Ry. Co. v. Carlton, 60 Tex. 397; Texas & N. O. R. Co. v. Crowder, 61 Tex. 262; Id., 63 Tex. 502; Id., 70 Tex. 222, 7 S. W. 709. But see § 35.

[26] Gay v. Winter, 34 Cal. 153; Noyes v. Southern Pac. R. Co. (Cal.) 24 Pac. 927; Bertelson v. Chicago, M. & St. P. Ry. Co., 5 Dak. 313, 40 N. W. 531; Rowland v. Cannon, 35 Ga. 105; Southwestern R. Co. v. Johnson, 60 Ga. 667; Berry v. Northeastern R. Co., 72 Ga. 137; Central R. Co. v. Thompson, 76 Ga. 770; Central Railroad & Banking Co. v. Kitchens, 83 Ga. 83, 9 S. E. 827; Pennsylvania R. Co. v. Zebe, 33 Pa. 318; Pennsylvania R. Co. v. Lewis, 79 Pa. 33; Pennsylvania R. Co. v. Bell, 122 Pa. 58, 15 Atl. 561; Helfrich v. Ogden City Ry. Co., 7 Utah, 186, 26 Pac. 295.

[27] Quinn v. New York, N. H. & H. R. Co., 56 Conn. 44, 12 Atl. 97, 7 Am. St. Rep. 284; Lane v. Central Iowa R. Co., 69 Iowa, 443, 29 N. W. 419; Newman v. Chicago, M. & St. P. Ry. Co., 80 Iowa, 672, 45 N. W. 1054; Beck v. Firmenich Manuf'g Co., 82 Iowa, 286, 48 N. W. 81; Knight v. Pontchartrain R. Co., 23 La. Ann. 462; Murray v. Pontchartrain R. Co., 31 La. Ann. 490; Weeks v. New Orleans & C. R. Co., 32 La. Ann. 615; Nashville & C. R. Co. v. Smith, 6 Heisk. (Tenn.) 174; Ryan v. Town of Bristol, 63 Conn. 26, 27 Atl. 309; Brown v. West Riverside Coal Co., 143 Iowa, 662, 120 N. W. 732, 28 L. R. A. (N. S.) 1260.

[28] Chicago, B. & Q. R. Co. v. Triplett, 38 Ill. 482; Chicago, B. & Q. R. Co. v. Payne, 49 Ill. 499; Toledo, W. & W. R. Co. v. O'Connor, 77 Ill. 391; Chicago & A. R. Co. v. Fietsam, 123 Ill. 518, 15 N. E. 169.

by "willful neglect," contributory negligence was no defense.[29]

The rule differs in different jurisdictions, in actions for personal injuries and consequently in actions for causing death, in respect to the burden of proof; in some jurisdictions the burden of showing that the plaintiff or the decedent was in the exercise of due care being upon the plaintiff, and in some jurisdictions the burden of proving contributory negligence being upon the defendant. In some states the general practice is regulated by statute. A consideration of the varying rules is beyond the scope of this book. The rule in respect to contributory negligence is also affected by the peculiar provisions of the death acts of some of the states, as well as by many of the employers' liability acts. Thus the federal employers' liability act, applicable to common carriers by railroads, provides that the fact that the employé may have been guilty of contributory negligence shall not bar a recovery, but the damages shall be diminished by the jury in proportion to the amount of negligence attributable to the employé.[30]

§ 66—1.   Deceased's violation of law as contributory cause

Since it is a defense in an action for personal injuries that the plaintiff's violation of law contributed directly and proximately to cause the injury, it follows that the same defense is open in the statutory action for death. Thus it was held that damages are not recoverable for the death of a boy under 15 years of age, who was killed through the negligence of his employer while operating a passenger elevator running at a speed of more than 100 feet a minute, in violation of a statute providing that such elevators shall

---

[29] See ante, § 41.   [30] Ante, § 59—1.

be operated only by competent persons not less than 18 years of age, and making its violation "by operating or causing an elevator to be operated" contrary to its provisions a penal offense.[81] "The illegal act of the plaintiff's intestate," said the court, "was the operation of the elevator. His injury occurred 'while he was engaged in the performance of his duties * * * in running and operating the said elevator.' The plaintiff's case stands like that of a street car conductor, who, while running a car on Sunday, was struck by a passing car negligently operated. Day v. Highland Street Railway, 135 Mass. 113, 44 Am. Rep. 447." Here the holding of the court rested upon the ground that the illegal act of the boy in operating the elevator contributed to the accident. On the other hand, in Kansas, in an action by a father for the negligent death of his son while employed in a factory, it was held that the fact that the father consented to such employment was not a bar to a recovery, notwithstanding that it was his duty under the statute to have his son at school.[82] "The defendant maintains that the plaintiff was guilty of contributory negligence," said the court, "in that he consented to his son's employment in the factory, thereby violating the statute requiring parents of children between 8 and 15 years of age to send them to school. The connection is too remote. The fact that the deceased was not at school was not the proximate cause of his injury. It, at most, merely produced a condition that made the accident possible. The defendant's argument is substantially the same as that upon which a few courts have held that a passenger traveling upon Sunday in violation of the law cannot re-

[81] Malloy v. American Hide & Leather Co. (C. C.) 148 Fed. 482.
[82] Smith v. Marion Fruit Jar & Bottle Co., 84 Kan. 551, 114 Pac. 845.

cover for an injury resulting from the negligence of the carrier. That argument has already been repudiated in this state (Kansas City v. Orr, 62 Kan. 61, 66, 61 Pac. 61, 50 L. R. A. 783), as well as in most others where it has been considered. The plaintiff's consent to his son's employment did not involve the assumption of any risk resulting from the company's negligence." While the principle that should govern such cases is conceded, there is much conflict in its application. "No case has been brought to our attention, and upon careful investigation we have found none, in which a plaintiff, whose violation of law contributed directly and proximately to cause him an injury, has been permitted to recover for it; and the decisions are numerous to the contrary. * * * While this principle is universally recognized, there is great practical difficulty in applying it. The best minds often differ upon the question whether, in a given case, illegal conduct of a plaintiff was a direct and proximate cause contributing, with others, to his injury, or was a mere condition of it; or, to state the question in another way, appropriate to the reason of the rule, whether or not his own illegal act is an essential element of his case as disclosed upon all the evidence. Upon this point it is not easy to reconcile the cases." [33]   A consideration of the questions involved, which are not peculiar to actions for death, is outside the scope of this book.

§ 67. Imputed negligence

It follows also from what has been said that, wherever the negligence of a third person would be imputed to the plaintiff in an action for personal injury, it will be equally

[33] Newcomb v. Boston Protective Department, 146 Mass. 596, 16 N. E. 555, 4 Am. St. Rep. 354.

imputed to the deceased in an action for his death. Indeed, the famous case of Thorogood v. Bryan,[34] which established the rule that the negligence of the carrier, contributing, with the negligence of a third person, to the injury of a passenger, will be imputed to the latter, was an action under Lord Campbell's act; and although Thorogood v. Bryan has been overruled in England,[35] and generally repudiated in the United States,[36] the rule of that case, in jurisdictions where it applies at all, applies to actions for death.[37]

§ 68. Imputed negligence in action for death of child

The question of imputed negligence arises most frequently in actions brought by or in behalf of persons non sui juris (who include children, idiots, and insane persons) for injuries to which the negligence of their legal custodians has contributed. In some jurisdictions it is held that, upon the theory of agency or identity, such contributory negligence should be imputed to the plaintiff; and in other jurisdictions this is denied. The leading authority in support of the rule which attributes the negligence of the parent or custodian to the child is the New York case of Hartfield v. Roper.[38] What is generally known as the rule of Hartfield v. Roper is that, in the case of a young child, the negligence of the parent or other person to whose care the child is intrusted has the same effect in preventing the maintenance

---

[34] 8 C. B. 115.

[35] The Bernina, L. R. 13 App. Cas. 1.

[36] See Beach, Contr. Neg. § 34 et seq.; Shearman & Redfield, Neg. § 66; Barrows, Neg. 56.

[37] Lockhart v. Lichtenthaler, 46 Pa. 151; Philadelphia & R. R. Co. v. Boyer, 97 Pa. 91; Payne v. Chicago, R. I. & P. R. Co., 39 Iowa, 523; Stafford v. City of Oskaloosa, 57 Iowa, 749, 11 N. W. 668.

[38] 21 Wend. 615, 34 Am. Dec. 273.

of an action by the child for an injury caused by negligence that the child's own want of care would have if he were an adult.[39]   In jurisdictions where Hartfield v. Roper is repudiated, the rule generally prevails that all that is required of a child is the exercise of care and prudence equal to his capacity, and that the negligence of his parent or custodian will not be imputed to him.[40]

In cases brought to recover damages for the death of persons non sui juris, where the injury from which death resulted was due in part to the contributory negligence of the parent or guardian of the deceased, in jurisdictions where the rule of Hartfield v. Roper prevails, there can of course be no recovery. In New York the rule of Hartfield v. Roper has frequently been applied in this class of cases.[41] Cases that hold that there can be no recovery by the executor or administrator for the death of an infant where the negligence of the parents contributed to the injury are also

[39] Beach, Contr. Neg. § 40; Shearman & R. Neg. § 74; Barrows, Neg. 64.

[40] Beach, Contr. Neg. § 43; Shearman & R. Neg. § 78; Barrows, Neg. 74 et seq.

[41] Ihl v. Forty-Second St. & G. St. Ferry R. Co., 47 N. Y. 317, 7 Am. Rep. 450; Kunz v. City of Troy, 104 N. Y. 344, 10 N. E. 442, 58 Am. Rep. 508; Birkett v. Knickerbocker Ice Co., 110 N. Y. 504, 18 N. E. 108; Ahern v. Steele, 48 Hun, 517, 1 N. Y. Supp. 259; Levey v. Dry Dock, E. B. & B. R. Co., 58 Hun, 610, 12 N. Y. Supp. 485; Williams v. Gardiner, 58 Hun, 508, 12 N. Y. Supp. 612; Huerzeler v. Central Cross-Town R. Co., 139 N. Y. 490, 34 N. E. 1101; Foley v. New York Cent. & H. R. R. Co., 78 Hun, 248, 28 N. Y. Supp. 816; Kennedy v. Hills Bros. Co., 54 App. Div 29, 66 N. Y. Supp. 280; Carr v. Merchants' Union Ice Co., 91 App. Div. 162, 86 N. Y. Supp. 368. Where plaintiff negligently drove in front of an engine on the defendant company's track, whereby his child, of 18 months, who was riding on its mother's lap, was thrown out and killed, the negligence of the father was not imputable to the child. Lewin v. Lehigh Val. R. Co., 52 App. Div. 69, 65 N. Y. Supp. 49.

to be found in Illinois,[42] Maryland,[43] Michigan,[44] Wisconsin,[45] and elsewhere,[46] and this application of the rule has

---

[42] A child four years old fell in a tank, and was drowned. An instruction that the jury must believe that the parents were not guilty of contributory negligence was held correct. City of Chicago v. Major, 18 Ill. 349, 68 Am. Dec. 553. A child six years old was killed by the fall of a counter leaning on a fence in the street. Held, that the negligence of the parents in permitting the child to roam the crowded thoroughfares of the city was even greater than that of the defendant, and that the plaintiff could not recover. City of Chicago v. Starr, 42 Ill. 174, 89 Am. Dec. 422. The parents of a boy nine years old intrusted him to a neighbor, and, as they were driving across the defendant's track, the wagon was struck, and the boy killed, by a train. The driver failed to use due care. Held, the plaintiff could not recover. Toledo, W. & W. Ry. Co. v. Miller, 76 Ill. 278. In an action for the death of a child 28 months old, the evidence was debatable whether the parents had exercised due care. The court charged that although the parents might be guilty of slight negligence in suffering the child to go beyond their sight, yet, if defendant was guilty of a greater degree of negligence, plaintiff might recover. Held, error, the rule being that where there is negligence on the part of the injured party, or, as in this case, on the part of those charged with the care of the injured party, contributing directly to produce the injury, there can be no recovery unless such negligence is slight, and that of defendant gross in comparison. Toledo, W. & W. Ry. Co. v. Grable, 88 Ill. 441. An instruction that children are required to exercise only the degree of care which persons of like age, capacity, and experience might rea-

---

[43] State, to Use of Coughlan, v. Baltimore & O. R. Co., 24 Md. 84, 87 Am. Dec. 600; Baltimore & O. R. Co. v. State, to Use of Fryer, 30 Md. 47.

[44] Apsey v. Detroit, L. & N. R. Co., 83 Mich. 432, 47 N. W. 319.

[45] Ewen v. Chicago & N. W. R. Co., 38 Wis. 613; Johnson v. Chicago & N. W. R. Co., 49 Wis. 529, 5 N. W. 886; Hoppe v. Chicago, M. & St. P. Ry. Co., 61 Wis. 357, 21 N. W. 227; Parish v. Town of Eden, 62 Wis. 272, 22 N. W. 399. See, also, Decker v. McSorley, 111 Wis. 91, 86 N. W. 554; O'Brien v. Wisconsin Cent. Ry. Co., 119 Wis. 7, 96 N. W. 424.

[46] Toner's Adm'r v. South Covington & C. St. R. Co., 109 Ky. 41, 58 S. W. 439, 22 Ky. Law Rep. 564; Mills' Adm'r v. Cavanaugh, 94 S. W. 651, 29 Ky. Law Rep. 685.

been approved in Minnesota.[47]   The rule of Hartfield v. Roper has also been applied in Indiana,[48] in actions by the parent for the death of a minor child, and in Massachusetts,[49] in actions by the administrator for personal injuries

sonably be expected to use, etc., provided the parents or persons having control of such children have not been guilty of want of ordinary care in allowing them to be placed under such circumstances, is proper. Illinois Cent. R. Co. v. Slater, 129 Ill. 91, 21 N. E. 575, 6 L. R. A. 418, 16 Am. St. Rep. 242. To leave out of the instructions, purporting to state the elements necessary to a right of recovery, the requirement of ordinary care on the part of the father, was prejudicial error. Chicago, M. & St. P. Ry. Co. v. Mason, 27 Ill. App. 450. And see City of Chicago v. Hesing, 83 Ill. 204, 25 Am. Rep. 378; Chicago & A. R. Co. v. Becker, 84 Ill. 483; Chicago City Ry. Co. v. Robinson, 27 Ill. App. 26, affirmed 127 Ill. 9, 18 N. E. 772, 4 L. R. A. 126, 11 Am. St. Rep. 87.

[47] O'Malley v. St. Paul, M. & M. Ry. Co., 43 Minn. 289, 45 N. W. 440.

[48] In an action by the father for the death of a child of tender years, the complaint is sufficient if it allege that the child was on defendant's track without the negligence of the parents. Pittsburgh, Ft. W. & C. Ry. Co. v. Vining's Adm'r, 27 Ind. 513, 92 Am. Dec. 269. The court says that the unnecessary exposure by the parents, or other person having the custody of a child incapable of exercising care and judgment, is an act of negligence, and is sufficient to defeat a recovery unless defendant's negligence is willful. This rule was applied in an action by the child in Lafayette & I. R. Co. v. Huffman, 28 Ind. 287, 92 Am. Dec. 318, and the above case was quoted as in point. In Jeffersonville, M. & I. R. Co. v. Bowen, 40 Ind. 545, s. c., 49 Ind. 154, which was an action by the father for the death of the child, the evidence did not show that the child was on the track without the negligence of the parents, as alleged in the complaint, and it was held that the action could not be maintained, the court citing both the above cases, as if they rested upon the same principle. In Evansville & C. R. Co. v. Wolf, 59 Ind. 89, an action by the father for the death of the child, where the child was suffered to wander unattended from its home to defendant's track, it was held that the facts showed such contributory negligence on the part of the parents that there could be no recovery unless defendant's negligence was willful.

[49] Wright v. Malden & M. R. Co., 4 Allen (Mass.) 283; Gibbons

/sustained by the intestate. In Kansas the question seems
to be undecided.[50]

Not all of these cases rest upon the rule of Hartfield v.
Roper, or, at any rate, rest exclusively on that ground. In
Maryland and Michigan, at least, the decisions are placed
rather upon the ground that the parents are the real parties
in interest, and that consequently no recovery can be had
if their negligence contributed to cause the death. Thus, in
a Maryland case,[51] where the child, when killed, was accompanied by her grandfather, under whose care her father had
placed her, and the judge charged that, if the jury should
find that the death resulted from the defendant's negligence,
the plaintiff could recover provided the accident could not
have been avoided by the exercise of due care and caution
on the part of the child, or of her father, or of the person
accompanying her, the court, in sustaining the charge, observed that to allow recovery in cases where the party entitled to the action was guilty of contributory negligence
would be to allow parties to take advantage of their own

---

v. Williams, 135 Mass. 333; Slattery v. O'Connell, 153 Mass. 94, 26
N. E. 430, 10 L. R. A. 653; Grant v. City of Fitchburg, 160 Mass. 16,
35 N. E. 84, 39 Am. St. Rep. 449; Walsh v. Loorem, 180 Mass. 18,
61 N. E. 222, 91 Am. St. Rep. 263.

[50] In Central Branch U. P. R. Co. v. Henigh, 23 Kan. 347, 33
Am. Rep. 167, which was an action by the administrator for the
death of a child, it was held that the facts did not show negligence
of the defendant. The court said: "Whether the negligence of his
parents or guardians could be imputed to him we do not now choose
to decide."

[51] Baltimore & O. R. Co. v. State, to Use of Fryer, 30 Md. 47.
In State, to Use of Coughlan, v. Baltimore & O. R. Co., 24 Md. 84,
87 Am. Dec. 600, the court observed that the same policy would require the plaintiff, in an action for injuries resulting in death, to
show that neither the party injured nor the parties for whose use
the action was brought had contributed by neglect or want of care
to the calamity complained of.

wrongful or negligent conduct. And in a Michigan case where the father, as administrator, sued for the death of a child, it was declared that, "if the parent is the real beneficiary, his contributory negligence will be imputed to the child." [52]

In Illinois the rule of Hartfield v. Roper was repudiated in Chicago City Ry. Co. v. Wilcox.[53] This was an action brought by an infant for personal injury and the court distinguishes such a case from an action by the administrator of an infant for death. Bailey, J., says: "It seems to be assumed by several of the writers that this court is committed to the doctrine that in a suit by a child to recover damages caused by the negligence of the defendant, the negligence of the plaintiff's parents or custodians may be imputed to the plaintiff in support of the defense of contributory negligence. While there is in some of the cases some foundation for this assumption, yet, in our opinion, the question has never been so considered or determined by

[52] Hurst v. Detroit City Ry. Co., 84 Mich. 539, 48 N. W. 44. The case was disposed of on other grounds. See, also, Green v. Chicago & W. M. Ry. Co., 110 Mich. 648, 68 N. W. 988; Miller v. Meade Tp., 128 Mich. 98, 87 N. W. 131.

[53] 138 Ill. 370, 27 N. E. 899, 21 L. R. A. 76. "In Chicago City Ry. Co. v. Wilcox, 138 Ill. 370, 27 N. E. 899, 21 L. R. A. 76, we held that, where a suit for damages caused by the negligence of the defendant is brought by a child of tender years, the negligence of his parents cannot be imputed to him in support of the defense of contributory negligence. Here, however, the suit is brought by the father as administrator of a deceased child. In such a case the contributory negligence of the parent, if it exists, may be shown in bar of the action. Chicago City Ry. Co. v. Wilcox, supra." City of Pekin v. McMahon, 154 Ill. 141, 39 N. E. 484, 27 L. R. A. 206, 45 Am. St. Rep. 114. See, also, West Chicago St. Ry. Co. v. Scanlan, 168 Ill. 34, 48 N. E. 149; True & True Co. v. Woda, 201 Ill. 315, 66 N. E. 369; Baltimore & O. S. W. Ry. Co. v. Pletz, 61 Ill. App. 161; City of Flora v. Pruett, 81 Ill. App. 161; Illinois Cent. R. Co. v. Bandy, 88 Ill. App. 629; McNulta v. Jenkins, 91 Ill. App. 309.

this court as to make it the settled rule in this state. Most
of the cases to which reference is made were suits brought
by a parent in his own right, or as the legal representative
of the child, where the death of the child was alleged to
have been caused by the negligence of the defendant. Such
was the case in City of Chicago v. Major, 18 Ill. 349, 68
Am. Dec. 553; City of Chicago v. Starr, 42 Ill. 174, 89 Am.
Dec. 422; Chicago & A. R. Co. v. Becker, 76 Ill. 25, Id., 84
Ill. 483; Hund v. Geier, 72 Ill. 393; City of Chicago v. Hesing, 83 Ill. 204, 25 Am. Rep. 378; and Toledo, W. & W. Ry.
Co. v. Grable, 88 Ill. 441.[54] Where an action for the negligent injury of an infant is brought by a parent, or for the
parent's own benefit, it is very justly held that the contributory negligence of such parent may be shown in bar of the
action. That is only a phase of the general rule that the
contributory negligence of the plaintiff is a defense."

And in an Indiana case, an action by the father, it was
held erroneous to charge that, if the child was capable of
exercising care and discretion, any question relating to the
parents' care was not to be considered. "If the child was
the plaintiff," said the court, "the negligence of the parent
would not be imputed to it; but the father is the plaintiff,
and seeks to recover because of the negligence of the defendant. In such case the negligence of the parents is a
proper question for the consideration of the jury." [55]

[54] Note 42, supra.
[55] Indianapolis St. Ry. Co. v. Antrobus, 33 Ind. App. 663, 71 N.
E. 971. See, also, Elwood Electric St. Ry. Co. v. Ross, 26 Ind. App.
258, 58 N. E. 535; City of Elwood v. Addison, 26 Ind. App. 28, 59
N. E. 47.

§ 69.   Contributory negligence of beneficiaries—In general

The question whether the contributory negligence of a beneficiary of the action is a bar to an action by him or on his behalf is most frequently presented in actions by or on behalf of parents for the death of a child. Where the doctrine of imputed negligence prevails, so that there could be no recovery by the child for personal injury if the negligence of the parent contributed to it, in such case there could, under acts similar to Lord Campbell's act, be no recovery for the death, for the reason that the right of recovery is limited to cases in which the person injured could have maintained an action if death had not ensued. The doctrine of imputed negligence being repudiated in most jurisdictions, however, the question is there presented whether the right of the party injured to maintain an action is the sole test of the right of the beneficiary to recover damages for the death, or whether it is merely one of the conditions of the right, and whether the right of action is not also conditional upon the beneficiary's freedom from contributory negligence. Against this view it has been urged that the statute in terms imposes no such condition, and that so to construe the statute is judicial legislation. Nevertheless the courts have almost unanimously held that the contributory negligence of the beneficiary is a bar, upon the general ground that one should not be allowed to profit by his own negligence.

§ 70.   Same—In action by beneficiaries

The question is presented in its simplest form where the right of action is given directly to the parent or next of kin, who bring the action in their own names without the intervention of a personal representative. Here the case is like that of an action by a father for loss of service of his child caused by personal injury, in which case the father's contributory negligence is a defense, and the cases are unanimous in so holding. Thus the distinction taken by the Illinois court in Chicago City Ry. Co. v. Wilcox [56] has also been taken in Pennsylvania [57] and Texas,[58] in

[56] Ante, § 68.

[57] In the suit of the parent for the death of a child the contributory negligence of the parent is a defense. Pennsylvania R. Co. v. James, *81 Pa. 194. Per Curiam: "A distinction is taken between the case of a father or mother bringing an action for the death of a child, and a child bringing an action for personal injury. In the former the contributing negligence of the parent may be used in defense, while in the latter case the negligence of an infant of tender years will not be available." The rule that the contributory negligence of the parents is a bar in actions by them for the death of the child is applied in Pittsburg, A. & M. Ry. Co. v. Pearson, 72 Pa. 169; Philadelphia & R. R. Co. v. Long, 75 Pa. 257; Pennsylvania R. Co. v. Lewis, 79 Pa. 33; Smith v. Hestonville, M. & F. Pass. R. Co., 92 Pa. 450, 37 Am. Rep. 705; Pennsylvania R. Co. v. Bock, 93 Pa. 427; Westerberg v. Kinzua, Creek & K. R. Co., 142 Pa. 471, 21 Atl. 878, 24 Am. St. Rep. 510; Borough of Birmingham v. Dorer, 3 Brewst. (Pa.) 69. In Smith v. Hestonville, M. & F. Pass. R. Co., Trunkey, J., says: "The argument of counsel is certainly ingenious in supporting his proposition that the negligence of the statutory plaintiff, arising from knowledge or direct act, cannot preclude a recovery where there has been no contributory negligence on the part of the deceased. However, this is not an open question." See, also, Del Rossi v. Cooney, 208 Pa. 233, 57 Atl. 514.

[58] In an action by the parent for the death of a child, the contributory negligence of the parent is a defense. Williams v. Texas, & P. Ry. Co., 60 Tex. 205. The court says that in a suit by a child for injuries resulting from the negligence of another, the child will be charged with only such discretion as a child of its years would exercise, and, if it be wanting in discretion, the fact that the negligence of its parents may have contributed to the injury can offer no excuse; yet, if the action be by the parent for the child's death, the contributory negligence of the parents is a defense, distinguishing the case from Galveston, H. & H. Ry. Co. v. Moore, 59

cases where the action was brought directly by the parents.
In these jurisdictions the rule of Hartfield v. Roper is denied.[59] That the contributory negligence of parents in actions by them for the death of a minor child is a defense is
also held in Missouri,[60] Arkansas,[61] Alabama,[62] Idaho,[63]

Tex. 64, 46 Am. Rep. 265, in which Hartfield v. Roper is expressly repudiated. The rule as to the negligence of the parents in an action
for death was applied in Texas Midland Ry. Co. v. Herbeck, 60 Tex.
602, and Cook v. Houston Direct Nav. Co., 76 Tex. 353, 13 S. W. 475,
18 Am. St. Rep. 52, and approved in San Antonio St. Ry. Co. v. Cailloutte, 79 Tex. 341, 15 S. W. 390.

[59] Smith v. O'Connor, 48 Pa. 218, 86 Am. Dec. 582; Kay v. Pennsylvania R. Co., 65 Pa. 269, 3 Am. Rep. 628; Galveston, H. & H. Ry.
Co. v. Moore, 59 Tex. 64, 46 Am. Rep. 265.

[60] Where a mother set a cup of milk before a child 16 months old,
and went into an adjoining room, and the child wandered out of the
house upon a railroad track, and was killed, held, that it is for the
jury to say, in an action by the parents, whether the mother was
guilty of contributory negligence. Reilly v. Hannibal & St. J. R.
Co., 94 Mo. 600, 7 S. W. 407. In an action by the parents for the
death of a child, held, that it was error to instruct the jury to find
for the plaintiffs, "if they believed that plaintiffs permitted their
son to wander from his home and go upon the turntable of defendant, and that the son was killed by the turntable, and was so young
and inexperienced as not to possess sufficient judgment to warn him
of the danger, and that he was killed by the negligence of defendant." Koons v. St. Louis & I. M. R. Co., 65 Mo. 592. In Boland v.
Missouri R. Co., 36 Mo. 484, an action by the parents for the death
of a child, it was held that there was no evidence of defendant's
negligence. The court says, however, that the same rigid rule, as
to contributory negligence, will not be applied to one infant as to
another, but all that is necessary to give a right of action to the
plaintiffs for an injury inflicted by the negligence of the defendant
is that the child should have exercised care and prudence equal to

---

[61] St. Louis, I. M. & S. Ry. Co. v. Freeman, 36 Ark. 41; St. Louis
Southwestern R. Co. v. Cochran, 77 Ark. 398, 91 S. W. 747.

[62] Alabama G. S. R. Co. v. Dobbs, 101 Ala. 219, 12 South. 770.
See, also, Alabama G. S. R. Co. v. Burgess, 116 Ala. 509, 22 South.
913.

[63] Holt v. Spokane & P. Ry. Co., 4 Idaho, 443, 40 Pac. 56.

and elsewhere.[64]   In Louisiana a distinction is drawn between the right of action for damages to the child which passes to the parents by inheritance and the right of action for damages from his death.   In respect to the former, the court say that their negligence would not be imputed to him, and therefore not to them; but, in respect to the lat-

his capacity. This case is sometimes cited as an authority to show that the rule of Hartfield v. Roper does not prevail in Missouri. But in Stillson v. Hannibal & St. J. R. Co., 67 Mo. 671, where a child of tender years, in the presence and by the direction of her father, attempted to cross defendant's track, and was injured, it was held in a suit by her for the personal injury that the father's negligence must be imputed to her. In Isabel v. Hannibal & St. J. R. Co., 60 Mo. 475, and Donahoe v. Wabash, St. L. & P. Ry. Co., 83 Mo. 543, it was held that a recovery by the parents for the death of a child would not be barred if their contributory negligence was not the proximate cause of the death. Though the parent was guilty of negligence in permitting the child to escape on the street, yet, if the death of the infant might have been avoided by the exercise of ordinary care on the part of the driver, plaintiff is entitled to recover. Czezewzka v. Benton-Bellefontaine Ry. Co., 121 Mo. 201, 25 S. W. 911. Where the death of plaintiffs' child was caused by his falling into an unguarded hole filled with water on premises occupied by them, and they knew of the danger, and could have removed it by covering the hole, they were guilty of contributory negligence. Wiese v. Remme, 140 Mo. 289, 41 S. W. 797. See, also, Levin v. Metropolitan St. Ry. Co., 140 Mo. 624, 41 S. W. 968; Jackson v. Kansas City, Ft. S. & M. R. Co., 157 Mo. 621, 58 S. W. 32, 80 Am. St. Rep. 650; Holmes v. Missouri Pac. Ry. Co., 190 Mo. 98, 88 S. W. 623; McGee v. Wabash R. Co., 214 Mo. 530, 114 S. W. 33; Day v. Consolidated Light, Power & Ice Co., 136 Mo. App. 274, 117 S. W. 81.

[64] Baltimore & O. R. Co. v. State, to Use of Fryer, 30 Md. 47. See, also, Fox v. Oakland Consol. St. Ry. Co., 118 Cal. 55, 50 Pac. 25, 62 Am. St. Rep. 216; Corbett v. Oregon Short Line R. Co., 25 Utah, 449, 71 Pac. 1065. In a suit by the mother in her own right, she is not chargeable with the contributory negligence of the father. Atlanta & C. Air Line Ry. Co. v. Gravitt, 93 Ga. 369, 20 S. E. 550, 26 L. R. A. 553, 44 Am. St. Rep. 145. Cf. Stamps v. Newton County, 8 Ga. App. 229, 68 S. E. 947.

ter, they say that the contributory negligence of the parents would be a defense.[65]

§ 71.   Same—In action by personal representative

Where the action is brought by the personal representative on behalf of the beneficiaries, the principle is the
same.   He is merely a formal plaintiff, and, although he
may be also a beneficiary, the vital question is: Who is entitled to the recovery?   Of course, the contributory negligence of an executor or administrator, if he is not a beneficiary, can have no effect at all.[66]   If he is the sole beneficiary, and is guilty of contributory negligence, the case
cannot be distinguished from one where the statute confers
upon him the right to sue in his own name, in which case,
as we have seen, he is barred by his own negligence.   This
is frequently the situation where a widowed parent is the
person solely entitled to the benefit of the action, as is the
case under most statutes when the action is brought for the
death of a minor child who leaves no issue.   It may, of
course, be that the sole beneficiary who is guilty of contributory negligence is not the personal representative, or that
he or some one else is the personal representative, but that
there are other negligent beneficiaries.   In all such cases the
principle is the same; that is, that the contributory negligence of the sole beneficial plaintiff or of all the beneficial
plaintiffs is a bar to recovery.[67]   "The underlying principle

[65] Westerfield v. Levis, 43 La. Ann. 63, 9 South. 52.   This case repudiates Hartfield v. Roper.

[66] Indiana Manuf. Co. v. Millican, 87 Ind. 87.

[67] Where the child is living and suing, the negligence of the father cannot be imputed to it to affect its action; but where the
child is dead, and the father is by law sole distributee of the child,
as he gets the recovery, and is guilty of the negligence producing

in the whole matter is that no one shall profit by his own
negligence, and to allow the father, who has been guilty of
negligence, to recover, notwithstanding that negligence,
when he brings the suit as administrator, although he could
not do so in his own right, would defeat this underlying
principle by a mere change of form, when the entire recovery, in either event, goes to him alone. Upon principle,
we think that, no matter how the suit is brought, whether
as administrator or as father, it can be defeated by the father's contributory negligence, when he is sole beneficiary." [68] "As the parent cannot recover for loss of services
when he himself contributed to the injury which caused the
loss, can the intervention of the personal representative,
who is a mere trustee, having no interest either for himself
or the estate he represents, shield him from the usual consequences of such negligence? I should say not. The damages for loss of services and those arising from the wrongful death are the same in principle, and should be governed
by the same rules as to defenses. The damages for wrongful death are such as are proportioned to the pecuniary injury resulting to the parent from death caused by such injury. Such is the provision of the statute. The damages
for loss of services are the same, being the pecuniary loss
resulting to the parent from the injury to the child. If the
parent, by his negligence, contributes towards the injury
which causes the death of the child, he is equally guilty with
the other party, who by his negligence caused the injury;
and when both parties, by their combined negligent acts,
bring about an injury, neither party can sustain an action

the accident, that will bar recovery, no matter who is administrator,
unless the defendant's act be willful or wanton. Gunn v. Ohio River
R. Co., 42 W. Va. 676, 26 S. E. 546, 36 L. R. A. 575.

[68] Bamberger v. Citizens' St. R. Co., 95 Tenn. 18, 31 S. W. 163, 28
L. R. A. 486, 49 Am. St. Rep. 909.

(158)

for damages against the other. To award damages to a parent guilty of contributory negligence in such cases would permit him to profit by his own wrong, and, besides, it would be in direct conflict with the universal rule as to contributory negligence." [69]

The position that there can be recovery in such cases has been taken in Iowa and New Hampshire, and was formerly, but is no longer, taken in Ohio and Virginia. In Connecticut,[70] New Jersey,[71] and Oregon [72] the question has been left undecided. In other states where the question has arisen it has been held that there can be no recovery.[73]

The cases which hold that the contributory negligence of

[69] Wolf v. Lake Erie & W. Ry. Co., 55 Ohio St. 517, 45 N. E. 708, 36 L. R. A. 812.

[70] In an action by an administrator of a child for damages for its death from being run over by a car of the defendant company, the negligence of the child's parents in allowing it to play in the street is an immaterial question, where it does not appear that the parents are in a position to be benefited by a participation in the distribution of the amount recovered. Murphy v. Derby St. Ry. Co., 73 Conn. 249, 47 Atl. 120.

[71] In the Supreme Court it was held not a defense to an action by a father, as administrator for the death of his son, that the death was in part occasioned by the carelessness of the father. The court of errors and appeals divided equally upon the question and reversed the judgment below on another ground. Consolidated Traction Co. v. Hone, 59 N. J. Law, 275, 35 Atl. 899.

[72] McDonald v. O'Reilly, 45 Or. 589, 78 Pac. 753 (holding that the negligence of the mother will not be imputed to the father).

[73] St. Louis, I. M. & S. Ry. Co. v. Dawson, 68 Ark. 1, 56 S. W. 46 (cf. Miles v. St. Louis, I. M. & S. R. Co., 90 Ark. 485, 119 S. W. 837; Nashville Lumber Co. v. Busbee [Ark.] 139 S. W. 301); Tucker v. Draper, 62 Neb. 66, 86 N. W. 917, 54 L. R. A. 321; O'Shea v. Lehigh Val. R. Co., 79 App. Div. 254, 79 N. Y. Supp. 890; Davis v. Seaboard Air Line R. Co., 136 N. C. 115, 48 S. E. 591, 1 Ann. Cas. 214; Harton v. Forest City Telephone City Co., 141 N. C. 455, 54 S. E. 299; Scherer v. Schlaberg, 18 N. Dak. 421, 122 N. W. 1000, 24 L. R. A. (N. S.) 520; Wolf v. Lake Erie & W. Ry. Co., 55 Ohio St. 517, 45 N. E. 708, 36 L. R. A. 812; Bamberger v. Citizens' St.

such beneficiary or beneficiaries is not a bar will now first be discussed.

In an Iowa case [74] the administrator sued for damages to the estate from the death of a child caused by the break- ing of a bridge over which the child was riding in a car- riage, with his parents, and it was held that their negligence would not defeat the action. The act was in terms a sur- vival act, and provided that the damages should be disposed of as personal property belonging to the estate of the de- ceased. The court repudiates the rule of Hartfield v. Roper, and says: "If his parents, by their negligence, contributed to his death, that does not seem to be a sufficient reason for denying his estate relief. Such negligence would prevent a recovery by the parents in their own right. * * * It is claimed that, * * * since they inherited his estate, the rule which would bar a negligent parent from recovering in such a case in his own right ought to apply. But plaintiff seeks to recover in the right of the child, and not for the

Ry. Co., 95 Tenn. 18, 31 S. W. 163, 28 L. R. A. 486, 49 Am. St. Rep. 909; Ploof v. Burlington Traction Co., 70 Vt. 509, 41 Atl. 1017, 43 L. R. A. 108; Lindsay v. Canadian Pac. Ry. Co., 68 Vt. 556, 35 Atl. 513; Richmond, F. & P. R. Co. v. Martin's Adm'r, 102 Va. 201, 45 S. E. 894; Vinnette v. Northern Pac. Ry. Co., 47 Wash. 320, 91 Pac. 975, 18 L. R. A. (N. S.) 328 (cf. Tecker v. Seattle R. & S. R. Co., 60 Wash. 570, 111 Pac. 791, Ann. Cas. 1912B, 842); Gunn v. Ohio River R. Co., 42 W. Va. 676, 26 S. E. 546, 36 L. R. A. 575 (cf. Bias v. Ches- apeake & O. Ry. Co., 46 W. Va. 349, 33 S. E. 240).

[74] Wymore v. Mahaska County, 78 Iowa, 396, 43 N. W. 264, 6 L. R. A. 545, 16 Am. St. Rep. 449. The court points out that it was assumed in Walters v. Chicago, R. I. & P. R. Co., 41 Iowa, 71, that in such a case the negligence of the parents would be imputed to the child, and, consequently, defeat the action by the administrator; but that in that case the point actually decided was, simply, that when the parents of a child two years old are unable to give him their personal care, and intrust him to a suitable person, the negligence of the latter cannot be imputed to the parents so as to defeat an ac- tion by the administrator for the death.

(160)

parents. It may be that a recovery in this case will result in conferring an undeserved benefit upon the father, but that is a matter which we cannot investigate. *If the facts are such that the child could have recovered had his injuries not been fatal, his administrator can recover the full amount of damages which the estate of the child sustained."* It is to be noted that, under the circumstances of this case, the amount recovered was not liable for the debts of the deceased, but belonged solely to the parents.

The same rule was formerly declared in Virginia, in a suit by the father as administrator of an infant.[75] "Such negligence," says the court, "is not imputable to the child, and is consequently not to be considered when the suit is by the child or his personal representative. * * * The doctrine of Hartfield v. Roper has been repudiated in this state. * * * Hence, *when the facts are such that the child could have recovered had his injuries not been fatal, his administrator may recover,* without regard to the negligence or presence of the parents at the time the injuries are received, and although the estate is inherited by the parents." The Virginia court has since pointed out that this language was not necessary to the decision, and has approved the rule which is now generally held.[76]

The question was presented in Ohio in Cleveland, C. & C. R. Co. v. Crawford [77] under peculiar circumstances. The

[75] Norfolk & W. R. Co. v. Groseclose's Adm'r, 88 Va. 267, 13 S. E. 454, 29 Am. St. Rep. 718.

[76] Where a father, through his agent, the custodian of child, is guilty of negligence contributing to cause its death, he cannot as administrator recover damages for its death in an action for his own benefit, under Code 1887, §§ 2903, 2905. Richmond, F. & P. R. Co. v. Martin's Adm'r, 102 Va. 201, 45 S. E. 894. See City of Newport News v. Scott's Adm'x, 103 Va. 794, 50 S. E. 266.

[77] 24 Ohio St. 631, 15 Am. Rep. 633.

administrator sued for the death of a father and mother killed by the collision of a wagon, in which they and three of their four children were driving, with the defendant's locomotive. The children were the sole next of kin. The defendant requested the court to charge that, if the persons for whose benefit the action was brought were guilty of contributory negligence, a recovery could not be had for their benefit. This request, the court held, was properly refused, because, first, the *statute gives the right of action to the personal representative upon the same conditions that would have entitled the party injured to an action if death had not ensued,* and because the right of action of the parents would not have been defeated, if they were free from negligence themselves, by the contributory negligence of the children. The court assigned as a second reason that the amount recovered is a gross sum to be distributed to the next of kin in the proportion provided by law, and that, if the contributory negligence of some would defeat a recovery as to them, it would also defeat it as to those who in no wise contributed to the injury. And in a later Ohio case [78] it was held that the contributory negligence of a husband in purchasing a drug to be used by his wife is not to be imputed to her, and would not defeat an action by her administrator against the dealer for her death, resulting from the use of a poisonous drug, which the dealer negligently delivered to the husband, instead of the drug requested, unless she constituted him her agent. Owen, C. J., says: "The plaintiff does not prosecute the action as husband, but as the administrator, of his wife. It is prosecuted for the benefit of the children, as well as the husband, of the intestate. The right of the beneficiaries, as well to

---

[78] Davis v. Guarnieri, 45 Ohio St. 470, 15 N. E. 350, 4 Am. St. Rep. 548.

a recovery as to the fruits of it, are to be tested by the statutes which the law would have ascribed to the wife and mother if she were alive and prosecuting her injury to her health or person." In a later case,[79] Cleveland, C. & C. R. Co. v. Crawford, it was in effect overruled, although the court distinguished it on the narrow ground of an amendment of the statute, requiring the jury to give such damages as they may think proportioned to the pecuniary injury resulting from the death to the beneficiaries "respectively." The court also distinguishes the cases in Iowa, Virginia, and Louisiana on the ground that the damages become a part of the estate of the deceased and are inherited from the estate by the beneficiaries as heirs, upon whom the estate is cast by operation of law. "But it is otherwise," the court says, "as to a recovery for damages under our statute. While the liability is created by the statute, the damages do not become a part of the estate, and are not cast as an estate by operation of law upon the beneficiaries, but must be sued for and recovered by action; and in such action the usual defenses, including contributory negligence, can be interposed, unless otherwise provided by statute. Our statute has no provision on the subject, and hence it would seem to irresistibly follow that the defense of contributory negligence may be made in such actions."

In New Hampshire [80] the action was brought by the administrator for the death of a child, under an act which provides that causes of action of tort for physical injury to the person shall survive, subject to the limitations of the act, and that the damages shall be distributed among persons

[79] Wolf v. Lake Erie & W. Ry. Co., 55 Ohio St. 517, 45 N. E. 708, 36 L. R. A. 812. The court also distinguishes Davis v. Guarnieri, supra. See, also, Cleveland, A. & C. Ry. Co. v. Workman, 66 Ohio St. 509, 64 N. E. 582, 90 Am. St. Rep. 602.

[80] Warren v. Manchester St. Ry., 70 N. H. 352, 47 Atl. 735.

specified ("if there be no child and no widow or widower, to the heirs at law of the deceased according to the laws of distribution"). In the case presented the parents were apparently the sole beneficiaries. It was held that the contributory negligence of the father was not a bar. The court rejects the rule of Hartfield v. Roper, and says: "This action, brought by the administrator of the child's estate, is for the benefit of the estate, and not, as the defendants claim, for the benefit of the father. The fact that the father will indirectly be benefited is only an incident of the suit. Had the child survived, the action would have been brought in its own name. The father's cause of action would have been what it is now—case for the loss of the child's service. The child's cause of action survived by reason of the statute, and the money recovered in it will be assets in the hands of its administrator, to be distributed in accordance with the special provisions of the statute. If the father's negligence barred his right to recover in the action, there would seem to be no reason why it would not bar him from recovering any property of the child's which he might inherit under the general provisions relating to descent and distribution; but this is not claimed to be, and is not, the law. The evidence of the father's negligence was properly excluded." The decision being that the father's negligence did not bar his right to recover, the question whether the negligence of one of the beneficiaries should bar the right of another (the mother) who was not negligent was not mentioned.

In Arkansas [81] an action was brought by the father as

---

[81] Nashville Lumber Co. v. Busbee (Ark.) 139 S. W. 301. See, also, Miles v. St. Louis, I. M. & S. R. Co., 90 Ark. 485, 119 S. W. 837 (cf. St. Louis, I. M. & S. Ry. Co. v. Dawson, 68 Ark. 1, 56 S. W. 46).

administrator for the death of his child and for the sole benefit of the estate, under a survival act which provides for an action to recover damages for the suffering of the intestate caused by personal injuries which resulted in his death, and it was held that the contributory negligence of the father could not defeat the action, although he was the sole distributee of the estate. The court distinguishes the case from one brought under the Arkansas death act (Lord Campbell's act), on the ground that under that act the administrator sues as trustee for those upon whom the act confers the right of recovery and not as representative of the estate, citing with approval the Iowa case above stated. "Our conclusion is," said the court, "that, where the right of the parent is derived from the child by inheritance under the statutes (sections 2636, 6285, Kirby's Dig.), contributory negligence is not a defense. To so hold is not, as some text-writers and judges loosely express it, magnifying form above substance, but rather is it carrying out the law as it is written. If the result is to confer an undeserved benefit upon one whose negligence has been partly instrumental in producing the estate sought to be recovered, that is a matter for the legislature to deal with, but not for the courts."

In Alabama, while it is held that in an action by the parent or by the personal representative on his behalf, under section 2485 of the Code (1907), to recover pecuniary compensation for the loss of service the contributory negligence of the parent is a defense,[82] it is also held that under section 2486, for the recovery of damages which the court has declared to be entirely punitive, the statute being intended to prevent homicides, that the contributory negligence of the parent administrator will not defeat a recovery, al-

[82] Alabama G. S. Ry. Co. v. Dobbs, 101 Ala. 219, 12 South. 770; Alabama G. S. R. Co. v. Burgess, 116 Ala. 509, 22 South. 913.

though he "may be one of the distributees, or entitled to all, or a part, of the proceeds of the judgment." [88]

In New York, in the appellate division of the supreme court, in an action brought by the father as administrator for the death of his child under the death act (Lord Campbell's act), it was held by a divided court that contributory negligence of the father, not being willful or intentional, would not defeat the action, although as next of kin he was entitled to the damages resulting.[84] The decision was based on the ground that by the express terms of the statute the decedent, if living, could have maintained an action, and that the statute contained no such limitation. "If the decedent had left several next of kin him surviving, all similarly situated as to him," said the opinion, "each would have been entitled, under the statute, to a pro rata share of any recovery which might be had. If the negligence of one of such next of kin contributed to the accident which resulted in the death, would such negligence prevent a recovery? Certainly the rights of those who were free from negligence ought not to be thus affected; and, if so, then, in such case, should a jury be instructed to deduct from its verdict the share of the one negligent? It is apparent that the rule contended for by defendant's counsel would lead to great confusion in the administration of the law in this class of cases, and ought not to be adopted, except for substantial reasons. There is nothing to indicate that the legislature intended that such construction should be placed upon the statute; but, on the contrary, its language would seem to forbid such an interpretation." In the court of appeals the judgment was affirmed, but it was said that the "interest-

---

[88] Southern Ry. Co. v. Shipp, 169 Ala. 327, 53 South. 150.

[84] Lewin v. Lehigh Val. R. Co., 52 App. Div. 69, 65 N. Y. Supp. 49, judgment affirmed 165 N. Y. 667, 59 N. E. 301.

ing question" as to the plaintiff's contributory negligence was not before the court. In a later case [85] in the appellate division, the above case was not approved, and it was held that the contributory negligence of the father in such case bars a recovery, he being the sole next of kin and solely entitled to the recovery.

It is to be observed that the case mentioned in this section on Iowa, New Hampshire, and Arkansas arose under acts which were in form survival rather than death acts, and in some of the cases which have declined to follow the rule adopted by them they have been distinguished on that ground, yet it seems that whatever the nature of the right of action which the statute gives to the survivors designated the same principle should be applicable; that is, that no one shall profit by his own negligence, and that if any beneficiary of the action has by his negligence contributed to the death there should be no recovery of damages for him.

§ 72.   Same—Where some but not all beneficiaries are negligent

The principle once established that there can be no recovery if the sole beneficiary or all the beneficiaries were guilty of contributory negligence, it logically follows that the contributory negligence of one or more of the beneficiaries cannot defeat a recovery by or on behalf of beneficiaries who were not negligent. The assessment of the damages in such cases, however, particularly where the statute provides for a recovery of a gross sum to be distributed among the beneficiaries, has seemed to some courts to present an insuperable difficulty to a denial of recovery to

[85] O'Shea v. Lehigh Val. R. Co., 79 App. Div. 254, 79 N. Y. Supp. 890.

some and an allowance to others.[86] But this difficulty is
more imaginary than real. In such cases the court may
properly leave it to the jury to assess the damages with
reference to the injury of the non-negligent beneficiaries
alone.[87] As was said in Ohio in Wolf v. Lake Erie & W.
R. Co.:[88] "In arriving at the total amount of damages to
be awarded under the statute as amended, the jury should
consider the pecuniary injury to each separate beneficiary
(not found guilty of contributory negligence), but return a
verdict for a gross sum, which sum should be distributed
among the beneficiaries not found guilty of contributory
negligence. As to beneficiaries found guilty of contributory negligence, no damages should be awarded on their account, and the jury should find in its verdict which, if any,
of the beneficiaries were guilty of such contributory negligence. This would no more complicate the trial than is

[86] Lewin v. Lehigh Val. R. Co., 52 App. Div. 69, 65 N. Y. Supp.
49 (but see O'Shea v. Lehigh Val. R. Co., 79 App. Div. 254, 79 N. Y.
Supp. 890); Cleveland, C. & C. R. Co. v. Crawford, 24 Ohio St. 631,
15 Am. Rep. 633; Davis v. Guarnieri, 45 Ohio St. 470, 15 N. E. 350,
4 Am. St. Rep. 548.

[87] Negligence of one of the next of kin of plaintiff's intestate contributing to her death is not a defense to the merits; at most, such
negligence will but bar right of such next of kin to damages. Chicago City Ry. Co. v. McKeon, 143 Ill. App. 598 (cf. Illinois Cent. R.
Co. v. Warriner, 229 Ill. 91, 82 N. E. 246). The question was referred
to, but not passed on, in Davis v. Seaboard Air Line Ry., 136 N. C.
115, 48 S. E. 591, 1 Ann. Cas. 214. In a suit by the mother in her
own right, she is not chargeable with the negligence of the father
because of the conjugal relation. Atlanta & C. Air Line Ry. Co. v.
Gravitt, 93 Ga. 369, 20 S. E. 550, 26 L. R. A. 553, 44 Am. St. Rep.
145.

[88] Wolf v. Lake Erie & W. R. Co., 55 Ohio St. 517, 45 N. E. 708,
36 L. R. A. 812. See, also, Cleveland, A. & C. Ry. Co. v. Workman,
66 Ohio St. 509, 64 N. E. 582, 90 Am. St. Rep. 602. See 2 Ill. Law
Rev. 487, "Contributory Negligence of the Beneficiary as a Bar to
an Administrator's Action for Death," by Prof. John H. Wigmore.

usual in trial for torts, in which it often occurs that some are discharged, and others held liable." It is true that in this case, in order to distinguish it from the earlier case of Cleveland, C. & C. R. Co. v. Crawford, the court, as already pointed out, laid stress on an intervening amendment of the statute requiring the jury to give damages proportioned to the injury to the beneficiaries "respectively," but under most statutes it is the damages that result to the beneficiaries that are recoverable, and the word "respectively" adds little if anything.

§ 73.   Instantaneous death

It follows from what has been said that under statutes of the general type of Lord Campbell's act, which create a new cause of action, and give damages for the injury resulting from the death, it is generally immaterial whether the death is or is not instantaneous.[89] This point seems too clear for argument, and that such is the law has been tacitly assumed in nearly all the cases which have arisen under these statutes, and in which death resulted immediately from the injury. In Brown v. Buffalo & S. L. R. Co.[90] the point was briefly disposed of. After referring to the first section of the New York act, the court says: "This provision

[89] Brown v. Buffalo & S. L. R. Co., 22 N. Y. 191; International & G. N. R. Co. v. Kindred, 57 Tex. 491; Roach v. Imperial Min. Co., 7 Fed. 698, 7 Sawy. 224; Reed v. Northeastern R. Co., 37 S. C. 42. 16 S. E. 289; Missouri, K. & T. Ry. Co. v. Elliott, 102 Fed. 96, 42 C. C. A. 188 (Arkansas statute); Malott v. Shimer, 153 Ind. 35, 54 N. E. 101, 74 Am. St. Rep. 278 (Illinois statute); Matz v. Chicago & A. R. Co. (C. C.) 85 Fed. 180 (Missouri damage act); Fink v. Garman, 40 Pa. 95; Perham v. Portland General Electric Co., 33 Or. 451, 53 Pac. 14, 24, 40 L. R. A. 799, 72 Am. St. Rep. 730; Sternenberg v. Mailhos, 99 Fed. 43, 39 C. C. A. 408 (Texas statute).

[90] 22 N. Y. 191.

settles the question, and leaves nothing for debate or doubt. No one would question the right of the intestate, in this case, if he had survived the injury, to have maintained an action for it. * * * The statute gives the action to the personal representative of the individual injured, when the injury causes his death, and it makes no distinction between cases where the death was immediate or instantaneous, or where it was consequential."

In some states, however, where there is a survival act as well as a death act, the latter is held to be limited to cases of instantaneous or immediate death, and cases where the death was not instantaneous or immediate are held to fall under the survival act. This is the construction which has been adopted in Maine and Michigan.[91] A different conclusion was reached in Massachusetts, under somewhat similar statutes, on the ground that under the death act there was no limitation to cases of instantaneous death in the express terms of the statute.[92] And in some other states where there are survival acts, the construction placed upon them is that the right of action survives only if death results from other causes than the injury, and consequently under the death acts in such states it is immaterial whether the death is or is not instantaneous.[93]

---

[91] Ante, §§ 43, 44—1.

[92] Commonwealth v. Metropolitan R. Co., 107 Mass. 236.

[93] Holton v. Daly, 106 Ill. 131; Chicago & E. I. R. Co. v. O'Connor, 19 Ill. App. 591; s. c., 119 Ill. 586, 9 N. E. 263; McCarthy v. Chicago, R. I. & P. R. Co., 18 Kan. 46, 26 Am. Rep. 742; Hulbert v. City of Topeka (C. C.) 34 Fed. 510; City of Eureka v. Merrifield, 53 Kan. 794, 37 Pac. 113; Lubrano v. Atlantic Mills, 19 R. I. 129, 32 Atl. 205, 34 L. R. A. 797; post, § 126.

§ 74.   Instantaneous death under statutes providing for survival of action

Under statutes which provide simply for a survival of causes of action for personal injury, and do not in terms or by implication provide for the recovery of damages for the injury resulting from the death, a different question is of course presented. These statutes suppose the person deceased to have been once entitled to an action for the injury, and either to have commenced the action and subsequently died, or, being entitled to bring it, to have died before exercising the right.[94] It follows that no action can be maintained by the personal representative if the death was instantaneous.

The question has frequently arisen in various forms in Massachusetts, under a statute which enacts that "the action for trespass on the case, for damages to the person, shall hereafter survive; so that, in the event of the death of the person entitled to bring such action, or liable thereto, the same may be prosecuted or defended by or against the executor or administrator in the same manner as if he were living." [95] Under this statute the rule has been repeatedly affirmed that no action can be maintained where the death was instantaneous.[96] The mere fact that there was evidence

---

[94] Hollenbeck v. Berkshire R. Co., 9 Cush. (Mass.) 478.

[95] Ante, § 44.

[96] Kearney v. Boston & W. R. Corp., 9 Cush. 108; Mann v. Boston & W. R. Corp., 9 Cush. 108. An action for personal injuries caused by falling 40 feet and resulting in instant death cannot be maintained. Moran v. Hollings, 125 Mass. 93. An action cannot be maintained for personal injuries resulting in death, if the evidence wholly fails to show whether or not death was instantaneous. Riley v. Connecticut River R. Co., 135 Mass. 292; Corcoran v. Boston & A. R. Co., 133 Mass. 507.

of some slight spasmodic action on the part of the deceased, where the other evidence tended to show that death was immediate, has been held not sufficient to prevent the court from directing a verdict for the plaintiff, on the ground that the death was instantaneous; [97] but where the injured party lived after the accident only 15 minutes, though in a state of unconsciousness, it was held that the action survived.[98]

[97] Kearney v. Boston & W. R. Corp., 9 Cush. (Mass.) 108. In discussing this question in that case, Shaw, C. J., says: "What constitutes that termination or period of life which is necessary to give the party's representatives a right of action? It is not necessary to go into a minute, metaphysical discussion of the question. We are to ascertain what the intent of the legislature was when they passed the law. It is not to be supposed that they intended to make a distinction between a case where death was so instantaneous that there was no manifestation of life whatever and a case where there might be some slight spasmodic action of the body of the sufferer to indicate that life was not quite extinct. * * * The statute must have a practical construction, and supposes a case where a cause of action accrued to the injured party in his lifetime, which, by force of the statute in question, devolved upon and vested in his personal representative, at his decease afterwards. * * * The question is, was the death instantaneous, or did the party injured live after the accident happened? It is in evidence that there was only a momentary, spasmodic struggle, and the death instantaneous." The deceased was last seen alive in the mill 10 or 15 minutes before the accident; three quarters of an hour after the accident his dead body was found about 20 feet below where he had been last seen, with no marks of injury upon it, surrounded by loose grain over his head. There was expert evidence that he died of suffocation, and that a person so situated would retain consciousness from 3 to 5 minutes. Held, that the jury were warranted in finding that the death was not instantaneous. Nourse v. Packard, 138 Mass. 307. In an action for injury to plaintiff's intestate by suffocation in a steamer in which the hatch had been closed to check fire, from the position of the body it was to be inferred that his death was not instantaneous, and that he lived in a state of conscious suffering for a greater or less time. Held, a proper case for the jury. Pierce v. Cunard S. S. Co., 153 Mass. 87, 26 N. E. 415.

[98] Bancroft v. Boston & W. R. Corp., 11 Allen (Mass.) 34. The de.

In the absence, however, of evidence of conscious suffering on the part of the deceased, or of expenses or loss incurred before the death by reason of the accident, only nominal damages can be recovered.[99]

In Maine and Michigan, likewise, as we have seen,[100] under statutes providing for the survival of the right of action for personal injury, it is held that no right of action survives where the death was instantaneous. And it is so held in Arkansas,[101] Mississippi,[102] Montana,[103] Wisconsin,[104] and Kentucky.[105]

ceased lived 15 or 20 hours, and there was some evidence that she manifested intelligence and consciousness, but it was held that, independently of this consideration, the action might be maintained. Hollenbeck v. Berkshire R. Co., 9 Cush. 478.

[99] Kennedy v. Standard Sugar Refinery, 125 Mass. 90, 28 Am Rep. 214; Tully v. Fitchburg R. Co., 134 Mass. 499; Mulchahey v. Washburn Car Wheel Co., 145 Mass. 281, 14 N. E. 106, 1 Am. St. Rep. 458.

[100] Ante, §§ 43, 44—1.

[101] A right of action for negligence resulting in death survives to the personal representative of deceased, if she lived after the act constituting the cause of action, though she never became conscious. St. Louis, I. M. & S. Ry. Co. v. Dawson, 68 Ark. 1, 56 S. W. 46. In an action for the death of a person thrown from a bridge by a train, evidence held to show that he was not instantly killed, but that he experienced an interval of pain and anguish after being struck. St. Louis, I. M. & S. Ry. Co. v. Stamps, 84 Ark. 241, 104 S. W. 1114. See, also, Texarkana Gas & Electric Light Co. v. Orr, 59 Ark. 215, 27 S. W. 66, 43 Am. St. Rep. 30.

[102] Illinois Cent. R. Co. v. Pendergrass, 69 Miss. 425, 12 South. 954; Beckman v. Georgia Pac. Ry. Co. (Miss.) 12 South. 956.

[103] Dillon v. Great Northern R. Co., 38 Mont. 485, 100 Pac. 960; ante, § 45—1.

[104] The length of time decedent survived is material only as to the damages recoverable. Brown v. Chicago & N. W. Ry. Co., 102 Wis. 137, 77 N. W. 748, 78 N. W. 771, 44 L. R. A. 579. See, also, Lehmann v. Farwell, 95 Wis. 185, 70 N. W. 170, 37 L. R. A. 333, 60 Am. St. Rep. 111.

[105] Hansford's Adm'x v. Payne, 11 Bush (Ky.) 380; Newport News & M. V. R. Co. v. Dentzel's Adm'r, 91 Ky. 42, 14 S. W. 958, 12 Ky. Law Rep. 626; ante, § 41.

§ 75. Instantaneous death—Connecticut, Iowa, Louisiana, Tennessee

The question, however, whether a right of action exists where death was instantaneous, even when the question arises under statutes which in terms provide for the survival of the action, necessarily depends. greatly upon the language and purpose of each particular enactment. In Connecticut, Iowa, Tennessee, and, it seems, in Louisiana, under statutes which so provide, it has been held that the fact that death was instantaneous is immaterial.

The question arose in Connecticut under the former statute, which provided that "actions for injury to the person, *whether the same do or do not result in death,* * * * shall survive." The court pointed out the difference between this language and that of the Massachusetts statute, and held that the right of action was not confined to cases where an interval of time intervened between the accident and the death.[106] The Connecticut statute was amended, to read: "Whether the same do or do not *instantaneously or otherwise* result in death."[107] The statute now provides

---

[106] Murphy v. New York & N. H. R. Co., 30 Conn. 184. Referring to the Massachusetts cases, Ellsworth, J., says: "These decisions obviously do not turn at all on the want of injury, * * * but upon the want of a perfect cause of action before death, which alone could bring the case within their statute. We think that construction rather nice and technical, and, were our statute the same as theirs, we are not prepared to say we should adopt it; but our statute is quite different. * * * Its language is merely 'whether the injury do or do not result in death.' This certainly puts an end to the application of the common-law maxim to this class of cases." The point was raised but not decided in Murphy v. New York & N. H. R. Co., 29 Conn. 496.

[107] See, Broughel v. Southern New England Tel. Co., 72 Conn. 617, 45 Atl. 435, 49 L. R. A. 404; Id., 73 Conn. 614, 48 Atl. 751, 84 Am. St. Rep. 176.

that in actions surviving or to be brought by an executor or administrator for injuries resulting in death, "whether in_ stantaneous or otherwise," the executor or administrator may recover just damages, not exceeding $10,000.[108]

In Iowa the statute enacts that "all causes of action shall survive, and may be brought, notwithstanding the death of the person entitled or liable to the same." In Conners v. Burlington, C. R. & N. Ry. Co.[109] the court, after quoting the various statutory provisions, says: "For many years before the enactment of the present Code, a statute was in force * * * which provided that, 'when a wrongful act produces death, the perpetrator is civilly liable for the injury.' When the present Code was enacted, the section in which that provision was contained was repealed, and the sections quoted above were enacted in lieu thereof. * * * But we think the effect of these provisions is the same as though that express language had been retained."

In Tennessee the statute enacts that "the right of action which a person who dies from injuries received from another, or whose death is caused by the wrongful act, omission, or killing by another, would have had against the wrongdoer in case death had not ensued, shall not abate or be extinguished by his death," etc. In respect to this section the supreme court of Tennessee has said: "It cannot be controverted that the language 'whose death is caused by the wrongful act or omission of another' includes cases of in-

---

[108] Pub. Acts 1903, c. 193, § 4, as amended by Pub. Acts 1911, c. 242. See post, § 132.

[109] 71 Iowa, 490, 32 N. W. 465, 60 Am. Rep. 814, followed in Worden v. Humeston & S. R. Co., 72 Iowa, 201, 33 N. W. 629. A husband is not entitled to recover from a railroad company for the instant killing of his wife in the absence of statute permitting such recovery. Seney v. Chicago, M. & St. P. Ry. Co., 125 Iowa, 290, 101 N. W. 76. See, also, Major v. Burlington, C. R. & N. Ry. Co., 115 Iowa, 309, 88 N. W. 815.

stantaneous death; and the language which immediately follows, 'would have had against the wrongdoer, in case death had not ensued, shall not abate and be extinguished by his death,' necessarily means that the representative of the deceased person shall have a right of action, whether the deceased person died after the injuries were received, or died simultaneously with the infliction of the injury which caused death." [110]

In Louisiana the statute reads: "Every act whatever that causes damage to another obliges him by whose fault it happened to repair it.. The right of this action shall survive in case of death in favor of the minor children or widow of the deceased," etc. Under this provision it seems that damages may be recovered although the death was instantaneous.[111]

---

[110] Nashville & C. R. Co. v. Prince, 2 Heisk. 580, overruling Louisville & N. R. Co. v. Burke, 6 Coldw. 45, and followed in Fowlkes v. N. & D. R. Co., 5 Baxt. 663; Haley v. Mobile & O. R. Co., 7 Baxt. 239; Kansas City, Ft. S. & M. R. Co. v. Daughtry, 88 Tenn. 721, 13 S. W. 698. The question whether deceased suffered mental or bodily pain, where death was instantaneous, is a question for the jury, where such pain is, under the statute, an element for which damages can be recovered. Western & A. R. Co. v. Roberson, 61 Fed. 592, 9 C. C. A. 646.

[111] Van Amburg v. Vicksburg, S. & P. R. Co., 37 La. Ann. 651, 55 Am. Rep. 517. This case was before the amendment which provides that the survivors may also recover the damages sustained by them by the death; and damages were recovered, although the court remarks that "the death was immediate, if not instantaneous." See, also, Hamilton v. Morgan's L. & T. R. & S. S. Co., 42 La. Ann. 824, 8 South. 586. In the latter case an infant child was instantly killed, and the father sued on the cause of action which accrued to the infant and survived to him. Punitive damages were awarded. Held, that though punitive damages were not recoverable, and there was no evidence of actual damages to the infant, the court would, in the exercise of its equitable powers, award the father compensatory damages in the nominal sum of $250, the circumstances of the injury having been such that the father had cause to seek a judicial

§ 76.   Proximate cause of death

It is of course necessary to the maintenance of the action that the death should have been caused by the wrongful act, neglect, or default; that is, that the death should have been the natural and proximate result.[112]   Thus, where,

investigation. But see Weeks v. New Orleans & C. R. Co., 32 La. Ann. 615, in which Levy, J., says that the article only subrogates the plaintiff to the right of action of the deceased, and that the plaintiff could only recover the damages suffered by the deceased himself. And see, also, The Corsair, 145 U. S. 335, 12 Sup. Ct. 949, 36 L. Ed. 727, where a vessel met with an accident, and sank 10 minutes later, drowning libelant's daughter, and it was held that an action for her suffering and fright during such 10 minutes, separate and apart from the cause of action arising out of her subsequent death, could not be maintained. In an action for negligence resulting in a man's drowning, his sufferings after he fell into the water, and before he drowned, cannot be taken into account, since they are substantially contemporaneous with his death. Cheatam v. Red River Line (C. C.) 56 Fed. 248.

112 If, having exercised reasonable prudence, considering the time, place, and circumstances, as also the condition of the drunken man himself, the conductor expels such passenger, who is afterwards run over and killed by another train, not in fault, the expulsion itself is not proximate cause of the death. Railway Co. v. Valleley, 32 Ohio St. 345, 30 Am. Rep. 601. Plaintiff's intestate was ejected from defendant's train, and left, in the nighttime, in a state of intoxication, near the track. Several hours after, at a distance of half a mile from where he was ejected, he was killed by another train. Verdict for plaintiff. Held that, to entitle plaintiff to recover, it should have been made to appear that the killing was the natural and proximate result of the ejectment; that the attention of the jury should have been called to the distance from the place where he was ejected to where he was killed, and to the question whether or not his faculties and power of locomotion had so far recovered as to enable him to understand and avoid the danger; and that the failure so to instruct the jury was ground for a new trial. Haley v. Chicago & N. W. Ry. Co., 21 Iowa, 15. Where deceased was driven from his home by defendants, and afterwards enlisted in the federal army, was captured and detained as a prisoner of war, and died in

prior to the injury, some cause, such as disease, existed, the question is whether the death resulted from the previously

prison, held, that the death was not the proximate result of defendants' acts. Wagner v. Woolsey, 1 Heisk. (Tenn.) 235. A. and B. fought, and B.'s son came to his father's rescue, and killed A. A.'s wife sued B. Held, that the homicide was not the natural and proximate result of B.'s wrong. White v. Conly, 14 Lea (Tenn.) 51, 52 Am. Rep. 154. The intestate was injured by a fall through defendant's negligence. By the fall he fractured his arm, and the broken bone developed a poisonous discharge, which, being absorbed into the blood, caused his death. Held, that death was the proximate result of the act. Ginna v. Second Ave. R. Co., 8 Hun, 494, affirmed 67 N. Y. 596. Deceased was driving on a street, and was thrown from his wagon by the wheel running into a hole by the side of a street-railway track, and was killed by striking his head on a loose rail and protruding spike. Held, that the railway company was liable for the death, its negligence in having its track in bad repair being the proximate cause of the accident, though the city was also negligent in permitting the hole to remain in the street; but that the negligence of the city was not the proximate cause of the death, and that the city was not liable. Cline v. Crescent City R. Co., 43 La. Ann. 327, 9 South. 122, 26 Am. St. Rep. 187. The declaration alleged that deceased, while in the office of defendant's agent for the transaction of business pertaining to the agency, was killed by the latter; that the agent was subject to aberration of mind which became at times homicidal mania; and that defendant employed him, knowing this fact. Held a good cause of action. Christian v. Columbus & R. Ry. Co., 79 Ga. 460, 7 S. E. 216. The negligent failure of a telephone company to connect a messenger, dispatched to call a doctor for a person who had sustained an accidental gunshot wound, with the doctor's telephone, thereby depriving such person of medical attention, is too remote to constitute it a proximate cause of the death; it not appearing that, but for the negligence, the death would not have resulted. Evans' Adm'r v. Cumberland Telephone & Telegraph Co., 135 Ky. 66, 121 S. W. 959, 135 Am. St. Rep. 444. An hour after a collision between a steamer and a schooner, in which the latter was injured, the steamer returned and offered to tow the schooner into port, 20 miles distant. The offer was refused, and some hours later, the wind and sea having increased, the schooner sprung a leak in consequence of the injury, and subsequently sank; the master and two seamen being drowned. Held, that the collision could not be deemed the proximate cause of their death.

existing cause or from the act complained of.[113] And it has been held that the fact that the death has been merely

The Onoko, 100 Fed. 477. If, while upon a pole, a person is so burned, shocked, and put in pain by a current of electricity as to lose his strength or consciousness and the control of his movements, and, in consequence, falls to the ground, and dies, his death is caused by the electric current. Atlanta Consol. St. Ry. Co. v. Owings, 97 Ga. 663, 25 S. E. 377, 33 L. R. A. 798. See, also, Randall v. New Orleans & N. E. R. Co., 45 La. Ann. 778, 13 South. 166; McLean v. Burbank, 11 Minn. 277 (Gil. 189); Coley v. City of Statesville, 121 N. C. 301, 28 S. E. 482; Bollinger v. Rader, 151 N. C. 383, 66 S. E. 314, 134 Am. St. Rep. 999; Seifter v. Brooklyn Heights R. Co., 169 N. Y. 254, 62 N. E. 349.

[113] Defendant requested the court to charge (1) that if, before the accident, plaintiff's intestate was taking or had incipient pneumonia, and that she died from such pneumonia, then the presumption is that the injury did not cause the death; (2) that if the jury believed that if she had been in ordinary health when the accident occurred, her injury would not have produced death, and that her death was the result of bad health at the time of the injury, then plaintiff cannot recover. The judge refused, and charged that if plaintiff's intestate was injured through the negligence of defendant, and such injury caused her to take pneumonia, or aggravated the pneumonia from which she was then suffering, so that death resulted on that account, the plaintiff was entitled to recover, unless she would have died from pneumonia, as an independent cause, if she had not received the injury. Held, that the refusal and the charge were correct. Louisville & N. R. Co. v. Jones, 83 Ala. 376, 3 South. 902. Where the jury was instructed to find whether or not the death was caused by defendant's act, held, that it was not error to refuse to instruct the jury that the injury could not be regarded as the proximate cause of the death, if the deceased had a tendency to insanity and disease, and the injury received by him producing death would not have produced the death of a well person. Jeffersonville, M. &. I. R. Co. v. Riley, 39 Ind. 568. Directly after the injury complained of decedent began to fail, and so continued, with but a slight change for the better, until about one year thereafter, when he died. Two or three years previous to the injury he had some ribs broken, but he fully recovered, and was a hearty man until the accident. The expert testimony differed as to the cause of the death. Held, that the evidence sustained the finding that the injury complained of was the cause. Sorenson v. Northern Pac. R. Co.

hastened by the injury is not sufficient.[114] Where the death is the proximate result, it is immaterial that there was concurrent negligence on the part of other persons.[115] The

(C. C.) 36 Fed. 166. An employer would be liable for the death of an employé whether it was caused solely by the wrongful assault of another employé, or whether such assault concurred with the effect of a surgical operation theretofore performed on decedent. Louisville & N. R. Co. v. Chamblee, 171 Ala. 188, 54 South. 681. Where an injury precipitated an attack of delirium tremens resulting in death, it was the proximate cause of the death. McCahill v. New York Transp. Co., 201 N. Y. 221, 94 N. E. 616, Ann. Cas. 1912A, 961. See, also, Turner v. Nassau Electric R. Co., 41 App. Div. 213, 58 N. Y. Supp. 490; McCahill v. New York Transp. Co., 135 App. Div. 322, 120 N. Y. Supp. 1; Briggs v. Minneapolis St. Ry. Co., 52 Minn. 36, 53 N. W. 1019.

[114] The fact that an injured person was, prior to his injuries, suffering from a disease of which he subsequently died, and that the injuries only hastened his death, does not preclude a recovery for his death. Strode v. St. Louis Transit Co., 197 Mo. 616, 95 S. W. 851, 7 Ann. Cas. 1084. See, also, Herke v. St. Louis & S. F. Ry. Co., 141 Mo. App. 613, 125 S. W. 822. Cf. Jackson v. St. Louis, I. M. & S. Ry. Co., 87 Mo. 422, 56 Am. Rep. 460. Plaintiff might recover, if a cause of the death was a disease, but the disease was accelerated and death hastened by the negligent act of defendant. Meekins v. Norfolk & S. R. Co., 134 N. C. 217, 46 S. E. 493. A charge relieving defendant of liability if the death was due to the effect of a disease to which decedent had previously been subject was properly refused, since defendant is liable if the injury aggravated a pre-existing tendency to disease in the injured person. Missouri, K. & T. Ry. Co. of Texas v. Smith (Tex. Civ. App.) 133 S. W. 482. Cf. Ellyson v. International & G. N. R. Co., 33 Tex. Civ. App. 1, 75 S. W. 868. See, also, Louisville & N. R. Co. v. Jones, 83 Ala. 376, 3 South. 902; Thompson v. Louisville & N. R. Co., 91 Ala. 496, 8 South. 406, 11 L. R. A. 146.

[115] Cline v. Crescent City R. Co., 43 La. Ann. 327, 9 South. 122, 26 Am. St. Rep. 187; Consolidated Ice Mach. Co. v. Keifer, 134 Ill. 481, 25 N. E. 799, 10 L. R. A. 696, 23 Am. St. Rep. 688; Quill v. New York Cent. & H. R. R. Co., 11 N. Y. Supp. 80. As all the parties in any way concerned with an unlawful killing by a mob are liable in solido, it is proper to join, as a party defendant with the individuals who participated in the killing, the city in which the act was

answer to the question whether the death was caused by the act or neglect complained of is, of course, generally determined by the same considerations that would determine the answer to the question whether the injury, if death had not ensued, was caused by the act or neglect in question.

In cases, however, where the death does not follow immediately after the injury, the question is often presented under somewhat peculiar circumstances. The question may arise whether the death was caused by the act or neglect complained of, or by some intervening cause. In such cases it must appear that the death was the result of the act or neglect, and not of the intervening cause.[116] But the death

committed, on the ground of its negligence in not preventing the killing. Comitez v. Parkerson (C. C.) 50 Fed. 170. See, also, Trauffler v. Detroit & Cleveland Nav. Co. (D. C.) 181 Fed. 256; Harrison v. Kansas City Electric Light Co., 195 Mo. 606, 93 S. W. 951, 7 L. R. A. (N. S.) 293; Strauhal v. Asiatic S. S. Co., 48 Or. 100, 85 Pac. 230.

[116] A passenger was so injured that he became insane, and eight months after the accident committed suicide. Held, that his own act was the proximate cause of his death. Scheffer v. Washington City, V. M. & G. S. R. Co., 105 U. S. 249, 26 L. Ed. 1070. The voluntary, willful act of suicide of an insane person, whose insanity was caused by a railroad accident, and who knows the purpose and physical effect of his act, is a new cause, so that his death is not by reason of the negligence of the railroad company. Daniels v. New York, N. H. & H. R. Co., 183 Mass. 393, 67 N. E. 424, 62 L. R. A. 751. An action is maintainable, when the death is self-inflicted, only where it is the result of an uncontrollable influence, or is accomplished in delirium or frenzy caused by defendant's negligent act or omission, and without conscious volition of a purpose to take life. Brown v. American Steel & Wire Co., 43 Ind. App. 560, 88 N. E. 80. It was a controverted question whether the intestate died of disease or from a fall in the street. The jury were instructed that plaintiff could not recover unless it was shown by a preponderance of the evidence that the injury received from the fall was the proximate cause of intestate's death, and there was no instruction in conflict with that one. Held, that the charge was not open to the objection that it was so framed as to sustain the theory of the defendant's liability,

will be referred to the act complained of, if it was sufficient to cause the death, unless it be shown that the death
must have resulted from the intervening cause, independently of the injury.[117] The mere fact that the party injured was unskillfully treated, or did not adopt the best
remedies, and that this contributed to his death, will not defeat the action, but the question should be left to the jury

notwithstanding the fact that the intestate died of disease. City of
Mt. Carmel v. Howell, 137 Ill. 91, 27 N. E. 77. See, also, Hoey v.
Metropolitan St. Ry. Co., 70 App. Div. 60, 74 N. Y. Supp. 1113; Koch
v. Zimmermann, 85 App. Div. 370, 83 N. Y. Supp. 339; Ostrander v.
Orange County Traction Co., 125 App. Div. 603, 110 N. Y. Supp.
15. See, also, Brashear v. Philadelphia Traction Co., 180 Pa. 392,
36 Atl. 914; McCafferty v. Pennsylvania R. Co., 193 Pa. 339, 44 Atl.
435, 74 Am. St. Rep. 690.

117 It was contended that the death was not the proximate result
of the injury, but of pneumonia. Held, that the death must be referred to the injury, unless it be shown that the death must have
resulted if the injury had not been done. Beauchamp v. Saginaw
Min. Co., 50 Mich. 163, 15 N. W. 65, 45 Am. Rep. 30. The evidence
showed that the immediate cause of death was peritonitis. Plaintiff's medical witnesses testified that that disease might be caused
in seven different ways. There was proof that a certain cause, which
the jury might competently find ensued from defendant's negligence,
already existed. The jury found for plaintiff. Held, that it was
no objection that there was no proof but that several causes which
could not be attributed to defendant's negligence existed in the case,
as, if a sufficient cause was shown, the presumption is that causes
not made to appear did not exist. Looram v. Third Ave. R. Co.,
6 N. Y. Supp. 504. The evidence tended to show that the child was
22 months old, and previously in good health; that defendant's
engine struck the child, and threw it 15 feet; that it was taken up
senseless, with one leg broken; that the leg was set, and the physician's directions followed; that a cough set in, and the child manifested great pain, etc; that in a few days it had an unnatural appearance in the eyes; that these symptoms increased until its death;
that about 8 days before its death it grew much worse; that a few
days before the death the physicians removed the splints and band-
ages; that the death occurred about a month after the injury.
Held, that the question whether the death was caused by the injury

whether or not the death was caused by the injury.[118]   In an Alabama case [119] the court went a step farther.   The intestate was injured in an accident, and afterwards, by

ought to have been left to the jury.   Jucker v. Chicago & N. W. Ry. Co., 52 Wis. 150, 8 N. W. 862.   Where plaintiff's evidence shows the negligent administration of an anæsthetic was the probable cause of the death, and defendant's evidence merely suggests the possibility of the existence of other causes, the cause of death is for the jury. Boucher v. Larochelle, 74 N. H. 433, 68 Atl. 870, 15 L. R. A. (N. S.) 416.   Where one who had been injured, while attending to her house-hold duties, lifted a wash boiler, which caused a hemorrhage from the original wound, resulting in death, the question whether her act was such negligence as to defeat recovery is for the jury.   Batton v. Public Service Corp. of New Jersey, 75 N. J. Law, 857, 69 Atl. 164, 18 L. R. A. (N. S.) 640, 127 Am. St. Rep. 855.   See, also, Illinois Cent. R. Co. v. Harris (Miss.) 29 South. 760.

[118] An instruction that, if the jury believed that the injury was the immediate cause of death, the fact that the person injured was unskillfully treated is no defense, is correct.   Nagel v. Missouri Pac. Ry. Co., 75 Mo. 653, 42 Am. Rep. 418.   It is no defense that the party injured did not adopt the best remedies, or follow explicitly the directions of the physician.   It should be left to the jury whether his conduct was reasonable, and whether the death was caused by the injury.   Texas & St. L. Ry. Co. v. Orr, 46 Ark. 182.   Where plaintiff's intestate, through the negligence of defendant, had received an injury which, without a surgical operation, would have caused death, and employed a competent surgeon, by whose mistake the operation was not successful, and the intestate died in consequence, held, that there was no error in refusing to charge that, if death was proximately caused by pressing the intestines into the abdominal cavity (the alleged mistake), the plaintiff could not recover.   Sauter v. New York Cent. & H. R. R. Co., 66 N. Y. 50, 23 Am. Rep. 18, affirming 6 Hun, 446.   The judge also charged that if death was produced by the error, ignorance, or maltreatment of the surgeon, the plaintiff could not recover, which the appellate court said was quite as favorable to the defendant as the case would warrant.   Plaintiff's intestate rejected the advice of his physician, and refused to submit his injured leg to amputation; the physician testifying that such an operation would merely "have improved the

[119] Thompson v. Louisville & N. R. Co., 91 Ala. 496, 8 South. 406, 11 L. R. A. 146.

mistake, poison was given him, sufficient to cause the death
of a well man, from the immediate effect of which he died.
There was evidence tending to show that the injuries received were mortal, and that they caused him to succumb
more quickly to the poison than if he had been well. It
was held that, under the provision of the Code giving a
right of action when the injury "results" in death, the action could be maintained against the original wrongdoer.
The reasoning of the court is to the effect that when the result is the necessary result of the first cause, and a cause
intervenes, sufficient, also, to produce the result, whose operation is, however, hastened by the concurrent operation of
the first cause, the latter may be regarded as a proximate
cause.

A person who aids and abets the wrongful act is equally
liable with the person who actually perpetrates it.[120]

---

chances" of recovery. Held, that the refusal could not, as a matter
of law, be said to be negligence. Sullivan v. Tioga R. Co., 112 N. Y.
643, 20 N. E. 569, 8 Am. St. Rep. 793. But where intestate was injured by defendant's negligence, but the injury was in no event fatal,
and intestate died solely because of the unnecessary and dangerous
act of the surgeon employed by intestate in giving him chloroform,
for which defendant was not responsible, though done in the course
or in connection with necessary surgical treatment, it was held that
the injury and anæsthetic were, at most, concurrent causes of the
death, for which defendant was not liable. Mella v. Northern S. S.
Co. (C. C.) 162 Fed. 499. A slight wound by a dog, greatly aggravated by imprudent treatment by a member of the family, will
not give rise to liability for damages, where both the attending
physicians trace the death to such treatment. Martinez v. Bern-
hard, 106 La. 368, 30 South. 901, 55 L. R. A. 671, 87 Am. St. Rep.
306. See, also, Caven v. City of Troy, 15 App. Div. 163, 44 N. Y.
Supp. 244; Louisville & N. R. Co. v. Simrall's Adm'r, 127 Ky. 55,
104 S. W. 1011, 31 Ky. Law Rep. 1269.

[120] Gray v. McDonald, 104 Mo. 303, 16 S. W. 398; Id., 28 Mo.
App. 477.

§ 77. Death resulting from neglect of statutory duty

It is immaterial that the injury causing death results from the neglect of a statutory duty, provided that the party injured thereby might have maintained an action if death had not ensued.[121] Thus railway companies are liable when

---

[121] Whether the act of a drug clerk in selling poison without labeling it was negligence on common-law principles, or was made so by the Minnesota statutes, the druggist is liable for the clerk's negligence committed in the course of his employment, and resulting in the death of the purchaser of the poison. Osborne v. McMasters, 40 Minn. 103, 41 N. W. 543, 12 Am. St. Rep. 698; Nugent v. Vanderveer, 39 Hun (N. Y.) 323. A recovery may be had for the death of an employé of a railroad company caused by failure of the company to comply with Act Cong. March 2, 1893, c. 196, 27 Stat. 531 (U. S. Comp. St. 1901, p. 3174), requiring railroad companies to maintain automatic couplers. Mobile, J. & K. C. R. Co. v. Bromberg, 141 Ala. 258, 37 South. 395. Whether failure by a mining company to provide an ambulance, as required by statute, whereby plaintiffs' son might have been promptly and carefully removed to his home after injury, was the cause of his death or his injury held for the jury. Lenahan v. Crescent Coal Mining Co., 225 Pa. 218, 74 Atl. 58. In an action for wrongful death alleging negligence generally, evidence showing defendant's failure to observe a federal or state statute, or a federal, state, or municipal regulation, is admissible to prove negligence. Beck v. Johnson (C. C.) 169 Fed. 154. New York City Building Code provides that the owner, builder, or contractor constructing or repairing buildings over a certain height shall maintain a shed over the work in front of the premises to protect persons using the street. The city charter and ordinance provide that the owner or general contractor constructing a building over a certain height shall build a temporary roof structure over the sidewalk of the building. Held, that the representatives of a person killed through failure to construct such covering have an action against the person liable for such failure, under the death act, though neither the Building Code nor the charter gives a new cause of action. Shields v. Paul B. Pugh & Co., 122 App. Div. 586, 107 N. Y. Supp. 604. See, also, Shannon v. Jefferson County, 125 Ala. 384, 27 South. 977.

the failure to give signals required by statute is the proximate cause of death.[122] So where a statute makes railroad companies liable for injuries to any employé, through the negligence of another employé, without contributory negligence, while engaged in operating, running, or switching cars, such company is liable under the death act, for the death of an employé injured by a coemployé occurring under such circumstances as would have entitled the decedent to recover under the former statute.[123] And where a statute gives a right of action to a person for injuries sustained while a passenger of a railroad company, except where the injury was occasioned by his own criminal negligence, or by his violation of some express rule

---

[122] Becke v. Missouri Pac. Ry. Co., 102 Mo. 544, 13 S. W. 1053, 9 L. R. A. 157; Crumpley v. Hannibal & St. J. R. Co., 98 Mo. 34, 11 S. W. 244; King v. Missouri Pac. Ry. Co., 98 Mo. 235, 11 S. W. 563. See Palmer v. New York Cent. & H. R. R. Co., 112 N. Y. 234, 19 N. E. 678; Rodrian v. New York, N. H. & R. Co., 125 N. Y. 526, 26 N. E. 741. It was held in Texas that Rev. St. art. 4232, which makes it negligence per se for an engineer to neglect to ring or whistle on approaching a crossing, and makes railroad companies liable "for all damages sustained by any person by reason of such neglect," does not give a right of action on account of an accident causing death. But this decision rests upon the law as it then stood, which gave a right of action for death in such case only when the negligence was "willful." Galveston, H. & S. A. Ry. Co. v. Cook (Tex.) 16 S. W. 1038. In an action to recover the statutory forfeiture for the death of a person occasioned by the negligence of a driver of a street car, the setting out in the petition of a city ordinance regulating the running of street cars, and prescribing the duties of those in charge of them, together with an allegation that the death of plaintiff was caused by a failure to observe such ordinance, is not a statement of a separate cause of action based upon a violation of the ordinance, but the pleading of such violation as furnishing proof of the negligence of the driver, the consequence of which, when resulting in a death, is fixed by the statute. Meyer v. Southern Ry. Co., 135 Mo. 512, 36 S. W. 367.

[123] Ean v. Chicago, M. & St. P. Ry. Co., 95 Wis. 69, 69 N. W. 997.

or regulation of the carrier actually brought to his notice, the statute creating a presumption of negligence where the case does not fall within the exceptions, the statute is applicable in an action brought by the administrator of a person injured while a passenger, under the death act. "The two statutes are not in conflict," said the court, "for the reason that one creates a liability in favor of the passenger himself, and obviates the necessity of proving the negligence of the carrier, while the other statute gives a right of action (where none existed before) to the personal representatives of a deceased person in all cases where such person could have recovered damages for his injury if death had not ensued." [124] Nor is it material that the statute creating a right of action for personal injury was enacted subsequently to the act creating a right of action for injuries resulting in death.[125] Thus, in a Michigan case,[126] it was held that the personal representative of a person whose death was caused by a bridge being allowed to be out of repair might maintain an action against the township whose duty it was under a certain statute to keep the bridge in repair, although the statute imposing such duty upon townships was passed subsequently to the act creating a right of action for injuries resulting in death, and although the later statute did not expressly provide that townships should be liable in case of death. The opinion was delivered by Cooley, C. J., who says: "The statute of 1848 [giving a remedy for injuries resulting in death] is in the strictest

124 Chicago, R. I. & P. Ry. Co. v. Zernecke, 59 Neb. 689, 82 N. W. 26, 55 L. R. A. 610, affirmed 183 U. S. 582, 22 Sup. Ct. 229, 46 L. Ed. 339.

125 Ean v. Chicago, M. & St. P. Ry. Co., 95 Wis. 69, 69 N. W. 997; Chicago, R. I. & P. Ry. Co. v. Young, 58 Neb. 678, 79 N. W. 556.

126 Merkle v. Bennington Tp., 58 Mich. 156, 24 N. W. 776, 55 Am. Rep. 666.

sense a remedial statute, and as such it should receive, not a strict, but a favorable, construction. * * * But a liberal construction of the statute is not necessary to make it applicable in these cases. * * * It is general, and applies 'whenever' a death has been caused under circumstances which would have given a cause of action had the person survived. It was not made for cases which might arise under the law as it then was, but it was enacted to establish a general and very wholesome rule, as applicable to causes of action that might arise under subsequent remedial statutes, and as to those arising under the common law or under statutes then existing." And in a later case [127] it was held by the same court that a city was liable under a later act rendering cities liable in damages to persons injured upon highways although the act provided that no municipality should be liable to any person for "bodily injury" sustained upon public highways except under the provisions of the act, and abrogated the common-law liability for such "bodily injuries," and made no provision for the recovery of damages in cases of death resulting therefrom. A different conclusion, however, was reached in South Carolina, where it was held that the act giving to the personal representative a right of action in case of death did not apply to a case under a subsequent statute, which gave a right of action "against a county for damages sustained by any one injured through a defect in the repair of a highway or bridge." The court rests its decision both upon the ground that the legislature could not have intended to embrace within the provisions of the earlier act new rights to be subsequently created by statute, and upon the ground that the right of action given by the later act was not based upon negligence, but upon a defect in the repair of the highway or bridge,

[127] Racho v. City of Detroit, 90 Mich. 92, 51 N. W. 360.

(188)

regardless of negligence, and that consequently the wrong complained of did not come within the words "wrongful act, neglect, or default." [128]

§ 78. Death resulting from liquor sold by defendant

Where the death of a person results from intoxication caused by liquor furnished him by the defendant, no action can, under ordinary circumstances, be maintained by the personal representative, since none could have been maintained by the party injured if death had not ensued.[129] But if, when the liquor is furnished, the decedent is already so intoxicated as to be incapable of intelligent action, a different question is presented, and it has been held that in such case the action can be maintained. Thus, where the decedent was a confirmed inebriate, and the defendants made a wager that he could not drink three pints of whisky, and persuaded him to try, and after drinking two pints he became helplessly intoxicated, but the defendants, although warned by a bystander that it would kill him, induced him to drink a third pint, which caused his death, it was held

[128] All v. Barnwell County, 29 S. C. 161, 7 S. E. 58.

[129] King v. Henkie, 80 Ala. 505, 60 Am. Rep. 119; Hackett v. Smelsley, 77 Ill. 109, per Sheldon, J. The facts that defendant furnished liquor to a third person while the latter was drunk, and failed to protect plaintiff's husband from such person, and that the latter killed plaintiff's husband in defendant's saloon, while defendant was present, deceased not being there as a guest, do not render defendant liable in damages for the killing, under Acts Ga. 1887, p. 45, allowing a recovery for death caused by crime, or "criminal or other negligence." Belding v. Johnson, 86 Ga. 177, 12 S. E. 304, 11 L. R. A. 53. Const. § 241, and the statute, giving a right of action for wrongful death, do not make one who unlawfully sells intoxicants liable for death of one killed by the buyer while intoxicated; the sale not being the proximate cause of the death. Waller's Adm'r v Collinsworth, 144 Ky. 3, 137 S. W. 766.

that the defendants were liable.[130] The court said that, whatever effect the consent of the decedent might otherwise have had in excusing the acts of the defendants, their conduct in persuading him to drink the third pint when he was in a helpless condition amounted to deception, and was equivalent to force. And in Pennsylvania, where the decedent was already intoxicated when the liquor was sold, it was held that there was not such concurrent negligence on the part of the deceased as to relieve the defendant from liability.[131] This case certainly goes to the extreme limit, and is opposed to a later Alabama case,[132] where it was held that, even if the action was within the purview of the statute, the contributory negligence of the decedent in becoming intoxicated would constitute a defense, notwithstanding the fact that he was already helplessly drunk when the liquor was sold. Where the wrongful act of the defendant who sold the liquor consisted in expelling the decedent from a saloon, late at night, after he had become helpless, it was held that the question of contributory negligence was not involved.[133]

The question whether an action can be maintained by the widow for loss of support caused by her husband's death under the so-called "civil damage acts" is, of course, totally distinct. The weight of authority is in favor of such an action,[134] although the contrary doctrine is also main-

---

[130] McCue v. Klein, 60 Tex. 168, 48 Am. Rep. 260.

[131] Fink v. Garman, 40 Pa. 95.

[132] King v. Henkie, 80 Ala. 505, 60 Am. Rep. 119.

[133] Weymire v. Wolfe, 52 Iowa, 533, 3 N. W. 541.

[134] Emory v. Addis, 71 Ill. 273; Hackett v. Smelsley, 77 Ill. 109; Schroder v. Crawford, 94 Ill. 357, 34 Am. Rep. 236; Flynn v. Fogarty, 106 Ill. 263; Rafferty v. Buckman, 46 Iowa, 195; Brockway v. Patterson, 72 Mich. 122, 40 N. W. 192, 1 L. R. A. 708; Roose v. Perkins, 9 Neb. 304, 2 N. W. 715, 31 Am. Rep. 409; Mead v. Stratton, 87 N. Y. 493, 41 Am. Rep. 386; Davis v. Standish, 26 Hun (N.

tained.[135] A consideration of the questions arising under
the diverse provisions of these statutes, in actions where
death results from their violation, is beyond the scope of
this book.[136]

§ 79. Felonious killing

Most of the acts, following Lord Campbell's act, provide
that the action may be maintained although the death has
been caused under such circumstances as amount in law to
felony.[137] This provision, however, has been omitted in

Y.) 608; McCarty v. Wells, 51 Hun, 171, 4 N. Y. Supp. 672; Black
on Intoxicating Liquors, §§ 310, 311. See, also, Triggs v. McIntyre,
215 Ill. 369, 74 N. E. 400; Homire v. Halfman, 156 Ind. 470, 60 N. E.
154; Bellison v. Apland, 115 Iowa, 599, 89 N. W. 22; League v.
Ehmke, 120 Iowa, 464, 94 N. W. 938; Mathe v. Story City Drug Co.,
130 Iowa, 111, 106 N. W. 368, 8 Ann. Cas. 275; Gardner v. Day, 95
Me. 558, 50 Atl. 892; Garrigan v. Kennedy, 19 S. D. 11, 101 N. W.
1081, 117 Am. St. Rep. 927, 8 Ann. Cas. 1125.

[135] Barrett v. Dolan, 130 Mass. 366, 39 Am. Rep. 456; Harrington
v. McKillop, 132 Mass. 567; Davis v. Justice, 31 Ohio St. 359, 27
Am. Rep. 514; Kirchner v. Myers, 35 Ohio St. 85, 35 Am. Rep. 598;
.Pegram v. Stortz, 31 W. Va. 220, 6 S. E. 485.

[136] See Smith v. People, 141 Ill. 447, 31 N. E. 425; Baker v. Sum-
mers, 201 Ill. 52, 66 N. E. 302; Stecher v. People, 217 Ill. 348, 75
N. E. 501; Deel v. Heiligenstein, 244 Ill. 239, 91 N. E. 429; Wall
v. State ex rel. Kendall, 10 Ind. App. 530, 38 N. E. 190; Boos v.
State ex rel. Sliney, 11 Ind. App. 257, 39 N. E. 197; McCarty v.
State ex rel. Boone, 162 Ind. 218, 70 N. E. 131; Dudley v. State
ex rel. Roe, 40 Ind. App. 74, 81 N. E. 89; Doty v. Postal, 87 Mich.
143, 49 N. W. 534; Bennett's Claim, In re, 160 Mich. 309, 125 N. W.
2; Weatherbee v. Byan, 160 Mich. 600, 125 N. W. 686; Curran v.
Percival, 21 Neb. 434, 32 N. W. 213; Sellars v. Foster, 27 Neb. 118,
42 N. W. 907; Roach v. Kelly, 194 Pa. 24, 44 Atl. 1090, 75 Am.
St. Rep. 685; Palmer v. Schurz, 22 S. D. 283, 117 N. W. 150.

[137] Arkansas, District of Columbia, Florida, Illinois, Maine, Maryland, Michigan, Nebraska, Nevada, New Jersey, New Mexico, North
Carolina, North Dakota, Rhode Island, South Carolina, Texas, Vermont, and Virginia. In New Hampshire, "although inflicted by a
person while committing a felony." In Rhode Island, "it shall not

(191)

many of the acts; and the failure to prosecute where felony was involved in the act complained of has never been allowed as a defense, and has seldom been raised. In a case under the Indiana act, which contained no such provision, it was held that failure to prosecute was no defense, the court observing that the common-law rule requiring prosecution of the felon before a civil action could be maintained did not prevail in the United States.[188] In Georgia the act formerly required, as a condition of the right to maintain the action,

be necessary first to institute criminal proceedings against the defendants." In Arizona, Ohio, West Virginia, and Wyoming, "although the death shall have been caused under such circumstances as amount in law to murder in the first or second degree or manslaughter." In Alabama, "though there has not been prosecution or conviction or acquittal of the defendant." In Iowa, New York, and and perhaps other states, the provision against the merger of the civil in the criminal offense is general. In Quebec, the act provides that the "actions are independent, and do not prejudice the criminal proceedings to which the parties may be subject."

[188] Lofton v. Vogles, 17 Ind. 105. In Lankford's Adm'r v. Barrett, 29 Ala. 700, it was said that the provision that the action must be brought within 12 months precludes any application of the common-law rule of merger. In Martin's Ex'x v. Martin, 25 Ala. 201, it was held that an action of trover for the conversion of a slave could not be maintained without instituting a prosecution for felony. See, also, Middleton v. Holmes, 3 Port. (Ala.) 424 (killing slave); Blackburn v. Minter, 22 Ala. 613. In Neal v. Farmer, 9 Ga. 555 (followed in Williams v. Fambro, 30 Ga. 232), it was held that, while in cases of felony the civil remedy is suspended, the killing of a slave was not felony. See, also, Adams v. Barrett, 5 Ga. 404. The rule of merger of the civil action in the felony is denied in the following cases: Blassingame v. Glaves, 6 B. Mon. (Ky.) 38; Nash v. Primm, 1 Mo. 178 (killing slave); Mann v. Trabue, 1 Mo. 709 (killing slave); White v. Fort, 10 N. C. 251. The plaintiff may commence a civil action without a previous acquittal or conviction of the felon. Pettingill v. Rideout, 6 N. H. 454, 25 Am. Dec. 473; Newell v. Cowan, 30 Miss. 492. In an action by an overseer for wages, defendant may recoup any damages he has sustained on account of the killing of his slave by plaintiff, if the killing was done negligently and without necessity. The rule of merger in felony has been changed

that, if the injury amounted to a felony, the person injured by the death must either simultaneously or concurrently or previously prosecute for the same, or allege a good excuse for failure to do so, except in cases of torts committed by corporations; [139] but this requirement has been repealed.[140]

by statute. Brunson v. Martin, 17 Ark. 270. See Hyatt v. Adams, 16 Mich. 180, for full discussion by Christiancy, J.

[139] Code 1882, § 2970; Allen v. Atlanta St. R. Co., 54 Ga. 503; Chick v. Southwestern R. Co., 57 Ga. 357; Southwestern R. Co. v. Johnson, 60 Ga. 667; Sawtell v. Western & A. R. Co., 61 Ga. 567; Western & A. R. Co. v. Sawtell, 65 Ga. 235. See Dodson v. McCauley, 62 Ga. 130; South Carolina R. Co. v. Nix, 68 Ga. 572.

[140] The act of August 27, 1879, entitled "An act to amend section 2970 of the Code" repealed the entire section. It was embodied in Code 1882, § 2970. "As no persons of any sort, either natural or artificial, were left, to whom the section could apply, the effect of the amending act was to strike it out entirely." Western & A. R. Co. v. Meigs, 74 Ga. 857.

TIFF.DEATH W.A.(2D ED.)—13   (193)

CHAPTER V

THE BENEFICIARIES

§ 80.   Existence of beneficiaries essential

The statutes which require the action to be brought in the name of the executor or administrator generally provide in express terms that the action shall be for the benefit of the widow and next of kin, or other members of the family, of the deceased, and that the amount recovered shall be divided among the persons for whose benefit the action is brought to the exclusion of creditors of the estate. The executor or administrator, as such, has no interest in the recovery, and he acts in effect as trustee for the persons beneficially entitled.[1] It follows that, unless the deceased left

---

[1] Leggott v. Great Northern Ry. Co., 1 Q. B. D. 599, 45 L. J. Q. B. 557, 35 L. T. (N. S.) 334; Bradshaw v. Lancashire & Y. Ry. Co., L. R. 10 C. P. 189, 44 L. J. C. P. 148, 31 L. T. (N. S.) 847; Kramer v. San Francisco Market St. R. Co., 25 Cal. 434; Lamphear v. Buckingham, 33 Conn. 237; City of Chicago v. Major, 18 Ill. 349, 68 Am. Dec. 553; Jeffersonville, M. & I. R. Co. v. Hendricks, 41 Ind. 49; Stewart v. Terre Haute & I. R. Co., 103 Ind. 44, 2 N. E. 208; Kansas Pac. Ry. Co. v. Cutter, 16 Kan. 568; Perry v. St. Joseph & W. R.

(194)

surviving some one of the persons entitled to the benefit of the action, no cause of action accrues; and that, unless it be alleged and proved that some such person survived, the action cannot be maintained.[2] The rule is the same where

Co., 29 Kan. 420; Dickins v. New York Cent. R. Co., 23 N. Y. 158; Yertore v. Wiswall's Ex'rs, 16 How. Prac. (N. Y.) 28; Hegerich v. Keddie, 99 N. Y. 258, 1 N. E. 787, 52 Am. Rep. 25.

[2] Lamphear v. Buckingham, 33 Conn. 237; Chicago, R. I. R. Co. v. Morris, 26 Ill. 400; Conant v. Griffin, 48 Ill. 410; Quincy Coal Co. v. Hood, 77 Ill. 68; Indianapolis, P. & C. R. Co. v. Keely's Adm'r, 23 Ind. 133; Jeffersonville, M. & I. R. Co. v. Hendricks, 41 Ind. 48; Stewart v. Terre Haute & I. R. Co., 103 Ind. 44, 2 N. E. 208; Clore v. McIntire, 120 Ind. 262, 22 N. E. 128; Missouri Pac. Ry. Co. v. Barber, 44 Kan. 612, 24 Pac. 969; Schwarz v. Judd, 28 Minn. 371, 10 N. W. 208; Barnum v. Chicago, M. & St. P. Ry. Co., 30 Minn. 461, 16 N. W. 364; Serensen v. Northern Pac. R. Co. (C. C.) 45 Fed. 407; Warren v. Englehart, 13 Neb. 283, 13 N. W. 401; Burlington & M. R. Co. v. Crockett, 17 Neb. 570, 24 N. W. 219; Dunhene v. Ohio Life Ins. & Trust Co., 1 Disn. (Ohio) 257; Conlin v. City Council of Charleston, 15 Rich. (S. C.) 201; Lilly v. Charlotte, C. & A. R. Co., 32 S. C. 142, 10 S. E. 932; Louisville & N. R. Co. v. Pitt, 91 Tenn. 86, 18 S. W. 118; East Tennessee, V. & G. Ry. Co. v. Lilly, 90 Tenn. 563, 18 S. W. 243; Westcott v. Central Vt. R. Co., 61 Vt. 438, 17 Atl. 745; Geroux's Adm'r v. Graves, 62 Vt. 280, 19 Atl. 987; Northern Pac. R. Co. v. Ellison, 3 Wash. 225, 28 Pac. 233; Woodward v. Chicago & N. W. R. Co., 23 Wis. 400; Wiltse v. Town of Tilden, 77 Wis. 152, 46 N. W. 234; Safford v. Drew, 3 Duer (N. Y.) 627; Lucas v. New York Cent. R. Co., 21 Barb. (N. Y.) 245; Webster v. Norwegian Min. Co., 137 Cal. 399, 70 Pac. 276, 92 Am. Dec. 181; Chicago & E. R. Co. v. La Porte, 33 Ind. App. 691, 71 N. E. 166; Pittsburg, C., C. & St. L. Ry. Co. v. Reed, 44 Ind. App. 635, 88 N. E. 1080; Walker v. Lake Shore & M. S. Ry. Co., 104 Mich. 606, 62 N. W. 1032; Topping v. Town of St. Lawrence, 86 Wis. 526, 57 N. W. 365; Brown v. Chicago & N. W. Ry. Co., 102 Wis. 137, 78 N. W. 771, 44 L. R. A. 579; Swift & Co. v. Johnson, 138 Fed. 867, 71 C. C. A. 619, 1 L. R. A. (N. S.) 1161. Some of the New York cases contain dicta that the action lies in every case where the party injured might have maintained an action (Oldfield v. New York & H. R. Co., 14 N. Y. 310; Quin v. Moore, 15 N. Y. 432; Keller v. New York Cent. R. Co., 2 Abb. Dec. [N. Y.] 480); but no New York case has decided that it lies where the deceased left surviving neith-

the remedy is by indictment,[3] or where, as in Maryland, the action is brought in the name of the state.[4] The beneficiary must be in existence when the action is brought.[5]

§ 81. Otherwise under some statutes

Under the Virginia statute, although the damages are given first to the husband or wife, parent or child, yet, if neither of these is alive, the damages are assets to be disposed of according to law. For this reason it is held that the existence of husband, wife, parent, or child is not necessary to the maintenance of the action.[6] The rule in West Virginia appears to be the same, although the statute expressly declares that the amount recovered shall not be subject to the debts and liabilities of the deceased, and the reason for the rule is not clear.[7] In North Carolina the same rule also prevails, for, though the amount recovered is not liable to be applied as assets, it is required to be paid, if it remains unclaimed for five years in the hands of the executor or administrator, to the state university.[8] In Oregon the amount recovered is to be administered as other per-

---

er widow, husband, nor next of kin. See, also, § 41, and cases cited in note. Muhl v. Southern M. R. Co., 10 Ohio St. 272; Little Rock & Ft. S. Ry. v. Townsend, 41 Ark. 382 (under the earlier act of 1875); and Kesler v. Smith, 66 N. C. 154, contra.

[3] Commonwealth v. Eastern R. Co., 5 Gray (Mass.) 473; Commonwealth v. Boston & A. R. Co., 121 Mass. 36; State v. Grand Trunk Ry. Co., 60 Me. 145; State v. Gilmore, 24 N. H. 461; State v. Manchester & L. R. R., 52 N. H. 528.

[4] State v. Baltimore & O. R. Co., 70 Md. 319, 17 Atl. 88.

[5] Woodward v. Chicago & N. W. R. Co., 23 Wis. 400; Wiltse v. Town of Tilden, 77 Wis. 152, 46 N. W. 234; State v. Baltimore & O. R. Co., 70 Md. 319, 17 Atl. 88; Westcott v. Central Vt. R. Co., 61 Vt. 438, 17 Atl. 745; Loague v. Memphis & C. R. Co., 91 Tenn. 458, 19 S. W. 430.

[6] See § 56.   [7] See § 58.   [8] See § 49.

sonal property of the decedent, and it is held that the action may be maintained although he left surviving no relatives or creditors.[9] "Under Lord Campbell's act, and similar statutes," said the court, "the damages recovered belong to the designated beneficiary, and are measured by the value of the life taken to the particular person entitled to the benefit of the statute, while under our statute they belong to the estate, and are coextensive with the value of the life lost, without regard to its value to any particular person. In the one case the object of the action is to recover the pecuniary loss sustained by the designated relatives, and in the other the value of the life lost, measured, as near as can be, by the earning capacity, thriftiness, and probable length of life of the deceased, and the consequent amount of probable accumulations during the expectancy of such life. Carlson v. Oregon Short Line & U. N. Ry. Co., 21 Or. 450, 28 Pac. 497. It follows, therefore, that, so far as the right to maintain the action is concerned, it is immaterial whether the deceased left surviving him any relatives or creditors whatever. The right of action is given by the statute to the administrator or executor in his representative capacity, and is in the nature of an asset of the estate. The heirs, creditors, or distributees have no interest in the recovery on account of any right of action for the pecuniary injury sustained by them, but only by virtue of being creditors or of kinship; and, if the expense of the administration and debts of the deceased equal or exceed the assets, including the

---

[9] Perham v. Portland General Electric Co., 33 Or. 451, 53 Pac. 14, 40 L. R. A. 799, 72 Am. St. Rep. 730. See, also, Olston v. Oregon Water Power & Ry. Co., 52 Or. 343, 96 Pac. 1095, 20 L. R. A. (N. S.) 915, rehearing denied 52 Or. 343, 97 Pac. 538, 20 L. R. A. (N. S.) 915. The personal representative of a minor child may bring action for its death, though it has a father, mother, or guardian. Schleiger v. Northern Terminal Co., 43 Or. 4, 72 Pac. 324.

amount of the recovery, the next of kin would receive no benefit whatever from the right of action." And so in Alaska, where the recovery is for the benefit of the husband, wife, or children, but if there be none is to be administered as other personal property of the decedent, it is held that, the act having been taken substantially from the Oregon Code after its construction in that state, in accordance with such construction, it is no defense that the decedent left no husband, wife, children, or family.[10] And in Arizona, where the statute provides that the jury shall give such damages as they shall deem fair and just, and that the recovery shall not be subject to the debts and liabilities of the deceased, and shall be distributed to the parties and in the proportions provided by law in relation to the distribution of the personal estate left by persons dying intestate, it is held that the plaintiff need not allege or prove the existence of beneficiaries, or the amount of damages suffered by them.[11]

§ 82. Widow and next of kin

Many of the statutes provide that the action may be brought for the benefit of the widow and next of kin. This provision does not mean, however, that the action is maintainable only when there are both widow and next of kin; it is sufficient if there be either.[12] Other statutes provide

[10] Jennings v. Alaska Treadwell Gold Mining Co., 170 Fed. 146, 95 C. C. A. 388.

[11] Southern Pac. Co. v. Wilson, 10 Ariz. 162, 85 Pac. 401. See Don Yan v. Ah You, 4 Ariz. 109, 77 Pac. 618.

[12] City of Chicago v. Major, 18 Ill. 349, 68 Am. Dec. 553; Oldfield v. New York & H. R. Co., 14 N. Y. 310; Quin v. Moore, 15 N. Y. 432; Tilley v. Hudson River R. Co., 24 N. Y. 471; McMahon v. City of New York, 33 N. Y. 642; Haggerty v. Central R. Co., 31 N. J. Law, 349.

that the action may be brought for the benefit of the widow, or widower, and next of kin; [13] and others, for the benefit of the widow and children, if any, or next of kin.[14] Fre_ quently it is also provided that the damages are to be dis_ tributed in the same manner as personal property of per_ sons dying intestate. In such case the "next of kin" comprehend those who would take the personal property of the deceased under the statute of descents and distributions.[15] This statement must be qualified, however, in accordance with the decisions in some jurisdictions, where the statute provides that the action is maintainable for the benefit of the widow, or widow and children, and next of kin, without expressly including the surviving husband, as explained in the following section.

[13] Where the statute provides that the damages shall inure to the exclusive benefit of the widow and children, if any, or next of kin, if deceased died leaving a widow, but no children, no right of action existed for the benefit of his brothers, who were his next of kin. Dillier v. Cleveland, C., C. & St. L. Ry. Co., 34 Ind. App. 52, 72 N. E. 271. Civ. Code 1870, art. 2315, as amended, giving to a widow the right to sue for damages for the death of the husband, is restricted to his lawful wife, and cannot be extended by construction so as to include his punitive wife by a bigamous marriage. Vaughan v. Dalton-Lard Lumber Co., 119 La. 61, 43 South. 926.

[14] Under a statute, providing that damages are for the benefit of decedent's husband or wife and next of kin, the right of action for an unmarried son's death belongs to the father, where the mother is dead and there are no heirs or next of kin. Doyle v. New York, O. & W. Ry. Co., 66 App. Div. 398, 72 N. Y. Supp. 936.

[15] Atchison, T. & S. F. Ry. Co. v. Ryan, 62 Kan. 682, 64 Pac. 603; Bolinger v. Beacham, 81 Kan. 746, 106 Pac. 1094; Mundt v. Glockner, 26 App. Div. 123, 50 N. Y. Supp. 190. Where the right of action is for the benefit of the widow and next of kin, and the damages are to be distributed to them in the same proportion as personal property of persons dying intestate, and deceased leaves no widow or child, since by the statute of descents and distributions the father in such case would take, the action is for his sole benefit, to the exclusion of a mother and sister. Swift & Co. v. Johnson,

(199)

§ 83. Whether husband is next of kin

Whether the husband is a beneficiary, under a statute providing that the action may be brought for the benefit of the widow and next of kin, is a question which has been answered differently by different courts. In some states it has been held adversely to the husband, on the ground that he is not expressly mentioned, and that he is not included among the next of kin.[16] Thus in New York the court said: "It is the pecuniary injury resulting to the wife and next of kin which is to be estimated; but the injury to the husband, when it is the wife whose death has been caused by the defendant's act, is not spoken of as a ground of damages. And the husband is not embraced within the description of next of kin of his wife. Husband and wife, as such, are not kin to each other in a legal sense." [17] And in Minnesota, where the statute also provided that the recovery was for the exclusive benefit of the widow and next of kin, "to be distributed to them in the same proportion as the personal property of deceased persons," the decision was

138 Fed. 867, 71 C. C. A. 619, 1 L. R. A. (N. S.) 1161. Where the statute provided for damages for the benefit of the next of kin, there could be no recovery for the death of a boy when the father, by his desertion of his family, had forfeited his right to his son's earnings, and had therefore sustained no pecuniary damages, and the mother, while entitled to his earnings, was not the next of kin, within the meaning of the statute. Thompson v. Chicago, M. & St. P. Ry. Co. (C. C.) 104 Fed. 845.

16 Dickins v. New York Cent. R. Co., 23 N. Y. 158. By the amendment of 1870, the law was changed so as to make him a beneficiary; but where a husband brought action as administrator before the amendment, and after its passage settled the suit, it was held that he was not entitled to share in the distribution. Drake v. Gilmore, 52 N. Y. 389. See, also, Johnson v. Seattle Electric Co., 39 Wash. 211, 81 Pac. 705.

17 Dickins v. New York Cent. R. Co., supra.

(200)

the same; the court saying that the words "next of kin" are limited in legal meaning to blood relations, and do not include husband or wife, unless accompanied by other words clearly manifesting an intention to extend their signification, and that, while the provision for distribution regulates the proportion in which the damages recoverable shall be distributed, the damages themselves by the express terms of the statute are for the benefit of the widow and next of kin.[18] And in New Jersey, where under a similar statute the same conclusion was reached, the court said: "This distribution is to be made in the same manner as the administrator would be required to distribute the fund, if it were a part of the intestate's estate, and the persons named in the act were the only persons legally entitled to share in its distribution under the statute of distribution."[19] In Nebraska, under a similar statute, the same conclusion was reached, but upon the ground that under the statute of descent and distribution the husband did not inherit his wife's personal estate.[20] In some states, on the other hand, it has been held that the husband is a beneficiary.[21] In Ohio, for the reason that he inherits under the statute of descent and distribution, he was held to be included.[22] And so in Tennessee.[23] And in Kansas, under a statute providing that the damages inure "to the exclusive benefit of the widow

[18] Watson v. St. Paul City Ry. Co., 70 Minn. 514, 73 N. W. 400. Under the present statute the damages are for the benefit of "the surviving spouse" and next of kin.

[19] Gottlieb v. North Jersey St. Ry. Co., 72 N. J. Law, 480, 63 Atl. 339.

[20] Warren v. Englehart, 13 Neb. 283, 13 N. W. 401.

[21] Rautman v. Chicago Consol. Traction Co., 156 Ill. App. 457.

[22] Steel v. Kurtz, 28 Ohio St. 191.

[23] Bream v. Brown, 5 Cold. (Tenn.) 168; Trafford v. Adams Ex. Co., 8 Lea (Tenn.) 96. In East Tennessee, V. & G. R. Co. v. Lilly, 90 Tenn. 563, 18 S. W. 243, it is suggested that these decisions may

and children, if any, or next of kin, to be distributed in the
same manner as personal property of the deceased," it was
held that the husband was next of kin of his wife, and entitled to recover damages for her death; the court holding
that the reference in the death act to the statute of descent
and distribution furnishes the rule for interpreting "next of
kin." [24] In a case under the Kansas statute, the federal
court had previously held that the husband is not included
in the next of kin.[25]

§ 84.   Posthumous child

The action may be maintained for the benefit of a posthumous child of the deceased.[26] And it has been held that a
brother of the deceased, born two months after the accident
is not one of the next of kin.[27]

---

rest on the ground that "widow" includes both feminine and masculine.

[24] Atchison, T. & S. F. Ry. Co. v. Townsend, 71 Kan. 524, 81 Pac.
205, 6 Ann. Cas. 191.

[25] Western Union Tel. Co. v. McGill, 57 Fed. 699, 6 C. C. A. 521,
21 L. R. A. 818.

[26] In a suit for limitation of liability instituted on behalf of the
owners of a vessel, an appearance was entered on behalf of a child
of one of the drowned men en ventre sa mere. The court reserved
leave to the child, if born within due time, to prefer its claim. The
George & Richard, L. R. 3 Ad. & Ecc. 466, 24 L. T. (N. S.) 717, 20
Wkly. R. 245. So held under a statute for the benefit of "the surviving children." Nelson v. Galveston, H. & S. A. Ry. Co., 78 Tex.
621, 14 S. W. 1021, 11 L. R. A. 391, 22 Am. St. Rep. 81; Texas &
P. Ry. Co. v. Robertson, 82 Tex. 657, 17 S. W. 1041, 27 Am. St. Rep.
929. See, also, Preble v. Wabash R. Co., 243 Ill. 340, 90 N. E. 716.

[27] Chicago & A. R. Co. v. Logue, 47 Ill. App. 292.

§ 85. Illegitimate child

A bastard is not a "child," within Lord Campbell's act.[28] Under the Pennsylvania statute, giving a right of action to the "parent," it was held that the mother of an illegitimate child could not recover.[29]　And so in Georgia, Louisiana and Mississippi.[30]　In South Carolina a mother cannot recover, as sole beneficiary, for the death of her illegitimate child.[31]　And under a Vermont statute, giving a right of action to one dependent on a person whose death is caused by intoxication from the use of liquor unlawfully sold, an illegitimate child cannot recover.[32]　On the other hand, in

[28] Dickinson v. Northeastern R. Co., 2 Hurl. & Colt. 735, 33 L. J. Ex. 91, 9 L. T. (N. S.) 299, 12 Wkly. R. 52.　The mother of an illegitimate child cannot recover.　Gibson v. Midland R. Co., 2 Ont. Rep. 658.　See. also, Clarke v. Carfin Coal Co. [1891] App. Cas. 412.

[29] Harkins v. Philadelphia & R. R. Co., 15 Phila. (Pa.) 286. Since Act July 10, 1901 (P. L. 639), making legitimate an illegitimate child and its heirs as to its mother and her heirs, the mother of an illegitimate child is entitled to recover for the negligent killing of the child.　Thompson v. Delaware, I. & W. R. Co., 41 Pa. Super. Ct. 617.

[30] Robinson v. Georgia R. & Banking Co., 117 Ga. 168, 43 S. E. 452, 60 L. R. A. 555, 97 Am. St. Rep. 156; Lynch v. Knoop, 118 La. 611, 43 South. 252, 8 L. R. A. (N. S.) 480, 118 Am. St. Rep. 391, 10 Ann. Cas. 807; Alabama & V. Ry. Co. v. Williams, 78 Miss. 209, 28 South. 853, 51 L. R. A. 836, 84 Am. St. Rep. 624; Illinois Cent. R. Co. v. Johnson, 77 Miss. 727, 28 South. 753, 51 L. R. A. 837; Runt v. Illinois Cent. R. Co., 88 Miss. 575, 41 South. 1 (Louisiana statute). Since Acts 1898, c. 65, giving a sister or brother a right of action for the wrongful or negligent death of a sister or brother, should be strictly construed as in derogation of the common law, it does not give a right of action to an illegitimate sister.　Illinois Cent. R. Co. v. Johnson, 77 Miss. 727, 28 South. 753, 51 L. R. A. 837.

[31] McDonald v. Southern Ry., 71 S. C. 352, 51 S. E. 138, 2 L. R. A. (N. S.) 640, 110 Am. St. Rep. 576.

[32] Good v. Towns, 56 Vt. 410, 48 Am. Rep. 799.

Ohio,[33] in an action by the personal representative, under an act providing that the recovery should be distributed among the widow and next of kin in the proportion provided by law in relation to the personal estate of intestates, the illegitimacy of a son of the deceased mother was not regarded as a bar to a recovery for his benefit, apparently on the ground that in that state an illegitimate child would take a share in the mother's estate. And in Missouri,[34] upon the ground that bastards are there by statute made capable of taking and transmitting inheritances on the part of the mother, and that she may inherit from her bastard child, it is held that such mother may sue for the wrongful killing of her bastard child, under a statute giving the right of action to the father or mother, when the deceased was a minor and unmarried; the court taking the view that, the principal incapacity of a bastard having been removed so far as he and his mother are concerned, the statute is to be regarded as applying to a mother and her illegitimate child. This decision has been approved and followed in Texas.[35] And in Illinois and Indiana, in view of similar statutory changes, it is held that under the death acts, which provide for a recovery for the benefit of the next of kin, the damages to be distributed as personal property of intestates, illegiti-

---

[33] Muhl's Adm'r v. Michigan Southern R. Co., 10 Ohio St. 272. The case seems to have been decided on the ground that the action might be maintained irrespective of the existence of next of kin.

[34] Marshall v. Wabash R. Co., 120 Mo. 275, 25 S. W. 179. Cf. Marshall v. Wabash R. Co. (C. C.) 46 Fed. 269.

[35] Since by the statute of descent and distribution illegitimates are placed on the same footing as legitimate children, with reference to the mother, the statute giving a right of action for the death of a mother to her children embraces her illegitimate children. Galveston, H. & S. A. Ry. Co. v. Walker, 48 Tex. Civ. App. 52, 106 S. W. 705.

mate children are included in the next of kin.[36] It is to
be observed that in Georgia, also, the incapacity of bastards
had been largely removed; but the court took the view
that the death act was to be strictly construed, and that
"child" prima facie meant legitimate child. And the same
observation applies to Louisiana.

§ 86. Aliens

There is nothing in the acts of the different states, with
one or two exceptions, to indicate an intention to limit their
application to beneficiaries who may be resident within the

---

[36] Under Act 1872, § 2, providing that the estate of an illegitimate
person shall descend to the widow or surviving husband and children as the estate of other persons, and under the death act, an
action can be maintained for the benefit of the mother of an illegitimate child as the next of kin of such child. Security Title &
Trust Co. v. West Chicago St. R. Co., 91 Ill. App. 332. The administrator of an illegitimate child brought action for his death for the
benefit of his "next of kin," consisting of his mother, his half-brothers, and his half-sister by his mother's subsequent marriage. Burns'
Ann. St. 1908, § 2998, provides that illegitimate children may inherit
from the mother as if legitimate, and through the mother, if dead,
any property or estate which she would, if living, have taken by
gift, devise, or descent, and by section 3002 the mother of an illegitimate child dying intestate without issue or other descendants inherits his estate; and, if such mother be dead, her descendants or
kindred shall inherit. Held, that the "next of kin" included such
persons as were entitled to inherit the personal property of the decedent, and that, under sections 2998 and 3002, the mother and the
half-brothers and the half-sister were the next of kin, and that the
administrator's action could be maintained for their benefit. L. T.
Dickason Coal Co. v. Liddil (Ind. App.) 94 N. E. 411 (distinguishing
Thornburg v. American Strawboard Co., 141 Ind. 443, 40 N. E. 1062,
50 Am. St. Rep. 334; McDonald v. Pittsburg, C., C. & St. L. R. Co.,
144 Ind. 459, 43 N. E. 447, 32 L. R. A. 309, 55 Am. St. Rep. 185;
Citizens' St. Ry. Co. v. Cooper, 22 Ind. App. 459, 53 N. E. 1092, 72
Am. St. Rep. 319); ante, § 39, note 32. See, also, Southern Ry. Co.
v. Hawkins, 35 App. D. C. 313, 21 Ann. Cas. 926.

state or citizens of the country. It has accordingly been held nearly unanimously that an action is maintainable although the next of kin or other persons entitled to the benefit of the action are residents of another state,[37] or citizens and resident of another country,[38] and although the decedent was himself an alien.[39] And the holding is of course

[37] Philpott v. Missouri Pac. Ry. Co., 85 Mo. 164; Luke v. Calhoun County, 52 Ala. 115; Chesapeake, O. & S. W. R. Co. v. Higgins, 85 Tenn. 620, 4 S. W. 47.

[38] Bonthron v. Phœnix Light & Fuel Co., 8 Ariz. 129, 71 Pac. 941, 61 L. R. A. 563; Kaneko v. Atchison, T. & S. F. Ry. Co. (C. C.) 164 Fed. 263 (California statute); Patek v. American Smelting & Refining Co., 154 Fed. 190, 83 C. C. A. 284, 21 L. R. A. (N. S.) 273 (Colorado statute); Szymanski v. Blumenthal, 3 Pennewill (Del.) 558, 52 Atl. 347; Kellyville Coal Co. v. Petraytis, 195 Ill. 215, 63 N. E. 94, 88 Am. St. Rep. 191; Cleveland, C., C. & St. L. Ry. Co. v. Osgood, 36 Ind. App. 34, 73 N. E. 285; Atchison, T. & S. F. Ry. Co. v. Fajardo, 74 Kan. 314, 86 Pac. 301, 6 L. R. A. (N. S.) 681; Lykiardopoulo v. New Orleans & C. R. Light & Power Co., 127 La. 309, 53 South. 575, Ann. Cas. 1912A, 976; Id., 127 La. 318, 53 South. 578; Mulhall v. Fallon, 176 Mass. 266, 57 N. E. 386, 54 L. R. A. 934, 79 Am. St. Rep. 309; Vetaloro v. Perkins (C. C.) 101 Fed. 393 (Massachusetts statute); Mascitelli v. Union Carbide Co., 151 Mich. 693, 115 N. W. 721; Renlund v. Commodore Min. Co., 89 Minn. 41, 93 N. W. 1057, 99 Am. St. Rep. 534; Mahoning Ore & Steel Co. v. Blomfelt, 163 Fed. 827, 91 C. C. A. 390 (Minnesota statute); Gaska v. American Car & Foundry Co., 127 Mo. App. 169, 105 S. W. 3; Philes v. Missouri Pac. Ry. Co., 141 Mo. App. 561, 125 S. W. 553 (Kansas statute); Cetofonte v. Camden Coke Co., 78 N. J. Law, 662, 75 Atl. 913, 27 L. R. A. (N. S.) 1058; Hirschkovitz v. Pennsylvania R. Co. (C. C.) 138 Fed. 438 (New Jersey statute); Alfson v. Bush Co., 182 N. Y. 393, 75 N. E. 230, 108 Am. St. Rep. 815; Pittsburg, C., C. & St. L. Ry. Co. v. Naylor, 73 Ohio St. 115, 76 N. E. 505, 3 L. R. A. (N. S.) 473, 112 Am. St. Rep. 701; Baltimore & O. R. Co. v. Baldwin, 144 Fed. 53, 75 C. C. A. 211 (Ohio statute); Anustasakas v. International Contract Co., 51 Wash. 119, 98 Pac. 93, 21 L. R. A. (N. S.) 267, 130 Am. St. Rep. 1089; Saveljich v. Lytle Logging & Mercantile Co., 173 Fed. 277, 97 C. C. A. 443 (Washington statute).

[39] Farrara v. Auric Min. Co., 43 Colo. 496, 95 Pac. 952, 17 L. R. A. (N. S.) 964; Rietveld v. Wabash R. Co., 129 Iowa, 249, 105 N. W.

the same, whether the statute provides that the action is to be brought by the personal representatives or may be maintained by the beneficiary in his own name.[40]

A different view has been taken in Pennsylvania, where in a leading case [41] it was held that a nonresident alien (an Italian) was not entitled to the benefit of the act. "No case has been cited to us," said the court, "nor are we aware of any, in which a nonresident alien, whether husband, widow, child, or parent of the deceased, has maintained a suit under the act of April 26, 1855, to recover damages for an injury causing death. Our legislation on this subject is in accord with the English statute of August 26, 1846, and therefore the decisions of the English courts construing this statute are often referred to in cases grounded upon our acts of April 15, 1851, and April 26, 1855. But no case has been brought to our notice in which an English court has held that a nonresident alien is entitled to the benefits conferred by the act of 1846. * * * No statute or law of Italy has been shown which authorizes such a suit. Our statute was not intended to confer upon nonresident aliens rights of action not conceded to them or to us by their own country, or to put burdens on our own citizens to be discharged for their benefit. It has no extraterritorial force, and the plaintiff is not within the purview of it. While it is possible that

515; Romano v. Capital City Brick & Pipe Co., 125 Iowa, 591, 101 N. W. 437, 68 L. R. A. 132, 106 Am. St. Rep. 323, 2 Ann. Cas. 678; Trotta's Adm'r v. Johnson, Briggs & Pitts, 121 Ky. 827, 90 S. W. 540, 28 Ky. Law Rep. 851, 12 Ann. Cas. 222; Cetofonte v. Camden Coke Co., 78 N. J. Law, 662, 75 Atl. 913, 27 L. R. A. (N. S.) 1058; Pocahontas Collieries Co. v. Rukas' Adm'r, 104 Va. 278, 51 S. E. 449; Low Moor Iron Co. v. La Bianca's Adm'r, 106 Va. 83, 55 S. E. 532, 9 Ann. Cas. 177.

40 See cases cited in two preceding notes.

41 Deni v. Pennsylvania R. Co., 181 Pa. 525, 37 Atl. 558, 59 Am. St. Rep. 676.

the language of the statute may admit of a construction which would include nonresident alien husbands, widows, children, and parents of the deceased, it is a construction so obviously opposed to the spirit and policy of the statute that we cannot adopt it." This case was adhered to in that state,[42] and of course followed in the federal courts in actions arising under the Pennsylvania statute.[48] By a recent amendment of the statute the rule in Pennsylvania has been made the same as that generally prevailing elsewhere by force of the decisions.[44] The Pennsylvania rule was fol-

[42] Under the treaty between the United States and Italy, securing to the citizens of Italy the same protection for their persons and property in the United States as the citizens of the United States enjoy, a nonresident alien who is a citizen of Italy has no standing to maintain an action under Act April 26, 1855, for the recovery of damages for injuries to another causing death.   Maiorana v. Baltimore & O. R. Co., 216 Pa. 402, 65 Atl. 1077, 21 L. R. A. (N. S.) 271, 116 Am. St. Rep. 778, affirmed 213 U. S. 268, 29 Sup. Ct. 424, 53 L. Ed. 792.

[48] Zeiger v. Pennsylvania R. Co. (C. C.) 151 Fed. 348; Id., 158 Fed. 809, 86 C. C. A. 69; Fulco v. Schuylkill Stone Co. (C. C.) 163 Fed. 124; Debitulia v. Lehigh & Wilkes-Barre Coal Co. (C. C.) 174 Fed. 886. The right of action is vested solely in the widow if living, and is single and indivisible, although the sum recovered is to be divided between herself and others in accordance with the law of distribution of personal estate, and, where there is a widow, the fact that she is incapacitated to sue by reason of being a nonresident alien does not vest a resident child with a right of action. Di Paolo v. Laquin Lumber Co. (C. C.) 178 Fed. 877. See, also, Gurofsky v. Lehigh Valley R. Co., 121 App. Div. 126, 105 N. Y. Supp. 514, affirmed 197 N. Y. 517, 90 N. E. 1159. The Pennsylvania rule was approved and applied to the Colorado statute in Brannigan v. Union Gold Min. Co. (C. C.) 93 Fed. 164; but this case was overruled by the Circuit Court of Appeals. Patek v. American Smelting & R. Co., 154 Fed. 190, 83 C. C. A. 284, 21 L. R. A. (N. S.) 273. The rule was also approved and applied to the Washington statute in Roberts v. Great Northern Ry. Co. (C. C.) 161 Fed. 239; but the Supreme Court of that state has not followed this case. See note 38, supra.

[44] Act June 7, 1911 (P. L. 678).

lowed in Wisconsin,[45] although even there an action was held to be maintainable for the benefit of a resident of another state, as distinguished from a nonresident alien.[46]

As to the point made in the leading Pennsylvania case that the English courts have not held that a nonresident alien is entitled to the benefits of Lord Campbell's act, it is to be said that a recent English decision has held that he is so entitled.[47] It is of course not necessary in this view that the act should have extraterritorial force. As observed by Holmes, C. J.: "It is true that legislative power is territorial, and that no duties can be imposed by statute upon persons who are within the limits of another state. But rights can be offered to such persons, and if, as is usually the case, the power that governs them makes no objection, there is nothing to hinder their accepting what is offered." [48] As to the contention that the more liberal construction is opposed to the spirit and policy of the statute, the weight of argument is certainly against this. As was said in a Minnesota case: "Turning, now, to the language of our own statute, there is not a word or expression indicating an intention to limit its application to persons residing within the state, or to residents of sister states. The object of the

---

[45] McMillan v. Spider Lake Sawmill & Lumber Co., 115 Wis. 332, 91 N. W. 979, 60 L. R. A. 589, 95 Am. St. Rep. 947. A sister is not debarred from suing because decedent left surviving him his nonresident father and mother. Pries v. Ashland Home Telephone Co., 143 Wis. 606, 128 N. W. 281. By a recent amendment (Laws 1911, c. 226) nonresident alien surviving relatives are entitled to the benefits of the action.

[46] Robertson v. Chicago, St. P., M. & O. Ry. Co., 122 Wis. 66, 99 N. W. 433, 66 L. R. A. 919, 106 Am. St. Rep. 925.

[47] Davidsson v. Hill [1901] 2 K. B. 606, disapproving Adams v. British, etc., S. S. Co. [1898] 2 Q. B. 430.

[48] Mulhall v. Fallon, 176 Mass. 266, 57 N. E. 386, 54 L. R. A. 934, 79 Am. St. Rep. 309.

statute was to remedy the harshness of the common law, and in some degree compensate those dependent upon the person killed. It would indicate an unnatural and selfish motive to draw a distinction between the dependent relatives who reside in another state or foreign government, and those residing in our own state; and, unless such intention is manifest, we are not at liberty to assume that the lawmakers were legislating upon any such basis." [49]   The anomalous consequences of a different construction were pointed out in England. "Here the plaintiff seeks to enforce her claim against an English subject, and I cannot see why she should not do so. If she has not the right, we should have the anomaly, as it seems to me, that, if a foreigner and an Englishman serving on the same ship were both drowned on the high seas by the same collision, negligently caused by an English vessel, the widow of the one could, and the widow of the other could not, obtain by suing the owners of the ship in fault in personam that reparation which our legislature in those statutes has declared to be a just reparation." [50]

§ 87.   Survival of right of beneficiary

The action for death, being an action for tort, is generally held to fall within the common-law rule that such actions do not survive the death of the party in whose favor the right of action existed. [51]   It is immaterial that the nominal

[49] Rehlund v. Commodore Min. Co., 89 Minn. 41, 93 N. W. 1057, 99 Am. St. Rep. 534.

[50] Davidsson v. Hill [1901] 2 K. B. 606.

[51] Frazier v. Georgia Railroad & Banking Co., 101 Ga. 77, 28 S. E. 662; Peebles v. Charleston & W. C. Ry. Co., 7 Ga. App. 279, 66 S. E. 953; Chivers v. Roger, 50 La. Ann. 57, 23 South. 100. See, also, Texas Loan Agency v. Fleming, 18 Tex. Civ. App. 668, 46 S. W. 63, reversed 92 Tex. 458, 49 S. W. 1039, 44 L. R. A. 279.

plaintiff is the personal representative. This has been decided in cases where the question was presented by the
death of the sole party in interest pending the suit.[52] Thus
under a Wisconsin statute, which provided that the damages
should go to the husband or widow, if such relative survive
the deceased, and otherwise to the descendants, etc., of the
deceased, it was held that where the husband died pending
the action it abated; the court saying that while it is apparent that under the English and New York statutes the
right of action vests at once for the benefit of all of the persons entitled to receive any part of the money recovered,
and may be maintained as long as any one of such persons
survives, it is equally apparent that by the Wisconsin statute the right of action vests solely for the benefit of the husband or widow, and for the benefit of descendants only if no
husband or widow survives.[53] Where this view prevails, it
follows that if there are several beneficiaries, upon the death
of one the action survives solely for the benefit of the others, to the exclusion of the estate of the beneficiary so
dying.[54] If, however, a beneficiary who at the time of the

[52] Dillier v. Cleveland, C., C. & St. L. Ry. Co., 34 Ind. App. 52, 72
N. E. 271: Doyle v. Baltimore & O. R. Co., 81 Ohio St. 184, 90 N.
E. 165, 135 Am. St. Rep. 775; Loague v. Memphis & C. R. Co., 91
Tenn. 458, 19 S. W. 430; Louisville & N. R. Co. v. Bean, 94 Tenn.
388, 29 S. W. 370; Sanders' Adm'x v. Louisville & N. R. Co., 111
Fed. 708, 49 C. C. A. 565 (Tennessee statute); Woodward v. Chicago
& N. W. Ry. Co., 23 Wis. 400; Schmidt v. Menasha Woodenware
Co., 99 Wis. 300, 74 N. W. 797. Under the Maryland statute provid-
ing that the action shall be for the benefit of the wife, husband, parent, and child, where the husband died pending the action it was
held that it abated, the Code, which provided for the survival of
personal actions, expressly excepting actions for personal injury.
(This was before Acts 1888, c. 262.) State v. Baltimore & O. R.
Co., 70 Md. 319, 17 Atl. 88.
   [53] Woodward v. Chicago & N. W. R. Co., 23 Wis. 400.
   [54] Taylor v. Western P. R. Co., 45 Cal. 323. Where an action for

decedent's death is the only party in interest dies, the cause of action is not thereby transferred to the beneficiaries of the next class, who would have been parties in interest had the former not survived the decedent.[55] Thus in a Tennessee case, under a statute providing that the right of action shall pass to the widow or to the personal representative for her benefit, or, if there is no widow, for the benefit of the next of kin, when pending an action for her benefit she died, it was held that the action could not be revived for the benefit of the surviving next of kin. "The widow having died," said the court, "the question now to be determined is whether the suit abates, or the administrator may still prosecute it, for the benefit of the father of deceased, who is the next of kin now surviving. We think the exclusive statutory beneficiary was that person or class of persons who were entitled to the recovery at the death of deceased, when the cause of action accrued. In this case it was the widow, and, in the language of the statute, the right of action passed to her, or to the administrator, for her benefit. The right of recovery having once vested in the widow, it did not pass upon her death to her personal representative, neither did it revest in the next of kin of deceased, for the reason that no provision is made in the

death is brought by several next of kin, the death of one before trial, though abating the action as to him, does not abate the action as to the others. Heald v. Wallace, 109 Tenn. 346, 71 S. W. 80. The action cannot be maintained if neither the widow nor any of the next of kin are in existence. Westcott v. Central Vt. R. Co., 61 Vt. 438, 17 Atl. 745. In Jeffersonville, M. & I. R. Co. v. Hendricks, 41 Ind. 48, the court says that children of a daughter of the deceased, dying since the commencement of the action, would inherit her share, but this was not involved in the decision. See Loague v. Memphis & C. R. Co., 91 Tenn. 458, 19 S. W. 430.

[55] Hammond v. Lewiston, A. & W. St. Ry., 106 Me. 209, 76 Atl. 672, 30 L. R. A. (N. S.) 78. Contra: Morris v. Spartanburg Ry. Gas & E. Co., 70 S. C. 279, 49 S. E. 854.

statute for such contingency. The cause of action, upon the death of the person to whom it survived, or for whose benefit it might be prosecuted, was thereby extinguished." [56]

In some states the law has been changed by statutes which provide for the survival of certain actions in addition to those which survive at common law. A provision that actions for damages for injury to the person shall survive does not include an action for death, since the action is to recover, not damages for the injury to the person of the decedent, but damages for the pecuniary loss which the beneficiaries have suffered.[57] A provision that actions for wrongs done to the property of another shall survive stands on a different footing, since the action for death is for the recovery of damages for the pecuniary injury suffered by the beneficiaries, and a statute which gives the right of action creates a property right, and it has accordingly been held in some states where actions for wrongs done to the property of another survive that this covers actions for death.[58] "As in the language of the statute," said

[56] Louisville & N. R. Co. v. Bean, 94 Tenn. 388, 29 S. W. 370.

[57] Schmidt v. Menasha Woodenware Co., 99 Wis. 300, 74 N. W. 797. Rev. St. Ind. § 282, provided that actions for personal injuries die with the party, "except in cases in which an action is given for an injury causing the death of any person," etc. Section 283 declared that all other causes of action survive to his representatives. Held, that an action by a father for the death of his child survives. Pennsylvania Co. v. Davis, 4 Ind. App. 51, 29 N. E. 425. See § 119. Cf. Dillier v. Cleveland, C., C. & St. L. R. Co., 34 Ind. App. 52, 72 N. E. 271.

[58] Cooper v. Shore Electric Co., 63 N. J. Law, 558, 44 Atl. 633; Meekin v. Brooklyn Heights R. Co., 164 N. Y. 145, 58 N. E. 50, 51 L. R. A. 235, 79 Am. St. Rep. 635; Mundt v. Glokner, 24 App. Div. 110, 48 N. Y. Supp. 940. Contra: Billingsley v. St. Louis, I. M. & S. Ry. Co., 84 Ark. 617, 107 S. W. 173, 120 Am. St. Rep. 95; Gilkeson v. Missouri Pac. R. Co., 222 Mo. 173, 121 S. W. 138, 24 L. R. A. (N. S.) 844, 17 Ann. Cas. 763. See, also, Bates v. Sylvester, 205 Mo. 493, 104 S. W. 73, 11 L. R. A. (N. S.) 1157, 120 Am. St. Rep. 761,

the New York court,[59] " 'the damages awarded to the plaintiff' are to be estimated on the basis of 'a fair and just compensation for the pecuniary injuries resulting from the decedent's death to the person or persons for whose benefit
the action is brought,' we think the injury is for a wrong
done to the property, rights, or interests of the beneficiary,
and that hence the cause of action survives; the recovery,
if any, being a part of his estate, the same as it would have
been if collected and paid over before his death." And in
a New Jersey case [60] it was said: "The controlling feature
of this legislation is that damages are made recoverable for
causing death as compensation for the pecuniary injury the
designated beneficiaries have sustained by reason of the
death. * * * It is also clear that the pecuniary injury
to be compensated for is that of the widow or persons who
are next of kin at the time of the death, * * * and that
the cause of action created by the statute inures to such
persons as a vested right. By this statute a property right
is created in the beneficiary. * * * The death of the
beneficiary pending suit will have a controlling influence
upon the quantum of recovery. The personal injury sustained would be limited in duration and extent to his lifetime. But the death of the beneficiary pending suit cannot
be made available to abrogate the liability of the wrongdoer

12 Ann. Cas. 457; Millar v. St. Louis Transit Co., 216 Mo. 99, 115
S. W. 521. Cf. Behen v. St. Louis Transit Co., 186 Mo. 430, 85 S.
W. 346. The right of a minor to care, support and maintenance was
not a property right, and the minor was not deprived of such a
right, but of a personal right by the wrongful killing of the parent,
and, where the minor dies before the damages are collected, his
cause of action does not survive. Gilkeson v. Missouri Pac. Ry. Co.,
supra.

59 Meekin v. Brooklyn Heights R. Co., supra. Cf. Hodges v. Web-
ber, 65 App. Div. 170, 72 N. Y. Supp. 508.

60 Cooper v. Shore Electric Co., supra.

incurred for the pecuniary injury already sustained. The right to compensation vested in the beneficiary immediately on the death of the deceased."

In some other states the survival of the action for the beneficiary has been held upon grounds that do not so clearly appear.[61] Under the peculiar provisions of the South Carolina statute it is held that, upon the death of the person who was the sole beneficiary when the action was begun, the action may be prosecuted, not for the benefit of his estate, but for the benefit of those who would have been the beneficiaries, had he not survived the decedent, and who stand next in the order of succession.[62]

§ 88. Assignment of right of beneficiary

In New York it has been held that the interest of a beneficiary in the damages to be recovered, having the essential attributes of property stands on the same footing as a distributive share in any other fund, and is assignable, and that the suit may be prosecuted, notwithstanding such assignment, by the sole beneficiary.[63]

[61] Fitzgerald v. Edison Electric Illuminating Co., 207 Pa. 118, 56 Atl. 350. An action by a father, as administrator, under Ky. St. § 6, to recover damages for the death of his child, did not abate upon the death of the father, but the action should have been revived in the name of his successor as administrator; the recovery, after the payment of funeral expenses, costs of administration, and costs of recovery, being for the benefit of the father's estate. Thomas' Adm'r v. Maysville Gas Co., 112 Ky. 569, 66 S. W. 398, 23 Ky. Law Rep. 1879.

[62] Morris v. Spartanburg Ry., Gas & Electric Co., 70 S. C. 279, 49 S. E. 854.

[63] Quin v. Moore, 15 N. Y. 432. See Blakeley v. Le Duc, 22 Minn. 476. That the only heirs of decedent had, prior to the commencement of the action, assigned all their interest in the cause of action to the administrator of deceased, who appeared as plaintiff, was no bar to the action, since the administrator was entitled to sue in his

§ 89.   Distribution

Lord Campbell's act provides that the amount recovered shall be divided among the parties for whose benefit the action is brought in such shares as the jury by their verdict shall find. This provision has been substantially followed in Maryland, Texas, and Virginia.[64] In Texas it has been held that the failure of the jury to apportion the damages assessed is error,[65] but, in the absence of objection, is not ground for reversal.[66] It is proper for the jury to exclude from the verdict a party who fails to prove pecuniary loss.[67]

It was enacted by 27 & 28 Vict. c. 95, that the defendant may pay money into court as compensation in one sum to all the persons entitled, without specifying the shares into which it is to be divided by the jury, and that if such sum is not accepted, and an issue is taken as to its sufficiency, and the jury shall think it sufficient, the defendant shall be en-

own right, and a recovery by him would have been a bar to any subsequent action. Fritz v. Western Union Tel. Co., 25 Utah, 263, 71 Pac. 209. See Hackett v. McIlwain, 158 Mich. 265, 122 N. W. 551.

[64] See Houston City St. Ry. Co. v. Sciacca, 80 Tex. 350, 16 S. W. 31; San Antonio St. R. Co. v. Mechler (Tex. Civ. App.) 29 S. W. 202; Missouri, K. & T. R. Co. of Texas v. Wall (Tex. Civ. App.) 110 S. W. 453. The manner in which the damages are to be distributed is for the jury, and their decision cannot be complained of by defendant. Norfolk & W. Ry. Co. v. Stevens, 97 Va. 631, 34 S. E. 525, 46 L. R. A. 367.

[65] Houston & T. C. Ry. Co. v. Moore, 49 Tex. 31, 30 Am. Rep. 98. See Galveston, H. & S. A. R. Co. v. Le Gierse, 51 Tex. 198.

[66] March v. Walker, 48 Tex. 372.

[67] Missouri Pac. Ry. Co. v. Henry, 75 Tex. 220, 12 S. W. 828. Where the evidence made it an issue whether each plaintiff had suffered loss, and the verdict for plaintiffs as a whole was not complained of as excessive, defendant cannot complain that the amount apportioned to one of plaintiffs was excessive. Houston & T. C. R. Co. v. Alexander, 102 Tex. 497, 119 S. W. 1135. See, also, International & G. N. R. Co. v. Munn, 46 Tex. Civ. App. 276, 102 S. W. 442.

titled to a verdict on that issue.[68] Where money has been
paid into court under this provision, and received by the
plaintiff, he is not liable therefor in an action at law, but
may be compelled as trustee to administer the fund in favor of all the persons entitled.[69] On a special case being
presented to the chancery division for advice as to the proper proportion in which such compensation should be divided, it was held that, by analogy of the statute of distribution, the widow should take one third and the children
two thirds;[70] but in such case the court may order the fund
distributed in the same manner as the jury could have done,
i. e. it may adjudge the individual claims separately, or may
fix an aggregate sum, and divide this among the persons entitled.[71]

The provisions for distribution differ in different states.[72]

Most of the acts in force in the United States, however,
provide, in substance, that the amount recovered shall be

[68] In an action by the widow, as administratrix, the defendants
paid money into court with their defense. The plaintiff admitted its
sufficiency, and joined issue, to enable the rights of all persons to
be determined. The father of the deceased applied to have his name
added as a party, for the purpose of establishing his claim to part of
the money. Application refused, but leave granted to appear and
tender evidence as to the amount of his share. Johnston v. Great
Northern Ry. Co., 20 L. R. Ir. 4.

[69] Condliff v. Condliff, 29 L. T. (N. S.) 831, 22 W. R. 325. In Shal-
low v. Verden, 9 Ir. Com. Law, 150, the widow was allowed to draw
the money out, on a consent signed by her being made a rule of
court, whereby she agreed to a division in a certain proportion.

[70] Sanderson v. Sanderson, 36 L. T. (N. S.) 847.

[71] Bulmer v. Bulmer, 25 Ch. D. 409, 53 L. J. Ch. 402, 32 W. R. 380.

[72] Under Code 1906, § 721, providing that in an action for the
death of a married man, leaving a wife and children, the damages
shall be distributed to the wife and children, whether the widow
joined in the action or not, she could not exclude the children from
participating, either by procuring the entry of judgment in favor of
herself alone or otherwise. Foster v. Hicks, 93 Miss. 219, 46 South.
533.

divided among the widow and next of kin, or other persons
entitled to the benefit of such action, in the proportion provided by law in relation to the distribution of the personal
property of persons dying intestate.[73] Creditors are by the
terms of most of the acts expressly excluded from the distribution.[74] In Iowa and Virginia they may participate if
there be no husband, wife, child, or parent.[75] In Oregon
and Washington it is held that they may participate.[76] In
North Carolina, if there are no next of kin entitled, the
amount recovered goes to the University.[77]

It was pointed out in a Michigan case[78] that there is a

[73] Under Rev. St. 1893, § 2316, providing that if there be no wife,
husband, or child the action shall be for the benefit of the parent
or parents, and that the amount recovered shall be divided between
the parties entitled in such shares as they would have been entitled
to if the deceased had died intestate and the amount had been personal
sonal assets, money paid to an administrator of a deceased unmarried son is equally divided between his father and mother, there
being no provision in the statute of distributions determining the
proportions in which the distribution shall be made when both father and mother are entitled and the statute of distributions being
therefore inapplicable. Childs v. Bolton, 69 S. C. 555, 48 S. E. 618.
The recovery given to the widow of deceased, or, if there be no
widow, to the children or personal representatives, for the benefit
of the widow or next of kin, free from claims of creditors, is personal property, distributable only under the provision for the distribution of personalty, and cannot pass by will of deceased, nor is
it an asset of the estate. Haynes v. Walker, 111 Tenn. 106, 76 S.
W. 902. See Toledo, St. L. & W. R. Co. v. Connolly, 149 Fed. 398,
79 C. C. A. 218 (Ohio).

[74] Revisal 1905, § 59, providing that recovery for negligent death
shall not be applied as assets in the payment of debts or legacies,
but shall be distributed as intestate property, refers to decedent's
creditors, and not the distributees'. Neill v. Wilson, 146 N. C. 242,
59 S. E. 674.

[75] See Casady v. Grimmelman, 108 Iowa, 695, 77 N. W. 1067.

[76] See § 144.

[77] Warner v. Western North Carolina R. Co., 94 N. C. 250. See
§ 49.

[78] Richmond v. Chicago & W. M. Ry. Co., 87 Mich. 374, 49 N. W.

seeming contradiction or inconsistency between the provision that the jury may give such damages as they shall deem fair and just with reference to the pecuniary injury resulting to the persons who may be entitled to the damages, and the provision that the amount recovered shall be distributed, not in proportion to the pecuniary injury severally suffered, but in the proportion provided by law in relation to the distribution of the personal property of persons dying intestate; since it might follow that some persons of a class would get more and some less than the share which they would receive upon the basis of pecuniary injury, or even that a person might participate in the distribution who had suffered no pecuniary injury at all. In that case the distribution of the fund was not in controversy, and it seems to be intimated that there would be no serious difficulty in the way of those of the next of kin who had suffered the pecuniary injury obtaining the amount of the recovery from the administrator to the exclusion of those of the next of kin who had suffered no pecuniary injury; but it is difficult to see how it could be shown who were entitled to participate and who not, even if any discrimination were possible within the terms of the statute.[79] "We are not insensible," said the court in a New York case,[80] "to the peculiar hardship of this case, where a widow, left with-

---

621, per Morse, J. To the same effect, opinion of Hoar, J., in Richardson v. New York Cent. R. Co., 98 Mass. 85.

[79] An action for the death of a father is properly brought in the name of all the children, the recovery being for the benefit of all, and not merely of those who prove actual damage. North Pennsylvania R. Co. v. Robinson, 44 Pa. 175. See opinion of Earl, J., in Murphy v. New York Cent. & H. R. R. Co., 88 N. Y. 445; St. Louis, I. M. & S. Ry. Co. v. Needham, 52 Fed. 371, 3 C. C. A. 129. See, also, Duzan v. Myers, 30 Ind. App. 227, 65 N. E. 1046, 96 Am. St. Rep. 341.

[80] Snedeker v. Snedeker, 164 N. Y. 58, 58 N. E. 4.

out means of support, is compelled to divide the net amount of the judgment she has recovered as administratrix with a man of means, possessed of considerable real and personal property. We must, however, construe the law as it is written, regardless of the seeming injustice inflicted in particular cases by the existing rule." The injustice of allowing participation by those who have suffered no pecuniary loss at the expense of those who have suffered such loss was recognized in a recent case in Nebraska; but the court held that, however much it might be in the interest of justice to make it the duty of the court or jury trying the case to determine the proportion in which the damages recovered should be distributed, the method of distribution enjoined by the statute must be followed.[81] In Pennsylvania, however, where the statute provided that the persons entitled to recover damages should be the husband, widow, children, or parents, and that the sum recovered should go to them on the proportion they would take in the decedent's personal estate in case of intestacy, it was held that, where the widow had recovered judgment, children of full age, whose family relations with the deceased had been severed, and who had suffered no direct pecuniary loss, were not entitled to share in the judgment.[82]

The distribution is governed by the law in force at the time of the death,[88] and of course, in an action under the statute of another state for death in that state, the distribution should be according to the law of the foreign state.[84]

[81] In re Griffin's Estate, 89 Neb. 733, 131 N. W. 1033.

[82] Lewis v. Hunlock's Creek & M. Turnpike Co., 203 Pa. 511, 53 Atl. 349, 93 Am. St. Rep. 774 (distinguishing North Pennsylvania R. Co. v. Robinson, supra); Allison v. Powers, 179 Pa. 531, 36 Atl. 333.

[88] Richmond v. Chicago & W. M. Ry. Co., supra.

[84] Dennick v. Central R. Co. of New Jersey, 103 U. S. 11, 26 L. Ed. 439; Weaver v. Baltimore & O. R. Co., 10 Mackey (D. C.) 499;

Where money is paid to the administrator by way of compromise, it is to be distributed in the same manner as if paid upon judgment, and may be recovered from him by the beneficiaries.[85] Although the amount recovered is not strictly assets, the sureties of the administrator are liable upon his bond for its proper application.[86] The shares of the distributees are subject to the payment of their proportionate part of the expenses of litigation.[87] In Minnesota it is held that, since the recovery does not inure to the benefit of the decedent's estate, but solely to the benefit of the beneficiaries, the distribution does not rest in the probate court appointing the administrator, but rests exclusively in the court in which the recovery is had.[88]

McDonald v. McDonald's Adm'r, 96 Ky. 209, 28 S. W. 482, 16 Ky. Law Rep. 412, 49 Am. St. Rep. 289; In re Degaramo's Estate, 86 Hun, 390, 33 N. Y. Supp. 502. ⸱Cf. Dronenburg v. Harris, 108 Md. 597, 71 Atl. 81. But see Hall v. Southern Ry. Co., 146 N. C. 345, 59 S. E. 879. Post, § 261.

[85] Goltra v. People to Use of Goltra, 53 Ill. 224; Perry v. Carmichael, 95 Ill. 519; Powell's Adm'x v. Powell, 84 Va. 415, 4 S. E. 744. See, also, Dronenburg v. Harris, 108 Md. 597, 71 Atl. 81.

[86] Goltra v. People, to Use of Goltra, supra.

[87] Baker v. Raleigh & G. R. Co., 91 N. C. 308; Matter of Snedeker, 95 App. Div. 149, 88 N. Y. Supp. 847. See, also, Louisville & N. R. Co. v. Perkins, 1 Ala. App. 376, 56 South. 105.

[88] Aho v. Republic Iron & S. Co., 104 Minn. 527, 116 N. W. 590; Mayer v. Mayer, 106 Minn. 484, 119 N. W. 217.

CHAPTER VI

PARTIES

§ 90.　Who may sue

Most of the statutes provide that the action may be prosecuted by the executor or administrator, or by the "personal representatives," though many provide that it may be prosecuted directly by the parties for whose benefit it is given. In certain cases in Massachusetts the remedy is by indictment. In Maryland, also, the action, though in all respects a civil proceeding, is brought in the name of the state. The peculiar provisions of the different acts, so far as they have been construed by the courts, will be considered before proceeding to the more general discussion of this subject.

§ 91.　Lord Campbell's act

By the amendment to Lord Campbell's act it is provided that if there be no executor or administrator, or if the executor or administrator fails to bring action within six months, the action may be brought by any or all the persons entitled to the benefit of it.

§ 92.　Alabama

Except in case of the death of a minor child, as provided in Code 1907, § 2485, the action must be brought by the personal representative.[1] For the death of a child no action can be brought by the father under the employés' act.[2]

---

[1] South & N. A. R. Co. v. Sullivan, 59 Ala. 272; Columbus & W. Ry. Co. v. Bradford, 86 Ala. 574, 6 South. 90; Stewart v Louisville & N. R. Co., 83 Ala. 493, 4 South. 373.

[2] Lovell v. De Bardelaben C. & I. Co., 90 Ala. 13, 7 South. 756; Williams v. South & N. A. R. Co., 91 Ala. 635, 9 South. 77. See Woodstock Iron Works v. Kline, 149 Ala. 391, 43 South. 362; ante, § 35.

§ 93. Arkansas

Kirby's Dig. § 6290, provides that the action shall be brought by the personal representatives, and, if there be no personal representatives, by the heirs at law. If there be a personal representative, the action may not be brought by the heirs at law.[3] The term "heirs at law" includes the widow and all other persons entitled to share in the distribution of the proceeds, and, if the action is brought by one of the heirs at law, all must be joined.[4]

§ 93—1. California

Code Civ. Proc. § 376, gives a right of action for the death of a minor child to the father, or in the case of his death or

---

[3] St. Louis, M. & S. E. R. Co. v. Garner, 76 Ark. 555, 89 S. W. 550.

[4] St. Louis, I. M. & S. Ry. Co. v. Needham, 52 Fed. 371, 3 C. C. A. 129; McBride v. Berman, 79 Ark. 62, 94 S. W. 913; Kansas City Southern Ry. Co. v. Henrie, 87 Ark. 443, 112 S. W. 967. A widow is one of the heirs at law. St. Louis, I. M. & S. Ry. Co. v. Oorman, 92 Ark. 102, 122 S. W. 116. Where the complaint sought a recovery for the benefit of the widow, but the evidence showed she had never been his lawful wife, an amendment, substituting decedent's mother was proper. St. Louis,. I. M. & S. Ry. Co. v. Block, 79 Ark. 179, 95 S. W. 155. Where decedent has left children, his mother is not an heir at law, and hence is not a proper party, though he contributed to her support. Kansas City Southern Ry. Co. v. Frost, 93 Ark. 183, 124 S. W. 748. An objection to the right of a portion of the heirs of a deceased to sue for his death under Kirby's Dig. § 6290, made for the first time on appeal, comes too late. St. Louis, I. M. & S. Ry. Co. v. Watson, 97 Ark. 560, 134 S. W. 949. See, also, St. Louis S. W. Ry. Co. v. Henson, 58 Fed. 531, 7 C. C. A. 349; Missouri, K. & T. Ry. Co. v. Foreman, 174 Fed. 377, 98 C. C. A. 281; Missouri, K. & T. Ry. Co. v. Elliott, 2 Ind. T. 407, 51 S. W. 1067.

desertion of his family to the mother,[5] and for the death of a ward to the guardian; and section 377 gives a right of action for the death of a person not being a minor to his heirs or personal representatives.[6]

§ 94. Colorado [7]

§ 94—1. Florida

Gen. St. 1906, §§ 3145, 3146, give a right of action for death, which shall be brought by and in the name of the widow or husband; and when there is neither, by the minor child or children; and when there are none of the above mentioned persons, by any person or persons dependent on the decedent for support; and when there is neither of the above classes of persons to sue, by the executor or ad-

---

[5] What constitutes desertion? Delatour v. Mackay, 139 Cal. 621, 73 Pac. 454.

[6] "Heirs" include all capable of inheriting from decedent generally, uncontrolled by limitation of statutes relating to distribution of community property, and hence includes minor children. Redfield v. Oakland Consol. St. Ry. Co., 110 Cal. 277, 42 Pac. 822, 1063. The widow is an heir of the deceased husband, and, under certain conditions, may be his sole heir. Knott v. McGilvray, 124 Cal. 128, 56 Pac. 789. In an action by heirs all should join as plaintiffs, but where the consent of one cannot be obtained he may be made a defendant. Salmon v. Rathjens, 152 Cal. 290, 92 Pac. 733. Where a child is unborn, and its existence is unknown to defendant in an action by its mother to recover for the death of her husband, the father of the child, at the time the judgment is rendered in favor of the widow or other heirs, such judgment is a bar to a subsequent action by such unborn child to recover for its father's death, notwithstanding Civ. Code, § 29, providing that an unborn child is deemed to be in existence so far as necessary for its interests in the event of its subsequent birth. Daubert v. Western Meat Co., 139 Cal. 480, 73 Pac. 244, 96 Am. St. Rep. 154.

[7] See § 103.

ministrator.[8] Section 3147 gives a right of action for the death of a minor child to the father, or if he be not living to the mother, as the legal representative of such child.[9]

§ 95. Georgia [10]

§ 96. Indiana [11]

§ 97. Iowa [12]

§ 97—1. Kansas

Gen. St. 1909, § 6014, provides for an action for death, to be brought by the personal representatives, the damages to

---

[8] The existence of the right of action in any of these named classes, commencing with the second, is wholly dependent on the fact whether there is no person in esse belonging to any one of the classes who are given the precedent right over him to maintain the action. Louisville & N. R. Co. v. Jones, 45 Fla. 407, 34 South. 246. See, also, Duval v. Hunt, 34 Fla. 85, 15 South. 876. The right of a minor sister, in the absence of a widow and minor child, to recover for the death of an older brother who was also a minor, rests on her dependence on such brother for support and on a reasonable expectancy of a continuation thereof. Louisville & N. R. Co. v. Jones, 50 Fla. 225, 39 South. 485. An administrator of a deceased minor can recover, where such minor leaves neither widow nor minor child, nor children, nor any person dependent on him for support. Bowden v. Jacksonville Electric Co., 51 Fla. 152, 41 South. 400, 7 Ann. Cas. 859.

[9] The damages are personal to the parents, and an action should be by the parent personally, and an administrator of the minor has no interest in such recovery; the term "legal representative" having reference to the parties benefited by the rights conferred and not to the administrator or executor of a decedent. Seaboard Air Line Ry. v. Moseley, 60 Fla. 186, 53 South. 718.

[10] See § 38. No action can be maintained by an administrator. Miller v. Southwestern R. Co., 55 Ga. 143.

[11] See § 39.   [12] See § 40.

inure to the benefit of the widow and children, if any, or next of kin, to be distributed in the same manner as personal property of the deceased.[13] Section 6015 provides that in all cases where the residence of the deceased is or has been at the time of his death in any other state or territory, or when, being a resident of the state, no personal representative is or has been appointed, the action may be brought by the widow, or, where there is no widow, by the next of kin.[14] The statute provides, also, that in addition to the actions which survive at common law actions for injuries to the person shall survive; but it is held that this enactment is applicable only to cases where death results from some other cause than the injury, and that if death results from the injury the only right of action is for the death.[15]

---

[13] "Next of kin" means those kin who inherit from the deceased under the statute of descents and distributions. Atchison, T. & S. F. Ry. Co. v. Ryan, 62 Kan. 682, 64 Pac. 603. See Charlton v. St. Louis & S. F. R. Co., 200 Mo. 413, 98 S. W. 529.

[14] This section (Laws 1889, c. 131, § 1) is not unconstitutional. Berry v. Kansas City, Ft. S. & M. R. Co., 52 Kan. 759, 34 Pac. 805, 39 Am. St. Rep. 371; Atchison, T. & S. F. R. Co. v. Napole, 55 Kan. 401, 40 Pac. 669. A nonresident, suing for the death of her husband, described herself in the petition as widow, and also as administratrix by appointment in another state. Held, that she might recover in her right as widow, though not entitled to maintain the action as administratrix. Chicago, R. I. & P. Ry. Co. v. Mills, 57 Kan. 687, 47 Pac. 834. Under section 6014, an action for death of a nonresident may still be brought by the Kansas administrator of his estate, notwithstanding the passage of Laws 1889, c. 131. Cox v. Kansas City, 86 Kan. 298, 120 Pac. 553. A parent, to recover as next of kin for death of a minor, a resident of the state, must prove that no personal representative has been appointed. Atchison, T. & S. F. Ry. Co. v. Judah, 10 Kan. App. 577, 62 P. 711; Atchison Water Co. v. Price, 9 Kan. App. 884, 59 Pac. 677. See Philes v. Missouri Pac. R. Co., 141 Mo. App. 561, 125 S. W. 553; Keele v. Atchison, T. & S. F. Ry. Co., 151 Mo. App. 364, 131 S. W. 730.

[15] McCarthy v. Chicago, R. I. & P. R. Co., 18 Kan. 46, 26 Am.

§ 98. Kentucky [16]

§ 99. Louisiana [17]

§ 100. Maryland

Code Pub. Civ. Laws, art. 67, § 2, provides that the action shall be for the benefit of the wife, husband, parent, and child, and shall be brought by and in the name of the state for the use of the person entitled to damages.

Except in respect to the provision as to who may sue, the statute is a close copy of Lord Campbell's act.[18] The state is merely a formal party.[19] The action is brought for the use of such of the beneficiaries as have been actually damaged, and others need not be joined.[20]

§ 101. Massachusetts [21]

§ 102. Mississippi [22]

Rep. 742; City of Eureka v. Merrifield, 53 Kan. 794, 37 Pac. 113; Martin v. Missouri Pac. Ry. Co., 58 Kan. 475, 49 Pac. 605. Cf. Missouri Pac. Ry. Co. v. Bennett's Estate, 5 Kan. App. 231, 47 Pac. 183, affirmed 58 Kan. 499, 49 Pac. 606; post, § 126.

[16] See § 41.

[17] See § 42.

[18] State, to Use of Coughlan, v. Baltimore & O. R. Co., 24 Md. 84, 87 Am. Dec. 600.

[19] State v. Baltimore & O. R. Co., 70 Md. 319, 17 Atl. 88. See Baltimore & O. R. Co. v. State, to Use of Allison, 62 Md. 479, 50 Am. Rep. 233.

[20] Deford v. State, to Use of Keyser, 30 Md. 179. In an action by a minor, the insertion of the name of a prochein ami, though not improper, is not required. Albert v. State, 66 Md. 325, 7 Atl. 697, 59 Am. Rep. 159.

[21] See § 44.   [22] See § 44—2.

§ 103. Missouri

Rev. St. §§ 5425–5427, provide that the action may be brought,[23] first, by the husband or wife; second, if there be no husband or wife, or if he or she fails to sue within six months after the death, by the minor children,[24] whether

[23] Where husband, wife, and children all perished in the same disaster, held, in an action by the wife's administrator, that no action could be maintained. Gibbs v. Hannibal, 82 Mo. 143.

[24] Where the deceased leaves widow and minor children, and the widow fails to sue within 6 months, her right is barred. Coover v. Moore, 31 Mo. 574. But the children must sue within 12 months after the cause of action accrued (the death). Kennedy v. Burrier, 36 Mo. 128. If the widow sues within 6 months, and is nonsuited, she may begin again after the 6 months. Shepard v. St. Louis, I. M. & S. Ry. Co., 3 Mo. App. 550. And, if she begins suit within 6 months, and dismisses it, the children cannot, after the 6 months, maintain an action. McNamara v. Slavens, 76 Mo. 329. If she sues after 6 months, she must aver and prove that there was no minor child. Barker v. Hannibal & St. J. R. Co., 91 Mo. 86, 14 S. W. 280. Cf. Hayes v. Williams, 17 Colo. 465, 30 Pac. 352. The right is not a concurrent one in the surviving husband or wife and the children, but during the first 6 months it is absolute in the husband or wife alone, and if he or she fails to sue within that time the right vests in the children only. The act of the widow in suing within 6 months is an election, and cuts off the children, though she sue the wrong defendant. Packard v. Hannibal & St. J. R. Co., 181 Mo. 421, 80 S. W. 951, 103 Am. St. Rep. 607. Where, in an action by minors for the death of their father, defendant alleged that a third person claiming to be decedent's widow had brought suit for his death, which suit was pending, but refused to prove that the third person was decedent's widow, the refusal of the court to admit in evidence the third person's petition was not erroneous; the minors not being estopped by the allegations in such petition. Penney v. St. Joseph Stockyards Co., 212 Mo. 309, 111 S. W. 79. In absence of a showing either way, it could not be presumed, in an action by the children, that the widow had previously sued. Fulwider v. Trenton Gas, Light & Power Co., 216 Mo. 582, 116 S. W. 508. Sufficiency of petition by minor children. Sharp v. Missouri Pac. Ry. Co., 213 Mo. 517, 111 S. W. 1154. The pendency of a suit

natural born or adopted, provided that, if adopted, they shall have been adopted according to the laws of adoption of the state where the person executing the deed of adoption resided; or, third, if the deceased be a minor [25] and unmarried,[26] whether natural born [27] or adopted, by the

by the widow could be pleaded in abatement of a subsequent suit by the children. Fulwider v. Trenton Gas, Light & Power Co., 216 Mo. 582, 116 S. W. 508.

[25] Under section 5425, the parents may sue although the child has been emancipated. The court says that the statute is penal as well as compensatory. Philpott v. Missouri Pac. Ry. Co., 85 Mo. 164. See, also, Matlock v. Williamsville, G. & St. L. R. Co., 198 Mo. 495, 95 S. W. 849, 115 Am. St. Rep. 484. The fact that decedent fraudulently represented himself to be of age in order to obtain the employment and that such representation was believed by defendant was no defense. Matlock v. Williamsville, G. & St. L. R. Co., supra. As the parents do not seek to recover by virtue of a relationship of master and servant, but sue in tort on the right which the child would have had if he had survived, the complainant need not aver that the child was the servant of the parents. Bellamy v. Whitsell, 123 Mo. App. 610, 100 S. W. 514.

[26] In a suit by the parents for the death of a minor child, it must be alleged and proved that he left neither wife nor children. McIntosh v. Missouri Pac. Ry. Co., 103 Mo. 131, 15 S. W. 80; Dulaney v. Missouri Pac. Ry. Co., 21 Mo. App. 597; Sparks v. Kansas City S. & M. R. Co., 31 Mo. App. 111; Case v. Cordell Zinc & Lead Min. Co., 103 Mo. App. 477, 78 S. W. 62. But in an action by a mother for the death of her sons, under the Colorado statute it is sufficient to allege that plaintiff is the sole heir of the decedents, without further averring that they were unmarried and childless; nor need she allege that she was dependent on them for support. Brennan v. Molly Gibson Consolidated Min. & Mill. Co. (C. C.) 44 Fed. 795. Where deceased was an infant of tender years, it was not necessary to instruct on the question of its being married. Czezewzka v. Benton-Bellefontaine Ry. Co., 121 Mo. 201, 25 S. W. 911. Under the New Mexico statute, giving to the parent a right of action if the deceased be a "minor and unmarried," the word "and" cannot be read "or." Isaac v. Denver & Rio Grande Ry. Co., 12 Daly (N. Y.) 340.

[27] "Natural born child" means no more than child. The mother of a bastard may sue, and the father need not join. Marshall v.

father and mother,[28] who may join in the suit, with an equal interest in the judgment, or, if either of them be dead, by the survivor,[29] or, fourth, if there be no husband, wife, minor child or minor children, natural born or adopted, or if the deceased be an unmarried minor and there be no father or mother, then suit may be instituted and recovery had by the administrator or executor, and the amount recovered shall be distributed according to the laws of descent.[30]

Wabash R. Co., 120 Mo. 275, 25 S. W. 179. Cf. Marshall v. Wabash R. Co. (C. C.) 46 Fed. 269.

[28] The father and mother may sue, though divorced before the death. Buel v. St. Louis Transfer Co., 45 Mo. 562; s. c., Crockett (late Buell) v. St. Louis Transfer Co., 52 Mo. 457. The penalty is indivisible, and all of it or none must be sued for, both parents joining prior to judgment, though they are divorced, and decedent has been in the exclusive custody of the mother, and, if the father refuses to join, the mother cannot recover by making him a coplaintiff against his consent. Clark v. Kansas City, St. L. & C. R. Co., 219 Mo. 524, 118 S. W. 40. A mother cannot support a separate action for the death of her minor child from whose father she has been divorced, unless the father joins as plaintiff, though she was awarded custody of the child. Clark v. Kansas City, St. L. & C. R. Co., 153 Mo. App. 689, 135 S. W. 979.

[29] Where both parents sue, and one of them dies before judgment, the entire right of action survives to the other, and the suit may be continued in his or her name alone for the full amount of the recovery authorized by law. Tobin v. Missouri Pac. Ry. Co., 18 S. W. 996. See, also, Senn v. Southern Ry. Co., 124 Mo. 621, 28 S. W. 66; Lee v. Publishers: Knapp & Co., 155 Mo. 610, 56 S. W. 458. On the death of a father, the mother, as survivor, alone has the right to maintain an action, and her second husband has no right to maintain the action. Hennessy v. Bavarian Brewing Co., 145 Mo. 104, 46 S. W. 966, 41 L. R. A. 385, 68 Am. St. Rep. 554.

[30] Rev. St. 1899, §§ 2865, 2866, adopted section 2864 as it originally existed, and the amendment of 1905 did not affect the sections, and the administrator of a decedent cannot maintain an action for his negligent death, especially in view of Laws 1907, p. 252, amending section 2866, so as to permit an action by the parties provided for in section 2864, as amended by Laws 1905, p. 135.

The Colorado statute,[31] in respect to who may sue, is the same as that of Missouri, omitting the fourth case, except that in the second case the action may be brought, if there be no husband or wife, or he or she fails to sue within one year after the death, by the heirs.[32] The Code of Civil Procedure (section 9) also provides that a father, or, in case of his death or desertion of his family, the mother, may maintain an action for the death of a child, or the guardian for the death of his ward.[33]

Crohn v. Kansas City Home Telephone Co., 131 Mo. App. 313, 109 S. W. 1068. The administrator may sue for the negligent death of one of mature age, unmarried, and childless. Pratt v. Missouri Pac. R. Co., 139 Mo. App. 502, 122 S. W. 1125.

[31] Rev. St. 1908, § 2056. The parties differ under the employers' liability act. Sess. Laws 1911, c. 113.

[32] The wife may maintain an action at any time before the expiration of the period of limitation (two years), provided there be no heirs, or provided the heirs, if any, have not instituted judicial proceedings, or where a bona fide action was instituted during the first year, which, having, through an excusable mistake, been brought against a wrong party, was ineffectual. Hayes v. Williams, 17 Colo. 465, 30 Pac. 352. The words "heir or heirs of deceased" mean "child or children," and limit the right of action to lineal descendants. Hindry v. Holt, 24 Colo. 464, 51 P. 1002, 39 L. R. A. 351, 65 Am. St. Rep. 235. If deceased left husband or wife, the sole right of action was in such survivor, save that as against children the right would be lost unless asserted within a year; if there was no surviving husband or wife, or the survivor failed to sue within a year, then the sole right would be in the children; and if there was neither surviving husband nor wife nor any children, then only would the right of action be in the father and mother, or the survivor; so that where an unmarried adult female is killed, and she leaves neither husband, child, nor mother, the right of action is in her surviving father. Hopper v. Denver & R. G. R. Co., 155 Fed. 273, 84 C. C. A. 21. If deceased be a minor, the father and mother may join, but either may sue alone. Pierce v. Conners, 20 Colo. 178, 37 Pac. 721, 46 Am. St. Rep. 279.

[33] Gen. St. §§ 2529, 2530, rendered children liable for the support of indigent parents. In a suit by the parents for the death of a son 25 years old, the court said that the action could be maintained

The New Mexico statute closely resembles that of Colo-rado.[34]

§ 103—1. Montana [35]

§ 104. New Mexico [36]

§ 104 —1. North Dakota

Rev. Codes 1905, §§ 7687–7689, provide that the jury shall give such damages as they think proportionate to the injury resulting to the persons entitled to the recovery; that the action shall be brought by the following persons in the order named: (1) The surviving husband or wife, if any; (2) the surviving children, if any; and (3) the personal repre-sentative; and that if any person entitled to bring the action refuses or neglects to do so for 30 days after demand of the person next in order, such person may bring the same; and that the amount recovered shall not be liable for the debts of the decedent, but shall inure to the exclusive benefit of the heirs at law in such shares as the judge before whom the case is tried shall fix in the order for judgment, and that for the purpose of fixing the shares he may make any in-vestigation which he deems necessary.[37]

for the recovery of substantial damages. Denver S. P. & P. R. Co. v. Wilson, 12 Colo. 20, 20 Pac. 340. Since the son was not a minor, the action would not be maintainable under sections 1030–1033, un-less they receive a different construction from that which appears to prevail in Missouri. Since the action was by both parents, it would not seem to be maintainable under Code Civil Proc. § 9. Cf. Brennan v. Molly Gibson Consolidated Min. & Mill. Co., supra, note 26.

[34] See Romero v. Atchison, T. & S. F. Ry. Co., 11 N. M. 679, 72 Pac. 37.

[35] See § 45—1.

[36] See § 103.

[37] The term "heirs at law" is not limited to the husband or wife or children of decedent, but includes his brothers and sisters, for

§ 105. Pennsylvania

The act of April 15, 1851, § 19,[38] provided that the widow, or, if no widow, the personal representatives, may sue; the act of April 26, 1855, § 1,[39] that the persons entitled to recover shall be the husband, widow, children, or parents.[40] By the earlier act the damages recovered were general assets of the estate, and available to creditors; by the later act the right of action was taken away from the personal representatives, and given, according to the circumstances of each case, to one of the four designated parties; [41] though

whose benefit an action may be maintained by the personal representative. Satterberg v. Minneapolis, St. P. & S. S. M. Ry. Co., 19 N. D. 38, 121 N. W. 70. Rev. Codes 1905, §§ 7686–7691, do not require a legal obligation by decedent towards surviving heirs to entitle them to recover. Id. Rev. Codes 1905, §§ 7686–7691, authorize a recovery for the benefit of an heir deprived of pecuniary aid which decedent was obliged to render, or which the heir had any reasonable expectation of receiving as a duty. Id. See, also, Stangeland v. Minneapolis, St. P. & S. S. M. R. Co., 105 Minn. 224, 117 N. W. 386.

[38] See Pepper & Lewis' 'Dig. p. 5332, par. 2.

[39] See Id. p. 5333, par. 3.

[40] The right vests in the widow solely where the deceased leaves surviving him a widow and parents, but no children; the parents, in such case, are entitled to no part of the damages which the widow may recover. Lehigh Iron Co. v. Rupp, 100 Pa. 95. A married woman who was deserted by her husband could sue in her own name for the death of their child. Kerr v. Pennsylvania R. R., 169 Pa. 95, 32 Atl. 96.

[41] Huntingdon & B. T. M. R. & Coal Co. v. Decker, 84 Pa. 419; Books v. Borough of Danville, 95 Pa. 158. An action for the death of a father is properly brought by all the children, not merely those who prove actual damage. North Pennsylvania R. Co. v. Robinson, 44 Pa. 175. Where the widow brings suit, joining the minor children, such joinder is not ground for reversal after verdict, no objection having been previously taken. Philadelphia, W. & B. R. Co. v. Conway, 112 Pa. 511, 4 Atl. 362; Borough of South Easton

the damages recovered are not necessarily to be retained by the plaintiff in his own right, but are to be distributed like personal estate in case of intestacy.[42] The act of 1855 is not changed by Const. art. 3, § 21.[43]

§ 106. Rhode Island *

§ 107. Tennessee

Shannon's Code, § 4025, provides that the right of action shall pass to the widow, and, in case there is no widow, to the children, or to the personal representative, for the benefit of the widow and next of kin, free from claims of creditors. Section 4026 provides that the action may be instituted by the personal representative, but, if he declines it, that the widow and children may use his name on giving bond for costs, or in the form prescribed for paupers. Section 4027 provides that the action may also be instituted by

v. Reinhart, 13 Wkly. Notes Cas. 389. Where decedent leaves widow and children, the action must be brought by her alone, though the damages are to be shared with the children. Haughey v. Pittsburg Rys. Co., 210 Pa. 367, 59 Atl. 1112. The widow, if living, is the person in whom the right of action is vested, and she may settle an action so brought by her, since she holds the amount recovered as trustee for all the persons interested therein. Conover v. Pennsylvania R. Co. (C. C.) 176 Fed. 638. See, also, Holmes v. Pennsylvania R. Co., 220 Pa. 189, 69 Atl. 597, 123 Am. St. Rep. 685.

[42] Huntingdon & B. T. M. R. & Coal Co. v. Decker, 84 Pa. 419. The amount recovered by a widow for the death of her husband is to be divided between herself and the children as in case of intestacy. Allison v. Powers, 179 Pa. 531, 36 Atl. 333. It is not necessary that plaintiff should have been dependent on or have had a legal claim on the services of deceased. Pennsylvania Co. v. Scofield, 161 Fed. 911, 88 C. C. A. 602. See, also, Marsh v. Western New York & P. Ry. Co., 204 Pa. 229, 53 Atl. 1001.

[43] Books v. Borough of Danville, 95 Pa. 158.

*Ante, § 52.

the widow in her own name, or, if there be no widow, by the children.[44] If there is a widow, the right to sue vests in her. If there are also children, they are not necessary parties, although the action is for their benefit, as well as hers;[45] and she may dismiss or compromise the action

[44] Sections 4025–4027 originated with the act of 1851, c. 17, and were sections 2291, 2292, in Code of 1858. Section 4028 originated with Code of 1858, § 2293. The original act provided that the right of action should pass to the personal representative for the benefit of the widow and next of kin. Code 1858, § 2291. The act of 1871, c. 78, amended Code 1858, § 2291, so that the language should be the same as that of section 4025 of the present Code; and also enacted that, in addition to the remedy existing by sections 2291, 2292, the widow, or, if no widow, the children, might institute the suit. The latter enactment is substantially section 4027 of the present Code. Webb v. East Tennessee, V. & G. R. Co., 88 Tenn. 119, 12 S. W. 428. Before the amendment of 1871 the action could be maintained only by the executor or administrator. Bledsoe v. Stokes, 1 Baxt. 314; Flatley v. Memphis & C. R. Co., 9 Heisk. 230. See Trafford v. Adams Exp. Co., 8 Lea, 96; Chambers v. Porter, 5 Coldw. 273. Where a widow brought suit after the amendment for the death of her husband, which occurred before its enactment, it was held that the action could be maintained, and that the act was not retroactive, since it only affected the remedy. Collins v. East Tennessee, V. & G. R. Co., 9 Heisk. 841. The action can be brought only by the personal representative, save in the excepted cases of widow and children, and hence an action by parents for the death of a minor child does not lie. Holston v. Dayton Coal & Iron Co., 95 Tenn. 521, 32 S. W. 486. The right to damages for the death of a married woman is vested in the surviving husband, to the exclusion of the next of kin, and the action is properly brought in the name of the administrator. Chattanooga Electric Ry. Co. v. Johnson, 97 Tenn. 667, 37 S. W. 558, 34 L. R. A. 442. Where deceased left no widow, children, or father, the contention that deceased's mother was his only next of kin, and that therefore it was error to admit evidence that he left a brother and sister, cannot be sustained. Freeman v. Illinois Cent. R. Co., 107 Tenn. 340, 64 S. W. 1.

[45] Collins v. East Tennessee, V. & G. R. Co., 9 Heisk. 841. See, also, Illinois Cent. R. Co. v. Davis, 104 Tenn. 442, 58 S. W. 296; Felton v. Spiro, 78 Fed. 576, 24 C. C. A. 321.

without their consent or that of their guardian.[46] But she may waive her right, and in such case the personal repre- · sentative may sue.[47] If she die pending the action by her, her administrator cannot revive and prosecute it.[48]

§ 108. Texas

Rev. St. 1895, art. 3021, provides that the action shall be for the benefit of the surviving husband, wife,[49] children,[50] and parents, and that the amount recovered shall not be liable for debts. Article 3022 provides that the action may be brought by the parties entitled thereto, or by any one of them for the benefit of all. Article 3023 provides that, if the parties entitled shall fail to commence action within three months after the death, it shall be the duty of the executor or administrator to commence action, unless requested by all parties entitled not to do so.[51]

[46] Greenlee v. East Tennessee, V. & G. R. Co., 5 Lea, 418; Stephens v. Nashville, C. & St. L. Ry., 10 Lea, 448.

[47] Webb v. East Tennessee, V. & G. R. Co., 88 Tenn. 119, 12 S. W. 428.

[48] Loague v. Memphis & C. R. Co., 91 Tenn. 458, 19 S. W. 430. See, also, Louisville & N. R. Co. v. Bean, 94 Tenn. 388, 29 S. W. 370.

[49] See Dallas & W. R. Co. v. Spicker, 61 Tex. 427, 48 Am. Rep. 297; International & G. N. Ry. Co. v. Kuehn, 70 Tex. 582, 8 S. W. 484; San Antonio St. Ry. Co. v. Cailloutte, 79 Tex. 341, 15 S. W. 390.

[50] An action may be brought by the guardian of minor children (Houston & T. C. R. Co. v. Bradley, 45 Tex. 171), or by their next friend (International & G. N. Ry. Co. v. Kuehn, 70 Tex. 582, 8 S. W. 484). See, also, International & G. N. R. Co. v. Sein, 11 Tex. Civ. App. 386, 33 S. W. 558; Taylor v. San Antonio Gas & Electric Co. (Civ. App.) 93 S. W. 674. A judgment awarding a recovery to his grandchildren is erroneous. Houston & T. C. R. Co. v. Harris (Civ. App.) 64 S. W. 227.

[51] Article 3023 does not limit the right to sue after three months

·The persons entitled must all be made parties, or else the petition must set forth the names of all who are entitled.[52] But a recovery by others will not bar a beneficiary who was

to the executor or administrator. Houston & T. C. R. Co. v. Brad-ley, 45 Tex. 171; March v. Walker, 48 Tex. 372.

[52] Galveston, H. & S. A. R. Co. v. Le Gierse, 51 Tex. 189; Dallas & W. R. Co. v. Spiker, 59 Tex. 435; Texas & N. O. R. Co. v. Berry, 67 Tex. 238, 5 S. W. 817; East Line & R. R. R. Co. v. Culberson, 68 Tex. 664, 5 S. W. 820; Missouri P. Ry. Co. v. Henry, 75 Tex. 220, 12 S. W. 828. A widow who has compromised her claim is not a necessary party in a suit in behalf of the children. Houston & T. C. R. Co. v. Bradley, 45 Tex. 171. Where certain beneficiaries were not mentioned in the original petition, and, after the expiration of the period of limitation, the plaintiff filed an amended petition in which they were mentioned, held, that the defendant could not object that the action was not brought for their benefit. Paschal v. Owen, 77 Tex. 583, 14 S. W. 203. The petition need not negative the existence of other beneficiaries than those named. Southern Cotton Press & Mfg. Co. v. Bradley, 52 Tex. 587. Where, in an action by a wife for the benefit of herself and child, for the death of her husband, it appears that both parents of deceased are living, a release by the parents before a notary of all claims by reason of the son's death constitutes no defense to defendant's motion for a new trial on the ground that the parents should have been made plaintiffs in the action. Ft. Worth & D. C. R. Co. v. Wilson, 85 Tex. 516, 22 S. W. 578. A widow may sue for the death of her husband, for herself and minor son, and also for the use of deceased's parents, without their knowledge, where she does so in good faith. San Antonio St. Ry. Co. v. Renken, 15 Tex. Civ. App. 229, 38 S. W. 829. An action for the death of a mother who left a husband and four daughters cannot be maintained by the husband and one daughter alone. San Antonio & A. P. R. Co. v. Mertink, 101 Tex. 165, 105 S. W. 485. In an action for the death of plaintiff's husband, where his father had not been dependent on him, and deceased had not contributed to his support, the father was not a necessary party. Texas Cent. Ry. Co. v. Frazier (Civ. App.) 34 S. W. 664. See, also, St. Louis, A. & T. Ry. Co. v. Taylor, 5 Tex. Civ. App. 668, 24 S. W. 975; Garcia v. Sanders (Civ. App.) 35 S. W. 52; Galveston, H. & S. A. Ry. Co. v. McCray (Civ. App.) 43 S. W. 275; El Paso & N. E. R. Co. of Texas v. Whatley (Civ. App.) 76 S. W. 589; De Garcia v. San Antonio & A. P. Ry. Co. (Civ. App.) 90 S. W. 670; International & G. N. R. Co. v. Howell

not included in the prior action.[53] Although by article 3022 parents are included among the parties entitled, they are not included in Const. art. 16, § 26, among the persons to whom the defendant is responsible in exemplary damages, and hence parents cannot maintain an action for exemplary damages.[54]

§ 108—1. Washington [55]

§ 109. Executor or administrator

"Personal representatives" means the executor or administrator.[56] The sole right of the personal representatives to maintain the action is not affected by the fact that the deceased was a married woman, and that the husband must

(Civ. App.) 105 S. W. 560; Houston & T. C. R. Co. v. Lemair, 55 Tex. Civ. App. 237, 119 S. W. 1162. An action for negligent death must be prosecuted in the name of all the beneficiaries, or in the name of one or more for the benefit of all. Vernon Cotton Oil Co. · v. Catron (Civ. App.) 137 S. W. 404.

[53] Nelson v. Galveston, H. & S. A. Ry. Co., 78 Tex. 621, 14 S. W. 1021, 11 L. R. A. 391, 22 Am. St. Rep. 81; Galveston, H. & S. A. R. Co. v. Kutac, 72 Tex. 643, 11 S. W. 127.

[54] Winnt v. International & G. N. Ry. Co., 74 Tex. 32, 11 S. W. 907, 5 L. R. A. 172; Gulf, C. & S. F. Ry. Co. v. Compton, 75 Tex. 667, 13 S. W. 667. See, also, Houston & T. C. Ry. Co. v. Cowser, 57 Tex. 306; International & G. N. R. Co. v. Kindred, 57 Tex. 496; Houston & T. C. Ry. Co. v. Baker, 57 Tex. 419. Whether article 2904 is constitutional, so far as it gives such a right of action to parents, quære. Texas & P. Ry. Co. v. Hall, 83 Tex. 675, 19 S. W. 121.

[55] See § 57.

[56] Dennick v. Central R. Co. of New Jersey, 103 U. S. 11, 26 L. Ed. 439. A statute authorizing maintenance of action by the personal representative, recovery to be for the benefit of decedent's widow and children, does not require the appointment of a special administrator to bring the suit, but authorizes suit by the general administrator of the estate. Lake Erie & W. R. Co. v. Charman, 161 Ind. 95, 67 N. E. 923.

have joined had the action been brought by her in her lifetime, as the condition that the act or neglect must be such
that the party injured might have maintained an action was
intended to declare the character of the act or neglect, and
not the person by whom the action could be maintained.[57]
A temporary or special administrator may sue.[58]

§ 110. Foreign administrator

Where the decedent was a resident of another state than
the state in which the injury occurred and in which the action is brought, the question arises whether it can be maintained by an executor or administrator elsewhere appointed.
As a general rule an executor or administrator appointed in
one state may not sue in another, letters testamentary or of
administration having no extraterritorial force, and it being the policy of the law to protect the creditors of the estates of decedents. On the other hand, it is true that the
claim of the personal representative under statutes similar
to Lord Campbell's act is not one for the benefit of the estate, but is for the benefit of the persons designated, among
whom creditors are not included. Nevertheless the rule
which precludes a foreign executor or administrator from
suing has frequently been applied in such cases, where the
foreign representative has not taken out ancillary letters,

[57] Green v. Hudson River R. Co., 31 Barb. (N. Y.) 260, affirming
s. c., 16 How. Prac. (N. Y.) 263 (Lynch v. Davis, 12 How. Prac. (N.
Y.) 323, overruled); Whiton v. Chicago & N. W. R. Co., 21 Wis.
310; Dimmey v. Wheeling & E. G. Ry. Co., 27 W. Va. 32, 55 Am.
Rep. 292; South & N. A. R. Co. v. Sullivan, 59 Ala. 272. See
Long v. Morrison, 14 Ind. 595, 77 Am. Dec. 72.

[58] Louisville & N. R. Co. v. Chaffin, 84 Ga. 519, 11 S. E. 891;
Houston & T. C. Ry. Co. v. Hook, 60 Tex. 403; Swan v. Norvell,
107 Wis. 625, 83 N. W. 934.

and where there is no statute specially authorizing such foreign representatives to sue.[59] The foreign representative may of course be excluded by the act which creates the right of action. Thus, in a recent case in North Carolina, the court dismissed the contention that the foreign administrator could sue because he must hold the proceeds of the recovery for those designated in the statute as beneficiaries of the fund upon the ground that the legislature in providing that the action should be brought by "the executor, administrator or collector of the decedent" clearly contemplated, nothing else appearing, a domestic representative.[60] In many states a more liberal interpretation of the statute has been adopted, and it is held that foreign representatives may sue.[61] In Wisconsin it has been held that the term

[59] Louisville & N. R. Co. v. Brantley's Adm'r, 96 Ky. 297, 28 S. W. 477, 49 Am. St. Rep. 291; Maysville Street Railroad & Transfer Co. v. Marvin, 59 Fed. 91, 8 C. C. A. 21; Brooks v. Southern Pac. Co. (C. C.) 148 Fed. 986. A Georgia statute authorized foreign executors and administrators to sue in cases where the decedent was not a citizen, and died without the state. Held, that an administrator appointed in Alabama could not maintain an action where deceased was killed in Georgia. Southwestern R. Co. v. Paulk, 24 Ga. 356. See Conner's Adm'x v. Paul, 12 Bush (Ky.) 144. Where the remedy is by indictment, it must allege that administration has been taken out in the state. Commonwealth v. Sanford, 12 Gray (Mass.) 174; Commonwealth v. East Boston Ferry Co., 13 Allen (Mass.) 589. An administrator appointed in another state cannot recover in New York for the death of his intestate without taking out ancillary letters; there being no New York statute authorizing foreign administrators as such to sue therein. J. B. & J. M. Cornell Co. v. Ward, 168 Fed. 51, 93 C. C. A. 473. See, also, Dodge v. Town of North Hudson (C. C.) 177 Fed. 986. An ancillary administrator may sue. Lang v. Houston, West St. & P. Ferry R. Co., 75 Hun, 90, 27 N. Y. Supp. 90, affirmed 144 N. Y. 717, 39 N. E. 858.

[60] Hall v. Southern Ry. Co., 146 N. C. 345, 59 S. E. 879. See, also, Hall v. Southern Ry. Co., 149 N. C. 108, 62 S. E. 899.

[61] St. Louis Southwestern Ry. Co. v. Graham, 83 Ark. 61, 102 S. W. 700, 119 Am. St. Rep. 112; Hodges v. Kimball, 91 Fed. 845,

"personal representative" is broad enough to include a foreign administrator.[62]   And upon the broad ground that the
act creates a new cause of action, in the enforcement of
which the executor or administrator is not suing as such
upon a claim of the decedent's estate, but is suing as trustee for the beneficiaries designated, it is held in some states
that the foreign representative may sue.[63]   "The statute,"
said the Indiana court, "was intended to provide a remedy
not only for the citizens of this state, but for the citizens
of other states while passing through or residing within the
state, and * * * such action may be maintained by a
foreign administrator. The fund, when recovered, * * *
is held by the personal representative, whether domestic or
foreign, as the trustee of an express trust. It must inure to
the benefit of the widow and children, if any, and, if not,
then to the next of kin. It would be an unjust reflection

34 C. C. A. 103; Chicago Transit Co. v. Campbell, 110 Ill. App. 366;
Kansas Pac. Ry. Co. v. Cutter, 16 Kan. 568 (but see Limekiller v.
Hannibal & St. J. R. Co., 33 Kan. 83, 5 Pac. 401, 52 Am. Rep. 523;
Hulbert v. City of Topeka [C. C.] 34 Fed. 510).

[62] Robertson v. Chicago, St. P., M. & O. R. Co., 122 Wis. 66, 99 N.
W. 433, 66 L. R. A. 919, 106 Am. St. Rep. 925.

[63] Jeffersonville R. Co. v. Hendricks, 26 Ind. 228, Id., 41 Ind.
48; Memphis & C. Packet Co. v. Pikey, 142 Ind. 304, 40 N. E. 527.
The Illinois statute authorizes foreign administrators to sue to enforce claims of the estate. Held, that a foreign administrator
could maintain an action to recover for the death of his intestate.
The court says that, while it may be that this is not in the strictest
sense a claim of the estate yet, in a broad and general sense, it is a
part of the estate. Wabash, St. L. & P. Ry. Co. v. Shacklett, 10
Ill. App. 404, affirmed 105 Ill. 364, 44 Am. Rep. 791; Union R. &
T. Co. v. Shacklet, 119 Ill. 232, 10 N. E. 896. A foreign administrator, who has brought action in Illinois, is not precluded from
filing a plea to the jurisdiction of the federal court, to which the
action has been removed, by a provision of the Illinois Statute that
no nonresident shall be appointed or act as administrator. Patch
v. Wabash R. Co., 207 U. S. 277, 28 Sup. Ct. 80, 52 L. Ed. 204, 12
Ann. Cas. 518.

upon the courts of Missouri [the state of the administra_
trix's appointment] to say that when money recovered in
such an action as this came into the hands of_the adminis_
tratrix, charged with a trust of the most high and sacred
character, they would not compel distribution as the law
under which it was recovered directs." [64]

The question of the right of a foreign representative to
sue may also be raised in an action under a foreign statute
for a death occurring in another state.[65] In such case it is
generally held that the question as to the proper plaintiff is
to be determined by the statute which creates the right of
action, and not by the lex fori, so that the action must be
brought by the personal representative of the decedent or
by the beneficiaries as the foreign statute may provide.[66]
When the statute provides that the action must be brought
by the personal representative, the same conflict in the decisions is found as in the preceding case. By some courts it
is held that the personal representative who is entitled to
sue is one appointed by authority of the state where the action is brought.[67] Other courts hold, upon the ground

[64] Memphis & C. Packet Co. v. Pikey, supra.

[65] See § 201, post.

[66] See § 201, post.

[67] Leonard v. Columbia Steam Nav. Co., 84 N. Y. 48, 38 Am.
Rep. 491. See, also, Bruce's Adm'r v. Cincinnati R. Co., 83 Ky. 174;
Illinois Cent. R. Co. v. Crudup, 63 Miss. 291. But a foreign administrator, held authorized, upon complying with certain formali-
ties, to sue in Georgia. South Carolina R. Co. v. Nix, 68 Ga. 573;
Central R. Co. v. Swint, 73 Ga. 651. It is not necessary that letters should have been taken out in the state where the death occurred. Gurney v. Grand Trunk Ry. Co., 59 Hun, 625, 13 N. Y.
Supp. 645. Under the New York statute, providing that foreign
corporations may be sued by residents, an action cannot be maintained by a nonresident who has been appointed administrator in
that state. Robinson v. Oceanic Steam Nav. Co., 112 N. Y. 315, 19
N. E. 625, 2 L. R. A. 636.

that the representative sues, not in his capacity as representative of the decedent's estate, but as a statutory trustee for the beneficiaries, that the foreign representative may sue, without taking out ancillary letters.[68] This was held in Pennsylvania in an action by a New Jersey administratrix for a death occurring in that state, notwithstanding a Pennsylvania act (Act of 1832 [P. L. 135]) providing that foreign letters testamentary or of administration should not confer any of the powers or authorities possessed by domestic executors or administrators. "The New Jersey statute," said the court, "confers the right of action in cases of this kind on the personal representative of the deceased. He acts, therefore, not by the authority which the probate court gave when it granted him the power to administer the estate of the deceased, but solely by virtue of the authority

---

[68] Boulden v. Pennsylvania R. Co., 205 Pa. 264, 54 Atl. 906; Connor v. New York, N. H. & H. R. Co., 28 R. I. 560, 68 Atl. 481, 18 L. R. A. (N. S.) 1252, 13 Ann. Cas. 1033. Under Code W. Va. 1906, c. 103, § 6, which provides that an action for death shall be brought by the personal representative, when an administrator has been appointed in another state, where decedent has his domicile, the right of action vests in him, and cannot be defeated by a release executed by an administrator subsequently appointed in West Virginia. Baltimore & O. R. Co. v. Evans, 188 Fed. 6, 110 C. C. A. 156. Under Rev. St. Ohio, § 6133, which authorizes an executor or administrator duly appointed in another state to maintain an action in the courts of Ohio in his official capacity, "in like manner and under like restrictions as a nonresident may be permitted to sue," and section 6134a, which provides that a right of action for death accruing under the laws of another state may be enforced in Ohio "in all cases where such other state * * * allows the enforcement in its courts of the statute of this state of like character," an administrator appointed in Indiana, where his decedent was killed, and who is given by the Indiana statute a right of action for the death in his official capacity, may maintain an action thereon in Ohio. Cincinnati, H. & D. R. Co. v. Thiebaud, 114 Fed. 918, 52 C. C. A. 538. See, also, Popp v. Cincinnati, H. & D. Ry. Co. (C. C.) 96 Fed. 465.

vested in him by the statute. It designated the personal representative of the deceased, whoever he might be, as the party to enforce the right of action given by the statute. In bringing this suit, therefore, the plaintiff does so, not as the personal representative of her deceased husband, and by virtue of the authority conferred upon her as such, but as the representative or trustee of the parties for whose benefit the action was instituted, and by the authority con_ ferred upon her by the statute. The right of action might have been conferred upon the beneficiaries themselves, or upon any private person or public official; and, if it had been, it is too clear for argument that there could be no question of the right of the person or official thus desig_ nated to maintain the action. The fact that the legisla-ture of New Jersey saw proper to invest the right to bring the action in the person acting as the personal represen-tative of the deceased, instead of conferring the authority upon some other person or official, does not make the per-son the representative of the deceased in prosecuting the case, and therefore bring him within the prohibition of the act of 1832." [69] Some courts have gone so far as to hold that the plaintiff must be the executor or administrator ap-pointed in the foreign state where the cause of action arose, upon the ground that the statute which creates the right confers the right of action upon him and upon him only.[70] It is generally held, however, that an administrator ap-pointed in the state where the action is brought is a proper plaintiff.[71]

[69] Boulden v. Pennsylvania R. Co., supra.

[70] Sanbo v. Union Pac. Coal Co. (C. C.) 130 Fed. 52. See, also, Connor v. New York, N. H. & H. R. Co., supra.

[71] Dennick v. Central R. Co. of New Jersey, 103 U. S. 11, 26 L. Ed. 439; Morris v. Chicago, R. I. & P. R. Co., 65 Iowa, 727, 23 N. W. 143, 54 Am. Rep. 39; Missouri Pac. Ry. Co. v. Lewis, 24 Neb.

§ 111. Appointment of administrator

When the jurisdiction of the probate court to appoint an administrator depends upon the existence of assets of the deceased to be administered, the question arises whether a claim for damages for his death constitutes such assets. Such a claim, although enforceable by the administrator, belongs in fact to the persons for whose benefit the right of action is given, and who do not include creditors of the estate; and, if the statutes which confer jurisdiction upon this ground are literally followed, jurisdiction in such cases cannot be obtained. This view has been taken in some states;[72] but it is generally held that the fact that this

848, 40 N. W. 401, 2 L. R. A. 67; Utah Savings & Trust Co. v. Diamond Coal & Coke Co., 26 Utah, 299, 73 Pac. 524; In re Lowham's Estate, 30 Utah, 436, 85 Pac. 445.

[72] Perry v. St. Joseph & W. R. Co., 29 Kan. 420. The Kansas statute provided that, upon the death of an inhabitant of the state, letters might be granted by the probate court of the county in which he was an inhabitant; and that, when any person should die intestate in any other state, leaving any estate to be administered in Kansas, administration might be granted in any county in which there was an estate to be administered. Whether the jurisdiction would depend on the existence of assets in the case of an inhabitant of the state, quære. Union Pac. Ry. Co. v. Dunden, 37 Kan. 1, 14 Pac. 501. By the Iowa statute, the court had authority to grant administration when deceased was an inhabitant of the county, or left property. Letters were issued by the clerk of the Iowa probate court upon the estate of a resident of Illinois, who had no property in Iowa. In a suit by the Iowa administrator in Illinois, where deceased was killed, held, that the action could not be maintained. The court says that the act of the clerk being ministerial, and not judicial, his authority was open to collateral attack. Illinois Cent. R. Co. v. Cragin, 71 Ill. 177; Marvin v. Maysville St. Railroad & Transfer Co. (C. C.) 49 Fed. 436. It is irrelevant to inquire as to assets where the jurisdictional fact recited is not bona notabilia, but residence in the county. Louisville & N. R. Co. v. Chaffin, 84 Ga. 519, 11 S. E. 891. Letters granted to an adminis-

right of action is given to the personal representative implies the right to appoint, if necessary, an administrator to enforce it, whether in the case of death occurring in the state where the appointment is made [73] or for the purpose of bringing an action for a death which occurred in another state.[74]

trator in another jurisdiction, without proof of any assets appearing in such jurisdiction, cannot defeat the right of an administrator appointed in New Jersey to recover in an action for death within that state. Pisano v. B. M. & J. F. Shanley Co., 66 N. J. Law, 1, 48 Atl. 618.

[73] Toledo, St. L. & K. C. R. Co. v. Reeves, 8 Ind. App. 667, 35 N. E. 199 (cf. Jeffersonville R. Co. v. Swayne's Adm'r, 26 Ind. 477); Brown's Adm'r v. Louisville & N. R. Co., 97 Ky. 228, 30 S. W. 639; Findlay v. Chicago & G. T. Ry. Co., 106 Mich. 700, 64 N. W. 732; Hutchins v. St. Paul, M. & M. Ry. Co., 44 Minn. 5, 46 N. W. 79; Missouri Pac. R. Co. v. Bradley, 51 Neb. 596, 71 N. W. 283; Mayo's Estate, In re, 60 S. C. 401, 38 S. E. 634, 54 L. R. A. 660; In re Lowham's Estate, 30 Utah, 436, 85 Pac. 445. See, also, Boston & M. R. R. v. Hurd, 108 Fed. 116, 47 C. C. A. 615, 56 L. R. A. 193. Where a nonresident suffers wrongful death in New York, the right of action for his death constitutes sufficient assets to entitle his domiciliary administrator to ancillary letters of administration in New York for the prosecution of such action. Dodge v. Town of North Hudson (C. C.) 177 Fed. 986. Decedent was killed in New Jersey, of which state she and her husband were residents, leaving money in a savings bank in New York deposited in the name of decedent and her husband, or either. The husband, instead of withdrawing all the money as he was entitled to do, withdrew half the principal and gave the bank book to a corporation as security for becoming surety on the bond of decedent's father, a resident of New York, as administrator. The next day the administrator commenced in New York an action for the death against defendant, a New Jersey corporation. Held to show a collusive effort to get the action into the New York courts, and to justify a refusal to entertain jurisdiction. Pietraroia v. New Jersey & H. R. Ry. & Ferry Co., 197 N. Y. 434, 91 N. E. 120. See, also, Hoes v. New York & N. H. & H. R. Co., 173 N. Y. 435, 66 N. E. 119.

[74] An administrator may be appointed in Iowa for the purpose of bringing an action to recover for the death of his decedent, which occurred in Illinois, although decedent left no property in Iowa.

In an action by the administrator for the death of his intestate his authority to sue cannot be questioned for mere
irregularity in his appointment.[75] Whether it can be questioned in such collateral proceeding on the ground that, by
reason of the nonexistence of assets, the probate court had
no jurisdiction to make the appointment, is a point which
has frequently been raised in cases in which the court did
not deem it necessary to pass upon it.[76] In a Kansas case
it has been decided that such a defense may be raised, upon
the ground that the appointment, being made without jurisdiction, is void for all purposes.[77] An opposite conclusion
was reached in a case in the United States district court for
Oregon, which decides that when the jurisdiction depends

Morris v. Chicago, R. I. & P. R. Co., 65 Iowa, 727, 23 N. W. 143,
54 Am. Rep. 39; Missouri Pac. Ry. Co. v. Lewis, 24 Neb. 848, 40
N. W. 401, 2 L. R. A. 67. Where a person was killed in Connecticut, held, that an administrator appointed in Maine, where intestate was domiciled, was entitled to an ancillary administration
in the former state, for the purpose of prosecuting the suit, and
that it was enough if the probate court was satisfied that there was
an apparent claim, and a bona fide intention to prosecute it. Hartford & N. H. R. Co. v. Andrews, 36 Conn. 213. See, also, Southern
Pac. Co. v. De Valleda Costa, 190 Fed. 689, 111 C. C. A. 417.

[75] The omission of the surrogate to require the administrator to
file a bond cannot be taken advantage of by the defendant. Sullivan v. Tioga R. Co., 44 Hun, 304; Id., 12 Civ. Proc. R. 301. Nor
irregular service of notice where the court had obtained jurisdiction. Chilton v. Union Pac. Ry. Co., 8 Utah, 47, 29 Pac. 963.

[76] Jeffersonville R. Co. v. Swayne's Adm'r, supra; Illinois Cent.
R. Co. v. Cragin, supra; Hutchins v. St. Paul, M. & M. Ry. Co.,
supra; Missouri Pac. Ry. Co. v. Lewis, supra; Louisville & N. R.
Co. v. Chaffin, supra. See In re Hardy, 35 Minn. 193, 28 N. W. 219;
Denver, S. P. & P. Ry. Co. v. Woodward, 4 Colo. 1.

[77] Perry v. St. Joseph & W. R. Co., 29 Kan. 420. In Union Pac.
Ry. Co. v. Dunden, 37 Kan. 1, 14 Pac. 501, the issue was raised and
evidence was introduced tending to show that the decedent left no
estate; but it was held that the evidence was not conclusive as
against the records and findings of the probate court, which made
a prima facie case, showing that decedent left "an estate of per-

upon the residence of the deceased in the county, and the decree expressly finds such residence, the decree cannot be attached on the ground of non-residence.[78] In Indiana it has been held that a railroad company against whom an ac_ tion is being prosecuted by the administrator has such an interest in his appointment as to enable it to maintain a petition to the probate court for a revocation of the letters, upon the ground that the decedent left no assets.[79] A per_ son against whom an administrator is entitled to bring suit for the killing of his intestate cannot appeal from the order appointing such administrator, under a provision that an appeal "can be taken by a party aggrieved."[80]

sonal articles," and that the jury had a right to pass upon the weight of the evidence. In Jacobs' Adm'r v. Louisville & N. R. Co., 10 Bush (Ky.) 263, plaintiff introduced in evidence the order appointing him, which did not set out the facts giving jurisdiction. Held, that the order was prima facie evidence, and that the burden of proving that there was no jurisdiction was on defendant, who raised the issue.

[78] Holmes v. Oregon & C. Ry. Co. (C. C.) 5 Fed. 523. Deceased, a child, was killed on his arrival in New York, where his father had lived for seven months. In an action by the father, who was appointed administrator in New York, held, that the evidence was sufficient to show prima facie that the deceased was domiciled there, and that, assuming that the point could be raised collaterally, the letters were properly issued. Kennedy v. Ryall, 67 N. Y. 379. See, also, Chicago, B. & Q. R. Co. v. Gould, 64 Iowa, 343, 20 N. W. 464; Missouri Pac. Ry. Co. v. Bradley, 51 Neb. 596, 71 N. W. 283.

[79] Jeffersonville R. Co. v. Swayne's Adm'r, 26 Ind. 477. Elliott, J., says that, the letters being void, a recovery would be no bar to a subsequent suit by the legal administrator, and that hence the company is interested in revoking the appointment. A similar petition was brought in Wheeler v. St. Joseph & W. Ry. Co., 31 Kan. 640, 3 Pac. 297, but it appeared that the deceased left sufficient estate, and the right of the company to maintain such a petition was not determined.

[80] In re Hardy, 35 Minn. 193, 28 N. W. 219.

§ 112. Widow

The right of a widow to sue, when the statute gives her the right, vests in her at the death of the husband, and is not divested by her subsequent marriage.[81] She is not prevented from maintaining the action by the fact that she had been living in separation from him.[82] She may recover, although she was married to the decedent after he received the injury causing his death.[83]

§ 113. Parents

In some states a right of action is given to the father or mother for the death of a child.[84] Under some statutes, as in Missouri,[85] adopted children are expressly included. Whether parents may recover for the death of an adopted child, where adopted children are not expressly included, is not clear.[86] Under the New Jersey death act, providing

---

[81] Georgia, R. & Banking Co. v. Garr, 57 Ga. 277, 24 Am. Rep. 492; International & G. N. Ry. Co. v. Kuehn, 70 Tex. 582, 8 S. W. 484; Crockett (late Buell) v. St. Louis Transfer Co., 52 Mo. 457 (affirming Buel v. Same, 45 Mo. 562). See § 176. In an action by an administrator to recover damages resulting to a wife from the death of her husband, the fact that she has subsequently remarried is immaterial. Chicago, St. P., M. & O. Ry. Co. v. Lagerkrans, 65 Neb. 566, 91 N. W. 358, 95 N. W. 2.

[82] Dallas & W. Ry. Co. v. Spicker, 61 Tex. 427, 48 Am. Rep. 297; Galveston, H. & S. A. Ry. Co. v. Murray (Tex. Civ. App.) 99 S. W. 144. Cf. Ft. Worth & D. C. R. Co. v. Floyd (Tex. Civ. App.) 21 S. W. 544. See, also, Abel v. Northampton Traction Co., 212 Pa. 329, 61 Atl. 915.

[83] Gross v. Electric Traction Co., 180 Pa. 99, 36 Atl. 424.

[84] See § 128.

[85] See § 103.

[86] See Citizens' St. R. Co. v. Willoeby, 15 Ind. App. 312, 43 N. E. 1058; Citizens' St. R. Co. v. Cooper, 22 Ind. App. 459, 53 N. E.

that the amount recovered shall be for the exclusive benefit of the widow and next of kin and shall be distributed in the proportions provided in relation to the personal property of intestates, it is held that the next of kin are those by blood, and that the act concerning the adoption of infants does not impress upon the term a different meaning so as to include the adopting parents.[87]

§ 114. Heirs [88]

§ 115. Guardian

Under the Indiana statute it has been held that the right of action of the guardian is limited to the recovery of damages to reimburse the estate of the ward for any actual loss.[89]

§ 116. Right to sue confined to statutory plaintiffs

The action is maintainable only by the person who is by the terms of the statute authorized to maintain it.[90] If

1092, 72 Am. St. Rep. 319. It seems that a stepfather may not maintain an action for the death of a stepchild. Thornburg v. American Strawboard Co., 141 Ind. 443, 40 N. E. 1062, 50 Am. St. Rep. 334.

[87] Heidecamp v. Jersey City, H. & P. St. Ry. Co., 69 N. J. Law, 284, 55 Atl. 239, 101 Am. St. Rep. 707.

[88] See §§ 41, 93.

[89] Louisville, N. A. & C. Ry. Co. v. Goodykoontz, 119 Ind. 111, 21 N. E. 472, 12 Am. St. Rep. 371. See § 39. The right to sue for the death of a ward is expressly given in a number of states.

[90] Salmon v. Rathjens, 152 Cal. 290, 92 Pac. 733; Kennedy v. Delaware Cotton Co., 4 Pennewill (Del.) 477, 58 Atl. 825; Louisville & N. R. Co. v. Jones, 45 Fla. 407, 34 South. 246; City of Eureka v. Merrifield, 53 Kan. 794, 37 Pac. 113; Clark v. Kansas City, St. L. & C. R. Co., 219 Mo. 524, 118 S. W. 40; Harshman v. North-

that person is the executor or administrator, the action cannot be brought by the beneficiaries; [91] and conversely, if the persons entitled to sue are those who are entitled to the benefit of the action, it cannot be maintained by the executor or administrator. [92]

§ 117. Joinder of parties

Whether it is necessary, under statutes providing that the action shall be brought directly by the persons in interest, to join all such persons, depends upon the requirements of the particular enactment. [93]

ern Pac. R. Co., 14 N. D. 69, 103 N. W. 412; Haughey v. Pittsburg Rys. Co., 210 Pa. 367, 59 Atl. 1112; Vaughn v. Bunker Hill & Sullivan Mining & Concentrating Co. (C. C.) 126 Fed. 895; Choctaw, O. & G. R. Co. v. Jackson (C. C.) 182 Fed. 342.

[91] Davis v. St. Louis, I. M. & S. Ry. Co., 53 Ark. 117, 13 S. W. 801, 7 L. R. A. 283; Kramer v. San Francisco Market St. R. Co., 25 Cal. 434; Covington St. Ry. Co. v. Packer, 9 Bush (Ky.) 455, 15 Am. Rep. 725; City of Chicago v. Major, 18 Ill. 349, 68 Am. Dec. 553; Hagen v. Kean, 3 Dill. 124, Fed. Cas. No. 5,899; Peru & I. R. Co. v. Bradshaw, 6 Ind. 146; Nash v. Tousley, 28 Minn. 5, 8 N. W. 875; Scheffler v. Minneapolis & St. L. Ry. Co., 32 Minn. 125, 19 N. W. 656; Wilson v. Bumstead, 12 Neb. 1, 10 N. W. 411; Worley v. Cincinnati, H. & D. R. Co., 1 Handy (Ohio) 481; Weidner v. Rankin, 26 Ohio St. 522; Goodwin v. Nickerson, 17 R. I. 478, 23 Atl. 12; Edgar v. Castello, 14 S. C. 20, 37 Am. Rep. 714; United States Electric Lighting Co. v. Sullivan, 22 App. D. C. 115; Baltimore & O. S. W. R. Co. v. Gillard, 34 Ind. App. 339, 71 N. E. 58; Major v. Burlington C. R. & N. Ry. Co., 115 Iowa, 309, 88 N. W. 815; Fitzhenry v. Consolidated Traction Co., 63 N. J. Law, 142, 42 Atl. 416; Sorenson v. Balaban, 11 App. Div. 164, 42 N. Y. S. 654; Howell v. Board of Com'rs of Yancey County, 121 N. C. 362, 28 S. E. 362; Killian v. Southern Ry. Co., 128 N. C. 261, 38 S. E. 873; Shaw v. City of Charleston, 57 W. Va. 433, 50 S. E. 527, 4 Ann. Cas. 515.

[92] Miller v. Southwestern R. Co., 55 Ga. 143; Gibbs v. City of Hannibal, 82 Mo. 143.

[93] See §§ 93, 100, 105, 107, 108.

§ 118. Who may be sued

The action being maintainable, according to the terms of most of the statutes, whenever the act or neglect causing death was such that the party injured might have maintained an action, the question who may be sued will in general depend in each case upon precisely the same considerations that would govern in an action for personal injury.[94] It has been held that the action could be maintained against the trustee or receiver of a corporation,[95] against the master of a vessel,[96] against the state,[97] and against a municipali-

[94] The legal representative of a prisoner who was murdered by a mob may maintain an action on the bond of the sheriff, in whose custody the deceased was at the time, for a failure of the sheriff to perform his official duty in protecting his prisoner, since deceased might have maintained an action had he lived. State of Indiana v. Gobin (C. C.) 94 Fed. 48.

[95] Texas & P. R. Co. v. Cox, 145 U. S. 593, 12 Sup. Ct. 905, 36 L. Ed. 829; Lamphear v. Buckingham, 33 Conn. 237; Meara's Adm'r v. Holbrook, 20 Ohio St. 137, 5 Am. Rep. 633; Little v. Dusenberry, 46 N. J. Law, 614, 50 Am. Rep. 445; McNulta v. Lockridge, 137 Ill. 270, 27 N. E. 452, 31 Am. St. Rep. 362. See Cardot v. Barney, 63 N. Y. 281, 20 Am. Rep. 533. Contra: Parker v. Dupree, 28 Tex. Civ. App. 341, 67 S. W. 185. In State v. Consolidated E. & N. A. Ry. Co., 67 Me. 479, it was held that a railroad corporation was not liable to indictment under the act, if it were in exclusive possession and control. See ante, § 55.

[96] Kennedy v. Ryall, 67 N. Y. 379; Ryall v. Kennedy, 40 N. Y. Super. Ct. 347.

[97] The fact that the statute giving a right of action for death omits to include actions against the state does not affect the right of an administratrix to proceed before the board of claims to recover damages for the drowning of her husband in the canal; the state assuming, under Laws 1870, c. 321, the same measure of liability incurred by individuals and corporations engaged in similar enterprises. Bowen v. State, 108 N. Y. 166, 15 N. E. 56; Splittorf v. State, 108 N. Y. 205, 15 N. E. 322. See Cannon v. Rowland, 34 Ga. 422.

ty,[98] and that it could not be maintained against a lessor.[99] Many of the statutes, in express terms, declare that corporations shall be liable; but, whether they are so included or not, the action is maintainable against them as much as against individuals.[100] Under a Minnesota statute, making vessels liable for all injuries done by them to persons or property, it has been held that an action is maintainable against a steamboat by the administrator of a person who was run down by the vessel and killed.[101] Joint tort-feasors may be joined as defendants.[102]

[98] City of Anniston v. Ivey, 151 Ala. 392, 44 South. 48; Merkle v. Bennington Tp., 58 Mich. 41, 24 N. W. 776, 55 Am. Rep. 666; Keever v. City of Mankato, 113 Minn. 55, 129 N. W. 158, 33 L. R. A. (N. S.) 339, Ann. Cas. 1912A, 216; Davis v. Town of Rumney, 66 N. H. 331, 29 Atl. 542; Murphy v. Board of Chosen Freeholders of Mercer County, 57 N. J. Law, 245, 31 Atl. 229; Rahe v. Cuyahoga County Com'rs, 26 Ohio Cir. Ct. R. 489. Cf. Hughes v. City of Auburn, 161 N. Y. 96, 55 N. E. 389, 46 L. R. A. 636. Contra: Ritz v. City of Austin, 1 Tex. Civ. App. 455, 20 S. W. 1029; Searight v. City of Austin (Tex. Civ. App.) 42 S. W. 857. See ante, § 77.

[99] Blackwell v. Wiswall, 14 How. Prac. 257; s. c., 24 Barb. 355; Norton v. Wiswall, 26 Barb. 618. But in Palmer v. Utah & N. Ry. Co., 2 Idaho (Hasb.) 382, 16 Pac. 553, it was held that a railroad company cannot avoid its liability by showing that its road and trains were operated by another company, without showing the consent of the power whence it obtained its franchise.

[100] Southwestern R. Co. v. Paulk, 24 Ga. 356; Chase v. American Steamboat Co., 10 R. I. 79; Donaldson v. Mississippi & M. R. Co., 18 Iowa, 280, 87 Am. Dec. 391; Fleming v. Texas Loan Agency, 87 Tex. 238, 27 S. W. 126, 26 L. R. A. 250; Lynch v. Southwestern Tel. & T. Co. (Tex. Civ. App.) 32 S. W. 776.

[101] Boutiller v. The Milwaukee, 8 Minn. 97 (Gil. 72).

[102] Oulighan v. Butler, 189 Mass. 287, 75 N. E. 726; Packard v. Hannibal & St. J. R. Co., 181 Mo. 421, 80 S. W. 951, 103 Am. St. Rep. 607; Mangan v. Hudson River Telephone Co., 50 Misc. Rep. 388, 100 N. Y. Supp. 539; Walton, Witten & Graham v. Miller's Adm'x, 109 Va. 210, 63 S. E. 458, 132 Am. St. Rep. 908.

§ 119.   Abatement on death of wrongdoer

The statutes which create a cause of action, with one or
two exceptions, do not undertake, either expressly or impliedly, to change the common-law rule which precludes
the maintenance of personal actions against the representatives of the wrongdoer. Accordingly, where the statute
makes no such exception, the right of action abates upon
the death of the offending party.[103] A different view was,
indeed, taken in the early New York case of Yertore v.
Wiswall's Ex'rs,[104] in which it was held that the right of
action survived by force of the statute of that state providing that actions for "wrongs done to the property rights or
interests of another" might be maintained against the executor or administrator. But this case was overruled in
Hegerich v. Keddie,[105] which holds that the "property

[103] Green v. Thompson, 26 Minn. 500, 5 N. W. 376; Hamilton v.
Jones, 125 Ind. 176, 25 N. E. 192 (cf. Pennsylvania Co. v. Davis, 4
Ind. App. 51, 29 N. E. 425); Johnson v. Farmer, 89 Tex. 610, 35 S.
W. 1062; Beavers' Adm'x v. Putnam's Curator, 110 Va. 713, 67 S.
E. 353.

[104] 16 How. Prac. 8. See, also, Doedt v. Wiswall, 15 How. Prac.
128, which held that an action might be maintained against the representatives of the wrongdoer, if the complaint stated facts constituting a cause of action founded on contract. The earliest New York
case was in accord with the later authorities. Norton v. Wiswall,
14 How. Prac. 42.

[105] 99 N. Y. 258, 1 N. E. 787, 52 Am. Rep. 25 (overruling s. c., 32
Hun, 141); Moriorty v. Bartlett, 99 N. Y. 651, 1 N. E. 794. Code
Civil Proc. § 764, provides that after verdict, report, or decision, in
an action for a personal injury, the action does not abate by the
death of a party. Held that, on the death of the defendant, the
plaintiff failing to show a verdict, etc., in her favor, the cause of
action abated under the decision in Hegerich v. Keddie. Pessini v.
Wilkins, 54 N. Y. Super. Ct. 146. Cf. Meekin v. Brooklyn Heights

rights or interests" referred to are those of. the deceased, and that the statute simply provides for the survival, in case of the death of either party, of causes of action which had previously accrued to the testator or intestate. The same conclusion was reached in Arkansas;[106] in Missouri,[107] under a substantially similar enactment; in Ohio,[108] where the statute provided for the survival of actions for injuries to the estate, real and personal; and in Pennsylvania,[109] where the statute provided that executors and administrators might prosecute and should be liable to be sued in "all personal actions which the decedent might have commenced, * * * except * * * actions for wrong done to the person." In the latter state it is held that a constitutional provision that the right of action for injuries resulting in death shall survive does not mean that it shall survive after the death of the wrongdoer.[110] On the other hand, in Illinois, where a statute provides "that actions to recover damages for an injury to the person" shall survive, it is held that an action for death may be maintained against the legal representative of the wrongdoer.[111] And so in Kentucky, under a statute providing that no right of action for personal injury, or injury to the real or personal estate, shall cease or die with the person injuring or injured, except actions for assault.[112]

R. Co., 164 N. Y. 145, 58 N. E. 50, 51 L. R. A. 235, 79 Am. St. Rep. 635. See § 87, ante.

[106] Davis v. Nichols, 54 Ark. 358, 15 S. W. 880.

[107] Bates v. Sylvester, 205 Mo. 493, 104 S. W. 73, 11 L. R. A. (N. S.) 1157, 120 Am. St. Rep. 761.

[108] Russell v. Sunbury, 37 Ohio St. 372, 41 Am. Rep. 523.

[109] Moe v. Smiley, 125 Pa. 136, 17 Atl. 228, 3 L. R. A. 341.

[110] Moe v. Smiley, supra.

[111] Devine v. Healy, 241 Ill. 34, 89 N. E. 251.

[112] Morehead's Adm'x v. Bittner, 106 Ky. 523, 50 S. W. 857, 20 Ky. Law Rep. 1986; Merrill v. Puckett's Curator (Ky.) 93 S. W. 912.

CHAPTER VII

STATUTES OF LIMITATION.

§ 120.　Limitation of time for commencing action

Lord Campbell's act contains a proviso that "every such action must be commenced within twelve calendar months after the death of such deceased person," and a similar provision is contained in a majority of the statutes, some limiting the time to one year and some to a longer period. Other statutes provide that the action must be commenced "within one year," or "within two years," or within a certain period after it accrues. Still other statutes limit the time from the act or neglect or from the injury. A few statutes [1] contain no special limitation, and leave the period to be determined by the general provisions regulating the limitation of actions so far as they may be applicable. The existence of the right of action cannot be made to depend, by analogy to the common-law rule in cases of murder, upon the dying of the injured person within a year and a day from the date of the injury.[2]

---

[1] See O'Kief v. Memphis & C. R. Co., 99 Ala. 524, 12 South. 454; Frazier v. Georgia Railroad & Banking Co., 101 Ga. 70, 28 S. E. 684; Atlantic, V. & W. R. Co. v. McDilda, 125 Ga. 468, 54 S. E. 140, 114 Am. St. Rep. 240; Robinson v. Baltimore & S. Mining & Reduction Co., 26 Wash. 484, 67 Pac. 274.

[2] Louisville, E. & St. L. R. Co. v. Clarke, 152 U. S. 230, 14 Sup. Ct.

§ 121.   Nature of limitation

These special limitations differ in some respects from those created by the ordinary statutes of limitation. Inasmuch as the act which creates the limitation also creates the action to which it applies, the limitation is not merely of the remedy, but is of the right of action itself.[3] The right is given subject to the limitation, and a subsequent change in the period of limitation will not extend the period so as to affect an existing right of action.[4] If the right is

579, 38 L. Ed. 422; Schlichting v. Wintgen, 25 Hun (N. Y.) 626; Purcell v. Laurer, 14 App. Div. 33, 43 N. Y. Supp. 988.

[3] Louisville & N. R. Co. v. Chamblee, 171 Ala. 188, 54 South. 681; Goodwin v. Bodcaw Lumber Co., 109 La. 1050, 34 South. 74; Poff v. New England Telephone & Telegraph Co., 72 N. H. 164, 55 Atl. 891; Gulledge v. Seaboard Air Line Ry. Co., 147 N. C. 234, 60 S. E. 1134, 125 Am. St. Rep. 544; Lambert v. Ensign Mfg. Co., 42 W. Va. 813, 26 S. E. 431. The declaration alleged the time of the death, which was within two years before the commencement of the action, without specifically alleging that it was within the two years. Held, that after verdict the declaration was good. Poland, C. J., says that the provision is not like an ordinary statute of limitation, which must be specially pleaded, but is an absolute bar, not removable by any of the ordinary exceptions or answers to the statute of limitations. Hill v. Town of New Haven, 37 Vt. 501, 88 Am. Dec. 613. The summons and complaint showed that the action was not brought within the year, and the defendant answered the statute of limitation. Held, that judgment should be ordered for defendant on the pleadings. The court says: "This is not strictly a statute of limitation. It gives a right of action that would not otherwise exist. * * * It must be accepted in all respects as the statute gives it. Why the action was not brought within the time does not appear, but any explanation in that respect would be unavailing; as there is no saving clause as to the time within which the action must be begun." Taylor v. Cranberry Iron & Coal Co., 94 N. C. 525. Approved in Best v. Town of Kinston, 106 N. C. 205, 10 S. E. 997.

[4] Pittsburg, C. & St. L. Ry. Co. v. Hine, 25 Ohio St. 629; Benjamin v. Eldridge, 50 Cal. 612. See Commonwealth v. Boston & W. R.

enforceable in another jurisdiction than that of the courts of the state which enacted the statute, the right will be en- forced subject to the limitation.[5] The statute of limitation need not be pleaded in defense, and, if the declaration shows that the action was not brought within the time lim-

Corp., 11 Cush. (Mass.) 512; Commonwealth v. East Boston Ferry, 13 Allen (Mass.) 589. See, also, O'Donnell v. Healy, 134 Ill. App. 187; Gruber v. La Salle County Carbon Coal Co., 150 Ill. App. 427; Bret- thauer v. Jacobson, 79 N. J. Law, 223, 75 Atl. 560.

[5] Boyd v. Clark (C. C.) 8 Fed. 849; Swanson v. Atlantic, Gulf & Pacific Co. (D. C.) 156 Fed. 977; Earnest v. St. Louis, M. & S. E. R. Co., 87 Ark. 65, 112 S. W. 141; Johnson v. Phœnix Bridge Co., 197 N. Y. 316, 90 N. E. 953; Cavanagh v. Ocean Steam Nav. Co. (Sup.) 13 N. Y. Supp. 540; Dowell v. Cox, 108 Va. 460, 62 S. E. 272. See, also, Stern v. La Compagnie Generale Transatlantique (D. C.) 110 Fed. 996; International Nav. Co. v. Lindstrom, 123 Fed. 475, 60 C. C. A. 649; Negaubauer v. Great Northern Ry. Co., 92 Minn. 184, 99 N. W. 620, 104 Am. St. Rep. 674, 2 Ann. Cas. 150; Dailey v. New York, O. & W. Ry. Co., 26 Misc. Rep. 539, 57 N. Y. Supp. 485; Dennis v. Atlantic Coast Line R. R., 70 S. C. 254, 49 S. E. 869, 106 Am. St. Rep. 746. If no limitation is made by the act which creates the ac- tion, the statute of limitations of the forum governs. Munos v. South- ern Pac. Co., 51 Fed. 188, 2 C. C. A. 163. If a suit in rem can be maintained in admiralty against a vessel for the recovery of dam- ages for the death of a human being, on the high seas, or on waters navigable from the sea, when an action at law is given by statute in the state where the wrong was done or where the vessel belonged, it must be commenced within the time prescribed by the statute. Chief Justice Waite observed: "The statute creates a new legal lia- bility, with the right to a suit for its enforcement, provided the suit is brought within twelve months, and not otherwise. The time within which the suit must be brought operates as a limitation of the lia- bility itself as created, and not of the remedy alone. It is a condi- tion attached to the right to sue at all. * * * If the admiralty adopts the statute as a rule of right to be administered within its own jurisdiction, it must take the right subject to the limitations which have been made a part of its existence. * * * The liability and the remedy are created by the same statutes, and the limita- tions of the remedy are, therefore, to be treated as limitations of the right." The Harrisburg, 119 U. S. 199, 7 Sup. Ct. 140, 30 L. Ed. 358; post, § 204.

ited, it is demurrable.[6] It is said that no exception can be alleged to excuse the delay;[7] but whether the disabilities and exceptions which in general prevent the running of the

[6] Hanna v. Jeffersonville R. Co., 32 Ind. 113. "Ordinarily," says Frazer, C. J., "statutes of limitations must be pleaded, though the facts appear by the averments of the complaint. The reason for this is that usually there are exceptions to the statute of limitations. * * * But in the case before us there are no exceptions." Approved in Jeffersonville, M. & I. R. Co. v. Hendricks, 41 Ind. 48. See, also, Radezky v. Sargent & Co., 77 Conn. 110, 58 Atl. 709; Lapsley v. Public Service Corp. of New Jersey, 75 N. J. Law, 266, 68 Atl. 1113; Dowell v. Cox, 108 Va. 460, 62 S. E. 272; George v. Chicago, M. & St. P. R. Co., 51 Wis. 603, 8 N. W. 374. .Contra: Wall v. Chesapeake & O. Ry. Co., 200 Ill. 66, 65 N. E. 632; Heimberger v. Elliot Frog & Switch Co., 245 Ill. 448, 92 N. E. 297. The petition must clearly show that the action is brought within the time. City of Eureka v. Merrifield, 9 Kan. App. 579, 58 Pac. 243. It is insufficient to lay a time under a videlicet which is necessarily within two years from the beginning of the action. Seitter v. West Jersey & S. R. Co., 79 N. J. Law, 277, 75 Atl. 435. The declaration need not allege that the action was brought within the two years prescribed; it being sufficient, prima facie, if it appears by the writ that the action was commenced within such time. Brothers' Adm'r v. Rutland R. Co., 71 Vt. 48, 42 Atl. 980. The burden of proving that the action was brought within the time was on the plaintiff. Poff v. New England Telephone & Telegraph Co., 72 N. H. 164, 55 Atl. 891. Where the complaint shows that the action was not begun in time, it shows affirmatively that plaintiff had no cause of action. Pernisi v. John Schmalz's Sons, 142 App. Div. 53, 126 N. Y. Supp. 880. See Kirton v. Atlantic Coast Line R. Co., 57 Fla. 79, 87, 49 South. 1024.

[7] Hill v. Town of New Haven, supra; Taylor v. Cranberry, I. & C. Co., supra; Hanna v. Jeffersonville R. Co., supra; George v. Chicago, M. & St. P. R. Co., supra. The provision of Code Civ. Proc. N. Y. § 401, that the time during which defendant is out of the state shall not be deemed part of the time limited for the commencement of actions, does not apply to an action for death under section 1902, for section 414 declares that the provisions of chapter 4 (which contains section 401) shall apply except where a different limitation is expressly prescribed by law. Londriggan v. New York, N. H. & H. R. Co., 5 Civ. Proc. R. 76. See, also, Bonnell v. Jewett, 24 Hun (N. Y.) 524. The limitation of two years is a condition to the right of

statute of limitations are or are not applicable to the special limitation in question will depend upon the language of the provisions creating such exceptions and disabilities.[8] What is to be deemed a commencement of suit must also depend upon the varying provisions of the statutes regulating practice.[9]

action, and is not extended by the pendency and dismissal of the former action, as provided in other cases. Rodman v. Missouri Pac. Ry. Co., 65 Kan. 645, 70 Pac. 642, 59 L. R. A. 704. Ann. Code 1892, § 2746, which contains a saving clause in favor of infants "in any of the personal actions before mentioned," applies only to actions mentioned in that chapter, and therefore an action by an infant for the death of its father, given by section 663, must be brought within one year after the death of the decedent, as required, though the infant at the time is not represented by any guardian, etc. Foster v. Yazoo & M. V. R. Co., 72 Miss. 886, 18 South. 380. See Rutter v. Missouri Pac. Ry. Co., 81 Mo. 169.

[8] See Heimberger v. Elliot Frog & Switch Co., 245 Ill. 448, 92 N. E. 297; Stephan v. Lake Shore & M. S. Ry. Co., 106 Ill. App. 13. The fact that at the time of the death one of the parties entitled to sue does not set the statute of limitations in motion against a posthumous child. Nelson v. Galveston, H. & S. A. Ry Co., 78 Tex. 621, 14 S. W. 1021, 11 L. R. A. 391, 22 Am. St. Rep. 81. But where the children are adults, the statute begins to run against them at once.

[9] Under section 2532 of the Iowa Code providing that "placing the notice in the hands of the sheriff for immediate service * * * shall, so far as the statute of limitations is concerned, be deemed the commencement of the action," the delivery of the notice to the sheriff, and not the filing of the petition, is the commencement of the action. Ewell v. Chicago & N. W. Ry. Co. (C. C.) 29 Fed. 57. The Wisconsin statute provided that "the presentment of any claim, in cases where by law such presentment is required, * * * to the board of audit of the proper town, * * * shall be deemed the commencement of an action within the meaning of any law limiting the time for the commencement of an action thereon." In an action against the town the notice was presented within two years from the death, but the summons was not served until after the two years. Held, that the action was not barred. Parish v. Town of Eden, 62 Wis. 272, 22 N. W. 399.

§ 122.   When the time begins to run

When the time is limited to a certain period "after the death," [10] or after the act or omission,[11] no question can

Paschal v. Owen, 77 Tex. 583, 14 S. W. 203. Gen. St. Ky. c. 71, art. 3, § 3, provided that an action for an injury to the person "shall be commenced within one year next after the cause of action accrues," and chapter 71, art. 4, § 2, provides that "if a person entitled to bring any of the actions mentioned * * * was, at the time the cause of action accrued, an infant, * * * the action may be brought within the like number of years after the removal of such disability." *Held*, that there was but one cause of action, and could be but one recovery for damages for death resulting from personal injury, and that such action must be brought within one year from the time the cause of action accrues; and that the statutory provision on behalf of infants, etc., was operative only where there was no person in esse, as a widow or administrator, who has a right to sue. Louisville & N. R. Co. v. Sanders, 86 Ky. 259, 5 S. W. 563, 9 Ky. Law Rep. 690. In Nelson v. Galveston, H. & S. A. Ry. Co., the court distinguishes this case on the ground that in Kentucky there can be but one action.

[10] See Nestelle v. Northern Pac. R. Co. (C. C.) 56 Fed. 261; O'Donnell v. Healy, 134 Ill. App. 187; Pickens v. Illinois Cent. R. Co., 92 Miss. 210, 45 South. 868. Where, at the time intestate died from an injury, an action brought within two years after the accident was pending for such injuries, an action for death, though not brought within such period, was not barred by limitations under the death act, providing that an action for death may be maintained if brought within twelve months after the death. Altzheimer v. Central R. R. of New Jersey, 75 N. J. Law, 424, 67 Atl. 1051. An action lies within two years after the death of the injured person, though such person had lost his right to sue by limitations before his death. Hoover's Adm'x v. Chesapeake & O. Ry. Co., 46 W. Va. 268, 33 S. E. 224. Revisal 1908, § 59, requires an action for death to be brought within one year after such death. Held that, where an action had been instituted within a year after decedent's death, the requirement was complied with, and the action was subject to section 370, declaring that if an action be commenced within the time pre-

[11] See Rugland v. Anderson, 30 Minn. 386, 15 N. W. 676; Winfree v. Northern Pac. Ry. Co., 173 Fed. 65, 97 C. C. A. 392.

arise as to the time when the statute begins to run. In such case the time is not extended to cover the appointment of an administrator.[12] Such limitations, however, as within a certain period after the cause of action "accrues," or "within two years," must be construed in connection with the other provisions of the particular statute.[13] Thus, under a former Connecticut statute, limiting the time "within one year after the cause of action shall have arisen," it was held that the cause of action did not exist, and that hence the time did not begin to run until after the appointment of an administrator.[14] And in New York, under a statute limiting the time within one year after the cause of action "shall have accrued," the same decision was reached by a

scribed therefor, and plaintiff is nonsuited, he may commence a new trial within a year after such nonsuit. Trull v. Seaboard Air Line Ry. Co., 151 N. C. 545, 66 S. E. 586.

[12] Rugland v. Anderson, supra. Under Code Civ. Proc. N. Y. § 1902, which gives a right of action for death, which must be commenced within two years after the death, the time is not extended to cover the appointment of an administrator. Williams v. Quebec S. S. Co. (D. C.) 126 Fed. 591. (Cf. Crapo v. City of Syracuse, infra.) Under Pub. Acts 1903, p. 114, c. 149 (Id. p. 149, c. 193, § 4), allowing recovery for death and providing that "no action shall be brought upon this statute but within one year from the neglect complained of," an action is barred if commenced more than one year after the death, although it be within one year from the appointment of the administrator who brings the action. Radezky v. Sargent & Co., 77 Conn. 110, 58 Atl. 709.

[13] Under the statute providing that an action for death by the personal representatives must be commenced within two years after the action has accrued, an action brought four years after deceased's death, is barred. Staeffler v. Menasha Wooden Ware Co., 111 Wis. 483, 87 N. W. 480.

[14] Andrews v. Hartford & N. H. R. Co., 34 Conn. 57. The Connecticut statute has been changed. Radezky v. Sargent & Co., supra. And, under the Iowa Code providing that such actions should be barred two years "after their causes accrue," a similar construction was approved. Sherman v. Western Stage Co., 24 Iowa, 515. The Iowa statute has been changed, infra.

divided court.[15] In this case it was held that where an administrator brings an action for death, under Code Civ. Proc. § 1902, which requires the action to be brought within two years after the death, it is an action for personal injuries within the meaning of Laws 1886, c. 572, providing that actions for damages for personal injuries, when brought against certain cities, must be commenced *within one year after the cause of action shall have accrued*, and that notice of the intent to bring the action and of the injuries must have been filed within six months *after the accrual of the cause of action;* that the cause of action for death does not accrue until appointment of an executor or administrator; and that where an administratrix was not appointed until sixteen months after the death, the filing of the notice within two months and commencement of the action within five months was a sufficient compliance with the statute. Cullen, C. J., who delivered the majority opinion, observed that such an action must be brought in compliance, not only with the statute of 1886, but with the provisions of the Code, which require an action by personal representatives for death to be brought within two years after the death, as was done in this case, and that this provision of the Code effectually cuts off stale claims. The dissenting opinion is based largely on the contention that the legislature could not have meant that the beneficiaries could thus, by delaying the appointment of an administrator, postpone the time when the action should accrue; but under a statute where only the personal representative may

---

[15] Crapo v. City of Syracuse, 183 N. Y. 395, 76 N. E. 465; Id., 184 N. Y. 561, 76 N. E. 1092. See, also, Barnes v. City of Brooklyn, 22 App. Div. 520, 48 N. Y. Supp. 36; Conway v. City of New York, 139 App. Div. 446, 124 N. Y. Supp. 660; Titman v. City of New York, 57 Hun, 469, 10 N. Y. Supp. 689; 19 Harv. Law Rev. 458. Cf. Williams v. Quebec S. S. Co. (D. C.) 126 Fed. 591.

sue the conclusion seems to follow necessarily that there can be no accrual of the action until his appointment. Different considerations must govern under a statute which limits the time from the accrual of the action, but which gives the right of action to the beneficiaries without the intervention of the personal representative as plaintiff.[16]

In Missouri, where the right of action is given directly to the persons interested, without the intervention of an administrator, under a provision that the action must be commenced within a year "after the cause of action shall accrue," it is held that the time begins to run at the death.[17] In Indiana a proviso that the action must be commenced "within two years" has been held to mean within two years from the death.[18]

In some states there are no limitations applicable solely to this class of actions, and the question has arisen under the general statute of limitations applicable to actions founded on injuries to the person. In Iowa, where the statute provides that "actions founded on injuries to the person" may be brought within two years "after their causes accrue," and the statute giving the action in case of death declares that "such action shall be deemed a continuing

---

[16] Western & A. R. Co. v. Bass, 104 Ga. 390, 30 S. E. 874; Glover v. Savannah, F. & W. Ry. Co., 107 Ga. 34, 32 S. E. 876.

[17] Kennedy v. Burrier, 36 Mo. 128; Jones v. Marble Head Lime Co., 152 Mo. App. 79, 132 S. W. 287.

[18] Hanna v. Jeffersonville R. Co., 32 Ind. 113. The court says that the widow and next of kin, to whom the action accrues, can procure administration when they wish; and that, in a class of actions that usually arise against corporations, whose business is performed by servants who are constantly being changed, the reason for a short period of limitation is imperative. See, also, Elliott v. Brazil Block Coal Co., 25 Ind. App. 592, 58 N. E. 736; Wilson v. Jackson Hill Coal & Coke Co. (Ind. App.) 95 N. E. 589; Louisville, E. & St. L. R. Co. v. Clarke, 152 U. S. 230, 14 Sup. Ct. 579, 38 L. Ed. 422.

one, and to have accrued to such representative or successor at the same time it did to the deceased if he had survived," it is held that the time begins to run from the injury.[19] In Tennessee, also, where the statute of limitations
provides that actions for injuries to the person shall be
brought within one year after the cause of action accrued,
it is held that the action which is given in case of death
accrues at the time of the injury, and is not suspended between the death and the qualification of the administrator.[20] But in Kentucky, under a similar limitation, the
time runs from the death and not from the time the administrator qualifies.[21]

[19] Ewell v. Chicago & N. W. Ry. Co. (C. C.) 29 Fed. 57. Sherman
v. Western Stage Co., supra, was decided before the amendment
declaring that the action shall be deemed to have accrued to the
representative at the same time as to the deceased. See, also, Sherman v. Western Stage Co., 22 Iowa, 556.

[20] Fowlkes v. Nashville & D. R. Co., 5 Baxt. (Tenn.) 663; Id., 9
Heisk. (Tenn.) 829. The question was raised, but not answered, in
Flatley v. Memphis & C. R. Co., 9 Heisk. (Tenn.) 230. See Bledsoe
v. Stokes, 1 Baxt. (Tenn.) 312. Plaintiff's infancy did not prolong the
time for suing, and the death did not stop limitations running, as
plaintiff's action was that of the parents, that had merely survived,
and was not a new cause of action in plaintiff's favor. Whaley v.
Catlett, 103 Tenn. 347, 53 S. W. 131.

[21] Act 1854 (1 Acts 1853–54, p. 175, c. 964) § 4, providing that actions for death shall be commenced within one year from the
time of such death, was not changed by embodying it in St. 1903,
§ 2516, declaring that an action for injury to the person shall be
commenced within one year after the cause of action accrued, under
the rule that, where a law has been settled, a mere change of phraseology in a revision will not be construed to change the law, unless
such phraseology purported to work a change. Louisville & N. R.
Co. v. Simrall's Adm'r, 127 Ky. 55; 104 S. W. 1011, 31 Ky. Law Rep.
1269, 104 S. W. 1199, 32 Ky. Law Rep. 240. See, also, Carden v.
Louisville & N. R. Co., 101 Ky. 113, 39 S. W. 1027, 19 Ky. Law Rep.
132; Chesapeake & O. Ry. Co. v. Kelley's Adm'r, 48 S. W. 993, 20
Ky. Law Rep. 1238; Van Vactor's Adm'x v. Louisville & N. R. Co.,
112 Ky. 445, 66 S. W. 4, 23 Ky. Law Rep. 1743. A cause of action

An amendment may be made after the expiration of the period of limitation, when it does not state a new cause of action.[22] ·

§ 123. Notice of claim and special limitation

Under some statutes it is provided that no action shall be maintained unless written notice, stating the particulars of the injury, be given to the defendant within a certain time.[23] Under most statutes the giving of such notice is a condition precedent of the right of action, and must be alleged in the complaint.[24]

In many states there are statutes which provide that actions for personal injuries shall not be brought against cities, villages, towns, etc., unless notice of the injury be served upon the defendant within a specified time after the injury, which often provide also as a prerequisite to the right of action that it must be begun within a specified time. If the statute which gives a right of action for death

against a railroad company for injuries to a servant, brought by the servant's administrator, accrued on the infliction of the injury, from which time the one-year statute of limitations began to run. Louisville & N. R. Co. v. Simrall's Adm'r, 127 Ky. 55, 104 S. W. 1011, 31 Ky. Law Rep. 1269.

[22] See § 187.

[23] Mitchell v. Colorado Milling & Elevator Co., 12 Colo. App. 277, 55 Pac. 736; Colorado Milling & Elevator Co. v. Mitchell, 26 Colo. 284, 58 Pac. 28. See Philes v. Missouri Pac. Ry. Co., 141 Mo. App. 561, 125 S. W. 553.

[24] Denver & R. G. R. Co. v. Wagner, 167 Fed. 75, 92 C. C. A. 527; Gmaehle v. Rosenberg, 83 App. Div. 339, 82 N. Y. Supp. 366. See, also, Swisher v. Atchison, T. & S. F. R. Co., 76 Kan. 97, 90 Pac.. 812; Gutierrez v. El Paso & N. E. R. Co., 102 Tex. 378, 117 S. W. 426. Gen. St. Conn. 1902, § 1130, which provides that no action shall be maintained against any railroad company for injury or death, unless notice shall have been served on defendant within four months after it was received, or unless the action is commenced within that time,

is merely a survival statute, as is the case in some states, the action may properly be called one for personal injuries, and the statute providing for notice is applicable.[25]   On the other hand, if the statute which gives a right of action for death, like Lord Campbell's act, creates a new cause of action, the action is not strictly one for personal injuries, and it is generally held that the statute providing for notice, and limiting the time within which the action may be brought, is not applicable.[26]   The statutes requiring such notice differ, and different courts have laid weight upon different provisions in reaching the conclusion that they do not apply, as that the notice is to be given by the "person injured," or that the statute makes a different period of limitation than that made by the death act.   In New York it has been held by a divided court that such a statute is applicable.[27]

as construed by the supreme court of the state, imposes a condition subsequent, and not a condition precedent, to the right of action, and plaintiff is not required to plead or prove the giving of notice, but failure to give it is a defense. Spinello v. New York, N. H. & H. R. Co., 183 Fed. 762, 106 C. C. A. 189. Cf. Brown v. New York, N. H. & H. R. Co. (C. C.) 136 Fed. 700. See § 44, ante.

[25] Sachs v. City of Sioux City, 109 Iowa, 224, 80 N. W. 336.

[26] Prouty v. City of Chicago, 250 Ill. 222, 95 N. E. 147; Maylone v. City of St. Paul, 40 Minn. 406, 42 N. W. 88; Orth v. Village of Belgrade, 87 Minn. 237, 91 N. W. 843; Senecal v. City of West St. Paul, 111 Minn. 253, 126 N. W. 826; Clark v. City of Manchester, 62 N. H. 577; Jewett v. Keene, 62 N. H. 701; Brown v. Salt Lake City, 33 Utah, 222, 93 Pac. 570, 14 L. R. A. (N. S.) 619, 126 Am. St. Rep. 828, 14 Ann. Cas. 1004. In Wisconsin the sufficiency of the notice has been considered in several cases, although the applicability of the statute requiring notice appears to be an open question. See Parish v. Town of Eden, 62 Wis. 272, 22 N. W. 399; McKeigue v. City of Janesville, 68 Wis. 50, 31 N. W. 298; Carpenter v. Town of Rolling, 107 Wis. 559, 83 N. W. 953; Hupfer v. National Distilling Co., 119 Wis. 417, 96 N. W. 809.

[27] Crapo v. City of Syracuse, 183 N. Y. 395, 76 N. E. 465; Id., 184 N. Y. 561, 76 N. E. 1092. See, also, cases cited note 15, supra.

CHAPTER VIII

MATTERS OF DEFENSE

§ 124. Release or recovery by party injured

If the deceased, in his lifetime, has done anything that would operate as a bar to a recovery by him of damages for the personal injury, this will operate equally as a bar in an action by his personal representatives for his death. Thus, a release by the party injured of his right of action,[1] or a

---

[1] Perry v. Philadelphia, B. & W. R. Co. (Del. Super.) 77 Atl. 725; Southern Bell Telephone & Telegraph Co. v. Cassin, 111 Ga. 575, 36 S. E. 881, 50 L. R. A. 694; Strode v. St. Louis Transit Co., 197 Mo. 616, 95 S. W. 851, 7 Ann. Cas. 1084; McGahey v. Nassau Electric R. Co., 166 N. Y. 617, 59 N. E. 1126, affirmed 51 App. Div. 281, 64 N. Y. Supp. 965; Solor Refining Co. v. Elliott, 15 Ohio Cir. Ct. R. 581; Hill v. Pennsylvania R. Co., 178 Pa. 223, 35 Atl. 997, 35 L. R. A. 196, 56 Am. St. Rep. 754; Brown v. Chattanooga Electric Ry. Co., 101 Tenn. 252, 47 S. W. 415, 70 Am. St. Rep. 666; Thompson v. Ft. Worth & R. G. Ry. Co., 97 Tex. 590, 80 S. W. 990, 1 Ann. Cas. 231; Blount v. Gulf, C. & S. F. Ry. Co. (Tex. Civ. App.) 82 S. W. 305. See, also, cases stated below. Contra: Donahue v. Drexler, 82 Ky. 157, 56 Am. Rep. 886 (under a highly penal statute). A plea of accord and satisfaction with the deceased in his lifetime is good. Read v. Great Eastern Ry. Co., 9 Best & S. 714, L. R. 3 Q. B. 555, 37 L. J. Q. B. 278, 18 L. T. (N. S.) 822, 16 Wkly. R. 1040. Deceased contracted with his employer, for himself and his representatives, and any person entitled in case of death, not to claim any compensation under the employers' liability act for personal injury, whether resulting

recovery of damages by him for the injury,[2] is a complete defense in the statutory action.

ₗBut, while the courts have agreed in their decisions; they have had difficulty in reconciling them with the express declaration of the statute that the action may be maintained

in death or not. Held, that his widow, suing under Lord Campbell's act, was bound by the contract. Griffiths v. Earl of Dudley, 9 Q. B. D. 357. Defendant steamship company issued to deceased a passenger ticket which contained a condition that the company would not be responsible for any loss or damage arising from the perils of the sea, etc. Held, in an action under Lord Campbell's act, that this condition exempted defendant. Haigh v. Royal Mail S. P. Co., 52 L. J. Q. B. 640, 49 L. T. (N. S.) 802, 5 Asp. M. C. 189 (affirming s. c., 52 L. J. Q. B. 395). Defendant introduced in evidence a receipt, signed by deceased, showing that defendant had settled with deceased in his lifetime, and paid his claim for the injury in full. Held, a bar to the action. Dibble v. New York & E. R. Co., 25 Barb.

---

[2] The answer alleged, and it was admitted on trial, that plaintiff's intestate brought suit against defendant for injuries sustained at the time and place mentioned in the complaint, and recovered judgment, which was paid. Held, that the action was properly dismissed by the court. Littlewood v. Mayor, etc., of City of New York, 89 N. Y. 24, 42 Am. Rep. 271 (this case overrules Schlichting v. Wintgen, 25 Hun [N. Y.] 626); Hecht v. Ohio & M. Ry. Co., 132 Ind. 507, 32 N. E. 302; Whitford v. Panama R. Co., 23 N. Y. 465, opinion of Comstock, C. J. See Barley v. Chicago & A. R. Co., 4 Biss. 430, Fed. Cas. No. 997, in which it was held that the recovery in a former action for medical attendance, expenses, and loss of service to time of death, does not affect the damages. The fact that a suit commenced by deceased was pending at his death is no bar. International & G. N. Ry. Co. v. Kuehn, 70 Tex. 582, 8 S. W. 484; Indianapolis & St. L. R. Co. v. Stout, 53 Ind. 143. Evidence of payment by the defendant of the expenses of support of the party injured and of his funeral expenses, not in satisfaction of the wrong, is inadmissible in bar or in mitigation of damages. Murray v. Usher, 117 N. Y. 542, 23 N. E. 564; Id., 46 Hun (N. Y.) 404. A judgment under St. 1887, c. 270, for personal injuries suffered by an employé, is no bar to a subsequent action, under Pub. St. c. 112, § 212, for death caused by such injuries. Clare v. New York & N. E. R. Co., 172 Mass. 211, 51 N. E. 1083.

whenever the act, neglect, or default is such that the party injured, if death had not ensued, might have maintained an action. The question has sometimes been discussed as if it depended on whether the statutory right of action is a new right of action, or only a continuation of the right of action of the party injured. Thus, in Read v. Great Eastern Ry. Co.,* Blackburn, J., found it necessary to qualify the

(N. Y.) 183. In Littlewood v. Mayor, infra, it is said that this case went before the court of appeals, but that the appeal does not appear ever to have been decided, though several times argued, the court having been divided. 21 How. Prac. (N. Y.) 593; 23 How. Prac. (N. Y.) 599. Deceased was killed while riding on a free pass exempting defendant from liability for the negligence of its agents. Held, in an action under the statute, that a charge that defendant would be liable for gross and culpable negligence, notwithstanding the exemption, was erroneous. Perkins v. New York Cent. R. Co., 24 N. Y. 196, 82 Am. Dec. 281. See Blair v. Erie Ry. Co., 66 N. Y. 313, 23 Am. Rep. 55. In Roesner v. Hermann (C. C.) 10 Biss. 486, 8 Fed. 782, a plea setting up a contract between deceased and his employer, releasing the employer from all liability for injury or death, was held bad, but on the ground that the contract was void. See, also, Rose v. Des Moines V. R. Co., 39 Iowa, 246; Annas v. Milwaukee & N. R. Co., 67 Wis. 46, 30 N. W. 282, 58 Am. Rep. 848. Where deceased, during his lifetime, released the wrongdoer, his administrator cannot maintain the action, unless he shows that the release was procured by fraud or duress. Gen. St. S. C. § 2186, which excludes a right of action in the administrator for a death by wrongful act where deceased, in his lifetime, has recovered a final judgment for the injury, does not imply that the administrator may maintain the action in every other case, but was only intended to prevent a double remedy in any case. Price v. Richmond & D. R. Co., 33 S. C. 556, 12 S. E. 413, 26 Am. St. Rep. 700. Under the Georgia statute giving a right of action in case of homicide, a contract between deceased and his employer, exempting the latter from liability for negligence is a bar in an action by the wife, if the deceased was killed under such circumstances as by his contract would have debarred him, if he had lived, from maintaining an action for personal injury. Western & A. R. Co. v. Strong, 52 Ga. 461; Hendricks v. Western & A. R. Co., 52 Ga. 467.

*Cited in note 1, supra.

declarations of the earlier cases on this point, and observes that "the action is not new in the sense that there is an independent cause of action vested in the representatives of the deceased in their own right." He concludes: "I think it [the statute] meant to say that, if the party injured had not in his lifetime received compensation, the defendant would be liable to an action by the executor or relatives for the loss which they had sustained from his death." And in Griffiths v. Earl of Dudley,[3] Field, J., says: "Read v. Great Eastern Ry. Co. is a clear decision that Lord Campbell's act did not give any new cause of action, but only substituted the right of the representative to sue in the place of the right which the deceased himself would have had if he had survived." In Littlewood v. Mayor, etc., of City of New York,† on the other hand, Rapallo, J., maintains that the statutory right of action is a new right, and not a mere continuation of the right of the deceased. He is of opinion, however, that this is not the point on which the case turns, and that the true question is whether, in enacting the statute, the legislature had in view a case, like that under his consideration, where the deceased, in his lifetime, had recovered damages. "The language of the act," he says, "plainly indicates, I think, that the framers had in view the maxim 'actio personalis,' etc., and that their main purpose was to deprive the wrongdoer of the immunity from civil liability afforded by that rule. * * * The form of expression employed in the act shows that the legislature had in mind the case of a party entitled to maintain an action, but whose right of action was by the rule of the common law extinguished by his death, and not the case of

---

[3] Cited in note 1, supra. See, also, remarks of Olds, J., in Hecht v. Ohio & M. Ry. Co., 132 Ind. 507, 32 N. E. 302.

†Cited in note 2, supra.

one who had maintained his action, or who had recovered damages. This still more strongly appears by reference to the words of the act which describe the wrongdoer against whom a right of action is given. He is not described in any language which is applicable to a party against whom judgment has been obtained by the deceased for the injury, but as 'the person who would have been liable if death had not ensued.' And the enactment is that this person shall be liable notwithstanding the death. It seems to me very evident that the only defense of which the wrongdoer was intended to be deprived was that afforded him by the death of the party injured. * * * The statute may well be construed as meaning that the party who, at the time of bringing the action, 'would have been liable if death had not ensued' shall be liable to an action notwithstanding the death."

In Georgia, where the statute did not contain the qualification that the act or neglect must be such as would have entitled the party injured to maintain an action, the court rested the defendant's liability upon still other grounds. "The substantial grounds on which the courts must hold that the husband's settlement bars the wife," said the court,[4] "are based upon the fact that the wife's right in the life of the husband is subordinate to what he himself has done with his life; that, as his negligence is imputable to her, so his ratification and condonation of the wrong done him estop her; that his acceptance of payment ratifies the act, and admits that he has been made whole of his injury; that thereafter the defendant can say he has not harmed the husband, but that payment, like pardon, relates back to the original act, and makes it as though it had not been. The

4 Southern Bell Telephone & Telegraph Co. v. Cassin, 111 Ga. 575, 36 S. E. 881, 50 L. R. A. 694.

settlement operates as a bar, upon considerations of a public policy encouraging compromises." It is hardly possible to place the general holding upon any very logical ground. The position taken by the courts is fairly enough summed up as follows: "Whether the right of action is a transmitted right or an original right, whether it be created by a survival statute or by a statute creating an independent right, the general concensus of opinion seems to be that the gist and foundation of the right in all cases is the wrongful act, and that for such wrongful act but one recovery should be had, and that if the deceased had received satisfaction in his lifetime, either by settlement and adjustment or by adjudication in the courts, no further right of action existed." [5]

Cases of a release of his claim by the party injured are to be distinguished from those of contracts entered into by him which undertake to abridge the right of the beneficiaries under a death act to recover damages in the event of his death. The question is frequently presented by contracts entered into by railway employés with railway relief associations, the contracts providing that benefits shall be paid in the event of injury or death, and that the acceptance of benefits from the relief fund shall operate as release of all claims for damages against the company arising from the injury or death. Under such contracts it is held that, while the acceptance by one of the beneficiaries under a death act of such a death benefit may bar that beneficiary, [6]

[5] Strode v. St. Louis Transit Co., 197 Mo. 616, 95 S. W. 851, 7 Ann. Cas. 1084.

[6] Payment by defendant of a sum of money, after the death of the injured person, to one whom he made his beneficiary under membership in a relief fund established by the defendant, was not a bar to a suit under the death act for the benefit of the widow and next of kin. "Whether the trial court, in case the plaintiff recovers in this

(274)

it does not bar a recovery by or for other beneficiaries.[7] Thus, where the person entitled to the relief was the employé's widow, and she accepted the benefit and released the company, and afterwards as administratrix brought suit under the death act on behalf of herself and the children, it was held that her acceptance and release operated to bar an action for her own benefit, but not to bar an action as administratrix on behalf of the children.[8] "The circumstances were such," said the Court, "that Wymore [the decedent] might have maintained an action, had he lived. He had not waived his right of action. He undertook to contract that the beneficiary named in the contract might waive it by accepting the benefit, but this action is not for the benefit of his estate, but for that of his widow and next of kin; and the measure of damages is, not what he might have recovered, had he lived, but their pecuniary loss by reason of his death. Whether or not he could, by a compromise after the accident, before his death, deprive them of their right of action, he could not contract away their right before the injury, and without their consent. Nor could he contract that the widow might, after his death, de-

---

suit," it was said, "should control the judgment, so that the share thereof of Nora McKeering, as one of the next of kin, will be held for the benefit of the defendant company, by reason of the payment made under the relief fund, need not now be considered." McKeering v. Pennsylvania R. Co., 65 N. J. Law, 57, 46 Atl. 715.

[7] Illinois Cent. R. Co. v. Cozby, 69 Ill. App. 256, affirmed 174 Ill. 109, 50 N. E. 1011; Pittsburgh, C., C. & St. L. Ry. Co. v. Hosea, 152 Ind. 412, 53 N. E. 419; Pittsburgh, C., C. & St. L. Ry. Co. v. Moore, 152 Ind. 345, 53 N. E. 290, 44 L. R. A. 638; Cowen v. Ray, 108 Fed. 320, 47 C. C. A. 352; Oyster v. Burlington Relief Department of Chicago, B. & Q. R. Co., 65 Neb. 789, 91 N. W. 699, 59 L. R. A. 291; Chicago, B. & Q. R. Co. v. Healy, 76 Neb. 783, 111 N. W. 598, 10 L. R. A. (N. S.) 198, 124 Am. St. Rep. 830. See, also, Gipe v. Pittsburgh, C., C. & St. L. Ry. Co., 41 Ind. App. 156, 82 N. E. 471.

[8] Chicago, B. & Q. R. Co. v. Wymore, 40 Neb. 645, 58 N. W. 1120.

prive the next of kin of their remedy. The children, of whom there were eight, were not beneficiaries in the contract, and his contract, and the widow's acceptance of a sum for her benefit, did not discharge the right of action on the children's behalf. The widow, in accepting her benefit, acted individually, and not as an administratrix. In maintaining this action, she proceeds in her representative capacity, and is not estopped, so far as the rights of others are concerned, by her acts as an individual."

From contracts of the character discussed in the preceding paragraph are to be distinguished those entered into between a railway company and a free passenger, whereby the company is exempted from liability for injury to the person of the passenger. Whether such an exemption, even from responsibility for injuries from ordinary negligence, is valid, is a question on which the cases conflict. Where the exemption is held to be valid, however, it operates, in case the death of the passenger results from an injury caused by such negligence, to exempt the company from liability to respond in damages to persons entitled to recover for death caused by wrongful act or neglect, not upon the ground that the injured person released his claim, but upon the ground that the death was not due to the omission on the part of the company of any duty owing to him, and hence cannot be considered wrongful or negligent.[9]

---

[9] Northern Pac. Ry. Co. v. Adams, 192 U. S. 440, 24 Sup. Ct. 408, 48 L. Ed. 513. See, also, Perry v. Philadelphia, B. & W. R. Co. (Del. Super.) 77 Atl. 725; Hodge v. Rutland R. Co., 112 App. Div. 142, 97 N. Y. Supp. 1107. Cf. Sewell v. Atchison, T. & S. F. Ry. Co., 78 Kan. 1, 96 Pac. 1007. A memorandum, on a season ticket issued by a railroad corporation, that "the corporation assumes no liability for any personal injury received, while in a train, to any season ticket holder," is no defense to an indictment of the corporation on Gen. St. c. 63, § 97, for causing the death of the ticket holder by gross

§ 125. Release or recovery by plaintiff or beneficiary

A release or compromise of his claim by the plaintiff is of course a defense to the action, and this, whether the release or compromise was by the administrator,[10] or other person authorized to prosecute the claim, either in a representative capacity [11] or for his own benefit,[12] or by a per-

---

negligence. Commonwealth v. Vermont & M. R. Co., 108 Mass. 7, 11 Am. Rep. 301.

[10] The administrator may stipulate for the dismissal of the action upon a settlement by which he receives less than the amount claimed. Henchey v. City of Chicago, 41 Ill. 136. Under Code Civ. Proc. § 1588, giving executors and administrators power to compromise, with the approval of the probate court, debts due decedent, the executor may compromise a suit for decedent's wrongful death. Hartigan v. Southern Pac. Co., 86 Cal. 142, 24 Pac. 851. The personal representative may compromise and settle without the consent of the next of kin, before or after action brought. Foot v. Great Northern Ry. Co., 81 Minn. 493, 84 N. W. 342, 52 L. R. A. 354, 83 Am. St. Rep. 395. A release of such claim fraudulently made by the administrator, the adverse party participating, is no bar to an action to enforce the claim by a succeeding administrator. Aho v. Jesmore, 101 Minn. 449, 112 N. W. 538, 10 L. R. A. (N. S.) 998. A release by the person appointed administrator, executed prior to his appointment, constitutes no defense. Snedeker v. Snedeker, 47 App. Div. 471, 63 N. Y. Supp. 580, order affirmed 164 N. Y. 58, 58 N. E. 4. See, also, Stuber v. McEntee, 142 N. Y. 200, 36 N. E. 878. A release by an administrator who was not appointed at the instance of the widow or next of kin, and not made with their approbation, is a nullity. Pisano v. B. M. & J. F. Shanley Co., 66 N. J. Law, 1, 48 Atl. 618.

[11] A suit brought by the widow, although for the benefit of her children as well as herself, may be dismissed by her over their objection. Greenlee v. East Tennessee, V. & G. R. Co., 5 Lea (Tenn.) 418; Stephens v. Nashville, C. & St. L. Ry. Co., 10 Lea (Tenn.) 448. A compromise by her in behalf of herself and children will bar all further claims. Holder v. Nashville, C. & St. L. R. Co., 92 Tenn. 141,

---

[12] See note 12 on following page.

son not authorized to prosecute the action as plaintiff, but actually entitled to the benefit of the action.[13]   A release by one of several persons so entitled is no bar, though it

20 S. W. 537, 36 Am. St. Rep. 77.   See, also, Smalling v. Kreech (Tenn. Ch. App.) 46 S. W. 1019; Prater v. Tennessee Producers' Marble Co., 105 Tenn. 496, 58 S. W. 1068.   Under Rev. Code 1880, § 1510, giving the widow the right to sue, and providing that, where she has children, the amount recovered "shall be distributed as personal property of the husband," the widow, pending an appeal by defendant, may compromise the case by accepting a certain sum in satisfaction of the judgment, and such compromise is binding on decedent's infant children.   Natchez C. M. Co. v. Mullins, 67 Miss. 672, 7 South. 542.   The acceptance of a verdict against one of the wrongdoers is not conclusive of a compromise of the claim, and it should be left to the jury to say whether such compromise had been actually effected, and the judgment accepted in satisfaction for the injury.   Owen v. Brockschmidt, 54 Mo. 285.   Under Act April 15, 1851, and Act April 26, 1855, on death of husband, the right of action is in widow, and her minor children are not necessary parties, and she has a right to compromise the claim when she does so in good faith, without the consent of the guardian of the children. Shambach v. Middlecreek Electric Co., 232 Pa. 641, 81 Atl. 802.   Cf. Houston & T. C. Ry. Co. v. Bradley, 45 Tex. 171; Southern Pac. Co. v. Tomlinson, 163 U. S. 369, 16 Sup. Ct. 1171, 41 L. Ed. 193.

   [12] In a suit by the widow, defendant, under a plea of accord and satisfaction, introduced a paper signed by both parties, which, after reciting that defendant had bought certain horses and mules of plaintiff, surrendered certain notes of her husband, and paid her a certain sum, stated that these were in full of all demands of every name and nature whatsoever from one party to the other.   Plaintiff testified that, at the time of signing, she knew she had a claim on account of the death.   Held, that a verdict for defendant was properly ordered.   Guldager v. Rockwell, 14 Colo. 459, 24 Pac. 556.

   [13] Kennedy v. Davis, 171 Ala. 609, 55 South. 104; Mattoon Gaslight & Coke Co. v. Dolan, 105 Ill. App. 1; Sykora v. J. I. Case Threshing Mach. Co., 59 Minn. 130, 60 N. W. 1008; McKeigue v. Chicago & N. W. Ry. Co., 130 Wis. 543, 110 N. W. 384, 11 L. R. A. (N. S.) 148, 118 Am. St. Rep. 1038, 10 Ann. Cas. 554; Mella v. Northern S. S. Co. (C. C.) 127 Fed. 416.   See, also, Doyle v. New York, O. & W. Ry. Co., 66 App. Div. 398, 72 N. Y. Supp. 936; Christe v. Chicago, R. I. & P. R. Co., 104 Iowa, 707, 74 N. W. 697 (cf. Dow.

might affect his interest in the distribution of the proceeds.[14]

§ 126. Cause of action of party injured survives by statute in some states

In many states the common-law rule has been changed by enactments which provide that the right of action for injury to the person shall survive. As the two causes of action are distinct—the one in favor of the estate to recover

ell v. Burlington, C. R. & N. R. Co., 62 Iowa, 629, 17 N. W. 901).
Contra: Yelton v. Evansville & I. R. Co., 134 Ind. 414, 33 N. E. 629, 21 L. R. A. 158. Cleveland, C., C. & St. L. Ry. Co. v. Osgood, 36 Ind. App. 34, 73 N. E. 285; City of Louisville v. Hart's Adm'r, 143 Ky. 171, 136 S. W. 212, 35 L. R. A. (N. S.) 207. A release given by the father of a minor child, whose death was caused by defendant's negligence, he being solely entitled to the proceeds of any recovery, is a bar to an action by the mother as administratrix. Stuebing v. Marshall, 10 Daly (N. Y.) 406. Plaintiff brought action for the recovery of securities executed by defendant in settlement of a cause of action for damages for the killing of plaintiff's husband. Held that, while the personal representative of the deceased was the proper party to sue for damages, yet, as plaintiff would be entitled to any damages recovered, she had authority to settle with defendant for these damages and to sue for the possession of the securities executed in settlement. Schmidt v. Deegan, 69 Wis. 300, 34 N. W. 83.

[14] A release by the husband, he not being the sole party entitled, is no bar to an action by the administrator. South & N. A. R. Co. v. Sullivan, 59 Ala. 272. An action by an administrator for the wrongful death of his intestate, "for the use and benefit of the widow and children," cannot be compromised by the widow without the consent of the children or administrator. Knoxville, C. G. & L. R. Co. v. Acuff, 92 Tenn. 26, 20 S. W. 348. Where, prior to the appointment of an administratrix or the commencement of action, defendant settles with one of the next of kin, the proper practice is to have that portion of the fund which would otherwise be distributed to the heir with whom the settlement was made applied pro tanto in settlement of the judgment. McVeigh v. Minneapolis & R. R. R. Co., 110 Minn. 184, 124 N. W. 971.

such damages as might have been recovered by the party injured, the other in favor of the surviving members of his family to recover damages for the pecuniary injury resulting to them from the death—it would logically follow that the administrator might, upon the same facts, avail himself of either remedy; and so it has been frequently held.[15] In Illinois, however, where the statute declares that, in addition to the actions which survive at common law, actions to recover damages for injury to the person shall survive, it is held that this enactment is applicable only to cases where death results from some other cause than the injury; and that, if death results from the injury, the only right of action is for the death.[16] A similar statute has received the same construction in Kansas[17] and Rhode Island.[18] In these states, therefore, the question whether the administrator might for the same injury avail himself of both remedies cannot arise. In some other states, where there is a survival act as well as a death act, the death act is held to be limited to cases of instantaneous or immediate death, and cases where the death was not instantaneous or imme-

---

[15] Davis v. St. Louis, I. M. & S. Ry. Co., 53 Ark. 117, 13 S. W. 801, 7 L. R. A. 283; Vicksburg & M. R. Co. v. Phillips, 64 Miss. 693, 2 South. 537; Needham v. Grand Trunk R. Co., 38 Vt. 294. See, also, Earl v. Tupper, 45 Vt. 275. But see Legg v. Britton, 64 Vt. 652, 24 Atl. 1016.

[16] Holton v. Daly, 106 Ill. 131; Chicago & E. I. R. Co. v. O'Connor, 119 Ill. 586, 9 N. E. 263; Id., 19 Ill. App. 591; Merrihew v. Chicago City Ry. Co., 92 Ill. App. 346.

[17] McCarthy v. Chicago, R. I. & P. R. Co., 18 Kan. 46, 26 Am. Rep. 742; Hulbert v. City of Topeka (C. C.) 34 Fed. 510; City of Eureka v. Merrifield, 53 Kan. 794, 37 Pac. 113. In Hulbert v. City of Topeka, supra, Brewer, J., doubted the correctness of McCarthy v. Chicago, R. I. & P. R. Co., but was constrained to follow it. See ante, § 97—1.

[18] Lubrano v. Atlantic Mills, 19 R. I. 129, 32 Atl. 205, 34 L. R. A. 797.

diate fall under the survival act, and consequently a recovery cannot be had under both acts.[19]

§ 127.   Concurrent actions by administrator

In other jurisdictions, whether the personal representative would be permitted to maintain both the action which survives by statute and the action for death is not entirely clear.[20]   It was said by Long, J., in Hurst v. Detroit City

[19] See ante. §§ 43, 44—1, 73.

[20] A recovery by the person injured through negligence, or a release of damages made by him after receiving the injuries, defeats an action for his death, since he could not, if living, have subsequently sued therefor. Perry v. Philadelphia, B. & W. R. Co. (Del. Super.) 77 Atl. 725. Gen. St. 1894, § 5912 (R. L. 1905, § 4502), declared that every cause of action arising out of an injury to the person dies with the person, except as provided in section 5913 (Rev. Laws 1905. § 4503), which provided that, when death is caused by the wrongful act or omission of another, the personal representatives of the deceased may maintain an action for the injury, if he could have done so if he had lived. Laws 1897. c. 261 (Rev. Laws 1905. § 4503),' provided that if an action had been commenced by such deceased person during his lifetime for such injury, which has not been finally determined, such action may be continued by the personal representative of the deceased for the benefit of the same person. Held to only authorize the personal representative to be substituted as plaintiff in the original action brought by him, and converted by amendment of the pleadings. if the facts warrant it, into an action for the benefit of the widow and next of kin. Anderson v. Fielding, 92 Minn. 42. 99 N. W. 357, 104 Am. St. Rep. 665. The right of action given to an administrator by Pub. St. c. 52, § 17, to sue for his intestate's loss of life, caused by a defect in a highway, for the benefit of the widow and children. is independent of the administrator's right to sue for damages suffered by the intestate during his lifetime from the injury which caused his death, under Pub. St. c. 165, § 1, and both actions may proceed at the same time. Bowes v. City of Boston, 155 Mass. 344. 29 N. E. 633, 15 L. R. R. A. 365. This case. however, arising under the Massachusetts statutes has little application.

Ry. Co.,[21] that the satisfaction of the claim for death
would be no bar to the other claim if such action could be
maintained.   In Leggott v. Great Northern Ry. Co.,[22] it
was held that a recovery by the administratrix in an action
under Lord Campbell's act was no bar to an action by her
(founded on the implied contract of the defendants as carriers) to recover for loss of time and expenses resulting
from personal injury to the intestate, who was a passenger
on the defendants' railway.   The opinions in that case point
out that the administratrix sued in a different right in each
case, and the principle of that decision is certainly equally
applicable to an action by the administrator on the cause of
action of his intestate for the personal injury, which is
made to survive by the enactments in question.   Whether
Leggott v. Great Northern Ry. Co. is reconcilable with the
cases which hold that a release or recovery by the party
injured is a bar to an action for the death, is perhaps ques-
tionable.   Certainly there is an apparent inconsistency in
holding that a recovery of judgment by the party injured is
a bar, and that a recovery by the administrator upon the
identical cause of action is no bar, in an action for the
death.[23]   Upon the ground that the two causes of action

[21] 84 Mich. 539, 48 N. W. 44. In Sweetland v. Chicago & G. T.
Ry. Co., 117 Mich. 329, 75 N. W. 1066, 43 L. R. A. 568, it is said
by Long, C. J., that the question was not involved in Hurst v. Detroit City R. Co., and that the language was mere dicta. It has
since been held in Michigan that a recovery cannot be had under
both acts. Ante, § 44–1.

[22] 1 Q. B. D. 599, 45 L. J. Q. B. 557, 35 L. T. (N. S.) 334. See Barnett v. Lucas, 6 Ir. C. L. 247. See § 18.

[23] The case of Legg v. Britton, 64 Vt. 652, 24 Atl. 1016, which disap-
proves the early case of Needham v. Grand Trunk Ry. Co., 38 Vt. 294,
above cited, in effect holds that an action by the administrator upon
the original cause of action would be a bar to an action for the death.
The case arose under R. L. Vt. § 2134, which provides that where
either party dies, pending an action for personal injuries, the ac-

arising under a survival act and under a death act are separate, distinct, and independent causes of action arising out of the same wrongful or negligent act, the damages in the one case being limited to such damages as the decedent himself might have recovered, and in the other being the pecuniary loss suffered by the persons entitled to the benefit of the action, it has been logically held in Maryland that a recovery in one action is not a bar to the other and that the two actions may be maintained concurrently.[24] And such appears to be the rule in Arkansas, Ohio, and Wisconsin.[25]

§ 128. Concurrent actions by parent or heirs and by administrator

The acts of many states give a right of action to the father or mother of a child, as well as a right of action to the

tion may be prosecuted to final judgment by or against the personal representative of decedent. It was held that where plaintiff, in an action for personal injuries, died from such injuries pending the action, and his administrator recovered judgment therein under section 2134, such judgment is a bar to an action by the administrator for the benefit of the widow and next of kin to recover for the injuries resulting from the death. Ross, C. J., who delivered the opinion says: "The construction we have placed on the act of 1849 gives the administrator or executor the right to sue and recover for the wife and next of kin, wherever the intestate, if he were living, could have maintained an action for such act causing the injury occasioning the death."

[24] Stewart v. United Electric Light & Power Co., 104 Md. 332, 65 Atl. 49, 8 L. R. A. (N. S.) 384, 118 Am. St. Rep. 410. Where decedent was killed and his horses and wagon were destroyed in a collision, an action by the administrator under the Ohio death act was not barred by a former recovery of the value of the horses and wagon in another action by the administrator. Peake v. Baltimore & O. R. Co. (C. C.) 26 Fed. 495.

[25] See, ante, §§ 35—3, 49—1, 58—1. In Kentucky the two causes of action cannot be united. Ante, § 41.

personal representative for the benefit of the widow and next of kin, or, as in Iowa, Oregon, and Washington, for the benefit of the estate. The right of the parents to recover is held to be confined to cases in which they were entitled to the child's services by reason of his minority, or because the relation of parent and child in fact continued after minority. Where, as in Indiana, the right of action of the personal representative is for the benefit of the widow and next of kin, it is difficult to see how a case could arise in which the parents would be entitled to recover for loss of the child's services, and in which all the damages that could result from the death would not be recoverable in an action by the parents; while, if the parents were not entitled to recover for the loss of the child's services, all the damages that could result would be recoverable in an action by the personal representative.[26] It would follow that in such jurisdictions the remedies of parent and of personal representative are practically exclusive, and that a recovery in an action by one would be a bar to an action by the other. In Alabama the act provides that a suit by the father or mother is a bar to a suit by the personal representative.

In Iowa and Washington, however, the recovery by the parent is confined to the loss of the child's services during minority, but the personal representative may recover for the loss to the child's estate after he should have attained his majority.[27] Upon this ground it has been held in Washington that a judgment in favor of the administrator is not a bar to an action by the father.[28] In Oregon, also, the

[26] See opinion of Mitchell, C. J,. in Mayhew v. Burns, 103 Ind. 328, 2 N. E. 793.

[27] See § 40 and § 57.

[28] Hedrick v. Ilwaco Ry. & Nav. Co., 4 Wash. 400, 30 Pac. 714.

measure of damages in an action by the personal representative is the loss to the estate. Where, however, the personal representative of a deceased adult recovered damages, it was held by a divided court that this was a bar to an action for the same death by the parent, although the child, who was married, continued to render services to him after majority, as well as before.[29]

In some acts it is provided that the action may be brought by the personal representative or heirs. In California it is held that a recovery by the executor is a bar to an action by the heirs.[30]

---

[29] Putman v. Southern Pac. Co., 21 Or. 230, 27 Pac. 1033.

[30] Hartigan v. Southern Pac. Co., 86 Cal. 142, 24 Pac. 851. See, also, St. Louis, I. M. & S. Ry. Co. v. Needham, 52 Fed. 371, 3 C. C. A. 129.

. CHAPTER IX

DAMAGES—THE STATUTES

§ 129. Classification of statutes

The distinguishing feature of Lord Campbell's act and of acts similar to it, in respect to damages, is that the damages to be recovered are solely such as result (1) from the

(286)

death (2) to the persons for whose benefit the action is given. This feature is common to all the acts in force in the United States, with the following exceptions:

1. The acts of Iowa, Kentucky, Oregon, and Rhode Island, as construed by the courts, provide that the damages, except in actions by parents, shall be such as result from the death to *the estate.*

2. The acts of North Carolina, Virginia, and West Virginia, as construed by the courts, provide for a recovery notwithstanding that there may be in existence no one of the relatives for whose benefit the action is primarily given.

3. The acts of Louisiana, Mississippi, and Tennessee provide, in effect, for the recovery both of such damages as result to the party injured from the injury and to the beneficiaries from the death.

4. The act of Georgia provides that the measure of damages shall be the full value of the life, without deduction for the expenses of the deceased had he lived.

5. The acts of Massachusetts provide for a forfeiture in certain cases to be recovered by indictment. A civil action may also be maintained under certain circumstances in which the damages are assessed with reference to the degree of culpability of the defendant.

The provisions of these states in respect to damages will be considered before proceeding to a general discussion of the subject of damages. Certain peculiar features in respect to damages in the acts of some other states will be considered in this chapter.

§ 130.   Alabama

Code, § 2486, as amended by Gen. Laws 1911, p. 484, provides that a personal representative may "recover such damages as the jury may assess" for the wrongful act, omission, or negligence of any person whereby the death was caused. Section 3910 (Employés' Act), as amended by Gen. Laws 1911, p. 485, provides that, if the injury results in death, the personal representative "is entitled to maintain an action therefor." Both sections provide that the damages are not subject to the payment of debts, but shall be divided according to the statute of distributions. Under section 2486 the damages are punitive, and the recovery is not confined to the pecuniary loss.[1] Under section 3912 the recovery is confined to the pecuniary loss,[2] and the

---

[1] Savannah & M. R. Co. v. Shearer, 58 Ala. 672; South & N. A. R. Co. v. Sullivan, 59 Ala. 272; see East Tennessee, V. & G. R. Co. v. King, 81 Ala. 177, 2 South. 152. This section is the act of Feb. 5, 1872, "An act to prevent homicides" (Code 1876, § 2641). The court has said that the purpose of the act is the prevention of homicide, and that this purpose it accomplishes by such pecuniary mulct as the jury "deem just." Richmond & D. R. Co. v. Freeman, 97 Ala. 289, 11 South. 800. The damages are entirely punitive, and evidence of loss of services, or mere pecuniary loss, and of mental suffering by parents of a deceased child, are immaterial. Alabama G. S. R. Co. v. Burgess, 116 Ala. 509, 22 South. 913. The amount rests in the discretion of the jury, whose verdict is not subject to review by the trial court for inadequacy. Louisville & N. R. Co. v. Street, 164 Ala. 155, 51 South. 306, 20 Ann. Cas. 877. It was the jury's duty on finding an electric railway company liable for the death of a pedestrian, struck by a car, to award an amount sufficient to punish for the wrong done. Randle v. Birmingham Ry., Light & Power Co., 169 Ala. 314, 53 South. 918. See, also, Kansas City, M. & B. R. Co. v. Sanders, 98 Ala. 293, 13 South. 57; Buckalew v. Tennessee Coal, I. & R. Co., 112 Ala. 146, 20 South. 606; Louisville & N. R. Co. v. Tegner, 125 Ala. 593, 28 South. 510; Western Ry. of Alabama v. Russell, 144 Ala. 142, 39 South. 311, 113 Am. St. Rep. 24; Smith v. Birmingham Ry., Light & Power Co., 147 Ala. 702, 41 South. 307; Kennedy v. Davis, 171 Ala. 609, 55 South. 104; Louisville & N. R. Co. v. Perkins, 1 Ala. App. 376, 56 South. 105; Louisville & N. R. Co. v. Lansford, 102 Fed. 62, 42 C. C. A. 160; McGhee v. McCarley, 103 Fed. 55, 44 C. C. A. 252.

[2] Columbus & W. Ry. Co. v. Bridges, 86 Ala. 448, 5 South. 864, 11 Am. St. Rep. 58; Louisville & N. R. Co. v. Orr, 91 Ala. 548, 8

measure of damage is the pecuniary value of the life to the persons entitled to inherit according to the statute of distributions.[3] Under section 2485, which gives a right of action for the death of a minor child, caused by wrongful act, omission, or negligence, to the father or in certain cases to the mother, and provides for a recovery of such

South. 360; Thompson v. Louisville & N. R. Co., 91 Ala. 496, 8 South. 406, 11 L. R. A. 146; Louisville & N. R. Co. v. Trammell, 93 Ala. 350, 9 South. 870.

[3] Louisville & N. R. Co. v. Orr, supra; James v. Richmond & D. R. Co., 92 Ala. 231, 9 South. 335; Richmond & D. R. Co. v. Hammond, 93 Ala. 181, 9 South. 577; Tennessee Coal, I. & R. Co. v. Herndon, 100 Ala. 451, 14 South. 287. See, also, Alabama Mineral R. Co. v. Jones, 114 Ala. 519, 21 South. 507, 62 Am. St. Rep. 121; Louisville & N. R. Co. v. Morgan, 114 Ala. 449, 22 South. 20; Louisville & N. R. Co. v. Brown, 121 Ala. 221, 25 South. 609; Decatur Car Wheel & Mfg. Co. v. Mehaffey, 128 Ala. 242, 29 South. 646; Louisville & N. R. Co. v. Jones, 130 Ala. 456, 30 South. 586; Tutwiler Coal, Coke & Iron Co. v. Enslen, 129 Ala. 336, 30 South. 600; Louisville & N. R. Co. v. Banks, 132 Ala. 471, 31 South. 573; McGhee v. Willis, 134 Ala. 281, 32 South. 301; Central Foundry Co. v. Bennett, 144 Ala. 184, 39 South. 574, 1 L. R. A. (N. S.) 1150, 113 Am. St. Rep. 13; Central of Georgia Ry. Co. v. Alexander, 144 Ala. 257, 40 South. 424; Reiter-Connolly Mfg. Co. v. Hamlin, 144 Ala. 192, 40 South. 280; Woodstock Iron Works v. Kline, 149 Ala. 391, 43 South. 362; Birmingham Ry., Light & Power Co. v. Mosely, 164 Ala. 111, 51 South. 424; Mobile Electric Co. v. Sanges, 169 Ala. 341, 53 South. 176, Ann. Cas. 1912B, 461; Louisville & N. R. Co. v. Young, 168 Ala. 551, 53 South. 213. This value, in an action for the benefit of wife or child or other dependent relative, when there were no net earnings, is such a sum as would yield, during the probable duration of the life of the deceased, a benefit equal to what such relative would have derived from its continuance. Louisville & N. R. Co. v. Trammell, supra. The measure of damages, where the heirs were in no relation of dependence on deceased for support, is such sum as, with legal interest during the period of his expectancy of life, would produce at the expiration of such period a sum equal to the accumulations of his earnings for the same period, estimated on the basis of his health, ability, habits of sobriety, industry, economy, gross earnings, and expenditures. McAdory v. Louisville & N. R. Co., 94 Ala. 272, 10 South. 507.

damages as the jury may assess, it has recently been held by the federal court that the plaintiff is not limited to the recovery of compensatory damages, but that he may recover such damages as the jury may assess under all the circumstances of the case, uninfluenced by passion, sympathy, or feeling.[4]

§ 130—1. Arkansas

When death is caused by wrongful act, neglect, or default, the personal representative can, as has been already stated, maintain two actions, one under the survival act for the benefit of the estate, and the other under the death act for the benefit of the next of kin.[5] Under the survival act the measure of damages is the same as if the action had been brought by the person injured.[6] Under the death act the measure of damages does not differ from that under Lord Campbell's act and similar statutes.[7] Section 6288,

[4] Sloss-Sheffield Steel & Iron Co. v. Drane, 160 Fed. 780, 88 C. C. A. 34. See, also, McGhee v. McCarley, 103 Fed. 55, 44 C. C. A. 252.

[5] Ante, § 35—3. See, also, cases cited in following note.

[6] A verdict awarding $1,000 to decedent's estate is sustained by evidence that, though he lived but a short time after the injury, he made exclamations showing conscious suffering. St. Louis S. W. Ry. Co. v. Mahoney, 67 Ark. 617, 55 S. W. 840. A verdict of $4,000 cannot stand; the interval of conscious suffering, if any, between the injury and death, being only for a moment. St. Louis, I. M. & S. Ry. Co. v. Dawson, 68 Ark. 1, 56 S. W. 46. See, also, St. Louis, I. M. & S. Ry. Co. v. Davis, 55 Ark. 462, 18 S. W. 628; St. Louis, I. M. & S. Ry. Co. v. Robbins, 57 Ark. 377, 21 S. W. 886; St. Louis, I. M. & S. Ry. Co. v. McCain, 67 Ark. 377, 55 S. W. 165; St. Louis, I. M. & S. Ry. Co. v. Block, 79 Ark. 179, 95 S. W. 155; St. Louis, I. M. & S. Ry. Co. v. Stamps, 84 Ark. 241, 104 S. W. 1114; St. Louis, I. M. & S. Ry. Co. v. Pate, 90 Ark. 135, 118 S. W. 260; Warren & O. V. R. Co. v. Waldrop, 93 Ark. 127, 123 S. W. 792.

[7] Decedent's widow's and children's pecuniary loss through his death is the probable aggregate amount of his contributions to them, reduced to present value. Kansas City Southern Ry. Co. v. Henrie,

Kirby's Dig., gives the husband a right of an action for the death of his wife, for the recovery of damages for her services and companionship in whatever sum the jury may consider he is entitled to.

§ 131.　Colorado [8]

§ 132.　Connecticut

Pub. Acts 1903, c. 193, §§ 1–5, as amended, provide in substance that actions for injuries to the person shall survive; that in actions surviving to or brought by an executor or administrator for injuries resulting in death, whether instantaneous or otherwise, the plaintiff may recover just damages, not exceeding $10,000, which shall be distributed

---

87 Ark. 443, 112 S. W. 967. While the amount of damages to be awarded to minor children for the loss of parental care caused by the death of their father is indeterminate, and is to be left to the sound discretion of the jury, yet the jury must proceed on the theory of compensation for pecuniary loss, and the court must see that the limit of such compensation is not exceeded. St. Louis & N. A. R. Co. v. Mathis, 76 Ark. 184, 91 S. W. 763, 113 Am. St. Rep. 85. See, also, St. Louis, I. M. & S. R. Co. v. Hitt, 76 Ark. 227, 88 S. W. 908, 990; St. Louis, I. M. & S. R. Co. v. Cleere, 76 Ark. 377, 88 S. W. 995; Choctaw, O. & G. R. Co. v. Doughty, 77 Ark. 1, 91 S. W. 768; St. Louis, I. M. & S. R. Co. v. Caraway, 77 Ark. 405, 91 S. W. 749; Choctaw, O. & G. R. Co. v. Baskins, 78 Ark. 355, 93 S. W. 757; St. Louis, I. M. & S. R. Co. v. Freeman, 89 Ark. 326, 116 S. W. 678; St. Louis, I. M. & S. R. Co. v. Garner, 90 Ark. 19, 117 S. W. 763; Kansas City Southern R. Co. v. Frost, 93 Ark. 183, 124 S. W. 748; Pulaski Gaslight Co. v. McClintock, 97 Ark. 576, 134 S. W. 1189, 1199, 32 L. R. A. (N. S.) 825; St. Louis, I. M. & S. R. Co. v. Evans, 137 S. W. 568; Memphis, D. & G. Ry. Co. v. Buckley, 138 S. W. 965. Sorrow caused by the death of a husband is not an element of damage by his death. Helena Gas Co. v. Rogers, 98 Ark. 413, 135 S. W. 904. Cf. St. Louis, I. M. & S. R. Co. v. Stamps, 84 Ark. 241, 104 S. W. 1114.

　[8] See § 139.

among the beneficiaries designated. It has been said that the object of this legislation was partly penal or punitive in character, but mainly to make compensation for loss of life, such compensation as part of the estate of the injured party to go to designated persons, that the loss of life is not to be estimated from the standpoint of the beneficiaries, but that the statute proceeds "in part at least, upon the theory that loss of earning capacity by death is a loss to a man's estate, which may be greater or less according to circumstances." In the case under consideration the death was instantaneous, and the court said that in such a case the loss thus measured would be the principal element to be considered in fixing the liability, and that hence evidence that the decedent was in good health and in the prime of life was properly received as showing the value of his life to himself.[9] Where the death is not instantaneous, it seems that the plaintiff may recover also damages measured by the same rule as if the action had been brought by the decedent in his lifetime.[10]

[9] Broughel v. Southern New England Tel. Co., 73 Conn. 614, 48 Atl. 751, 84 Am. St. Rep. 176. See, also, Id., 72 Conn. 617, 45 Atl. 435, 49 L. R. A. 404.

[10] In an action for the death of a child, plaintiff, if entitled to recover at all, may recover on the same grounds damages measured by the same rule as if the action had been brought by decedent in his lifetime. Wilmot v. McPadden, 79 Conn. 367, 65 Atl. 157, 19 L. R. A. (N. S.) 1101. See, also, Wilmot v. McPadden, 78 Conn. 284, 61 Atl. 1069. The evidence tended to show that deceased was a man of average size, and in good condition mentally and physically, and that he lived for some minutes, and suffered some pain. Held, that it was not error to award the full statutory damages; it appearing that there was little or no contest as to the quantum of damages, and the attention of the court not having been called to the matter, save by a somewhat ambiguous claim of law that no judgment could be rendered for more than nominal damages. Hesse v. Meriden, S. & C. Tramway Co., 75 Conn. 571, 54 Atl. 299. See, also, Murphy v. New York & N. H. R. Co., 29 Conn. 496; Id., 30 Conn. 184; Good_

§ 133. Georgia

Civ. Code 1910, § 4425,[11] provides that the plaintiff may recover "the full value of the life of the deceased, as shown by the evidence," which "is the full value of the life of the deceased, without any deduction for necessary or other personal expenses of the deceased had he lived." [12]

In estimating the value of the life, age, habits, health, occupation, expectation of life,[13] ability to labor, probable

sell v. Hartford & N. H. R. Co., 33 Conn. 51; Waldo v. Goodsell, 33 Conn. 432; Lamphear v. Buckingham, 33 Conn. 237; Carey v. Day, 36 Conn. 152.

[11] Prior to Act Dec. 16, 1878, amending section 2971 of Code of 1873, the statute provided no measure of damages. Macon & W. R. Co. v. Johnson, 38 Ga. 409. This act is constitutional. Georgia R. Co. v. Pittman, 73 Ga. 325.

[12] Before the amendment of 1887, enacting that there should be no deduction for the expenses of the deceased, it was held that such deduction should be made. Central R. Co. v. Rouse, 77 Ga. 393, 3 S. E. 307; Id., 80 Ga. 442, 5 S. E. 627; Augusta & K. R. Co. v. Killian, 79 Ga. 234, 4 S. E. 165; Savannah, F. & W. Ry. Co. v. Flannagan, 82 Ga. 579, 9 S. E. 471, 14 Am. St. Rep. 183; Georgia R. Co. v. Pittman, 73 Ga. 325.

[13] See. also, Bussey v. Charleston & W. C. R. Co., 78 S. C. 352, 58 S. E. 1015: Central of Georgia Ry. Co. v. Minor, 2 Ga. App. 804, 59 S. E. 81. Where there is no proof as to probable duration of life, a verdict should be directed for defendant. Savannah, F. & W. Ry. Co. v. Stewart, 71 Ga. 427. Life tables may be used, but are not conclusive. Id.; Georgia R. & Banking Co. v. Oaks, 52 Ga. 410; Georgia R. Co. v. Pittman, 73 Ga. 325; Central R. Co. v. Crosby, 74 Ga. 737, 58 Am. Rep. 463; Central R. Co. v. Thompson, 76 Ga. 770. Nevertheless, in Central R. Co. v. Crosby, where life tables were introduced, and the value of the services of the deceased proved, and after a verdict in excess of the damages proved plaintiff voluntarily wrote off a part of the verdict, so as to bring the amount within the measure of damages proved, it was held that the refusal to grant a new trial was not error. The court said that the life tables were not conclusive, yet that they established a fixed criterion of damages.

increase or diminution of that ability with lapse of time,[14] rate of wages, etc., should be considered.[15] In actions against railroad companies for the death of passengers, evidence of the negligence of the deceased may be shown in mitigation of damages.[16]

[14] It should be left to the jury to determine how far age would have diminished the capacity for labor. Georgia R. Co. v. Pittman, 73 Ga. 325; Central R. v. Thompson, 76 Ga. 770.

[15] Central R. Co. v. Rouse, supra; Savannah, F. & W. Ry. Co. v. Flannagan, supra; Atlanta & W. P. R. Co. v. Newton, 85 Ga. 517, 11 S. E. 776. The measure of damages is not affected by the wants of the family, but depends solely on the value of the life. Central R. Co. v. Rouse, 77 Ga. 393, 3 S. E. 307; Id., 80 Ga. 442, 5 S. E. 627. Prior to the amendment of 1878 it had been held that the measure of damages was the amount that would be a reasonable support. Macon & W. R. Co. v. Johnson, 38 Ga. 409; David v. Southwestern R. Co., 41 Ga. 223; Atlanta & R. A. L. R. Co. v. Ayers, 53 Ga. 12; Atlanta & W. P. R. R. Co. v. Venable, 67 Ga. 697. Where the widow died pending suit, and the action survived to the children, held that the recovery should be for the damages to them, not to her. David v. Southwestern R. Co., supra. When a widow is entitled to recover for the homicide of her husband, the measure of her damages is the full value of his life, although she and he were living in a state of separation at the time of his death. Central of Georgia Ry. Co. v. Bond, 111 Ga. 13, 36 S. E. 299. See, also, Boswell v. Barnhart, 96 Ga. 521, 23 S. E. 414; Western & A. R. Co. v. Hyer, 113 Ga. 776, 39 S. E. 447; Brunswick & W. R. Co. v. Wiggins, 113 Ga. 842, 39 S. E. 551, 61 L. R. A. 513; Savannah Electric Co. v. Bell, 124 Ga. 663, 53 S. E. 109; Western Union Telegraph Co. v. Harris, 6 Ga. App. 260, 64 S. E. 1123. Mental anguish occasioned by the bereavement is not also recoverable. Glawson v. Southern Bell Telephone & Telegraph Co., 9 Ga. App. 450, 71 S. E. 747. A child of 1 year and 8 months being incapable of rendering valuable services, the father may not recover for loss of service, but may recover the expenses necessarily and reasonably incurred in the burial of the child, including compensation for the loss of such time as was needed for this purpose. Southern Ry. Co. v. Covenia, 100 Ga. 46, 29 S. E. 219, 40 L. R. A. 253, 62 Am. St. Rep. 312.

[16] Macon & W. R. Co. v. Johnson, 38 Ga. 409; Atlanta & R. A. L. R. Co. v. Ayers, 53 Ga. 12. But not where deceased was an employé. Western & A. R. Co. v. Meigs, 74 Ga. 857. In an action for a homi_

§ 134. Iowa

Under the provisions of the Iowa Code, which are peculiar, it is held that the action lies, not for the benefit of the
next of kin, but of the estate,[17] and that the measure of
damages is the sum necessary to compensate the estate for
the loss occasioned by the death; [18] hence all facts are admissible which show what his accumulations would probably have been.[19] In an action by the parent for the death

cide committed in resisting a battery where deceased was the assail-
ant, this fact will go in mitigation of damages. Weekes v. Cottingham, 58 Ga. 559.

[17] See § 40.

[18] Donaldson v. Mississippi & M. R. Co., 18 Iowa, 290, 87 Am. Dec.
391; Sherman v. Western Stage Co., 24 Iowa, 515; Coates v. Burling-
ton, C. R. & N. R. Co., 62 Iowa, 486, 17 N. W. 760; McMarshall v.
Chicago, R. I. & P. Ry. Co., 80 Iowa, 757, 45 N. W. 1065, 20 Am. St.
Rep. 445; Kelley v. Central Railroad of Iowa, 5 McCrary, 653, 48
Fed. 663.

[19] The jury may consider the expectancy of the life of deceased,
the nature of his calling, the wages he was receiving, and his phys-
ical condition and habits of industry. Wheelan v. Chicago, M. & St.
P. Ry. Co., 85 Iowa, 167, 52 N. W. 119; Van Gent v. Chicago, M.
& St. P. R. Co., 80 Iowa, 526, 45 N. W. 913; Kelley v. Central Railroad of Iowa (C. C.) 48 Fed. 663; Morris v. Chicago, M. & St. P. Ry.
Co. (C. C.) 26 Fed. 22; Lowe v. Chicago, St. P., M. & O. Ry. Co., 89
Iowa, 420, 56 N. W. 519; McKelvy v. Burlington, C. R. & N. Ry.
Co., 58 N. W. 1068; Fish v. Illinois Cent. Ry. Co., 96 Iowa, 702, 65
N. W. 995; Spaulding v. Chicago, St. P. & K. C. Ry. Co., 98 Iowa,
205, 67 N. W. 227; Hammer v. Janowitz, 131 Iowa, 20, 108 N. W.
109. But not the number of his family or the amount of property
he left. Beems v. Chicago, R. I. & P. R. Co., 58 Iowa, 150, 12 N. W.
222. Nor can damages be given for the sufferings of deceased or the
grief of his family. Kelley v. Central Railroad of Iowa, supra;
Dwyer v. Chicago, St. P., M. & O. Ry. Co., 84 Iowa, 479, 51 N. W. 244,
35 Am. St. Rep. 322. Cf. Muldowney v. Illinois Cent. R. Co., 36 Iowa,
462. The damages accruing to the estate of a married woman are not
to be assessed as though she were unmarried. Stulmuller v. Cloughly,
58 Iowa, 738, 13 N. W. 55. Deceased was 24 years old, without family,

of a minor, the damages are measured by the loss of service during minority.[20]

temperate and industrious, and his net earnings were $263 a year. Held, that a verdict of $10,000 should be reduced to $5,000. Rose v. Des Moines Val. R. Co., 39 Iowa, 246. Where the expectancy of life of deceased is 42 years, and his earnings about $650 annually, a verdict of $10,000 is not excessive. McDermott v. Iowa Falls & S. C. Ry. Co., 47 N. W. 1037. See Walter v. C. D. & M. R. Co., 39 Iowa, 33. In an action to recover for the negligent killing of a boy such damages as his estate may have sustained, an instruction calling attention to his expectancy of life, character, intelligence, business experience, etc., and telling the jury to make the best possible estimate therefrom of the loss, is not, considering the youth of deceased, and the meagerness of the data from which his future might have been estimated, objectionable for indefiniteness in failing to point out a specific method of calculating the probable amount of his accumulations, or in providing an abatement of interest therefrom so as to arrive at the present worth, but is as definite as practicable. Andrews v. Chicago, M. & St. P. Ry. Co., 86 Iowa, 677, 53 N. W. 399. In an action for the death of a girl 8 years of age, evidence that her stepfather was a school teacher, and as to the amount of salary paid women school teachers in the township, was not objectionable on the ground that, decedent's mother being a housewife, the presumption was that the daughter would follow her mother's avocation, and not that of her stepfather, since, in view of contemporaneous history, the majority of school teachers are women, and there was a slight probability that deceased would have chosen that occupation. Eginoire v. Union County, 112 Iowa, 558, 84 N. W. 758. The mere fact that a married woman was not pursuing an independent occupation, does not defeat a recovery for damages to her estate where she had been prevented, by a temporary illness from which she had recovered, from pursuing such occupation, and where but for her death she would have pursued it. Myers v. Chicago, B. & Q. R. Co., 152 Iowa, 330, 131 N. W. 770. There can be no recovery for the pain and suffering of decedent. Dwyer v. Chicago, St. P., M. & O. Ry. Co., 84 Iowa, 479, 51 N. W. 244, 35 Am. St. Rep. 322; Jacobs v. Glucose Sugar Refining Co. (C. C.) 140 Fed. 766.

[20] See § 40.

§ 135. Kentucky [21]

§ 136. Louisiana

Under Rev. Civil Code, art. 2315, as amended, a recovery may be had (1) of such damages as the party injured could have recovered, and (2) of damages for the death.[22] No rule seems to be laid down in respect to the measure of damages under either cause of action, except that the damages are compensatory.[23] Louisiana is peculiar in allow-

---

[21] Ante, § 41.   [22] See § 42.

[23] In a case under the amendment of 1855 the court said that, in cases where no exact computation of damages can be made, discretion in fixing the amount is left to the judge and jury. Frank v. New Orleans & C. R. Co., 20 La. Ann. 25.

In an action by the father and mother of a son 18 years old, it appeared that the father was a policeman earning $50 a month, with 5 children, 3 of whom he provided for; that the son was earning $25 a month, which he devoted to the family. Held, that a verdict of $25,000 should be reduced to $2,000. Bermudez, C. J., said: "It is for the deprivation of his presence and support that his father and mother are entitled to relief. While we * * * admit that it is almost impossible, systematically, to figure out by items what may amount to an adequate relief, we think, under a somewhat instinctive appreciation, considering that, as it is a probability that in course of time the circumstances of E. M. might have changed, had he lived, an allowance of $2,000 would not be unreasonable." Myhan v. Louisiana Electric Light & Power Co., 41 La. Ann. 964, 6 South. 799, 7 L. R. A. 172, 17 Am. St. Rep. 436. Deceased was 22 years old, and contributed somewhat to the support of his family, consisting of his mother, the plaintiff, with whom he lived, and her two daughters, the younger 16 years old. She had property of no great value, and was in debt. Plaintiff sued upon both causes of action. Held, that a verdict of $7,500 should be reduced to $6,000. Breaux, J., said: "The object is not benefit, but compensation. * * * We will not particularize the damages, and we will not dissect the purest sentiments, and the kindest impulses, to establish how much is allowed for each particular item of suffering." McFee v. Vicksburg, S. & P.

ing damages, not merely for the pecuniary loss, but for the mental suffering, of the beneficiaries.[24]   Punitive damages cannot be recovered.[25]

R. Co., 42 La. Ann. 790, 7 South. 720. In an action by the surviving parents of a daughter who has been drowned, the damages may include expenses in finding the body, loss of service, and also the amount which the daughter was entitled to recover at the moment of her death. Le Blanc v. Sweet, 107 La. 355, 31 South. 766, 90 Am. St. Rep. 303. The amount of property which the father might have possibly earned up to the date of his probable natural death, which his children might have inherited, cannot be considered. Eichorn v. New Orleans & C. R., Light & Power Co., 114 La. 712, 38 South. 526, 8 Ann. Cas. 98. Though the parent in case of need has the right to look to the child for support, such right cannot be considered in a suit by the parent for the death of the child, where it does not appear that the parent is in need, or likely to be so. Bourg v. Brownell-Drews Lumber Co., 120 La. 1009, 45 South. 972, 124 Am. St. Rep. 448. In assessing damages claimed by a widow for the negligent killing of her husband, employed in a hazardous occupation, the pecuniary loss is impossible of determination on any scientific basis, and the courts can only exercise a sound discretion and award such amount as may seem just and not unduly oppressive to either litigant. Dobyns v. Yazoo & M. V. R. Co., 119 La. 72, 43 South. 934. See, also, Hamilton v. Morgan's L. & T. R. & S. S. Co., 42 La. Ann. 824, 8 South. 586; Cline v. Crescent City R. Co., 43 La. Ann. 327, 9 South. 122, 26 Am. St. Rep. 187; Westerfield v. Levis, 43 La. Ann. 63, 9 South. 52; Mattise v. Consumers' Ice Mfg. Co., 46 La. Ann. 1535, 16 South. 400, 49 Am. St. Rep. 356; McGuire v. Vicksburg, S. & P. R. Co., 46 La. Ann. 1543, 16 South. 457; Bland v. Shreveport Belt R. Co., 48 La. Ann. 1057, 20 South. 284, 36 L. R. A. 114; Rice v. Crescent City R. Co., 51 La. Ann. 108, 24 South. 791; Cherry v. Louisiana & A. R. Co., 121 La. 471, 46 South. 596, 17 L. R. A. (N. S.) 505, 126 Am. St. Rep. 323; Moren v. New Orleans Ry. & Light Co., 125 La. 944, 52 South. 106, 136 Am. St. Rep. 344; Burvant v. Wolfe, 126 La. 787, 52 South. 1025, 29 L. R. A. (N. S.) 677; Blackburn v. Louisiana Ry. & Nav. Co., 128 La. 319, 54 South. 865.

[24] Parker v. Crowell & Spencer Lumber Co., 115 La. 463, 39 South. 445; Dobyns v. Yazoo & M. V. R. Co., 119 La. 72, 43 South. 934; Bourg v. Brownell-Drews Lumber Co., 120 La. 1009, 45 South. 972,

[25] Hamilton v. Morgan's L. & T. R. & S. S. Co., 42 La. Ann. 824, 8 South. 586.

§ 137. Maine

Under the death act an action can be maintained only where the death was instantaneous; and if the death was not instantaneous, the action must be brought under the survival act.[26] Under the death act the jury may give such damages as they shall deem fair and just compensation, not exceeding $5,000, with reference to the pecuniary injuries resulting from the death, to the beneficiaries, and the measure of damages is the same as under Lord Campbell's act and similar enactments.[27] Under the survival act plaintiff may recover only such damages as the deceased sustained in his lifetime, nothing being allowed for the loss of life, nor for what he might have earned, had he lived longer.[28]

§ 138. Massachusetts [29]

§ 138—1. Michigan

Under the death act an action can be maintained only where the death was instantaneous; and if the death was

124 Am. St. Rep. 448; Wooten v. United Irrigation & Rice Milling Co., 128 La. 294, 54 South. 824; Robertson v. Town of Jennings, 128 La. 795, 55 South. 375; Underwood v. Gulf Refining Co. of Louisiana, 128 La. 968, 55 South. 641.

[26] Ante, § 43.

[27] McKay v. New England Dredging Co., 92 Me. 454, 43 Atl. 29. Damages cannot be awarded for the physical pain and suffering of the deceased, nor for the grief and sorrow of the beneficiary, as the sum given must be the present worth of the probable future pecuniary benefits of which the beneficiary has been deprived. Oakes v. Maine Cent. R. Co., 95 Me. 103, 49 Atl. 418. See, also, Conley v. Maine Cent. R. Co., 95 Me. 149, 49 Atl. 668; Ward v. Maine Cent. R. Co., 96 Me. 136, 51 Atl. 947.

[28] Ramsdell v. Grady, 97 Me. 319, 54 Atl. 763. Cf. Welch v. Maine Cent. R. Co., 86 Me. 552, 30 Atl. 116, 25 L. R. A. 658.

[29] See § 44.

not instantaneous, the action must be brought under the survival act.[30] Under the death act the jury may give such damages as they shall deem fair and just, with reference to the pecuniary injury resulting from the death, to the beneficiaries, and the measure of damages is the same as under Lord Campbell's act and similar enactments.[31] Under the survival act, the plaintiff may recover, not only such damages as the decedent sustained in his lifetime, such as damages for physical and mental suffering, but also damages for the decedent's loss sustained by reason of being deprived, by his injuries, of the ability to labor during the time he would probably have lived had he not been injured.[32]

[30] Ante, § 44—1.

[31] Rouse v. Detroit Electric Ry., 128 Mich. 149, 87 N. W. 68.

[32] Oliver v. Houghton County St. R. Co., 134 Mich. 367, 96 N. W. 434, 104 Am. St. Rep. 607, 3 Ann. Cas. 53. Plaintiff may recover the amount decedent would have earned during the period he would probably have lived, without any deduction for what it would probably have cost him for food, clothing, and other personal expenditures. Olivier v. Houghton County St. R. Co., 138 Mich. 242, 101 N. W. 530. See, also, Miller v. Sadowsky, 138 Mich. 502, 101 N. W. 621. An instruction that, if the jury found for plaintiff, their verdict should be for all damages sustained in consequence of the injury to and death of decedent, which would comprise a reasonable amount for pain and suffering he endured, and such sums as he would probably have earned during the time he would probably have lived, but for the injury, without reference to the amount he probably would have saved, and that the jury should estimate the present worth of his probable earnings during the time that he would probably have lived, at 5 per cent. simple interest, etc., stated the correct rule of damages. Davis v. Michigan Cent. R. Co., 147 Mich. 479, 111 N. W. 76. Pub. Acts 1905, No. 89, making the measure of damages substantially the same as that under the death act, was repealed by Pub. Acts 1907, No. 217. See Norblad v. Minneapolis, St. P. & S. S. M. R. Co., 156 Mich. 697, 118 N. W. 595. See, also, Kyes v. Valley Tel. Co., 132 Mich. 281, 93 N. W. 623; Ingersoll v. Detroit & M. Ry. Co., 163 Mich. 268, 128 N. W. 227, 32 L. R. A. (N. S.) 362.

§ 138—2. Mississippi

Formerly the statute provided that the jury might give such damages as might be fair and just with reference to the injury of the parties suing. The present statute provides that "the party or parties suing shall recover such damages as the jury may determine to be just, taking into consideration all the damages of every kind to the decedent and all damages of every kind to any and all of the parties interested in the suit." [33] There may now be a recovery of damages for the physical and mental suffering endured by a decedent between the injury and death, however short the time may be, and for such sum as the decedent might have recovered as the present value of his own expectancy, as well as of the damages which are to be assessed with reference to pecuniary injury resulting from the death to the beneficiaries. [34]

---

[33] Ante, § 44—2.

[34] A parent suing for the death of a minor child, may recover, not only the value of his services until majority, but such damages as the jury may award for the physical and mental suffering endured by the child between the injury and death, with such gratuities as the evidence may show the parent had a reasonable expectation of receiving before or after the child's majority, and such sum as the son might have recovered as the present value of his own expectancy. Cumberland Telephone & Telegraph Co. v. Anderson, 89 Miss. 732, 41 South. 263. A mother, suing for the death of a minor son, could not recover the value of his prospective earnings before majority, in absence of proof as to her age, health, constitution, etc. Mississippi Oil Co. v. Smith, 95 Miss. 528, 48 South. 735. See Cumberland Telephone & Telegraph Co. v. Pitchford (Miss.) 30 South. 41; Yazoo & M. V. R. Co. v. Farr, 94 Miss. 557, 48 South. 520.

§ 139. Missouri

In case of a recovery under Rev. St. 1909, § 5425, that section now provides that the defendant "shall forfeit and pay *as a penalty* for every such person, employé or passenger so dying the sum of *not less than $2,000 and not exceeding $10,000, in the discretion of the jury.*" [35] The section was amended in 1905 by adding the words in italics, and by changing the amount from $5,000 to the sum now provided. Under the section in its earlier form it was held that if the plaintiff established a right to recover he was entitled to the full sum of $5,000.[36] The section is remedial as well as penal, and the jury may consider, not only the negligence of the defendant, but the pecuniary loss to the plaintiff caused by the death.[37] The section "does not call

[35] See § 45.

[36] Le May v. Missouri Pac. R. Co., 105 Mo. 361, 16 S. W. 1049. See, also, Anderson v. Missouri Pac. R. Co., 196 Mo. 442, 93 S. W. 394, 113 Am. St. Rep. 748; Mangan v. Foley, 33 Mo. App. 250; Gormley v. St. Louis Transit Co., 126 Mo. App. 405, 103 S. W. 1147; King v. St. Louis & S. F. R. Co., 130 Mo. App. 368, 109 S. W. 859. An instruction that the jury cannot take into consideration the anguish or suffering of the deceased or of the plaintiff is properly refused. Tobin v. Missouri Pac. Ry. Co., 18 S. W. 996. The sum is not intended as a penalty, but as compensatory damages liquidated by the statute. Coover v. Moore, 31 Mo. 574. A petition, in an action under said section, failing to demand the full penalty prescribed, was defective. Casey v. St. Louis Transit Co., 205 Mo. 721, 103 S. W. 1146.

[37] Boyd v. Missouri Pac. Ry. Co,. 236 Mo. 54, 139 S. W. 561. See, also, Young v. St. Louis, I. M. & S. R. Co., 227 Mo. 307, 127 S. W. 19; Murphy v. Wabash R. Co., 228 Mo. 56, 128 S. W. 481; Ellis v. Metropolitan St. Ry. Co., 234 Mo. 657, 138 S. W. 23; Potter v. St. Louis & S. F. R. Co., 136 Mo. App. 125, 117 S. W. 593; Pratt v. Missouri Pac. R. Co., 139 Mo. App. 502, 122 S. W. 1125; Williams v. Metropolitan St. R. Co., 141 Mo. App. 625, 125 S. W. 522; Childress v. Southwest Missouri R. Co., 141 Mo. App. 667, 126 S. W. 169; Hartzler v.

for any measure of damages. It provides for a minimum and a maximum, and the exercise of the discretion by the jury between the two extremes. * * * As the statute has a remedial side to it, the jury may consider the extent of the injury to be remedial; and as it has a penal side, the jury have the right to consider the facts of the negligence in determining the amount to be allowed under that phase of the case." [38]

In case of recovery under section 5426, section 5427 provides that the jury may give such damages, not exceeding $10,000 (formerly $5,000), as they may deem fair and just with reference to the necessary injury resulting from such death to the surviving parties who may be entitled to sue, and also having regard to the mitigating and aggravating circumstances attending such wrongful act, neglect, or default.

In actions under section 5427 the words "having regard to the mitigating and aggravating circumstances" authorize exemplary damages, when the circumstances justify the award.[39] But, in the absence of circumstances justifying

Metropolitan St. R. Co., 140 Mo. App. 665, 126 S. W. 760; Johnston v. St. Louis & S. F. R. Co., 150 Mo. App. 304, 130 S. W. 413.

[38] Boyd v. Missouri Pac. Ry. Co., 236 Mo. 54, 139 S. W. 561.

[39] Owen v. Brockschmidt, 54 Mo. 285; Gray v. McDonald, 104 Mo. 303, 16 S. W. 398. What circumstances will mitigate or aggravate is a question of law, and, if any such exist, they should be pointed out by proper instructions. Rains v. St. Louis, I. M. & S. Ry. Co., 71 Mo. 164, 36 Am. Rep. 459; Nichols v. Winfrey, 79 Mo. 544. A general instruction that the jury should have regard to the mitigating and aggravating circumstances is bad, but, if there are no mitigating circumstances, the defendant cannot complain of the instruction for its generality. Nagel v. Missouri Pac. Ry. Co., 75 Mo. 653, 42 Am. Rep. 418; Smith v. Wabash, St. L. & P. Ry. Co., 92 Mo. 360, 4 S. W. 129, 1 Am. St. Rep. 729. Such an instruction is erroneous where there are no aggravating circumstances. Stoher v. St. Louis, I. M. & S. Ry. Co., 91 Mo. 509, 4 S. W. 389; Parsons v. Mis-

exemplary damages, only such damages can be recovered as will compensate the plaintiff for the pecuniary injury necessarily resulting from the death.[40]

The Missouri statute is peculiar in confining the right of action of a parent to the death of a minor child, and the

souri Pac. Ry. Co., 94 Mo. 286, 6 S. W. 464. Evidence of contributory negligence will not justify an instruction based on mitigating circumstances. McGowan v. St. Louis Ore & Steel Co., 16 S. W. 236. See Foppiano v. Baker, 3 Mo. App. 560. Where there are no aggravating circumstances, evidence of the financial condition of defendant is inadmissible. Morgan v. Durfee, 69 Mo. 469, 33 Am. Rep. 508. To authorize the recovery of exemplary damages, defendant must have acted maliciously or wantonly, or have been guilty of negligence so gross as to evince a conscious disregard of the rights of others, and the complaint must allege such facts. A mere allegation that defendant's negligence was gross is not sufficient. Otto Kuehne Preserving Co. v. Allen, 148 Fed. 666, 78 C. C. A. 418, 8 Ann. Cas. 746.

[40] McGowan v. St. Louis Ore & Steel Co., 16 S. W. 236; Id., 109 Mo. 518, 19 S. W. 199. It seems that "necessary" is equivalent to "pecuniary." Id., 109 Mo. 518, 19 S. W. 199, per Thomas, J. Morgan v. Durfee, 69 Mo. 469, 33 Am. Rep. 508, per Sherwood, J. Hickman v. Missouri Pac. Ry. Co., 22 Mo. App. 344. But an instruction to the jury that if they find for the plaintiffs they will assess the damages in such sum as they believe will compensate them for the pecuniary injury sustained by them in the death of deceased, not in excess of the sum of $5,000, is erroneous, as not furnishing the jury with a sufficiently definite rule for the measure of damages; although it is harmless error, where the verdict is only for $5,000, and the plaintiffs are four minor children, and deceased was only 40 years old, and was earning $3 a day. McGowan v. St. Louis Ore & Steel Co., 109 Mo. 518, 19 S. W. 199 (reversing on this point Id., 16 S. W. 236). See Schultz v. Moon, 33 Mo. App. 329. Where the essential elements of the damages are given to the jury in the language of the statute, its generality does not constitute reversible error; defendant being bound to point out, in its own instructions, the elements limiting the damages. Barth v. Kansas City El. Ry. Co., 142 Mo. 535, 44 S. W. 778. See, also, Browning v. Wabash Western R. Co., 124 Mo. 55, 27 S. W. 644; Geismann v. Missouri-Edison Electric Co., 173 Mo. 654, 73 S. W. 661; Sipple v. Laclede Gaslight Co., 125 Mo. App. 81, 102 S. W. 608. Cf. Coleman v. Himmelberger-Harrison Land & Lumber Co., 105 Mo. App. 254, 79 S. W. 981. The measure of damages in an

measure of damages, apart from exemplary damages, is the pecuniary benefit the parent could have hoped to derive from the child during minority.[41] And, conversely, the right of action for the death of a parent is confined to minor children, and the damages are restricted to compensation for the loss of the parent's support, etc., during minority.[42]

action by a parent for the death of his minor son does not include loss of comfort and society of the son; the words "necessary injury" meaning "pecuniary injury," and confining damages to property loss. Marshall v. Consolidated Jack Mines Co., 119 Mo. App. 270, 95 S. W. 972. See. also, Calcaterra v. Iovaldi, 123 Mo. App. 347, 100 S. W. 675. Cf. Sharp v. National Biscuit Co., 179 Mo. 553, 78 S. W. 787. Plaintiff is entitled also to compensation for prospective or proximate losses. Barth v. Kansas City El. Ry. Co., 142 Mo. 535, 44 S. W. 778. See, also, Haines v. Pearson, 107 Mo. App. 481, 81 S. W. 645; Young v. Waters-Pierce Oil Co., 185 Mo. 634, 84 S. W. 929; McCarty v. St. Louis Transit Co., 192 Mo. 396, 91 S. W. 132; Hach v. St. Louis. I. M. & S. R. Co., 208 Mo. 581, 106 S. W. 525; Overby v. Mears Min. Co., 144 Mo. App. 363, 128 S. W. 813.

[41] Parsons v. Missouri Pac. Ry. Co., 94 Mo. 286, 6 S. W. 464; Rains v. St. Louis, I. M. & S. Ry. Co., 71 Mo. 164, 36 Am. Rep. 459. In an action by parents for the death of a child, the court instructed that the measure of damages was what the child would have earned until he became 21, minus the cost of his support, clothes, and maintenance. Held, that inasmuch as the parents were entitled to damages for the loss of the comfort, society, and love of the child, which they were not given by the instruction, it was more favorable to defendant than it was entitled to. Sharp v. National Biscuit Co., 179 Mo. 553, 78 S. W. 787. But see Calcaterra v. Iovaldi, 123 Mo. App. 347, 100 S. W. 675; Dando v. Home Telephone Co., 126 Mo. App. 242, 103 S. W. 103. The measure of damages is the value of the child's services during minority, and burial and other expenses, if any, incurred by his death or sickness, less the expense of his support and maintenance during that time. Leahy v. Davis, 121 Mo. 227, 25 S. W. 941. See, also, Leahy v. Davis, 121 Mo. 227, 25 S. W. 941; Lee v. Publishers: Knapp & Co., 155 Mo. 610, 56 S. W. 458; Stumbo v. Duluth Zinc Co., 100 Mo. App. 635, 75 S. W. 185; Barnes v. Columbia Lead Co., 107 Mo. App. 608, 82 S. W. 203.

[42] McPherson v. St. Louis, I. M. & So. Ry. Co., 97 Mo. 253, 10 S. W.

The provisions of the Colorado [48] and New Mexico [44] statutes closely resemble that of Missouri. But in Colorado a different construction is put upon the words "hav-

846; McGowan v. St. Louis Ore & Steel Co., 16 S. W. 236; Id., 109 Mo. 518, 19 S. W. 199. The jury are not confined to nominal damages, though the earnings of the father are not shown. The loss of care in the education, maintenance, and support have a pecuniary value. Stoher v. St. Louis, I. M. & S. Ry. Co., 91 Mo. 509, 4 S. W. 389. In an action by a child for the death of her father, plaintiff may recover damages for the loss of support, education, and maintenance, and also for the loss of intellectual and moral instruction, and in estimating this latter element of damage, the jury is not confined to an exact calculation, but is vested with considerable discretion, with which the court will not interfere unless such discretion is abused. Gamache v. Johnston Tin Foil & Metal Co., 116 Mo. App. 596, 92 S. W. 918.

[48] Rev. St. 1908, §§ 2056–2059. The act of February 8, 1872, gave an action when death was caused by wrongful act, etc., to be brought by the personal representatives, for the benefit of the husband, wife, children, parents, etc. The measure of damages was held to be the estimated accumulations of the deceased during the probable remainder of his life, having reference to his age, occupation, habits, health, and ability. Kansas Pac. Ry. Co. v. Lundin, 3 Colo. 94; Denver, S. P. & P. Ry. Co. v. Woodward, 4 Colo. 1 (modifying Kansas Pac. Ry. Co. v. Miller, 2 Colo. 442). This is also held to be the measure of damages under the present statute. Hayes v. Williams, 17 Colo. 465, 30 Pac. 352. In an action for the death of a minor son, the complaint stated the relationship, age, occupation, amount of earnings, etc., and alleged damages to plaintiff in a certain sum. Held, that the complaint was sufficient to permit the recovery of such damages as naturally result from the death, without alleging special damages. Orman v. Mannix, 17 Colo. 564, 30 Pac. 1037, 17 L. R. A. 602, 31 Am. St. Rep. 340. In a suit by a parent for the death of a minor child, the measure of recovery is a sum equal to the net pecuniary benefit which plaintiff might have reasonably ex_

[44] The measure of compensatory damages is the present worth of the life of deceased, determined from the evidence as to age, earning capacity, health, habits, and probable duration of life, but with noth_ ing added by way of solatium to the distributees, and nothing for suffering by deceased. Cerrillos Coal R. Co. v. Deserant, 9 N. M. 49, 49 Pac. 807.

ing reference to the mitigating and aggravating circumstances," and it is held that they do not authorize exemplary damages.[45]

pected to receive. Pierce v. Conners, 20 Colo. 178, 37 Pac. 721, 46 Am. St. Rep. 279. A parent may recover damages for the death of a child, although the child never contributed to his support. Mollie Gibson Consolidated Mining & Milling Co. v. Sharp, 5 Colo. App. 321, 38 Pac. 850. Under section 2058 the recovery is limited to the resulting pecuniary loss, and an instruction which permits the jury to find any amount which they deem just, not exceeding $5,000, regardless of whether plaintiff suffered pecuniary loss, is erroneous. Denver & R. G. R. Co. v. Spencer, 25 Colo. 9, 52 Pac. 211. Where children in no manner dependent on their father seek to recover for his death, their recovery must be limited to the sum which he by his personal exertions, less his necessary personal expenses and those of his wife during her life, would have added to his estate. Denver & R. G. R. Co. v. Spencer, 27 Colo. 313, 61 Pac. 606, 51 L. R. A. 121. In an action by a husband for the death of his wife, damages can only be awarded for his pecuniary loss. Denver & R. G. R. Co. v. Gunning, 33 Colo. 280, 80 Pac. 727.

[45] "Taken in connection with the preceding language of the section, we are constrained to hold that the words 'mitigating and aggravating circumstances attending such wrongful act,' etc., contemplate circumstances not relating to the wrongful act itself, but such as affect the actual damages suffered by the surviving party entitled to sue, either by way of diminishing or enhancing the same. Hence the section allows compensatory damages only." Moffatt v. Tenney, 17 Colo. 189, 30 Pac. 348, approved in Hayes v. Williams, 17 Colo. 465, 30 Pac. 352, where the court intimates, however, that punitive damages may perhaps be recovered in actions of this kind under Act Feb. 19, 1889 (Mills' Ann. St. § 1512). An instruction that the damages should be such a sum as would compensate plaintiff "in a pecuniary sense for the loss," and that "in arriving at this sum" they might take into consideration mitigating or aggravating circumstances connected with the neglect or injury complained of, was proper, it not being necessary that the court should enumerate each and every aggravating or mitigating circumstance. Hayes v. Williams, 17 Colo. 465, 30 Pac. 352.

§ 139—1. Montana

Rev. Codes 1907, § 6485, provides that the father, or, in certain cases, the mother, may maintain an action for the death of a minor child, and a guardian for the death of a ward. Section 6486 gives a right of action, where the death of a person, not being a minor, is caused by wrongful act, neglect, or default, to the heirs or personal representatives of the decedent, and provides that under this and the preceding section "such damages may be given as under all the circumstances of the case may be just." While under this death act the damages are compensatory, in view of the broad language of the statute the rule appears to be applied with a good deal of liberality.[46] A provision of the Code, that in an action for tort, where the defendant has been guilty of oppression, malice, etc., the jury may give damages by way of punishment, has been held to apply to actions under section 6486.[47] Sections 5248–5250 make mine operators liable for damages to an employé through the negligence of coemployés and provide that in case of death

---

[46] The quantum of damages is for the jury. Hollingsworth v. Davis-Daly Estates Copper Co., 38 Mont. 143, 99 Pac. 142. The jury may take into consideration pecuniary loss decedent's widow sustained on account of being deprived of his comfort, society, and companionship. Mize v. Rocky Mountain Bell Telephone Co., 38 Mont. 521, 100 Pac. 971, 129 Am. St. Rep. 659, 16 Ann. Cas. 1189. In action for death of minor son, jury may fix damages at sum required to purchase annuity equal to amount that minor might reasonably be expected to contribute yearly to plaintiff during his expectancy of life. Gilman v. G. W. Dart Hardware Co., 42 Mont. 96, 111 Pac. 550. See, also, Yergy v. Helena Light & R. Co., 39 Mont. 213, 102 Pac. 310, 18 Ann. Cas. 1201; Neary v. Northern Pac. R. Co., 41 Mont. 480, 110 Pac. 226.

[47] Olsen v. Montana Ore Purchasing Co., 35 Mont. 400, 89 Pac. 731.

(308)

in consequence of injury or damages so sustained the right of action shall survive and may be prosecuted by the heirs and personal representatives. Under these sections the scope of recovery is the same as it would have been but for the death, including damages for the pain and suffering of the decedent, if he survived for any length of time, and also for his diminished earning capacity for the period of his natural expectancy.[48] Sections 5251, 5252, make persons and corporations operating railways and railroads liable for damages sustained by employés in consequence of the neglect, mismanagement, or willful wrongs, of omission or commission, of other employés, etc., and provide that in case of death the right of action shall survive and may be prosecuted by the heirs or personal representatives. Those sections, like the preceding, merely revive an action existing in favor of the employé, and do not create a new cause of action for damages sustained by the heirs, and consequently no action lies if the death was instantaneous.[49]

§ 140.   New Hampshire [50]

§ 141.   New Mexico [51]

§ 142.   North Carolina

"The plaintiff may recover such damages as are a fair and just compensation for the pecuniary injury resulting from" the death, and the amount recovered is to be dis-

[48] Beeler v. Butte & London Copper Development Co., 41 Mont. 465, 110 Pac. 528.

[49] Ante, § 45—1   [50] See § 47.   [51] See § 139.

tributed in the same manner as personal property in case
of intestacy.[52] The statute thus differs from Lord Campbell's act and other enactments which in substance provide
for damages to be measured by the pecuniary loss resulting
to the beneficiaries of the action. "The English statute,"
the supreme court has said,[53] "required the jury to apportion the damages among the beneficiaries as therein provided, and that made it necessary to take proof of the number, names, ages, etc., of the children. * * * It will be
observed that, under our statute, the pecuniary injury is
the measure. That means the value of the labor or amount
of the earnings of the deceased, if he had lived, without
regard to the number of the recipients of his labor; and
the jury, in arriving at such value, are allowed to know
by proofs whether he was an industrious or an idle man,
honest or dishonest, drinking or sober man, and the like,
and in that way the jury may work out the pecuniary
damage sustained by the family." The measure of damages
is the present value of the decedent's net income, to be ascertained by deducting his expenditure from his gross income, and by estimating the present value of the accumulation from such net income, based upon his expectation
of life; and in estimating the reasonable expectation of
pecuniary advantage from the continuance of his life, his

[52] See § 49.

[53] Bradley v. Ohio River & C. R. Co., 122 N. C. 972, 30 S. E. 8.
See, also, Collier v. Arrington's Ex'rs, 61 N. C. 356; Kesler v. Smith,
66 N. C. 154; Burton v. Wilmington & W. R. Co., 82 N. C. 504; Pickett v. Wilmington & W. R. Co., 117 N. C. 616, 23 S. E. 264, 30 L. R. A.
257, 53 Am. St. Rep. 611. A father may not recover damages for
mental anguish or for loss of services. Ballinger v. Rader, 153 N. C.
488, 69 S. E. 497; Byrd v. Southern Exp. Co., 139 N. C. 273, 51 S. E.
851. No punitive or exemplary damages can be recovered. Western
Union Telegraph Co. v. Catlett, 177 Fed. 71, 100 C. C. A. 489.

age, habits, industry, skill, and reasonable expectation of life should be considered.[54]

§ 144. Oregon

L. O. L. 1910, § 380, provides that, when death is caused by wrongful act or omission, the personal representative may maintain an action, and that the damages "shall be administered as other personal property of the deceased person." The statute does not further define the persons for whose benefit the action shall be brought, or exempt the amount recovered from the claims of creditors. It is accordingly held that the measure of damages is the pecuniary loss *to the estate,* which consists in what the deceased would probably have accumulated for the benefit of his estate during the residue of his life, taking into con-

---

[54] Benton v. North Carolina R. Co., 122 N. C. 1007, 30 S. E. 333; Watson v. Seaboard A. L. R. Co., 133 N. C. 188, 45 S. E. 555. After the gross income or earnings which deceased would have made is determined, there should be deducted therefrom only his reasonably necessary personal expenses, taking into consideration his age, manner of living, and business, and not the total expenditures which deceased might have made for family and other expenses. Carter v. North Carolina R. Co., 139 N. C. 499, 52 S. E. 642. The recovery is what deceased would have earned, reduced only by what his personal expenses would have been, and not in addition by what his expenses for his family and dependants would have been. Roberson v. Greenleaf Johnson Lumber Co., 154 N. C. 328, 70 S. E. 630. Acts 1905, p. 366, c. 347, prescribing the method for determining the present value of an annuity, does not establish a rule for estimating the present value of the probable future earnings. Poe v. Raleigh & A. Air Line R. Co., 141 N. C. 525, 54 S. E. 406. In an action for the death of a child 5 months old, the measure of damages is the difference between such infant's probable gross income, based on his life expectancy, and the probable cost of his living. Russell v. Windsor Steamboat Co., 126 N. C. 961, 36 S. E. 191. See, also, Davis v. Seaboard Air Line R. Co., 136 N. C. 115, 48 S. E. 591, 1 Ann. Cas. 214.

sideration his age, ability, and disposition to labor, and his habits of living and expenditure.[55]

§ 145. Pennsylvania

The act of April 15, 1851, § 19,[56] provides that the widow, or, if no widow, the personal representatives, may recover "damages for the death." The act of April 4, 1868, § 2,[57] provides that, in actions against common carriers and railroad corporations, "only such compensation for loss or damage shall be recovered as the evidence shall clearly prove to have been pecuniarily suffered or sustained."

The latter section simply declared the law as previously

---

[55] Holmes v. Oregon & C. R. Co. (D. C.) 5 Fed. 75, 6 Sawy. 262; Carlson v. Oregon Short Line & U. N. Ry. Co., 21 Or. 450, 28 Pac. 497; Skottowe v. Oregon, S. L. & U. N. Ry. Co., 22 Or. 430, 30 Pac. 222, 22 L. R. A. 593; Mullen v. Same, 22 Or. 430, 30 Pac. 222, 16 L. R. A. 593; Ladd v. Foster (D. C.) 31 Fed. 827; Holland v. Brown (D. C.) 35 Fed. 43. See, also, Perham v. Portland General Electric Co., 33 Or. 451, 53 Pac. 14, 24, 40 L. R. A. 799, 72 Am. St. Rep. 730; Schleiger v. Northern Terminal Co., 43 Or. 4, 72 Pac. 324; Staats v. Twohy Bros. Co. (Or.) 123 Pac. 909; The Aurora (D. C.) 178 Fed. 587.

[56] Pepper & Lewis' Dig. p. 5331, par. 2.

[57] 2 Bright. Purd. Dig. p. 1268, § 7. This act limited the liability of common carriers and railroad corporations in case of death to $5,000, and provided that, upon acceptance of the provisions of the act by any corporation, the same should become part of its act of incorporation. The act, so far as it limited the liability, was held to be avoided by Const. 1874, art. 3, § 21. See appendix. Lewis v. Hollahan, 103 Pa. 425. It was also held that the act did not constitute a contract between the state and an accepting corporation, having a previously granted charter whose road was not constructed on the faith of it. Pennsylvania R. Co. v. Bowers, 124 Pa. 183, 16 Atl. 836, 2 L. R. A. 621, overruling Pennsylvania R. Co. v. Langdon, 92 Pa. 21, 37 Am. Rep. 651. See, also, Kay v. Pennsylvania R. Co., 65 Pa. 269, 3 Am. Rep. 628.

decided,[58] damages being confined to such loss on the part of the surviving family as is capable of pecuniary estimate.[59]

§ 145—1. Rhode Island

The death act provides that the amount recovered "shall one-half thereof go to the husband or widow, and one-half thereof to the children of the deceased, and if there be no children the whole shall go to the husband or widow, and, if there be no husband or widow, to the next of kin, in the proportion provided by law in relation to the distribution of personal property left by persons dying intestate." The statute thus distributes the total amount recovered according to a fixed rule, and without regard to the greater or less damage suffered by any beneficiary, and the action is considered as though brought in behalf of the estate of the decedent for the damage caused to the estate by the death.[60]

---

[58] Pennsylvania R. Co. v. Keller, 67 Pa. 300. See Cleveland & P. R. Co. v. Rowan, 66 Pa. 393.

[59] Pennsylvania R. Co. v. Zebe, 33 Pa. 318. The court distinguishes this case, which was under the act of April 26, 1855, from Pennsylvania R. Co. v. McCloskey's Adm'r, 23 Pa. 526, which was under the act of April 15, 1851, on the ground that the later act changed the law by confining the recovery to the persons therein named. See, also, Pennsylvania R. Co. v. Butler, 57 Pa. 335; Pennsylvania R. Co. v. Henderson, 51 Pa. 315; Pennsylvania Tel. Co. v. Varnau, 15 Atl. 624. See, also, Schnatz v. Philadelphia & R. R. R., 160 Pa. 602, 28 Atl. 952.

[60] McCabe v. Narragansett Electric Lighting Co., 27 R. I. 1, 61 Atl. 667. See, also, Wilson v. New York, N. H. & H. R. R. Co., 29 R. I. 146, 69 Atl. 364; Underwood v. Old Colony St. R. Co., 33 R. I. 319, 80 Atl. 390; McLaughlin v. Hebron Mfg. Co. (C. C.) 171 Fed. 269. The measure of damages is the pecuniary loss sustained, to be ascertained by first finding the gross amount of the prospective income or earnings, deducting therefrom what deceased would have

§ 145—2. South Carolina

Civ. Code 1902, § 2852, provides that the action shall be for the benefit of the wife or husband or child or children, and if there be none such, for the benefit of the parent or parents, and if there be none such, for the benefit of the heirs at law or distributees of the decedent who may be dependent on him for support, and that "the jury may give such damages, *including exemplary damages where such wrongful act, neglect or default was the result of recklessness, willfulness or malice,* as they may think proportioned to the injury resulting from such death to the parties respectively for whom and for whose benefit such action shall be brought." The words in italics were not originally in the statute, but were inserted in 1902, and before the amendment exemplary damages were not recoverable.[61] But before the amendment and since the provision that the jury may give such damages as they think proportioned to the injury resulting from the death to the beneficiaries was given a broad construction; it being held that the measure

---

to lay out, as a producer, to render the service or to acquire the money that he might be expected to produce, computing such expenses according to his station in life and his means and personal habits, and then reducing the net result so obtained to its present value. McCabe v. Narragansett Electric Lighting Co., 26 R. I. 427, 59 Atl. 112; Reynolds v. Narragansett Electric Lighting Co., 26 R. I. 457, 59 Atl. 393.

[61] Nohrden v. Northeastern R. Co., 54 S. C. 492, 32 S. E. 524; Garrick v. Florida Cent. & P. R. Co., 53 S. C. 448, 31 S. E. 334, 69 Am. St. Rep. 874. Under Civ. Code 1902, §§ 2851, 2852, giving a right to recover exemplary damages, the amount is left to the discretion of the jury. Brickman v. Southern Ry., 74 S. C. 306, 54 S. E. 553. See, also, Osteen v. Southern Ry., 76 S. C. 368, 57 S. E. 196.

of damages is not confined to the pecuniary loss,[62] and that damages for the mental anguish of the beneficiaries may be recovered.[63]

§ 147. Tennessee

Shannon's Code, 1896, § 4025,[64] provides that the right of action which a person who dies from injuries received from another, or whose death is caused by the wrongful act, omission, or killing by another, would have had in case death had not ensued, shall pass to his widow, or, in case there is no widow, to his children or his personal representative, for the benefit of his widow or next of kin. Section 4029 [65] provides that the plaintiff may recover for

---

[62] Strother v. South Carolina & G. R. Co., 47 S. C. 375, 25 S. E. 272; Trimmier v. Atlanta & C. A. L. Ry., 81 S. C. 203, 62 S. E. 209; Turbyfill v. Atlanta & C. A. L. Ry. Co., 86 S. C. 379, 68 S. E. 687. A pecuniary loss need not be shown in an action for death of an infant. Mason v. Southern Ry. Co., 58 S. C. 70, 36 S. E. 440, 53 L. R. A. 913, 79 Am. St. Rep. 826. Where there is no evidence of pecuniary loss, it is not error to instruct the jury that they should consider all the elements of compensatory damages, except that based on pecuniary loss. Barksdale v. Seaboard Air Line Ry., 76 S. C. 183, 56 S. E. 906. No recovery can be had for the negligent or wanton exposure of decedent's dead body. Pinson v. Southern Ry., 85 S. C. 355, 67 S. E. 464.

[63] Brown v. Southern R. Co., 65 S. C. 260, 43 S. E. 794. See, also, Nohrden v. Northeastern R. Co., 59 S. C. 87, 37 S. E. 228, 82 Am. St. Rep. 826; Stuckey v. Atlantic Coast Line R. Co., 60 S. C. 237, 38 S. E. 416, 85 Am. St. Rep. 842. A wife and child may recover for mental anguish and loss of companionship. Brickman v. Southern Ry., 74 S. C. 306, 54 S. E. 553.

[64] Sections 3130, 3131 are Acts 1851, c. 17.

[65] Section 4029 is act of 1883, c. 186. Before this act only such damages were recoverable as the deceased might have recovered if he had lived. Nashville & C. R. Co. v. Smith, 9 Lea, 471; East Tennessee, V. & G. R. Co. v. Toppins, 10 Lea, 58; Louisville & N. R. Co. v. Conley, 10 Lea, 531; Chicago, St. L. & N. O. R. Co. v. Pounds, 11 Lea, 130; Trafford v. Adams Exp. Co., 8 Lea, 96; East

(315)

the mental and physical suffering, loss of time, and necessary expenses resulting to the deceased from the personal injuries, and also the damages resulting to the parties for whose benefit the action survives from the death.

The right of action, whether the death was instantaneous or not, passes with all its incidents to the personal representative,[66] and, if fraud, malice, gross negligence, or oppression upon the part of the defendant be shown, exemplary damages may be recovered.[67]

The contributory negligence of the deceased may be shown in mitigation of damages.[68] In estimating the damages, the jury must consider the value of the life, as determined by the age, condition, capacity for earning money, and expectation of life of the deceased, and also the amount of compensation due for the physical or mental sufferings; but the principal inquiry is, how much negligence was dis-

Tennessee, V. & G. R. Co. v. Gurley, 12 Lea, 46. Though the earlier cases had held that damages for the loss caused by the death were also recoverable. Nashville & C. R. Co. v. Prince, 2 Heisk. 580; Nashville & C. R. Co. v. Smith, 6 Heisk. 174; Nashville & C. R. Co. v. Stevens, 9 Heisk. 12; Collins v. East Tennessee, V. & G. R. Co., 9 Heisk. 841; East Tennessee, V. & G. R. Co. v. Mitchell, 11 Heisk. 400. Cf. Louisville & N. R. Co. v. Burke, 6 Cold. 45.

[66] See note, § 75.

[67] Haley v. Mobile & O. R. Co., 7 Baxt. 239; Kansas City, Ft. S. & M. R. Co. v. Daughtry, 88 Tenn. 721, 13 S. W. 698. An instruction that, if the negligence was gross or wanton, "you shall make proper additions" by way of punitive damages, is erroneous, in making the assessment of punitive damages compulsory, and not discretionary. Louisville & N. R. Co. v. Satterwhite, 112 Tenn. 185, 79 S. W. 106.

[68] Louisville & N. R. Co. v. Burke, 6 Cold. 45; Nashville & C. R. Co. v. Smith, 6 Heisk. 174; Louisville & N. R. Co. v. Howard, 90 Tenn. 144, 19 S. W. 116. See, also, Jenkins v. Hankins, 98 Tenn. 545, 41 S. W. 1028; Artenberry v. Southern Ry. Co., 103 Tenn. 266, 52 S. W. 878; Louisville & N. R. Co. v. Satterwhite, 112 Tenn. 185, 79 S. W. 106.

played by the defendant, and to what extent did the negligence of the deceased contribute? [69]

[69] Deceased was 57 years old, in declining health, his monthly
earnings $25, and his sufferings had not been extreme; the neg-
ligence of defendant was not gross, and there was evidence of contributory negligence. Held, that a verdict of $12,000 was excessive.
Snodgrass, J., said: "The principal inquiry is not what is the value
of the life taken. It is whether and how much negligence was dis-
played in taking it, and whether and to what extent the negligence
of the deceased caused or contributed to it, and, from the reasonable and just compensation to be given upon determining the first
inquiry against the negligent wrongdoer, what amount should be
deducted on account of the contributing fault of the deceased.".
Louisville & N. R. Co. v. Stacker, 86 Tenn. 343, 6 S. W. 737, 6 Am.
St. Rep. 840. The statute but preserved the right of action accruing to deceased, and did not create a new cause of action in the
widow, or child, or personal representative; and in the prosecution
of that action damages were recoverable for the physical and mental
suffering, loss of time, etc., to deceased in consequence of his injuries, and accruing up to the time of his death, and also damages
to compensate the widow or next of kin for the pecuniary loss sustained by them by the death of deceased, which latter are equivalent to those accruing for loss of earning capacity to one totally dis-
abled; and hence an instruction permitting a recovery for deceased's loss of earning capacity and also for pecuniary damages
sustained by his widow and child was erroneous. 'Davidson Bene-
dict Co. v. Severson, 109 Tenn. 572, 72 S. W. 967 (reviewing decisions). A widow cannot recover for her mental or physical suffering occasioned by the death. Knoxville, C. G. & L. R. Co. v. Wy-
rick, 99 Tenn. 500, 42 S. W. 434. A widow's loss of her husband's
aid, other than pecuniary, such as aid of advice and counsel, and
her loss of comfort and of his society, are not elements of damages. Illinois Cent. R. Co. v. Bentz, 108 Tenn. 670, 69 S. W. 317,
58 L. R. A. 690, 91 Am. St. Rep. 763. See, also, Tennessee, Coal &
R. Co. v. Roddy, 85 Tenn. 400, 5 S. W. 286; Chesapeake, O. & S. W.
R. Co. v. Hendricks, 88 Tenn. 710, 13 S. W. 696, 14 S. W. 488;
Loague v. Memphis & C. R. Co., 91 Tenn. 458, 19 S. W. 430; Illinois Cent. R. Co. v. Spence, 93 Tenn. 173, 23 S. W. 211, 42 Am. St.
Rep. 907; Southern Queen Mfg. Co. v. Morris, 105 Tenn. 654, 58
S. W. 651; Freeman v. Illinois Cent. R. Co., 107 Tenn. 240, 64 S.
W. 1; Stuber v. Louisville & N. R. Co., 113 Tenn. 305, 87 S. W.
411; Memphis St. R. Co. v. Berry, 118 Tenn. 581, 102 S. W. 85;

§ 148.   Texas [70]

§ 148—1.   Utah

Comp. Laws 1907, §§ 2911, 2912, provide for an action when death is caused by wrongful act or neglect, to be brought by the father, or, in certain cases, the mother, in case of the death of a minor child, by a guardian in case of the death of a ward, and by the heirs or personal representatives of the decedent for their benefit in case of the death of a person not a minor, and that "such damages may be given as under all the circumstances may be just." The statute contemplates damages for the pecuniary injury or loss resulting from the death to the beneficiaries, which include damages for loss of society and comfort, while excluding damages for sorrow, grief, or anguish of the beneficiaries and for the pain or suffering of the decedent.[71]

Memphis Consol. Gas & Electric Co. v. Letson, 135 Fed. 969, 68 C. C. A. 453.

[70] See § 55.

[71] Pool v. Southern Pac. Co., 7 Utah, 303, 26 Pac. 654; Hyde v. Union Pac. Ry. Co., 7 Utah, 356, 26 Pac. 979; Wells v. Denver & R. G. W. Ry. Co., 7 Utah, 482, 27 Pac. 688; Chilton v. Union Pac. Ry. Co., 8 Utah, 47, 29 Pac. 963; Corbett v. Oregon Short Line R. Co., 25 Utah, 449, 71 Pac. 1065. Cf. Spiking v. Consolidated Ry. & Power Co., 33 Utah, 313, 93 Pac. 838; Evans v. Oregon Short Line R. Co., 37 Utah, 431, 108 Pac. 638, Ann. Cas. 1912C, 259. The damages in an action by parents for the death of an adult child are not limited to the probable contributions of money which the parents would have received during the child's lifetime, but may also consist of the elements entering into the domestic relations of parent and child living in one family, or otherwise. Rogers v. Rio Grande Western Ry. Co., 32 Utah, 367, 90 Pac. 1075, 125 Am. St. Rep. 876. A judgment for damages for negligent death, supported by some legitimate and competent proof, will not be disturbed on appeal merely because it is excessive, as, under the constitution, the de-

§ 149.　Virginia

The statute provides that the jury "may award such damages as to it may seem fair and just, not exceeding $10,-000," and that they may direct in what proportion it may be distributed to the beneficiaries named, and that if there be none such the amount shall be assets in the hands of the personal representative, to be disposed of according to law.[72] The jury is not confined to the pecuniary loss, but may give damages for the loss of society, and by way of solace and comfort for the sorrow, suffering, and mental anguish occasioned by the death.[73]

§ 150.　Washington

The statute gives a right of action when the death of a person is caused by the wrongful act or neglect of another

termination of the amount of a verdict rests entirely with the trial court and jury. Corbett v. Oregon Short Line R. Co., supra.

[72] See § 56.

[73] Matthews v. Warner's Adm'r, 70 Va. 570, 26 Am. Rep. 396; Baltimore & O. R. Co. v. Noell's Adm'r, 73 Va. 394; Simmons v. McConnell, 86 Va. 494, 10 S. E. 838; Bertha Zinc Co. v. Black's Adm'r, 88 Va. 303, 13 S. E. 452; Portsmouth St. R. Co. v. Peed's Adm'r, 102 Va. 662, 47 S. E. 850. Seē, also, Chesapeake & O. R. Co. v. Rodgers' Adm'x, 100 Va. 324, 41 S. E. 732; Norfolk & W. Ry. Co. v. Munsell's Adm'r, 109 Va. 417, 64 S. E. 50. In Matthews v. Warner, supra, the court rests its decision on the language of the act that the jury "may award such damages as to it may seem fair and just," which it says differs from that of other states in not expressly or impliedly limiting the damages to pecuniary loss. In an action for the death of plaintiff's husband, she was entitled to recover compensation for the loss of his care, attention, and society, and such sum as may be deemed fair and just by way of comfort for the sorrow, suffering, and mental anguish occasioned by the death. Norfolk & W. R. Co. v. Cheatwood's Adm'r, 103 Va. 356, 49 S. E. 489.

in favor of designated beneficiaries, and provides that "the jury may give such damages as under all the circumstances of the case may to them seem just." [74] In spite of the broad language used, the measure of damages appears to be substantially the same as under statutes more closely resembling Lord Campbell's act, being the pecuniary loss resulting to beneficiaries from the death, without any allowance by way of solatium.[75]

§ 151. West Virginia

Under the statute of this state,[76] which resembles that of Virginia, and which provides that the jury "may give such damages as they shall deem fair and just, not exceeding $10,000," the jury are not confined to compensative damages for mere pecuniary loss, but may consider the

[74] See § 57, § 144.

[75] Walker v. McNeill, 17 Wash. 582, 50 Pac. 518. See, also, Harris v. Puget Sound Electric Ry., 52 Wash. 289, 100 Pac. 838; Ohrstrom v. City of Tacoma, 57 Wash. 121, 106 Pac. 629; Walters v. Spokane International Ry. Co., 58 Wash. 293, 108 Pac. 593; Tecker v. Seattle, R. & S. Ry. Co., 60 Wash. 570, 111 Pac. 791, Ann. Cas. 1912B, 842; Cox v. Wilkeson Coal & Coke Co., 61 Wash. 343, 112 Pac. 231; Northern Pac. R. Co. v. Freeman, 83 Fed. 82, 27 C. C. A. 457; Seattle Electric Co. v. Hartless, 144 Fed. 379, 75 C. C. A. 317. Evidence showing the age of decedent, his life expectancy, and his earning capacity was sufficient to enable the jury to assess the damages. Archibald v. Lincoln County, 50 Wash. 55, 96 Pac. 831. A husband can recover for funeral expenses resulting directly from the wrongful death of his wife. Philby v. Northern Pac. Ry. Co., 46 Wash. 173, 89 Pac. 468, 9 L. R. A. (N. S.) 1193, 123 Am. St. Rep. 926, 13 Ann. Cas. 742. See, also, Dean v. Oregon R. & Nav. Co., 44 Wash. 564, 87 Pac. 824. While loss of decedent's society, protection, and guidance is an element of damage, it is only the pecuniary, and not the sentimental, value thereof for which recovery may be had. Felt v. Puget Sound Electric Ry. (C. C.) 175 Fed. 477.

[76] See § 58.

sorrow, mental distress, and bereavement of the beneficiaries,[77] and may also give punitive or exemplary damages.[78]

§ 152.   Limit of recovery

Many statutes provide that the amount that may be recovered as damages shall not exceed a certain sum. This sum is limited to $5,000 in Colorado, Connecticut, Illinois, Maine, and Wyoming; to $7,500 in Minnesota and Oregon; to $7,000 in New Hampshire; to $10,000 in Alaska, Connecticut, the District of Columbia, Illinois, Indiana, Kansas, Missouri, Ohio, Oklahoma, South Dakota, Virginia, West Virginia, and Wisconsin. In some states a minimum as well as a maximum limit is imposed, and in some different amounts are fixed for the different rights of action which are created. · In many states the statutes impose no limit.

[77] Kelley v. Ohio River R. Co., 58 W. Va. 216, 52 S. E. 520, 2 L. R. A. (N. S.) 898. See, also, Searle v. Kanawha & O. R. Co., 32 W. Va. 370, 9 S. E. 248; Chesapeake & O. R. Co. v. Hawkins, 174 Fed. 597, 98 C. C. A. 443, 26 L. R. A. (N. S.) 309; Baltimore & O. R. Co. v. Taylor, 186 Fed. 828, 109 C. C. A. 172. In Kelley v. Ohio River R. Co., supra, the court points out that the case is clearer than in Virginia, since in the original act the damages were to be assessed "with reference to the pecuniary injury resulting from such death," and these words were subsequently eliminated. The verdict of a jury in an action for death from wrongful act cannot be set aside for excessiveness in an amount under $10,000, their assessment being final, unless the verdict be the result of passion, prejudice, partiality, or corruption on the part of the jury. Thomas v. Wheeling Electrical Co., 46 W. Va. 395, 46 S. E. 217. See, also, Sample v. Consolidated Light & Ry. Co., 50 W. Va. 472, 40 S. E. 597, 694, 57 L. R. A. 186.

[78] Turner v. Norfolk & W. R. Co., 40 W. Va. 675, 22 S. E. 83.

TIFF.DEATH W.A.(2D ED.)—21   (321)

CHAPTER X

DAMAGES

§ 153. Measure of damages under statutes similar to Lord Campbell's act—Pecuniary loss to beneficiaries

Lord Campbell's act provides that the jury may assess such damages as they may think proportioned to the in-

(322)

jury resulting from the death to the parties respectively for whose benefit the action shall be brought. This language has been substantially followed in the District of Columbia, Maryland, Mississippi, North Dakota, South Carolina, South Dakota, and Texas, although in Texas exemplary damages may also be given.

A more common form of language is that of the original New York act, viz. that the damages may be such a sum as the jury shall deem a fair and just compensation, with reference to the *pecuniary* injuries resulting from the death to the wife and next of kin. This language has been substantially followed in Arkansas, Illinois, Maine, Michigan, Nebraska, New Jersey, Ohio, Vermont, and Wisconsin, and (with certain important qualifications) in Colorado, Missouri, Nevada, and New Mexico.

In other states the language is broader, viz.: Alabama, "such damages as the jury may assess;" California, Idaho, Montana, and Utah, "such damages as, under all the circumstances of the case, may be just;" Arizona and Wyoming, "such damages as they shall deem fair and just;" Florida, "such damages as the parties * * * may have sustained;" Pennsylvania, "damages for the death;" Delaware, "damages for the death and loss thus occasioned."

In Indiana, Kansas, Minnesota, and Oklahoma, there is no express provision as to the measure of damages, except that limiting the amount of recovery.

In spite of these differences in phraseology, it is believed that the principles applicable to the measure of damages under all these acts is generally the same, viz., that *the damages are measured by the pecuniary loss resulting to the beneficiaries of the action from the death.*[1] This statement, however, is subject to the qualification that certain

---

[1] As to other acts, see the preceding chapter.

of the acts authorize exemplary, in addition to compensatory, damages.

§ 154.   No damages for solatium

In Blake v. Midland Ry. Co.,[2] which is perhaps the leading case upon the measure of damages, Coleridge, J., said: "The title of this act may be some guide to its meaning; and it is 'An act for compensating the families of persons killed,' not for solacing their wounded feelings;" and in that case it was held that, in assessing damages, the jury could not take into consideration the mental sufferings of the plaintiff for the loss of her husband, and that, as the damages exceeded any loss sustained by her admitting of a *pecuniary* estimate, they must be considered excessive. As has been stated, the New York act, and some others which have been modeled upon it, require the damages to be assessed with reference to the "pecuniary" injuries. But, irrespective of the use of "pecuniary" in the various enactments, the construction adopted in Blake v. Midland Ry. Co. has been almost universally followed, and it is held that the jury are confined to the pecuniary loss, and that nothing can be allowed by way of solatium for the grief and wounded feelings of the beneficiaries,[3] or to compen-

---

[2] 18 Q. B. 93, 21 L. J. Q. B. 233, 16 Jur. 562.

[3] This principle is expressly declared in nearly every case in which the measure of damages is discussed. It is sufficient to cite the following: Illinois Cent. R. Co. v. Barron, 5 Wall. 95, 18 L. Ed. 591; Barron v. Illinois Cent. R. Co., 1 Biss. 412, Fed. Cas. No. 1052; Id., 1 Biss. 453, Fed. Cas. No. 1053; Whiton v. Chicago & N. W. R. Co., 2 Biss. 282, Fed. Cas. No. 17,597; Chicago & N. W. R. Co. v. Whitton, 13 Wall. 270, 20 L. Ed. 571; Little Rock & Ft. S. Ry. Co. v. Barker, 33 Ark. 350, 34 Am. Rep. 44; City of Chicago v. Major, 18 Ill. 349, 68 Am. Dec. 553; Conant v. Griffin, 48 Ill. 410; City of Chicago v. Scholten, 75 Ill. 468; Chicago City Ry. Co. v. Gillam, 27 Ill.

sate them for the mere loss of society or of companionship which they have suffered.[4] A different rule was once de-

App. 386; Barley v. Chicago & A. R. Co., 4 Biss. 430, Fed. Cas. No. 997; Brady v. Chicago, 4 Biss. 448, Fed. Cas. No. 1,796; Kansas Pac. Ry. Co. v. Cutter, 19 Kan. 83; State to Use of Coughlan v. Baltimore & O. R. Co., 24 Md. 84, 87 Am. Dec. 600; Mynning v. Detroit, L. & N. R. Co., 59 Mich. 257, 26 N. W. 514; Hutchins v. St. Paul, M. & M. Ry. Co., 44 Minn. 5, 46 N. W. 79; Collins v. Davidson (C. C.) 19 Fed. 83; Hardy v. Minneapolis & St. L. R. Co. (C. C.) 36 Fed. 657; Schaub v. Hannibal & St. J. R. Co., 106 Mo. 74, 16 S. W. 924; McGowan v. St. Louis, Ore & Steel Co. (Mo.) 16 S. W. 236; Atchison, T. & S. F. R. Co. v. Wilson, 48 Fed. 57, 1 C. C. A. 25; Besenecker v. Sale, 8 Mo. App. 211; Anderson v. Chicago, B. & Q. R. Co., 35 Neb. 95, 52 N. W. 840; Oldfield v. New York & H. R. Co., 14 N. Y. 310; Tilley v. Hudson River R. Co., 29 N. Y. 252, 86 Am. Dec. 297; s. c., 24 N. Y. 471; Wise v. Teerpenning, 8 N. Y. Leg. Obs. 153; Dorman v. Broadway R. Co., 1 N. Y. Supp. 334; Steel v. Kurtz, 28 Ohio St. 191; Au v. New York, L. E. & W. R. Co. (C. C.) 29 Fed. 72; Pennsylvania R. Co. v. Zebe, 33 Pa. 318; Cleveland & P. R. Co. v. Rowan, 66 Pa. 393; Pennsylvania R. Co. v. Butler, 57 Pa. 335; March v. Walker, 48 Tex. 375; Southern Cotton Press & Mfg. Co. v. Bradley, 52 Tex. 587; City of Galveston v. Barbour, 62 Tex. 172, 50 Am. Rep. 519; Galveston, H. & S. A. Ry. Co. v. Matula, 79 Tex. 577, 15 S. W. 573; Taylor, B. & H. Ry. Co. v. Warner, 84 Tex. 122, 19 S. W. 449; McGown v. International & G. N. R. Co., 85 Tex. 289, 20 S. W. 80; Webb v. Denver & R. G. W. Ry. Co., 7 Utah, 17, 24 Pac. 616; Hyde v. Union Pac. Ry. Co., 7 Utah, 356, 26 Pac. 979; Wells v. Denver & R. G. W. Ry. Co., 7 Utah, 482, 27 Pac. 688; Needham v. Grand Trunk R. Co., 38 Vt. 294; Potter v. Chicago & N. W. Ry. Co., 21 Wis. 372, 94 Am. Dec. 548. Under the Scotch law the jury may administer a solatium. Patterson v. Wallace, 1 Macq. H. L. Cas. 748. See, also, Howey v. New England Nav. Co., 83 Conn. 278, 76 Atl. 469 (New York statute); Smith v. Cissel, 22 App. D. C. 318; Florida Cent. & P. R. Co. v. Foxworth, 41 Fla. 1, 25 South. 338, 79 Am. St. Rep. 149; O'Fallon Coal & Mining Co. v. Laquet, 198 Ill. 125, 64 N. E. 767; Chicago & E. I. R. Co. v. Rains, 203 Ill. 417, 67 N. E. 840; Johnson County v. Carmen, 71 Neb. 682, 99 N. W. 502; Kountz v. Toledo, St. L. & W. R. Co. (C. C.) 189 Fed. 494 (Ohio statute); Gulf, C. & S. F. R. Co. v. Farmer, 102 Tex. 235, 115 S. W. 260; Texas & N. O. R. Co. v. Green, 42 Tex. Civ. App. 216, 95 S. W. 694.

[4] Gillard v. Lancashire & Y. Ry. Co., 12 L. T. 356; Schaub v. Hannibal & St. J. R. Co., 106 Mo. 74, 16 S. W. 924; Atchison, T. & S.

clared in Indiana.[5]　In California,[6] Idaho,[7] and Florida,[8] in estimating the pecuniary loss, the jury may take into con-

---

F. R. Co. v. Wilson, 48 Fed. 57, 1 C. C. A. 25; Green v. Hudson River R. Co., 2 Abb. Dec. (N. Y.) 277, affirming s. c., 32 Barb. 27; Taylor, B. & H. Ry. Co. v. Warner, 84 Tex. 122, 19 S. W. 449; Mc-Gown v. International & G. N. Ry. Co., 85 Tex. 289, 20 S. W. 80, and cases in preceding note. In an action by the husband, the court charged that damages should be given as a pecuniary compensation, the jury measuring plaintiff's loss by a just estimate of the wife's services and companionship; that is, by their value in a pecuniary sense, nothing being allowed for plaintiff's wounded feelings. Held, no error, companionship evidently being intended to express service. Pennsylvania R. Co. v. Goodman, 62 Pa. 329. See, also, Wabash R. Co. v. Smith, 162 Ill. 583, 44 N. E. 856; Wood v. City of Omaha, 87 Neb. 213, 127 N. W. 174; Smith v. Lehigh Valley R., 177 N. Y. 379, 69 N. E. 729; International & G. N. Ry. Co. v. McVey, 99 Tex. 28, 87 S. W. 328; International & G. N. R. Co. v. Glover (Tex. Civ. App.) 88 S. W. 515; Texas & N. O. R. Co. v. Walker (Tex. Civ. App.) 125 S. W. 99; Lazelle v. Town of Newfane, 70 Vt. 440, 41 Atl. 511.

[5] Long v. Morrison, 14 Ind. 595, 77 Am. Dec. 72. This case, so far as it holds that damages for anything but the pecuniary injury can be recovered, was disapproved in Jeffersonville R. Co. v. Swayne's Adm'r, 26 Ind. 477. Louisville, N. A. & C. Ry. Co. v. Rush, 127 Ind. 545, 26 N. E. 1010. See, also, Ohio & M. R. Co. v. Tindall, 13 Ind. 366, 74 Am. Dec. 259. See, also, Commercial Club of Indianapolis v. Hilliker, 20 Ind. App. 239, 50 N. E. 578.

[6] Beeson v. Green Mountain Gold Min. Co., 57 Cal. 20; McKeever v. Market St. R. Co., 59 Cal. 294; Cook v. Clay St. Hill R. Co., 60 Cal. 604; Nehrbas v. Central Pac. R. Co., 62 Cal. 320; Cleary v. City R. Co., 76 Cal. 240, 18 Pac. 269. In Morgan v. Southern Pac. Co., 95 Cal. 510, 30 Pac. 603, 17 L. R. A. 71, 29 Am. St. Rep. 143, all the cases were reviewed, and it was there held that the recovery

---

[7] In an action by a father for the death of his daughter, the degree of intimacy existing between them and the loss of comfort and happiness and her companionship may be considered in determining the amount of damages. Anderson v. Great Northern Ry. Co., 15 Idaho, 513, 99 Pac. 91. See, also, Holt v. Spokane & P. R. Co., 3 Idaho (Hasb.) 703, 35 Pac. 39.

[8] Florida Cent. & P. R. Co. v. Foxworth, 41 Fla. 1, 25 South. 338, 79 Am. St. Rep. 149; Florida Cent. & P. R. Co. v. Foxworth, 45 Fla. 278, 34 South. 270.

sideration the loss of society and support. In Virginia[9] and West Virginia[10] the jury are not confined to the pecuniary loss, but may give damages for the loss of society, and by way of solace and comfort for the sorrow, suffering, and mental anguish occasioned by the death. And so in South Carolina.[11] The general rule obtains also in states like Iowa[12] and Oregon,[13] where the measure of damages is the pecuniary injury to the estate.

---

is limited to the actual pecuniary loss. Munro v. Pacific Coast Dredging & Reclamation Co., 84 Cal. 515, 24 Pac. 303, 18 Am. St. Rep. 248. Under the original California act, exemplary damages were expressly provided for. Myers v. City and County of San Francisco, 42 Cal. 215. See, also, Pepper v. Southern Pac. Ry. Co., 105 Cal. 389, 38 Pac. 974; Harrison v. Sutter St. Ry. Co., 116 Cal. 156, 47 Pac. 1019; Green v. Southern Pac. Co., 122 Cal. 563, 55 Pac. 577; Wales v. Pacific Electric Motor Co., 130 Cal. 521, 62 Pac. 932; Keast v. Santa Ysabel Gold Min. Co., 136 Cal. 256, 68 Pac. 771; Hale v. San Bernadino Valley Traction Co., 156 Cal. 713, 106 Pac. 83; Valente v. Sierra Ry. Co. of California, 158 Cal. 412, 111 Pac. 95; Simoneau v. Pacific Electric Ry. Co., 159 Cal. 494, 115 Pac. 320; Peters v. Southern Pac. Co., 160 Cal. 48, 116 Pac. 400. An instruction that in estimating the pecuniary loss the jury had a right to take into consideration the loss of society, comfort, and care suffered by them in the death of the husband and father was proper. Dyas v. Southern Pac. Co., 140 Cal. 296, 73 Pac. 972. In an action for death of a minor daughter it was error to limit the consideration of the pecuniary loss suffered by reason of plaintiff's deprivation of the comfort and society of the deceased "for the remainder of her minority," since a parent may enjoy the comfort and society of a child after minority. Quill v. Southern Pac. Co., 140 Cal. 268, 73 Pac. 991.

[9] Ante, § 149.

[10] Ante, § 151.

[11] Ante, § 145—2.

[12] Donaldson v. Mississippi & M. R. Co., 18 Iowa, 280, 87 Am. Dec. 391; Kelley v. Central Railroad of Iowa (C. C.) 48 Fed. 663. See § 134.

[13] Holmes v. Oregon & C. Ry. Co. (C. C.) 5 Fed. 523; Carlson v. Oregon Short Line & U. N. Ry. Co., 21 Or. 450, 28 Pac. 497; Ladd v. Foster (D. C.) 31 Fed. 827. See § 144.

§ 155. Exemplary damages

It follows from the rule that damages must be assessed with reference to the pecuniary loss to the beneficiaries that exemplary or punitive damages cannot be given.[14] They are, however, expressly authorized by the acts of Kentucky, Missouri, Nevada, South Carolina, Texas, and, it seems, New Mexico. In Connecticut,[15] where the right of action of the party injured survives; in Tennessee,[16] under the peculiar statutes of that state; and in Alabama,[17] under the "Act to prevent homicides"—they may be given. They may also be given in West Virginia,[18] and, it seems, Virginia,[19] under the anomalous construction there adopted. But, even where exemplary damages are authorized, they are not to be given in every case where a recovery of pecuniary damages would be proper.[20] Thus, in Texas,[21] the statute confines them to cases of "willful act or omission or gross negligence of the defendant." In Missouri [22] they cannot be given unless there are "aggravating circumstances."

[14] See cases cited in note 3, supra, and note 24, infra. See, also, Lange v. Schoettler, 115 Cal. 388, 47 Pac. 139; Atchison, T. & S. F. Ry. Co. v. Townsend, 71 Kan. 524, 81 Pac. 205, 6 Ann. Cas. 191; Oakes v. Maine Cent. R. Co., 95 Me. 103, 49 Atl. 418; Gray v. Little, 127 N. C. 304, 37 S. E. 270; Palmer v. Philadelphia, B. & W. R. Co., 218 Pa. 114, 66 Atl. 1127.

[15] Murphy v. New York & N. H. R. Co., 29 Conn. 496. See § 132.

[16] See § 147.

[17] See § 130.

[18] Ante, § 151.

[19] Matthews v. Warner's Adm'r, 70 Va. 570, 26 Am. Rep. 396. And see note 9, supra; ante, § 149.

[20] Klepsch v. Donald, 4 Wash. 436, 30 Pac. 991, 31 Am. St. Rep. 936.

[21] See § 55.

[22] See § 139. The language of the Colorado and New Mexico stat.

§ 156. No damages for injury to deceased

It was observed by Pollock, C. B., in Franklin v. South Eastern Ry. Co.,[23] that the only way to ascertain what Lord Campbell's act did mean was to show what it did not mean. Inasmuch as these acts do not transfer the right of action of the party injured to his personal representative, but give a new right of action, in which the damages are to be assessed with reference to the injury resulting from the death to the beneficiaries, nothing can be allowed on account of the physical or mental suffering, or other injury, to the deceased.[24] The rule is otherwise under the acts of Connecticut,[25] Mississippi,[26] New Hampshire,[27] and

utes is similar, but in Colorado it is held that the existence of "aggravating" circumstances does not authorize exemplary damages.

[23] 3 Hurl. & N. 211, 4 Jur. (N. S.) 565.

[24] Blake v. Midland Ry. Co., supra; Illinois Cent. R. Co. v. Barron, 5 Wall. 90, 18 L. Ed. 591; Chicago & N. W. R. Co. v. Whitton, 13 Wall. 270, 20 L. Ed. 571; Donaldson v. Mississippi & M. R. Co., 18 Iowa, 280, 87 Am. Dec. 391; Dwyer v. Chicago, St. P., M. & O. Ry. Co., 84 Iowa, 479, 51 N. W. 244, 35 Am. St. Rep. 322; Kelley v. Central Railroad of Iowa (C. C.) 48 Fed. 663; Kansas Pac. Ry. Co. v. Cutter, 19 Kan. 83; Oldfield v. New York & H. R. Co., 14 N. Y. 310; Whitford v. Panama R. Co., 23 N. Y. 465, 469; Pennsylvania R. Co. v. Zebe, 33 Pa. 318; Pennsylvania R. Co. v. Henderson, 51 Pa. 315; Brady v. Chicago, 4 Biss. 448, Fed. Cas. No. 1,796; Southern Cotton Press & Mfg. Co. v. Bradley, 52 Tex. 587; Potter v. Chicago & N. W. Ry. Co., 21 Wis. 372, 94 Am. Dec. 548; and cases cited in note 3, supra. See, also, St. Louis & S. F. Ry. Co. v. Hicks, 79 Fed. 262, 24 C. C. A. 563 (Arkansas statute); Florida Cent. & P. R. Co. v. Foxworth, 41 Fla. 1, 25 South. 338, 79 Am. St. Rep. 149; West Chicago St. R. Co. v. Foster, 175 Ill. 396, 51 N. E. 690; O'Fallon Coal & Mining Co. v. Laquet, 198 Ill. 125, 64 N. E. 767; Dillon v. Great Northern Ry. Co., 38 Mont. 485, 100 Pac. 960; McLaughlin v. Hebron Mfg. Co. (C. C.) 171 Fed. 269 (Rhode Island statute).

[25] See § 132.　　　[26] Ante, § 138—2　　　[27] Ante, § 47.

Tennessee,[28] where the statutes authorize the jury to consider the suffering of the deceased.

§ 157. Medical and funeral expenses

Since the damages are based solely upon the injury which results from the death, it would logically follow that in an action for death the expenses of nursing, medical attendance, etc., which result, not from the death, but from the injury causing it, cannot be recovered. It has been frequently held, however, usually in actions by parents for the death of minor children, that these expenses may be included.[29] As to funeral expenses, it has been held in England that they cannot be included.[30] "The subject-

---

[28] See § 147.

[29] Little Rock & Ft. S. Ry. Co. v. Barker, 33 Ark. 350, 34 Am. Rep. 44; Pennsylvania Co. v. Lilly, 73 Ind. 252; Rains v. St. Louis, I. M. & S. Ry. Co., 71 Mo. 164, 36 Am. Rep. 459; Roeder v. Ormsby, 13 Abb. Prac. (N. Y.) 334; Id., 22 How. Prac. 270; Pennsylvania R. Co. v. Zebe, 33 Pa. 318; Pennsylvania R. Co. v. Bantom, 54 Pa. 495; Cleveland & P. R. Co. v. Rowan, 66 Pa. 393; Lehigh Iron Co. v. Rupp, 100 Pa. 95; City of Galveston v. Barbour, 62 Tex. 172, 50 Am. Rep. 519; Brunswig v. White, 70 Tex. 504, 8 S. W. 85. In an action for death of plaintiff's wife, the husband was entitled to recover the cost of medical expenses necessarily incurred by reason of such injuries. International & G. N. R. Co. v. Boykin, 32 Tex. Civ. App. 72, 74 S. W. 93. Contra: Holland v. Brown (D. C.) 35 Fed. 43. Surgical expenses incurred by the father of a minor child, who is also next of kin, in consequence of an injury which caused the death of such minor, are not recoverable. Hutchinson v. West Jersey & S. R. Co. (C. C.) 170 Fed. 615 (New Jersey statute). In an action by heirs for the death of their ancestor, money expended in medical treatment of the decedent, if it can ever be a proper element of damage, is not such where the charges therefor have not been paid by plaintiffs, and where they are not liable therefor. Salmon v. Rathjens, 152 Cal. 290, 92 Pac. 733. Cf. Jackson v. Pittsburg, C. C. & St. L. Ry. Co., 140 Ind. 241, 39 N. E. 663, 49 Am. St. Rep. 192.

[30] Dalton v. South Eastern R. Co., 4 C. B. (N. S.) 296, 4 Jur. (N. S.)

matter of the statute," says Willes, J., in Dalton v. South
Eastern R. Co., "is compensation for injury by reason of
the relative not being alive." In that case the action was
for the benefit of a father on account of the death of a
minor son, and the verdict was reduced by the amount of
the funeral and mourning expenses which the father had
paid. And there are decisions to the same effect in this
country.[31] In the United States, however, funeral expenses
are generally held to be a legitimate element of damages, at
least when paid by one of the beneficiaries who was under
obligation to pay them.[32] The Minnesota act provides that,
out of the money recovered, "funeral expenses and any demand for the support of the deceased, duly allowed by the
probate court, shall be first deducted and paid."[33] In New

711, 27 L. J. C. P. 227. See Boulter v. Webster, 13 Wkly. R. 289.
See, also, Clarke v. London General Omnibus Co., [1906] 2 K. B. 648.

[31] St. Louis, I. M. & S. Ry. Co. v. Sweet, 57 Ark. 287, 21 S. W. 587
(cf. St. Louis, I. M. & S. Ry. Co. v. Sweet, 63 Ark. 563, 40 S. W.
463); Consolidated Traction Co, v. Hone, 60 N. J. Law, 444, 38 Atl.
759;· Wilcox v. Wilmington City Ry. Co., 2 Pennewill (Del.) 157, 44
Atl. 686. See, also, Trow v. Thomas, 70 Vt. 580, 41 Atl. 652.

[32] Owen v. Brockschmidt, 54 Mo. 285; Murphy v. New York Cent.
& H. R. R. Co., 88 N. Y. 445 (affirming s. c., 25 Hun, 311;) Petrie v.
Columbia & G. R. Co., 29 S. C. 303, 7 S. E. 515, and cases cited in
note 29 supra; Gulf, C. & S. F. Ry. Co. v. Southwick (Tex. Civ. App.)
30 S. W. 592; Dean v. Oregon R. & Nav. Co., 44 Wash. 564, 87 Pac.
824; Secard v. Rhinelander Lighting Co., 147 Wis. 614, 133 N. W.
45. In Holland v. Brown, supra, it was held that they did not result from the death. In Gay v. Winter, 34 Cal. 153, it was held that
if recoverable they must be specially pleaded. See Bunyea v. Metropolitan R. Co., 19 D. C. 76. Where, in an action by a father for
loss of services and expenses connected with an injury to his minor
daughter, the narr. did not allege expenses incurred for funeral services made necessary by the daughter's death, they were not recoverable. Baldwin v. People's Ry. Co., 7 Pennewill (Del.) 81, 76 Atl.
1088.

[33] This does not make the fund subject to all debts incurred by the
deceased for the support of himself and family, but only to such as

York the act now provides that "the plaintiff may deduct from the recovery the reasonable expenses of the action, the reasonable funeral expenses of the decedent, and his commissions upon the residue, which shall be allowed by the surrogate upon notice." [84]

§ 158. Meaning of "pecuniary"

The use of "pecuniary" to designate the kind of loss for which recovery can be had is misleading, for the damages are by no means confined to the loss of money, or of what can be estimated in money. As will be seen, damages are recoverable for the loss of the services of husband, wife, and child, and also for the loss by a child of the care, education, and counsel which he might have received from his parents. The word has been used rather for the purpose of excluding from the recovery damages to the feelings and affections than of confining the damages strictly to those injuries which are "pecuniary," according to the ordinary definition. As was observed by Denio, J., in Tilley v. Hudson River R. Co.: [85] "The word 'pecuniary' was used in distinction to those injuries to the affections and sentiments which arise from the death of relatives, and which, though

were incurred in consequence of, or after, the injury. State v. Probate Court of Dakota County, 51 Minn. 241, 53 N. W. 463. The value of services performed by the father and mother of deceased during his last illness, and the board for nurses in attendance, where there was no evidence as to the reasonable value of either, is not recoverable. Sieber v. Great Northern Ry. Co., 76 Minn. 269, 79 N. W. 95. See, also, Sykora v. J. I. Case Threshing Mach. Co., 59 Minn. 130, 60 N. W. 1008.

[84] See In re McDonald's Estate, 51 Misc. Rep. 318, 101 N. Y. Supp. 275.

[85] 24 N. Y. 471; s. c., 29 N. Y. 252, 86 Am. Dec. 297. See, also, Carter v. West Jersey & S. R. Co., 76 N. J. Law, 602, 71 Atl. 253, 19 L. R. A. (N. S.) 128, 16 Ann. Cas. 929.

painful and grievous to be borne, cannot be measured or recompensed by money. It excludes, also, those losses which result from the deprivation of the society and companionship, which are equally incapable of being defined by any recognized measure of value." The meaning would be better expressed by "material," as was suggested by Patterson, J. A., in an opinion in which he carefully reviews all the English decisions.[36] The construction placed upon the word by the courts can only be ascertained by an examination of the various rules which have been evolved for measuring the damages, and which differ, according as the action is brought for the benefit of husband, wife, minor child, or parent of minor child, for the loss of services or support to which the beneficiary was legally entitled, or is brought for the benefit of a person whose damages consist only in the loss of a prospective benefit to which he was not legally entitled.

§ 159. Reasonable expectation of benefit

The loss which a man suffers by the death of a relative may be the loss of something which he was legally entitled to receive, or may be the loss of something which it was merely reasonably probable he would receive. The first description of loss is principally [37] confined to a husband's loss of his wife's services, a wife's loss of her hus-

---

[36] Lett v. St. Lawrence & O. Ry. Co., 11 Ont. Ap. 1; Patterson, Railway Accident Law, § 401. See, also, Hunt v. Conner, 26 Ind. App. 41, 59 N. E. 50.

[37] But not exclusively. Thus where the deceased had covenanted to pay his mother an annuity during their joint lives, this, of course, furnished a basis for damages. Rowley v. London & N. W. Ry. Co., L. R. 8 Ex. 221, 42 L. J. Ex. 153, 29 L. T. (N. S.) 180. And, where the deceased was a child of 8, and his mother lost by his death a pension of $2 a month, which under the pension laws she drew on

band's support and services, a parent's loss of the services of a minor child, and a minor child's loss of the support of a parent. But the statutes do not confine the benefit of the action to husbands, wives, minor children, and parents of minor children; and hence a person entitled to the benefit of the action may recover damages for the loss of a pecuniary benefit to which he was not legally entitled, but which it is reasonably probable he would have received except for the death.[88] The second description of loss includes the loss by the beneficiary of any pecuniary benefit which he might reasonably have expected to receive during the lifetime of the deceased by gift, and also the loss of any accumulations which it is probable that the deceased would have added to his estate had he lived out his natural life, and which the beneficiary would probably have received by inheritance. Thus the second description of loss may be divided into (1) losses of prospective gifts, and (2) losses of prospective inheritances. The loss sustained by a husband, wife, minor child, and parent of a minor child may be of both descriptions. The loss sustained by an adult child, parent of an adult child, or collateral relative can only be of the latter description. The measure of damages can most conveniently be considered by classifying the cases according as the action is brought for the benefit of (1) a husband, (2) wife, (3) minor child, (4) parent of a minor child, or for the benefit of (5) one seeking to recover for the loss of prospective gifts, or (6) of a prospective inheritance.

his account, it was held that she could recover damages on account of its loss. Ewen v. Chicago & N. W. Ry. Co., 38 Wis. 613.

[88] See, Swift & Co. v. Johnson, 138 Fed. 867, 71 C. C. A. 619, 1 L. R. A. (N. S.) 1161; McKay v. New England Dredging Co., 92 Me. 454, 43 Atl. 29; Greenwood v. King, 82 Neb. 17, 116 N. W. 1128; Boyden v. Fitchburg R. Co., 70 Vt. 125, 39 Atl. 771.

§ 160. Death of husband and father of minor

The pecuniary loss which a wife sustains by the death of a husband, and which a minor child sustains by the death of a father, necessarily includes the loss of support which the deceased owed them respectively.[39] The measure of damages is the amount which the deceased would probably have earned during his life for their benefit, taking into consideration his age, ability, and disposition to work, and habits of living and expenditure.[40] To this may be added,

---

[39] Illinois Cent. R. Co. v. Welden, 52 Ill. 290; Chicago, R. I. & P. R. Co. v. Austin, 69 Ill. 426; Chicago & A. R. Co. v. May, 108 Ill. 288. Evidence, not merely of the fact that deceased had contributed nothing to the widow's support for 15 years, but that during all such time she had lived in adultery and prostitution, relieving him of liability to support her, is admissible. Orendorf v. New York Cent. & H. R. R. Co., 119 App. Div. 638, 104 N. Y. Supp. 222. Evidence of the remarriage and as to the habits and moral character of decedent's widow are properly excluded. Consolidated Stone Co. v. Morgan, 160 Ind. 241, 66 N. E. 696. Intestate was in good health, about 30 years of age, and was married to a girl whom he had been compelled to marry after he had seduced her, and whom he had abandoned. Held, that the question of whether she had suffered any pecuniary injury, by reason of any contribution to her support which he might have made or might have been compelled to make, was a question for the jury. Ingersoll v. Detroit & M. Ry. Co., 163 Mich. 268, 128 N. W. 227, 32 L. R. A. (N. S.) 362. Where a wife has not, by her own acts, forfeited the right to support by her husband, she may recover damages, though he has not for a long time fulfilled that duty. De Garcia v. San Antonio & A. P. Ry. Co. (Tex. Civ. App.) 77 S. W. 275.

[40] Pennsylvania R. Co. v. Butler, 57 Pa. 335; Pennsylvania Tel. Co. v. Varnau (Pa.) 15 Atl. 624; Hudson v. Houser, 123 Ind. 309, 24 N. E. 243; Baltimore & O. R. Co. v. State, to Use of Kelly, 24 Md. 271. Schaub v. Hannibal & St. J. R. Co., 106 Mo. 74, 16 S. W. 924; Hogue v. Chicago & A. R. Co. (C. C.) 32 Fed. 365; Shaber v. St. Paul, M. & M. Ry. Co., 28 Minn. 103, 9 N. W. 575; Bolinger v. St. Paul & D. R. Co., 36 Minn. 418, 31 N. W. 856, 1 Am. St. Rep. 680;

according to some cases, the amount which he would probably have accumulated, and which they might reasonably

Burton v. Wilmington & W. R. Co., 82 N. C. 504; s. c., 84 N. C. 192;
Blackwell v. Lynchburg & D. R. Co., 111 N. C. 151, 16 S. E. 12, 17
L. R. A. 729, 32 Am. St. Rep. 786; Pool v. Southern Pac. Co.,
7 Utah, 303, 26 Pac. 654; Wells v. Denver & R. G. W. Ry. Co., 7
Utah, 482, 27 Pac. 688; Baltimore & O. R. Co. v. Wightman's Adm'r,
70 Va. 431, 26 Am. Rep. 384; St. Louis, I. M. & S. Ry. Co. v. Sweet,
60 Ark. 550, 31 S. W. 571; MacFeat v. Philadelphia, W. & B. R. Co.,
5 Pennewill (Del.) 52, 62 Atl. 898. See, also, Wood v. Philadelphia,
B. & W. R. Co., 1 Boyce (Del.) 336, 76 Atl. 613; Cox v. Wilmington
City Ry. Co., 4 Pennewill (Del.) 162, 53 Atl. 569; O'Fallon Coal &
Mining Co. v. Laquet, 198 Ill. 125, 64 N. E. 767; Malott v. Shimer,
153 Ind. 35, 54 N. E. 101, 74 Am. St. Rep. 278; Jones v. Kansas City,
Ft. S. & M. R. Co., 178 Mo. 528, 77 S. W. 890, 101 Am. St. Rep. 434;
Soyer v. Great Falls Water Co., 15 Mont. 1, 37 Pac. 838; Ward v.
Dampskibsselskabet Kjoebenhavn (D. C.) 144 Fed. 524; Baltimore &
P. R. Co. v. Mackey, 157 U. S. 72, 15 Sup. Ct. 491, 39 L. Ed. 624. Opportunities of acquiring wealth by change of circumstances in life
are not to be considered. Mansfield Coal & Coke Co. v. McEnery, 91
Pa. 185, 36 Am. Rep. 662; Atlantic & W. P. R. Co. v. Newton, 85 Ga.
517, 11 S. E. 776. See Christian v. Columbus & R. Ry. Co., 90 Ga.
124, 15 S. E. 701. Deceased was a fireman, and evidence was introduced to prove that firemen on defendant's road, when they had acquired sufficient experience and skill, were sometimes promoted to be
engineers at increased wages. Held that, as it was not shown that
deceased possessed the skill to be an engineer, the admission was error. Brown v. Chicago, R. I. & P. R. Co., 64 Iowa, 652, 21 N. W.
193. The court refused to charge that, if deceased was largely in.
debted, the plaintiff would have no pecuniary interest in his life until
his debts were paid, and that the jury must fix a period when he
would have acquired property beyond his debts. Held no error.
Pennsylvania R. Co. v. Henderson, 51 Pa. 315. But in Texas it is
held that it is proper to show what were the deceased's chances of
promotion. St. Louis, A. & T. Ry. Co. v. Johnston, 78 Tex. 536, 15
S. W. 104; Texas & P. Ry. Co. v. Robertson, 82 Tex. 657, 17 S. W.
1041, 27 Am. St. Rep. 929. And that the standard is not to be fixed
by what he was earning when he died. International & G. N. R. Co.
v. Ormond, 64 Tex. 485; East Line & R. R. Ry. Co. v. Smith, 65
Tex. 167. The measure of the damages is the present value of the
probable earnings of deceased that would have gone to the support
of the family. Irwin v. Pennsylvania R. Co., 226 Pa. 156, 75 Atl. 19.

have expected to inherit.[41] The damages to the widow should be calculated upon the basis of their joint lives; the damages to the minor children, for the loss of support, should be confined to their minority.[42] The pecuniary value of the support of the head of a family cannot be limited to the amount of his wages earned for the benefit of his family, but his daily services, attention, and care on their behalf may be considered.[43] The testimony in such cases,

The recovery should be limited to such sum as, put to interest, will each year, by taking a part of the principal and adding to the interest, yield an amount sufficient for plaintiff's support during the time deceased would probably have lived, together with such other sum as she could reasonably have expected to have received from his earnings. Rudiger v. Chicago, St. P., M. & O. Ry. Co., 101 Wis. 292, 77 N. W. 169. See, also, Hackney v. Delaware & A. Telegraph & Telephone Co., 69 N. J. Law, 335, 55 Atl. 252.

[41] Lake Erie & W. R. Co. v. Mugg, 132 Ind. 168, 31 N. E. 564; Catawissa R. Co. v. Armstrong, 52 Pa. 282; Castello v. Landwehr, 28 Wis. 522; Bauer v. Richter, 103 Wis. 412, 70 N. W. 404; Ryan v. Oshkosh Gaslight Co., 138 Wis. 466, 120 N. W. 264; post, § 171.

[42] The court charged that the jury should estimate the reasonable probabilities of the life of deceased, and give plaintiffs such pecuniary damages as they had suffered, or would suffer, as the direct consequence of deceased's death; that for the children these prospective damages should be estimated to their majority, "and as to the widow, to such probability of life as the jury may find reasonable." Held, that this was correct, and, no objection being made to the part relating to the widow, it would be assumed that it was understood by the jury as meaning the probable duration of the joint lives of herself and her husband. Baltimore & R. Turnpike Road v. State, 71 Md. 573, 18 Atl. 884; Baltimore & O. R. Co. v. State, to Use of Trainor, 33 Md. 542; Baltimore & O. R. Co. v. State, to Use of Woodward, 41 Md. 268. See Duval v. Hunt, 34 Fla. 85, 15 South. 876.

[43] Bolinger v. St. Paul & D. R. Co., 36 Minn. 418, 31 N. W. 856, 1 Am. St. Rep. 680; Anthony Ittner Brick Co. v. Ashby, 198 Ill. 562, 64 N. E. 1109; Indianapolis Traction & Terminal Co. v. Romans, 40 Ind. App. 184, 79 N. E. 1068; Johnson v. C. A. Smith Lumber Co., 99 Minn. 343, 109 N. W. 810; Voelker v. Hill-O'Meara Const. Co., 153 Mo. App. 1, 131 S. W. 907; Galveston, H. & S. A. Ry. Co. v. Currie,

as also in actions for the death of a minor child, necessarily takes a wider range than when the question is simply whether the beneficiaries have suffered a pecuniary loss, in a strict sense.[44] Provided that it appears that the deceased was apparently able to provide for the support of his family, the court will be slow to set aside a verdict for lack of

100 Tex. 136, 96 S. W. 1073, 10 L. R. A. (N. S.) 367; Kountz v. Toledo, St. L. & W. R. Co. (C. C.) 189 Fed. 494.

[44] Staal v. Grand Rapids & I. R. Co., 57 Mich. 239, 23 N. W. 795. Testimony as to the household and living expenses of decedent's family, by one who had kept the accounts, is competent to show the loss to decedent's family because of his death. Hudson v. Houser, 123 Ind. 309, 24 N. E. 243. Evidence that deceased had been in the habit of turning his wages over to his wife, was properly admitted for the purpose of showing the loss sustained by deceased's family. Lake Erie & W. R. Co. v. Mugg, 132 Ind. 168, 31 N. E. 564. As having reference to the question of the reasonable expectation of pecuniary benefit to the widow, an instruction to the jury that they might consider his capacity to earn money, the injury to his business, his health, and general condition in life, as disclosed by the evidence, is not erroneous. Clapp v. Minneapolis & St. L. Ry. Co., 36 Minn. 6, 29 N. W. 340, 1 Am. St. Rep. 629. Evidence showing what property deceased had when he came to the state 20 years before, what occupation he had followed, how much he had accumulated, and what he was worth at the time of his death, held admissible. Phelps v. Winona & St. P. R. Co., 37 Minn. 485, 35 N. W. 273, 5 Am. St. Rep. 867. Evidence of the pecuniary value of deceased's services, or the profits which he derived from his business, need not be given; but a sufficient basis for the damages may be found in the character, habits, capacity, business, and condition of the deceased, as well as the age, sex, circumstances, and condition in life of the next of kin. Missouri Pac. Ry. Co. v. Moffatt, 60 Kan. 113, 55 Pac. 837, 72 Am. St. Rep. 343. It is competent for plaintiff to show the relation existing between deceased and his family, as bearing upon the question of pecuniary injury. Union Pac. Ry. Co. v. Sternberger, 8 Kan. App. 131, 54 P. 1101. The presumption of the dependence of the wife and children on the husband and father during his lifetime is rebuttable, and evidence in support of it, before it is known whether defendant will present evidence to overcome, is competent and material. Standard Oil Co. v. Parkinson, 152 Fed. 681, 82 C. C. A. 29. See, also, Hollingsworth v. Davis-Daly Estates Copper Co., 38 Mont. 143, 99 Pac. 142.

exact proof.[45] Thus, it is not essential that the deceased should have been actually earning wages at the time of his death;[46] but, in default of such proof, the amount of the verdict will doubtless be more carefully scrutinized.[47]

---

[45] Deceased left a wife and three children, two of them minors. He was a strong, healthy man, 48 years old, accustomed to earn good wages as a day laborer. Held, that a verdict of $5,000 was not clearly excessive. Bolinger v. St. Paul & D. R. Co., 36 Minn. 418, 31 N. W. 856, 1 Am. St. Rep. 680. The deceased was a laboring man, sober and industrious, who provided for his family as best he could under the circumstances, and was 36 years old. He left a widow and six young children. Held, that a verdict of $5,000 was not excessive. Board Com'rs Howard County v. Legg, 110 Ind. 479, 11 N. E. 612. The deceased was the head of a family, 39 years old, able to perform the duties of fireman, and always at work. Held, that the jury were authorized to find more than nominal damages, and that a verdict of $3,500 was not excessive. Smith v. Wabash, St. L. & P. R. Co., 92 Mo. 364, 4 S. W. 129, 1 Am. St. Rep. 729. It is not necessary to show that deceased would have been able to continue to earn what he was receiving at the time of his death, or what part of his earnings he expended for the benefit of his family, or what part of his time he spent with his family, or what part he took in raising and educating his sons, in order to entitle his widow to more than nominal damages. Malott v. Shimer, 153 Ind. 35, 54 N. E. 101, 74 Am. St. Rep. 278.

[46] Evidence was given of the age, habits, health, and occupation of the deceased, and of the condition of his family, etc., but there was no evidence of the specific wages paid him at the time of his death. Held, that the jury were not confined to nominal damages. Baltimore & O. R. Co. v. State, 24 Md. 271. Averments showing that deceased was a laboring man, working for defendant (without alleging that he was receiving any compensation for his labor) and that he left no widow, but left a child three years old, held, on demurrer, to show sufficiently that such child suffered pecuniary damage by the father's death. Kelley v. Chicago, M. & St. P. Ry. Co., 50 Wis. 381, 7 N. W. 291. See, also, Ruppel v. United Railroads of San Francisco, 1 Cal. App. 666, 82 Pac. 1073.

[47] The deceased was a common laborer, who left a widow and several minor children, but what wages he received was not shown. Held, that a verdict of $5,000 was excessive, in view of the absence

The amount of verdict which will be sustained differs considerably in different jurisdictions.[48]

of evidence that he earned annually so much as the interest on one half that sum. Illinois Cent. R. Co. v. Welden, 52 Ill. 290.

[48] Deceased earned $1 a day, which he always brought home and spent on his wife. The probable duration of his life was 27 years. Held, that a verdict of $2,500 should be reduced to $1,650. Louisville & N. R. Co. v. Trammell, 93 Ala. 350, 9 South. 870. A verdict of $10,000 will not be set aside as excessive, in view of testimony that deceased was a "stout, healthy, and sober" laborer, about 35 years old, earning $1.25 a day, and that he left a widow and two infant children. Missouri Pac. Ry. Co. v. Lehmberg, 75 Tex. 61, 12 S. W. 838. The deceased was a healthy and robust man 29 years old, an engineer, and earning $125 a month. Held, that a verdict in favor of his wife for $10,000 was not excessive. Texas & P. Ry. Co. v. Geiger, 79 Tex. 13, 15 S. W. 214. Where plaintiff's husband was a healthy man, 55 years old, who earned from $500 to $1,200 a year, and who had always supported plaintiff, a verdict for $6,250 actual damages held not excessive. Paschal v. Owen, 77 Tex. 583, 14 S. W. 203. Decedent was 26 years old, was employed in a hardware store at a salary of $75 a month, had the full confidence of his employers, and was considered well acquainted with the hardware business for one of his experience. Held, that in an action by his widow and child a judgment for $12,000 will not be reversed as excessive. Hale v. San Bernardino Valley Traction Co., 156 Cal. 713, 106 Pac. 83. $30,000 is not excessive recovery for negligent death of a locomotive engineer, in a suit for the benefit of his widow and two minor children. Peters v. Southern Pac. Co., 160 Cal. 48, 116 Pac. 400. A verdict for $10,000 is not excessive where deceased was of the age of 38, in good health, earning from $125 to $130 per month, and left a widow and a child of the age of 7. Smith v. Chicago, P. & St. L. Ry. Co., 143 Ill. App. 128. Where decedent was 32 years of age, and was in the mail service, under civil service rules, earning $1,000 a year, a verdict of $9,500 was not excessive. Malott v. Central Trust Co. of Greencastle, 168 Ind. 428, 79 N. E. 369, 11 Ann. Cas. 879. Where deceased was a city fireman 46 years old, healthy, and able to work, with a life expectancy of 24 years, and receiving a salary of $1,000 a year, had accumulated property worth $2,000, and had no source of income aside from his personal earnings, a verdict for $8,250 was excessive, and was reduced to $6,000. Engvall v. Des Moines City Ry. Co., 145 Iowa, 560, 121 N. W. 12. Where deceased was a freight conductor, 32 years old, of good health and habits, and earning $1,200

§ 161.   Death of husband—Evidence of number of children

Where the children are included among the beneficiaries, as is the case under most statutes, evidence of their num-

a year, a verdict of $25,000 for his widow was reduced to $10,000. Dobyns v. Yazoo & M. V. R. Co., 119 La. 72, 43 South. 934. Where decedent was 73 years old, a laborer working at odd jobs for only part of the time, and earning not more than $225 per annum, a verdict for $1,600 is excessive. Conley v. Maine Cent. R. Co., 95 Me. 149, 49 Atl. 668. Where deceased was 51 years old, healthy, steady, and industrious, and left a widow and five children, a verdict of $5,000 is not excessive. McCarthy v. Claflin, 99 Me. 290, 59 Atl. 293. Where deceased was an assistant lighthouse keeper, earning $450 a year, but in the line of promotion under the civil service rules, strong and healthy, and had a life expectancy of 35.33 years, and left a wife 31 years of age, and a child of 7 months, a verdict assessing the loss at $8,000 was excessive, and should be reduced to $5,000. King v. Ann Arbor R. Co., 144 Mich. 65, 107 N. W. 868. Where decedent was 47 years of age, and was not earning over $10 a week, and that his wife was 40 years of age, and his two children 18 and 14 years of age, a verdict for $7,000 is excessive, since recovery is limited to damages. Geiger v. Worthen & Aldrich Co., 66 N. J. Law, 576, 49 Atl. 918. See, also, Garbaccio v. Jersey City H. & P. St. Ry. Co. (N. J.) 53 Atl. 707. In an action for a widow's sole benefit, a recovery of $5,000 is excessive, where he was 65 years of age and earned but $12.50 per week. Swanson v. Union Stock Yards Co. of Omaha, 89 Neb. 361, 131 N. W. 594. An award of $25,000 made to libelant on behalf of herself and children for the death of her husband, a physician, 39 years old, industrious, of good health and habits, and high standing in his profession, and assistant quarantine physician, receiving a salary and perquisites amounting to $3,000 per year; his personal expenditures being estimated at $1,000 per year. Ward v. Dampskibsselskabet Kjoebenhavn (D. C.) 144 Fed. 524. Where deceased was a strong, healthy man 32 years of age, employed as a teamster, a verdict held excessive above $10,000. Gorman v. Hand Brewing Co., 28 R. I. 180, 66 Atl. 209. A verdict for $10,000 is not excessive for damages to the wife and children by the death of a strong and active business man, 57 years old, and earning $300 or $400 a month, though he had failed in business, and was trading in his wife's name, it appearing that such failure did not result from

ber and ages is, of course, necessary.[49] Where, however, the
action is to be brought by the widow in her own name, the
question arises whether such evidence is proper. In Pennsylvania, where the widow sues for the benefit of the children, as well as of herself, and the declaration must state
who are the parties entitled, such evidence is required.[50] In
Missouri, on the other hand, and in some other states, the
action, when brought by the widow, is for her sole benefit.
It is held, nevertheless, that, as the burden of supporting
minor children is imposed upon her, evidence of their number and ages is admissible to show the extent of the burden
cast upon her by the death.[51] So, in Wisconsin, although

mismanagement. Rosenbaum v. Shoffner, 98 Tenn. 624, 40 S. W. 1086.
In an action for the death of a locomotive engineer, brought by his
widow and two children, it appeared that he was earning $150 per
month, was sober and industrious, and had good business ability,
and that his expectancy of life was 38 years. Held, that a verdict
for $40,000 was excessive to the extent of $15,000. Walker v. Mc-
Neill, 17 Wash. 582, 50 Pac. 518. See, also, Halverson v. Seattle
Electric Co., 35 Wash. 600, 77 Pac. 1058. A verdict of $9,000 for the
death of a man 48 years old, of good health and habits, earning from
$100 to $125 per month, and leaving a wife and son, 35 and 11 years
of age, respectively, both entirely dependent on him, will not be disturbed as excessive. McHolm v. Philadelphia & Reading Coal &
Iron Co., 147 Wis. 381, 132 N. W. 585.

[49] Breckenfelder v. Lake Shore & M. S. Ry. Co., 79 Mich. 560, 44
N. W. 957; Bonato v. Peabody Coal Co., 156 Ill. App. 196; Id., 248
Ill. 422, 94 N. E. 69; Simpson v. Foundation Co., 201 N. Y. 479, 95
N. E. 10, Ann. Cas. 1912B, 321; Baltimore & P. R. Co. v. Mackey,
175 U. S. 72, 15 Sup. Ct. 491, 39 L. Ed. 624. See, also, Felton v.
Spiro, 78 Fed. 576, 24 C. C. A. 321; ante, § 80. Otherwise in an action for personal injuries by an administrator, under the survival
act. Oliver v. Houghton County St. Ry. Co., 138 Mich. 242, 101
N. W. 530. Evidence that deceased had made an arrangement
whereby he had agreed to adopt two children of plaintiff's by her
first husband was inadmissible. Philip v. Heraty, 135 Mich. 446,
97 N. W. 963, rehearing denied Id., 135 Mich. 446, 100 N. W. 186.

[50] Huntingdon & B. T. M. R. & Coal Co. v. Decker, 84 Pa. 419.

[51] Tetherow v. St. Joseph & D. M. R. Co., 98 Mo. 74, 11 S. W.

the action is for the sole benefit of the widow, and hence an instruction that damages may be allowed to the widow and children is erroneous,[52] the fact that the deceased left children who will be dependent on her may be considered in estimating her damages.[53] This ruling has been followed in other jurisdictions.[54]

§ 162. Death of parent of minor—Loss of education and personal training

The damages for loss of support suffered by a minor child include the loss of such comforts, conveniences, and also of such education as the parent might have been expected to bestow upon him. In Pym v. Great Northern Ry. Co.,[55] Cockburn, C. J., said: "We are of opinion that, as

310, 14 Am. St. Rep. 617; Soeder v. St. Louis, I. M. & S. Ry. Co., 100 Mo. 673, 13 S. W. 714, 18 Am. St. Rep. 724; Atchison, T. & S. F. R. Co. v. Wilson, 48 Fed. 57, 1 C. C. A. 25. Under Rev. St. 1889, § 4425, such evidence is, of course, improper. Schlereth v. Missouri Pac. R. Co., 19 S. W. 1134. See, also, Fisher v. Central Lead Co., 156 Mo. 479, 56 S. W. 1107; Ogan v. Missouri Pac. R. Co., 142 Mo. App. 248, 126 S. W. 191; Brinkman v. Gottenstroeter, 153 Mo. App. 351, 134 S. W. 584.

[52] Schadewald v. Milwaukee, L. S. & W. Ry Co., 55 Wis. 569, 13 N. W. 458; Liermann v. Chicago, M. & St. P. Ry. Co., 82 Wis. 286, 52 N. W. 91, 33 Am. St. Rep. 37. It is error to direct the jury to give damages to recompense the estate of deceased, for such instruction in effect directs them to compensate the children as well as the widow. Gores v. Graff, 77 Wis. 174, 46 N. W. 48.

[53] Mulcairns v. City of Janesville, 67 Wis. 24, 29 N. W. 565; Abbot v. McCadden, 81 Wis. 563, 51 N. W. 1079, 29 Am. St. Rep. 910; Hamann v. Milwaukee Bridge Co., 136 Wis. 39, 116 N. W. 854.

[54] Escambia County Electric Light & Power Co. v. Sutherland, 61 Fla. 167, 55 South. 83; Claffy v. Chicago Dock & Canal Co., 249 Ill. 210, 94 N. E. 551; Cook v. Big Muddy-Carterville Min. Co., 249 Ill. 41, 94 N. E. 90 (mining act); Spiro v. Felton (C. C.) 73 Fed. 91 (Tennessee).

[55] 2 Best & S. 759, 10 Wkly. R. 737, 31 L. J. Q. B. 249, affirmed 4 B. & S. 396, 11 Wkly. R. 922, 32 L. J. Q. B. 377.

the benefit of education, and the enjoyment of the greater
comforts and conveniences of life, depend on the possession
of pecuniary means to procure them, the loss of these advantages is one which is capable of being estimated in money—in other words, is a pecuniary loss—and therefore the
loss of such advantages arising from the death of a father
whose income ceases with his life is an injury in respect
of which an action can be maintained on the statute." It
has frequently been held, however, that damages are not
confined to the loss of such education as is procurable only
by pecuniary means, but that they may be given for the
loss of the personal care, training, and instruction of a parent, and even of a mother, where the father still survives.[56]

[56] Tilley v. Hudson River R. Co., 24 N. Y. 471; s. c., 29 N. Y. 252,
86 Am. Dec. 297; Board of Com'rs of Howard County v. Legg, 93
Ind. 523, 47 Am. Rep. 390; Stoher v. St. Louis, I. M. & S. Ry. Co., 91
Mo. 509, 4 S. W. 389; Dimmey v. Wheeling & E. G. R. Co., 27 W.
Va. 32, 55 Am. Rep. 292; Searle v. Kanawha & O. Ry. Co., 32 W.
Va. 370, 9 S. E. 248; Baltimore & O. R. Co. v. Wightman's Adm'r,
70 Va. 431, 26 Am. Rep. 401; St. Louis, I. M. & S. Ry. Co. v. Mad-
dry, 57 Ark. 306, 21 S. W. 472. See, also, St. Louis & N. A. R. Co.
v. Mathis, 76 Ark. 184, 91 S. W. 763, 113 Am. St. Rep. 85; St.
Louis, I. M. & S. Ry. Co. v. Standifer, 81 Ark. 275, 99 S. W. 81;
Redfield v. Oakland Consol. St. Ry. Co., 110 Cal. 277, 42 Pac. 822;
Johnson v. Southern Pac. R. Co., 154 Cal. 285, 97 Pac. 520; Valente
v. Sierra Ry. Co. of California, 158 Cal. 412, 111 Pac. 95; Anthony
Ittner Brick Co. v. Ashby, 198 Ill. 562, 64 N. E. 1109; Goddard v.
Enzler, 222 Ill. 462, 78 N. E. 805; Hunt v. Conner, 26 Ind. App. 41,
59 N. E. 50; Cleveland, C., C. & St. L. Ry Co. v. Starks (Ind. App.)
89 N. E. 602; Omaha Water Co. v. Schamel, 147 Fed. 502, 78 C.
C. A. 68 (Nebraska); Sternfels v. Metropolitan St. Ry. Co., 73 App.
Div. 494, 77 N. Y. Supp. 309, affirmed 174 N. Y. 512, 66 N. E. 1117;
Hoadley v. International Paper Co., 72 Vt. 79, 47 Atl. 169. In Illinois Cent. R. Co. v. Welden, 52 Ill. 290, it was held that while,
on principle, an instruction that the jury might consider the loss
of instruction and physical, moral, and intellectual training of the
father was correct, it should not have been given, because there was
no evidence tending to show that the deceased was fitted by education or by disposition to furnish it. Followed in Chicago, R.

A leading case on this subject is Tilley v. Hudson River R. Co., which was an action brought by a father as administrator for the benefit of children for the death of their mother. On the first appeal it was held that the value of the mother's earnings, and the probability that the children would have received an estate increased by such earnings on the death and intestacy of the father, could not be considered; but, upon the second appeal, it was held that evidence of the mother's capacity to bestow upon her children such training, instruction, and education as would be pecuniarily serviceable to them was admissible, and that, as indicating such capacity on her part, it was not improper to admit evidence of her capacity to conduct business and save money. "It is certainly possible," said Hogeboom, J., "and not only so, but highly probable, that a mother's nurture, instruction, and training, if judiciously administered, will operate favorably upon the worldly prospects and pecuniary

I. & P. R. Co. v. Austin, 69 Ill. 426. An instruction that the jury may consider the loss of the moral and intellectual training of the deceased father is erroneous, in the absence of evidence that he was fitted to furnish such training. St. Louis & S. F. Ry. Co. v. Townsend, 69 Ark. 380, 63 S. W. 994. It is error to allow the jury to consider damages sustained by decedent's children from the loss of nurture, instruction, and moral and physical training received from the father, of the value of which there was no evidence. Walker v. Lake Shore & M. S. Ry. Co., 111 Mich. 518, 69 N. W. 1114. See, also, Id., 104 Mich. 606, 62 N. W. 1032; May v. West Jersey & S. R. Co., 62 N. J. Law, 63, 42 Atl. 163. In an action on behalf of a minor for the death of his mother, under a statute authorizing such damages "as under all the circumstances of the case may be just," the recovery is not limited to the pecuniary loss suffered by the minor prior to his majority, and the jury may consider evidence tending to show that he was deprived of a home, was dependent on her earnings for his education, and that she intended to send him to college and earned sufficient to have enabled her to do so. Butte Electric R. Co. v. Jones, 164 Fed. 308, 90 C. C. A. 240, 18 L. R. A. (N. S.) 1205.

interests of the child. * * * If they acquire health, knowledge, and a sound bodily constitution, and ample intellectual development, under the judicious training and discipline of a competent and careful mother, it is very likely to tell favorably upon their pecuniary interests." In Rhode Island, on the other hand, where the action, in relation to the question of damages, is considered as though it were brought on behalf of the estate of the decedent for the damages caused to the estate by the death, and the damages are thus distributed without regard to the damage suffered by any beneficiary,[57] damages for the loss to a child of the parental care of a father are not recoverable.[58]

§ 163.   Death of wife—Loss of service

The pecuniary injury to a husband from the death of a wife necessarily includes the loss of her services, and the measure of damages is their reasonable value.[59] Thus, in Whiton v. Chicago & N. W. Ry. Co.,[60] a case arising in the circuit court, under the Wisconsin statute, the plaintiff

[57] Ante, § 145—1.

[58] McCabe v. Narragansett Electric Lighting Co., 27 R. I. 272, 61 Atl. 667.

[59] Chicago & N. W. R. Co. v. Whitton, 13 Wall. 270, 20 L. Ed. 571; s. c., Whiton v. Chicago & N. W. R. Co., 2 Biss. 282, Fed. Cas. No. 17,597; Chant v. South Eastern Ry. Co., Weekly Notes (Eng.) 1866, p. 134; Pennsylvania R. Co. v. Goodman, 62 Pa. 329; Delaware, L. & W. R. Co. v. Jones, 128 Pa. 308, 18 Atl. 330; Lett v. St. Lawrence & O. Ry. Co., 11 Ont. App. 1, reversing s. c., 1 Ont. R. 548; Denver & R. G. R. Co. v. Gunning, 33 Colo. 280, 80 Pac. 727; Nelson v. Lake Shore & M. S. Ry. Co., 104 Mich. 582, 62 N. W. 993. The measure of damages was the value of the services lost, less the cost of her maintenance. Gorton v. Harmon, 152 Mich. 473, 116 N. W. 443, 15 Ann. Cas. 461; Fisher v. Waupaca Electric Light & Ry. Co., 141 Wis. 515, 124 N. W. 1005.

[60] Supra, note 59.

proved that his wife was a superior woman, as wife, mother, and member of society. The court charged the jury (after stating that the damages were confined to the pecuniary loss; that it was impossible to lay down any fixed rule; and that the matter largely rested with the sound reason and discretion of the jury) that, taking all the facts and circumstances into consideration, they might consider the personal qualities, the ability to be useful, of the deceased, and also her capacity to earn money. The jury rendered a verdict of $5,000, which was held not to be excessive. The defendant having brought the case to the supreme court, the charge was approved, Mr. Justice Field, who delivered the opinion, declaring it to be clear and explicit as to the character of the damages which the jury were authorized to consider. Proof that the deceased actually rendered services is not necessary, but may be inferred by the jury. Thus, in Chant v. South Eastern Ry. Co.,[61] which was an action by a gardener, owing to the fact that the plaintiff, the only witness, broke down in course of his examination, no evidence was given of the pecuniary loss, but the jury gave a verdict of £200. This was moved against in the exchequer chamber, on the ground that there was no evidence of pecuniary assistance; but the court thought that, in the absence of evidence to the contrary, it must be assumed that she was a person of average health, industry, and good character, and that to a poor man such a wife gave pecuniary assistance in keeping house, etc., and declined to grant a new trial. So, in Delaware, L. & W. R. Co. v.

---

61 Supra, note 59. But see Mitchell v. New York Cent. & H. R. R. Co., 2 Hun (N. Y.) 535, where a verdict for $4,000 was set aside as unauthorized by the proof, the only pecuniary loss shown being what might be inferred from the fact that deceased was a married woman and aged 20.

Jones,[62] the plaintiff introduced evidence to show that the deceased was 66 years old and had always been healthy, and rested. The court refused to rule that this evidence did not show a pecuniary loss, or that the plaintiff could only recover nominal damages; and in the supreme court the lower court was sustained, Sterrett, J., observing that the jury might infer that she was an ordinarily industrious and useful wife. In Pennsylvania R. Co. v. Goodman [63] it is said that the frugality, industry, usefulness, attention, and tender solicitude of a wife and the mother of children, inasmuch as they render her services more valuable than those of an ordinary servant, are elements which are not to be excluded from the jury in making their estimate of value.

§ 164. Death of minor child—Loss of service

In an action for the benefit of a parent for the death of a minor child the damages necessarily include the loss of the child's services during minority,[64] and the measure of

[62] Supra, note 59. See, also, Waechter v. Second Ave. Traction Co., 198 Pa. 129, 47 Atl. 967.

[63] 62 Pa. 329. The court charged that damages should be given as a pecuniary compensation, the jury measuring the plaintiff's loss by a just estimate of the services and companionship of the wife; that is, by their value in a pecuniary sense, nothing being allowed for the plaintiff's wounded feelings. The charge was sustained, on the ground that "companionship" was evidently used to express the relation of the deceased in the character of the services performed.

[64] Little Rock & Ft. S. Ry. Co. v. Barker, 33 Ark. 350, 34 Am. Rep. 44; Chicago v. Keefe, 114 Ill. 222, 2 N. E. 267, 55 Am. Rep. 860; Illinois Cent. R. Co. v. Slater, 129 Ill. 91, 21 N. E. 575, 6 L. R. A. 418, 16 Am. St. Rep. 242; McGovern v. New York Cent. & H. R. R. Co., 67 N. Y. 417; City of Galveston v. Barbour, 62 Tex. 172, 50 Am. Rep. 519; Rains v. St. Louis, I. M. & S. Ry. Co., 71 Mo. 164, 36 Am. Rep. 459; Pennsylvania R. Co. v. Zebe, 33 Pa. 318; Caldwell v. Brown, 53 Pa. 453; Southern Indiana Ry. Co. v. Moore (Ind. App.) 71 N. E. 516; Id., 34 Ind. App. 154, 72 N. E. 479; Mc.

damages is the value of the services less the probable cost of support and maintenance.[65]

It is not essential that the child should ever have earned anything. Thus, in Duchworth v. Johnson,[66] a father, who was a working man, sued for the death of a son 14 years of age, who had earned 4s. a week for a year or more, but who, at the time of his death, was without employment. There was no evidence of the cost of boarding and clothing him, and the judge left it to the jury to say whether the plaintiff had sustained any pecuniary loss by the death; and, the jury having found a verdict of £20, it was held that the plaintiff was entitled to retain it. In Bramall v. Lees [67]

Cahill v. Detroit City Ry., 96 Mich. 156, 55 N. W. 668; Snyder v. Lake Shore & M. S. R. Co., 131 Mich. 418, 91 N. W. 643; Scherer v. Schlaberg, 18 N. D. 421, 122 N. W. 1000, 24 L. R. A. (N. S.) 520. A widowed mother may recover notwithstanding that she has no right to the services of a minor child, since the act gives her a right of action. Pennsylvania R. Co. v. Bantom, 54 Pa. 495. Abandonment by the father recalls his right to the child's services and earnings. Swift & Co. v. Johnson, 138 Fed. 867, 71 C. C. A. 619, 1 L. R. A. (N. S.) 1161.

[65] Rockford, R. I. & St. L. R. Co. v. Delaney, 82 Ill. 198, 25 Am. Rep. 308; Rajnowski v. Detroit, B. C. & A. R. Co., 74 Mich. 15, 41 N. W. 849; Pennsylvania Co. v. Lilly, 73 Ind. 252; Brunswig v. White, 70 Tex. 504, 8 S. W. 85; City of Elwood v. Addison, 26 Ind. App. 28, 59 N. E. 47. The value of the services is to be without regard to any peculiar value which the parent might attach to them. St. Louis, I. M. & S. Ry. Co. v. Freeman, 36 Ark. 41. It is proper to instruct that the parent could not recover the value of the child's services independent of the expense of caring for and maintaining him during minority. Cleveland, C., C. & St. L. Ry. Co. v. Miles, 162 Ind. 646, 70 N. E. 985. Some proof of the probable cost of maintenance during minority is indispensable, in order that the item should be deducted from his probable earnings, to establish the real damages. Peters v. Bessemer & L. E. R. Co., 225 Pa. 307, 74 Atl. 61.

[66] 4 Hurl. & N. 653, 29 L. J. Ex. 25, 5 Jur. (N. S.) 630.

[67] 29 L. T. 111. See Chapman v. Rothwell, 4 Jur. (N. S.) 1180, where Crompton, J., comments upon the case with approval.

a father recovered £15 for the death of a daughter 12 years
old, who had never actually earned anything, but who
might, if she had lived, have obtained work in a factory.
So, in Condon v. Great Southern & W. Ry. Co.,[68] a widow
recovered £10 for the death of a son of 14, who had never
earned anything, but whose capabilities were valued at 6d.
a day.

In no English case does it appear that damages have
been given for the death of a child of such tender years as
to be incapable of earning wages. But in the United
States it is well settled that substantial damages may be
recovered in such cases. Ihl v. Forty-Second St. & G. St.
Ferry R. Co.[69] is a leading case in point. The action was
brought for the death of a child three years old, and the
verdict was $1,800. The court of appeals sustained the
lower court in refusing to nonsuit the plaintiff, or to direct

---

[68] 16 Ir. Com. Law, 415. See Burke v. Cork, etc., R. Co., 10
Cent. Law J. 48. In an action by a father for the death of his
daughter, aged 10, it was proved that deceased lived with her parents, and was maintained by them, rendering services which enabled
them to dispense with a servant. No evidence was given of the
exact value of her services, or as to the cost of her maintenance.
Held, that there was evidence for the jury, but a verdict for £150
should be reduced to £50. Wolfe v. Great Northern Ry. Co., 26 L.
R. Ir. 548. The plaintiff's father and stepmother were killed simultaneously. An action for the loss of the father had been instituted
in which £100 was obtained; but 1s. only was allocated to plaintiff,
who sued in a second action for the death of her stepmother. The
parties were in humble life. The stepmother earned 6s. a week besides her food, which earnings were applied to the support of the
family. Plaintiff resided with her father and stepmother. For
six months preceding the death she earned 5s. a week, but previously had not been able to work from weakness of health. Held
that a verdict in the former case was no bar; also that there was
evidence of pecuniary loss sufficient to sustain the action. Johnston
v. Great Northern Ry. Co., 26 L. R. Ir. 691.

[69] 47 N. Y. 317, 7 Am. Rep. 450.

a verdict for nominal damages, for absence of proof of pecuniary damages to the next of kin. "It was within the province of the jury," said Rapallo, J., "who had before them the parents, their position in life, the occupation of the father, and the age and sex of the child, to form an estimate of the damages with reference to the pecuniary injury, present or prospective, resulting to the next of kin. Except in very rare instances, it would be impracticable to furnish direct evidence of any specific loss occasioned by the death of a child of such tender years; and to hold that, without such proof, the plaintiff could not recover, would, in effect, render the statute nugatory in most cases of this description. It cannot be said, as a matter of law, that there is no pecuniary damage in such a case, or that the expense of maintaining and educating the child would necessarily exceed any pecuniary advantage which the parents could have derived from his services had he lived. These calculations are for the jury, and any evidence on the subject beyond the age and sex of the child, the circumstances and condition in life of the parents, or other facts existing at the time of the death or trial, would necessarily be speculative and hypothetical, and would not aid the jury in arriving at a conclusion." He adds that the amount of damages could have been reviewed in the court below, but could not in the court of appeals; the only question for the higher court being whether any, or more than nominal, damages could be recovered.[70]

---

[70] In Lehman v. City of Brooklyn, 29 Barb. (N. Y.) 234, a stricter construction of the statute was adopted; but this decision is opposed to the decisions earlier and later. Indeed, in actions for the death of minor children, as in other actions under the statute, the New York courts have gone farther than those of any other state in yielding the question of damages to the discretion of the jury. Thus in Oldfield v. New York & H. R. Co., 14 N. Y. 310, affirming

However far the courts have gone in allowing the jury to speculate upon the supposed pecuniary value to the par-

s. c., 3 E. D. Smith, 103, which was an action for the death of a daughter six years old, the judge charged that the plaintiff could recover whatever pecuniary loss the next of kin (the mother) might be supposed to incur in consequence of the loss of the child, and qualified this by adding that the jury were to give what they should deem fair and just, with reference to the pecuniary injury resulting from the death. The judge also excluded all considerations arising from the suffering of the child or the anguish of the parents, and confined the rule of damages exclusively to indemnification for a pecuniary loss. This instruction was sustained by the court of appeals, Wright, J., observing that it was only another way of instructing the jury that the damages were a sum which, in their opinion, taking into consideration all the circumstances of the case, would be the pecuniary loss to the next of kin. "This," he concludes, "was right, *unless the statute limits the recovery to the actual loss proved at the trial. We think it does not.*" See Quin v. Moore, 15 N. Y. 432. In O'Mara v. Hudson River R. Co., 38 N. Y. 445, 98 Am. Dec. 61, the jury rendered a verdict of $1,500 for a boy 11 years old. The defendant moved for a new trial on the ground that there was no evidence of the pecuniary value of the life, which was denied, and in the court of appeals the lower court was sustained, Hunt, C. J., observing that the jury woul⌐ have the right, acting upon their own knowledge, and without proof, to say that the services of a boy from 11 until 21 years of age were valuable to his father, and to estimate their value. The court went to the extreme length in Houghkirk v. Delaware & H. Canal Co., 92 N. Y. 219, 44 Am. Rep. 370; s. c., 28 Hun, 407 (general term); Houghkirk v. Delaware & H. Canal Co., 11 Abb. N. C. 72, 63 How. Prac. 328 (special term)—in which case a verdict of $5,000 was rendered for an only child 6 years old, intelligent and healthy, the daughter of a market gardener—these facts and the circumstance of her death constituting the only .evidence. The general term declined to set the verdict aside as excessive, and the court of appeals declared that it was impossible to say that error had been committed thereby, although it granted a new trial on another ground. In the opinion of the court at general term the difficulty of any court called upon to review the damages in such cases is clearly set forth as follows: "The court in that case" [Ihl v. Forty-Second St. & G. St. Ferry R. Co.] "says that the damages could be reviewed in this court. But the difficulty is, by what test are we to review

ents of the life of young children, the line is drawn at living
children, to the exclusion of prospective offspring with

them? If it is a matter of guesswork, the jury can guess as well
as we. If we are to review them by the test of the evidence, then
the difficulty is that there is no direct evidence proving the amount
of loss. The facts to which the consideration of the jury is limited by the case cited would be, in the present case, substantially
and in brief: A girl of six years, healthy and bright, only child
of a gardener and his wife, both of whom survived her. Given
her death; what is their pecuniary loss?" Referring to the position taken by the general term, that the doctrine of the court of
appeals leaves it impossible for a court to say in any instance that
damages are excessive, Finch, J., who delivered the opinion of the
court of appeals, says: "The damages to the next of kin * * *
are necessarily indefinite, prospective, and contingent. They cannot be proved with even an approach to accuracy, and yet they
are to be estimated and awarded, for the statute has so com-
manded. But even in such case there is, and there must be, some
basis in the proof for the estimate, and that was given here, and
always has been given. Human lives are not all of the same value
to the survivors. The age and sex, the general health and intelligence, of the person killed, the situation and condition of the survivors, and their relation to the deceased,—these elements furnish
some basis for judgment. That it is slender and inadequate is true;
but it is all that is possible, and, while that should be given, more
cannot be required. Upon that basis and from such proof the jury
must judge; and, having done so, it is possible, though not entirely
easy, for the general term to review such judgment, and set it
aside if it appears excessive, or the result of sympathy and prejudice." In Ahern v. Steele, 48 Hun, 517, 1 N. Y. Supp. 257, in sustaining a verdict of $4,500 for a child of six, Van Brunt, P. J., re-
marked: "The damages appear to be excessive, as it does not seem
that there can be any pecuniary damage resulting from the death
of so young a child; * * * but as recoveries have been sustained, based on the death of much younger children, we see no
reason for interference with the verdict upon this account." Gorham v. New York Cent. & H. R. R. Co., 23 Hun, 449; Huerzeler v.
Central Cross T. R. Co., 1 Misc. Rep. 136, 20 N. Y. Supp. 676. But
in Carpenter v. Buffalo, N. Y. & P. R. Co., 38 Hun, 116, it was held
that a verdict could not be sustained on evidence merely of the
relationship, age, and habits of the child, when there was no evidence of the condition, pecuniary and physical, of the parents or

which a mother whose death has been caused by wrongful
act was pregnant.[71]

of their age. See, also, Gill v. Rochester & P. R. Co., 37 Hun, 107;
Birkett v. Knickerbocker Ice Co., 110 N. Y. 504, 18 N. E. 108. See,
also, Heinz v. Brooklyn Heights R. Co., 91 Hun, 640, 36 N. Y.
Supp. 675. The tendency of the later cases seems to be to restrain
the verdicts in such cases within more reasonable limits. A verdict in favor of a father, a laboring man, for $4,000 for the death
of a daughter 16 years old, who, since her mother's death, had
taken care of her father's house, is excessive, where there is no
evidence as to the relations which existed between plaintiff and
decedent, or of his or her character or capabilities. Dinnihan v.
Lake Ontario Beach Imp. Co., 8 App. Div. 509, 40 N. Y. Supp. 764.
For the death of a healthy, strong, bright, and studious boy eight
years of age, a verdict in favor of his father for $5,250 was excessive,
and should be reduced to $3,000. Connaughton v. Sun Printing & Pub-
lishing Ass'n, 73 App. Div. 316, 76 N. Y. Supp. 755. A verdict for
$3,500 in an action by parents for a bright, healthy girl 8½ years
of age, who lived with her mother apart from the father and husband, was excessive, and should be reduced to $2,500. Wells v.
New York Cent. & H. R. R. Co., 78 App. Div. 1, 78 N. Y. Supp. 991.
A verdict for $2,500 for the death of a girl 3½ years old is exces-
sive and must be reduced to $1,500. Barretto v. Mouquin-Offerman-
Wells Coal Co., 142 App. Div. 504, 126 N. Y. Supp. 1009. Verdict
of $600 for death of a child under six years of age cannot be set
aside as inadequate. Terhune v. Joseph W. Cody Contracting Co.,
72 App. Div. 1, 76 N. Y. Supp. 255. Where a jury awarded a verdict of $200 for the wrongful killing of an infant six years of age,
the trial court was not justified in setting it aside as inadequate.
Gubbitosi v. Rothschild, 75 App. Div. 477, 78 N. Y. Supp. 286. Cf.
Morris v. Metropolitan St. Ry. Co., 51 App. Div. 512, 64 N. Y. Supp.
878. See, also, Howell v. Rochester Ry. Co., 24 App. Div. 502, 49
N. Y. Supp. 17; Schaffer v. Baker Transfer Co., 29 App. Div. 459,
51 N. Y. Supp. 1092; Twist v. City of Rochester, 37 App. Div. 307,
55 N. Y. Supp. 850.

[71] Butler v. Manhattan Ry. Co., 143 N. Y. 417, 38 N. E. 454, 26
L. R. A. 46, 42 Am. St. Rep. 738. "The speculation," said the
court, "which, in the present case, the jury were permitted to make,
had not even these safeguards, slight as they are. They were allowed to estimate the pecuniary interest which a husband had in
the chance that an embryo, not yet quickened into life, would become a living child. The sex could not be known, and, if born

In conformity with the views expressed in Ihl v. Forty-Second St. & G. St. Ferry R. Co., it is generally held that the jury may infer the amount of loss from proof of the age, sex, and condition in life of the deceased child, and that testimony as to the value of the services is unnecessary,[72] though perhaps not improper.[73] It would seem, however, that such proof would not dispense with the ne-

alive, the infant might have been destitute of some faculty, or so physically infirm as to have made it a helpless charge. There are no elements whatever upon which a jury could base any conclusion that a pecuniary injury had been suffered by the plaintiff from the loss of the unborn child, and this inquiry should have been excluded from the consideration of the jury as too remote and speculative to form an element in the recovery."

[72] Little Rock & Ft. S. Ry. Co. v. Barker, 39 Ark. 491; City of Chicago v. Major, 18 Ill. 349, 68 Am. Dec. 553; City of Chicago v. Scholten, 75 Ill. 468; City of Chicago v. Hesing, 83 Ill. 204, 25 Am. Rep. 378; Union Pac. Ry. Co. v. Dunden, 37 Kan. 1, 14 Pac. 501; Nagel v. Missouri Pac. Ry. Co., 75 Mo. 653, 42 Am. Rep. 418; Grogan v. Broadway Foundry Co., 87 Mo. 321; Brunswig v. White, 70 Tex. 504, 8 S. W. 85; New York, C. & St. L. R. Co. v. Mushrush, 11 Ind. App. 192, 38 N. E. 871; Atchison, T. & S. F. Ry. Co. v. Fajardo, 74 Kan. 314, 86 Pac. 301, 6 L. R. A. (N. S.) 681; Black v. Michigan Cent. R. Co., 146 Mich. 568, 109 N. W. 1052; Russell v. Windsor Steamboat Co., 126 N. C. 961, 36 S. E. 191; Davis v. Seaboard Air Line Ry., 136 N. C. 115, 48 S. E. 591, 1 Ann. Cas. 214; Hoon v. Beaver Valley Traction Co., 204 Pa. 369, 54 Atl. 270; Schnable v. Providence Public Market, 24 R. I. 477, 53 Atl. 634; Atrops v. Costello, 8 Wash. 149, 35 Pac. 620. Cf. Dinnihan v. Lake Ontario Beach Imp. Co., 8 App. Div. 509, 40 N. Y. Supp. 764; Swift & Co. v. Johnson, 138 Fed. 867, 71 C. C. A. 619, 1 L. R. A. (N. S.) 1161.

[73] Rajnowski v. Detroit, B. C. & A. R. Co., 74 Mich. 15, 41 N. W. 849; Id., 74 Mich. 20, 41 N. W. 847; Pennsylvania Coal Co. v. Nee (Pa.) 13 Atl. 841; Pennsylvania R. Co. v. Henderson, 51 Pa. 315. See, also, Klanowski v. Grand Trunk Ry. Co., 57 Mich. 525, 24 N. W. 801; Pressman v. Mooney, 5 App. Div. 121, 39 N. Y. Supp. 44. Defendant may show the expense of educating and maintaining the child, and the probable value of his earnings. Atrops v. Costello, 8 Wash. 149, 35 Pac. 620.

cessity of evidence showing the expectancy of life of the parents.[74] It is said in some of the cases that where the deceased is a minor, and leaves a parent entitled to his services, the law presumes a loss for which more than nominal damages can be recovered.[75] Such damages may be enhanced by proof of the personal characteristics, capacity to render service, and habits of industry.[76] The jury may take into account the services which the child might reasonably have performed in the family, including acts of kindness and attention which would administer to the com-

---

[74] Carpenter v. Buffalo, N. Y. & P. R. Co., 38 Hun (N. Y.) 116.

[75] Bradley v. Sattler, 156 Ill. 603, 41 N. E. 171; McKechney v. Redmond, 94 Ill. App. 470; Nordhaus v. Vandalia R. Co., 147 Ill. App. 274; Id., 242 Ill. 166, 89 N. E. 974; Bonato v. Peabody Coal Co., 156 Ill. App. 196, affirmed 248 Ill. 422, 94 N. E. 69; Youngquist v. Minneapolis St. R. Co., 102 Minn. 501, 114 N. W. 259; Luessen v. Oshkosh Electric Light & Power Co., 109 Wis. 94, 85 N. W. 124; Thompson v. Johnston Bros. Co., 86 Wis. 576, 57 N. W. 298. Where the next of kin are collateral kindred of the deceased, and have not received pecuniary aid from him, proof of such relationship will warrant a recovery of nominal damages only; but where the deceased is a minor, and leaves a father entitled to his services, the law presumes there has been a pecuniary loss. City of Chicago v. Scholten, 75 Ill. 468; City of Chicago v. Hesing, 83 Ill. 204, 25 Am. Rep. 378. Deceased was a brakeman over 20 years old, whose next of kin was a father, living in Germany. Held, that the plaintiff was entitled to more than nominal damages. The court says that while the measure of recovery would be affected by proof, or by the absence of it, of facts showing the value of the life to the survivors, the law presumes some value. Robel v. Chicago, M. & St. P. Ry. Co., 35 Minn. 84, 27 N. W. 305. It is not competent for the defendant to prove that the child's services were of no value. Foppiano v. Baker, 3 Mo. App. 560. Where a minor leaves a father entitled to his services, loss is presumed, and the fact that the minor worked for his father and received pay for his services does not show that he was "an expense, and not a benefit." Chicago & E. I. R. Co. v. Huston, 196 Ill. 480, 63 N. E. 1028, affirming 95 Ill. App. 350.

[76] City of Chicago v. Scholten, 75 Ill. 468.

fort of the family.[77] From the nature of the case, juries cannot be held to fixed and precise rules in estimating damages in case of the death of young children.[78] Nevertheless, as in other cases, the courts exercise their right to set aside and reduce excessive verdicts, though upon what principle the limit is determined it is often difficult to understand. The extent and character of the supervision exercised is illustrated in the cases collected in the subjoined note.[79]

[77] Louisville, N. A. & C. Ry. Co. v. Rush, 127 Ind. 545, 26 N. E. 1010.

[78] Potter v. Chicago & N. W. R. Co., 22 Wis. 615; Ewen v. Chicago & N. W. Ry. Co., 38 Wis. 613. See, also, Decker v. McSorley, 111 Wis. 91. 86 N. W. 554.

[79] The mother was a widow, poor, and kept boarders. Deceased was a boy, an only child, healthy, intelligent, and obedient. The physician's bills and funeral expenses were $290. On the first trial the jury gave $4,500, which was set aside as excessive. Little Rock & Ft. S. Ry. Co. v. Barker, 33 Ark. 350, 34 Am. Rep. 44. On the second trial the jury gave $3,500, of which the plaintiff remitted $1,235. Held, that a third trial would not be granted on the ground of excessive damages. Id., 39 Ark. 491. A verdict for $4,800 for the death of a boy, 4 years and 4 months old, strong, healthy, and intelligent, was not excessive. De Amado v. Friedman, 11 Ariz. 56, 89 Pac. 588. A verdict for $6,000, for the death of a boy of 4½ years, ordinarily bright, healthy, affectionate, and obedient, whose expectancy of life, if realized, would have carried him considerably beyond the age of majority, was excessive. Fox v. Oakland Consol. St. Ry., 118 Cal. 55, 50 Pac. 25, 62 Am. St. Rep. 216. See, also, Clark v. Tulare Lake Dredging Co., 14 Cal. App. 414, 112 Pac. 564; Bond v. United Railroads of San Francisco, 159 Cal. 270, 113 Pac. 366, Ann. Cas. 1912C, 50. A verdict of $5,000 for a bright active boy, 16 years of age, for nearly 3 years a general clerk in a grocery store, is not excessive. Nelson v. Branford Lighting & Water Co., 75 Conn. 548, 54 Atl. 303. A verdict of $2,000 for a child 4 years old is not excessive. York v. Pacific & N. Ry. Co., 8 Idaho, 574, 69 Pac. 1042. Deceased was a son 6 or 7 years old. Held, that a verdict of $2,000 was not so excessive as to justify the court to interfere. Chicago & A. R. Co. v. Becker, 84 Ill. 483. Whether the damages were excessive is a question of fact which will not be reviewed in the supreme court. City of Joliet v. Weston, 123 Ill. 641, 14 N. E. 665;

A more logical, if less humanitarian, view is taken in New Jersey, where the courts refuse to lose sight of the fact that under the statutes the recovery is confined to the

Id., 22 Ill. App. 225; City of Salem v. Harvey, 29 Ill. App. 483; Id., 129 Ill. 344, 21 N. E. 1076. A verdict for $5,000 for the death of an infant 4 years of age is not excessive. United States Brewing Co. v. Stoltenberg, 113 Ill. App. 435, judgment affirmed 211 Ill. 531, 71 N. E. 1081. See, also, West Chicago St. R. Co. v. Mabie, 77 Ill. App. 176; Cicero & P. St. Ry. Co. v. Boyd, 95 Ill. App. 510; Chicago G. W. Ry. Co. v. Root, 106 Ill. App. 164; Chicago Terminal Transfer R. Co. v. O'Donnell, 114 Ill. App. 345, affirmed 213 Ill. 545, 72 N. E. 1133; Illinois Cent. R. Co. v. Johnson, 123 Ill. App. 300, affirmed 221 Ill. 42, 77 N. E. 592; Chicago City R. Co. v. Strong, 129 Ill. App. 511, affirmed 230 Ill. 58, 82 N. E. 335; Savage v. Hayes Bros. Co., 142 Ill. App. 316. For the death of a child about 7 years old, a verdict for $1,000 is not excessive. Indianapolis Traction & Terminal Co. v. Beckman, 40 Ind. App. 100, 81 N. E. 82. For an ordinarily bright boy, 4 years and 4 months of age, a verdict for $6,000 is excessive, and should only be allowed to stand to the extent of $3,000. Hively v. Webster County, 117 Iowa, 672, 91 N. W. 1041. See, also, Ellis v. Republic Oil Co., 133 Iowa, 11, 110 N. W. 20; Farrell v. Chicago, R. I. & P. Ry. Co., 123 Iowa, 690, 99 N. W. 578; Eginoire v. Union County, 112 Iowa, 558, 84 N. W. 758. A judgment for $3,000 for a minor, who was 11 years and 8 months old, intelligent, healthy, and promising, and left surviving him a father, earning $700 or $800 a year as an engineer, and having a wife and 3 children, is not grossly excessive. Union Pac. Ry. Co. v. Dunden, 37 Kan. 1, 14 Pac. 501. Deceased was 18 years old, and was employed at $1.40 a day. His next of kin were a father and brother. Held, that a verdict of $3,400 was excessive, as it would realize a perpetual income equal to more than three quarters of his annual earnings. Chicago & N. W. Ry. Co. v. Bayfield, 37 Mich. 205. For the death of plaintiff's son, aged 7 years and 1 month, healthy and intelligent, and of excellent disposition, a verdict for $1,500 was not excessive. Black v. Michigan Cent. R. Co., 146 Mich. 568, 109 N. W. 1052. See, also, Kalis v. Detroit United Ry., 155 Mich. 485, 119 N. W. 906. Deceased was 6 years old, in good health, and of ordinary intelligence and promise. His father and sole heir was working on a salary, and was 40 years old. The jury gave a verdict of $5,000, which the trial court reduced to $3,-000. Held, that it should be set aside as excessive. Gunderson v. Northwestern Elevator Co., 47 Minn. 161, 49 N. W. 694. Cf.

pecuniary injury sustained by the beneficiaries by reason of
the death, and, while not requiring strict proof of pecuniary
loss, exercise more rigidly the right to set aside or reduce

O'Malley v. St. Paul, M. & M. Ry. Co., 43 Minn. 289, 45 N. W. 441.
In Strutzel v. St. Paul City Ry. Co., 47 Minn. 543, 50 N. W. 690,
it was held, "though not without some hesitancy," that a verdict
of $2,300 for a boy of 6 years should not be disturbed. $4,500 is
excessive for the death of a minor ·17 years of age, who contributed to his father not more than $90 per year. Kerling v. G.
W. Van Dusen & Co., 109 Minn. 481, 124 N. W. 235; Id., 109
Minn. 481, 124 N. W. 372. See, also, Gray v. St. Paul City Ry.
Co., 87 Minn. 280, 91 N. W. 1106; Kerling v. G. W. Van Dusen
& Co., 113 Minn. 501, 129 N. W. 1048; Healy v. Hoy, 115 Minn.
321, 132 N. W. 208; Erdner v. Chicago & N. W. Ry. Co., 115
Minn. 392, 132 N. W. 339. A verdict of $4,000 for a boy of 8 years
held excessive, and reduced to $2,000. City of Vicksburg v. Mc-
Lain, 67 Miss. 4. 6 South. 774. A verdict of $5,000 for a son 18
years old, employed as a brakeman, where there is no evidence of
the amount of his earnings, and no aggravating circumstances exist, is excessive. Parsons v. Missouri Pac. Ry. Co., 94 Mo. 286, 6
S. W. 464. For the death of a boy of 7 years, a verdict for $1,525
is not so excessive as to require a reversal. City of Omaha v. Bow-
man, 63 Neb. 333, 88 N. W. 521. See, also, Post v. Olmsted, 47
Neb. 893, 66 N. W. 828; City of Omaha v. Richards, 49 Neb. 244,
68 N. W. 528. Verdicts of $936 and $1,056 for two sons, aged 13
and 15, respectively, held excessive. Telfer v. Northern R. Co., 30
N. J. Law, 188. For the death of a 16 year old son, who resided
with his father, and, being on the eve of graduation, was in position greatly to aid him in business, a verdict for $7,500 will not
be disturbed as excessive. Judgment (1901) 63 App. Div. 78, 71 N.
Y. Supp. 321, affirmed. Morris v. Metropolitan St. Ry. Co., 170 N.
Y. 592, 63 N. E. 1119. A verdict of $1,518 for the death of
a boy 6 years old is not excessive. Hoon v. Beaver Valley Traction
Co., 204 Pa. 369, 54 Atl. 270.   A verdict of $2,500 for a 6 year
old child is not excessive. Sweet v. Providence & S. R. Co., 20 R.
I. 785, 40 Atl. 237. A verdict for $750 for a boy of 5 years will not
be disturbed on appeal as inadequate. Schnable v. Providence Public Market, 24 R. I. 477, 53 Atl. 634. A verdict of $5,000 for a 7
year old boy held excessive by $2,000. Riley v. Salt Lake Rapid
Transit Co., 10 Utah, 428, 37 Pac. 681.   A verdict for $2,160.20
for a one year old child was not excessive, in the absence of anything indicating prejudice or passion. Abby v. Wood, 43 Wash.

excessive verdicts.[80]   Thus in a case in New Jersey,[81] in which a verdict of $5,000 for the death of a four year old child was set aside, the court said : "Children are more often an expense, than a pecuniary benefit, to the father. If, at the father's death, an account were stated showing, on the one side, the moneys expended by him in the education, maintenance, and support of the child, and, on the other side, the moneys received by the father from his child, in a majority of every 100 cases the moneys expended for the benefit of the child would be found to be far in excess of the amount received from him. And yet, on the theory upon which this verdict is based, the larger a man's family is, the more likely is he to die rich. In the present case, if the father of the decedent had a reasonable expectation of

379, 86 Pac. 558. Deceased was 7 years old. His father was poor, troubled with rheumatism, and sawed wood for a living, and his mother at times worked out. Held, that a verdict of $2,500 was not excessive. Johnson v. Chicago & N. W. Ry. Co., 64 Wis. 425, 25 N. W. 223. A verdict of $2,000 for a boy 18 months old held not excessive. Schrier v. Milwaukee, L. S. & W. Ry. Co., 65 Wis. 457, 27 N. W. 167. A verdict of $3,000, reduced by the trial court to $2,500, for a boy 10 years old, leaving a father, was not excessive. Lomoe v. Superior Water, Light & Power Co., 147 Wis. 5, 132 N. W. 623.

[80] Graham v. Consolidated Traction Co., 62 N. J. Law, 90, 40 Atl. 773. See, also, Graham v. Consolidated Traction Co., 64 N. J. Law, 10, 44 Atl. 964; Graham v. Consolidated Traction Co., 65 N. J. Law, 539, 47 Atl. 453; Rowe v. New York & N. J. Tel. Co., 66 N. J. Law, 19, 48 Atl. 523; Cook v. American E. C. & Schultze Gunpowder Co., 70 N. J. Law, 65, 56 Atl. 114. Verdicts of $963 and $1,056 for two sons, aged 13 and 15 respectively, held excessive. Telfer v. Northern R. Co., 30 N. J. Law, 188. In an action for the death of a girl 5 years and 8 months old, in the absence of any evidence showing that her father had any reasonable expectation of receiving benefit, in case she had lived, to the extent of $2,000, a verdict for that amount was excessive by $1,000. Fleming v. Lobel, 59 Atl. 27.

[81] Graham v. Consolidated Traction Co., supra.

(360)

being benefited in dollars and cents to the extent of $5,000 by the continuance of the life of his deceased child, a family of 10 sons would justify the assumption that, at his death he would be better off by $50,000 than he would be if he had never had issue. The mere statement of such an assumption makes its absurdity apparent. The verdict in this case is so excessive as to make it clear that it is not the result of the dispassionate, unprejudiced action of the jury."

§ 165. Death of minor child—Expectancy of benefit after majority

Damages for the death of an adult child, as will be seen, are usually confined, except where they are based upon the loss of a prospective inheritance, to cases where the child has manifested his willingness to assist his parents by actually doing so. In accordance with the principle of these cases, it is logically held in Arkansas,[82] Maryland,[83] Michigan,[84] Pennsylvania,[85] and Rhode Island [86] that, in an action for the death of a minor child of tender years, damages are limited to the loss of service during the child's minority, and that the chances of his surviving his parents

[82] Little Rock & Ft. S. Ry. Co. v. Barker, 33 Ark. 350, 34 Am. Rep. 44; St. Louis, I. M. & S. Ry. Co. v. Freeman, 36 Ark. 41.

[83] State, to Use of Coughlan, v. Baltimore & O. R. Co., 24 Md. 84, 87 Am. Dec. 600.

[84] Cooper v. Lake Shore & M. S. Ry. Co., 66 Mich. 261, 33 N. W. 306, 11 Am. St. Rep. 482; Hurst v. Detroit City Ry. Co., 84 Mich. 539, 48 N. W. 44. See, also, Moers v. Michigan United Rys. Co., 158 Mich. 659, 123 N. W. 602.

[85] Pennsylvania R. Co. v. Zebe, 33 Pa. 318; Caldwell v. Brown, 53 Pa. 453; Lehigh Iron Co. v. Rupp, 100 Pa. 95; Deninger v. American Locomotive Co., 185 Fed. 22, 107 C. C. A. 126.

[86] Schnable v. Providence Public Market, 24 R. I. 477, 53 Atl. 634.

and of his ability and willingness to assist them after that period, should be excluded from consideration. In Maryland [87] the same rule has been held to apply, although the minor is old enough to be self-supporting, and has actually contributed to the support of the parent; and the rule as declared in Pennsylvania would cover such a case.[88] But in Arkansas the rule does not apply where the minor has shown himself able and willing to make his own living, and to contribute to the support of his parents.[89]

In Missouri and some other states the right of action is confined by the terms of the statute to the death of a minor child.

In New York, Kansas,[90] Texas,[91] and Wisconsin, damages are not limited to the value of the services during minority.[92] And this rule now obtains in many other ju-

---

[87] No expectation of pecuniary benefit to the father from the continuance of the life, after minority, of a son 19 years old, can be considered, although the son had been emancipated 2 years before his death, and had paid to his father the greater part of his earnings, and had promised to help him after becoming of age. Agricultural & Mech. Ass'n of Washington County v. State, 71 Md. 86, 18 Atl. 37, 17 Am. St. Rep. 507.

[88] Lehigh Iron Co. v. Rupp, 100 Pa. 95.

[89] St. Louis, I. M. & S. Ry. Co. v. Davis, 55 Ark. 462, 18 S. W. 628.

[90] Missouri Pac. Ry. Co. v. Peregoy, 36 Kan. 424, 14 Pac. 7; Atchison, T. & S. F. R. Co. v. Cross, 58 Kan. 424, 49 Pac. 599; Fidelity Land & Improvement Co. v. Buzzard, 69 Kan. 330, 76 Pac. 832; Atchison, T. & S. F. Ry. Co. v. Fajardo, 74 Kan. 314, 86 Pac. 301, 6 L. R. A. (N. S.) 681.

[91] Gulf, C. & S. F. Ry. Co. v. Compton, 75 Tex. 667, 13 S. W. 667. See Houston & T. R. Co. v. Nixon, 52 Tex. 19. See, also, San Antonio Traction Co. v. White, 94 Tex. 468, 61 S. W. 706; St. Louis S. W. R. Co. v. Shiflet, 98 Tex. 102, 81 S. W. 524; Texas & P. R. Co. v. Wilder, 92 Fed. 953, 35 C. C. A. 105. Cf. San Antonio Traction Co. v. White, 94 Tex. 468, 61 S. W. 706.

[92] In an action by the administrator for the death of a child 18 months old, owing to the fact that another action had been (erroneously) begun by the father to recover for the loss of services of the

risdictions.[93]   In New York [94] the right of action, even in case of the death of an adult child or of a collateral relative, is not confined to cases where there is evidence of past benefits upon which to base a reasonable probability of future benefits; and it is accordingly held that in an action for the death of a minor child the jury are not confined to a consideration of the benefits which would have resulted to the parents during minority, but may consider the probable, and even possible, benefits which might have resulted to them from his life, modified by the chances of failure and misfortune.   In Wisconsin [95] it is held that the jury may take into consideration the reasonable expectation of pecun-

child during minority, only such damages were claimed as would accrue to the father or next of kin by reason of the loss of such pecuniary benefit as he might have received after the minority. A new trial was granted for error in the instructions, but the court intimates that the action might be maintained. Scheffler v. Minneapolis & St. L. Ry. Co., 32 Minn. 518, 21 N. W. 711. Although the father had given his time to the deceased (a minor son,) the parents may recover more than nominal damages. St. Joseph & W. R. Co. v. Wheeler, 35 Kan. 185, 10 Pac. 461.

[93] Bond v. United Railroads of San Francisco, 159 Cal. 270, 113 Pac. 366, Ann. Cas. 1912C, 50; Pierce v. Conners, 20 Colo. 178, 37 Pac. 721, 46 Am. St. Rep. 279; United States Electric Lighting Co. v. Sullivan, 22 App. D. C. 115; Holt v. Spokane & P. Ry. Co., 3 Idaho, 703, 35 Pac. 39; United States Brewing Co. v. Stoltenberg, 211 Ill. 531, 71 N. E. 1081; Illinois Cent. R. Co. v. Warriner, 229 Ill. 91, 82 N. E. 246; Gilman v. G. W. Dart Hardware Co., 42 Mont. 96, 111 Pac. 550; Draper v. Tucker, 69 Neb. 434, 95 N. W. 1026; Crabtree v. Missouri Pac. R. Co., 86 Neb. 33, 124 N. W. 932, 136 Am. St. Rep. 663; Morhart v. North Jersey St. Ry. Co., 64 N. J. Law, 236, 45 Atl. 812; Beaman v. Martha Washington Min. Co., 23 Utah, 139, 63 Pac. 631.

[94] Birkett v. Knickerbocker Ice Co., 110 N. Y. 504, 18 N. E. 108. See, also, Connaughton v. Sun Printing & Publishing Ass'n, 73 App. Div. 316, 76 N. Y. Supp. 755.

[95] Potter v. Chicago & N. W. R. Co., 22 Wis. 615; s. c., 21 Wis. 372, 94 Am. Dec. 548. Cf. Seaman v. Farmers' Loan & Trust Co., 15 Wis. 578. See, also, Thompson v. Johnston Bros. Co., 86 Wis. 576,

iary advantage that would have resulted from the child living beyond minority; but that it must be shown that the circumstances were such as to render it probable that the
parents might need the services of the child, or aid from
him, after majority; and that a sufficient foundation for
such damages is laid by showing that the physical or pecuniary circumstances of the parents were such as to show
that they might need such services or aid.

In Iowa [96] and Washington [97] two actions may be maintained—one by the personal representative to recover damages to the estate for the loss of benefits that would have
accrued after majority, and one by the parent for loss of
services during minority.

§ 166.   Loss of prospective gifts and inheritance

The measure of damages in actions where the pecuniary
injury consists in loss of services and of support, or of
other benefits which are peculiar to the mutual relation of
husband and wife, and of parent and of minor child, have
been considered. It remains to consider what other damages may be recovered, as well in actions which involve
these peculiar relations, as in cases which do not involve
them. As has been stated, such damages may be recovered
(1) for the loss of prospective gifts, and (2) for the loss of
a prospective inheritance.

§ 167.   Loss of prospective gifts

The cases in which, upon the facts, damages are recoverable for the loss of prospective gifts, are commonly actions

57 N. W. 298; Hayes v. Chicago, M. & St. P. R. Co., 131 Wis. 399,
111 N. W. 471.
   [96] See § 40.   [97] See § 57.

by parents for the death of adult children, although cases also arise in which such damages may be recovered for the benefit of adult children on account of the death of a parent, or for the benefit of brothers and sisters and other collateral relatives. As has been said, such damages are not confined to cases of these descriptions, but may be recovered, where the facts furnish a proper basis, in addition to damages for loss of services, support, etc., in actions for the benefit of husbands, wives, minor children,[98] and in some jurisdictions at least, of parents of minor children.

In order to lay a foundation for the recovery of damages for the loss of prospective gifts, it is usually held necessary, except in New York, for the plaintiff to show that the deceased, during his life, gave assistance to the beneficiaries, by way of money, services, or other material benefits, which, in reasonable probability would have continued but for the death.[99] In Illinois, however, the rule is established that, where the next of kin sustain a lineal relation to the deceased, the law presumes some substantial damages from the relationship alone, and it is not essential to show that they received pecuniary assistance from the deceased,[100] although it is of course competent to show that such assistance was given.[101]

[98] Pym v. Great Northern Ry. Co., 2 B. & S. 759, 4 B. & S. 396.

[99] Cases cited in notes to sections 168–170.

[100] Dukeman v. Cleveland, C., C. & St. L. R. Co., 237 Ill. 104, 86 N. E. 712; Chicago, P. & St. L. R. Co. v. Woolridge, 174 Ill. 330, 51 N. E. 701; Cleveland, C., C. & St. L. Ry. Co. v. Dukeman, 130 Ill. App. 105. Cf. Chicago & W. I. R. Co. v. Ptacek, 171 Ill. 9, 49 N. E. 191. The law presumes damage to have resulted to adult children from the death of their mother. Rautman v. Chicago Consol. Traction Co., 156 Ill. App. 457.

[101] Prendergast v. Chicago City Ry. Co., 114 Ill. App. 156; Nordhaus v. Vandalia R. Co., 147 Ill. App. 274.

§ 168.   Loss of prospective gifts—Death of adult child

Thus, in Dalton v. South Eastern Ry. Co.,[102] where it appeared that the plaintiff's son, who was 27 years old and unmarried, and lived away from his parents, had in the last 7 or 8 years been in the habit of making them occasional presents of provisions and money, amounting to about £20 a year, it was held that the jury were warranted in inferring that the father had such a reasonable expectation of pecuniary benefit from his son's life as to entitle him to recover damages. And in Franklin v. South Eastern Ry. Co.[103] it appeared that the father was old and infirm, and that the son, who was young and earning good wages, assisted him in some work, for which he was paid 3s. 6d. a week; and, the jury having found that the father had a reasonable expectation of benefit from the continuance of the son's life, it was held that the action was maintainable, although the verdict of £75 was excessive. In Sykes v. North Eastern Ry. Co.,[104] on the contrary, where the deceased was a bricklayer, and received from his father the wages of a skilled workman, and was of great assistance to his father, who was also a bricklayer, and who, owing to the loss of assistance from the deceased, could not take the contracts which he had done during his son's life, it was held that, inasmuch as the benefit which the father derived

---

[102] 4 C. B. (N. S.) 296, 4 Jur. (N. S.) 711, 27 L. J. C. P. 227.

[103] 3 Hurl & N. 211, 4 Jur. (N. S.) 565. The plaintiff was 59 years old, nearly blind, injured in his leg and hands, and unable to work as formerly. Some 5 or 6 years before the death of his son, when the plaintiff was out of work for 6 months, the son had assisted the father pecuniarily, but had not done so since. Held, that there was evidence of pecuniary injury. Hetherington v. North Eastern Ry. Co., 9 Q. B. D. 160.

[104] 44 L. J. C. P. 191, 32 L. T. (N. S.) 199, 23 Wkly. R. 473.

accrued, not from the relationship, but from a contract, and there was no evidence that he paid his son less than the usual wages, he had suffered no pecuniary loss from the death.[105]

The distinction taken in the English cases has generally been observed in the United States; [106] that is, the plaintiff must show that the decedent gave assistance to the parent or that the parent had reasonable expectation of pecuniary benefit from the continued life of the child. The proper

[105] The injury to the sons of deceased by the dissolution of a partnership between him and them cannot be considered. Demarest v. Little, 47 N. J. Law, 28.

[106] St. Louis, M. & S. E. R. Co. v. Garner, 76 Ark. 555, 89 S. W. 550; Hillebrand v. Standard Biscuit Co., 139 Cal. 233, 73 Pac. 163; Colorado Coal & Iron Co. v. Lamb, 6 Colo. App. 255, 40 Pac. 251; Louisville, N. A. & C. Ry. Co. v. Wright, 134 Ind. 509, 34 N. E. 314; Diebold v. Sharpe, 19 Ind. App. 474, 49 N. E. 837; Pittsburg Vitrified Pav. & Bldg. Brick Co. v. Fisher, 79 Kan. 576, 100 Pac. 507; McKay v. New England Dredging Co., 92 Me. 454, 43 Atl. 29; Greenwood v. King, 82 Neb. 17, 116 N. W. 1128; Holmes v. Pennsylvania R. Co., 220 Pa. 189, 69 Atl. 597, 123 Am. St. Rep. 685; Texas Portland Cement & Lime Co. v. Lee, 36 Tex. Civ. App. 482, 82 S. W. 306; Brush Electric Light & Power Co. v. Lefevre (Tex. Civ. App.) 55 S. W. 396; Gulf, C. & S. F. R. Co. v. Brown, 33 Tex. Civ. App. 269, 76 S. W. 794; St. Louis Southwestern Ry. Co. of Texas v. Huey (Tex. Civ. App.) 130 S. W. 1017; Fritz v. Western Union Tel. Co., 25 Utah. 263, 71 Pac. 209; Southern Pac. Co. v. Lafferty, 57 Fed. 536, 6 C. C. A. 474; In an action for the benefit of a father for the death of an unmarried son 22 years of age, plaintiff can recover only by showing that deceased gave assistance to his father, contributed money to his support, or that the father had reasonable expectation of pecuniary benefit from the continued life of the son, the reasonable character of this expectation to appear from the facts in proof. In the absence of such proof, only nominal damages can be recovered. Fordyce v. McCants, 51 Ark. 509, 11 S. W. 694, 4 L. R. A. 296, 14 Am. St. Rep. 69. A verdict of $10,000 should be set aside, it appearing that the next of kin entitled to the benefit of the verdict was a mother in comfortable pecuniary circumstances, who had derived no profit from the earnings of her son, and was not likely to profit by his earnings had he lived. Atchison, T. & S. F. R. Co. v.

measure of damages is the present worth of the amount which it is reasonably probable the deceased would have contributed to the support of the parent during the latter's

Brown, 26 Kan. 443. The son lived apart from his parents, but was unmarried. No proof was offered of the parents' financial condition, or that they had ever received any actual pecuniary benefits from him during his lifetime; nor was there any evidence showing a reasonable probability of pecuniary advantage to them from the continuance of the son's life. Held, that no more than nominal damages should have been recovered. Cherokee & P. Coal & Min. Co. v. Limb, 47 Kan. 469, 28 Pac. 181. The deceased contributed to the support of his mother and invalid sister, but not of his other brothers and sisters. Held, that damages should be allowed only on account of the first two. Richmond v. Chicago & W. M. Ry. Co., 87 Mich. 374, 49 N. W. 621. Damages for the death of a son must be shown by evidence regarding the earnings of deceased and other circumstances, unless such evidence is not accessible. A verdict for $9,000, based on no evidence showing the value of deceased's life to plaintiff, set aside. Houston & T. C. Ry. Co. v. Cowser, 57 Tex. 293. The petition must show that the son supported plaintiff, or contributed to his support, or that there was some expectation of pecuniary benefit to be derived from deceased; and a mere allegation that plaintiff, "as his sole surviving parent, had been damaged $10,000 actual damages," is insufficient. Winnt v. International & G. N. Ry. Co., 74 Tex. 32, 11 S. W. 907, 5 L. R. A. 172. But see Johnson v. Missouri Pac. Ry. Co., 18 Neb. 690, 26 N. W. 347, where the father lived in Sweden, and had received no aid from the deceased since his coming to the United States, a short time before the death, and it was held that the evidence should have been submitted to the jury. In Pennsylvania it is said that "parents" and "children," as used in the act, indicate the family relation in point of fact as the foundation of the right of action, without regard to age. Pennsylvania R. Co. v. Adams, 55 Pa. 499. If the child was of age and the family relation existed, damages may be recovered for the loss of the reasonable expectation of pecuniary advantage, if any, from the continuance of the relation. Pennsylvania R. Co. v. Adams, supra; Pennsylvania R. Co. v. Keller, 67 Pa. 300; North Pennsylvania R. Co. v. Kirk, 90 Pa. 15. But if the family relation has ceased, and the child does not contribute to his parents' support, no damages can be recovered. Lehigh Iron Co. v. Rupp, 100 Pa. 95. Loss of the expectation of the payment of a debt due from the son to the father is a proper element of damage. Stangeland v. Minneapolis, St. P. & S. S.

expectancy of life, in proportion to the amount he was contributing at the time of his death, not exceeding his expectancy of life; [107] though it would seem that the rule is not to be applied with mathematical strictness, and that the jury may properly take into consideration the increasing wants of the parent, and the increasing ability of the child to supply them.[108] In some cases, indeed, the evidence has been held sufficient to sustain a finding that there was a reasonable expectation of pecuniary benefit, although the evidence fell short of showing that assistance was actually furnished.[109] In Hutchins v. St. Paul, M. & M. Ry. Co.,[110]

M. R. Co., 105 Minn. 224, 117 N. W. 386. Evidence that during his minority the son paid all his earnings to the father is incompetent. Bonnet v. Galveston, H. & S. A. Ry. Co., 89 Tex. 72, 33 S. W. 334. Evidence to the effect that the deceased had agreed to reimburse his father for the expense of his education by assisting in the education of his sisters is evidence which tends to establish pecuniary loss to such father. Huff v. Peoria & E. Ry. Co., 127 Ill. App. 242. Where, after deceased was married, he contributed nothing to the support of his parents, and there was no evidence that they needed, or had any reasonable expectation of receiving, any pecuniary benefit from him thereafter had he lived, their mere relationship was insufficient to sustain a recovery for his death. Standard Light & Power Co. v. Muncey, 33 Tex. Civ. App. 416, 76 S. W. 931.

[107] Richmond v. Chicago & W. M. Ry. Co., supra. But in Virginia, in an action for the benefit of a widowed mother for the death of an unmarried son, who lived with and cared for her, it was held that the jury might allow such sum as would be equal to his probable earnings during his and her expectancy of life. Baltimore & O. R. R. Co. v. Noell's Adm'r, 73 Va. 394.

[108] International & G. N. R. Co. v. Kindred, 57 Tex. 491; Texas & P. Ry. Co. v. Lester, 75 Tex. 56, 12 S. W. 955. See Hetherington v. Northeastern Ry. Co., 9 Q. B. D. 160. It is error to instruct the jury as to the disposition of the child to help, since the question is, did he help? Chicago & N. W. R. Co. v. Swett, 45 Ill. 197, 92 Am. Dec. 206.

[109] Hopper v. Denver & R. G. R. Co., 155 Fed. 273, 84 C. C. A. 21; Sieber v. Great Northern Ry. Co., 76 Minn. 269, 79 N. W. 95.

[110] 44 Minn. 5, 46 N. W. 79. In that case the verdict was $3,500,

TIFF.DEATH W.A.(2D ED.)—24   (369)

it was said: "The proper estimate can usually be arrived at with approximate accuracy by taking into account the calling of the deceased, and the income derived therefrom; his health, age, talents, habits of industry; his success in life in the past, as well as the amount of aid in money or services which he was accustomed to furnish the next of kin; and, if the verdict is greatly in excess of the sum thus arrived at, the court will set it aside or cut it down." [111] The application of the rules in actions for the death of adult children, particularly with reference to the amount of the verdict, is illustrated in the cases in the subjoined note.[112]

while the evidence showed that the contributions of the son to his mother did not exceed $50 a year, and that her expectancy of life was only 7½ years. The court reduced the verdict to $2,000. Opsahl v. Judd, 30 Minn. 126, 14 N. W. 575.

[111] The jury may consider the circumstances of the son, his occupation, age, health, habits of industry, sobriety, and economy, his annual earnings, and his probable duration of life at the time of the accident; also the amount of property, age, health, and probable duration of plaintiff's life, and the amount of assistance he had a reasonable expectation of receiving from the son. Hall v. Galveston, H. & S. A. R. Co. (C. C.) 39 Fed. 18. Though the true measure of damages for the killing of plaintiff's son is "a sum equal to the pecuniary benefit the parent had a reasonable expectation of receiving from her child had he not died," it is not misleading to charge that the damages are "such sum as you may, under the evidence, reasonably believe plaintiff might have received from the assistance of deceased had he not been killed; and you may, in estimating such sum, if any, consider, under the evidence before you, the age of deceased, the time he might have lived, the age of the plaintiff, the time she may probably live, and any other evidence tending to show what damages, if any, she may have suffered by the killing of deceased. You will find for plaintiff such damages, under the instructions heretofore given, as you may think will compensate her for the loss, if any, she may have sustained by the killing." Missouri Pac. R. Co. v. Lee, 70 Tex. 496, 7 S. W. 857.

[112] Deceased contributed to the support of his mother and her invalid daughter $30 to $50 a month, and gave his sister $5 to $20 a month when necessary. He was healthy, and his expectancy of life

§ 169. Loss of prospective gifts—Death of parent of adult child

Although the benefit of the action, unless, as in Missouri, the statute otherwise provides, is not confined to minor

was 32½ years. His mother was 59 years old, and her expectancy was 14¾ years. His sister was 19 years old, and her expectancy 42 years. He earned $100 to $150 a month. Held, that a verdict for $6,500 was not excessive; and that the jury were at liberty to consider that, in aiding the daughter, who belonged to his mother's family, the son was contributing to the support of his mother, who was his next of kin. Little Rock & Ft. S. Ry. Co. v. Voss (Ark.) 18 S. W. 172. Deceased first received $25 and afterwards $35 per month and board; his services were constantly increasing in value; his living expenses were about $125 a year, and the balance of his wages was sent to his parents. His father was poor, and dependent on his relatives for support, and his expectancy of life was about 17 years. Held, that a judgment of $2,391.50 was not excessive. Fordyce v. McCants, 55 Ark. 384, 18 S. W. 371. When deceased was 23 years old, of good habits, and the sole support of his mother and her minor children, to whom he gave from $40 to $50 per month, a verdict for $3,000 is not excessive. O'Callaghan v. Bode, 84 Cal. 489, 24 Pac. 269. The father was 50 years old, and had little property besides his homestead. When not on the road the son lived with him and contributed to the support of the family. There was a policy of insurance on the life of the father for the benefit of the mother, upon which the son paid the premium, and he had promised to keep it paid. Held, that a verdict for $2,000 was not excessive. Chicago & A. R. Co. v. Shannon, 43 Ill. 338. Deceased left, surviving her, a father, mother, two brothers, and a sister. She lived with her father, mother and sister, and had contributed to the support of her family as well as she could, and was under an engagement to teach school. Held, that a verdict of $1,500 was not excessive. City of Salem v. Harvey, 29 Ill. App. 483; affirmed 129 Ill. 344, 21 N. E. 1076. In an action by a widowed mother 54 years old for the death of an unmarried son 24 years old, who was her sole support, contributing about $150 annually, an award of $4,000 damages was excessive. Chicago & E. I. R. Co. v. Vester, 47. Ind. App. 141, 93 N. E. 1039. See, also, Commercial Club of Indianapolis v. Hilliker, 20 Ind. App. 239, 50 N. E. 578; Chicago & E. I. R. Co. v. Stephen-

children,[118] cases in which the facts warrant a recovery of
damages by adult children for the loss of pecuniary benefits
in the nature of prospective gifts are rare. The recovery

son, 33 Ind. App. 95, 69 N. E. 270. Intestate was 23 years old and
a stonecutter, his wages being $2 a day. His parents were advanced
in years and infirm. He paid $20 a month for board, and received
15 cents an hour; he not having steady work, and at times being
unable to obtain any work. Held, that a verdict for the parents for
$2,000 should be reduced to $750. McKay v. New England Dredging
Co., 92 Me. 454, 43 Atl. 29. Where a son was 22, his mother 51, and
his father 61 years of age, and the son was a sober, industrious man,
had contributed regularly to his mother's support from $250 to $350
a year, and had saved several hundred dollars, and was earning
over $1,000 a year, with prospects of early promotion, a recovery
of $3,750 was not excessive. McVeigh v. Minneapolis & R. R. R. Co.,
113 Minn. 450, 129 N. W. 852. See, also, Swanson v. Oakes, 93 Minn.
404, 101 N. W. 949; Holden v. Great Northern Ry. Co., 103 Minn.
98, 114 N. W. 365; McVeigh v. Minneapolis & R. R. R. Co., 110
Minn. 184, 124 N. W. 971. Where deceased had a life expectancy of
25 years and earned $60 a month, and spent about $100 on clothing
and personal expenses annually, and the balance of her wages was
turned over to her mother whose life expectancy was between 11 and
12 years, a verdict for $4,500 was not excessive. Smith v. Coon, 89
Neb. 776, 132 N. W. 535. See, also, Chicago, R. I. & P. R. Co. v.
Young, 67 Neb. 568, 93 N. W. 922. A verdict of $10,000 for the death
of a laborer 30 years old, earning $3 a day, is excessive, where it
does not appear that he contributed anything to his parents, nor that
they are in need of assistance, and there is no proof of the expectancy of life of the decedent or beneficiaries except their ages. Christensen v. Floriston Pulp & Paper Co., 29 Nev. 552, 92 Pac. 210. Deceased was 22 years old, and left as next of kin a mother aged 42,
able to support herself by the needle, and two brothers aged 16 and
19. The evidence of his assistance to his mother was only of a general character. Held, that a verdict of $3,000 was excessive. Paul-
mier v. Erie R. Co., 34 N. J. Law, 151. Deceased was industrious
and economical, and, at the age of 26 years, earning $1,000 a year,
out of which he was furnishing plaintiff, his mother, then 51 years
old, $200 per annum. Held, that a verdict of $4,200 would not be
disturbed. Texas & P. Ry. Co. v. Lester, 75 Tex. 56, 12 S. W. 955.
Where a mother who is 60 years old, and in good health, had for

----

[118] Baltimore & O. R. Co. v. State, to Use of Hauer, 60 Md. 449.

(372)

must, of course, be based upon evidence of pecuniary benefits conferred by the deceased during his life, the contin-

many years been supported by her son, aged 22½ years, and who at the time of his death was earning from $60 to $65 per month, one-half of which he had been in the habit of giving to his mother, a verdict for $3,550 is not excessive. Missouri Pac. Ry. Co. v. Henry, 75 Tex. 220, 12 S. W. 828. A verdict for $4,995 was not so excessive as to justify reversal, where decedent, at the time of his death, was a strong, healthy man 28 years old, of good habits, and earning $1.75 per day. Webb v. Denver & R. G. Ry. Co., 7 Utah, 363, 26 Pac. 981. Deceased was industrious, 21 years old, earning $40 per month, with board and room. His father was 54 years old, in fairly good health, earning $40 a month. His mother was 43 years old, in poor physical condition. Two sisters were 20 and 18 years old, respectively, and a brother of 15 was not self-supporting. There was evidence that deceased had promised to take care of his parents, and that he did not expect to marry soon. Held, that a verdict for $2,500 was not excessive. Leque v. Madison Gas & Electric Co., 133 Wis. 547, 113 N. W. 946. Where a fireman contributed to the support of his parents $250 per year, that they had furnished him with a home, and that the youngest parent was 51 years old, a verdict of $4,500 was excessive by $2,000, as being a larger sum than the parents in all probability would have ever received from the son. Hackett v. Wisconsin Cent. Ry. Co., 141 Wis. 464, 124 N. W. 1018. See, also, Innes v. City of Milwaukee, 103 Wis. 582, 79 N. W. 783. Deceased was 27 years of age, had been in the United States from 2½ to 5 years, was a common laborer, employed at $1.50 per day as a car cleaner, and was unmarried. There was evidence that he sent from $20 to $25 per month to his father in Roumania, who was 65 years of age. Held, that a verdict for $3,500 was excessive, and should be reduced to $2,500. Hirschkovitz v. Pennsylvania R. Co. (C. C.) 138 Fed. 438. An unmarried son, 30 years old, lived with his parents, to whom he had given his services for a number of years, the estimated value of which was from $4,000 to $7,000 a year, receiving from them only about $500 a year to meet his personal expenses, having assured his father that he would continue so to work until the father had paid off an indebtedness. Held, that the parents' reasonable expectation of the continuance of such services could not extend more than a year or two ahead at any time and that a verdict awarding them $17,000 was excessive. Scofield v. Pennsylvania Co. (C. C.) 149 Fed. 601. See, also, St. Louis, I. M. & S. Ry. Co. v. Block, 79 Ark. 179, 95 S. W. 155; Chicago & A. R. Co. v. Adler, 28 Ill. App. 102; Illi-

uance of which might reasonably have been expected.[114]
Nothing can be allowed for the loss of a father's counsel

nois Steel Co. v. Paige, 136 Ill. App. 410; Casey v. Kelly-Atkinson
Const. Co., 146 Ill. App. 551; St. Louis & S. F. Ry. Co. v. French,
56 Kan. 584, 44 Pac. 12; Flaherty v. New York, N. H. & H. R. Co.
(R. I.) 35 Atl. 308; Texas & N. O. R. Co. v. Scarborough (Tex. Civ.
App.) 104 S. W. 408; Mexican Nat. Ry. Co. v. Finch, 8 Tex. Civ.
App. 409, 27 S. W. 1028; International & G. N. R. Co. v. McNeel
(Tex. Civ. App.) 29 S. W. 1133; Texas & P. Ry. Co. v. Spence (Tex.
Civ. App.) 52 S. W. 562; Lindstrom v. International Nav. Co. (C. C.)
117 Fed. 170; Baker v. Philadelphia & R. Ry. Co. (C. C.) 149 Fed.
882; Stockton v. Pennsylvania R. Co. (C. C.) 182 Fed. 282.

114 Schnatz v. Philadelphia & R. R. Co., 160 Pa. 602, 28 Atl. 952;
San Antonio & A. P. Ry. Co. v. Long, 87 Tex. 148, 27 S. W. 113, 24 L.
R. A. 637, 47 Am. St. Rep. 87; International & G. N. R. Co. v. DeBa-
jligethy, 9 Tex. Civ. App., 108, 28 S. W. 829; St. Louis S. W. Ry.
Co. of Texas v. Bishop, 14 Tex. Civ. App. 504, 37 S. W. 764; Texas
& N. O. Ry. Co. v. Brown, 14 Tex. Civ. App. 697, 39 S. W. 140;
San Antonio & A. P. Ry. Co. v. Long, 19 Tex. Civ. App. 649, 48 S.
W. 599; Texas Pac. R. Co. v. Martin, 25 Tex. Civ. App. 204, 60 S.
W. 803; Procter v. San Antonio St. Ry. Co., 26 Tex. Civ. App. 148,
62 S. W. 938, 939; Galveston, H. & S. A. Ry. Co. v. Polk (Tex. Civ.
App.) 63 S. W. 343; Rader v. Galveston, H. & S. A. Ry. Co. (Tex. Civ.
App.) 137 S. W. 718. In an action for the benefit of two sons and a
daughter, all married and of age, it appeared that the deceased lived
with her daughter, thus enabling the latter to work and earn $6 a
week, and that the deceased also frequently assisted in nursing the
sick in her sons' families; but it did not appear how often she
went, how long she stayed, or what was the value of such services.
Held (1) that, as the services rendered by the mother constituted the
pecuniary benefit which the daughter had a right to expect from
the continuance of the life, the value of such services, and not what
the daughter might earn, was the measure of damages; (2) that
there was no evidence sufficient to warrant the jury in finding any
pecuniary loss to the sons. Baltimore & O. R. Co. v. State, to Use
of Mahone, 63 Md. 135. The deceased lived with one married daughter, and was in the habit of rendering services (the value of which
did not appear) to her and to her husband, who was an invalid, and
to her other adult children. Held, that a nonsuit was properly denied. Petrie v. Columbia & G. R. Co., 29 S. C. 303, 7 S. E. 515.
The court lays stress on the absence of the word "pecuniary" from
the statute. A married daughter and son, nearly 21 years old, nei.

and services, except so far as they can be estimated in money.[115]

§ 170. Loss of prospective gifts—Death of collateral relative

The same rules apply to the recovery of damages for the death of collateral relations, who may be next of kin or otherwise included among the beneficiaries, that is, there may be a recovery of substantial damages if it appears that the decedent gave assistance to the beneficiary, or if there are other circumstances indicating an intention to give assistance, so that there was a reasonable expectation of pe-

tner of them supported by their father, who left also a widow and dependent minor children, have no right to damages. St. Louis, A. & T. Ry. Co. v. Johnston, 78 Tex. 536, 15 S. W. 104. In an action by a daughter for the death of her mother, it appeared that deceased lived with plaintiff, who was a laundress, and by whom she was maintained, the deceased assisting her in the laundry, etc. It was not shown that the value of the services of the deceased exceeded her support. Held, that a verdict for plaintiff should be set aside. Hull v. Great Northern Ry. Co., 26 L. R. Ir. 289. Where there was some evidence that deceased earned money with which she aided her married daughters, such evidence was properly submitted to the jury to be considered in the assessment of damages. Omaha Water Co. v. Schamel, 147 Fed. 502, 78 C. C. A. 68. The right of adult children to recover damages for the death of their father, who made them a yearly allowance, is not affected by the fact of their inheriting his estate. Stahler v. Philadelphia & R. Ry. Co., 199 Pa. 383, 49 Atl. 273, 85 Am. St. Rep. 791. Where the only aid plaintiffs in an action to recover such compensation received from deceased during her life was a part of the income of property, defendant may show that plaintiffs have received such property by devise or descent from the estate of deceased, for the purpose of reducing damages. San Antonio & A. P. Ry. Co. v. Long, 87 Tex. 148, 27 S. W. 113, 24 L. R. A. 637, 47 Am. St. Rep. 87.

115 Demarest v. Little, 47 N. J. Law, 28.

cuniary benefit from a continuance of life; [116] while otherwise there can be a recovery, at most, of only nominal

[116] Deceased had a sister and two brothers living in Denmark. He
was a bridge carpenter, and received $2 a day. He had been at
work three or four months, and had sent some money to his sister
(how much did not appear). There was no evidence as to his age
or his capacity for earning and saving money, or as to the expectation of pecuniary benefit to be derived by the next of kin from
his estate if he had lived longer. Held, that a verdict of $1,750
should be set aside as excessive. Serensen v. Northern Pac. R. Co.
(C. C.) 45 Fed. 407. Where the deceased was a young, unmarried
man, and left an only sister, who was an orphan, and had been
partly supported by him, the failure of the evidence to show the
extent of her pecuniary loss did not restrict the jury to nominal
damages. Ohio & M. Ry. Co. v. Wangelin, 152 Ill. 138, 38 N. E. 760.
See, also, Chicago & E. I. R. Co. v. Beaver, 199 Ill. 34, 65 N. E.
144; Terminal R. Ass'n of St. Louis v. Condon, 128 Ill. App. 335.
Where intestate left her two brothers and a nephew, with whom she
lived, they contributing their earnings in consideration of her services to the support of the family, they were entitled to recover,
though there was no legal obligation resting on her to render such
services, arising on contract or otherwise. Smith v. Michigan Cent.
R. Co., 35 Ind. App. 188, 73 N. E. 928. See, also, Pittsburg, C., C.
& St. L. Ry. Co. v. Reed, 44 Ind. App. 635, 88 N. E. 1080; Henry v.
Prendergast (Ind. App.) 94 N. E. 1015. Where intestate was a single
woman, who kept house for her three brothers and a sister, receiving as compensation her board, clothing, etc., and a share in the
savings of the family, a verdict for $5,000 was excessive. Rafferty
v. Erie R. Co., 66 N. J. Law, 444, 49 Atl. 456. In an action by decedent's brother and only next of kin, the jury could consider, on
the question of damages, the fact that decedent might have died,
married, given his money to another, or spent it on himself, so that
plaintiff would never have received anything. Conklin v. Central
New York Telephone & Telegraph Co., 130 App. Div. 308, 114 N. Y.
Supp. 190. The next of kin of decedent, a scowman, were two sisters who supported themselves; but it was shown that deceased had
promised to take them back to Norway to live and to supply the
money required. Held, that such evidence was sufficient to warrant damages in the sum of $500. The O. L. Hallenbeck (D. C.) 119
Fed. 468.

damages.[117] In an Illinois case,[118] the court said: "If, then, the next of kin are collateral kindred of the deceased and have not been receiving from him pecuniary assistance, and are not in a situation to require it, it is immaterial how near the relationship may be, only nominal damages can

---

[117] Where decedent was addicted to the use of intoxicating liquors, was careless in his work, and did not save his earnings, his brothers and sisters, to whose support he had never contributed, were entitled to nominal damages only. Anderson v. Chicago, B. & Q. R. Co., 35 Neb. 95, 52 N. W. 840. But see Grotenkemper v. Harris, 25 Ohio St. 510. Where the next of kin are collateral kindred, and have not received pecuniary aid from him, and are not in a situation to require it, only nominal damages can be recovered. Rhoads v. Chicago & A. R. Co., 227 Ill. 328, 81 N. E. 371, 11 L. R. A. (N. S.) 623, 10 Ann. Cas. 111. See, also, Locher v. Kluga, 97 Ill. App. 518; Chicago Bridge & Iron Co. v. La Mantia, 112 Ill. App. 43; Chicago Electric Transit Co. v. Kinnare, 115 Ill. App. 115; Romeo v. Western Coal & Min. Co., 157 Ill. App. 67. Deceased was 32 years of age, and left as his sole heirs at law two older brothers, who were able to support themselves, and to whose support he had not contributed. There was no evidence of a deprivation of a pecuniary advantage which the brothers had reasonable ground to anticipate from their kinship with deceased. Held, that the administrator was not entitled to any damages whatever. Wabash R. Co. v. Cregan, 23 Ind. App. 1, 54 N. E. 767. See, also, Cleveland, C., C. & St. L. Ry. Co. v. Drumm, 32 Ind. App. 547, 70 N. E. 286. When brought in behalf of the next of kin to whose support deceased was under no legal obligation to contribute, an action can be maintained for substantial damages only by proof that he was in the habit of contributing to their support or education, and might be reasonably expected to continue such habit, or by proof of declarations, acts, conduct or relevant circumstances reasonably tending to show an intention on his part to make such contributions of support or education. Atchison, T. & S. F. Ry. Co. v. Ryan, 62 Kan. 682, 64 Pac. 603. Where deceased was 66 years of age, unmarried, a farmer living on leased land, who owned only a small amount of personal property, and plaintiffs were his nephews and nieces in comfortable circumstances, to whom he had made casual gifts, a verdict of $7,000 was excessive. Missouri, K. & T. Ry. Co. v. McLaughlin, 73 Kan. 248, 84 Pac. 989.

[118] Chicago & A. R. Co. v. Shannon, 43 Ill. 338.

be given, because there has been no pecuniary injury. If, on the other hand, the next of kin have been dependent on the deceased for support, in whole or in part, it is immaterial how remote the relationship may be, there has been a pecuniary loss, for which compensation under the statute must be given."

§ 171. Loss of prospective inheritance

Where the evidence shows that it is probable that the decedent, but for his death, would have accumulated property, which, if he had died intestate, would have been inherited by the beneficiaries of the action, these facts constitute such a reasonable expectation of pecuniary benefit as to authorize a recovery of damages for its loss.[119]

In Pym v. Great Northern Ry. Co.,[120] where the party killed was in possession of personalty to the amount of £3,400, and was tenant for life of an estate in land worth nearly £4,000 a year, with remainder to his eldest son in tail, and, by settlement, a jointure of £1,000 a year was settled on his wife, and £20,000 secured to the younger children on his death, and the deceased died intestate, it was held that the widow and younger children had a sufficient expectation of pecuniary benefit to render its loss a ground for action. Cockburn, C. J., after observing that the loss of education and the greater comforts and enjoyments of

[119] Pym v. Great Northern Ry. Co., 2 Best & S. 759, 31 L. J. Q. B. 249, 8 Jur. (N. S.) 819, 10 Wkly. R. 737, 6 L. T. (N. S.) 1537; affirmed in 4 Best & S. 396, 32 L. J. Q. B. 377, 10 Jur. (N. S.) 199, 11 Wkly. R. 922; Illinois Cent. R. Co. v. Barron, 5 Wall. 90, 18 L. Ed. 591; Lake Erie & W. R. Co. v. Mugg, 132 Ind. 168, 31 N. E. 564; Castello v. Landwehr, 28 Wis. 522. The loss of the chance to be endowed out of her husband's accumulations is a pecuniary injury to the wife. Catawissa R. Co. v. Armstrong, 52 Pa. 282.

[120] 2 B. & S. 759, 4 B. & S. 396.

life arising from the death of a father whose income ceases with his life is an injury in respect of which an action can be maintained, continues as follows: "A fortiori, the loss of a pecuniary provision, which fails to be made owing to the premature death. * * * It is true that it must always remain matter of uncertainty whether the deceased person would have applied the necessary portion of income in securing to his family the social and domestic advantages of which they are said to have been deprived by his death; still more, whether he would have laid by any and what portion of his income to make provision for them at his death. But * * * it is for the jury to say, under all the circumstances, taking into account all the uncertainties and contingencies of the particular case, whether there was such a reasonable and well-founded expectation of pecuniary benefit as can be estimated in money." The jury having given £13,000—£1,000 to the widow, and £1,500 to each of the younger children—it was held that the latter sum ought in each case to be reduced to £1,000.

In Illinois Cent. R. Co. v. Barron,[121] an action brought under the Illinois statute, the testator was a bachelor, 35 years old, and had an estate of $35,000, which he left by will to his father. He was an attorney, but for four years prior to his death had been a judge. His term of office having expired, he was about to resume his profession, with a fair promise of doing as well as before he was elected judge, when his professional income had been about $3,000 a year. The action was for the benefit of his father, brothers, and sisters, one of whom had formerly received some assistance from him for support. The court refused to charge that it was necessary that the beneficiaries should have a legal interest in the life, but charged, among other things, that

[121] 5 Wall. 90, 18 L. Ed. 591.

the jury had a right, in estimating the amount of pecuniary injury, to take into consideration the relations between the deceased and his next of kin, the amount of his property, the character of his business, and the prospective increase of wealth likely to accrue to a man of his age with the business and means which he had, the possibility that his estate would have dècreased rather than increased, and the contingency that he might have married, and his property descended in another channel. The verdict and judgment were for $3,750; and, the case coming before the supreme court on exceptions to the charge, and on the refusal to charge as requested, the judgment was affirmed. The opinion was delivered by Mr. Justice Nelson, who said: "The damages in these cases, whether the suit is in the name of the injured party, or, in case of his death, under the statute, by the legal representative, must depend very much on the good sense and sound judgment of the jury, upon all the facts and circumstances of the particular case. If the suit is brought by the party, 'there can be no fixed measure of compensation for the pain and anguish of body and mind, nor for the loss of time and care in business, or the permanent injury to health and body. So, when the suit is brought by the representative, the pecuniary injury resulting from the death to the next of kin is equally uncertain and indefinite. If the deceased had lived, they may not have been benefited, and, if not, then no pecuniary injury could have resulted to them from his death. But the statute in respect to the measure of damages seems to have been enacted upon the idea that, as a general fact, the personal assets of the deceased would take the direction given them by the law, and hence the amount recovered is to be distributed to the wife and next of kin in the proportion provided for in the distribution of personal property left

(380)

by a person dying intestate. If the person injured had survived and recovered, he would have added so much to his personal estate, which the law, on his death, if intestate, would have passed to his wife and next of kin. In case of his death by the injury, the equivalent is given by a suit in the name of his representative."

The cases in which this element of damages have been allowed are rare. It has been pointed out that any such benefit depends on three contingencies: That the decedent would have increased his estate, that he would not have made a will disinheriting the beneficiaries, and that they would survive him.[122] If such damages are to be allowed, there must at least be evidence tending to show that the decedent would probably have accumulated property had he lived;[123] and the verdict will, of course, be set aside if the amount is grossly out of proportion to the reasonable probabilities of the case.[124] In Illinois it seems that no

[122] Sutherland, Dam. (3d Ed.) § 1276, quoted with approval in Rhoads v. Chicago & A. R. Co., 227 Ill. 328, 81 N. E. 371, 11 L. R. A. (N. S.) 623, 10 Ann. Cas. 111.

[123] In an action for the benefit of brothers and sisters, where the deceased had accumulated nothing, held, that only nominal damages should be awarded. Howard v. Delaware & H. Canal Co. (C. C.) 40 Fed. 195, 6 L. R. A. 75. But in Grotenkemper v. Harris, 25 Ohio, 510, where the deceased was only 4 or 5 years old, and the beneficiaries were a brother and sisters, it was held not to be error to charge that the reasonable expectation of pecuniary benefit may consist of what a person may give to his next of kin while living, as well as what they may inherit from him at his death. See, also, Missouri, K. & T. Ry. Co. v. McLaughlin, 73 Kan. 248, 84 Pac. 989.

[124] The injury claimed was the deprivation of the probable accumulations of deceased in his business. The jury gave a verdict of $27,500. To reach this result, they must have found that deceased, who had already acquired a competence, would have continued in business for his full expectancy of life; would have retained sufficient health and vigor of mind to enable him to do so as successfully as before; would have avoided business losses; would have

such recovery can be had on behalf of collateral relatives.[125] And in Pennsylvania it seems that an expectation of inheritance cannot be considered as an element of damages to adult children from their father's death. Thus where the trial court charged: "The loss to the children, of course, was one from whom [sic] they might expect some inheritance, if you think the business was such as to warrant them in that hope," the supreme court said: "This statement presented to the consideration of the jury an element in measuring the damages which is extremely vague. The possi-

safely invested his accumulations; and that the children would have received them at his death. Held, that the verdict should be set aside, unless the plaintiff would consent to a reduction to $15,000. Demarest v. Little, 47 N. J. Law, 28. In an action by a widow for the death of her husband, where it appeared that plaintiff was 20 years old and her husband 22 at the time of his death, and that his wages up to that time had been entirely consumed in the expenses of his household, it was error to charge that, if the jury believed the widow's expectancy of life was greater than her husband's, they should allow her the present value of any property she would probably have received from her husband as dower if he had not been killed, as the realization of any sum as dower depended on too many remote contingencies. St. Louis, I. M. & S. Ry. Co. v. Needham, 52 Fed. 371, 3 C. C. A. 129. Decedent was a widow 61 years old, who had done a profitable business as a boardinghouse keeper, and had made some money, beside supporting a daughter, and occasionally gave small amounts to a son. Held that, as the jury were authorized to take into consideration the reasonable expectation of her property being increased for the benefit of her children, who were of age, and the reasonable expectation of pecuniary benefit to them by support or otherwise, a verdict of $1,000 was sustained by the evidence. Tuteur v. Chicago & N. W. R. Co., 77 Wis. 505, 46 N. W. 897. Decedent was a widower, 73 years old, strong and vigorous, and actively engaged in business. The children were of age, and not dependent on him. Held, that $1,000 was not excessive. City of Wabash v. Carver, 129 Ind. 552, 29 N. E. 25, 13 L. R. A. 851.

[125] Rhoads v. Chicago & A. Ry. Co., 130 Ill. App. 145, affirmed 227 Ill. 328, 81 N. E. 371, 11 L. R. A. (N. S.) 623, 10 Ann. Cas. 111. See also cases cited note 117, supra.

bility of accumulating an estate by the decedent was very remote. The testimony did not show any accumulation up to the time of his death, and whether or not he could have succeeded in gathering more than would have provided for his own wants during the remainder of his life was purely conjectural. If the subject were considered at all by the jury in making up the verdict, it could only result in confusion and speculation. An expectation of inheritance is not properly one of the elements of loss to children in a case of this kind, and should not be allowed to enter into the question in any way whatever." [126]

§ 172. Rule of damages in New York

A looser rule in respect to the measure of damages prevails in New York than elsewhere, under similar statutory provisions; for in that state it is held in all cases that it is enough for the plaintiff to show the age, sex, condition, physical and mental, and the circumstances and situation in life of the deceased, and the age, circumstances, and condition of the next of kin, and that, provided such evidence is introduced, it is for the jury to estimate the "pecuniary injuries," present and prospective, to the next of kin.[127] This rule differs little, if at all, from the rule elsewhere applied in actions brought by parents for the death of young children, but in New York the rule is also applied in cases in which the only possible basis for damages would seem to be the loss of prospective gifts, or of a prospective inheritance—cases in which, in other jurisdictions, some evidence

[126] Wiest v. Electric Traction Co., 200 Pa. 148, 49 Atl. 891, 58 L. R. A. 666.

[127] See note 70, supra.

either of past gifts, or of the probability of future accumulations, is usually required.[128]

Thus, in Tilley v. Hudson River R. Co.,[129] it was held that damages for the loss of the training, instruction, and education of a mother were not confined to minor children. The opinion by Hogeboom, J., upon the measure of damages, is frequently referred to with approval.[130] The jury, he says, "are to give such damages as they shall deem a fair and just compensation, with reference to the pecuniary injuries resulting from such death. They are not tied down to any precise rule. Within the limit of the statute, as to the amount and the species of injury sustained, the matter is to be submitted to their sound judgment and sense of justice. They must be satisfied that pecuniary injuries resulted. If so satisfied, they are at liberty to allow them from whatever source they actually proceeded, which could produce them. If they are satisfied, from the history of the family, or the intrinsic probabilities of the case, that they were sustained by the loss of bodily care or intellectual

---

[128] The jury may consider the prospect of the next of kin of inheriting from decedent. Johnson v. Long Island R. Co., 80 Hun, 306, 30 N. Y. Supp. 318. In an action on behalf of a mother and adult brothers and sisters, it is not necessary to show that decedent contributed to their support. Kane v. Mitchell Transp. Co., 90 Hun, 65, 35 N. Y. Supp. 581.

[129] 29 N. Y. 252, 86 Am. Dec. 297; Id., 24 N. Y. 471.

[130] McIntyre v. New York C. R. Co., 37 N. Y. 287, affirming 47 Barb. 515. In this case the deceased was a widow about 48 years old, who left three children, all of age, one a married daughter with whom she lived. She was a seamstress, capable of earning $1 a day above her board, and left only a small amount of property. She had been in the habit of making small articles of clothing for her children from time to time. A verdict for $3,500 was reduced to $1,500, and an appeal sustained for that amount. A nonsuit was granted at a former trial, and overruled in 43 Barb. 532. See, also, Keller v. New York Cent. R. Co., 2 Abb. Dec. 480, 24 How. Prac. 172, affirming 17 How. Prac. 102, 28 Barb. 44, note.

culture or moral training which the mother had before supplied, they are at liberty to allow for it. *The statute has
set no bounds to the sources of these pecuniary injuries."*

In Dickens v. New York Cent. R. Co.[181] the plaintiff
sued as administrator of his wife, for the benefit (the action being prior to the act of 1870) of brothers and sisters
and nephews and nieces. The court refused to charge, as
requested, that the plaintiff could only recover nominal
damages, on the ground that, as the deceased had left neither child nor parent, the only loss incurred by her next
of kin would be the chance of her accumulating a separate
estate and dying intestate, or making a will in their favor,
and that this would be too remote a contingency to be of
any substantial value to them. The court charged, in the
language of the statute, that the only damages the jury
could give were such as they might deem a fair and just
compensation, not exceeding $5,000, with reference to the
pecuniary damages resulting from the death to the next of
kin; and that whether more than nominal damages, and,
if so, how much, resulted to the next of kin, were questions
for the jury. The defendant excepted, and requested the
judge to charge that there was no evidence of any pecuniary
injury, and that the relation of brother and sister did not
raise a presumption of pecuniary loss, which was refused.
The jury rendered a verdict for $500. The court of ap-
peals held the charge correct, within Tilley v. Hudson
River R. Co. Hogeboom, J., in delivering the opinion, says:
"I think the defendants cannot successfully assail the
charge * * * unless it is a case for limiting the plain-

---

[181] 1 Abb. Dec. 504. At a former trial the plaintiff obtained judgment, which was sustained by the general term (28 Barb. 41), but reversed in the court of appeals (23 N. Y. 158), on the ground that the
verdict included damages to the husband for loss of service. Thomas
v. Utica & B. R. R. Co., 6 Civ. Proc. R. 353.

tiff to nominal damages. We are not at liberty to lay down any such restricted rule, without violating the statute and the current of former decisions. * * * It is not always easy to see how the death of a particular individual, *and she a wife,* will operate to the pecuniary injury of *collateral relatives,* and, if so, to what extent. But as the law does not require direct and precise proof on this subject, and has committed to the jury a liberal discretion in its actual disposition, we cannot say, in view of the not very extravagant sum assessed by the jury in this particular case, if any sum whatever were to be allowed, that any principle of law has been violated."

In Lockwood v. New York, L. E. & W. R. Co.[182] the court of appeals seems to recognize that it has gone beyond the courts of other states in its rulings upon this subject. The deceased was 68 years old, and left seven children, all

---

[182] 98 N. Y. 523. Lustig v. New York, L. E. & W. R. Co., 65 Hun, 547, 20 N. Y. Supp. 477. It was improper to refuse to instruct that nominal damages only might be awarded if the next of kin, who were adult children, sustained no actual money loss through the death. Wagner v. H. Clausen & Son Brewing Co., 146 App. Div. 70, 130 N. Y. Supp. 584. Cf. Predmore v. Consumers' Light & Power Co., 99 App. Div. 551, 91 N. Y. Supp. 118. Evidence of the financial circumstances of the next of kin is admissible on the question of damages. Fowler v. Buffalo Furnace Co., 41 App. Div. 84, 58 N. Y. Supp. 223. Evidence of the wages which plaintiff earns is not admissible in an action for death of his child. Terhune v. Joseph W. Cody Contracting Co., 72 App. Div. 1, 76 N. Y. Supp. 255. In an action by a father for the death of his son, who left no widow and children, the father being the sole next of kin, it was error to admit evidence as to the poverty of the brothers and sisters and other relatives of deceased, who are not next of kin. Lipp v. Otis Bros. & Co., 161 N. Y. 559, 56 N. E. 79. While evidence was admissible as to damages to show the age of decedent's children and that they depended on him for support, evidence that one was in an orphan asylum was inadmissible. Harrison v. New York Cent. & H. R. R. Co., 195 N. Y. 86, 87 N. E. 802.

of age, self-supporting, and living away from home, except an unmarried daughter, who lived with him and did household work, in consideration of her board, and a married son, who lived with him, but worked for himself, and used his own earnings. The plaintiff, against objection, was permitted to prove that the children had no property, and that the daughter who lived at home had a disease which prevented her from working, as she could otherwise have done. The court refused to charge that where the children are of full age, and living away from home, and self-supporting, no such pecuniary loss has been sustained by them as can be recovered. The opinion of the court of appeals was delivered by Earl, J., who said: *"Whatever the rule may be in other states,* there are many cases in this which in principle sustain the rulings of the trial judge. * * * In but few cases arising under this act is the plaintiff able to show direct, specific pecuniary loss, * * * and generally the basis for the allowance of damages has to be found in the proof of the character, qualities, capacity, and condition of the deceased, and in the age, sex, circumstances, and condition of the next of kin. The proof may be unsatisfactory, and the damages may be quite uncertain and contingent; yet the jurors in each case must take the elements thus furnished, and make the best estimate of damages they can. There seems to be no other mode of administering the statute referred to, and protection against excessive damages must be found in the power of courts in some of the modes allowed by law to revise or set aside the verdicts of juries." [133]

[133] How slight is the protection thus afforded is illustrated by Pineo v. New York Cent. & H. R. R. Co., 34 Hun, 80, which was an action brought by the brother as administrator of a girl of 14, whose next of kin was supposed to be her father, who had abandoned his family years before, and concerning whom it was not known whether

In Bierbauer v. New York Cent. & H. R. R. Co.,[184] the intestate was 21 years old, earning $25 a month. He was unmarried, but left, as next of kin, a father, aged 65, residing in Germany. The court declined to set aside as excessive a verdict for $5,000. Bockes, J., observed: "It is admissible to permit a reduction of the damages as alterna-

he was alive or dead. It was held that a refusal to charge that there was no evidence that the life of deceased had any pecuniary value to her father was not error, and that a verdict of $3,500 should not be set aside as excessive. In a dissenting opinion, Barker, J., pertinently remarks: "If we uphold this verdict, we do, in effect, say that the jury are omnipotent in this class of cases, and that there is no rule of law to be observed by them in assessing damages."

[184] 15 Hun, 559, affirmed 77 N. Y. 588. The deceased was an engineer, industrious and faithful to his mother, who was his next of kin. Held, that a verdict for $5,000 was not excessive. Erwin v. Neversink Steamboat Co., 23 Hun, 573; Quinn v. Power, 29 Hun, 183. Decedent was a single woman 36 years old, without other near relatives than her parents, who were 66 and 58 years old. Both were poor, and the father infirm, and, for 20 years decedent had contributed $300 or $400 per annum to their support. She was in good health, and receiving a salary of $8 or $9 per week. Held, that a verdict for $4,000 damages was not excessive. Bowles v. Rome, W. & O. R. Co., 46 Hun, 324. In Kelly v. Twenty-Third St. Ry. Co., 14 Daly, 418, the only relatives of the deceased were a brother and sister in Ireland, and three nephews in New York. There was no evidence that he ever did anything to assist them, nor was it shown what the proceeds of his business were, nor what, if anything, was the value of his life to his next of kin. A verdict of $1,000 was held not excessive. The court points out that the courts of New York have not discriminated between the immediate and collateral kindred, and that in other states proof is necessary that the relatives had received or were likely to receive support from the deceased. But where no facts appeared except that the deceased was a married woman aged 20 years, and a verdict of $4,000 was rendered, it was held that a new trial should be granted. Mitchell v. New York Cent. & H. R. R. Co., 2 Hun, 535. It was error to admit evidence showing the number of next of kin's children, and services and expenditures rendered and made by decedent for the benefit of the children. Murphy v. Erie R. Co., 202 N. Y. 242, 95 N. E. 699.

(388)

tive to the granting of a new trial. In my judgment, this is a proper case for the exercise of a fair discretion in that regard; but my associates are of opinion that the court should not trench upon the right of the jury to determine the damages to be awarded in cases of this character, unless it can be plainly seen that some improper element was considered and allowed in their estimate, or that they were influenced by passion, partiality, prejudice, or corrupt motives. In this view of the case, the verdict must be allowed to stand."

In Countryman v. Fonda, J. & G. R. Co.,[135] the intestate was a woman 53 years old, leaving a daughter aged 22, and a son aged 25, and the mother supported herself, as did the children. The trial court dismissed the complaint, saying that there did not seem to be any property loss on the part of the next of kin, that the intestate was a woman without any children to whom she owed any duty, without the power to accumulate property, simply earning her own living by housework, and that to say that the children had suffered a property loss in dollars and cents on these facts and to leave it to the jury as pure guesswork was something the courts did not permit. The judgment of the appellate division, affirming the trial court, was reversed by the court of appeals, which said: "In the case at bar it is a question for the jury to determine, in the exercise of a reasonable discretion, what damages the next of kin of the intestate have suffered, if any, considering the situation as proved. * * * It is for the jury to consider, if the health of the daughter should fail, whether the mother might not take her to her own home, and nurse and care for her indefinitely. The same might be true of the son. In other words, they are permitted to consider, in a reason-

[135] 166 N. Y. 201, 59 N. E. 822, 82 Am. St. Rep. 640.

able way, those prospective and indefinite damages arising from the death of a mother under these circumstances, in addition to the actual money damages as proved."

Nevertheless, while the damages are indefinite and the discretion of the jury is very wide, the courts exercise the right to set aside and reduce excessive verdicts, as well as to set aside inadequate verdicts, although upon what principle the limit is determined it is often impossible to determine. In a recent case,[186] in which a considerable verdict on behalf of a widow and minor children was sustained, the appellate division of the supreme court said: "This court has reduced verdicts in such cases, where in its opinion there was no substantial basis for the same, reversing the judgment of the jury in that regard. Indeed, it is made the duty of this court, when the matter is properly presented, to determine whether or not a verdict rendered by a jury is inadequate or excessive, and it has unhesitatingly exercised its power in that regard, as it believed justice and the rights of the parties required." The extent and character of the supervision exercised is illustrated in the cases collected in the subjoined note.[187]

---

[186] Conrad v. New York Cent. & H. R. R. Co., 137 App. Div. 372, 121 N. Y. Supp. 774.

[187] A railroad fireman 34 years old, in good health, left a wife, son, and daughter, aged 32, 10, and 8 years, respectively. Defendant had employed him for 3 years, paying $1.75 per day the first year, $1.85 the second, and $2 the third. Held, that a verdict of $15,000, for his death was excessive. Cooper v. New York, O. & W. Ry. Co., 25 App. Div. 383, 49 N. Y. Supp. 481. A verdict of $9,000 is not excessive, where deceased was 43 years of age, in good health, received a salary of $1,250 a year, and left five dependent children. Wallace v. Third Ave. R. Co., 36 App. Div. 57, 55 N. Y. Supp. 132. Where the death of an active business man, 61 years old, deprived the wife of home and support, a judgment for $10,000 was not excessive, since the jury could find that good health and exceptional activity promised him a long life. Beecher v. Long Island R. Co., 53

§ 173. Evidence of pecuniary condition of beneficiaries

As a general rule, it is inadmissible to introduce evidence of the poverty [138] or bad health [139] or of other facts tending

App. Div. 324, 65 N. Y. Supp. 642. See, also, Douglass v. Northern Cent. Ry. Co., 59 App. Div. 470, 69 N. Y. Supp. 370; Stevens v. Un-

---

[138] Illinois Cent. R. Co. v. Baches, 55 Ill. 379; Chicago & N. W. Ry. Co. v. Moranda, 93 Ill. 302, 34 Am. Rep. 168; Chicago & N. W. R. Co. v. Howard, 6 Ill. App. 569; Heyer v. Salsbury, 7 Ill. App. 93; Chicago, R. I. & P. R. Co. v. Henry, Id. 322; Beard v. Skeldon, 13 Ill. App. 54; Illinois Cent. R. Co. v. Slater, 28 Ill. App. 73, affirmed 129 Ill. 91, 21 N. E. 575, 6 L. R. A. 418, 16 Am. St. Rep. 242; Overholt v. Vieths, 93 Mo. 422, 6 S. W. 74, 3 Am. St. Rep. 557; Chicago & N. W. Ry. Co. v. Bayfield, 37 Mich. 205; Hunn v. Michigan Cent. R. Co., 78 Mich. 513, 44 N. W. 502, 7 L. R. A. 500; Central R. R. v. Rouse, 77 Ga. 393, 3 S. E. 307; Central R. R. v. Moore, 61 Ga. 151; Green v. Southern Pac. Co., 122 Cal. 563, 55 Pac. 577; Mahoney v. San Francisco & S. M. Ry. Co., 110 Cal. 471, 42 Pac. 968; Consolidated Gas, Electric Light & Power Co. v. State, to Use of Smith, 109 Md. 186, 72 Atl. 651; Gundy v. Nye-Schneider-Fowler Co., 89 Neb. 599, 131 N. W. 964. See, also, South Omaha Water-Works Co. v. Vocasek, 62 Neb. 710, 87 N. W. 536; Chicago, R. I. & P. R. Co. v. Hambel, 2 Neb. (Unof.) 607, 89 N. W. 643; Same v. Holmes, 68 Neb. 826, 94 N. W. 1007. The Illinois cases on this subject are somewhat modified by Pennsylvania Co. v. Keane, 143 Ill. 172, 32 N. E. 260, in which it was held that, in an action by the widow as administratrix, it is proper to allow her to testify that the deceased was at the time of her death her sole support. The opinion says: "We take it that the rule deducible from the cases is substantially this: that it is not competent to show what the pecuniary circumstances of the widow, family, or next of kin are or have been since the decease of the intestate, but that it is competent to show that the wife, children, or next of kin were dependent upon him for support before and at the time of his death." See, also, Swift & Co. v. Foster, 163 Ill. 50, 44 N. E. 837; Economy Light & Power Co. v. Stephen, 187 Ill. 137, 58 N. E. 359; Pittsburgh, C., C. & St. L. R. Co. v. Kinnare, 203 Ill. 388, 67 N. E. 826; Brennen v. Chicago & Carterville Coal Co., 241 Ill. 610, 89 N. E. 756; Preble v. Wabash R. Co., 243 Ill. 340, 90 N. E. 716.

[139] See note 139 on following page.

to show the necessities of the beneficiaries, since such facts do not tend to prove that they have suffered a pecu‐ niary loss. "If the moral obligation to support near rela‐

ion Ry. Co., 176 N. Y. 607, 68 N. E. 1125. Deceased was 62 years old, in robust health, and had a life expectancy of 13 years. He had been a successful business man, and had accumulated considerable property, and expended for his own and family's support about $5,000 a year. Held, that a verdict of $25,000 was not excessive. Judgment 73 App. Div. 494, 77 N. Y. Supp. 309, affirmed. Sternfels v. Metropolitan St. Ry. Co., 174 N. Y. 512, 66 N. E. 1117. For the death of a dentist 37 years old, having a family of four children and earning an income of from $17,000 to $20,000 a year, a verdict for $40,000 was not excessive. Morhard v. Richmond Light & R. Co., 111 App. Div. 353, 98 N. Y. Supp. 124. Decedent was 46 years of age and in perfect health, save shortsightedness and a slight deaf‐ ness. He left a widow and two children, aged respectively, 3½ years and 21 months, earned from $75 to $100 a week, from which he gave his wife $72 to $75, and was an excellent musician. Held, that a verdict of $30,000 was not excessive. Zucker v. Whitridge, 143 App. Div. 191, 128 N. Y. Supp. 233. See, also, Cunningham v. Mu‐ tual Reserve Life Ins. Co., 125 App. Div. 688, 109 N. Y. Supp. 1070; Boyce v. New York City Ry. Co., 126 App. Div. 248, 110 N. Y. Supp. 393; Clancy v. New York, N. H. & H. R. Co., 133 App. Div. 119, 117 N. Y. Supp. 233; Conrad v. New York Cent. & H. R. R. Co., 137 App. Div. 372, 121 N. Y. Supp. 774. Where intestate was a longshore‐ man and fruit vender, engaged in keeping a fruit and vegetable stand, in which his wife assisted him, and it did not appear that the business was discontinued at his death, a verdict for $27,306 was ex‐ cessive. Scarpati v. Metropolitan St. Ry. Co., 69 App. Div. 609, 74 N. Y. Supp. 499. Deceased was 37 years old, and left a wife and four children, the oldest 4½ years of age, and the youngest 3½

---

139 Illinois Cent. R. Co. v. Baches, supra; Benton v. Chicago, R. I. & P. R. Co., 55 Iowa, 496, 8 N. W. 330; Seattle Electric Co. v. Hartless, 144 Fed. 379, 75 C. C. A. 317; Simoneau v. Pacific Electric Ry. Co., 159 Cal. 494, 115 Pac. 320; Evarts v. Santa Barbara Con‐ sol. Ry. Co., 3 Cal. App. 712, 86 Pac. 830. In an action on behalf of deceased's widow and children, evidence as to the condition of such children, and as to one of them being an invalid needing care, is admissible, as bearing on the damages recoverable. Hunt v. Con‐ ner, 26 Ind. App. 41, 59 N. E. 50. See, also, Evans v. Oregon Short Line R. Co., 37 Utah, 431, 108 Pac. 638, Ann. Cas. 1912C, 259.

tives," says Cooley, C. J., in Chicago & N. W. R. Co. v. Bayfield, "were to be the criterion, we might take their poverty into account; * * * but as this may or may not have been recognized,. and, if recognized, may have been

months. The evidence was indefinite as to the amount he earned. His wife testified that she received from him from $20 to $25 a week for herself and children. Held, that a verdict for $22,000 was excessive. Coolidge v. City of New York, 99 App. Div. 175, 90 N. Y. Supp. 1078, affirmed Parks v. Miller, 185 N. Y. 529, 77 N. E. 1192. A verdict for $20,000 for a healthy, sober, and industrious man 43 years old, earning $60 per month used in the support of his family, consisting of a wife and six children, the oldest 12 years, is excessive, though the jury are not concluded by the annuities table showing the pecuniary value of his life, based on earnings, at $8,213.14, and may consider the pecuniary value of the father's advice and care to his children, and the verdict should be reduced to $15,000. O'Doherty v. Postal Telegraph Cable Co., 134 App. Div. 298, 118 N. Y. Supp. 871. For a woman 49 years of age and in good health, who left a husband 48 years of age, and two sons 21 and 18, respectively, a verdict of $10,000 was excessive, and the judgment should be reversed, unless plaintiff stipulated to reduce it to $7,000. Smith v. Lehigh Val. R. Co., 61 App. Div. 46, 69 N. Y. Supp. 1112. For the death of a wife, who had been living apart from her husband, and successfully conducting an independent business, it was error to limit his recovery to nominal damages, where there was some evidence of pecuniary injury offered, showing decedent's earning capacity, expectancy of life, etc. Austin v. Metropolitan St. Ry. Co., 108 App. Div. 249, 95 N. Y. Supp. 740. A verdict for $6,000 for the death of plaintiff's daughter is excessive, where the only evidence as to damages is that plaintiff was 61 years old, and his daughter 19, that plaintiff was a machinist, and his daughter was an industrious girl, earning $7 a week, which she gave her mother to be used in supporting the family. Seeley v. New York Cent. & H. R. R. Co., 8 App. Div. 402, 40 N. Y. Supp. 866. For an only daughter, 20 years of age, well developed physically and mentally, a successful musician, who assisted her mother in housekeeping and her father occasionally in his store, a verdict for $9,500 to compensate the father held excessive. Kellogg v. Albany & H. Ry. & Power Co., 72 App. Div. 321, 76 N. Y. Supp. 85. A verdict of $800 for a woman 70 years of age, who was supported by her children, but who was in fair health, and rendered

very imperfectly responded to, it is manifest that it can be no measure of the pecuniary injury the family received, or was likely to receive, from the death." But an exception to this rule is generally recognized where damages are based upon the loss of prospective gifts, and especially in cases for the benefit of parents on account of the death of minor children, as tending to show the probability that such gifts

assistance to her daughter, with whom she lived, held not excessive. Phalen v. Rochester Ry. Co., 31 App. Div. 448, 52 N. Y. Supp. 836. A verdict for $10,000 for the death of a man 73 years of age, successful in business, apparently in good financial circumstances, leaving a wife and adult children, to none of whom he gave financial aid except to the wife, was excessive, and should be reduced to $5,000. Stillings v. Metropolitan St. Ry. Co., 84 App. Div. 201, 82 N. Y. Supp. 726. A verdict for more than $2,500 was excessive, where defendant was only liable for the damage to decedent's mother, who resides abroad, and the evidence as to what he paid towards her support was indefinite. Rice v. Interurban St. Ry. Co., 121 App. Div. 714, 106 N. Y. Supp. 463. Where the only evidence as to damages was that deceased was unmarried, 22 years old, that for 12 months prior to his death, while living with his father and mother, he had worked for $9 a week, which he brought to his mother, and that his next of kin were father, mother, one sister, and four brothers, a verdict of $600 was not so small as to justify setting it aside as shocking to the moral sense, or as having been rendered in palpable disregard of the elements of damage presented to the jury. Swanton v. King, 72 App. Div. 578, 76 N. Y. Supp. 528. The next of kin of an unmarried woman 32 years old, consisted of two married sisters and a brother, two of whom were her seniors, for whose support she had never contributed. She was a seamstress at $9 a week. While she lived with a married sister she paid $4 a week for her board. She left no estate. Held, that a verdict for the amount of the funeral expenses was improperly set aside as inadequate, and the absence of any showing that the jury were improperly influenced. De Luna v. Union Ry. Co. of New York City, 130 App. Div. 386, 114 N. Y. Supp. 893. $3,000 was excessive for death of a man 72 years old who earned only $300 a year, and whose next of kin were all adult children. Wagner v. H. Clausen & Son Brewing Co., 146 App. Div. 70, 130 N. Y. Supp. 584.

would have been made.[140] In Wisconsin,[141] New York,[142] and some other jurisdictions,[143] such evidence seems to be admissible in all cases.

§ 174. Expectation of life—Life tables

In order to show the expectation of life of the deceased and of the beneficiaries the Carlisle, Northampton, and other standard life tables may be introduced;[144] though

[140] Potter v. Chicago & N. W. Ry. Co., 21 Wis. 373, 94 Am. Dec. 548; Id., 22 Wis. 615; Ewen v. Chicago & N. W. Ry. Co., 38 Wis. 613; Johnson v. Chicago & N. W. Ry. Co., 64 Wis. 425, 25 N. W. 223; Wiltse v. Town of Tilden, 77 Wis. 152, 46 N. W. 234; Staal v. Grand Rapids & I. R. Co., 57 Mich. 239, 23 N. W. 795; Cooper v. Lake Shore & M. S. Ry. Co., 66 Mich. 261, 33 N. W. 306, 11 Am. St. Rep. 482; Missouri Pac. R. Co. v. Peregoy, 36 Kan. 424, 14 Pac. 7; Little Rock, M. R. & T. Ry. Co. v. Leverett, 48 Ark. 333, 3 S. W. 50, 3 Am. St. Rep. 230; International & G. N. R. Co. v. Kindred, 57 Tex. 491; Illinois Cent. R. Co. v. Crudup, 63 Miss. 291. See City of Chicago v. Powers, 42 Ill. 169, 89 Am. Dec. 418. See, also, United States Electric Lighting Co. v. Sullivan, 22 App. D. C. 115; Coffeyville Mining & Gas Co. v. Carter, 65 Kan. 565, 70 Pac. 635; Crabtree v. Missouri Pac. R. Co., 86 Neb. 33, 124 N. W. 932, 136 Am. St. Rep. 663; Cincinnati St. Ry. Co. v. Altemeier, 60 Ohio St. 10, 53 N. E. 300. On a question of pecuniary injury sustained by a minor daughter because of the mother's death, evidence of the father's financial condition was admissible, as showing what aid the daughter would probably have received from the mother had she lived. Gulf, C. & S. F. Ry. Co. v. Younger, 90 Tex. 387, 38 S. W. 1121.

[141] Annas v. Milwaukee & N. R. Co., 67 Wis. 46, 30 N. W. 282, 58 Am. Rep. 848; McKeigue v. City of Janesville, 68 Wis. 50, 31 N. W. 298; Thoresen v. La Crosse City Ry. Co., 94 Wis. 129, 68 N. W. 548; Hamann v. Milwaukee Bridge Co., 136 Wis. 39, 116 N. W. 854.

[142] See last section.

[143] Lazelle v. Town of Newfane, 70 Vt. 440, 41 Atl. 511.

[144] Donaldson v. Mississippi & M. R. R. Co., 18 Iowa, 280, 87 Am. Dec. 391; Coates v. Burlington, C. R. & N. R. Co., 62 Iowa, 486, 17 N. W. 760; Worden v. Humeston & S. R. Co., 76 Iowa, 310,

such tables are not conclusive, since the jury should consider them with the other evidence in the case,[145] and may
determine the probable length of life solely upon evidence

41 N. W. 26; Gorman v. Minneapolis & St. L. Ry. Co., 78 Iowa,
509, 43 N. W. 303; Louisville, C. & L. R. Co. v. Mahony's Adm'x,
7 Bush (Ky.) 235; Cooper v. Lake Shore & M. S. Ry. Co., 66 Mich.
261, 33 N. W. 306, 11 Am. St. Rep. 482; Hunn v. Michigan Cent.
R. Co., 78 Mich. 513, 44 N. W. 502, 7 L. R. A. 500; Sellars v. Foster,
27 Neb. 118, 42 N. W. 907; Sauter v. New York Cent. & H. R. R.
Co., 66 N. Y. 50, 23 Am. Rep. 18; Mississippi & T. R. Co. v. Ayres,
16 Lea (Tenn.) 725; San Antonio & A. P. Ry. Co. v. Bennett, 76
Tex. 151, 13 S. W. 319; St. Louis, I. M. & S. Ry. Co. v. Hitt, 76
Ark. 227, 88 S. W. 908; Valente v. Sierra R. Co. of California, 151
Cal. 534, 91 Pac. 481; Calvert v. Springfield Electric Light & Power
Co., 231 Ill. 290, 83 N. E. 184, 14 L. R. A. (N. S.) 782, 12 Ann. Cas.
423; Pittsburgh, C., C. & St. L. Ry. Co. v. Rogers, 45 Ind. App.
230, 87 N. E. 28; Southern R. Co. v. Adkins' Adm'r, 133 Ky. 219,
117 S. W. 321; Little v. Bousfield & Co., 165 Mich. 654, 131 N. W.
63; O'Mellia v. Kansas City, St. J. & C. B. R. Co., 115 Mo. 205, 21
S. W. 503. It was improper to admit mortuary tables, where decedent was an asthmatic and asthmatics were not embraced by
such tables. Mississippi Oil Co. v. Smith, 95 Miss. 528, 48 South.
735.

145 Scheffler v. Minneapolis & St. L. Ry. Co., 32 Minn. 518, 21 N.
W. 711; McKeigue v. City of Janesville, 68 Wis. 50, 31 N. W. 298;
Georgia R. & Banking Co. v. Oaks, 52 Ga. 410; Georgia R. R. v.
Pittman, 73 Ga. 325; Central R. R. v. Crosby, 74 Ga. 737, 58 Am.
Rep. 463; Central R. R. v. Thompson, 76 Ga. 770; Louisville & N.
R. Co. v. Anderson, 150 Ala. 350, 43 South. 566; Northern Ala-
bama Ry. Co. v. Key, 150 Ala. 641, 43 South. 794; Harrison v. Sut-
ter St. Ry. Co., 116 Cal. 156, 47 Pac. 1019; Philadelphia, B. & W.
R. Co. v. Tucker, 35 App. D. C. 123; Central of Georgia R. Co. v.
Minor, 2 Ga. App. 804, 59 S. E. 81; Atchison, T. & S. F. R. Co. v.
Hughes, 55 Kan. 491, 40 Pac. 919; Jones v. McMillan, 129 Mich.
86, 88 N. W. 206; Chambers v. Kupper-Benson Hotel Co., 154 Mo.
App. 249, 134 S. W. 45; Memphis St. R. Co. v. Berry, 118 Tenn.
581, 102 S. W. 85. It was an invasion of the province of the jury
to charge that if deceased was, at the time of his death, in good
health and of sober habits, and was 48 years old, his expectancy
of life was as much as 18 years. Alabama Mineral R. Co. v. Jones,
114 Ala. 519, 21 South. 507, 62 Am. St. Rep. 121. Mortality tables
prepared for life insurance purposes afford little aid in determining

of the age, health, habits, etc., of the person.[146] The computation should be made from the death of the deceased;[147] and where, as in Iowa, the action is brought for the death of a minor to recover damages for the loss of benefits that would have accrued to the estate after his majority, it is error to compute the expectation from the age of 21.[148] The calculation of the amount of pecuniary loss should be based upon the joint lives of the deceased and of the beneficiary.[149]

the duration of life in actions to recover damages for death, and especially where the deceased was a colored person. The Saginaw, 139 Fed. 906; The Hamilton, Id.; In re Clyde S. S. Co., Id.

[146] Beems v. Chicago, R. I. & P. Ry. Co., 67 Iowa, 435, 25 N. W. 693; Deisen v. Chicago, St. P., M. & M. Ry. Co., 43 Minn. 454, 45 N. W. 864; Gulf, C. & S. F. Ry. Co. v. Compton, 75 Tex. 667, 13 S. W. 667; Warren & O. V. R. Co. v. Waldrop, 93 Ark. 127, 123 S. W. 792; St. Louis, I. M. & S. R. Co. v. Evans (Ark.) 137 S. W. 568; Boswell v. Barnhart, 96 Ga. 521, 23 S. E. 414; Western & A. R. Co. v. Clark, 117 Ga. 548, 44 S. E. 1; Farrell v. Chicago, R. I. & P. Ry. Co., 123 Iowa, 690, 99 N. W. 578; Coffeyville Mining & Gas Co. v. Carter, 65 Kan. 565, 70 Pac. 635; Texas Mexican Ry. Co. v. Higgins, 44 Tex. Civ. App. 523, 99 S. W. 200; Norfolk & W. Ry. Co. v. Phillips' Adm'r, 100 Va. 362, 41 S. E. 726. Where the court erroneously gives positive directions for ascertaining the damages by certain mathematical calculations, the error is not cured by the subsequent statement that in the end the whole matter of damages is left entirely to the sound judgment of the jury as to what is proper under all the circumstances. St. Louis, I. M. & S. Ry. Co. v. Needham, 52 Fed. 371, 3 C. C. A. 129.

[147] Plaintiff's intestate being only 5 years old at the time of his death, it was error to admit in evidence tables giving no expectancy of life for any age under 10 years. Rajnowski v. Detroit, B. C. & A. R. Co., 74 Mich. 15, 41 N. W. 849; Id., 74 Mich. 20, 41 N. W. 847. See, also, Goodes v. Lansing & Suburban Traction Co., 150 Mich. 494, 114 N. W. 338.

[148] Walters v. Chicago, R. I. & P. R. Co., 41 Iowa, 71; Wheelan v. Chicago, M. & St. P. Ry. Co., 85 Iowa, 167, 52 N. W. 119. See, also, Valente v. Sierra R. Co. of California, 158 Cal. 412, 111 Pac. 95.

[149] Rowley v. London & N. W. Ry. Co., L. R. 8 Ex. 221, 42 L. J.

§ 175.   Interest as damages

While the jury may, perhaps, take into account the time which has elapsed since the death, as affecting the amount of damages, it is improper for them, after computing the amount of damages, to add interest upon that sum.[150] The New York act provides that the amount recovered shall draw interest from the death which interest shall be added to the verdict, and inserted in the entry of judgment. This provision is not unconstitutional.[151] The rate of interest is governed by the statute regulating interest in force at the time of the verdict.[152] The interest is to be added and inserted by the clerk.[153]

Ex. 153, 29 L. T. (N. S.) 180; Illinois Cent. R. Co. v. Crudup, 63 Miss. 291; The Dauntless (D. C.) 121 Fed. 420; George B. Swift Co. v. Gaylord, 229 Ill. 330, 82 N. E. 299; Baltimore & L. Turnpike Road v. State, 71 Md. 573, 18 Atl. 884. Contra: Emery v. City of Philadelphia, 208 Pa. 492, 57 Atl. 977. Where decedent left his father, as his sole next of kin, who died before trial, the damages were limited to the pecuniary injuries sustained by the father between the death of the son and his own death. Pitkin v. New York Cent. & H. R. R. Co., 94 App. Div. 31, 87 N. Y. Supp. 906.

150 Central R. R. v. Sears, 66 Ga. 499; Cook v. New York Cent. & H. R. R. Co., 10 Hun (N. Y.) 426 (before act of 1870). Plaintiff was entitled to interest on the amount of damages from the date of death to the date of recovery. St. Louis, I. M. & S. Ry. Co. v. Cleere, 76 Ark. 377, 88 S. W. 995.

151 Cornwall v. Mills, 44 N. Y. Super. Ct. 45.

152 Salter v. Utica & B. R. R. Co., 86 N. Y. 401; Id., 23 Hun (N. Y.) 533, overruling Erwin v. Neversink Steamboat Co., 23 Hun (N. Y.) 578.

153 See Manning v. Port Henry Iron Ore Co. of Lake Champlain, 91 N. Y. 665, reversing Id., 27 Hun (N. Y.) 219. An extra allowance should be computed on the sum awarded by the jury plus the interest inserted in the entry of judgment. Boyd v. New York Cent. & H. R. R. Co., 6 Civ. Proc. R. (N. Y.) 222; Bord v. New York Cent. & H. R. R. Co., 1 How. Prac. (N. S. N. Y.) 1. Sinne v. City of New York, 8 Civ. Proc. R. (N. Y.) 252, note, contra. Plaintiff may waive

§ 176. Reduction of damages

Where the beneficiary acquires property by descent or otherwise upon the death of the deceased, it is not proper for the jury to reduce the damages on that account; for it may fairly be assumed that the beneficiary would, in the natural course of events, have acquired the property ultimately, and his damages are for the loss of benefits which he might have received during the remainder of the life of the deceased, or of the accumulations which the deceased might have added to his estate, and which the beneficiary would have acquired, in addition to the estate existing at the time of the premature death. Thus, in Terry v. Jewett,[154] it was held that it was not error to refuse to charge the jury that they might take into consideration that the plaintiff would be entitled to the property of the deceased as next of kin. A distinction was suggested in Grand Trunk Ry. Co. of Canada v. Jennings,[155] by Lord Watson, who said: "Money provisions made by a husband for the maintenance of a widow, in whatever form, are mat-

the interest. Robostelli v. New York, N. H. & H. R. Co. (C. C.) 34 Fed. 719.

[154] 78 N. Y. 338; Id., 17 Hun (N. Y.) 395. It is error to permit the plaintiff to show that her intestate left no property. Koosorowska v. Glasser (Super. Buff.) 8 N. Y. Supp. 197. That intestate may have saved money out of his earnings, which his widow had at the time of his death, would not reduce the amount of recovery. Sloss-Sheffield Steel & Iron Co. v. Holloway, 144 Ala. 280, 40 South. 211.

[155] 13 App. Cas. 800, 58 L. J. P. C. 1, 59 L. T. (N. S.) 679, 37 Wkly. R. 403. See Pym v. Great Northern Ry. Co., supra. Where the only aid plaintiffs received from decedent was part of the income of property, defendant might show that plaintiffs had received such property by devise or descent. San Antonio & A. P. Ry. Co. v. Long, 87 Tex. 148, 27 S. W. 113, 24 L. R. A. 637, 47 Am. St. Rep. 87.

ters proper to be considered by the jury in estimating her loss; but the extent, if any, to which these ought to be imputed in reduction of damages, must depend upon the nature of the provision, and the position and means of the deceased. When the deceased did not earn his own living, but had an income from property, one half of which had been settled upon his widow, a jury might reasonably come to a conclusion that, to the extent of that half, the widow was not a loser by his death, and might properly confine their estimate of her loss to the interest which she might probably have had in the other half."

Similarly, where the beneficiary receives money on account of an insurance policy on the life of the deceased, this fact is not to be considered in reduction of damages.[156]

---

[156] Althorf v. Wolfe, 22 N. Y. 355; Kellogg v. New York Cent. & H. R. R. Co., 79 N. Y. 72; Sherlock v. Alling, 44 Ind. 184; Carroll v. Missouri Pac. Ry. Co., 88 Mo. 239, 57 Am. Rep. 382; North Pennsylvania R. Co. v. Kirk, 90 Pa. 15; Baltimore & O. R. Co. v. Wightman, 70 Va. 431, 26 Am. Rep. 384; Western & A. R. Co. v. Meigs, 74 Ga. 857; Clune v. Ristine, 94 Fed. 745, 36 C. C. A. 450; Illinois Cent. R. Co. v. Prickett, 210 Ill. 140, 71 N. E. 435; Coulter v. Pine Tp., 164 Pa. 543, 30 Atl. 490; Lipscomb v. Houston & T. C. Ry. Co., 95 Tex. 5, 64 S. W. 923, 55 L. R. A. 869, 93 Am. St. Rep. 804; Houston & T. C. R. Co. v. Lemair, 55 Tex. Civ. App. 237, 119 S. W. 1162. See, also, Spaulding v. Chicago, St. P. & K. C. Ry. Co., 98 Iowa, 205, 67 N. W. 227. See Harding v. Town of Townshend, 43 Vt. 536, 5 Am. Rep. 304; Beckett v. Grand Trunk Ry. Co., 8 Ont. Rep. 601, 13 Ont. App. 174, contra. In estimating damages of the widow and children, that they might under certain conditions receive a government pension in consequence of the death cannot be considered. St. Louis, I. M. & S. Ry. Co. v. Maddry, 57 Ark. 306, 21 S. W. 472. In assessing damages for the death of one employed in a city fire department, the jury should not consider the pension his widow is receiving from the city. Geary v. Metropolitan St. Ry. Co., 73 App. Div. 441, 77 N. Y. Supp. 54. In an action for the death of a railroad employé defendant cannot show, in mitigation of damages, that the mother of deceased would receive from the relief department of the road, of which deceased

In England, however, it has been held that the jury may properly take into consideration the probable amount of future premiums which would have been payable during the life of the deceased.[157] Says Lord Watson in Grand Trunk Ry. Co. v. Jennings: "The pecuniary benefit which accrued to the respondent from his premature death consisted in the accelerated receipt of a sum of money, the consideration of which had been paid by him out of his earnings. In such case the extent of the benefit may fairly be taken to be represented by the use and interest of the money during the period of acceleration; and it was upon that footing that Lord Campbell, in Hicks v. Newport, A. & H. Ry. Co., suggested to the jury that, in estimating the widow's loss, the benefit which she derived from acceleration might be compensated by deducting from their estimate of the future earnings of the deceased the amount of the premiums which, if he had lived, he would have had to pay."

Since the right of action vests upon the death of the deceased, it is not permissible to show that pecuniary benefits have, from another source, subsequently accrued to the beneficiary, which are equivalent to those of which he has been deprived. Thus, in an action for the death of a wife and mother, evidence that the husband had again married, and that his second wife performed like services to those performed by the deceased, is inadmissible in mitigation of damages.[158] And so in an action by a widow for the death

---

was a member, certain death benefits. Boulden v. Pennsylvania R. Co., 205 Pa. 264, 54 Atl. 906.

[157] Hicks v. Newport A. & H. Ry. Co., 4 Best & S. 403, note. See Bradburn v. Great Western R. Co., 44 L. J. Ex. 9, L. R. 10 Ex. 1, per Bramwell, B.; Grand Trunk Ry. Co. v. Jennings, supra; Jennings v. Grand Trunk Ry. Co., 15 Ont. App. 477. The law in this regard was changed by 8 Edw. VII, c. 7. See Appendix.

[158] Davis v. Guarnieri, 45 Ohio St. 470, 15 N. E. 350, 4 Am. St. Rep. 548; Georgia R. & Banking Co. v. Garr, 57 Ga. 277, 24 Am.

of her husband her remarriage is not to be considered as affecting the damages.[159]

§ 177. Discretion of jury—Instructions

From the indefinite nature of the proof of pecuniary loss possible in such cases, much is left to the discretion and judgment of the jury, and it is not improper to instruct them to that effect.[160] But such an instruction should not be given without charging them definitely upon the proper measure of damages in the particular case,[161] and instructing them that the damages must be based upon the evidence,[162] and upon the pecuniary injury to the benefici-

Rep. 492. It is improper on cross-examination to ask the husband if he is not engaged to be married again. Dimmey v. Wheeling & E. G. R. Co., 27 W. Va. 32, 55 Am. Rep. 292. See, also, Chicago & E. I. R. Co. v. Driscoll, 107 Ill. App. 615, affirmed 207 Ill. 9, 69 N. E. 620; Philpott v. Pennsylvania R. Co., 175 Pa. 570, 34 Atl. 856; Gulf, C. & S. F. Ry. Co. v. Younger, 90 Tex. 387, 38 S. W. 1121.

[159] St. Louis, I. M. & S. Ry. Co. v. Cleere, 76 Ark. 377, 88 S. W. 995; O. S. Richardson Fueling Co. v. Peters, 82 Ill. App. 508; Consolidated Stone Co. v. Morgan, 160 Ind. 241, 66 N. E. 696.

[160] Illinois Cent. R. Co. v. Barron, 5 Wall. 90, 18 L. Ed. 591; Chicago & N. W. Ry. Co. v. Whitton, 13 Wall. 270, 20 L. Ed. 571; Pennsylvania R. Co. v. Ogier, 35 Pa. 60, 78 Am. Dec. 322; City of Vicksburg v. McLain, 67 Miss. 4, 6 South. 774; Kansas Pac. R. Co. v. Cutter, 19 Kan. 83; Terminal R. Ass'n of St. Louis v. Condon, 128 Ill. App. 335; Illinois Cent. R. Co. v. Spence, 93 Tenn. 173, 23 S. W. 211, 42 Am. St. Rep. 907.

[161] Pennsylvania R. Co. v. Ogier, supra; Pennsylvania R. Co. v. Vandever, 36 Pa. 298; Catawissa R. Co. v. Armstrong, 52 Pa. 282; Parsons v. Missouri Pac. Ry. Co., 94 Mo. 286, 6 S. W. 464; Pittsburgh, C., C. & St. L. Ry. Co. v. Sudhoff, 173 Ind. 314, 90 N. E. 467; McHugh v. Schlosser, 159 Pa. 480, 28 Atl. 291, 23 L. R. A. 574, 39 Am. St. Rep. 699; Hunt v. Kile, 98 Fed. 49, 38 C. C. A. 641. The fact that the damages are larger than would probably upon the testimony have been found by the court is not ground for reversal. Missouri Pac. Ry. Co. v. Lee, 70 Tex. 496, 7 S. W. 857.

[162] Chicago & N. W. Ry. Co. v. Swett, 45 Ill. 197, 92 Am. Dec.

aries;[163] though, as has been shown, much is left, especially in actions for the death of minor children, to the jury's knowledge and experience.[164]

§ 178. Excessive verdict—Reduction of amount

In cases where the amount of the verdict is deemed by the court to be excessive, it is a common practice to allow the verdict to stand upon condition that the plaintiff remit a part of the sum awarded.[165] In Wisconsin, however, it

206; Chicago & A. R. Co. v. Shannon, 43 Ill. 338; North Chicago R. M. Co. v. Morrissey, 111 Ill. 646; Chicago, M. & St. P. Ry. Co. v. Dowd, 115 Ill. 659, 4 N. E. 368. And see Chicago, B. & Q. R. Co. v. Sykes, 96 Ill. 162; Chicago, R. I. & P. R. Co. v. Austin, 69 Ill. 426; Conant v. Griffin, 48 Ill. 410; Lake Shore & M. S. R. Co. v. Parker, 131 Ill. 557, 23 N. E. 237; Jacksonville Electric Co. v. Bowden, 54 Fla. 461, 45 South. 755, 15 L. R. A. (N. S.) 451; Florida Cent. & P. R. Co. v. Sullivan, 120 Fed. 799, 57 C. C. A. 167, 61 L. R. A. 410; Callison v. Brake, 129 Fed. 196, 63 C. C. A. 354; Muren Coal & Ice Co. v. Howell, 204 Ill. 515, 68 N. E. 456; Illinois Cent. R. Co. v. Johnson, 221 Ill. 42, 77 N. E. 592; Cleveland, C., C. & St. L. Ry. Co. v. Drumm, 32 Ind. App. 547, 70 N. E. 286.

[163] Chicago & A. R. Co. v. Becker, 76 Ill. 25; Chicago, B. & Q. R. Co. v. Harwood, 80 Ill. 88; Denver & R. G. R. Co. v. Spencer, 25 Colo. 9, 52 Pac. 211; Illinois Cent. R. Co. v. Hicks, 122 Ill. App. 349; Illinois Cent. R. Co. v. Whiteaker, 122 Ill. App. 333; Consolidated Stone Co. v. Staggs, 164 Ind. 331, 73 N. E. 695.

[164] City of Chicago v. Scholten, 75 Ill. 468; Ohio & M. Ry. Co. v. Voight, 122 Ind. 288, 23 N. E. 774; Denver & R. G. R. Co. v. Gunning, 33 Colo. 280, 80 Pac. 727; Baltimore & O. S. W. Ry. Co. v. Then, 159 Ill. 535, 42 N. E. 971; Chicago & A. R. Co. v. Kelly, 182 Ill. 267, 54 N. E. 979.

[165] Pym v. Great Northern Ry. Co., 2 Best & S. 759, 31 L. J. Q. B. 249, 10 Wkly. R. 737, 6 L. T. (N. S.) 537, 8 Jur. (N. S.) 819; s. c., 4 Best & S. 396, 32 L. J. Q. B. 377, 11 Wkly. R. 922, 10 Jur. (N. S.) 199; Little Rock & Ft. S. Ry. Co. v. Barker, 39 Ark. 491; Central R. R. v. Crosby, 74 Ga. 737, 58 Am. Rep. 463; Rose v. Des Moines Val. R. Co., 39 Iowa, 246; Hutchins v. St. Paul, M. & M. Ry. Co., 44 Minn. 5, 46 N. W. 79; Smith v. Wabash, St. L. & P. Ry. Co., 92 Mo. 360, 4 S. W. 129, 1 Am. St. Rep. 729; Demarest

has been held that this practice is allowable only when the illegal portion of the judgment is readily severable from the rest, and hence that there can be no remittitur in actions for death;[166] and this view has been in several cases maintained in dissenting opinions.[167]

§ 179. Inadequate verdict

Where the damages are inadequate, the court may, in its discretion, set the verdict aside, and order a new trial.[168]

v. Little, 47 N. J. Law, 28; McIntyre v. New York Cent. R. Co., 37 N. Y. 287; McDonald v. Champion Iron & Steel Co., 140 Mich. 401, 103 N. W. 829; Little v. Bousfield & Co., 165 Mich. 654, 131 N. W. 63; Bremer v. Minneapolis, St. P. & S. S. M. Ry. Co., 96 Minn. 469, 105 N. W. 494; May v. West Jersey & S. R. Co., 62 N. J. Law, 67, 42 Atl. 165; Vowell v. Issaquah Coal Co., 31 Wash. 103, 71 Pac. 725; Felt v. Puget Sound Electric Ry. (C. C.) 175 Fed. 477. Where the action is brought by one for the benefit of several, plaintiff may not remit damages allotted to some, so as to reduce to nominal damages the sums allotted to them. Southern Pac. Co. v. Tomlinson, 163 U. S. 369, 16 Sup. Ct. 1171, 41 L. Ed. 193.

[166] Potter v. Chicago & N. W. R. Co., 22 Wis. 615.

[167] Little Rock & Ft. S. Ry. Co. v. Barker; Central R. R. v. Crosby; Rose v. Des Moines Val. R. Co., supra, note 165.

[168] Mariani v. Dougherty, 46 Cal. 27; Wolford v. Lyon Gravel Gold Min. Co., 63 Cal. 483; James v. Richmond & D. R. Co., 92 Ala. 231, 9 South. 335. See Springett v. Balls, 7 Best & S. 477, 4 Fost. & F. 472; Draper v. Tucker, 69 Neb. 434, 95 N. W. 1026; Meyer v. Hart, 23 App. Div. 131, 48 N. Y. Supp. 904; Willsen v. Metropolitan St. Ry. (Sup.) 74 N. Y. Supp. 774. See next section. An award of $5,000 damages in a suit in admiralty held too small, and increased to $7,500. The San Rafael, 141 Fed. 270, 72 C. C. A. 388.

§ 180. Nominal damages

Since the damages are based upon the pecuniary loss of the beneficiaries, it would seem on principle to follow that, if there is no pecuniary loss, the action cannot be maintained for the recovery even of nominal damages. This has been intimated in England,[169] and held in Michigan,[170] Texas,[171] Vermont,[172] and Wisconsin.[173] Thus, in Duckworth v. Johnson, Pollock, C. B., said: "If there was no damage the action is not maintainable. It appears to me that it was intended by the act to give compensation for damage sustained, and not to enable persons to sue in respect of some imaginary damage, and so punish those who are guilty of negligence by making them pay costs." And in

[169] Duckworth v. Johnson, 4 Hurl. & N. 653, 29 L. J. Ex. 25, 5 Jur. (N. S.) 630. See Boulter v. Webster, 13 Wkly. R. 289, 11 L. T. (N. S.) 598. In the earlier case of Chapman v. Rothwell, E. B. & E. 168, Crompton, J., had said that section 1 of Lord Campbell's act appears to contemplate giving damages, wherever the party injured could have recovered them, whether nominal or not. The jury found a verdict of £1 for the widow, and 10s. for each of the children. The court granted a new trial, without imposing costs on the plaintiff, on the ground that the jury had shrunk from their duty of deciding the issue. Springett v. Balls, 7 Best & S. 477, 4 Fost. & F. 472.

[170] Hurst v. Detroit City Ry. Co., 84 Mich. 539, 48 N. W. 44; Van Brunt v. Cincinnati, J. & M. R. Co., 78 Mich. 530, 44 N. W. 321; Charlebois v. Gogebic & M. R. R. Co., 91 Mich. 59, 51 N. W. 812. Cf. Ingersoll v. Detroit & M. R. Co., 163 Mich. 268, 128 N. W. 227, 32 L. R. A. (N. S.) 362.

[171] McGown v. International & G. N. Ry. Co., 85 Tex. 289, 20 S. W. 80; Rader v. Galveston, H. & S. A. Ry. Co. (Tex. Civ. App.) 137 S. W. 718.

[172] Lazelle v. Town of Newfane, 70 Vt. 440, 41 Atl. 511.

[173] Regan v. Chicago, M. & St. P. Ry. Co., 51 Wis. 599, 8 N. W. 292. The burden of proof as to damages is on plaintiff. Hupfer v. National Distilling Co., 127 Wis. 306, 106 N. W. 831.

Hurst v. Detroit City Ry. Co., Long, J., said: "The statute does not imply that damages and pecuniary loss necessarily flow from the negligent killing." On the other hand, it has been held, or rather intimated, in a great number of cases, that damages do necessarily flow from the negligent killing, and that whenever there is proof of the negligence of the defendant, and of the existence of next of kin, the action lies for at least nominal damages; [174] although the question of nominal damages has in few cases been actually involved

[174] Chicago & A. R. Co. v. Shannon, 43 Ill. 338; Chicago & N. W. Ry. Co. v. Swett, 45 Ill. 197, 92 Am. Dec. 206; City of Chicago v. Scholten, 75 Ill. 468; Quincy Coal Co. v. Hood, 77 Ill. 68; Quin v. Moore, 15 N. Y. 432; Dickens v. New York Cent. R. Co., 1 Abb. Dec. (N. Y.) 504; Ihl v. Forty-Second St. & G. St. Ferry R. Co., 47 N. Y. 317, 7 Am. Rep. 450; Lehman v. City of Brooklyn, 29 Barb. (N. Y.) 234; Atchison, T. & S. F. R. Co. v. Weber, 33 Kan. 543, 6 Pac. 877, 52 Am. Rep. 543; In re California Nav. & Imp. Co. (D. C.) 110 Fed. 670; Falkenau v. Rowland, 70 Ill. App. 20; Howard v. Delaware & H. Canal Co. (C. C.) 40 Fed. 195, 6 L. R. A. 75. See, also, Alabama Mineral R. Co. v. Jones, 121 Ala. 113, 25 South. 814; Central of Georgia R. Co. v. Alexander, 144 Ala. 257, 40 South. 424; Scherer v. Schlaberg, 18 N. D. 421, 122 N. W. 1000, 24 L. R. A. (N. S.) 769. In an action by a father for death of his minor child, the father's right to the child's services being infringed by defendant's act, he is entitled to recover at least nominal damages. Seaboard Air Line Ry. v. Moseley, 60 Fla. 186, 53 South. 718. No more than nominal damages can be recovered where it is not shown that the next of kin sustained pecuniary loss, unless the relation of husband and wife or parent and child existed between the deceased and such next of kin, in which case pecuniary loss is presumed of law. Chicago Bridge & Iron Co. v. La Mantia, 112 Ill. App. 43. Where there was evidence that some of the next of kin sustained a pecuniary loss, more than nominal damages were recoverable. Grace & Hyde Co. v. Strong, 224 Ill. 630, 79 N. E. 967. Where an action for the death of a minor son is prosecuted for the sole benefit of the father, who is conclusively shown to have lost his legal right to the services and earnings of the son during his minority, and where, apart from this legal right, there is no substantial evidence of a reasonable expectation of pecuniary benefit to the father from the continued life of the son, the recovery should

in the decision.[175] Nominal damages will be awarded in admiralty.[176]

be limited to nominal damages. Swift & Co. v. Johnson, 138 Fed. 867, 71 C. C. A. 619, 1 L. R. A. (N. S.) 1161.

[175] Johnston v. Cleveland & T. R. Co., 7 Ohio St. 336, 70 Am. Dec. 75; Kenney v. New York Cent. & H. R. R. Co., 49 Hun, 535, 2 N. Y. Supp. 512; Korrady v. Lake Shore & M. S. Ry. Co., 131 Ind. 261, 29 N. E. 1069; Burk v. Arcata & M. R. R. Co., 125 Cal. 364, 57 Pac. 1065, 73 Am. St. Rep. 52 (cf. Hillebrand v. Standard Biscuit Co., 139 Cal. 233, 73 Pac. 163).

[176] In re California Nav. & Imp. Co. (D. C.) 110 Fed. 670.

CHAPTER XI

PLEADING AND PRACTICE

§ 181.   The wrongful act or neglect

It is not necessary, unless the action is based upon a foreign statute,[1] that the declaration or complaint should refer to the statute under which the action is brought, but it is sufficient to allege facts that bring the case within the statute.[2] Nor is it necessary to allege that the act or neglect of the defendant was such that, if death had not ensued, the person injured might have maintained an action.[3] The complaint must, of course, show that the death was caused by the act or neglect.[4] Since it is a part of the plaintiff's

---

[1] See §§ 195, 202.

[2] Brown v. Harmon, 21 Barb. (N. Y.) 508; Kennayde v. Pacific R. Co., 45 Mo. 255; White v. Maxcy, 64 Mo. 552; Westcott v. Central Vt. R. Co., 61 Vt. 438, 17 Atl. 745; Morrisey v. Hughes, 65 Vt. 553, 27 Atl. 205; Ervin v. St. Louis, I. M. & S. Ry. Co., 158 Mo. App. 1, 139 S. W. 498.

[3] Philadelphia, W. & B. R. Co. v. State, to Use of Bitzer, 58 Md. 372.

[4] Kansas City, M. & B. R. Co. v. Matthews, 142 Ala. 298, 39 South. 207; Pierce v. Seaboard Air Line Ry., 122 Ga. 664, 50 S. E. 468; Coy v. Indianapolis Gas Co., 146 Ind. 655, 46 N. E. 17, 36 L. R. A.

(408)

case to show that the act or neglect by which death was caused was such that the party injured, had death not ensued, might have maintained an action, the complaint must, of course, allege the facts which would have been necessary to establish a cause of action in the party injured in the same manner as would have been required in an action by him. So far as concerns the allegations of the complaint necessary to establish a cause of action in the party injured, it must be tested by the rules of pleading that would be applicable in an action for personal injury.[5]

§ 182.   Existence of beneficiaries

The existence of some person entitled to the benefit of the recovery being under most acts essential to the maintenance of the action,[6] the existence of such person must be

535; Storrs v. City of Grand Rapids, 110 Mich. 483, 68 N. W. 258; Norfolk & W. Ry. Co. v. Stegall's Adm'x, 105 Va. 538, 54 S. E. 19.

[5] See, by way of illustration, Louisville & N. R. Co. v. Jones, 83 Ala. 376, 3 South. 902; Brown v. St. Louis, I. M. & S. Ry. Co., 52 Ark. 120, 12 S. W. 203; Brown v. Central Pac. R. Co., 68 Cal. 171, 7 Pac. 447; 8 Pac. 828; Davies v. Oceanic S. S. Co., 89 Cal. 280, 26 Pac. 827; Central R. Co. v. Hubbard, 86 Ga. 623, 12 S. E. 1020; Pennsylvania Co. v. O'Shaughnessy, 122 Ind. 588, 23 N. E. 675; Mobile & O. R. Co. v. Stroud, 64 Miss. 784, 2 South. 171; Sullivan v. Missouri Pac. Ry. Co., 97 Mo. 113, 10 S. W. 852; Pope v. Kansas City C. Ry. Co., 99 Mo. 400, 12 S. W. 891; Parker v. Providence & S. Steamboat Co., 17 R. I. 376, 22 Atl. 284, 14 L. R. A. 414, 33 Am. St. Rep. 869; San Antonio St. Ry. Co. v. Cailloutte, 79 Tex. 341, 15 S. W. 390; Norfolk & W. R. Co. v. Harman's Adm'r, 83 Va. 553, 8 S. E. 251; Searle v. Kanawha & O. Ry. Co., 32 W. Va. 370, 9 S. E. 248; Fitts v. Waldeck, 51 Wis. 567, 8 N. W. 363. A cause of action is not stated by a complaint merely alleging that on a certain day defendant "wrongfully and negligently killed" plaintiff's intestate. Chattanooga Cotton-Oil Co. v. Shamblin, 101 Tenn. 263, 47 S. W. 496.

[6] In Alabama it is held that the existence of heirs is a collateral fact which will be presumed. Columbus & W. Ry. Co. v. Bradford, 86 Ala. 574, 6 South. 90; Alabama & F. R. Co. v. Waller, 48 Ala. 459;

alleged in the complaint.[7] But it seems that it is unnecessary to set forth the names of the beneficiaries,[8] although,

Woodstock Iron Works v. Kline, 149 Ala. 391, 43 South. 362. Under the statute providing for payment of the sum recovered to certain relatives, and, if there be no such relatives, then to the heirs of deceased, it is not necessary to name the heirs, or aver that there are any. Budd v. Meriden Electric R. Co., 69 Conn. 272, 37 Atl. 683. See, also, East Tennessee Telephone Co. v. Simms' Adm'r, 99 Ky. 404, 36 S. W. 171, 18 Ky. Law Rep. 761; Roach v. Imperial Min. Co. (C. C.) 7 Fed. 698; Harper v. Norfolk & W. R. Co. (C. C.) 36 Fed. 102.

[7] See cases cited ante, § 80, note 2. See, also, Webster v. Norwegian Min. Co., 137 Cal. 399, 70 Pac. 276, 92 Am. St. Rep. 181; St. Luke's Hospital v. Foster, 86 Ill. App. 282; West Chicago St. R. Co. v. Mable, 77 Ill. App. 176; Village of Assumption v. Campbell, 95 Ill. App. 521; Toledo, St. L. & W. R. Co. v. Lander (Ind. App.) 95 N. E. 319; Oulighan v. Butler, 189 Mass. 287, 75 N. E. 726; Bartley v. Boston & N. St. Ry. Co., 198 Mass. 163, 83 N. E. 1093; Vander Wegen v. Great Northern Ry. Co., 114 Minn. 118, 130 N. W. 70; Chicago, B. & Q. R. Co. v. Oyster, 58 Neb. 1, 78 N. W. 359; Pizzi v. Reid, 36 Misc. Rep. 123, 72 N. Y. Supp. 1053; Southern Ry. Co. v. Maxwell, 113 Tenn. 464, 82 S. W. 1137; Archibald v. Lincoln County, 50 Wash. 55, 96 Pac. 831; Davidow v. Pennsylvania R. Co. (C. C.) 85 Fed. 943. A complaint alleging that deceased left surviving him a certain person as his next of kin and heir at law, without stating the relation of this person, or that the deceased left no widow, is good as against demurrer. Lahti v. Oliver Iron Min. Co., 106 Minn. 241, 118 N. W. 1018. If the existence of the surviving minor children of the decedent is averred, the omission to allege whether he left a widow will not render the pleading bad on demurrer. Chicago, B. & Q. R. Co. v. Oyster, 58 Neb. 1, 78 N. W. 359. Allegations from which it can be inferred that the suit is for the benefit of the next of kin are sufficient, without a direct averment to that effect. Hamilton v. Bordentown Electric Light & Motor Co., 68 N. J. Law 85, 52 Atl. 290; Zipple v. Sandford & Harris Co. (N. J. Sup.) 58 Atl. 176.

[8] In Conant v. Griffin, 48 Ill. 410, it was held unnecessary to allege the names; but in Quincy Coal Co. v. Hood, 77 Ill. 68, where the declaration limited the next of kin to the father, it was held error to admit proof that deceased left a father, mother, and brothers and sisters. The court observed that if the complaint had simply alleged that the deceased left a widow, or next of kin, without naming them,

as the action is based solely upon the pecuniary loss to the beneficiaries, it would not be unreasonable to require the plaintiff to allege the names of the persons damaged.[9] A few of the acts require the plaintiff to furnish a full particular of the persons for whom the action is brought.[10] If the act gives a right of action first to a designated class of beneficiaries, and if there be none of that class then to another class, in an action on behalf of beneficiaries of the latter class the nonexistence of beneficiaries of the first class must be averred.[11] Thus in an action by a mother under a

no question of variance could have been raised. In Indianapolis, P. & C. R. Co. v. Keely's Adm'r, 23 Ind. 133, it was said that the names and relationship should be stated, but in Jeffersonville, M. & I. R. Co. v. Hendricks, 41 Ind. 48, the court declares that this is unnecessary. See, also, Pennsylvania Co. v. Coyer, 163 Ind. 631, 72 N. E. 875. A declaration which sets forth adequately the right of a personal representative to recover is sufficient without alleging specifically the rights of the respective distributees. Howard v. Delaware & H. Canal Co. (C. C.) 40 Fed. 195, 6 L. R. A. 75. The fact that the administrator fails to name all the legal beneficiaries will not bar any distributee not named from receiving his distributive share of the judgment. Oyster v. Burlington Relief Department of Chicago, B. & Q. R. Co., 65 Neb. 789, 91 N. W. 699, 59 L. R. A. 291. See, also, Chicago, B. & Q. R. Co. v. Oyster, 58 Neb. 1, 78 N. W. 359; Chicago, B. & Q. R. Co. v. Bond, 58 Neb. 385, 78 N. W. 710.

[9] In Barnum v. Chicago, M. & St. P. Ry. Co., 30 Minn. 461, 16 N. W. 364, a complaint which set forth the names of the next of kin, and how they were related, with an allegation of damage to them, was held sufficient, the court observing that upon it the plaintiff could recover all the damages which could be recovered in such an action. A variance between the allegations of the petition and the proof as to the sex of the minor children, brothers and sisters of deceased, is not material. O'Callaghan v. Bode, 84 Cal. 489, 24 Pac. 269. The declaration need not negative the existence of any relatives other than those named. Barnes v. Ward, 9 C. B. 392. See Peers v. Nevada Power, Light & Water Co. (C. C.) 119 Fed. 400.

[10] See § 185.

[11] Louisville E. & St. L. Consolidated R. Co. v. Lohges, 6 Ind. App. 288, 33 N. E. 449; Barker v. Hannibal & St. J. R. Co., 91 Mo.

statute authorizing her, if the father be dead, to sue for the death of a minor child, the complaint must show that the father is not in being.[12] Where the proceeding is by indictment, it must be averred that the deceased left widow

86, 14 S. W. 280; McIntosh v. Missouri Pac. Ry. Co., 103 Mo. 131, 15 S. W. 80; Nohrden v. Northeastern R. Co., 54 S. C. 492, 32 S. E. 524. See ante, § 103. In action by a widower for the death of his wife, a demurrer to the petition is properly sustained, where it fails to show there are no children, under a statute providing that damages must inure to the benefit of the widow and children, if any, or next of kin. Bartlett v. Chicago, R. I. & P. Ry. Co., 21 Okl. 415, 96 Pac. 468. A complaint, alleging that decedent's father and mother and two sisters named are the persons who survive him negatives the idea that other persons survive him, and sufficiently shows that he left no widow or children. Pries v. Ashland Home Telephone Co., 143 Wis. 606, 128 N. W. 281. In order for a parent to recover for the death of his minor son, he must, under a statute giving the right of action in such case to the next of kin when no personal representative has been appointed, allege and prove that there has been no such appointment. Atchison Water Co. v. Price, 9 Kan. App. 884, 59 Pac. 677. In an action by a widow for the death of her husband, who was a resident of the state, an allegation that no personal representative of his estate had been appointed is put in issue by the unverified denial, and without proof of such fact a demurrer to the evidence is rightfully sustained. Vaughn v. Kansas City N. W. R. Co., 65 Kan. 685, 70 Pac. 602. In an action by the widow and heirs of a decedent for causing his death, plaintiff must plead, and prove, that there has been no administration. Choctaw, O. & G. R. Co. v. Jackson (C. C.) 182 Fed. 342.

[12] An allegation that the mother was next of kin held sufficient after verdict, as it could have been sustained only by showing that the father was dead. David v. Waters, 11 Or. 448, 5 Pac. 748. It is not sufficient to allege that the plaintiff is a widow, since it is consistent with this allegation that she may have been divorced and remarried, and that her first husband is still alive. St. Louis, I. M. & S. Ry. Co. v. Yocum, 34 Ark. 493. A petition by a mother to recover for the death of her son should negative the existence of minor children and a widow of deceased. Blackburn v. Louisiana Ry. & Nav. Co., 128 La. 319, 54 South. 865. Cf. Davis v. Arkansas Southern R. Co., 117 La. 320, 41 South. 587. See ante, § 103.

or heirs;[13] and in Maine, where the forfeiture was payable directly to them, and not, as in Massachusetts, to the administrator, it was held that their names must be set out.[14]

§ 183. Appointment of executor or administrator

Where the statute requires the action to be brought in the name of the personal representative, the complaint must allege the appointment of the plaintiff as executor or administrator. Thus, where suit was brought by the widow, and on her motion an order was made substituting as plaintiff a person who was represented to be the administrator, it was held that failure to amend the complaint so as to show that the substituted plaintiff was administrator of the estate of the deceased was a fatal defect.[15] But where the complaint was in the name of the plaintiff "as administratrix," and in the body of the complaint the deceased was referred to as "plaintiff's intestate," it was held that the representative capacity of the plaintiff sufficiently appeared.[16] The ap-

[13] Commonwealth v. Boston & W. R. Corp., 11 Cush. (Mass.) 512; Commonwealth v. Eastern R. Co., 5 Gray (Mass.) 473; Commonwealth v. Boston & A. R. Co., 121 Mass. 36; State v. Gilmore, 24 N. H. 461.

[14] State v. Grand Trunk Ry. Co. of Canada, 60 Me. 145.

[15] City of Atchison v. Twine, 9 Kan. 350; Hagerty v. Hughes, 4 Baxt. (Tenn.) 222. But where the allegations of the administrator's appointment, etc., were sufficient, although the plaintiff averred that by the death of the intestate "he is damaged," the complaint was held good. Clore v. McIntire, 120 Ind. 262, 22 N. E. 128. A petition alleging that plaintiff sues as administratrix, naming the next of kin and praying for damages, is sufficient to indicate plaintiff's authority to maintain the action. Board of Com'rs of Hardin County v. Coffman, 18 Ohio Cir. Ct. R. 254, 10 O. C. D. 91.

[16] Louisville & N. R. Co. v. Trammell, 9 South. 870. See, also, Kansas City, M. & B. R. Co. v. Matthews, 142 Ala. 298, 39 South. 207; Bowler v. Lane, 3 Metc. (Ky.) 311.

pointment of the administrator is not put in issue by a general denial, but that issue must be raised by a special plea or denial.[17] Where the administrator had authority when the action was begun, a subsequent revocation of his authority is not put in issue by a denial of his authority to maintain the action, but must be specially pleaded.[18]

§ 184. Allegations of damages

As has been stated, it is held in some jurisdictions that the statute necessarily implies pecuniary loss to the beneficiaries from the death, and that the action can consequently be maintained in the absence of pecuniary loss for at least nominal damages; while in other jurisdictions it is held that, without pecuniary loss, the action is not maintainable, even for nominal damages.[19] In the latter jurisdictions it appears to be necessary to allege in the complaint the facts showing pecuniary loss. Thus, in Michigan it is said that the damages are special, and that it must be made to appear by proper allegations that pecuniary loss necessarily resulted.[20] And in Wisconsin it is held that the

[17] Ewen v. Chicago & N. W. Ry. Co., 38 Wis. 613; Union R. & T. Co. v. Shacklet, 119 Ill. 232, 10 N. E. 896; Chicago & A. R. Co. v. Smith, 180 Ill. 453, 54 N. E. 325. See, also, Hughes v. Richter, 161 Ill. 409, 43 N. E. 1066, affirming 60 Ill. App. 616. A plea to the merits admits the representative character in which the plaintiff sues. Hanley v. West Virginia Cent. & P. Ry. Co., 59 W. Va. 419, 53 S. E. 625. Where the answer admits that plaintiff is administrator, and the case is reached for trial more than two years after death, and defendant asks leave to amend by denial of the appointment and qualifications of plaintiff to interpose the two-year bar of the statute, the amendment will be denied. Archdeacon v. Cincinnati Gas & Electric Co., 76 Ohio St. 97, 81 N. E. 152.

[18] Burlington & M. R. Co. v. Crockett, 17 Neb. 570, 24 N. W. 219.

[19] See § 180.

[20] Hurst v. Detroit City Ry., 84 Mich. 539, 48 N. W. 44. See, also, Rouse v. Detroit Electric Ry., 128 Mich. 149, 87 N. W. 68.

complaint must allege facts showing that loss, present or prospective, has resulted,[21] although in the latter state, where the complaint showed that the deceased was a laboring man, working for the defendant (without alleging that he received any compensation), and that he left a child of three years, it was held on demurrer that it sufficiently showed that the child had suffered pecuniary loss.[22]

On the other hand, in jurisdictions where it is held that nominal damages necessarily result from the death, it seems that a complaint is good on demurrer although it does not allege more than the death and the survival of beneficiaries.[23] Thus, in New York, in an action for the benefit of a widow, the complaint was held good on demurrer notwithstanding that it contained no allegations that damages had been sustained, although the court declined to express an opinion whether, without further allegations, proof of substantial damages would be admissible.[24] And, in an

---

[21] Regan v. Chicago, M. & St. P. Ry. Co., 51 Wis. 599, 8 N. W. 292. But in Ewen v. Chicago & N. W. R. Co., 38 Wis. 613, where an element in the pecuniary injury was the loss of a pension cut off by the death of deceased, it was held unnecessary to allege this fact in order to admit proof of it. Where, in an action for death of plaintiff's son, it was alleged that deceased was an intelligent boy of 17 years, in good health, and capable of earning considerable money, and unmarried, the complaint necessarily implied that plaintiff was deprived of the reasonable value of deceased's services for the balance of his minority. Luessen v. Oshkosh Electric Light & Power Co., 109 Wis. 94, 85 N. W. 124. See Lounsbury v. Davis, 124 Wis. 432, 102 N. W. 941.

[22] Kelley v. Chicago, M. & St. P. Ry. Co., 50 Wis. 381, 7 N. W. 291.

[23] Salem Bedford Stone Co. v. Hobbs, 11 Ind. App. 27, 38 N. E. 538.

[24] Kenney v. New York Cent. & H. R. R. Co., 49 Hun, 535, 2 N. Y. Supp. 512. Nominal damages at least are presumed, and a complaint is sufficient without alleging the facts constituting damages. Pizzi v. Reid, 72 App. Div. 162, 76 N. Y. Supp. 306.

Indiana case, a complaint which showed that the deceased
left a widow and infant children surviving was held good
on demurrer although it did not directly allege that the
beneficiaries sustained actual damages; the court saying
that the legal presumption is that the infant children and
wife are entitled to the services of a father and husband,
and that such services are valuable to them.[25] In order to
allow proof of damages in these jurisdictions, it appears to
be sufficient to allege that the beneficiaries have sustained
damages in a certain amount.[26] It has been held in Indiana,

[25] Korrady v. Lake Shore & M. S. Ry. Co., 131 Ind. 261, 29 N. E.
1069. See, also, Chicago & E. R. Co. v. Thomas (Ind.) 55 N. E. 861;
Chicago & E. R. Co. v. Thomas, 155 Ind. 634, 58 N. E. 1040; Cleveland, C., C. & St. L. R. Co. v. Starks, 174 Ind. 345, 92 N. E. 54.

[26] Safford v. Drew, 3 Duer (N. Y.) 627; Louisville, N. A. & C. Ry.
Co. v. Buck, 116 Ind. 566, 19 N. E. 453, 2 L. R. A. 520, 9 Am.
St. Rep. 883; Barron v. Illinois Cent. R. Co., 1 Biss. 412, Fed. Cas.
No. 1052; Serensen v. Northern Pac. R. Co. (C. C.) 45 Fed. 407;
Barnum v. Chicago, M. & St. P. Ry. Co., 30 Minn. 461, 16 N. W. 364.
See, also, Westcott v. Central Vt. R. Co., 61 Vt. 438, 17 Atl. 745;
Ewen v. Chicago & N. W. Ry. Co., supra; Kenney v. New York Cent.
& H. R. R. Co., supra; Bond v. United Railroads of San Francisco,
159 Cal. 270, 113 Pac. 366, Ann. Cas. 1912C, 50; Peters v. Southern
Pac. Co., 160 Cal. 48, 116 Pac. 400; Seaboard Air Line Ry. v. Mose-
ley, 60 Fla. 186, 53 South. 718; Commercial Club of Indianapolis v.
Hilliker, 20 Ind. App. 239, 50 N. E. 578; Elwood Electric St. Ry.
Co. v. Ross, 26 Ind. App. 258, 58 N. E. 535; Cleveland, C., C. & St.
L. Ry. Co. v. Henry (Ind. App.) 80 N. E. 636; Cleveland, C., C. &
St. L. Ry. Co. v. Henry, 170 Ind. 94, 83 N. E. 710; Erb v. Morasch, 8
Kan. App. 61, 54 Pac. 323; Kansas City v. Siese, 71 Kan. 283, 80
Pac. 626; Norfolk & W. Ry. Co. v. Stevens' Adm'r, 97 Va. 631, 34
S. E. 525, 46 L. R. A. 367; Peers v. Nevada Power, Light & Water
Co. (C. C.) 119 Fed. 400. The declaration averred that by the death
the widow and minor children were deprived of their support and
the children of their means of education, to the damage, etc. Held,
that such averments were sufficient to admit evidence of the ability
of deceased to earn money. Chicago & A. Ry. Co. v. Carey, 115 Ill.
115, 3 N. E. 519. Where the complaint shows that deceased left a
widow and minor children of tender years, no specific allegations

however, in an action by a father for the death of a minor child, that, in order to recover for loss of services beyond the date of the beginning of suit, such damages must be specially averred.[27] And a California case has held that damages for funeral expenses, if recoverable at all, must be specially alleged.[28] In some cases a distinction is drawn between actions on behalf of beneficiaries who are so related to the decedent that the law imposes upon him a duty to support them and actions on behalf of collaterals or other beneficiaries not legally dependent upon him, and it is held that in actions of the first class it is enough if the complaint show the existence of such beneficiaries, the pecuniary injury being thereby sufficiently averred,[29] but that

showing that such widow and children suffered pecuniary damages by the loss of such life are required. Haug v. Great Northern Ry. Co., 8 N. D. 23, 77 N. W. 97, 42 L. R. A. 664, 73 Am. St. Rep. 727. A general allegation of damages to a stated amount is sufficient to allow proof of the age of deceased and his expectancy of life, and the dependency of plaintiff on him for support. International & G. N. Ry. Co. v. Knight, 91 Tex. 660, 45 S. W. 556. While, in an action for death of plaintiff's wife, damages for loss of her services generally may be recovered as general damages, yet where her services are not such as are usually performed by a wife, or are of peculiar value to him in his trade or profession, they should be pleaded and proved. Gulf, C. & S. F. Ry. Co. v. Younger (Tex. Civ. App.) 40 S. W. 423. A petition stating the extent of decedent's earnings for services rendered, and alleging that plaintiffs have lost his services and earnings, and also alleging his death, his character, his relation to plaintiffs, and their ages, and concluding with the averment that, "by reason of the premises," plaintiffs have been damaged in a certain sum, was sufficient to authorize the recovery of all damages legally recoverable, including allowance for assistance, care, and nurture of husband and father. Houston & T. C. R. Co. v. Davenport, 102 Tex. 369, 117 S. W. 790.

[27] Pennsylvania Co. v. Lilly, 73 Ind. 252.

[28] Gay v. Winter, 34 Cal. 153.

[29] Kearney Electric Co. v. Laughlin, 45 Neb. 390, 63 N. W. 941; City of Friend v. Burleigh, 53 Neb. 674, 74 N. W. 50; Tucker v.

in actions of the second class the complaint must allege facts showing an actual pecuniary interest in the life of the decedent.[30]

§ 185. Bill of particulars

Lord Campbell's act provides that the plaintiff must, together. with the declaration, deliver to the defendant full particular of the person or persons for whom the action is brought, and of the nature of the claim in respect to the damages sought to be recovered. The Maryland and New Jersey acts contain similar provisions, the particular in the latter state to be furnished on request. Under Lord Campbell's act, the omission to furnish particulars has been held ground for setting aside the service of the writ, but not the writ itself.[31] In Maryland, where the declaration fully stated the nature and amount of the claim, and the defendant pleaded without demanding a particular, the failure to furnish a particular was held no objection.[32] The particular

---

Draper, 62 Neb. 66, 86 N. W. 917, 54 L. R. A. 321. A petition which alleges that deceased left a widow and next of kin, describing them, on whom the law confers the right to be supported by the person killed, sufficiently avers pecuniary loss, and in that respect states a cause of action. Omaha & R. V. R. Co. v. Crow, 54 Neb. 747, 74 N. W. 1066, 69 Am. St. Rep. 741. See, also, Peden v. American Bridge Co., 120 Fed. 523.

[30] Orgall v. Chicago, B. & Q. R. Co., 46 Neb. 4, 64 N. W. 450; Chicago, B. & Q. R. Co. v. Van Buskirk, 58 Neb. 252, 78 N. W. 514; Chicago, B. & Q. R. Co. v. Bond, 58 Neb. 385, 78 N. W. 710; Chicago, R. I. & P. Ry. Co. v. Young, 58 Neb. 678, 79 N. W. 556; Union Pac. R. Co. v. Roeser, 69 Neb. 62, 95 N. W. 68; Greenwood v. King, 82 Neb. 17, 116 N. W. 1128; Thompson v. Chicago, M. & St. P. R. Co. (C. C.) 104 Fed. 845 (Nebraska).   ·

[31] McCabe v. Guinness, 9 Ir. R. Com. Law, 510.

[32] Philadelphia, W. & B. R. Co. v. State, to Use of Bitzer, 58 Md. 372.

is intended for the same purpose as in other cases.[33] In a New York case, a bill of particulars was denied, the court saying that it would be unreasonable to require the plaintiff to state, by anticipation, all the items and amounts that would properly enter into a computation of damages.[34] But in a Vermont case it was intimated that, where the damages are not sufficiently set forth, the court would order suitable specifications.[35]

§ 186. Indictment

The proceeding by indictment provided for by the statutes of Massachusetts, and formerly of Maine and New Hampshire, though criminal in form, is to be treated in its main features as a civil action for the recovery of damages, and the same rules of evidence and principles of law are to be applied as in civil cases.[36] Thus, the indictment may be discontinued, with leave of court, by a nolle prosequi, entered by the prosecutor while the cause is on trial, against the objection of the defendant.[37]

§ 187. Amendment

The complaint or declaration may be amended as in other actions where the amended pleading does not state a new

[33] Baltimore & O. R. Co. v. State, to Use of Woodward, 41 Md. 279; Telfer v. Northern R. Co., 30 N. J. Law, 188.

[34] Murphy v. Kipp, 1 Duer (N. Y.) 659. See Manning v. International Nav. Co., 24 App. Div. 143, 49 N. Y. Supp. 182; Causullo v. Lenox Const. Co., 106 App. Div. 575, 94 N. Y. Supp. 639; Heslin v. Lake Champlain & M. R. Co., 109 App. Div. 814, 96 N. Y. Supp. 761; Rosney v. Erie R. Co. (C. C.) 124 Fed. 90.

[35] Westcott v. Central Vt. R. Co., 61 Vt. 438, 17 Atl. 745.

[36] State v. Grand Trunk Ry. Co. of Canada, 58 Me. 176, 4 Am. Rep. 258; State v. Manchester & L. R. R., 52 N. H. 528. See § 44.

[37] State v. Maine Cent. R. Co., 77 Me. 244.

cause of action; and such amendment, although made after the expiration of the period of limitation, will relate back to the commencement of the suit.[88] Thus, an amendment may be made which merely adds more particular [89] or different [40] allegations in respect to the defendant's negligence; or which otherwise sets forth a more complete statement of the original cause of action; [41] or which alleges that the deceased was killed while being carried as an employé, instead

[88] Where under Code § 25, neither father nor mother could bring an action for injuries to a minor child resulting in death, and a mother, as administratrix of a minor, brought action as alleged "under the provisions of section 25 of the Code," plaintiff could amend by striking out the words quoted, leaving a right of action good under section 27. Louisville & N. R. Co. v. Robinson, 141 Ala. 325, 37 South. 431. Otherwise, where no cause of action was stated. Bell v. Central R. R., 73 Ga. 520; Smith v. East & West R. Co., 84 Ga. 183, 10 S. E. 602; Lilly v. Charlotte, C. & A. R. Co., 32 S. C. 142, 10 S. E. 932.

[89] Jeffersonville, M. & I. R. Co. v. Hendricks, 41 Ind. 48; Kuhns v. Wisconsin, I. & N. Ry. Co., 76 Iowa, 67, 40 N. W. 92; Moody v. Pacific R. Co., 68 Mo. 470; Mills' Adm'r v. Cavanaugh, 94 S. W. 651, 29 Ky. Law Rep. 685.

[40] Harris v. Central R. Co., 78 Ga. 525, 3 S. E. 355; Muren Coal & Ice Co. v. Howell, 217 Ill. 190, 75 N. E. 469; Roseberry's Adm'r v. Newport News & M. V. R. Co., 39 S. W. 407, 19 Ky. Law Rep. 194. A declaration in a suit by an administrator, in one count stated a cause of action for personal injuries of the intestate good at common law, and imperfectly stated a cause of action under the statute for the benefit of the minor children of the intestate for his death. Held, that it was not error to allow plaintiff to amend by stating the latter cause of action correctly, and then, the actions not being proper to join in one suit, to allow plaintiff to strike out his original count. Daley v. Boston & A. R. Co., 147 Mass. 101, 16 N. E. 690. An amendment which charges defendant railroad company with the negligent killing of intestate, by charging, instead, a willful and wanton killing, is not a departure from the original cause of action, and it will not be stricken out. Central of Georgia Ry. Co. v. Foshee, 125 Ala. 199, 27 South. 1006.

[41] Deninger v. American Locomotive Co., 185 Fed. 22, 107 C. C. A. 126; Chicago, R. I. & P. R. Co. v. Young, 67 Neb. 568, 93 N. W. 922.

of as a passenger;[42] or which adds an allegation that the deceased left a wife and children;[43] or which alleges that one of two joint defendants was solely guilty of the negligence charged (the action being dismissed as to the other defendant);[44] or which makes a party coplaintiff who was originally made defendant,[45] or joins a coplaintiff when the right of action is in both;[46] or, if the action is based upon a foreign statute, which alleges the provisions of such statute.[47] On the other hand, where the proposed amendment states a new cause of action, it cannot be allowed,[48]

---

[42] Kansas Pac. Ry. Co. v. Salmon, 14 Kan. 512.

[43] South Carolina R. Co. v. Nix, 68 Ga. 572; Haynie v. Chicago & A. R. Co., 9 Ill. App. 105. See, also, Van Pelt v. Chattanooga, R. & C. R. Co., 89 Ga. 706, 15 S. E. 622; Central of Georgia Ry. Co. v. Henson, 121 Ga. 462, 49 S. E. 278; Chicago Terminal Transfer R. Co. v. Helbreg, 99 Ill. App. 563; Blackburn v. Louisiana Ry. & Nav. Co., 128 La. 319, 54 South. 865.

[44] Lottman v. Barnett, 62 Mo. 159; Reed v. Northeastern R. Co., 37 S. C. 42, 16 S. E. 289.

[45] Buel v. St. Louis Transfer Co., 45 Mo. 562.

[46] Where an action is brought by a father for the death of his son, after the period of limitations the record may be amended so as to make the mother a party; the right of action being in both parents. Holmes v. Pennsylvania R. Co., 220 Pa. 189, 69 Atl. 597, 123 Am. St. Rep. 685.

[47] Lustig v. New York, L. E. & W. R. Co., 65 Hun, 547, 20 N. Y. Supp. 477; South Carolina R. Co. v. Nix, 68 Ga. 572; Louisville & N. R. Co. v. Pointer's Adm'r, 113 Ky. 952, 69 S. W. 1108, 24 Ky. Law Rep. 772. But see Selma, R. & D. R. Co. v. Lacey, 49 Ga. 106.

[48] Randolph's Adm'r v. Snyder, 139 Ky. 159, 129 S. W. 562. A declaration in an action by an administrator in the New Hampshire circuit court stated a cause of action against a railroad company at common law for injuries to plaintiff's intestate, coupled, also, with allegations which might have been intended to include damages for a death, given by the New Hampshire statutes. By an amendment he subsequently declared under the Massachusetts statute authorizing actions for death, and limiting the action to one year from the injury. Held, that the amendment was a change of the ground of

although the decisions are not entirely harmonious on the
application of the rule. Thus an amendment which substi-
tutes another beneficiary in place of the one named in the
declaration, when the effect of the substitution is to change
the amount of the recovery, the direct pecuniary injury to
the beneficiary being an element of the damages, states a
different cause of action, and is subject to the plea of the
statute of limitations.[49] And so where the amendment
changes the capacity in which the plaintiff sues, as from
the individual capacity of the plaintiff to his capacity as
administrator, or vice versa, if the effect of the change is to
introduce a different cause of action, as where the death
occurred in another state, and the purpose of the amendment is to bring the action within the foreign statute.[50]

action and that the action was barred. Boston & M. R. R. v. Hurd,
108 Fed. 116, 47 C. C. A. 615, 56 L. R. A. 193.

[49] Atlanta, K. & N. Ry. Co. v. Hooper, 92 Fed. 820, 35 C. C. A. 24.
See, also, Flatley v. Memphis & C. R. Co., 9 Heisk. (Tenn.) 230;
Lilly v. Charlotte, C. & A. R. Co., 32 S. C. 142, 10 S. E. 932.

[50] Where a widow of an employé of an interstate railroad company brought suit against such company in a state court of Florida
in her capacity as widow to recover for the death of her husband,
such action was necessarily based on the state statute, and an amendment of her declaration, changing the capacity in which she sued
to that of administratrix, introduced a new and different cause of
action based on the federal statute, and was, in effect, the bringing
of a new action thereunder, which was begun, for the purpose of
limitation, when the amendment was filed, and did not relate back
to the time of the commencement of the original action. Hall v.
Louisville & N. R. Co. (C. C.) 157 Fed. 464. Where a foreign
statute gave a right of action for death only to the consort and descendant and ascendant relations of deceased, and plaintiff, in an
action for death of her husband, sued as administratrix, an amendment making it appear that the action was brought by her individually and as guardian ad litem for her children, etc., was improper;
an action by one as administrator being in a capacity distinct from
one as an individual. Johnson v. Phœnix Bridge Co., 133 App. Div.
807, 118 N. Y. Supp. 88. Under a statute giving a right of action

So where the declaration is improperly based upon a common-law liability, and the amendment would state a cause of action under the death act.[51] But where the mistake

for death, to be brought within a year thereafter by decedent's personal representative, where a foreign administrator who had commenced an action thereafter qualified as a domestic administrator, and became a party to the action by amendment, but not until after a year from decedent's death, the action by him, as domestic administrator, was barred. Hall v. Southern Ry. Co., 149 N. C. 108, 62 S. E. 899. A declaration for a death in Pennsylvania, where the right of action is vested in the widow, and not in the personal representative, cannot be amended so as to make it appear that plaintiff is prosecuting the action as widow, and not as personal representative. Rankin v. Central R. Co. of New Jersey, 77 N. J. Law, 175, 71 Atl. 55. See, also, Lower v. Segal, 60 N. J. Law, 99, 36 Atl. 777. Where a widow sued in her own right for the death of her husband, which occurred in New Jersey, she could not amend so as to sue as executrix, as required by the New Jersey statute, after the limitation had expired. Le Bar v. New York & S. W. R. Co., 218 Pa. 261, 67 Atl. 413. But where an action for death occurring in Pennsylvania was erroneously brought in the name of the administrator, instead of by the widow, as provided by the Pennsylvania statute, an amendment substituting the name of decedent's widow was held not to constitute the commencement of a new cause of action, or work a discontinuance of the original suit. Leman v. Baltimore & O. R. Co. (C. C.) 128 Fed. 191. See, also, Van Doren v. Pennsylvania R. Co., 93 Fed. 260, 35 C. C. A. 282.

[51] Plaintiff brought an action in which he stated a common-law liability for loss of services of his daughter, but the averments were insufficient to constitute a statutory liability for her death. More than two years after the negligent injury, he obtained leave to amend his petition, so as to state a cause of action for death under the statute. Held, that the amendment constituted a new cause of action, which was barred by limitations. City of Kansas City v. Hart, 60 Kan. 684, 57 Pac. 938. See, also, Sawyer v. Perry, 88 Me. 42, 33 Atl. 660; All v. Barnwell County, 29 S. C. 161, 7 S. E. 58. In an action by a husband for the death of his wife, it is not permissible to amend the complaint so as to allow plaintiff to sue as administrator of his deceased wife's estate. Walker v. Lansing & S. Traction Co., 144 Mich. 685, 108 N. W. 90. A cause of action for death cannot be set up by amendment to an action brought by decedent himself for the injuries which ultimately resulted in such

arose, not in regard to the nature of the action, but merely in supposing that the administrator, and not the next of kin, was the party in whose name the action should be brought, it has been held that an amendment substituting the proper parties is allowable.[52]

§ 188.   Liability of personal representative for costs

Whether the liability of the personal representative for costs in case the action fails should be governed by the same rules as if he were suing as representative of the estate has been differently answered. Thus, in New Jersey, where the statute provided that, if the plaintiff prosecute a suit in the right of his intestate, no costs can be recovered against him, it was held that the same rule applied to an administrator suing for the death.[53] And in Indiana it was held

death.   Bolick v. Southern Ry. Co., 138 N. C. 370, 50 S. E. 689. Where an action has been improperly commenced by a father, as such, to recover damages for loss of services caused by the wrongful death of his son, an amendment substituting the personal representative as plaintiff, under the death act, will not be allowed, where the statutory period in which an action under the death act could be brought has expired.   Fitzhenry v. Consolidated Traction Co., 63 N. J. Law, 142, 42 Atl. 416.   But where the declaration in an action for negligence resulting in injury to plaintiff's minor son alleged a permanent disability, and a total loss of services, an amended declaration, setting up the death of the child as a result of the injury, and claiming damages for the loss of services resulting from the death, was allowed.   Bradford City v. Downs, 126 Pa. 622, 17 Atl. 884.

[52] Silva v. New England Brick Co., 185 Mass. 151, 69 N. E. 1054; Herlihy v. Little, 200 Mass. 284, 86 N. E. 294.   Where an action was erroneously commenced by intestate's widow and children, who were the only parties in interest, instead of by the personal representative, it was error not to allow an amendment of the complaint substituting the widow in her capacity as administratrix.   Pugmire v. Diamond Coal & Coke Co., 26 Utah, 115, 72 Pac. 385.

[53] Kinney v. Central R. Co., 34 N. J. Law, 273.

erroneous to direct that, if there be no property of the decedent, costs should be levied out of the property of the administrator personally.[54] But in Alabama, it was held that because he was suing as trustee of the beneficiaries, and not as representative of the estate, the judgment should be de bonis propriis, and not de bonis intestati, and that consequently the sureties on the administrator's bond were not liable for his failure to pay such judgment out of the assets of the estate.[55]

[54] Evans v. Newland, 34 Ind. 112.
[55] Hicks v. Barrett, 40 Ala. 291.

CHAPTER XII

EVIDENCE

§ 189. Character of evidence in actions for death

The questions of evidence that arise in actions for death are, for the most part, the same as those that arise in ordinary personal injury cases. Questions of evidence that are peculiar to such actions have been referred to in the preceding chapters. As in other actions, the burden of proof is upon the plaintiff to establish his case, including the fact that the death was caused by the wrongful act or neglect of the defendant, by a preponderance of evidence.[1] It is

---

[1] Weatherly v. Nashville, C. & St. L. Ry., 166 Ala. 575, 51 South. 959; St. Louis & S. F. Ry. Co. v. Townsend, 69 Ark. 380, 63 S. W. 994; Wood v. Philadelphia, B. & W. R. Co., 1 Boyce, 336, 76 Atl. 613; Southern Ry. Co. v. Webb, 116 Ga. 152, 42 S. E. 395, 59 L. R. A. 109; Hart v. St. Louis & S. F. R. Co., 80 Kan. 699, 102 Pac. 1101; Warner v. St. Louis & M. R. R. Co., 178 Mo. 125, 77 S. W. 67; Piper v. Boston & M. R. R., 75 N. H. 228, 75 Atl. 1041; Suburban Electric Co. v. Nugent, 58 N. J. Law, 658, 34 Atl. 1069, 32 L. R. A. 700; Potter v. New York Cent. & H. R. R. Co. (Super. N. Y.) 19 N. Y. Supp. 862; Morhard v. Richmond Light & R. Co., 111 App. Div. 353, 98 N. Y. Supp. 124; Hanley v. West Virginia Cent. & P. Ry. Co., 59 W. Va. 419, 53 S. E. 625; Rutherford v. Foster, 125 Fed. 187, 60 C. C. A. 129; Northern Pac. Ry. Co. v. King, 181 Fed. 913, 104 C. C. A. 351. Where the injury was occasioned by one of two causes, for one of which defendant is responsible, and for the other not, plaintiff must fail if his

to be observed, however, that, by reason of the death of the person injured, it is often impossible to prove the facts and circumstances immediately surrounding the injury, and especially the absence of contributory negligence of the deceased, with the same precision and fullness that would be required in an action in which the person injured was alive and able to testify. For this reason, courts incline to greater liberality in this class of cases in allowing the questions of the negligence of the defendant, and of the contributory negligence of the plaintiff, to go to the jury, upon slight evidence; [2] although, if there is no evidence reason-

evidence does not show it was produced by the former, or if it is just as probable it was caused by one as by the other. Chester v. Cape May Real Estate Co., 78 N. J. Law, 131, 73 Atl. 836, 138 Am. St. Rep. 614. See, also, Kelly v. Union Pac. R. Co., 141 Mo. App. 490, 125 S. W. 818. The rule that the jury cannot be permitted to determine by conjecture between two equally probable causes of an injury, for one only of which defendant is liable, has no application, unless the existence of a sufficient cause for the injury, aside from the negligence charged, is conceded or conclusively proved. Boucher v. Larochelle, 74 N. H. 433, 68 Atl. 870, 15 L. R. A. (N. S.) 416.

[2] Central R. R. v. Rouse, 77 Ga. 393, 3 S. E. 307; Chicago, B. & Q. R. Co. v. Gregory, 58 Ill. 272; Missouri Furnace Co. v. Abend, 107 Ill. 44, 47 Am. Rep. 425; Chicago, R. I. & P. Ry. Co. v. Clark, 108 Ill. 113; Chicago & A. Ry. Co. v. Carey, 115 Ill. 115, 3 N. E. 519; McDermott v. Iowa Falls & S. C. Ry. Co. (Iowa) 47 N. W. 1037; Louisville & N. R. Co. v. Brooks' Adm'x, 83 Ky. 129, 4 Am. St. Rep. 135; Northern Cent. Ry. Co. v. State, to use of Price, 29 Md. 420, 96 Am. Dec. 545; Maguire v. Fitchburg R. Co., 146 Mass. 379, 15 N. E. 904; Kelly v. Hannibal & St. J. R. Co., 70 Mo. 604; Buesching v. St. Louis Gaslight Co., 73 Mo. 219, 39 Am. Rep. 503; Soeder v. St. Louis, I. M. & S. Ry. Co., 100 Mo. 673, 13 S. W. 714, 18 Am. St. Rep. 724; Galvin v. Mayor, etc., of New York, 112 N. Y. 223, 19 N. E. 675; Jones v. New York Cent. & H. R. R. Co., 62 How. Prac. (N. Y.) 450; Flanagan v. New York, N. H. & H. R. Co., 55 Hun, 611, 8 N. Y. Supp. 744; Atkinson v. Abraham, 45 Hun (N. Y.) 238; Phillips v. Milwaukee & N. R. Co., 77 Wis. 349, 46 N. W. 543, 9 L. R. A. 521; Schafer v. City of New York, 154 N. Y.

ably tending to show that the death was due to the defendant's wrongful act or negligence, a verdict for the defendant should be directed.[3]   Where there were no eyewitnesses, the negligence of the defendant and the freedom from negligence of the decedent may be proved by showing circumstances from which their existence may reasonably be inferred.[4]   Some courts, indeed, hold that where there were no eyewitnesses the decedent is presumed, prima facie, to have been in the exercise of due care;[5] some courts,

466, 48 N. E. 749; Harrison v. New York Cent. & H. R. R. Co., 195 N. Y. 86, 87 N. E. 802; Braun v. Buffalo General Electric Co., 200 N. Y. 484, 94 N. E. 206, 35 L. R. A. (N. S.) 1089, 140 Am. St. Rep. 645, 21 Ann. Cas. 370; Carpenter v. Town of Rolling, 107 Wis. 559, 83 N. W. 953. See Sweeney v. New York Steam Co., 15 Daly, 312, 6 N. Y. Supp. 528, per Larremore, C. J., and Mulligan v. New York Cent. & H. R. R. Co., 58 Hun, 602, 11 N. Y. Supp. 452, per Dwight, P. J.

[3] See Newell v. Rahn, 64 Ill. App. 249; Pearson v. Wilcox, 109 Iowa, 123, 80 N. W. 228; Cochran's Adm'r v. Krause, 144 Ky. 202, 137 S. W. 1053; United Electric Light & Power Co. v. State, to use of Lusby, 100 Md. 634, 60 Atl. 248; Powers v. Pere Marquette R. Co., 143 Mich. 379, 106 N. W. 1117; Southern Ry. Co. in Mississippi v. Miller (Miss.) 30 South. 68; Lee v. Reliance Mills Co., 21 R. I. 549, 45 Atl. 554; Mt. Marion Coal Min. Co. v. Holt, 54 Tex. Civ. App. 411, 118 S. W. 825; Armstrong v. Cosmopolis, 32 Wash. 110, 75 Pac. 1038.

[4] Hotchkiss Mt. Mining & Reduction Co. v. Bruner, 42 Colo. 305, 94 Pac. 331; Illinois Cent. R. Co. v. Cozby, 174 Ill. 109, 50 N. E. 1011; United States Brewing Co. v. Stoltenberg, 211 Ill. 531, 71 N. E. 1081; Prince v. Lowell Electric Light Corp., 201 Mass. 276, 87 N. E. 558; Yongue v. St. Louis & S. F. R. Co., 133 Mo. App. 141, 112 S. W. 985; Voelker v. Hill-O'Meara Const. Co., 153 Mo. App. 1, 131 S. W. 907; Fejdowski v. President, etc., of Delaware & H. Canal Co., 12 App. Div. 589, 43 N. Y. Supp. 84; Boyle v. Degnon-McLean Const. Co., 47 App. Div. 311, 61 N. Y. Supp. 1043; Waters-Pierce Oil Co. v. Deselms, 18 Okl. 107, 89 Pac. 212.

[5] Cameron v. Great Northern Ry. Co., 8 N. D. 124, 77 N. W. 1016; Kunkel v. Minneapolis, St. P. & S. S. M. Ry. Co., 18 N. D. 367, 121 N. W. 830; Whaley v. Vidal (S. D.) 132 N. W. 242; Baker v. Philadelphia & R. Ry. Co. (C. C.) 149 Fed. 882.

that where there were no eyewitnesses, and the negligence
of the defendant is shown, it will be presumed, in the absence of evidence to the contrary, that the decedent used due
care; [6] some courts, that where there is no direct evidence
as to the surrounding circumstances it is to be presumed,
prima facie, that the decedent, prompted by the instinct
of self-preservation, exercises due care, although if there
is such direct evidence, the presumption does not obtain; [7]
some courts, that if there were no eyewitnesses the plaintiff may establish the exercise of due care on the part of
the decedent by the highest proof of which the case is capable, including the habits of the decedent, and that in determining the question the jury may take into consideration
the instinct of self-preservation, although the right to take
into consideration the instinct of self-preservation is limited to cases where there were no eyewitnesses; [8] and oth-

[6] Adams v. Iron Cliffs Co., 78 Mich. 271, 44 N. W. 270, 18 Am. St.
Rep. 441; Gilbert v. Ann Arbor R. Co., 161 Mich. 73, 125 N. W. 745.
Plaintiff is not relieved from the burden of proving the negligence of
defendant, and that the death was caused by his negligence, merely
because it is presumed that decedent exercised due care. Powers v.
Pere Marquette R. Co., 143 Mich. 379, 106 N. W. 1117.

[7] Dalton v. Chicago, R. I. & P. Ry. Co., 104 Iowa, 26, 73 N. W.
349; Ames v. Waterloo & C. F. Rapid Transit Co., 120 Iowa, 640, 95
N. W. 161; Brown v. West Riverside Coal Co., 143 Iowa, 662, 120 N.
W. 732, 28 L. R. A. (N. S.) 1260. The presumption is of fact, and
it becomes a question for the jury whether that presumption has been
overcome by other proof in the case. Gray v. Chicago, R. I. & P. R.
Co., 143 Iowa, 268, 121 N. W. 1097. See, also, Korab v. Chicago, R.
I. & P. Ry. Co., 149 Iowa, 711, 128 N. W. 529; Wilson v. Illinois
Cent. R. Co., 150 Iowa, 33, 129 N. W. 340, 34 L. R. A. (N. S.) 687;
Rich v. Chicago, M. & St. P. Ry. Co., 149 Fed. 79, 78 C. C. A. 663;
Cogdell v. Wilmington & W. R. Co., 132 N. C. 852, 44 S. E. 618.

[8] Chicago & A. R. Co. v. Wilson, 225 Ill. 50, 80 N. E. 56, 116 Am.
St. Rep. 102; Collison v. Illinois Cent. R. Co., 239 Ill. 532, 88 N. E.
251; Stollery v. Cicero & P. St. Ry. Co., 243 Ill. 290, 90 N. E. 709;
Illinois Cent. R. Co. v. Kief, 111 Ill. App. 354; Casper v. Illinois
Cent. R. Co., 149 Ill. App. 588; Cook v. Chicago, R. I. & P. Ry. Co.,

er courts, that while if there were no eyewitnesses less evidence to prove the decedent's freedom from negligence is
required, there must be some evidence tending to prove
freedom from contributory negligence, the burden being
upon the plaintiff to introduce some evidence upon the
point.[9] A discussion of the cases cited under this paragraph, involving, as it would, a consideration of the varying rules that prevail in different jurisdictions in respect to
the burden of proof as to contributory negligence, and in
respect to kindred questions of negligence, is beyond the
scope of this book.

§ 190.   Defendant as witness

Notwithstanding the general abrogation of the common-
law rule disqualifying parties and persons interested from
testifying, the statutes in force in most of the states provide that, in actions by or against executors or administrators, neither party shall be allowed to testify against the
other, this exclusion being commonly confined, however, to
the testimony of such persons as to transactions with or
statements by the testator or intestate. Whether these
statutes exclude the parties to an action for death must,
of course, depend much upon the terms of the particular
statute. But where the action is brought, not in the name

153 Ill. App. 596. The jury may infer due care from evidence that
the deceased was sober, industrious, careful, and of good habits.
Dallemand v. Saalfeldt, 175 Ill. 310, 51 N. E. 645, 48 L. R. A. 753,
67 Am. St. Rep. 214.

[9] Kauffman v. Cleveland, C., C: & St. L. R. Co., 144 Ind. 456, 43
N. E. 446; Jones v. Ryan, 125 App. Div. 282, 109 N. Y. Supp. 156;
Gallagher v. New York City Ry. Co., 124 App. Div. 868, 109 N. Y.
Supp. 515; Nichols v. Searle Mfg. Co., 134 App. Div. 62, 118 N. Y.
Supp. 651; Zaun v. Long Island R. Co., 139 App. Div. 719, 124 N. Y.
Supp. 511, affirmed, 201 N. Y. 599, 95 N. E. 1142.

of the personal representative, but directly in the name of the beneficiary, such statutes have been held not to exclude the defendant.[10] And in Missouri, where the statute provided that, in actions where one of the original parties to the contract or cause of action is dead, the other party shall not be allowed to testify in his own favor, it was held, in an action by a widow, that the defendant was a competent witness, since the plaintiff was not suing on a contract or cause of action to which the deceased was a party.[11] On the other hand, where the action is brought in the name of the executor or administrator, it has been held in Illinois[12] and Indiana[18] that the defendant is incompetent—in the former state under a statute excluding parties and persons interested from testifying in suits by executors and administrators; and in the latter state under a statute providing that in suits in which an executor or administrator is a party, involving matters which occurred during the lifetime of the decedent, where a judgment may be rendered for or against the estate, any person who is a necessary party to the issue or record, whose interest is adverse to such estate, shall not be a competent witness as to such matters against the estate. In Tennessee, on the contrary, although the statute made evidence as to transactions with or statements by the decedent incompetent in all cases in which judgment might be rendered for or against the administrator, it was held in an action by the widow, in the name of the administrator,

10 Mann v. Weland, *81 Pa. 243; Wallace v. Stevens, 74 Tex. 559, 12 S. W. 283; McEwen v. Springfield, 64 Ga. 159.

11 Entwhistle v. Feighner, 60 Mo. 214.

12 Forbes v. Snyder, 94 Ill. 374. The president, who is also a stockholder, of a defendant corporation is incompetent. Consolidated Ice Mach. Co. v. Keifer, 134 Ill. 481, 25 N. E. 799, 10 L. R. A. 696, 23 Am. St. Rep. 688.

18 Hudson v. Houser, 123 Ind. 309, 24 N. E. 243; Sherlock v. Alling, 44 Ind. 184.

who refused to act, for the benefit of herself and an infant child, that the defendant might testify; the court observing that the administrator was only a nominal party, and had no interest in the suit, no judgment being capable of affecting the estate.[14]

§ 191. Beneficiary as witness

Where the beneficiary sues in his own name, the same rule would, of course, apply to his competency as a witness as to that of the defendant.[15] Whether, in an action by the administrator, the beneficiary would be competent to testify under a statute excluding parties in such case, does not appear to have been expressly decided, although in an Indiana case it was intimated that he would not be deemed a party, and would be competent.[16] And in New York, under a provision that the exemption should not apply to a party to the action, nor to any person for whose immediate benefit the action is prosecuted or defended, it was held that the beneficiary was not incompetent, the rule only applying to a person into whose hands the money would go immediately when collected, and hence not to a case where it would go first into the hands of the administrator.[17] But in Wisconsin, where the only statutory exception to the common-law rule—that the husband and wife may not be witnesses for or against each other—was a provision that

[14] Hale v. Kearly, 8 Baxt. (Tenn.) 50.

[15] A husband, who is coplaintiff with his wife in an action for the death of their son, is competent. Bell v. Hannibal & St. J. Ry. Co., 86 Mo. 599; Reilly v. Hannibal & St. J. R. Co., 94 Mo. 600, 7 S. W. 407. See, also, Owen v. Brockschmidt, 54 Mo. 285.

[16] Louisville, N. A. & C. Ry. Co. v. Thompson, 107 Ind. 442, 8 N. E. 18, 9 N. E. 357, 57 Am. Rep. 120. See Yates v. Huntsville Hoop & Heading Co. (Ala.) 39 South. 647.

[17] Quin v. Moore, 15 N. Y. 432.

a party to a civil action or proceeding may be examined as a witness, it was held, in an action by the husband as administrator, for the benefit of himself and wife, on account of the death of a son, that the wife, being a real party in interest, was a competent witness.[18]

§ 192. Testimony of deceased witness

It has been held that, in an action under the statute, it is admissible to prove the testimony of a deceased witness in a suit by the intestate for the personal injury which abated on his death, upon the ground that the causes of action were the same, and that the admissibility of such evidence turns rather upon the right to cross-examine than upon the precise nominal identity of the parties.[19] But the testimony of a deceased witness at a coroner's inquest, where the plaintiff had no opportunity to cross-examine, is inadmissible, as well upon that ground [20] as upon the ground that the inquest is not a judicial proceeding.[21]

[18] Strong v. City of Stevens Point, 62 Wis. 255, 22 N. W. 425. In suit by a widow as administratrix, declarations of plaintiff during her husband's lifetime as to the circumstances of the accident are admissible to contradict her testimony, but not for the purpose of proving negligence of the deceased, plaintiff not having been the party interested adversely to defendant at the time of such declarations. Fitzgerald v. Town of Weston, 52 Wis. 354, 9 N. W. 13.

[19] Indianapolis & St. L. R. Co. v. Stout, 53 Ind. 143. See Greenl. Ev. § 164. Where deceased began suit for the injury, and afterwards an action was brought for the death, under a statute which provided that the testimony taken in one action might be used in another if the parties and issues were substantially the same, it was held that answers by deceased to interrogatories taken in the suit by him were admissible. Atlanta & W. P. R. Co. v. Venable, 67 Ga. 697.

[20] Jackson v. Crilly, 16 Colo. 103, 26 Pac. 331.

[21] Cook v. New York Cent. R. Co., 5 Lans. (N. Y.) 401. See Erwin v. Neversink Steamboat Co., 88 N. Y. 184.

§ 193. Verdict of acquittal—Coroner's verdict

A verdict of not guilty upon an indictment for the homicide is inadmissible.[22] A fortiori the verdict of a coroner's jury, the inquest not being a judicial proceeding, is inadmissible in favor of either party.[23]

§ 194. Declarations and admissions of the deceased

The declarations of the deceased, although made under such circumstances as would, upon an indictment for homicide, render them admissible as dying declarations, are inadmissible on that ground.[24] Whether the declarations of the deceased are admissible in favor of the plaintiff will depend upon whether they were made under such circum-

[22] March v. Walker, 48 Tex. 372; Cottingham v. Weeks, 54 Ga. 275; Gray v. McDonald, 104 Mo. 303, 16 S. W. 398. In an action against a railroad company for the death of an engineer, caused by a misplaced switch, it is not competent for the company to put in evidence the conviction of a trespasser under an indictment for the murder of the engineer by tampering with the switch, nor can the company prove confessions made by the accused. Miller v. Southern Pac. R. Co., 20 Or. 285, 26 Pac. 70; Guthrie v. Same (Or.) 26 Pac. 76.

[23] State, to Use of Grice, v. Cecil County Com'rs, 54 Md. 426; Memphis & C. R. Co. v. Womack, 84 Ala. 149, 4 South. 618; Central R. Co. v. Moore, 61 Ga. 151; Rowe v. Such, 134 Cal. 573, 66 Pac. 862, 67 Pac. 760; Sullivan v. Seattle Electric Co., 51 Wash. 71, 97 Pac. 1109, 130 Am. St. Rep. 1082. Contra: Stollery v. Cicero & P. St. Ry. Co., 148 Ill. App. 499; Id., 243 Ill. 290, 90 N. E. 709. Cf. Callaway v. Spurgeon, 63 Ill. App. 571; O'Donnell v. Chicago & A. Ry. Co., 127 Ill. App. 432.

[24] East Tennessee, V. & G. R. Co. v. Maloy, 77 Ga. 237, 2 S. E. 941; Louisville & N. R. Co. v. Stacker, 86 Tenn. 343, 6 S. W. 737, 6 Am. St. Rep. 840; Friedman v. Railroad Co., 7 Phila. (Pa.) 203; Chicago & N. W. Ry. Co. v. Howard, 6 Ill. App. 569; Bionto v. Illinois Cent. R. Co., 125 La. 147, 51 South. 98, 27 L. R. A. (N. S.) 1030.

stances as to form part of the res gestæ.[25] It would seem that such declarations, if not admissible as part of the res gestæ, are not admissible in favor of the defendant as admissions, since the plaintiff in such case does not claim in the right of the deceased, but upon a new cause of action; but the point has been decided both in the affirmative [26] and in the negative.[27]

[25] Brownell v. Pacific R. Co., 47 Mo. 240; Entwhistle v. Feighner, 60 Mo. 214; Stoeckman v. Terre Haute & I. R. Co., 15 Mo. App. 503; Galveston, City of, v. Barbour, 62 Tex. 172, 50 Am. Rep. 519; McKeigue v. City of Janesville, 68 Wis. 50, 31 N. W. 298; Merkle v. Bennington Tp., 58 Mich. 156, 24 N. W. 776, 55 Am. Rep. 666; Chicago & N. W. Ry. Co. v. Howard, 6 Ill. App. 569; Waldele v. New York Cent. & H. R. R. Co., 95 N. Y. 274, 47 Am. Rep. 41; Richmond & D. R. Co. v. Hammond, 93 Ala. 181, 9 South. 577; Little Rock, M. R. & T. Ry. Co. v. Leverett, 48 Ark. 333, 3 S. W. 50, 3 Am. St. Rep. 245; Fordyce v. McCants, 51 Ark. 509, 11 S. W. 694, 4 L. R. A. 296, 14 Am. St. Rep. 69; Poole v. East Tennessee, V. & G. Ry. Co., 92 Ga. 337, 17 S. E. 267; Armil v. Chicago, B. & Q. R. Co., 70 Iowa, 130, 30 N. W. 42; Fish v. Illinois Cent. R. Co., 96 Iowa, 702, 65 N. W. 995; Texas & P. Ry. Co. v. Hall, 83 Tex. 675, 19 S. W. 121.

[26] Perigo v. Chicago, R. I. & P. R. Co., 55 Iowa, 326, 7 N. W. 621; Lord v. Pueblo Smelting & Refining Co., 12 Colo. 390, 21 Pac. 148; Lax v. Forty-Second St. & Grand St. F. R. Co., 46 N. Y. Super. Ct. 448 (semble).

[27] City of Bradford v. Downs, 126 Pa. 622, 17 Atl. 884; Pennsylvania Co. v. Long, 94 Ind. 250; Louisville, E. & St. L. C. R. Co. v. Berry, 2 Ind. App. 427, 28 N. E. 714; Id., 9 Ind. App. 63, 35 N. E. 565, 36 N. E. 646. In Stein v. Railway Co., 10 Phila. (Pa.) 440, such an admission was said to be admissible, but it was also held that the declaration was part of the res gestæ. In an action by a widow for injuries received by her husband at a railroad crossing, and which resulted in his death, the exclusion of declarations made by deceased after the accident, though not part of the res gestæ, on the ground that they were not made by a party to the suit, was error, since plaintiff derived her cause of action from decedent. Hughes v. President, etc., of Delaware & H. Canal Co., 176 Pa. 254, 35 Atl. 190. Evidence of previous threats of the deceased communicated to the defendants before the murder are inadmissible, where there is no evidence to show that the killing was done in self-defense. Forbes v. Snyder, 94 Ill. 374.

CHAPTER XIII

JURISDICTION OF STATE COURTS—CONFLICT OF LAWS

§ 195.   Statute has no extraterritorial force

It is a general rule that for the purpose of redress it is immaterial where a tort was committed; in other words, the wrong being personal, the action is transitory, and may be brought wherever the wrongdoer may be found. But to support an action the act must have been wrongful where it was committed.

Where the wrong complained of was one for which an action is given by the common law, it will be presumed, in the absence of proof to the contrary, that the common law was in force in the place where the wrong was committed. But, where the wrong is one for which the right of action is purely statutory, no presumption arises that such statute is in force outside the state which enacted it. Since the right of action for death is statutory, it follows that, if the wrongful act or neglect by which the death was caused occurred outside of the state which enacted the statute, no action can

(436)

be maintained by virtue of it.[1]   No doubt it would be within the competency of the legislature of a state to declare that any wrong which might be committed against its citizens abroad might be redressed at home, according to the principles of its law, if the wrongdoer could be found there, so as to subject him to the jurisdiction of its courts;[2] but such a construction has never been placed upon any of the acts in question.

Thus, where the death was caused in New Grenada, it was held that no action was maintainable in New York, although the defendant was a corporation of that state.[3]   So, also, it has been held where the death occurred on the high seas,[4] and in a state where no right of action existed.[5]   And, if the action is based upon the foreign law, it cannot be maintained if that law is not alleged and proved.[6]

---

[1] Louisville & N. R. Co. v. Williams, 113 Ala. 402, 21 South. 938; Runt v. Illinois Cent. R. Co., 88 Miss. 575, 41 South. 1; Vaughn v. Bunker Hill & Sullivan Mining & Concentrating Co. (C. C.) 126 Fed. 895.

[2] Whitford v. Panama R. Co., 23 N. Y. 465, per Denio, J.

[3] Whitford v. Panama R. Co., 23 N. Y. 465 (affirming 3 Bosw. 67); Crowley v. Panama R. Co., 30 Barb. (N. Y.) 99.

[4] Armstrong v. Beadle, 5 Sawy. 484, Fed. Cas. No. 541.

[5] Needham v. Grand Trunk R. Co., 38 Vt. 294; Campbell v. Rogers, 2 Handy (Ohio) 110; Willis v. Missouri Pac. Ry. Co., 61 Tex. 432, 48 Am. Rep. 301; Hover v. Pennsylvania Co., 25 Ohio St. 667; Davis v. New York & N. E. R. Co., 143 Mass. 301, 9 N. E. 815, 58 Am. Rep. 138.

[6] Vanderwerken v. New York & N. H. R. Co., 6 Abb. Prac. (N. Y.) 239; Beach v. Bay State S. Co., 30 Barb. (N. Y.) 433, 10 Abb. Prac. 71 (reversing 6 Abb. Prac. 415, 16 How. Prac. 1, 27 Barb. 248); Debevoise v. New York, L. E. & W. R. Co., 98 N. Y. 377, 50 Am. Rep. 683; Kahl v. Memphis & C. R. Co., 95 Ala. 337, 10 South. 661; Selma, R. & D. R. Co. v. Lacy, 43 Ga. 461; Chicago & W. I. R. Co. v. Schroeder, 18 Ill. App. 328; Hyde v. St. L. & P. Ry. Co., 61 Iowa, 441, 16 N. W. 351, 47 Am. Rep. 820; State, to Use of Allen, v. Pittsburgh & C. R. Co., 45 Md. 41; Nashville & C. R. Co. v. Eakin, 6 Cold. (Tenn.) 582; Jackson v. Pittsburgh, C. C. & St. L. Ry. Co., 140 Ind.

§ 196. Action based on foreign statute—Jurisdiction sustained

But, although these statutes have no extraterritorial force, it is held by the greater weight of authority that, if a right of action is given by a statute of the state in which occurred the wrongful act or neglect by which the death was caused, the remedy may be enforced in any tribunal having jurisdiction of the defendant, provided, at least, according to the generally prevailing statement of the rule, that such statute is not in substance inconsistent with the statutes or public policy of the state of the tribunal.[7] A leading case on

241, 39 N. E. 663, 49 Am. St. Rep. 192; Wabash R. Co. v. Hassett, 170 Ind. 370, 83 N. E. 705; Murray's Adm'x v. Louisville & N. R. Co., 132 Ky. 336, 110 S. W. 334, 33 Ky. Law Rep. 545; Stewart v. Great Northern R. Co., 103 Minn. 156, 114 N. W. 953, 123 Am. St. Rep. 318; Lee v. Missouri Pac. Ry. Co., 195 Mo. 400, 92 S. W. 614; Geoghegan v. Atlas S. S. Co., 3 Misc. Rep. 224, 22 N. Y. Supp. 749; Rankin v. Central R. Co. of New Jersey, 77 N. J. Law, 175, 71 Atl. 55. Cf. Lemon's Adm'r v. Louisville & N. R. Co., 137 Ky. 276, 125 S. W. 701.

[7] Dennick v. Central R. Co. of New Jersey, 103 U. S. 11, 26 L. Ed. 439; Texas & P. Ry. Co. v. Cox, 145 U. S. 593, 12 Sup. Ct. 905, 36 L. Ed. 829; South Carolina R. Co. v. Nix, 68 Ga. 572; Central R. Co. v. Swint, 73 Ga. 651; Shedd v. Moran, 10 Ill. App. 618; Burns v. Grand Rapids & I. R. Co., 113 Ind. 169, 15 N. E. 230; Cincinnati, H. & D. R. Co. v. McMullen, 117 Ind. 439, 20 N. E. 287, 10 Am. St. Rep. 67; Morris v. Chicago, R. I. & P. R. Co., 65 Iowa, 727, 23 N. W. 143, 54 Am. Rep. 39 (see, also, Boyce v. Wabash Ry. Co., 63 Iowa, 70, 18 N. W. 673, 50 Am. Rep. 730); Bruce's Adm'r v. Cincinnati R. Co., 83 Ky. 174 (overruling Taylor's Adm'r v. Pennsylvania Co., 78 Ky. 348, 39 Am. Rep. 244); Louisville & N. R. Co. v. Shivell's Adm'x, 18 S. W. 944, 13 Ky. Law Rep. 902; Wintuska's Adm'r v. Louisville & N. R. Co., 20 S. W. 819, 14 Ky. Law Rep. 579; Chicago, St. L. & N. O. R. Co. v. Doyle, 60 Miss. 977; Illinois Cent. R. Co. v. Crudup, 63 Miss. 291; Missouri Pac. Ry. Co. v. Lewis, 24 Neb. 848, 40 N. W. 401, 2 L. R. A. 67; Leonard v. Columbia Steam Nav. Co., 84 N. Y. 48, 38 Am. Rep. 491; Wooden v. Western N. Y. & P. R. Co., 126 N. Y.

this subject is Dennick v. Central R. Co. of New Jersey,⁸ decided in the supreme court of the United States in 1880. The plaintiff, as administratrix appointed in New York, brought suit in that state to recover damages for the death of her husband in New Jersey. The defendant removed the case into the circuit court of the United States, on the ground of citizenship, and judgment was rendered for the defendant, on the ground that the liability of the defendant under the New Jersey statute could be enforced by no one but a personal representative of the deceased, appointed by

10, 26 N. E. 1050, 13 L. R. A. 458, 22 Am. St. Rep. 803 (affirming 12 N. Y. Supp. 908); Stallknecht v. Pennsylvania R. Co., 13 Hun (N. Y.) 451 (affirming 53 How. Prac. 305); Gurney v. Grand Trunk Ry. Co., 59 Hun, 625, 13 N. Y. Supp. 645; Lustig v. New York, L. E. & W. R. Co., 65 Hun, 547, 20 N. Y. Supp. 477; Knight v. West Jersey R. Co., 108 Pa. 250, 56 Am. Rep. 200 (see, also, Patton v. Pittsburgh, C. & St. L. Ry. Co., 96 Pa. 169); Nashville & C. R. Co. v. Sprayberry, 9 Heisk. (Tenn.) 852; Mississippi & T. R. Co. v. Ayres, 16 Lea (Tenn.) 725; Nelson v. Chesapeake & O. Ry. Co., 88 Va. 971, 14 S. E. 838, 15 L. R. A. 583. See, also, Northern Pac. R. Co. v. Babcock, 154 U. S. 190, 14 Sup. Ct. 978, 38 L. Ed. 958; Stewart v. Baltimore & O. R. Co., 168 U. S. 445, 18 Sup. Ct. 105, 42 L. Ed. 537; McCarty v. New York, L. E. & W. R. Co. (C. C.) 62 Fed. 437; Theroux v. Northern Pac. R. Co., 64 Fed. 84, 12 C. C. A. 52; Boston & M. R. Co. v. McDuffey, 79 Fed. 934, 25 C. C. A. 247; Davidow v. Pennsylvania R. Co. (C. C.) 85 Fed. 943; Law v. Western Ry. of Alabama (C. C.) 91 Fed. 817; Van Doren v. Pennsylvania R. Co., 93 Fed. 260, 35 C. C. A. 282; Erickson v. Pacific Coast S. S. Co. (C. C.) 96 Fed. 80; Smith v. Empire State-Idaho Mining & Development Co. (C. C.) 127 Fed. 462; Leman v. Baltimore & O. R. Co. (C. C.) 128 Fed. 191; Southern Pac. Co. v. De Valle Da Costa, 190 Fed. 689, 111 C. C. A. 417; St. Louis, I. M. & S. Ry. Co. v. Haist, 71 Ark. 258, 72 S. W. 893, 100 Am. St. Rep. 65; Nicholas v. Burlington, C. R. & N. Ry. Co., 78 Minn. 43, 80 N. W. 776; Harrill v. South Carolina & G. E. R. Co. of North Carolina, 132 N. C. 655, 44 S. E. 109; Utah Savings & Trust Co. v. Diamond Coal & Coke Co., 26 Utah, 299, 73 Pac. 524; In re Lowham's Estate, 30 Utah, 436, 85 Pac. 445; McLeod v. Connecticut & P. R. R. Co., 58 Vt. 727, 6 Atl. 648.

⁸ 103 U. S. 11, 26 L. Ed. 439.

the authority of that state. This judgment was reversed in the supreme court, upon the broad ground that wherever, either by the common law or by the statute law of a state, a right of action has become fixed, and a legal liability incurred, that liability may be enforced or the right of action pursued in any court which has jurisdiction of such matters, and can obtain jurisdiction of the parties. Mr. Justice Miller, who delivered the opinion, says: "The action in the present case is in the nature of trespass to the person, always held to be transitory, and the venue immaterial. * * * We do not see how the fact that it was a statutory right can vary the principle. A party legally liable in New Jersey cannot escape that liability by going to New York. * * * It would be a very dangerous doctrine to establish that, in all cases where the several states have substituted the statute for the common law, the liability can be enforced in no other state but that where the statute was enacted and the transaction occurred." The court also considers the objection that the right of action was limited to the personal representative appointed in New Jersey, and amenable to its jurisdiction, and holds that the statute could not be construed as confining the right of action to a personal representative so appointed; distinguishing the case from that of an administrator appointed in one state, suing in that character in the courts of another state, without authority from the latter. As to the objection that the administrator is not responsible to the courts of New Jersey, the opinion says: "But the courts of New York are as capable of enforcing the rights of the widow and next of kin as the courts of New Jersey, and, as the court which renders the judgment for damages in favor of the administratrix can only do so by virtue of the New Jersey statute, so any court having control of her can compel distribution

(440)

of the amount received in the manner prescribed by that statute." Again, as to the objection that, by virtue of her appointment in New York, the administratrix could only act upon or administer that which was the estate of the deceased in his lifetime, the opinion says: "No reason is perceived why the specific direction of the law on this subject may not invest the administrator with the right to receive or recover by suit, and impose on him the duty of distributing under that law."

It is to be observed that the gist of the action is the wrongful act, neglect, or default, although death must result therefrom to give rise to a right of action, and an action is maintainable under the statute of another state, if the wrongful act, neglect, or default occurred there, whether the death also occurred there or occurred without the state.[9]

---

[9] Louisville & N. R. Co. v. Williams, 113 Ala. 402, 21 South. 402; Van Doren v. Pennsylvania R. Co., 93 Fed. 260, 35 C. C. A. 282. See, also, Slater v. Mexican Nat. R. Co., 194 U. S. 120, 24 Sup. Ct. 581, 48 L. Ed. 900. Contra: Hoodmacher v. Lehigh Val. R. Co., 218 Pa. 21, 66 Atl. 975 (holding that, though the act or neglect occurred in another state, if the death occurred in Pennsylvania, a recovery may be had under the Pennsylvania statute). And see Ryley v. Philadelphia & R. R. Co. (D. C.) 173 Fed. 839. The Illinois statute provides that on death by wrongful act the person or corporation which would have been liable for the injury, if death had not ensued, shall be liable notwithstanding the death of the person injured. By Laws 1903, p. 217, a proviso was added, declaring that no action should be brought or prosecuted in Illinois to recover damages for a death occurring outside the state. *Held*, that the proviso should be construed to prohibit actions in Illinois only where the act by which the death was caused occurred in another state, and did not prohibit an action where the wrongful act was committed in Illinois, because such act resulted in the decedent's death in Indiana. Crane v. Chicago & W. I. R. Co., 233 Ill. 259, 84 N. E. 222. An action for death by wrongful act, under the Wisconsin statute, if brought for a death caused in the state, will lie whenever the wrongful act, negligence, or default causing death occurred in the state, irrespective of the

§, 197. Whether a similar statute must exist in the state of the tribunal

In Dennick v. Central R. Co. of New Jersey the opinion notices the fact that a statute like that of New Jersey existed in New York, but it is not there said to be essential to the maintenance of the action that a similar statute should exist in the state of the tribunal. In Nashville & C. R. Co. v. Sprayberry,[10] decided in Tennessee in 1872, no such limitation was suggested. In Leonard v. Columbia Steam Nav. Co.,[11] however, decided in New York about the same time as Dennick v. Central R. Co. of New Jersey and cited in the opinion, it is laid down that this is essential. In that case Miller, J., refers to the fact that in McDonald v. Mallory[12] such a rule had been laid down, although the point was not there involved; and he says that the rule is just and reasonable. "It is not essential," he observes, "that the statute should be precisely the same, * * * but merely requires that it should be of a similar import and character." The case held that the statute of Connecticut was sufficiently similar to that of New York. And in Wooden v. Western N. Y. & P. R. Co.[13] the rule was ap-

place of death. Rudiger'v. Chicago, St. P., M. & O. Ry. Co., 94 Wis. 191, 68 N. W. 661.

[10] 9 Heisk. 852. Courts of Tennessee will not decline to entertain an action for death based on the Alabama statute, because of dissimilarity between its provisions as to damages and those of Tennessee on the same subject. Whitlow v. Nashville, C. & St. L. R. Co., 114 Tenn. 344, 84 S. W. 618, 68 L. R. A. 503.

[11] 84 N. Y. 48, 38 Am. Rep. 491.

[12] 77 N. Y. 546, 33 Am. Rep. 664.

[13] 126 N. Y. 10, 26 N. E. 1050, 13 L. R. A. 458, 22 Am. St. Rep. 803. See, also, Boyle v. Southern Ry. Co., 36 Misc. Rep. 289. 73 N. Y. Supp. 465; Strauss v. New York, N. H. & H. R. Co., 91 App. Div. 583, 87 N. Y. Supp. 67; Howlan v. New York & N. J. Telephone Co.,

(442)

proved, and it was held that the Pennsylvania statute was sufficiently similar, notwithstanding that by it the action could, upon the facts, be maintained only by the widow, instead of by the personal representative, as required by the New York statute; and that the amount of recovery by the former statute was unlimited, and by the latter was limited to $5,000. The latter provision was held to pertain to the remedy, rather than to the right, and to indicate the public policy of New York as to the extent of the remedy, and to be a limit upon the amount which might be recovered in the action. The difference between the rule as laid down in Dennick v. Central R. Co. of New Jersey and in Leonard v. Columbia Steam Nav. Co. has been referred to in several subsequent cases, in which the court did not deem it necessary to pass upon the question for the reason that the statutes under consideration were sufficiently similar. This was held to be the case in Bruce's Adm'r v. Cincinnati R. Co.,[14] brought in Kentucky, under the statute of Tennessee; in Morris v. Chicago, R. I. & P. R. Co.,[15] brought in Iowa, under the statute of Illinois; and in Burns v. Grand Rapids & I. R. Co.,[16] brought in Indiana, under the statute of Michigan—although in the latter case the court observes that the better view seems to be that taken in Leonard v. Columbia Steam Nav. Co. In Shedd v. Moran,[17] brought in Illinois, under the statute of Indiana, it was said that the law of Illinois had no application, except as showing that the foreign statute was not repugnant to the public policy

131 App. Div. 443, 115 N. Y. Supp. 316. Cf. Pietraroia v. New Jersey & H. R. Ry. & Ferry Co., 197 N. Y. 434, 91 N. E. 120. The foreign statute must be similar. Zeikus v. Florida East Coast R. Co., 144 App. Div. 91. 128 N. Y. Supp. 933.

14 83 Ky. 174.

15 65 Iowa, 727. 23 N. W. 143, 54 Am. Rep. 39.

16 113 Ind. 169, 15 N. E. 230.　　17 10 Ill. App. 618.

of that state. And in Knight v. West Jersey R. Co.,[18] brought in Pennsylvania, under the statute of New Jersey, Trunkey, J., says: "If the statute of New Jersey * * * is similar to the statute of this state upon the same subject, it is plain that the law sought to be enforced is not contrary to the public policy of this state, or prejudicial to its interests." The opinion in Chicago, St. L. & N. O. R. Co. v. Doyle,[19] brought in Mississippi, under the statute of Tennessee, is to the same effect. In the following cases also, the right to sue under the foreign statute was maintained: South Carolina R. Co. v. Nix,[20] brought in Georgia, under the statute of South Carolina; Central R. R. v. Swint,[21] in the same state, under the statute of Alabama; Missouri Pac. Ry. Co. v. Lewis,[22] in Nebraska, under the statute of Kansas; Nashville & C. R. Co. v. Sprayberry,[23] in Tennessee, under the statute of Mississippi; Mississippi & T. R. Co. v. Ayres,[24] in Tennessee, under the statute of Mississippi; Nelson v. Chesapeake & O. Ry. Co.,[25] in Virginia, under the statute of West Virginia; Cincinnati, H. & D. R. Co. v. McMullen,[26] in Indiana, under the statute of Ohio; Louisville & N. R. Co. v. Shivell's Adm'x,[27] in Kentucky, under the statute of Alabama.

The question was brought before the supreme court of the United States for a second time in Texas & P. Ry. Co.

[18] 108 Pa. 250, 56 Am. Rep. 200. Cf. Usher v. West Jersey R. Co., 126 Pa. 206, 17 Atl. 597, 4 L. R. A. 261, 12 Am. St. Rep. 863.
[19] 60 Miss. 977.
[20] 68 Ga. 572.
[21] 73 Ga. 651.
[22] 24 Neb. 848, 40 N. W. 401, 2 L. R. A. 67.
[23] 9 Heisk. 852.
[24] 16 Lea, 725.
[25] 88 Va. 971, 14 S. E. 838, 15 L. R. A. 583.
[26] 117 Ind. 439, 20 N. E. 287, 10 Am. St. Rep. 67.
[27] 18 S. W. 944, 13 Ky. Law Rep. 902.

v. Cox,[28] in an action brought in the circuit court for the eastern district of Texas, under the statute of Louisiana. It was held, affirming the judgment of the lower court, that the action could be maintained. The opinion was delivered by the Chief Justice, who, after citing Dennick v. Central R. Co. of New Jersey, says: "And, notwithstanding some contrariety of decision upon the point, the rule thus stated is generally recognized and applied *where the statute of the state in which the cause of action arose is not in substance inconsistent with the statutes or public policy of the state in which the right of action is sought to be enforced.* The statutes of these two states on this subject are not essentially dissimilar, and it cannot be successfully asserted that the maintenance of jurisdiction is opposed to a settled public policy of the state of Texas." [29] In construing these same statutes, the Texas court, in Texas & P. Ry. Co. v. Richards,[30] had arrived at an opposite conclusion, but the Chief Justice says that the question is one of general law, and settled by Dennick v. Central R. Co. of New Jersey.

In Herrick v. Minneapolis & St. L. Ry. Co.,[31] it was held that an action which accrued in Iowa under a statute which made railroad corporations liable for damages sustained by employés in consequence of the negligence of co-employés might be maintained in Minnesota, where there was no such statute. "The statute of another state has, of course, no extraterritorial force," said Mitchell, J., "but rights acquired

[28] 145 U. S. 593, 12 Sup. Ct. 905, 36 L. Ed. 829.

[29] Where the lex loci and lex fori in respect to actions for death by negligent act give the same remedy to the same persons, that the former places no restrictions upon the transitory nature of the action, while the latter does, does not affect the policy of the latter, so far as it recognizes the cause of action and its enforcement. Christensen v. Floriston Pulp & Paper Co., 29 Nev. 552, 92 Pac. 210.

[30] 68 Tex. 375, 4 S. W. 627.

[31] 31 Minn. 11, 16 N. W. 413, 47 Am. Rep. 771.

under it will always, in comity, be enforced, if not against
the public policy of the laws of the former. In such cases
the law of the place where the right was acquired, or the
liability was incurred, will govern as to the right of action;
while all that pertains merely to the remedy will be controlled by the law of the state where the action is brought.
And we think the principle is the same whether the right
of action be ex contractu or ex delicto. The defendant admits the general rule to be as thus stated, but contends
that, as to statutory actions like the present, it is subject
to the qualification that, to sustain the action, the law of
the forum and the law of the place where the right of action accrued must concur in holding that the act done gives
a right of action. We admit that some text writers—nota-
bly, Rorer on Interstate Law—seems to lay down this rule,
but the authorities cited generally fail to sustain it. * * *
But it by no means follows that, because the statute of one
state differs from the law of another state, therefore it would
be held contrary to the policy of the laws of the latter state.
* * * To justify a court in refusing to enforce a right
of action which accrued under the law of another state because against the policy of our laws, it must appear that it
is against good morals or natural justice, or that, for some
other such reason, the enforcement of it would be prejudicial
to the general interests of our own citizens. If the state of
Iowa sees fit to impose this obligation upon those operating railroads within her bounds, and to make it a condition
of the employment of those who enter their service, we see
nothing in such a law repugnant either to good morals or
natural justice, or prejudicial to the interests of our own
citizens." This language was quoted with approval by the
Supreme Court of the United States in Northern Pac. R.
Co. v. Babcock.[32]

[32] 154 U. S. 190, 14 Sup. Ct. 978, 38 L. Ed. 958.

(446)

The question was again considered in the same court in Stewart v. Baltimore & O. R. Co.,[33] and it was held that an action may be maintained in the District of Columbia to recover damages for a death caused by negligence in Maryland, since in both jurisdictions the statutes have removed the common-law obstacle to such a suit, and permitted a recovery for the benefit of the near relatives of the deceased, and that the fact that in Maryland the action must be brought in the name of the state, while in the District it is brought in the name of the personal representatives, or the fact that the Maryland statute names as beneficiaries the wife, husband, parent, and child of the deceased, while the District statute provides for a distribution of a recovery according to the statute of distribution, does not show such an inconsistency between the two statutes as would prevent the maintenance of the suit. "Such statutes are not penal," said the court, "but remedial, for the benefit of the persons injured by the death. An action to recover damages for a tort is not local, but transitory, and can, as a general rule, be maintained wherever the wrongdoer can be found. * * * It may well be that, where a purely statutory right is created, the special remedy provided by the statute for the enforcement of that right must be pursued; but, where the statute simply takes away a common-law obstacle to a recovery for an admitted tort, it would seem not unreasonable to hold that an action for that tort can be maintained *where the statute of the state in which the cause of action arose is not, in substance, inconsistent with the statutes or public policy of the state in which the right of action is sought to be enforced.* * * * We can-

---

[33] 168 U. S. 445, 18 Sup. Ct. 105, 42 L. Ed. 537. See post, § 201. See, also, Florida Cent. & P. R. Co. v. Sullivan, 120 Fed. 799, 57 C. C. A. 167, 61 L. R. A. 410.

not think that these differences are sufficient to render the statute of Maryland, in substance, inconsistent with the statute or public policy of the District of Columbia; and so, within the rule heretofore announced in this court, it must be held that the plaintiff was entitled to maintain this action in the courts of the District for the benefit of the persons designated in the statute of Maryland."

On the other hand, in Slater v. Mexican National R. Co.,[34] the same court recognized that the right of recovery given by the foreign statute may be so dissimilar to that given by the lex fori, and so incapable of enforcement through any procedure provided by its law, with regard to the rights of the defendant, that the court would be without jurisdiction of an action for the enforcement of such right of recovery. In this case it was held by a divided court that a circuit court of the United States in the state of Texas was without jurisdiction of a common-law action founded on the liability for death by wrongful act created by the Mexican laws, because of its lack of power to make a decree of the kind required by such laws, which demanded that the damages be awarded as support in the nature of alimony or pension, by a decree which contemplated periodical payments, and which was subject to modification from time to time, as the circumstances changed. "As Texas has statutes which give an action for wrongfully causing death," said the court, "of course there is no general objection of policy to enforcing such a liability there, although it arose in another jurisdiction. * * * But when such a liability is enforced in a jurisdiction foreign to the place of the wrongful act, obviously that does not mean that the act in any degree is subject to the lex fori, with regard to either

[34] 194 U. S. 120, 24 Sup. Ct. 581, 48 L. Ed. 900, affirming Mexican Nat. R. Co. v. Slater, 115 Fed. 593, 53 C. C. A. 239.

its quality or its consequences. On the other hand, it equally means that the law of the place of the act is operative outside its own territory. The theory of the foreign suit is that, although the act complained of was subject to no law having force in the forum, it gave rise to an obligation, an obligation, which, like other obligations, follows the person, and may be enforced wherever the person may be found. * * * But as the only source of this obligation is the law of the place of the act, it follows that that law determines not merely the existence of the obligation, * * * but equally determines its extent. It seems to us unjust to allow a plaintiff to come here absolutely depending on the foreign law for the foundation of his case, and yet to deny the defendant the benefit of whatever limitations on his liability that law would impose. * * * We may lay on one side as quite inadmissible the notion that the law of the place of the act may be resorted to so far as to show that the act was a tort, and then may be abandoned, leaving the consequences to be determined according to the accident of the place where the defendant may happen to be caught. * * * The present action is a suit at common law, and the court has no power to make a decree of this kind contemplated by the Mexican statutes. What the circuit court did was to disregard the principles of the Mexican statute altogether and to follow the Texas statute. This clearly was wrong. * * * But we are of opinion, further, that justice to the defendant would not permit the substitution of a lump sum, however estimated, for the periodical payments which the Mexican statute required."

§ 198. Action based on foreign statute—Jurisdiction denied

The right of an administrator appointed in the state of the tribunal to maintain an action based on the foreign statute has been denied, upon grounds that do not rest upon the dissimilarity of particular statutes, in Ohio, Massachusetts, and Kansas.[35] The right to maintain the action has also been denied, in cases that turned to a greater or less extent upon the dissimilarity of the statutes involved, in Missouri, Maryland, and Texas.[36]

In Woodard v. Michigan, S. & N. I. R. Co.,[37] which is the earliest case in point, it was held that an Ohio adminis-

[35] Woodard v. Michigan S. & N. I. R. Co., 10 Ohio St. 121; Richardson v. New York Cent. R. Co., 98 Mass. 85 (see, also, Davis v. New York & N. E. R. Co., 143 Mass. 301, 9 N. E. 815, 58 Am. Rep. 138; but see Higgins v. Central N. E. & W. R. Co., 155 Mass. 176, 29 N. E. 534, 31 Am. St. Rep. 544); McCarthy v. Chicago, R. I. & P. R. Co., 18 Kan. 48, 26 Am. Rep. 742. In Mackay v. Central R. R. of New Jersey, 14 Blatchf. 65, 4 Fed. 617, it was held in the circuit court, southern district of New York, that an administrator appointed in New York could not recover for a death which occurred in New Jersey under the statute of that state; but this case may be considered as overruled by Dennick v. Central R. Co. of New Jersey, 103 U. S. 11, 26 L. Ed. 439. Taylor's Adm'r v. Pennsylvania Co., 78 Ky. 348, 39 Am. Rep. 244, which held that an action could not be maintained in Kentucky under the statute of Indiana, where the death occurred, was overruled by Bruce's Adm'r v. Cincinnati R. Co., 83 Ky. 174. See Anderson v. Milwaukee & St. P. Ry. Co., 37 Wis. 321.

[36] Vawter v. Missouri Pac. Ry. Co., 84 Mo. 679, 54 Am. Rep. 105; Oates v. Union Pac. Ry. Co., 104 Mo. 514, 16 S. W. 487, 24 Am. St. Rep. 348; Ash v. Baltimore & O. R. Co., 72 Md. 144, 19 Atl. 643, 20 Am. St. Rep. 461; Texas & P. Ry. Co. v. Richards, 68 Tex. 375, 4 S. W. 627; St. Louis, I. M. & S. Ry. Co. v. McCormick, 71 Tex. 660, 9 S. W. 540, 1 L. R. A. 804.

[37] 10 Ohio St. 121. See, also, Hover v. Pennsylvania Co., 25 Ohio St. 667; Wabash R. Co. v. Fox, 64 Ohio St. 133, 59 N. E. 888,

trator could not maintain an action in that state under the statute of Illinois. The two main grounds of decision were that the Illinois statute had no extraterritorial force, and that the jurisdiction of the Ohio statute under which the administrator was appointed did not extend to trusts to be carried out in pursuance of the law of another state; but the court also questioned whether the petition sufficiently showed that the act was one for which the deceased, had he lived, might have maintained an action.

The next case was Richardson v. New York Cent. R. Co.,[88] which held that an action could not be maintained under the New York statute in Massachusetts. Hoar, J., who delivered the opinion, took the view that the statute was penal, but rested the decision on the ground that the right of action of the administrator, who was appointed in Massachusetts, was confined to actions which accrued to his intestate, or which grew out of his rights of property or those of his creditors; and that the right of action which the New York statute gave to the personal representative was not a right of property passing as assets to the decedent, but a specific power to sue, which was created by the law of that state, and which consequently did not pass to the plaintiff as administrator. This objection, which is similar to that raised in the Ohio case, was discussed in Dennick v. Central R. Co. of New Jersey. It is to be observed that no statute similar to that of New York existed in Massachusetts, though the decision was not placed on that ground. In a later Massachusetts case,[89] where the deceased was instantly killed in Connecticut, it was held that

83 Am. St. Rep. 739. Cf. Baltimore & O. R. Co. v. Chambers, 73 Ohio St. 16, 76 N. E. 91, 11 L. R. A. (N. S.) 1012.

88 98 Mass. 85. See Davis v. New York & N. E. R. Co., 143 Mass. 301, 9 N. E. 815, 58 Am. Rep. 138.

89 Higgins v. Central N. E. & W. R. Co., 155 Mass. 176, 29 N. E.

an action might be maintained under the statute of that state, which provided that "all actions for injury to the person, whether the same do or do not instantaneously or otherwise result in death," should survive. The court distinguishes the case from Richardson v. New York Cent. R. Co., on the ground that in that case the right of action was not one that passed to the administrator by succession; but in spite of the fact that the Connecticut statute provides, in terms, that the right of action, even in case of an instantaneous death, shall "survive," it creates, in effect, a new right of action for the benefit of certain designated persons; and the distinction drawn between these two cases is a very narrow one.

In Lyon v. Boston & M. R. Co.[40] it was held that although a cause of action for death, which by the New Hampshire statute survived to the administrator, was transitory, the survival was wholly where the right was, and local, and that, the right to sue arising solely in New Hampshire, where the accident causing death occurred, it was not carried by that statute to a Vermont administrator, endeavoring to sue the defendant in Vermont; the court saying that if the statute had given a new cause of action to the administrator, it could have been brought wherever jurisdiction of the defendant could be had, but that, as the

534, 31 Am. St. Rep. 544. Followed in Chandler v. New York, N. H. & H. R. Co., 159 Mass. 589, 35 N. E. 89.

[40] 107 Fed. 386. Such cause of action would not survive, as authorized by the New Hampshire statute, in any place where an administrator should be appointed merely for the purpose of recovering damages for such wrongful death as an asset of decedent's estate, but survived only in the state where deceased had his domicile at the time of his death, where the cause of action accrued; and where intestate was domiciled in Vermont at the time he was killed in New Hampshire, the cause of action accrued to him in Vermont. Stockwell v. Boston & M. R. Co. (C. C.) 131 Fed. 153.

cause of action came to an administrator by survival only, the administrator must be such a one as it would survive to.

In McCarthy v. Chicago, R. I. & P. R. Co.,[41] it was held that a Kansas administrator could not recover for a death that occurred in Missouri. The petition does not appear to have alleged the Missouri law, but the court discusses the question as if such were the case, and reasons substantially in accordance with the opinions in Woodard v. Michigan, S. & N. I. R. Co. and Richardson v. New York Cent. R. Co. It is also pointed out that the two statutes are in many respects dissimilar.

In Vawter v. Missouri Pac. Ry. Co.[42] it was held, conversely, that a Missouri administrator could not recover for a death that occurred in Kansas. The reasoning of Woodard v. Michigan, S. & N. I. R. Co. and Richardson v. New York Cent. R. Co. is approved, but the court also lays stress on the fact that the statutes are dissimilar, and especially on the fact that by the Missouri statute it is ex-

[41] 18 Kan. 46, 26 Am. Rep. 742. In Hamilton v. Hannibal & St. J. R. Co., 39 Kan. 56, 18 Pac. 57, the court declined to enter upon a re-examination of the question, because the complaint did not show that the suit was begun within the time prescribed by the Missouri statute. Cf. Dale v. Atchison, T. & S. F. R. Co., 57 Kan. 601, 47 Pac. 521; Matheson v. Kansas City, Ft. S. & M. R. Co., 61 Kan. 667, 60 Pac. 747.

[42] 84 Mo. 679, 54 Am. Rep. 105. In Stoeckman v. Terre Haute & I. R. Co., 15 Mo. App. 503, it had been held that an administrator appointed in Missouri could maintain an action under the Illinois statute. While this case is not in terms overruled, it is not easy to reconcile it with Vawter v. Missouri Pac. Ry. Co. In Oates v. Union Pac. Ry. Co., 104 Mo. 514, 16 S. W. 487, 24 Am. St. Rep. 348, it was held that where a resident of Missouri was killed in Kansas no action could be maintained in Missouri by the wife, though no administrator could be appointed in Kansas, because the deceased left no estate there, and though no action could be brought in either state by an administrator appointed in Missouri. Cf. Wilson v. Tootle (C. C.) 55 Fed. 211.

pressly provided that the action shall not be brought by the personal representative.

In Ash v. Baltimore & O. R. Co.[48] it was held that a Maryland administrator could not maintain an action under the statute of West Virginia. The court adopts the reasoning of the Ohio and Massachusetts cases, but distinguishes the case from Dennick v. Central R. Co. of New Jersey, on the ground that the statutes of Maryland and West Virginia are essentially different—in respect to the beneficiaries, the period of limitation, the amount of recovery, and the nominal plaintiff. Whether an action could be maintained under a foreign statute similar to that of Maryland the court declines to say.

In Texas & P. Ry. Co. v. Richards [44] it was held that an action could not be maintained in Texas under the Louisiana statute, upon the ground that the latter statute provided that the cause of action should survive, but created no new cause of action. Again, in St. Louis, I. M. & S. Ry. Co. v. McCormick,[45] the court declined to entertain an action by a Texas administrator under the Arkansas statute. The decision, which leaves the main question open, is placed upon the dissimilarity of the statutes.

Without discussing in detail the questions of the similarity and dissimilarity of the various statutes involved in the foregoing decisions, it is enough to say that the dissimilarity was not greater in any of them, except, perhaps, in the cases involving the Missouri statute, than that between the

[48] 72 Md. 144, 19 Atl. 643, 20 Am. St. Rep. 461.

[44] 68 Tex. 375, 4 S. W. 627. In an action begun in the circuit court involving the same statutes, an opposite conclusion was reached by the supreme court. Texas & P. Ry. Co. v. Cox, 145 U. S. 593, 12 Sup. Ct. 905, 36 L. Ed. 829; ante, § 198.

[45] 71 Tex. 660, 9 S. W. 540, 1 L. R. A. 804.

statutes involved in many of the cases cited in the preceding section, in which the jurisdiction was sustained.

In some states it has been enacted that no action shall be brought for death if the wrongful act or neglect occurred without the state. In Ohio by statute the right to maintain an action for a death caused in another state is limited to cases where the decedent was a citizen of Ohio,[46] and it has been held by the supreme court of the United States that the privileges and immunities of citizens in the several states, secured by the federal constitution to the citizens of each state, are not denied by this provision.[47]

§ 198—1. Action based on penal statute

If the foreign statute is penal, it is conceded that it cannot be enforced in another jurisdiction. Thus it has been held that when the injury was received in Massachusetts, where an action for death was maintainable to recover damages to be assessed with reference to the culpability of the defendant, an action could not be maintained in another state whose statutes had no such penal feature.[48] So it has

[46] Under an amendment of the statutes providing that whenever the death of a citizen of the state has been caused by wrongful act in another state, for which a right to maintain an action in respect thereof is given by a statute of such other state, such right of action may be enforced in the state, no action can be maintained in the courts of the state on a cause of action for wrongful death occurring in another state, except where the person wrongfully killed was a citizen of the state of Ohio. Baltimore & O. R. Co. v. Chambers, 73 Ohio St. 16, 76 N. E. 91, 11 L. R. A. (N. S.) 1012.

[47] Chambers v. Baltimore & O. R. Co., 207 U. S. 142, 28 Sup. Ct. 34, 52 L. Ed. 143.

[48] O'Reilly v. New York & N. E. R. Co., 16 R. I. 388, 17 Atl. 906, 5 L. R. A. 364, 6 L. R. A. 719 (cf. O'Reilly v. New York & N. E. R. Co. [R. I.] 19 Atl. 244); Adams v. Fitchburg R. Co., 67 Vt. 76, 30 Atl. 687, 48 Am. St. Rep. 800. See, also, Lyman v. Boston & A. R. Co. (C.

been held that when the injury·was received in Missouri, where an action for death was maintainable under a statute providing that the wrongdoer should forfeit and pay for any person so dying the sum of $5,000, an action thereon cannot be maintained in another state whose statutes had no penal feature.[49]

§ 199. Death on navigable waters within the state

The constitution of the United States declares that "the judicial power shall extend * * * to all cases of admiralty, and maritime jurisdiction"; and the ninth section of the judiciary act of 1789 (chapter 20, 1 Stat. 77)[50] enacted that "the district courts shall have exclusive original cognizance of all civil causes of admiralty and maritime jurisdiction, *saving to suitors in all cases the right of a common-law remedy where the common law is adequate to give it."* By reason of the above saving clause, the state courts have jurisdiction to entertain an action under the statutes giving a right of action for injuries resulting in death, although the death occurred on navigable waters of the United States, provided, of course, that it occurred within the territorial limits of the state under whose stat-

C.) 70 Fed. 409; Perkins v. Boston & A. R. Co. (C. C.) 90 Fed. 321. Contra: Boston & M. R. R. v. Hurd, 108 Fed. 116, 47 C. C. A. 615, 56 L. R. A. 193; Malloy v. American Hide & Leather Co. (C. C.) 148 Fed. 482.

[49] Marshall v. Wabash R. Co. (C. C.) 46 Fed. 269; Raisor v. Chicago & A. R. Co., 215 Ill. 47, 74 N. E. 69, 106 Am. St. Rep. 153, 2 Ann. Cas. 802; Matheson v. Kansas City, Ft. S. & M. R. Co., 61 Kan. 667, 60 Pac. 747; Dale v. Atchison, T. & S. F. R. Co., 57 Kan. 601, 47 Pac. 521.

[50] The same provision is contained in the recent judiciary act. Act March 3, 1911, c. 231, § 24, subd. 3, 36 Stat. 1091 (U. S. Comp. St. Supp. 1911, p. 136).

ute the remedy is sought.[51]   Thus, in American Steamboat Co. v. Chace,[52] where the death occurred on Narragansett bay, within the state of Rhode Island, the supreme court decided that the action was maintainable under the Rhode Island statute, in the courts of that state. The opinion was delivered by Mr. Justice Clifford, who held that the state court had jurisdiction, irrespective of the question whether the case was or was not also within the jurisdiction of the admiralty courts, which was not decided. "Attempt is made," he observes, "to deny the right to such a remedy in this case, upon the ground that the operation of the saving clause must be limited to such causes of action as were known to the common law at the time of the passage of the judiciary act; and the argument is that the cause of action alleged was not known to the common law at that period, which cannot be admitted, as actions to recover damages for personal injuries, prosecuted in the name of the injured party, were well known even in the early history of the common law. Such actions, it must be admitted, did not ordinarily survive, but nearly all the states have passed laws to prevent such a failure of justice, and the validity of such laws has never been questioned." The decision of the same court in Sherlock v. Alling[53] is to the

51 American Steamboat Co. v. Chace, 16 Wall. 522, 21 L. Ed. 369; Chase v. American Steamboat Co., 9 R. I. 419, 11 Am. Rep. 274; Sherlock v. Alling, 93 U. S. 99, 23 L. Ed. 819; Id., 44 Ind. 184; Mahler v. Norwich & N. Y. Transp. Co., 35 N. Y. 352 (reversing 45 Barb. 226; s. c., 30 How. Prac. 237); Dougan v. Champlain Transp. Co., 56 N. Y. 1 (affirming 6 Lans. 430); Opsahl v. Judd, 30 Minn. 126, 14 N. W. 575; Chicago Transit Co. v. Campbell, 110 Ill. App. 366; Lennan v. Hamburg-American S. S. Co., 73 App. Div. 357, 77 N. Y. Supp. 60.

52 16 Wall. 522, 21 L. Ed. 369; Chase v. American Steamboat Co., 9 R. I. 419, 11 Am. Rep. 274.

53 93 U. S. 99, 23 L. Ed. 819; Id., 44 Ind. 184. See, also, Memphis & C. Packet Co. v. Pikey, 142 Ind. 304, 40 N. E. 527.

same effect. In that case the deceased was killed by a collision of two steamboats on the Ohio river, between the states of Kentucky and Indiana, but above low-water mark on the Indiana side. It was admitted that the territorial limits of Indiana included the place in question. The decision held that the legislation of Indiana could be enforced with respect to any matter occurring on the river within the state limits, as much as with respect to any matter occurring on the land; and that, although the colliding boats were engaged in carrying on interstate commerce under the laws of the United States, until congress made some regulation touching the liabilities of parties for maritime torts resulting in death, the statute of Indiana applied, and constituted no encroachment upon the commercial power of congress. So, where the legislation of congress, and the constitutions of Minnesota and Wisconsin, adopted in conformity therewith, gave concurrent jurisdiction to both states on the St. Croix river, it was held that an action might be ·maintained in the state courts of Minnesota for an injury causing the death of the decedent while navigating that river, and that the jurisdiction was not affected by the fact that the boat, at the time of the accident, was on the Wisconsin side of the stream.[54]

§ 200.　Death on high seas on vessel owned in state

Although the statute of a state has no extraterritorial force extending over the high seas,[55] it has been held in New York, in a case[56] where the death occurred on the

[54] Opsahl v. Judd, 30 Minn. 126, 14 N. W. 575.

[55] Armstrong v. Beadle, 5 Sawy. 484, Fed. Cas. No. 541; The E. B. Ward, Jr. (C. C.) 16 Fed. 255.

[56] McDonald v. Mallory, 77 N. Y. 546, 33 Am. Rep. 664 (reversing 44 N. Y. Super. Ct. 80). See, also, Cavanagh v. Ocean Steam Nav.

high seas, in a vessel owned and registered in a port of that state, that an action might be maintained under the New York statute. The case is placed upon the authority of the decision of the United States supreme court in Crapo v. Kelly.[57] The decision rests upon the ground that, in respect to matters not committed by the constitution exclusively in the federal government, or legislated upon by congress, but which are regulated entirely by state laws, a state to which a vessel belongs can be regarded as the sovereignty whose laws follow her until she comes within the jurisdiction of some other government, and that hence such vessel, while on the high seas, is to be regarded, so far as concerns the operation of such laws, as a portion of the territory of the state.

§ 200—1.   Action under foreign statute—Substantive rights

Where an action is maintainable based upon a foreign statute, that statute of course governs, so far as it affects the extent of the defendant's obligation and the substantive

Co., 13 N. Y. Supp. 540. This reasoning was approved by Pardee, J., in The E. B. Ward, Jr. (C. C.) 17 Fed. 456. See Old Dominion S. S. Co. v. Gilmore, 207 U. S. 398, 28 Sup. St. 133, 52 L. Ed. 264. A steamship owned by a New Jersey corporation is a vessel of that state, and subject to its laws, notwithstanding the vessel's registry in New York. International Nav. Co. v. Lindstrom, 123 Fed. 475, 60 C. C. A. 649, reversing Lindstrom v. International Nav. Co. (C. C.) 117 Fed. 170.

[57] 16 Wall. 610, 21 L. Ed. 430 (reversing Kelly v. Crapo, 45 N. Y. 86, 6 Am. Rep. 35). In this case the vessel was owned and registered in Massachusetts, and, while she was on the high seas and bound for the port of New York, an involuntary transfer of all the property of her owner was executed to an assignee by the Massachusetts insolvency court. In a suit between the assignee and the sheriff of New York, who had attached the vessel on her arrival in that port,

rights of the parties.[58] Thus the foreign statute governs the effect of contributory negligence upon the right of recovery,[59] and the distribution among the beneficiaries of the amount recovered.[60] If the statute imposes a limitation of time to which the right of action is subject, that limitation, and not the statute of limitation of the forum, controls.[61]

it was held that, for the purposes of the suit, the ship, though on the high seas, was a portion of the territory of Massachusetts, and that the assignment by the insolvency court passed the title to her with like effect as if she had been physically within the bounds of that state, and that the prior right was with the assignee as against the attaching creditor.

[58] Slater v. Mexican Nat. R. Co., 194 U. S. 120, 24 Sup. Ct. 581, 48 L. Ed. 900; Cowen v. Ray, 108 Fed. 320, 47 C. C. A. 352 (effect of release). Interest on the recovery will not be allowed, under Code Civ. Proc. § 1904, providing that the clerk must add to the judgment interest from decedent's death, where the accident occurred in Canada, the law of which makes no provision for interest on judgments in such cases. Kiefer v. Grand Trunk Ry. Co., 12 App. Div. 28, 42 N. Y. Supp. 171, affirmed 153 N. Y. 688, 48 N. E. 1105. See, also, Frounfelker v. Delaware, L. & W. R. Co., 73 App. Div. 350, 76 N. Y. Supp. 745; Gurofsky v. Lehigh Valley R. Co., 121 App. Div. 126, 105 N. Y. Supp. 514. In an action in Indiana against a railroad company, plaintiff was entitled to the benefit of a statute of Illinois, where the accident happened, relative to the use of whistles and bells on locomotive engines, and an ordinance of the city where the accident occurred concerning the maintenance of gates at street crossings, etc. Baltimore & O. R. Co. v. Ryan, 31 Ind. App. 597, 68 N. E. 923.

[59] Louisville & N. R. Co. v. Whitlow's Adm'r, 105 Ky. 1, 114 Ky. 470, 43 S. W. 711, 19 Ky. Law Rep. 1931, 41 L. R. A. 614.

[60] Denver & R. G. R. Co. v. Warring, 37 Colo. 122, 86 Pac. 305; In re Coe's Estate, 130 Iowa, 307, 106 N. W. 743, 4 L. R. A. (N. S.) 814, 114 Am. St. Rep. 416, 8 Ann. Cas. 148 ; In re Williams' Estate, 130 Iowa, 553, 107 N. W. 608; Hartley v. Hartley, 71 Kan. 691, 81 Pac. 505, 114 Am. St. Rep. 519 ; McDonald v. McDonald's Adm'r, 96 Ky. 209, 28 S. W. 482, 49 Am. St. Rep. 289. See, also,

[61] Ante, § 121.

§ 201.   Who may sue under a foreign statute

The proper party plaintiff in an action under the foreign statute is the person thereby authorized to sue. Thus, if the statute provides that the action shall be brought by the personal representative, only he is entitled to sue; and this, notwithstanding that the statute of the state where the remedy is sought requires the action to be brought by the beneficiaries.[62] On the other hand, if the right to sue is given by the foreign statute directly to the beneficiaries, they only are entitled to sue, notwithstanding that the statute of the state of the tribunal gives the right of action to the personal representative.[63] Whether the personal represent-

Kelly v. Union Pac. R. Co., 141 Mo. App. 490, 125 S. W. 818; Florida Cent. & P. R. Co. v. Sullivan, 120 Fed. 799, 57 C. C. A. 167, 61 L. R. A. 410.

[62] Usher v. West Jersey R. Co., 126 Pa. 206, 17 Atl. 597, 4 L. R. A. 261, 12 Am. St. Rep. 863; Patton v. Pittsburgh, C. & St. L. Ry. Co., 96 Pa. 169; Selma, R. & D. R. Co. v. Lacey, 49 Ga. 106; Western & A. R. Co. v. Strong, 52 Ga. 461; Illinois Cent. R. Co. v. Crudup, 63 Miss. 291; Fabel v. Cleveland, C., C. & St. L. Ry. Co., 30 Ind. App. 268, 65 N. E. 929; McGinnis v. Missouri Car & Foundry Co., 174 Mo. 225, 73 S. W. 586, 97 Am. St. Rep. 553; Thorpe v. Union Pac. Coal Co., 24 Utah, 475, 68 Pac. 145. See, also, Atlanta, K. & N. R. Co. v. Smith, 1 Ga. App. 162, 58 S. E. 106; Jones v. Kansas City, Ft. S. & M. R. Co., 178 Mo. 528, 77 S. W. 890, 101 Am. St. Rep. 434; Lee v. Missouri Pac. Ry. Co., 195 Mo. 400, 92 S. W. 614; Keele v. Atchison, T. & S. F. R. Co., 151 Mo. App. 364, 131 S. W. 730; Hoodmacher v. Lehigh Val. R. Co., 218 Pa. 21, 66 Atl. 975; Wilson v. Tootle (C. C.) 55 Fed. 211. Under the Oklahoma statute, authorizing actions by the personal representatives of decedent, or, in case he was a nonresident or, being a resident, no personal representative had been appointed, by the widow or next of kin, the widow of a resident of Oklahoma, having been appointed as his administratrix, cannot sue in Missouri in her individual capacity for the death of her husband. Casey v. Hoover, 197 Mo. 62, 94 S. W. 982.

[63] Wooden v. Western N. Y. & P. R. Co., 126 N. Y. 10, 26 N. E. 1050, 13 L. R. A. 458, 22 Am. St. Rep. 803 (affirming 12 N. Y. Supp.

ative who is entitled to sue is one appointed by authority
of the state where the action is brought or the foreign representative has already been considered.[64] The cases above
cited under this paragraph rest upon the ground that the
question as to the proper plaintiff is not a question of remedy, determinable by the lex fori, but of right, and that the
right, being created by statute, can be enforced only by the
statutory plaintiff.   Hardly to be reconciled with these cases is Stewart v. Baltimore & O. R. Co.,[65] in which it was
held by the supreme court of the United States that an action in the name of the personal representative might be
maintained in the District of Columbia for a death caused
in Maryland, although the Maryland statute provided that
the action should be brought in the name of the state, while
the statute of the District provided that the action should
be brought in the name of the personal representative.
"Neither the state in the one case nor the personal repre-

908); Nashville & C. R. Co. v. Sprayberry, 9 Heisk. (Tenn.) 852; Id.,
8 Baxt. (Tenn.) 342, 35 Am. Rep. 705; Lower v. Segal, 60 N. J. Law,
99, 36 Atl. 777; Stone v. Groton Bridge & Mfg. Co., 77 Hun, 99,
28 N. Y. Supp. 446. Under Civil Code of Lower Canada, giving a
right of recovery for death to decedent's consort and his ascendant
and descendant relations, but providing that no more than one action can be brought in behalf of those entitled to indemnity, and
that the judgment shall determine the proportion of such indemnity
which each is to receive, the right given such persons is individual
and personal, and not representative, so that the action cannot be
brought by decedent's administratrix. Johnson v. Phœnix Bridge
Co., 197 N. Y. 316, 90 N. E. 953. But in South Carolina it was held
that, though the Georgia statute, authorizing a widow to recover
for the negligent killing of her husband, designates the beneficiaries,
it did not prescribe the mode of procedure, so that suit in South
Carolina for death in Georgia should be brought in the name of
the personal representatives of the decedent in accordance with the
procedure of South Carolina. Bussey v. Charleston & W. C. R.
Co., 73 S. C. 215, 53 S. E. 165.

64 Ante, § 110.

65 168 U. S. 445, 18 Sup. Ct. 105, 42 L. Ed. 537; ante, § 197.

sentative in the other," said the court, "has any pecuniary interest in the recovery. Each is simply a nominal plaintiff. While in the District the nominal plaintiff is the personal representative of the deceased, the damages recovered do not become part of the assets of the estate, or liable for the debts of the deceased, but are distributed among certain of his heirs. By neither statute is there any thought of increasing the volume of the deceased's estate, but in each it is the award to certain. prescribed heirs of the damages resulting to them from the taking away of their relative. For purposes of jurisdiction in the federal courts, regard is had to the real, rather than the nominal, party. * * * In such an action it is evident that the real party in interest is not the nominal plaintiff, but the party for whose benefit the recovery is sought; and the courts of either jurisdiction will see that the damages awarded pass to such party." This decision has been adversely criticised on the ground that it confused two questions—one, whether the right of action on the statute is transitory and enforceable by the right person in the foreign jurisdiction; the other, whether the personal representative is the right person to enforce it in that jurisdiction [66]—and the criticism has much force. Indeed, the opinion concedes that "it may well be that, where a purely statutory right is created, the special remedy provided by the statute for the enforcement of that right must be pursued," and makes the distinction, which is hardly to be supported, that the statute is one "which simply takes away a common-law obstacle to

[66] See opinion of Cochran, J., in Williams v. Camden Interstate R. Co. (C. C.) 138 Fed. 571, affirmed Camden Interstate Ry. Co. v. Williams, 140 Fed. 985, 72 C. C. A. 680. See, also, comments upon the principal cases in Cincinnati, H. & D. R. Co. v. Thiebaud, 114 Fed. 918, 52 C. C. A. 538; Sanbo v. Union Pac. Coal Co. (C. C.) 130 Fed. 52.

a recovery for an admitted tort," saying that in such case it would not seem unreasonable to hold that an action for that tort can be maintained in any state where the common-law obstacle has been removed." While the courts have sometimes felt it necessary, in order to explain a particular decision, to say that statutes like Lord Campbell's act give only a substituted right of the representative to sue in the place of the right which the deceased himself would have had if he had survived,[67] that position is clearly untenable, and there is no logical escape from the conclusion that the statutes create a new right.[68] This criticism in no wise involves the correctness of the decision that the right of action given by the statutes is enforceable by the right person in the foreign jurisdiction.

§ 202. Pleading foreign statute

The plaintiff whose right of action arises under a foreign statute must allege and prove it.[69] Where the declaration sets out a good cause of action, according to the law of the forum, without alleging that the killing was in the state, the declaration will be held good, as setting out a cause of action arising within the state.[70] If the declaration fails to allege the foreign statute, an amendment alleging it is not open to the objection that it sets up a new cause of action,[71]

[67] Ante, § 124.   [68] Ante, § 23.

[69] Gurney v. Grand Trunk Ry. Co., 59 Hun, 625, 13 N. Y. Supp. 645. It is sufficient to set out its substance in effect. St. Louis, I. M. & S. Ry. Co. v. Haist, 71 Ark. 258, 72 S. W. 893, 100 Am. St. Rep. 65; cases cited note 6, supra.

[70] Hobbs v. Memphis & C. R. Co., 12 Heisk. (Tenn.) 526. See Woodward v. Chicago & N. W. R. Co., 21 Wis 309.

[71] Lustig v. New York, L. E. & W. R. Co., 65 Hun, 547, 20 N. Y. Supp. 477; ante, § 187.

although the period of limitation prescribed by the foreign statute has elapsed.[72]

[72] South Carolina R. Co. v. Nix, 68 Ga. 572. But in Selma, R. & D. R. Co. v. Lacey, 49 Ga. 106, where the suit was originally brought in the name of the wife for the death of her husband in Alabama, and the declaration did not allege the laws of that state, it was held that an amendment after the year limited by the Alabama statute, setting up the laws of that state, could not be allowed, because it set up a new cause of action, but also because by the Alabama law the action was not maintainable by the wife.

CHAPTER XIV

JURISDICTION OF FEDERAL COURTS AND IN ADMIRALTY

§ 203. Jurisdiction of federal courts

An action for injuries resulting in death may be brought in or removed into the proper federal court, if the citizenship of the parties is such as to confer jurisdiction upon that ground.[1] And notwithstanding the provision of the Wisconsin statute "that such actions shall be brought for a death caused in this state, and in some court established by the constitution and laws of the same," it was held in Chicago & N. W. Ry. Co. v. Whitton [2] that a nonresident plaintiff might remove an action, begun by him in the state

---

[1] Chicago & N. W. Ry. Co. v. Whitton, 13 Wall. 270, 20 L. Ed. 571; Dennick v. Central R. Co. of New Jersey, 103 U. S. 11, 26 L. Ed. 439; American Steamboat Co. v. Chace, 16 Wall. 522, 21 L. Ed. 369, per Clifford, J. See Lung Chung v. Northern Pac. R. Co. (D. C.) 19 Fed. 254; Texas & P. R. Co. v. Cox, 145 U. S. 593, 12 Sup. Ct. 905, 36 L. Ed. 829; Burrell v. Fleming, 109 Fed. 489, 47 C. C. A. 598. See, also, Lung Chung v. Northern Pac. Ry. Co. (D. C.) 19 Fed. 254; Atchison, T. & S. F. Ry. Co. v. Phillips, 176 Fed. 663, 100 C. C. A. 215.

[2] 13 Wall. 270, 20 L. Ed. 571. See, also, Bigelow v. Nickerson, 70 Fed. 113, 17 C. C. A. 1, 30 L. R. A. 336.

court, into the circuit court. If the administrator is a citizen of another state, he may bring the action in the federal court, although the deceased was a citizen of the state where the cause of action arose, and the beneficiaries and the defendant are also citizens of the same state.[3] Nor does the fact that a citizen of another state is selected as administrator, for the purpose of conferring jurisdiction on the federal court, defeat that jurisdiction.[4]

§ 204. Suit in admiralty for death not maintainable independently of statute

The rule of the common law that no suit can be maintained to recover damages for the death of a human being also prevails in admiralty.[5]

Whether such a suit might not be maintained in the admiralty courts of the United States independently of any statute was a question in respect to which much doubt existed [6] until it was set at rest by the decision of the su-

[3] Harper v. Norfolk & W. R. Co. (C. C.) 36 Fed. 102. See, also, Boston & M. R. Co. v. Hurd, 108 Fed. 116, 47 C. C. A. 615, 56 L. R. A. 193; Cincinnati, H. & D. R. Co. v. Thiebaud, 114 Fed. 918, 52 C. C. A. 538; Bishop v. Boston & M. R. R. (C. C.) 117 Fed. 771.

[4] Goff's Adm'r v. Norfolk & W. R. Co. (C. C.) 36 Fed. 299.

[5] The Harrisburg, 119 U. S. 199, 7 Sup. Ct. 140, 30 L. Ed. 358 (overruling Id. [C. C.] 15 Fed. 610); The Alaska, 130 U. S. 201, 9 Sup. Ct. 461, 32 L. Ed. 923; Williams v. Quebec S. S. Co. (D. C.) 126 Fed. 591.

[6] The jurisdiction of the admiralty courts, independently of statute, was sustained in the following cases: The Sea Gull, Chase, 145, Fed. Cas. No. 12,578; The Towanda, 34 Leg. Int. 394, Fed. Cas. No. 14,109; s. c., under the name of Coggins v. Helmsley, 5 Cent. Law J. 418, Fed. Cas. No. 14,109; The Charles Morgan, 2 Flip. 274, Fed. Cas. No. 2,618; The David Reeves, 5 Hughes, 89, Fed. Cas. No. 6,625; The E. B. Ward, Jr. (C. C.) 17 Fed. 456; The E. B. Ward, Jr. (C. C.) 23 Fed. 900; The Columbia (D. C.) 27 Fed. 704. The following cases contained dicta to the same effect: Plummer

preme court in The Harrisburg.[7] In that case a suit in rem was brought in the eastern district of Pennsylvania, against the steamer Harrisburg, by the widow and child of the first officer of the schooner Marietta Tilton, to recover damages for his death in a collision between the two vessels, which occurred in a sound of the sea embraced between the islands of Martha's Vineyard and Nantucket, parts of the state of Massachusetts. The steamer was engaged in the coasting trade, and belonged to the port of Philadelphia, where she was duly enrolled, according to the laws of the

v. Webb, 1 Ware, 75, Fed. Cas. No. 11,234; Cutting v. Seabury, 1 Spr. 522, Fed. Cas. No. 3,521; The Epsilon, 6 Ben. 378, Fed. Cas. No. 4,506; The Highland Light, Chase, 150, Fed. Cas. No. 6,477; Holmes v. Oregon & C. Ry. Co. (D. C.) 6 Sawy. 262, 5 Fed. 75; The Garland (D. C.) 5 Fed. 924; The Manhasset (D. C.) 18 Fed. 918. See, also, In re Long Island, N. S., P. & F. Transp. Co. (D. C.) 5 Fed. 599; The Clatsop Chief (D. C.) 8 Fed. 163; The Cephalonia (D. C.) 29 Fed. 332; Id. (D. C.) 32 Fed. 112; Ladd v. Foster (D. C.) 31 Fed. 827. In The City of Brussels, 6 Ben. 370, Fed. Cas. No. 2,745, Mr. Justice Blatchford, then judge of the district court, sustained a libel by an administrator of an infant child who took passage from Liverpool to New York, and while on the voyage was poisoned by the carelessness of the officers of the vessel. He placed the decision, however, on the ground of a breach of the contract of carriage. The jurisdiction was denied in The Sylvan Glen (D. C.) 9 Fed. 335; The E. B. Ward, Jr. (C. C.) 16 Fed. 255. In Ex parte Gordon, 104 U. S. 515, 26 L. Ed. 814, the supreme court refused to issue a writ of prohibition to a district court sitting in admiralty, wherein a libel claiming damages was filed against a steamer for drowning certain seamen of a vessel with which, as she was navigating Chesapeake bay, the steamer, as was alleged, wrongfully collided. The supreme court held that the district court, having jurisdiction of the steamer and of the collision, was competent to pass upon the question whether, under the circumstances, it might estimate the damages which one person had sustained by the killing of another, and that the proper way to raise the question was by appeal. To the same effect Ex parte Detroit River Ferry Co., 104 U. S. 519, 26 L. Ed. 815. See 20 Am. Law Reg. 742, note, The Garland (D. C.) 5 Fed. 924.

[7] 119 U. S. 199, 7 Sup. Ct. 140, 30 L. Ed. 358.

United States. The district court entered a decree in favor of the libelants, which was affirmed in the circuit court. This decree was reversed in the supreme court, after an elaborate consideration of the authorities, in an opinion delivered by Chief Justice Waite. The questions for decision were stated by the chief justice as follows:

1. Can a suit in admiralty be maintained in the courts of the United States to recover damages for the death of a human being on the high seas, or waters navigable from the sea, caused by negligence, in the absence of an act of congress or a statute of a state giving a right of action therefor?

2. If not, can a suit in rem be maintained in admiralty against an offending vessel for the recovery of such damages, when an action at law has been given therefor by statute in the state where the wrong was done, or where the vessel belonged?

3. If it can, will the admiralty courts permit such a recovery in a suit begun nearly five years after the death, when the statute which gives the right of action provides that the suit shall be brought within one year?

The opinion answers the first branch of the question in the negative, and concludes: "The argument everywhere in support of such suits in admiralty has been, not that the maritime law, as actually administered in common-law countries, is different from the common law in this particular, but that the common law is not founded on good reason, and is contrary to 'natural equity and the general principles of law.' Since, however, it is now established that in the courts of the United States no action at law can be maintained for such a wrong in the absence of a statute giving the right, and it has not been shown that the maritime law, as accepted and received by maritime nations gen-

(469)

erally, has established a different rule for the government
of the courts of admiralty from those which govern courts
of law in matters of this kind, we are forced to the conclusion that no such action will lie in the courts of the United
States under the general maritime law." As to the second
branch of the question, the court expressed no opinion, since
it was satisfied that the suit under the limitation common
to both the Massachusetts and the Pennsylvania statutes
was begun too late.

The question decided in The Harrisburg was brought before the supreme court a second time in The Alaska.[8] In
that case the libel was filed to recover damages for the loss
of the pilot boat Columbia, and the personal effects of her
crew, in consequence of a collision with the steamer Alaska,
in which the pilot boat was sunk, and all the men on board
were drowned. A supplemental libel was filed to recover
damages for the death of the persons lost, on behalf of their
respective widows. In the circuit court it was held that the
supplemental libel was properly dismissed, and in the supreme court the decree of the lower court was affirmed.
The opinion was delivered by Mr. Justice Blatchford, who
said: "It is admitted by the counsel for the libelants that
the statute of New York on the subject of actions for death
by negligence does not apply to the present case, because
the deaths did not occur within the state of New York, or
in waters subject to its jurisdiction. * * * A distinction is sought to be drawn between the present case and
that of The Harrisburg, on the ground that in that case
the vessel was owned in Pennsylvania, while here the Alaska is a British vessel, and that in that case the wrongful
killing occurred in the waters of the state of Massachusetts,

[8] 130 U. S. 201, 9 Sup. Ct. 461, 32 L. Ed. 923.

while here it occurred on the high seas. But we see no sound distinction between the two cases."

§ 205. Jurisdiction in admiralty under state statutes—In rem where statute creates no lien

In The Harrisburg the question was left unanswered whether a suit in rem could be maintained in admiralty against an offending vessel for the recovery of damages for the death of a human being, where an action therefor had been given, in the state where the wrong was done, or where the vessel belonged. Prior to that decision a number of libels founded upon state statutes, both in rem and in personam, had been brought for loss of life, in the courts of the different districts, and, as a rule, the jurisdiction in personam was sustained,[9] as it has since been sustained,[10] though the weight of authority was against the maintenance

---

[9] Holmes v. Oregon & C. Ry. Co. (D. C.) 5 Fed. 75, 6 Sawy. 262; The Clatsop Chief (D. C.) 8 Fed. 163; Holland v. Brown (D. C.) 35 Fed. 43; In re Long Island, N. S., P. & F. Transp. Co. (D. C.) 5 Fed. 599; Ladd v. Foster (D. C.) 31 Fed. 827; Grimsley v. Hankins (D. C.) 46 Fed. 400.

[10] In re Humboldt Lumber Manufacturers' Ass'n (D. C.) 60 Fed. 428, affirmed 73 Fed. 239, 19 C. C. A. 481, 46 L. R. A. 264; State of Maryland v. Miller (D. C.) 180 Fed. 796; State of Maryland v. Hamburg-American Steam Packet Co. (D. C.) 190 Fed. 240, affirmed Atlantic Transport Co. of West Virginia v. State of Maryland, 193 Fed. 1019, 113 C. C. A. 408. A libel in personam may be maintained for damages for death, under statutes like Lord Campbell's act, where the death occurred in navigable waters within the state. The Norwalk (D. C.) 55 Fed. 98; The Transfer No. 4, 61 Fed. 364, 9 C. C. A. 521; Robinson v. Detroit & C. Steam Nav. Co., 73 Fed. 883, 20 C. C. A. 86. See, also, Bigelow v. Nickerson, 70 Fed. 113, 17 C. C. A. 1, 30 L. R. A. 336; The Jane Gray (D. C.) 95 Fed. 693; Stern v. La Compagnie Générale Transatlantique (D. C.) 110 Fed. 996; Trauffler v. Detroit & Cleveland Nav. Co. (D. C.) 181 Fed. 256.

of a libel in rem where no lien was created by the statute.[11] The question left open in The Harrisburg, however, was determined by the supreme court in the negative in The Corsair,[12] which decides that no action in rem for loss of life is maintainable where no lien is expressly created by the local law. The libel was in rem against the tug Corsair by the mother of a passenger whose death was caused by the tug running against the bank of the Mississippi river within the state of Louisiana. The suit was founded on article 2315, Rev. Civil Code of Louisiana, as amended by the Laws of 1884, and was upon two causes of action— one for damages for the pains and sufferings endured by the deceased, and the other for damages sustained by the mother in the loss of the life of her daughter. Exceptions were sustained, upon the ground that a suit in rem would not lie for injuries resulting in death; but leave was given to amend, by proceeding in personam against the owner of the tug. Exceptions were also sustained as to the amended libel, and the suit was dismissed. Upon appeal to the su-

---

[11] The Sylvan Glen (D. C.) 9 Fed. 335; The Manhasset (D. C.) 18 Fed. 918; Welsh v. The North Cambria (D. C.) 40 Fed. 655; Oleson v. The Ida Campbell (D. C.) 34 Fed. 432. See, also, The Wydale (C. C.) 37 Fed. 716. But see The Garland (D. C.) 5 Fed. 924; The E. B. Ward, Jr. (C. C.) 17 Fed. 456. The death statutes of both Illinois and Wisconsin give a right of action in behalf of the next of kin of the deceased. The water craft statutes of both states make a vessel liable for all damages arising from injuries done to person or property by such vessel. Held, that such water craft laws were not intended to give a lien in favor of the next of kin of persons killed by the negligent navigation of a vessel, but only in favor of those directly injured in person or property, and that a suit in rem for wrongful death of a person killed as the result of a collision, based upon the statute of either state, cannot be maintained in a court of admiralty against the vessel charged with being in fault for the collision. The Onoko, 107 Fed. 984, 47 C. C. A. 111.

[12] 145 U. S. 335, 12 Sup. Ct. 949, 36 L. Ed. 727.

preme court, it was held that the decree of dismissal was proper, so far as it operated upon the amended libel, (1) because the amendment by introducing new parties was in violation of admiralty rule 15, which prohibits joining the ship and her owner in the same suit, and (2) because, if the amended libel be considered as an independent libel against the owners in personam, it was defective, in failing to aver that the respondents were the owners at the time of the accident. As to the dismissal of the original libel, the opinion, which was delivered by Mr. Justice Brown, says: "An important question arises in connection with the dismissal of the original libel, which has never been squarely presented to this court before, and that is as to the power of the district court to entertain a libel in rem for damages incurred by loss of life, where, by the local law, a right of action survives to the administrator or relatives of the deceased, but no lien is expressly created by the act. * * * A maritime lien is said by writers upon maritime law to be the foundation of every proceeding in rem in the admiralty. In much the larger class of cases the lien is given by the general admiralty law, but in other instances—such, for example, as insurance, pilotage, wharfage, and materials furnished in the home port of the vessel—the lien is given, if at all, by the local law. As we are to look, then, to the local law in this instance for the right to take cognizance of this class of cases, we are bound to inquire whether the local law gives a lien upon the offending thing. If it merely gives a right of action in personam for a cause of action of a maritime nature, the district court may administer the law by proceedings in personam, as was done with a claim for half pilotage dues under the law of New York, in the case of Ex parte McNiel, 13 Wall. 237, 20 L. Ed. 624; but, unless a lien be given by the local law, there is no lien to

(473)

enforce by proceedings in rem in the court of admiralty. The Louisiana act declares, in substance, that the right of action for every act of negligence which causes damage to another shall survive, in case of death, in favor of the minor children or widow of the deceased, and, in default of these, in favor of the surviving father or mother; and that such survivors may also recover the damages sustained by them by the death of the parent, child, husband, or wife. Evidently nothing more is here contemplated than an ordinary action, according to the course of the law as it is administered in Louisiana. There is no intimation of a lien or privilege upon the offending thing, which, as we have already held, is necessary to give a court of admiralty jurisdiction to proceed in rem." [13] As to the question whether a libel in rem would lie upon the first cause of action for injuries, suffered by the deceased before her death, the court did not find it necessary to express an opinion, because there was no averment from which it could be gathered that the pains and sufferings were not substantially contemporaneous with her death, and inseparable, as matter of law, from it.

§ 206. Jurisdiction in personam—In rem where statute creates lien

It was intimated in The Corsair that, if the state statute gives a right of action in personam for a cause of action of a maritime nature, the district court may administer the law by proceedings in personam; and that, if the statute

---

[13] Such a lien was not created by Rev. Civ. Code La. art. 3237, subd. 12, creating a privilege for loss or damage caused to person or property by negligent management of a vessel, as this was not intended to apply to actions for damages resulting in death. The Albert Dumois, 177 U. S. 240, 20 Sup. Ct. 595, 44 L. Ed. 751.

gives a lien, it may be enforced by proceedings in rem. Nevertheless, in Butler v. Boston & S. S. S. Co.[14] it was intimated that it was still an open question whether, under such circumstances, a court of admiralty would entertain a suit at all. In that case the opinion, delivered by Mr. Justice Bradley, concludes: "We have no question, therefore, in saying that the limited liability act applies to the present case, notwithstanding the disaster happened within the technical limits of a county of Massachusetts, and notwithstanding the liability itself may have arisen from a state law. It might be a much more serious question *whether a state law can have force to create a liability in a maritime case at all*, within the dominion of the admiralty and maritime jurisdiction, where neither the general maritime law nor an act of congress has created such a liability. On this subject we prefer not to express an opinion." [15]

The question on which the court in Butler v. Boston & S. S. S. Co. declined to express an opinion was recently determined by the supreme court in the affirmative in The Hamilton,[16] in which it was held that applying to a claim for death on the high seas, due to a tortious collision of two vessels belonging to Delaware corporations the provisions of the Delaware act, authorizing personal representatives to maintain an action to recover damages for death occasioned by unlawful violence or negligence, does not render such provisions repugnant either to the commerce

---

[14] 130 U. S. 527, 9 Sup. Ct. 612, 32 L. Ed. 1017.

[15] Doubts of a similar nature were expressed in The A. W. Thompson (D. C.) 39 Fed. 115; Jones v. The St. Nicholas (D. C.) 49 Fed. 671. The power of a state to creat a maritime lien in such cases was seriously questioned in The Sylvan Glen (D. C.) 9 Fed. 335; The Manhasset (D. C.) 18 Fed. 918; The North Cambria (C. C.) 40 Fed. 655.

[16] 207 U. S. 398, 28 Sup. Ct. 133, 52 L. Ed. 264.

or admiralty clauses of the federal constitution, where congress has not legislated upon the subject; and that the liability created by the act will be enforced in a proceeding in admiralty for the limitation of liability arising out of such collision. The principal question discussed was whether the Delaware statute applied to a claim for death on the high seas, arising purely from tort, in proceedings in admiralty. The opinion was delivered by Mr. Justice Holmes, who said that, apart from the subordination of the state to the federal constitution, there was no doubt that the state would have power to make its statute applicable to the case, and that the question was narrowed to whether there is anything in the structure of the national government and under the federal constitution that qualifies the authority that otherwise the state would possess—the question that was considered doubtful in Butler v. Boston & S. S. S. Co.

"The question," said the court, "has two branches: First, whether the state law is valid for any purpose; and, next, whether, if valid, it will be applied in the admiralty. * * * The power of congress to legislate upon the subject has been derived both from the power to regulate commerce and from the clause in the constitution extending the judicial power to 'all cases of admiralty and maritime jurisdiction.' Const. art. 3, § 2; 130 U. S. 557, 9 Sup. Ct. 612, 32 L. Ed. 1017. The doubt in this case arises as to the power of the states where congress has remained silent. That doubt, however, cannot be serious. The grant of admiralty jurisdiction, followed and construed by the judiciary act of 1789, 'saving to suitors, in all cases, the right of a common law remedy where the common law is competent to give it,' leaves open the common-law jurisdiction of the state courts over torts committed at sea. This, we believe, always has been admitted. * * * And as the state courts in their decisions would follow their own notions about the law and might change them from time to time, it would be strange if the state might not make changes by its other mouthpiece, the legislature. The same argument that deduces the legislative power of congress from the jurisdiction of the national courts tends to establish the legislative power of the state where congress has not acted. Accordingly, it has been held that a statute giving damages for death caused by a tort might be enforced in a state court, although the tort was committed at sea. American S. B. Co. v. Chace, 16 Wall. 522, 21 L. Ed. 369. So far as the objection to the state law is founded on the admiralty clause in the constitution, it would seem not to matter whether the accident happened near shore or in mid-ocean, notwithstanding some expressions of doubt. The same conclusion was reached in McDonald v. Mallory, 77 N. Y. 546, 33 Am. Rep. 664, where the death occurred on the high seas. Sherlock v. Alling, 93 U. S. 99, 23 L. Ed. 819, reinforces Chace's Case, and answers any argument based on the power of congress over commerce. * * * Without further recapitulation of the authorities, we are of opinion that the statute is valid. See Workman v. New York, 179 U. S. 552, 563, 21 Sup. Ct. 212, 45 L. Ed. 314, 321. We should add, what has been assumed thus far, as it had to be assumed in order to raise the question discussed, that we construe the statute as intended to govern all cases which it is competent to govern, or, at least, not to be confined to deaths occasioned on land. McDonald v. Mallory, supra. If it touches any case at sea, it controls this. See The Belgenland (The Belgenland v. Jenson) 114 U. S. 355, 370, 5 Sup. Ct. 860, 29 L. Ed. 152, 157. Whether it is to be taken to offer a similar liability of Delaware owners to foreign subjects (Mulhall v. Fallon, 176 Mass. 266, 57 N. E. 386, 54

L. R. A. 934, 79 Am. St. Rep. 309), need not be determined
now.

"We pass to the other branch of the first question—
whether the state law, being valid, will be applied in the
admiralty.   Being valid, it created an obligatio—a personal
liability of the owner of the Hamilton to the claimants.
Slater v. Mexican Nat. R. Co., 194 U. S. 120, 126, 24 Sup.
Ct. 581, 48 L. Ed. 900, 902.   This, of course, the admiralty
would not disregard, but would respect the right when
brought before it in any legitimate way.   Ex parte McNiel,
13 Wall. 236, 243, 20 L. Ed. 624, 626.   It might not give
a proceeding in rem, since the statute does not purport to
create a lien.   It might give a proceeding in personam.
The Corsair (Barton v. Brown) 145 U. S. 335, 347, 12 Sup.
Ct. 949, 36 L. Ed. 727, 731.   If it gave the latter, the result
would not be, as suggested, to create different laws for different districts.   The liability would be recognized in all.
Nor would there be produced any lamentable lack of uniformity.   Courts constantly enforce rights arising from and
depending upon other laws than those governing the local
transactions of the jurisdiction in which they sit.   But we
are not concerned with these considerations.   In this case
the statutes of the United States have enabled the owner
to transfer its liability to a fund and to the exclusive jurisdiction of the admiralty, and it has done so.   That fund is
being distributed. · In such circumstances all claims to
which the admiralty does not deny existence must be recognized, whether admiralty liens or not."

The doctrine of The Hamilton was followed in La Bourgogne,[17] in which case it was held that the law of France,

---

[17] 210 U. S. 95, 28 Sup. Ct. 664, 52 L. Ed. 973.   In a suit in personam, in the district court for the northern district of Illinois, by
an administrator to recover damages for the death by drowning

(478)

which authorizes a recovery for loss of life against a vessel in fault, will be enforced by the courts of the United States in a proceeding to limit the liability of claims against a French vessel found to be at fault for a collision in a fog on the high seas, although the French courts, in applying to the facts the international rule as to the speed of vessels in a fog, might not have held such vessel to be at fault.

It is thus settled by The Hamilton and La Bourgogne that a state law can have force to create a liability in a maritime case, within the dominion of the admiralty and maritime jurisdiction, where neither the general maritime law nor an act of congress has created such a liability. What the cases specifically decide, indeed, is that, if the owner of the vessel takes proceedings to obtain the benefit of the limited liability act, persons entitled to an action for death under the laws of the ship's domicile or flag may share in the fund thereby created. It follows that an action in personam for a death on the high seas will lie where such right of action is given by the law of the ship's domicile.[18]

of a passenger, as the result of the same disaster, against owners of La Bourgogne, the libel was dismissed. Rundell v. La Compagnie Générale Transatlantique (D. C.) 94 Fed. 366. The decree was affirmed in the circuit court of appeals upon the ground that it did not appear that the death occurred upon the steamship, a ground which seems untenable (see ante, § 196), and upon the further ground that in cases arising in tort upon the high seas the district court, sitting in admiralty, cannot enforce the local law of France, even if in terms it applied to the case, which did not appear, but that such cases must be adjudged and governed by the general maritime and admiralty law as understood and administered by the United States courts. Id., 100 Fed. 655, 40 C. C. A. 625, 49 L. R. A. 92. For a valuable discussion of the questions involved in this case, see "Enforcement of a Right of Action Acquired under Foreign Law for Death upon the High Seas," by G. Philip Wardner, 21 Harv. Law Rev. 1–22, 75–91.

[18] The Kentucky death act confers a right of action against a

Whether, if a state statute creates a lien upon the ship, it will be enforced in admiralty by an action in rem, seems to be still an open question in the supreme court, but the jurisdiction has frequently been sustained in the lower federal courts.   In The Oregon [19] the jurisdiction in rem was sustained upon the ground that a lien was created by the Oregon statute.   After citing the section of the Oregon statute which gives the right of action, Deady, J., says: "It is admitted that the right of action conferred by this section on the personal representative of the deceased is not accompanied by any privilege or lien on the offending thing, if any; and therefore, although it may, as in this case, arise out of a marine tort, it can only be asserted in admiralty in personam.   But the statute also gives this privilege or lien.   Section 3690 [Comp. Laws 1887] provides: 'Every boat or vessel used in navigating the waters of this state * * * shall be liable and subject to a lien * * * for all * * * damages or injuries done to persons or property by such boat or vessel.'   The Oregon was being used to navigate the waters of this state, and the injury com-

corporation, a citizen of that state, for death of another resulting from the corporation's negligence, while operating a vessel on the high seas. "The Hamilton, we think," said the court, "directly supports this ruling." Southern Pac. Co. v. De Valle 'Da Costa, 190 Fed. 689, 111 C. C. A. 417. See The Lotta (D. C.) 150 Fed. 219; Fisher v. Boutelle Transportation & Towing Co. (D. C.) 162 Fed. 994. A right of action for death given by a state statute may be enforced in admiralty in proceedings in personam, the death occurring on navigable waters of the state (citing The Hamilton, supra). Monongahela River Consol. Coal & Coke Co. v. Schinnerer (C. C. A.) 196 Fed. 375.

[19] 45 Fed. 62. See, also, The Premier (D. C.) 59 Fed. 797; The Willamette, 70 Fed. 874, 18 C. C. A. 366, 31 L. R. A. 715; The Oregon (D. C.) 73 Fed. 847; Laidlaw v. Oregon Ry. & Nav. Co., 81 Fed. 876, 26 C. C. A. 665; The Jane Gray (D. C.) 95 Fed. 693; The Aurora (D. C.) 163 Fed. 633.

plained of was suffered thereon, and she is clearly within the purview of the statute. A state may give a lien for building a ship (Edwards v. Elliott, 21 Wall. 532, 22 L. Ed. 487), or for materials furnished in the home port (The Lottawanna, 21 Wall. 558, 22 L. Ed. 654), and such liens may be enforced in admiralty."

In The Glendale,[20] it was held that the Virginia statute, which gives a right of action for death, and provides also for a libel in rem against a vessel, creates a lien, which may be enforced in the federal courts, when the tort occurred on the navigable waters of the state.

§ 207. Contributory negligence

Notwithstanding that the admiralty courts have their own doctrine on the subject of contributory negligence, such negligence reducing, but not defeating, recovery,[21] the right of action arising under a death statute, being conferred upon the condition that the decedent if living might have maintained an action, is barred even in admiralty by the decedent's contributory negligence.[22]

§ 208. Jurisdiction of admiralty in England

The English cases throw little light upon the jurisdiction of the courts of admiralty in the United States in such cases, since the jurisdiction of the admiralty division is de-

---

[20] 77 Fed. (D. C.) 906.

[21] Hughes, Admiralty, 208.

[22] The A. W. Thompson (D. C.) 39 Fed. 115; The City of Norwalk (D. C.) 55 Fed. 98; Robinson v. Detroit & C. Steam Nav. Co., 73 Fed. 883, 20 C. C. A. 86; Gretschmann v. Fix (D. C.) 189 Fed. 716.

rived from an act of parliament,[23] which gives "jurisdiction over any claim of damage done by any ship." Under the construction placed upon these words, it is held that the admiralty division cannot entertain an action in rem for loss of life under Lord Campbell's act.[24] But, while the denial of jurisdiction is based upon the construction of the statute, it has been pointed out that the purpose of Lord Campbell's act was to give the parties a right to compensation, to be recovered according to the procedure of the common law; and that a transfer of jurisdiction to the admiralty would not only deprive parties of the common-law procedure and mode of trial, but would materially alter their rights and relative positions.[25]

The admiralty division has jurisdiction, however, as a branch of the high court, to entertain an action under Lord Campbell's act in personam; but such a suit is not an admiralty action, and the admiralty rule as to half damages does not apply.[26]

---

[23] Admiralty Court Act 1861 (24 Vict. c. 10, § 7).

[24] Seward v. The Vera Cruz, 10 App. Cas. 59, affirming 9 P. D. 96, which reversed Id. 88. Prior to the decision of this case a conflict of authority had existed. The jurisdiction had been maintained in The Guldfaxe, 38 L. J. (N. S.) Adm. 12, L. R. 2 A. & E. 325, and in The Explorer, 40 L. J. (N. S.) Adm. 41, L. R. 3 A. & E. 289. In Smith v. Brown, L. R. 6 Q. B. 729, however, the court of queen's bench, by writ of prohibition, restrained the court of admiralty from proceeding with such a suit, on the ground that it had no jurisdiction to entertain it. The court of admiralty again asserted its jurisdiction in The Franconia, 2 P. D. 163, and was sustained in the court of appeal by a divided court. The question was discussed in Monaghan v. Horn, 7 Can. Sup. Ct. 409, but the case was determined on other grounds.

[25] Smith v. Brown, L. R. 6 Q. B. 729, per Cockburn, C. J. See, also, remarks of Lindley, L. J., in The Bernina, 12 P. D. 58.

[26] The Bernina, 13 App. Cas. 1 (affirming 12 P. D. 58, which, upon this point, affirmed 11 P. D. 31). See Roche v. London & S. W. Ry.

§ 209.   Jurisdiction under limited liability act

The limited liability act,[27] which provides that the liability of the shipowner "for any loss, damage, or injury by collision, or for any act, matter, or thing, [loss,] damage, or forfeiture, done, occasioned or incurred without the privity or knowledge" of the owner, shall in no case exceed the value of the interest of the owner, applies to damages for loss of life; and, where the owner has taken appropriate proceedings to obtain the benefit of that act, the person injured is barred of the right to maintain a separate action for such injuries.[28] The act applies notwithstanding that the death was caused within the technical limits of a state, and that the liability sought to be enforced arose from the state law.[29] The question whether the state law can have

Co., [1899] 2 Q. B. 502, C. A. In Adam v. British & Foreign S. S. Co. Ltd., [1898] 2 Q. B. 430, it was held that the act did not apply where the person killed was a foreigner. Contra: Davidsson v. Hill, [1901] 2 K. B. 606.

[27] Rev. St. §§ 4283–4285 (U. S. Comp. St. 1901, pp. 2943, 2945).

[28] Butler v. Boston & S. S. S. Co., 130 U. S. 527, 9 Sup. Ct. 612, 32 L. Ed. 1017; The City of Columbus (D. C.) 22 Fed. 460; The Epsilon, 6 Ben. 378, Fed. Cas. No. 4,506; In re Long Island, N. S. P. & F. Transp. Co. (D. C.) 5 Fed. 599; The Albert Dumois, 177 U. S. 240, 20 Sup. Ct. 595, 44 L. Ed. 751. See, also, The Northern Queen (D. C.) 117 Fed. 906. The limitation of liability may be set up in defense in a state court. Loughin v. McCaulley, 186 Pa. 517, 40 Atl. 1021, 48 L. R. A. 33, 65 Am. St. Rep. 872 (notwithstanding the prohibition of limitation of amount of recovery for injuries resulting in death, contained in the Pennsylvania constitution). Cf. The S. A. McCaulley (D. C.) 99 Fed. 302. See, also, The Rosa (D. C.) 53 Fed. 132; The Lotta (D. C.) 150 Fed. 219; Seese's Adm'x v. Monongahela River, Consol. Coal & Coke Co. (C. C.) 155 Fed. 507; Hughes, Admiralty, 329. Contra: Duffy v. Gleason, 26 Ind. App. 180, 58 N. E. 729.

[29] See Butler v. Boston & S. S. S. Co., supra; Jones v. The St.

(483)

force to create any liability at all in such a case, within the
dominion of the admiralty and maritime jurisdiction, has
now been determined in the affirmative.[30]

Nicholas (D. C.) 49 Fed. 671. In England, damages for an action
arising under Lord Campbell's act may be ascertained and awarded
in a proceeding to limit the liability of the shipowner. Glaholm v.
Barker, L. R. 2 Eq. 598, affirmed L. R. 1 Ch. App. 223.

[30] The Hamilton, 207 U. S. 398, 28 Sup. Ct. 133, 52 L. Ed. 264; La
Bourgogne, 210 U. S. 95, 28 Sup. Ct. 664, 52 L. Ed. 973; ante, § 206.

APPENDIX

STATUTES GIVING A RIGHT OF ACTION FOR IN-JURIES RESULTING IN DEATH IN FORCE IN ENGLAND AND THE UNITED STATES

ENGLAND

9 and 10 Vict. c. 93

[An act for compensating the families of persons killed by accidents.]

Whereas, no action at law is now maintainable against a person who, by his wrongful act, neglect, or default, may have caused the death of another person, and it is oftentimes right and expedient that the wrongdoer in such case should be answerable in damages for the injury so caused by him: Be it therefore enacted, * * * that whensoever the death of a person shall be caused by wrongful act, neglect, or default, and the act, neglect, or default is such as would, if death had not ensued, have entitled the party injured to maintain an action and recover damages in respect thereof then, and in every such case, the person who would have been liable if death had not ensued shall be liable to an action for damages, notwithstanding the death of the person injured, and although the death shall have been caused under such circumstances as amount in law to felony.

Sec. 2. And it be enacted, that every such action shall be for the benefit of the wife, husband, parent, and child of the person whose death shall have been so caused, and shall be brought by and in the name of the executor or administrator of the person deceased; and in every such action the jury may give such damages as they may think proportioned to the injury resulting from such death to the parties, respectively, for whom and for whose benefit such action shall be brought; and the amount so recovered, after deducting the costs not recovered from the defendant, shall be divided amongst the before-mentioned parties in such shares as the jury, by their verdict, shall find and direct.

Sec. 3. Provided, always, and be it enacted, that not more than one action shall lie for and in respect of the same subject-matter of complaint; and that every such action shall be commenced within twelve calendar months after the death of such deceased person.

Sec. 4. And be it enacted, that in every such action the plaintiff on the record shall be required, together with the declaration, to deliver to the defendant or his attorney a full particular of the person or persons for whom and on whose behalf such action shall be brought, and of the nature of the claim in respect of which damages shall be sought to be recovered.

Sec. 5. And be it enacted, that the following words and expressions are intended to have the meanings hereby assigned to them, respectively, so far as such meanings are not excluded by the context or by the nature of the subject-matter, that is to say: Words denoting the singular number are to be understood to apply also to a plurality of persons or things; and words denoting the masculine gender are to be understood to apply also to persons of the feminine gender; and the word "person" shall apply to bodies politic and corporate; and the word "parent" shall include father and mother, and grandfather and grandmother, and stepfather and stepmother; and the word "child" shall include son and daughter, and grandson and granddaughter, and stepson and stepdaughter.

Sec. 6. And be it enacted, that this act shall come into operation from and immediately after the passing thereof, and that nothing therein contained shall apply to that part of the United Kingdom called "Scotland."

Sec. 7. And be it enacted, that this act may be amended or repealed by any act to be passed in this session of parliament.

27 and 28 Vict. c. 95

[An act to amend the act 9 and 10 Vict. c. 93.]

Section 1. If and so often as it shall happen, at any time or times hereafter, in any of the cases intended and provided for by the said act, that there shall be no executor or administrator of the person deceased, or that, there being such executor or administrator, no such action as in the said act mentioned shall within six calendar months after the death of such deceased person, as therein mentioned, have been brought by and in the name of his or her executor or administrator, then, and in every such case, such action may be brought by and in the name or names of all or any of the persons (if more than one) for whose benefit such action would have been if it had been brought by and in the name of such executor or administrator, and every action so to be brought shall be for the benefit of the same person or persons, and shall be subject to the same regulations and procedure as nearly as may be, as if it were brought by and in the name of such executor or administrator.

Sec. 2. It shall be sufficient, if the defendant is advised to pay money into court, that he pay it as a compensation in one sum to all persons entitled under the said act for his wrongful act, neglect, or default, without specifying the shares into which it is to be divided by the jury; and if the said sum be not accepted, and an issue is taken by the plaintiff as to its sufficiency, and the jury shall think the same sufficient, the defendant shall be entitled to the verdict upon that issue.

Sec. 3. This act and the said act shall be read together as one act.

8 Edw. VII, c. 7

[An act to amend the law with respect to the assessment of damages under the Fatal Accidents Acts.]

Section 1. In assessing damages in any action, whether commenced before or after the passing of this act, under the Fatal Accidents Act, 1846, as amended by any subsequent enactment, there shall not be taken into account any sum paid or payable on the death of the deceased under any contract of assurance or insurance, whether made before or after the passage of this act.

ALABAMA

Code 1907

Sec. 2484. A father, or in case of his death or desertion of his family, or of his imprisonment for a term of two years or more, under a conviction for crime, or of his confinement in an insane asylum, or if he has been declared of unsound mind, the mother may sue for an injury to a minor child, a member of the family.

Sec. 2485. When the death of a minor child is caused by the wrongful act, or omission, or negligence of any person or persons, or corporation, his or their servants or agents, the father, or the mother, in cases mentioned in the preceding section; or if the father and mother are both dead, or if they decline to bring the action or fail to do so within six months from the death of the minor, the personal representative of such minor may sue, and in any case shall recover such damages as the jury may assess; but a suit by any one of them for the wrongful death of the minor shall be a bar to another action, either under this section or under the succeeding section.

Sec. 2486. A personal representative may maintain an action, and recover such damages as the jury may assess, in a court of competent jurisdiction within the state of Alabama and not elsewhere, for the wrongful act, omission, or negligence of any person or persons, or corporation, his or their servants or agents, whereby the death of his testator or intestate was caused, if the testator or intestate could have maintained an action for such wrongful act, omission, or negligence, if it had not caused death; such action shall not abate by the death of the defendant, but may be revived against his personal representative; and may be maintained, though there has not been prosecution, or conviction, or acquittal of the defendant for the wrongful act, or omission or negligence; and the damages recovered are not subject to the payment of the debts or liabilities of the testator or intestate, but must be distributed according to the statute of distributions. Such action must be brought within two years from and after the death of the testator or intestate. (As amended Gen. Laws 1911, p. 484.)

Sec. 3910. When a personal injury is received by a servant or employé in the service or business of the master or employer, the master or employer is liable to answer in damages to such servant or employé, as if he were a stranger, and not engaged in such service or employment, provided such liability is enforced in a court of competent jurisdiction within the state of Alabama, and not elsewhere, in the cases following: (1) When the injury is caused by reason of any defect in the condition of the wages, works, machinery, or plant connected with, or used in the business of, the master or employer. (2) When the injury is caused by reason of the negligence of any person in the service or employment of the master or employer who has any superintendence intrusted to him whilst in the exercise of such superintendence. (3) When such injury is caused by reason of the negligence of any person in the service or employment of the master or employer, to whose orders or directions the servant or employé at the time of the injury, was bound to conform, and did conform, if such injuries resulted from his having so conformed. (4) When such injury is caused by reason of the act or omission of any person in the service or employment of the master or employer, done or made in obedience to the rules and regulations or by-laws of the master or employer, or in obedience to particular instructions given by any person delegated with the authority of the master or employer in that behalf. (5) When such injury is caused by reason of the negligence of any person in the service or employment of the master or employer, who has the charge or control of any signal, points, locomotive, engine, electric motor, switch, car, or train upon a railway, or of any part of the track of a railway. The master or employer is not liable under this section, if the servant or employé knew of the defect or negligence causing the injury and failed in a reasonable time to give information thereof to the master or employer, or to some person superior to himself engaged in the service or employment of the master or employer, unless the master or employer, or such superior, already knew of such defect or negligence; nor is the master or employer liable under subdivision 1, unless the defect therein mentioned arose from, or had not been discovered or remedied owing to the negligence of the master or employer, or of some person in the service of the master or employer, and intrusted by him with the duty of seeing that the ways, works, machinery, or plant were in proper condition; provided, that in no event shall it be contributory negligence or an assumption of the risk on the part of a servant to remain in the employment of the master or employer after knowledge of the defect or negligence, causing the injury, unless he be a servant whose duty it is to remedy the defect or who committed the negligent act causing the injury complained of. (As amended Gen. Laws 1911, p. 486.)

Sec. 3911. Damages recovered by the servant or employé, of and from the master or employer, are not subject to the payment of debts, or any legal liabilities incurred by him.

Sec. 3912. If such injury results in the death of the servant or employé, his personal representative is entitled to maintain an action therefor, in a court of competent jurisdiction within the state of Alabama and not elsewhere, and the damages recovered are not subject to the payment of debts or liabilities, but shall be distributed according to the statute of distributions. (As amended Gen. Laws 1911, p. 483.)

Sec. 3913. No contract of employment, insurance, relief benefit, or indemnity for injury or death entered into by or on behalf of any employé, nor the acceptance of any such insurance, relief benefit, or indemnity by the person entitled thereto, shall constitute any bar or defense to any action brought to recover damages for personal injuries to or death of such employé; but upon the trial of such action against any employer, the defendant may set off therein any sum he (or it) has contributed toward any such insurance, relief benefit, or indemnity that may have been paid to the injured employé, or, in case of death, to his personal representative.

ALASKA
Carter's Ann. Code Civil Proc.

Sec. 353. When the death of a person is caused by the wrongful act or omission of another, the personal representatives of the former may maintain an action therefor against the latter, if the former might have maintained an action, had he lived, against the latter for an injury done by the same act or omission. Such action shall be commenced within two years after the death, and the damages therein shall not exceed ten thousand dollars, and the amount recovered, if any, shall be exclusively for the benefit of the decedent's husband or wife and children when he or she leaves a husband, wife, or children, him or her surviving; and when any sum is collected it must be distributed by the plaintiff as if it were unbequeathed assets left in his hands, after payment of all debts and expenses of administration, and when he or she leaves no husband, wife, or children, him or her surviving, the amount recovered shall be administered as other personal property of the deceased person; but the plaintiff may deduct therefrom the expenses of the action, to be allowed by the proper court upon notice, to be given in such manner and to such persons as the court deems proper.

ARIZONA
Civil Code 1901

Par. 2764. Whenever the death of any person shall be caused by wrongful act, neglect or default and the act, neglect or default is such as would, if death had not ensued, have entitled the party injured to maintain an action to recover damages in respect thereof, then, and in every such case, the person who or the corporation which would have been liable if death had not ensued, shall be liable to an action for damages, notwithstanding the death of the person injured, and although the death shall have been caused under such circumstances as amount in law to murder in the first or second degree or manslaughter.

Par. 2765. Every such action shall be brought by and in the name of the personal representative of such deceased person; and, provided, that the father, or in the case of his death or desertion of his family, the mother, may maintain the action for the death of a child, and the guardian for the death of his ward; and the amount recovered in every such action shall be distributed to the parties and in the proportions provided by law in relation to the distribution of personal estate left by persons dying intestate.

Par. 2766. In every case the jury shall give such damages as they shall deem fair and just, and the amount so recovered shall not be subject to any debts and liabilities of the deceased: Provided, that every action shall be commenced within one year after the death of such deceased person. If the defendant in any such action die pending the suit, his executor or administrator may be made a party and the suit be prosecuted to judgment as though such defendant had continued alive. The judgment in such case, if rendered in favor of the plaintiff, shall be paid in due course of administration. (As amended Laws 1909, c. 16, § 1.[1])

ARKANSAS

Const. art. 5

Sec. 31. No act of the general assembly shall limit the amount to be recovered for injuries resulting in death, or for injuries to persons or property, and in case of death from such injuries, the right of action shall survive, and the general assembly shall prescribe for whose benefit such action shall be prosecuted.

Kirby's Dig. 1904

Sec. 6285. For wrongs done to the person or property of another, an action may be maintained against the wrong-doers, and such action may be brought by the person injured, or, after his death, by his executor or administrator against such wrong-doer, or, after his death, against his executor or administrator, in the same manner and with like effect in all respects as actions founded on contracts.

Sec. 6287. When any adult person be killed by railroad trains running in this state, the husband may sue for damages to a wife. If the adult be wounded he may sue in his own name.

Sec. 6288. When a wife be killed in this state by the wrongful act, neglect or default of any person, company or corporation, the husband may have a cause of action therefor against such wrong-doer, and be entitled to damages for the services and companionship of his said wife in whatever amount the jury trying the cause may consider he is entitled to; provided, suit be brought within two years from the time said cause of action occurs, which action may be brought by and in the name of the husband.

[1] Section 1 repeals all acts and parts of acts in conflict with this act.

Sec. 6289. Whenever the death of a person shall be caused by wrongful act, neglect or default, and the act, neglect or default is such as would, if death had not ensued, have entitled the party injured to maintain an action and recover damages in respect thereof, then, and in every such case, the person who, or company or corporation which, would have been liable if death had not ensued, shall be liable to an action for damages, notwithstanding the death of the person injured, and although the death shall have been caused under such circumstances as amount in law to a felony.

Sec. 6290. Every such action shall be brought by, and in the name of, the personal representatives of such deceased person, and if there be no personal representatives, then the same may be brought by the heirs at law of such deceased person; and the amount recovered in every such action shall be for the exclusive benefit of the widow and next of kin of such deceased person, and shall be distributed to such widow and next of kin in the proportion provided by law in relation to the distribution of personal property left by persons dying intestate; and, in every such action, the jury may give such damages as they shall deem a fair and just compensation, with reference to the pecuniary injuries resulting from such death, to the wife and next of kin of such deceased person: Provided, every such action shall be commenced within two years after the death of such person.

CALIFORNIA

Code Civil Proc.

Sec. 376. A father, or in case of his death or desertion of his family, the mother, may maintain an action for the injury or death of a minor child, and a guardian for the injury or death of his ward, when such injury or death is caused by the wrongful act or neglect of another. Such action may be maintained against the person causing the injury, or death, or if such person be employed by another person who is responsible for his conduct, also against such other person.

Sec. 377. When the death of a person not being a minor is caused by the wrongful act or neglect of another, his heirs or personal representatives may maintain an action for damages against the person causing the death, or if such person be employed by another person, who is responsible for his conduct, then also against such other person. In every action under this and the preceding section such damages may be given as, under all the circumstances of the case, may be just.

Sec. 335. The periods prescribed for the commencement of actions other than for the recovery of real property are as follows:

*　*　*　*　*　*　*　*　*　*

Sec. 340. Within one year:

*　*　*　*　*　*　*　*　*　*

3. An action * * * for the death of one caused by the wrongful act or neglect of another.

COLORADO

Rev. St. 1908

Sec. 2056. Whenever any person shall die from any injury resulting from or occasioned by the negligence, unskillfulness or criminal intent of any officer, agent, servant or employé, whilst running, conducting or managing any locomotive, car or train of cars, or of any driver of any coach or other public conveyance whilst in charge of the same as a driver, and when any passenger shall die from any injury resulting or occasioned by any defect or insufficiency in any railroad or any part thereof, or in any locomotive or car, or in any stage coach, or other public conveyance, the corporation, individual or individuals in whose employ any such officer, agent, servant, employé, master, pilot, engineer or driver shall be at the time such injury is committed, or who owns any such railroad, locomotive, car, stage coach or other public conveyance at the time any such injury is received, and resulting from or occasioned by defect or insufficiency above described, shall forfeit and pay for every person and passenger so injured the sum of not exceeding five thousand dollars, and not less than three thousand dollars, which may be sued for and recovered:

First—By the husband or wife of deceased; or

Second—If there be no husband or wife, or he or she fails to sue within one year after such death, then by the heir or heirs of the deceased, or

Third—If such deceased be a minor or unmarried, then by the father or mother who may join in the suit, and each shall have an equal interest in the judgment; or if either of them be dead, then by the survivor. In suits instituted under this section it shall be competent for the defendant for his defense to show that the defect or insufficiency named in this section was not a negligent defect of insufficiency. If the action under this section shall be brought by the husband or wife of deceased, the judgment obtained in said action shall be owned by such persons as are heirs at law of said deceased under the statutes of descents and distributions, and shall be divided among such heirs at law in the same manner as real estate is divided according to said statute of descents and distributions.

Sec. 2057. Whenever the death of a person shall be caused by a wrongful act, neglect or default of another, and the act, neglect or default is such as would (if death had not ensued) have entitled the party injured to maintain an action and recover damages in respect thereof, then, and in every such case, the person who, or the corporation which, would have been liable if death had not ensued, shall be liable to an action for damages notwithstanding the death of the party injured.

Sec. 2058. All damages accruing under the last preceding section shall be sued for and recovered by the same parties and in the same manner as provided in the first section of this act, and in every such action the jury may give such damages as they may deem fair and just, not exceeding five thousand dollars, with reference to the necessary injury resulting from such death, to the surviving parties who may be entitled to sue; and also having regard to the mitigating or aggravating circumstances attending any such wrongful act, neglect, or default.

Sec. 2059. All actions provided for by this act shall be brought within two years from the commission of the alleged negligence resulting in the death for which suit is brought.

Code Civil Proc.

Sec. 9. A father, or in case of his death or desertion of his family, the mother, may maintain an action for the injury or death of a child, and a guardian for the injury or death of his ward.

Sess. Laws 1911, c. 113

Section 1. That every corporation or company which or individual who may employ agents, servants or employés, such agents, servants or employés being in the exercise of due care, shall be liable to respond in damages for injuries or death sustained by any such agent, servant or employé resulting from the carelessness, omission of duty or negligence of such employer, or which may have resulted from the carelessness, omission of duty or negligence of any other agent, servant or employé of the said employer, in the same manner and to the same extent as if the carelessness, omission of duty or negligence causing the injury or death was that of the employer.

Sec. 2. Whenever the death of a person shall be caused by an act of carelessness, omission of duty or negligence as provided in the preceding section, then, and in every such case, the corporation or company which, or individual who, would have been liable, if death had not ensued, shall be liable to an action for the damages, notwithstanding the death of the party injured, and in every such case the jury may give such damages as they deem fair and just, not exceeding the sum of five thousand dollars, with reference to the necessary injury resulting from such death, to the party or parties who may be entitled to sue hereunder.

Sec. 3. Every such action shall in case of death be maintained,

First, by the husband or wife of the deceased, or

Second, if there be no husband or wife, or if he or she fails to sue within one year after such death, then by the children of the deceased or their descendants, or

Third, if such deceased be a minor or unmarried, without issue, then by the father or mother, or by both jointly, or

Fourth, if there be no such person entitled to sue, then by such other next of kin of the deceased as may be dependent upon deceased for support.

Every such action, in case of death, may be maintained by any such person entitled to sue, for the use and benefit of the other or others so entitled to sue, as well as for the plaintiff so suing, and the verdict of the jury and the judgment of the court shall, in such case, specify the amount of damages awarded to each such person, and if any such actions be separately brought, the same be consolidated with the action so first commenced in the court that shall have jurisdiction of said actions, when so consolidated.

Sec. 4. All actions provided for by this act shall be brought within two years from the time of the accident causing the injury, if death does not ensue, or within two years from the time of death, in case of injury resulting in death. The amount of compensation recoverable under this act in case of personal injury resulting solely from the negligence of a co-employé shall not exceed the sum of five thousand dollars.

Sec. 5. An act entitled "An act concerning damages sustained by agents, servants or employés," approved April 8, 1893, and an act entitled "An act to give a right of action against an employer for injuries or death resulting to his agents, employés or servants, either from the employer's negligence or from the negligence of some of his other employés, servants or agents, and to repeal all acts and parts of acts in conflict herewith," approved March 28, 1901, and all acts and parts of acts in conflict herewith are hereby repealed: Provided, however, this act shall not affect any cause of action which shall have accrued at the time this act takes effect.

Approved May 27th, 1911.

CONNECTICUT

Gen. St. 1902

Sec. 399. All damages recovered under § 1094 shall be distributed, after deducting the costs and expenses of suit, as follows: Half to the husband, or widow, and half to the lineal descendants of the decedent, per stirpes; but if there be no such descendants, the whole shall go to the husband or widow, and if there be no husband or widow, to the heirs, according to the law regulating the distribution of intestate personal estate.

Sec. 1119. No action against a municipal or other corporation, to recover damages for injury to the person, or for causing the death of any person, or for an injury to personal property caused by negligence, shall be brought but within one year from the date of such injury, or from the decease of such person, as the case may be.

Sec. 1130. No action to recover damages for an injury to, or for the death of, any person, or for an injury to personal property, caused by negligence, shall be maintained against any electric, cable, or street railway company, or against any steam railroad company, unless written notice containing a general description of the injury and of the time, place, and cause of its occurrence, as nearly as the same can be ascertained, shall have been given to the defendant within four months after the neglect complained of, unless the action itself is commenced within said period of four months. Such notice may be given to the secretary, or to any agent or executive officer of the company in fault.

Sec. 1136. If an action to recover damages for a personal injury which causes death, be pending at the time of such death, and the decedent's executor or administrator enters and prosecutes such action to final judgment, the damages so recovered shall be distributed as directed in § 399.

Pub. Acts 1903, c. 193

Section 1. No cause or right of action shall be lost or destroyed by the death of any person, but shall survive in favor of or against the executor or administrator of such deceased person.

Sec. 2. No civil action or proceeding shall abate by reason of the death of any party thereto, but may be continued by or against the executor or administrator of such decedent. In case of the death of any party plaintiff, his executor or administrator may enter within six months thereafter, and prosecute the suit in the same manner as his testator or intestate might have done if he had lived; and in case of the death of any party defendant, the plaintiff may have a writ of scire facias against said decedent's executor or administrator to show cause why judgment should not be rendered against him, which shall be served at least twelve days before the day upon which it is returnable, and upon its return the action may proceed.

Sec. 3. The provisions of this act shall not apply to any cause or right of action or to any civil action or proceeding the purpose or object of which is defeated or rendered useless by the death of any party thereto; nor to any civil action or proceeding whose prosecution or defense depends upon the continued existence of the persons who are plaintiffs or defendants; nor to any civil action upon a penal statute.

Sec. 4. In all actions surviving to or brought by an executor or administrator for injuries resulting in death, whether instantaneous or otherwise, such executor or administrator may recover, from the party legally in fault for such injuries, just damages, not exceeding ten thousand dollars. No action shall be brought upon this statute but within one year from the neglect complained of. (As amended Pub. Acts 1911, c. 242, § 1.²)

Sec. 5. All damages recovered under this act shall be distributed as directed in section 399 of the General Statutes.

Sec. 6. Sections 1094 and 1131 of the General Statutes and all acts and parts of acts inconsistent herewith are hereby repealed.

DELAWARE

Laws 1866 (13 Del. Laws) c. 31

Section 1. That no action hereafter brought to recover damages for injuries to the person by negligence or default, shall abate by reason of the death of the plaintiff; but the personal representatives of the deceased may be substituted as plaintiff and prosecute the suit to final judgment and satisfaction.

Sec. 2. Whenever death shall be occasioned by unlawful violence or negligence, and no suit be brought by the party injured to recover damages during his or her life, the widow or widower of any such deceased person, or if there be no widow or widower the personal representatives may maintain an action for and recover damages for the death and loss thus occasioned. (As amended Laws 1901–03 [22 Del. Laws] c. 210.)

---

² Sec. 2. The passage of this act shall in no way affect causes of action arising before this act takes effect. Approved September 12, 1911.

TIFF.DEATH W.A.(2D ED.)—32

DISTRICT OF COLUMBIA
Act Cong. Feb. 17, 1885 (23 Stat. p. 307, c. 126)

Whenever, by an injury done or happening within the limits of the District of Columbia, the death of a person shall be caused by the wrongful act, neglect, or default of any person or corporation, and the act, neglect, or default is such as would, if death had not ensued, have entitled the party injured, or if the person injured be a married woman, have entitled her husband, either separately or by joining with the wife, to maintain an action and recover damages, the person who, or corporation which, would have been liable if death had not ensued, shall be liable to an action for damages for such death, notwithstanding the death of the person injured, even though the death shall have been caused under circumstances which constitute a felony; and such damages shall be assessed with reference to the injury resulting from such act, neglect, or default causing such death, to the widow and next of kin of such deceased person: Provided, that in no case shall the recovery under this act exceed the sum of ten thousand dollars: And provided, further, that no action shall be maintained under this act in any case when the party injured by such wrongful act, neglect, or default has recovered damages therefor during the life of such party.

Sec. 2. Every such action shall be brought by and in the name of the personal representative of such deceased person, and within one year after the death of the party injured.

Sec. 3. The damages recovered in such action shall not be appropriated to the payment of the debts or liabilities of such deceased person, but shall inure to the benefit of his or her family, and be distributed according to the provisions of the statute of distributions in force in the said District of Columbia.

FLORIDA
Gen. St. 1906

Sec. 3145. Whenever the death of any person in this state shall be caused by the wrongful act, negligence, carelessness or default of any individual or individuals, or by the wrongful act, negligence, carelessness, or default of any corporation or by the wrongful act, negligence, carelessness, or default of any agent of any corporation, acting in his capacity of agent of such corporation and the act, negligence, carelessness or default is such as would, if death had not ensued, have entitled the party injured thereby to maintain an action for damages in respect thereof, then and in every such case, the person or persons who or corporation which would have been liable in damages, if death had not ensued, shall be liable to an action for damages, notwithstanding the death shall have been caused under such circumstances as make it in law amount to a felony.

Sec. 3146. Every such action shall be brought by and in the name of the widow or husband, as the case may be, and where there is neither widow nor husband surviving the deceased, then the minor child or children may maintain an action; and where there is neither widow nor husband, nor minor child or children, then the action may be maintained by any person or persons dependent on such person killed for a support; and where there is neither of the above class of persons to sue then the action may be maintained by the executor or administrator as the case may be, of the person so killed; and in every such action the jury shall give such damages as the party or parties entitled to sue may have sustained by reason of the death of the party killed. Any action instituted under this article by or in behalf of a person or persons under twenty-one years of age, shall be brought by and in the name of a next friend.

Sec. 3147. Whenever the death of any minor child shall be caused by the wrongful act, negligence, carelessness or default of any private association of persons, or by the wrongful act, negligence, carelessness or default of any officer, agent or employé, or by the wrongful act, negligence, carelessness or default of any corporation, or by the wrongful act, negligence, carelessness or default of any officer, agent or employé of any corporation acting in his capacity as such officer, agent or employé, the father of such minor child, or if the father be not living, the mother, as the legal representative of such deceased minor child, may maintain an action against such individual, private association of persons or corporation, and may recover not only for the loss of service of such minor child, but in addition thereto such sum for the mental pain and suffering of the parent or parents as the jury may assess.

Sec. 1375. All actions for personal injuries shall die with the person, to-wit: Assault and battery, slander, false imprisonment, and malicious prosecution; all other actions shall and may be maintained in the name of the representatives of the deceased.

Sec. 1725. Actions other than those for the recovery of real property can only be commenced as follows:

＊　　＊　　＊　　＊　　＊　　＊　　＊　　＊　　＊

7. Within one year:—

＊　　＊　　＊　　＊　　＊　　＊　　＊　　＊　　＊

An action arising upon account of an act causing the wrongful death, and on account of wrongful death, of child.

GEORGIA

Civil Code 1910

Sec. 4421. No action for a tort shall abate by the death of either party where the wrongdoer received any benefit from the tort complained of; nor shall any action of tort for the recovery of damages for homicide, injury to person, or injury to property abate by the death of either party; but such cause of action, in case of the death of the plaintiff, shall, in the event there is no right of survivorship in any other person, survive to the personal representative of the deceased plaintiff, and, in case of the death of the defendant, shall survive against said defendant's personal representative.

Sec. 4424. A widow, or, if no widow, a child or children, may recover for the homicide of the husband or parent; and if suit be brought by the widow or children, and the former or one of the latter dies pending the action, the same shall survive in the first case to the children, and in the latter case to the surviving child or children. The husband may recover for the homicide of his wife, and if she leaves child or children surviving, said husband and children shall sue jointly, and not separately, with the right to recover the full value of the life of the deceased, as shown by the evidence, and with the right of survivorship as to said suit if either die pending the action. A mother, or, if no mother, a father, may recover for the homicide of a child, minor or sui juris, upon whom she or he is dependent, or who contributes to his or her support, unless said child leave a wife, husband, or child. Said mother or father shall be entitled to recover the full value of the life of said child.

Sec. 4425. The word "homicide," used in the preceding section, shall be held to include all cases where the death of a human being results from a crime or from criminal or other negligence. The plaintiff, whether widow, or child, or children, may recover the full value of the life of the deceased, as shown by the evidence. In the event of a recovery by the widow she shall hold the amount recovered subject to the law of descents, just as if it had been personal property descending to the widow and children from the deceased; and no recovery had under the provisions of this section shall be subject to any debt or liability of any character of the deceased husband or parent. The full value of the life of the deceased, as shown by the evidence, is the full value of the life of the deceased without deduction for necessary or other personal expenses of the deceased had he lived.

Séc. 4426. If the plaintiff by ordinary care could have avoided the consequences to himself caused by the defendant's negligence, he is not entitled to recover. But in other cases the defendant is not relieved, although the plaintiff may in some way have contributed to the injury sustained.

Sec. 4460. A person who knowingly or carelessly sells to another unwholesome provisions of any kind, the defect being unknown to the purchaser, and damage results to the purchaser, or his family, or his property, such person shall be liable in damages for such injury.

Sec. 4461. A person who, knowingly or carelessly, by himself or his agents, sells to another adulterated drugs or liquors, by the use of which damage accrues to the purchaser, or his patients, or his family, or his property, shall be liable in damages for the injury done.

Sec. 4462. If a vendor of drugs and medicines, by himself or his agent, either knowingly or negligently furnishes the wrong article or medicine, and damage accrues from the use of the drug or medicine furnished, to the purchaser, or his patients, or his family, or his property, the vendor shall respond in damages for the injury done. If death ensues to the purchaser, in any case arising under this or the two foregoing paragraphs, the right of action shall be to the widow or children, as prescribed in cases of physical injuries.

IDAHO

Rev. Codes 1908

Sec. 4099. A father, or in case of his death or desertion of his family, the mother, may maintain an action for the injury or death of a minor child, and a guardian for the injury or death of his ward, when such injury or death is caused by the wrongful act or neglect of another. Such action may be maintained against the person causing the injury or death, or if such person be employed by another person, who is responsible for his conduct, also against such other person.

Sec. 4100. When the death of a person, not being a minor, is caused by the wrongful act or neglect of another, his heirs or personal representatives may maintain an action for damages against the person causing the death; or if such person be employed by another person, who is responsible for his conduct, then also against such other person. In every action under this and the preceding section such damages may be given as, under all the circumstances of the case, may be just.

Sec. 4050. The periods prescribed for the commencement of actions other than for the recovery of real property are as follows:

*   *   *   *   *   *   *   *   *

Sec. 4055. Within two years:

*   *   *   *   *   *   *   *   *

4. An action to recover damages for injury to the person, or for the death of one caused by the wrongful act or neglect of another.

ILLINOIS

Hurd's Rev. St. 1911, c. 70

Section 1. Whenever the death of a person shall be caused by wrongful act, neglect or default, and the act, neglect or default is such as would, if death had not ensued, have entitled the party injured to maintain an action and recover damages in respect thereof, then and in every such case the person who or company or corporation which would have been liable if death had not ensued, shall be liable to an action for damages, notwithstanding the death of the person injured, and although the death shall have been caused under such circumstances as amount in law to felony.

Sec. 2. Every such action shall be brought by and in the names of the personal representatives of such deceased person and the amount recovered in every such action shall be for the exclusive benefit of the widow and next of kin of such deceased person, and shall be distributed to such widow and next of kin in the proportion provided by law. In relation to the distribution of personal property left by persons dying intestate; and in every such action the jury may give such damages as they shall deem a fair and just compensation with reference to the pecuniary injuries resulting from such death to the wife and next of kin of such deceased person not exceeding the sum of ten thousand dollars: Provided, that every such action shall be commenced within one year after the death of such person. Provided further, that no action shall be brought or prosecuted in this state to recover damages for a death occurring outside of this state, and that the increase from five thousand to ten thousand dollars in the amount hereby authorized to be recovered shall apply only in cases when death hereafter occurs.

Chapter 3

Sec. 122. In addition to the actions which survive by the common law, the following shall also survive: Actions of replevin, actions to recover damages for an injury to the person, (except slander and libel), actions to recover damages for any injury to real or personal property, or for the detention or conversion of personal property, and actions against officers for misfeasance, malfeasance or nonfeasance of themselves or their deputies, and all actions for fraud or deceit.

Chapter 93

Sec. 29 (c). For any injury to person or property, occasioned by any wilful violation of this act,[3] or wilful failure to comply with any of its provisions, a right of action shall accrue to the party injured, for any direct damages sustained thereby; and in case of loss of life by reason of such wilful violation or wilful failure as aforesaid, a right of action shall accrue to the personal representatives of the person so killed for the exclusive benefit of the widow and next of kin of such person and to any other person or persons who were, before such loss of life, dependent for support on the person or persons so killed, for a like recovery of damages for the injuries sustained by reason of such loss of life or lives not to exceed the sum of ten thousand dollars: Provided, that every such action for damages in case of death shall be commenced within one year after the death of such person: And, provided further, that the amount recovered by the personal representative of the person so killed shall be distributed to the widow and next of kin of such person in the proportion provided by law in relation to the distribution of personal property left by persons dying intestate: Provided, that if and when ever there shall be in force in this state, a statute or statutes providing for compensation to workmen for all injuries received in the course of their employment, the provisions thereof shall apply in lieu of the right of action for damages provided in this act.

Chapter 48

Sec. 126. That any employer covered by the provisions of this act in this state may elect to provide and pay compensation for injuries sustained by any employé arising out of and in the course of the employment according to the provisions of this act, and thereby relieve himself from any liability for the recovery of damages, except as herein provided. If, however, any such employer shall elect not to provide and pay the compensation to any employé who has elected to accept the provisions of this act, according to

---

[3] An act to provide for the health and safety of persons employed in coal mines.

the provisions of this act he shall not escape liability for injuries sustained by such employé arising out of and in the course of his employment because

1. The employé assumed the risks of the employer's business.

2. The injury or death was caused in whole or in part by the negligence of a fellow servant.

3. The injury or death was proximately caused by the contributory negligence of the employé, but such contributory negligence shall be considered by the jury in reducing the amount of damages.

Sec. 128. No common law or statutory right to recover damages for injury or death sustained by any employé while engaged in the line of his duty as such employé other than the compensation herein provided shall be available to any employé who has accepted the provisions of this act or to any one wholly or partially dependent upon him or legally responsible for his estate: Provided, that when the injury to the employé was caused by the intentional omission of the employer, to comply with statutory safety regulations, nothing in this act shall affect the civil liability of the employer. If the employer is a partnership, such omission must be that of one of the partners thereof, and if a corporation, that of any elective officer thereof.

Sec. 129. The amount of compensation which the employer who accepts the provisions of this act shall pay for injury to the employé which results in death, shall be:

a. If the employé leaves any widow, child or children, or parents or other lineal heirs to whose support he had contributed within five years previous to the time of his death, a sum equal to four times the average annual earnings of the employé, but not less in any event than one thousand five hundred dollars, and not more in any event than three thousand five hundred dollars. Any weekly payments, other than necessary medical or surgical fees, shall be deducted in ascertaining such amount payable on death.

b. If the employé leaves collateral heirs dependent upon his earnings, such a percentage of the sum provided in section "a" as the contributions which deceased made to the support of these dependents, bore to his earnings.

c. If the employé leaves no widow or child or children, parents or lineal or collateral heirs dependent upon his earnings, a sum not to exceed one hundred and fifty dollars for burial expenses.

d. All compensation provided for in this section to be paid in case injury results in death, shall be paid in installments equal to one-half the average earnings, at the same intervals at which the wages or earnings of the employé were paid while he was living; or if this shall not be feasible, then the installments shall be paid weekly.

e. The compensation to be paid for injuries which result in death, as provided for in this section, shall be paid to the personal representative of the deceased employé and shall be distributed by such personal representative to the beneficiaries entitled thereto, in accordance with the laws of this state relating to the descent and distribution of personal property.

INDIANA

Burns' Ann. St. 1908

Sec. 267. A father (or, in case of his death, or desertion of his family, or imprisonment, the mother) may maintain an action for the injury or death of a child, and a guardian for the injury or death of his ward. But, when the action is brought by the guardian for an injury to his ward, the damages shall inure to the benefit of his ward.

Sec. 283. A cause of action arising out of an injury to the person dies with the person of either party, except in cases in which an action is given for an injury causing the death of any person, and actions for seduction, false imprisonment, and malicious prosecution.

Sec. 285. When the death of one is caused by the wrongful act or omission of another, the personal representatives of the former may maintain an action therefor against the latter, if the former might have maintained an action, had he or she (as the case may be) lived, against the latter for an injury for the same act or omission. The action shall be commenced within two years. The damages can not exceed ten thousand dollars; and must inure to the exclusive benefit of the widow, or widower (as the case may be), and children, if any, or next of kin, to be distributed in the same manner as personal property of the deceased.

Sec. 286. That whoever has a claim for personal injuries and obtains judgment for the same against any person, company or corporation in any trial court of this state, and from which judgment any person, company or corporation, against whom or which the same was obtained, shall appeal to the supreme or appellate court of this state, and such judgment be reversed by such supreme or appellate court, and a new trial be granted to appellant thereon; and if the person who obtained such judgment should die, pending such appeal, or before a new trial after such reversal can be had; such claim for personal injuries shall survive and may be prosecuted by the personal representatives of such decedent, as other claims are prosecuted for and on behalf of decedents' estates.

Sec. 362. That hereafter in all actions for damages brought on account of the alleged negligence of any person, copartnership or corporation for causing personal injuries, or the death of any person, it shall not be necessary for the plaintiff in such action to allege or prove the want of contributory negligence on the part of the plaintiff, or on the part of the person for whose injury or death the action may be brought. Contributory negligence, on the part of the plaintiff, or such other person, shall be a matter of defense, and such defense may be proved under the answer of general denial: Provided, that this act shall not affect pending litigation.

Sec. 8597. For any injury to person or persons or property occasioned by any violation of this act,[4] or any wilful failure to comply with any of its provisions, a right of action against the operator shall accrue to the party injured for the direct injury sustained thereby; and in case of loss of life, by reason of such violation, a right of action shall accrue; first, to the widow, if any; second, if no widow, to the children, or adopted children (if any), jointly; third, if neither the foregoing classes, then to the parents jointly, or parent; fourth, or to any person or persons jointly, who were, before such loss of life, dependent for support on the person or persons killed, for like recovery of damages for the injury sustained by reason of such loss of life or lives.

Acts 1911, c. 88

Section 1. That any person, firm or corporation while engaged in business, trade or commerce within this state, and employing in such business, trade or commerce five or more persons shall be liable and respond in damages to any person suffering injury while in the employ of such person, firm or corporation, or in the case of death of such employé, then to his or her personal representative, for the benefit of the surviving widow or husband and children of such employé; and if none, then to such employé's parents; and if none then to the next of kin dependent upon such employé, where such injury or death resulted in whole or in part from the negligence of such employer or his, its or their agents, servants, employés or officers, or by reason of any defect, mismanagement or insufficiency, due to his, its or their carelessness, negligence, fault or omission of duty.

Sec. 2. In any action prosecuted under the provisions of this act, the burden of proving that such injured or killed employé did

---

[4] An act regulating the operation of coal mines.

not use due care and diligence at the time of such injury or death, shall be upon the defendant, but the same may be proved under the general denial. No such employé who may have been injured or killed shall be held to have been guilty of negligence or contributory negligence by reason of the assumption of the risk thereof in any case where the violation by the employer or his, its or their agents or employés, of any ordinance or statute enacted, or of any rule, regulation or direction made by any public officer, bureau or commission, was the cause of the injury or death of such employé. In actions brought against any employer under the provisions of this act for the injury or death of any employé, it shall not be a defense that the dangers or hazards inherent or apparent in the employment in which such injured employé was engaged, contributed to such injury. No such injured employé shall be held to have been guilty of negligence or contributory negligence where the injury complained of resulted from such employé's obedience or conformity to any order or direction of the employer or of any employé to whose orders or directions he was under obligation to conform or obey, although such order or direction was a deviation from other rules, orders or directions previously made by such employer.

Sec. 3. That in any action brought against any employer under or by virtue of this act to recover damages for injuries or the death of, any of his, its or their employés, such employé shall not be held to have assumed the risks of the employment in any case where the violation of such employer or his, its or their agents or employés of any ordinance or statute enacted, or of any rule, direction or regulation made by any public officer or commission, contributed to the injury or death of such employé; nor shall such injured employé, be held to have assumed the risk of the employment where the injury complained of resulted from his obedience to any order or direction of the employer or of any employé to whose orders or directions he was under obligations to conform or obey although such order or direction was a deviation from other orders or directions or rules previously made by such employer. In any action brought against any employer under the provisions of this act to recover damages for injuries to or the death of, any of his, its or their employés, such employé shall not be held to have assumed the risk of any defect in the place of work furnished to such employé, or in the tool, implement or appliance furnished him by such employer, where such defect was, prior to such injury, known to such employer or by the exercise of ordinary care might have been known to him in time to have repaired the same or to have discontinued the use of such defective working place, tool, implement or appliance. The burden of proving that such employer did not know of such defect, or that he was not chargeable with knowledge thereof in time to have repaired the same or to have discontinued the use of such working place, tool, implement or appliance, shall be on the defendant, but the same may be proved under the general denial.

Sec. 4. The damages recoverable under this act shall be commensurate with the injuries sustained, and in case death results from such injury, the action shall survive: Provided, that where any such injured person recovers a judgment under the provisions of this act and an appeal is taken from such judgment, and pending such appeal, the injured person dies and said judgment be thereafter reversed; or where such injured person dies after said judgment is reversed and before trial, the right of action of such person shall survive to his or her personal representative, and such action may be continued in the name of such personal representative, for the benefit of the person entitled under this act to receive the same.

Sec. 5. That any contract, rule, regulation, by-law, or device whatsoever, the purpose, intent, or effect of which would be to enable any employer to exempt himself or itself from any liability created by this act, shall to that extent be void: Provided, that in any action brought against any such employer under or by virtue of any of the provisions of this act, such employer may set off therein by special plea any sum such employer has contributed or paid to any insurance, relief benefit, or indemnity for and on behalf of such injured employé that may have been paid to him or to the person entitled thereto on account of the injury or death for which said action is brought, but in no event shall the amount of such set-off exceed the amount paid to such employé or other person entitled thereto out of such insurance, relief benefit or indemnity fund.

Sec. 6. That where any action is brought on account of the death of any person under this act, the liability of any such employer shall not exceed $10,000, and the provisions of the law now in force as to parties plaintiff shall apply.

Sec. 7. All questions of assumption of risk, negligence or contributory negligence shall be questions of fact for the jury to decide, unless the cause is being tried without a jury in which case, such questions shall be questions of fact for the court.

Sec. 8. That no action shall be maintained under this act unless the same is commenced within two years from the date the cause of action accrued.

Sec. 9. That the terms "employer," "persons," "firm," and "corporation" shall include receivers or other persons charged with the duty of managing, conducting or operating business, trade or commerce.

Sec. 10. This act shall not apply to injuries received by any employé before the passage of the same nor affect any suit or legal proceedings pending in any court at the time of its passage.

Sec. 11. This act shall be construed as supplemental to all laws and parts of laws now in force concerning employers and employés, and shall repeal only such laws and parts of laws as are in direct conflict with the provisions of this act. That nothing in this act shall be held to limit the duty or liability of employers or to impair the rights of their employés under the common law or any other existing statute or to affect the prosecution of any pending proceeding or right of action now existing.

Sec. 12. Whereas, an emergency exists for the immediate taking effect of this act, this act shall be in force from and after its passage.

IOWA

Code 1897

Sec. 3443. All causes of actions shall survive, and may be brought, notwithstanding the death of the person entitled or liable to the same.

Sec. 3444. The right of civil remedy is not merged in a public offense, but may in all cases be enforced independently of and in addition to the punishment of the latter.

Sec. 3445. Any action contemplated in the two preceding sections may be brought, or the court, on motion, may allow the action to be continued, by or against the legal representatives or successors in interest of the deceased. Such action shall be deemed a continuing one, and to have accrued to such representative or successor at the same time it did to the deceased if he had survived. If such is continued against the legal representative of the defendant, a notice shall be served on him as provided for service of original notices.

Sec. 3471. A father, or, in case of his death or imprisonment or desertion of his family, the mother, may as plaintiff maintain an action for the expenses and actual loss of service resulting from the injury or death of a minor child.

Sec. 3313. The avails of any life or accident insurance, or other sum of money made payable by any mutual aid or benevolent society upon the death or disability of a member thereof, are not subject to the debts of the deceased, except by special contract or arrangement, and shall be disposed of like other property left by the deceased. When a wrongful act produces death, damages recovered therefor shall be disposed of as personal property belonging to the estate of the deceased, but if the deceased leaves a husband, wife, child or parent, it shall not be liable. for the payment of debts. The words "heirs," or "legal heirs" or other equivalent words used to designate the beneficiaries in any life insurance policy or certificate of membership in any mutual aid or benevolent association, where no contrary intention is expressed in such instrument, shall be construed to include the surviving husband or wife of the insured, and the share of such survivor in the proceeds of such policy or certificate made payable as aforesaid shall be the same as that provided by law for the distribution of the personal property of intestates.

Sec. 3447. Actions may be brought within the times herein limited, respectively, after their causes accrue, and not afterwards, except when otherwise specially declared:

*　　*　　*　　*　　*　　*　　*　　*　　*

3. Those founded on injuries to the person or reputation, including injuries to relative rights, whether based on contract or tort, or for a statute penalty, within two years.

*　　*　　*　　*　　*　　*　　*　　*　　*

KANSAS

Gen. St. 1909

Sec. 6012. In addition to the causes of action which survive at common law, causes of action for mesne profits, or for an injury to the person, or to real or personal estate, or for any deceit or fraud shall also survive; and the action may be brought, notwithstanding the death of the person entitled or liable to the same.

Sec. 6014. When the death of one is caused by the wrongful act or omission of another, the personal representatives of the former may may maintain an action therefor against the latter, if the former might have maintained an action had he lived, against the latter for an injury for the same act or omission. The action must be commenced within two years: The damages cannot exceed ten thousand dollars, and must inure to the exclusive benefit of the widow and children, if any, or next of kin, to be distributed in the same manner as personal property of the deceased.

Sec. 6015. That in all cases where the residence of the party whose death has been or hereafter shall be caused as set forth in the next preceding section is or has been at the time of his death in any other state or territory, or when, being a resident of this state, no personal representative is or has been appointed, the action provided in said section may be brought by the widow, or, where there is no widow, by the next of kin of such deceased.

KENTUCKY

Constitution

Sec. 54. The general assembly shall have no power to limit the amount to be recovered for injuries resulting in death, or for injuries to person or property.

Sec. 241. Whenever the death of a person shall result from an injury inflicted by negligence or wrongful act, then, in every such case, damages may be recovered for such death, from the corporations and persons so causing the same. Until otherwise provided by law, the action to recover such damages shall in all cases be prosecuted by the personal representative of the deceased person. The General Assembly may provide how the recovery shall go and to whom belong; and until such provision is made the same shall form part of the personal estate of the deceased person.

Ky. St. 1909

Sec. 4. The widow and minor child, or either or both of them, of a person killed by the careless, wanton or malicious use of firearms, or by any weapon popularly known as colts, brass knuckles, or slung-shots, or other deadly weapon, or sand-bag or any imitation or substitute therefor, not in self-defense, may have an action against the person who committed the killing, and all others aiding or promoting, or any one or more of them; and in such actions the jury may give vindictive damages.

Sec. 5. The widow and minor child of a person killed in a duel, or either of them, may have an action against the surviving principal, the seconds, and all others aiding or promoting the duel, or against any one or more of them, for reparation of the injury; and in such action the jury may give punitive damages. The failure to include any of the persons mentioned as defendants in the action shall discharge them from liability.

Sec. 6. Whenever the death of a person shall result from an injury inflicted by negligence or wrongful act, then in every such case, damages may be recovered for such death from the person or persons, company, or companies, corporation or corporations, their agents or servants, causing the same, and when the act is wilful or the negligence is gross, punitive damages may be recovered, and the action to recover such damages shall be prosecuted by the personal representative of the deceased. The amount recovered, less funeral expenses and the cost of administration, and such costs about the recovery, including attorney fees as are not included in the recovery from the defendant, shall be for the benefit of and go to the kindred of the deceased in the following order, viz.:

1. If the deceased leaves a widow or husband, and no children or their descendants, then the whole to such widow or husband.

2. If the deceased leaves either a widow and children or a husband and children, then one-half to such widow or husband and the other one-half to the children of the deceased.

3. If the deceased leaves a child or children, but no widow or husband, then the whole to such child or children. If the deceased leaves no widow, husband or child, then such recovery shall pass to the mother and father of deceased, one moiety each, if both be living; if the mother be dead and the father be living, the whole thereof shall pass to the father; and if the father be dead and the mother living, the whole thereof shall go to the mother; and if both father and mother be dead, then the whole of the recovery shall become a part of the personal estate of the deceased; and after the payment of his debts, the remainder, if any, shall pass to his kindred more remote than those above named, as is directed by the general law on descent and distribution.

Sec. 10. No right of action for personal injury or injury to real or personal estate shall cease or die with the person injuring or injured, except actions for assault, slander, criminal conversation, and so much of the action for malicious prosecution as is intended to recover for the personal injury; but for any injury other than those excepted, an action may be brought or revived by the personal representative, or against the personal representative, heir or devisee, in the same manner as causes of action founded on contract.

Sec. 2516. An action for an injury to the person of the plaintiff, or of his wife, child, ward, apprentice, or servant, or for injuries to person, cattle, or stock, by railroads, or by any company or corporation; an action for a malicious prosecution, conspiracy, arrest, seduction, criminal conversation, or breach of promise of marriage; an action for libel or slander; an action for the escape of a prisoner arrested or imprisoned on civil process, shall be commenced within one year next after the cause of action accrued, and not thereafter.

LOUISIANA

Rev. Civil Code, 1909

Art. 2315. Every act whatever of man that causes damage to another, obliges him by whose fault it happened to repair it; the right of this action shall survive in case of death in favor of the children or widow of the deceased or either of them, and in default of these in favor of the surviving father and mother or either of them, and in default of any of the above persons, then in favor of the surviving brothers and sisters or either of them for the space of one year from the death: Provided, that should the deceased leave a widow together with minor children, the right of action shall accrue to both the widow and minor children; Provided further, that the right of action shall accrue to the major children only in those cases where there [is] no surviving widow or minor child or children.

The survivors above mentioned may also recover the damages sustained by them by the death of the parent or child or husband or wife or brothers or sisters, as the case may be.

MAINE

Rev. St. 1903, c. 89

Sec. 8. In addition to those surviving by the common law, the following actions survive: Replevin, trover, assault and battery, trespass, trespass on the case, and petitions for and actions of review; and these actions may be commenced by or against an executor or administrator or when the deceased was a party to them, may be prosecuted or defended by them.

Sec. 9. Whenever the death of a person shall be caused by wrongful act, neglect or default, and the act, neglect or default, is such as would, if death had not ensued, have entitled the party injured to maintain an action and recover damages in respect thereof, then, and in every such case, the person who, or the corporation which, would have been liable if death had not ensued, shall be liable to an action for damages, notwithstanding the death of the person injured, and although the death shall have been caused under such circumstances as shall amount to a felony.

Sec. 10. Every such action shall be brought by and in the names of the personal representatives of such deceased person, and the amount recovered in every such action shall be for the exclusive benefit of his widow, if no children, and of the children, if no widow, and if both, then of her and them equally, and, if neither, of his heirs. The jury may give such damages as they shall deem a fair and just compensation not exceeding five thousand dollars, with reference to the pecuniary injuries resulting from such death to the persons for whose benefit such action is brought, provided, that such action shall be commenced within two years after the death of such person.

TIFF.DEATH W.A.(2D ED.)—33

Chapter 23

Sec. 76. Whoever receives any bodily injury, or suffers damage in his property, through any defect or want of repair or sufficient railing, in any highway, townway, causeway or bridge, may recover for the same in a special action on the case to be commenced within one year from the date of receiving such injury or suffering damage, of the county or town obliged by law to repair the same, if the commissioners of such county, or the municipal officers or road commissioners of such town, or any person authorized by any commissioner of such county or any municipal officer, or road commissioner of such town, to act as a substitute for either of them, had twenty-four hours' actual notice of the defect or want of repair; but not exceeding two thousand dollars in case of a town; and if the sufferer had notice of the condition of such way previous to the time of the injury, he cannot recover of a town unless he has previously notified one of the municipal officers of the defective condition of such way; and any person who sustains injury or damage, as aforesaid, or some person in his behalf, shall within fourteen days thereafter, notify one of the county commissioners of such county, or of the municipal officers of such town, by letter or otherwise, in writing, setting forth his claim for damages and specifying the nature of his injuries and the nature and location of the defect which caused such injury. If the life of any person is lost through such deficiency, his executors or administrators may recover of such county or town liable to keep the same in repair, in an action on the case, brought for the benefit of the estate of the deceased, such sum as the jury may deem reasonable as damages, if the parties liable had said notice of the deficiency which caused the loss of life; at the trial of any such action the court may, on motion of either party, order a view of the premises where the defect or want of repair is alleged, when it would materially aid in a clear understanding of the case.

MARYLAND

Ann. Code Pub. Civ. Laws 1911, art. 67

Section 1. Whenever the death of a person shall be caused by wrongful act, neglect or default, and the act, neglect or default is such as would (if death had not ensued) have entitled the party injured to maintain an action and recover damages in respect thereof, the person who would have been liable if death had not ensued shall be liable to an action for damages, notwithstanding the death of the person injured, and although the death shall have been caused under such circumstances as amount in law to felony.

Sec. 2. Every such action shall be for the benefit of the wife, husband, parent and child of the person whose death shall have been so caused, and shall be brought by and in the name of the state of Maryland for the use of the person entitled to damages; and in every such action the jury may give such damages as they may think proportioned to the injury resulting from such death to the parties respectively for whom and for whose benefit such action shall be brought, and the amount so recovered, after deducting the costs not recovered from the defendant, shall be divided amongst the above-mentioned parties in such shares as the jury by their verdict shall find and direct: Provided, that not more than one action shall lie for and in respect of the same subject-matter of complaint; and that every such action shall be commenced within twelve calendar months after the death of the deceased person.

Sec. 3. In every such action the equitable plaintiff on the record shall be required, together with the declaration, to deliver to the defendant or his attorney a full particular of the persons for whom and on whose behalf such action shall be brought, and of the nature of the claim in respect of which damages shall be sought to be recovered.

Sec. 4. The word "person" shall apply to bodies politic and corporate, and all corporations shall be responsible under this article for the wrongful acts, neglect or default of all agents employed by them.

Article 93

Sec. 104. Executors and administrators shall have full power to commence and prosecute any personal action whatever, at law or in equity, which the testator or intestate might have commenced and prosecuted, except actions for slander; and they shall be liable to be sued in any court of law or equity, in any action (except for slander and injuries to the person) which might have been maintained against the deceased. * * *

MASSACHUSETTS

Rev. Laws 1902, c. 171

Section 1. In addition to the actions which survive by the common law, the following shall also survive: Actions of replevin, tort for assault, battery, imprisonment or other damage to the person, for goods taken and carried away or converted or for damage to real or personal property, and actions against sheriffs for the misconduct or negligence of themselves or their deputies.

Sec. 2. If a person or corporation by his or its negligence, or by the negligence of his or its agents or servants while engaged in his or its business, causes the death of a person who is in the exercise of due care and not in his or its employment or service, he or it shall be liable in damages in the sum of not less than five hundred nor more than ten thousand dollars to be assessed with reference to the degree of his or its culpability or of that of his or its agents or servants, to be recovered in an action of tort, commenced within two years after the injury which caused the death, by the executor or administrator of the deceased, one-half thereof to the use of the widow and one-half to the use of the children of the deceased; or, if there are no children, the whole to the use of the widow; or, if there is no widow, the whole to the use of the next of kin. (As amended St. 1907, c. 375.)

Rev. Laws Supp. 1902–1908, p. 958 (St. 1906, c. 463, pt. 1, § 63, as amended St. 1907, c. 392)

Sec. 63. [Amended by St. 1907, c. 392.] If a corporation which operates a railroad or a street railway, by reason of its negligence or by reason of the unfitness or gross negligence of its agents or servants while engaged in its business, causes the death of a passenger, or of a person who is in the exercise of due care and who is not a passenger or in the employ of such corporation, it shall be punished by a fine of not less than five hundred nor more than five thousand dollars which shall be recovered by an indictment prosecuted within one year after the time of the injury which caused the death, and shall be paid to the executor or administrator, one half thereof to the use of the widow and one half to the use of the children of the deceased; or, if there are no children, the whole to the use of the widow; or if there is no widow, the whole to the use of the next of kin; but a corporation which operates a railroad shall not be so liable for the death of a person while walking or being upon its railroad contrary to law or to the reasonable rules and regulations of the corporation. Such corporation shall also be liable in damages in the sum of not less than five hundred nor more than five thousand dollars, which shall be assessed with reference to the degree of culpability of the corporation or of its servants or agents, and shall be recovered in an action of tort, begun within one year after the injury which caused the death, by the executor or administrator of the deceased for the use of the persons hereinbefore specified in the case of an indictment. If an employé of a railroad corporation.

being in the exercise of due care, is killed under such circumstances as would have entitled him to maintain an action for damages against such corporation if death had not resulted, the corporation shall be liable in the same manner and to the same extent as it would have been if the deceased had not been an employé. But no executor or administrator shall, for the same cause, avail himself of more than one of the remedies given by the provisions of this section.

Rev. Laws Supp. 1902–1908, p. 1012 (St. 1906, c. 463, pt. 2, § 245)

Sec. 245. If a person is injured in his person or property by collision with the engines or cars of a railroad corporation at a crossing such as is described in section one hundred and forty-seven, and it appears that the corporation neglected to give the signals required by said section, and that such neglect contributed to the injury, the corporation shall be liable for all damages caused by the collision, or to a fine recoverable by indictment as provided in section sixty-three of part 1, or, if the life of a person so injured is lost to damages recoverable in an action of tort as provided in said section, unless it is shown that in addition to a mere want of ordinary care the person' injured or the person who had charge of his person or property was, at the time of the collision, guilty of gross or wilful negligence, or was acting in violation of the law, and that such gross or wilful negligence or unlawful act contributed to the injury.

Rev. Laws Supp. 1902–1908, p. 993 (St. 1906, c. 463, pt. 2, § 147)

Sec. 147. Every railroad corporation shall cause a bell of at least thirty-five pounds in weight, and a steam whistle, to be placed on each locomotive engine passing upon its railroad; and such bell shall be rung or at least three separate-and distinct blasts of such whistle sounded at the distance of at least eighty rods from the place where the railroad crosses upon the same level any highway, town way or travelled place over which a signboard is required to be maintained as provided in sections one hundred and forty-nine and one hundred and fifty; and such bell shall be rung or such whistle sounded continuously or alternately until the engine has crossed such way or traveled place. The provisions of this section shall not affect the authority conferred upon the board of railroad commissioners by the provisions of the following section.

Rev. Laws 1902, c. 70

Sec. 6. If the proprietor of a steamboat or stage coach or a common carrier of passengers, except a railroad corporation or street railway company, by reason of his or its negligence, or by reason of the unfitness or gross negligence or carelessness of his or its servants or agents, causes the death of a passenger, he or it shall be liable in damages in the sum of not less than five hundred nor more than five thousand dollars which shall be assessed with reference to the degree of culpability of the proprietor or common carrier liable, or of his or its servants or agents, and shall be recovered in an action of tort, commenced within one year after the injury which caused the death, by the executor or administrator of the deceased, one-half to the use of the widow and one-half to the use of the children of the deceased; or, if there are no children, the whole to the use of the widow; or, if there is no widow, the whole to the use of the next of kin.

Chapter 51

Sec. 17. If the life of a person is lost by reason of a defect or a want of repair of or a want of a sufficient railing in or upon a way, causeway or bridge, the county, city or town or person by law obliged to repair the same shall, if it or he had previous reasonable notice of the defect or want of repair or want of railing, be liable in damages not exceeding one thousand dollars, which shall be assessed with reference to the degree of culpability of the defendant and recovered in an action of tort, commenced within one year after the injury causing the death by the executor or administrator of the deceased person, for the use of the widow and children of the deceased in equal moieties, or, if there are no children, to the use of the widow, or, if there is no widow, to the use of the next of kin.

St. 1909, c. 514

Sec. 127. If personal injury is caused to an employé, who, at the time of the injury, is in the exercise of due care by reason of:

First. A defect in the condition of the ways, works or machinery connected with or used in the business of the employer, which arose from, or had not been discovered or remedied in consequence of, the negligence of the employer or of a person in his service who had been entrusted by him with the duty of seeing that the ways, works or machinery were in proper condition; or,

Second. The negligence of a person in the service of the employer who was entrusted with and was exercising superintendence and whose sole or principal duty was that of superintendence, or, in the absence of such superintendent, of a person acting as superintendent with the authority or consent of such employer; or,

Third. The negligence of a person in the service of the employer who was in charge or control of a signal, switch, locomotive engine, elevated train or train upon a railroad or elevated railway;

The employé, or his legal representatives, shall, subject to the provisions of the nine following sections, have the same rights to compensation and of action against the employer as if he had not been an employé, nor in the service, nor engaged in the work, of the employer.

A car which is in use by, or which is in possession of, a railroad corporation, or an elevated car which is in use by or which is in possession of an elevated railway corporation, shall be considered as a part of the ways, works or machinery of the corporation which uses or has it in possession, within the meaning of clause one of this section, whether it is owned by such corporation or by some other company or person. One or more cars which are in motion, whether attached to an engine or not, shall constitute a train within the meaning of clause three of this section, and whoever, as a part of his duty for the time being, physically controls or directs the movements of a signal, switch, locomotive engine, elevated train or train shall be deemed to be a person in charge or control of a signal, switch, locomotive engine, elevated train or train within the meaning of said clause.

Sec. 128. If the injury described in the preceding section results in the death of the employé, and such death is not instantaneous or is preceded by conscious suffering, and if there is any person who would have been entitled to bring an action under the provisions of the following section, the legal representatives of said employé may, in the action brought under the provisions of the preceding section, recover damages for the death in addition to those for the injury; and in the same action under a separate count at common law, may recover damages for conscious suffering resulting from the same injury.

Sec. 129. If, as the result of the negligence of an employer himself, or of a person for whose negligence an employer is liable under the provisions of section one hundred and twenty-seven, an employé is instantly killed, or dies without conscious suffering, his widow or, if he leaves no widow, his next of kin, who, at the time of his death, were dependent upon his wages for support, shall have a right of action for damages against the employer.

Sec. 130. If an action is brought under the provisions of the preceding section by the widow of the employé, or by the next of kin, who may have such right of action, or if the action is brought under the provisions of section one hundred and twenty-seven by the legal representatives, such action shall not fail by reason of the fact that it should have been brought under the other section, but may be so amended as to provide against such failure at any time prior to final judgment.

Sec. 131. If under the provisions of sections one hundred and twenty-eight and one hundred and twenty-nine damages are awarded for the death, they shall be assessed with reference to the degree of culpability of the employer or of the person for whose negligence the employer is liable.

The amount of damages which may be awarded in an action under the provisions of section one hundred and twenty-seven for a personal injury to an employé, in which no damages for his death are awarded under the provisions of section one hundred and twenty-eight shall not exceed four thousand dollars.

The amount of damages which may be awarded in such action, if damages for his death are awarded under the provisions of section one hundred and twenty-eight shall not exceed five thousand dollars for both the injury and the death, and shall be apportioned by the jury between the legal representatives of the employé and the persons who would have been entitled under the provisions of section one hundred and twenty-nine to bring an action for his death if it had been instantaneous or without conscious suffering.

The amount of damages which may be awarded in an action brought under the provisions of section one hundred and twenty-nine shall not be less than five hundred nor more than five thousand dollars.

Sec. 132. No action for the recovery of damages for injury or death under the provisions of the five preceding sections shall be maintained unless notice of the time, place and cause of the injury is given to the employer within sixty days, and the action is commenced within one year, after the accident which causes the injury or death. Such notice shall be in writing, signed by the person injured or by a person in his behalf; but if, from physical or mental incapacity it is impossible for the person injured to give the notice within the time provided in this section, he may give it within ten days after such incapacity has been removed, and if he dies without having given notice and without having been for ten days at any time after his injury of sufficient capacity to give it, his executor or administrator may give such notice within sixty days after his appointment.

A notice given under the provisions of this section shall not be held invalid or insufficient solely by reason of an inaccuracy in stating the time, place or cause of the injury if it is shown that there was no intention to mislead, and that the employer was not in fact misled thereby.

MICHIGAN

⁙ *Comp. Laws 1897*

Sec. 10,427. Whenever the death of a person shall be caused by wrongful act, neglect or default, and the act, neglect or default is such as would (if death had not ensued) have entitled the party injured to maintain an action, and recover damages in respect thereof, then and in every such case the person who, or the corporation which would have been liable, if death had not ensued, shall be liable to an action for damages, notwithstanding the death of the person injured, and although the death shall have been caused under such circumstances as amount in law to felony.

Sec. 10,428. Every such action shall be brought by, and in the names of, the personal representatives of such deceased person, and the amount recovered in every such action, shall be distributed to the persons and in the proportions provided by law in relation to the distribution of personal property left by persons dying intestate; and in every such action the jury may give such damages as they shall deem fair and just, with reference to the pecuniary injury resulting from such death, to those persons who may be entitled to such damages when recovered.

Sec. 6308. Whenever the death of a person shall be caused by wrongful act, neglect, or default of any railroad company, or its agents, and the act, neglect, or default is such as would (if death had not ensued) entitle the party injured to maintain an action and recover damages in respect thereof, then and in every such case, the railroad corporation which would have been liable if death had not ensued shall be liable to an action on the case for damages notwithstanding the death of the person so injured, and although the death shall have been caused under such circumstances as amount in law to felony.

Sec. 6309. Every such action shall be brought by and in the names of the personal representatives of such deceased person, and the amount recovered in any such action shall be distributed to the persons, and in the proportion provided by law in relation to the distribution of personal property left by persons dying intestate; and in every such action the jury may give such amount of damages as they shall deem fair and just, to the persons who may be entitled to such damages when recovered: Provided, nothing herein contained shall affect any suit or proceedings heretofore commenced and now pending in any of the courts of this state.

Sec. 6389. Whenever the death of a person shall be caused by wrongful act, neglect, or default of any such company [5] or its agents, and the act, neglect, or default is such as would (if death had not ensued) entitle the party injured to maintain an action and recover damages in respect thereof, then and in every such case the corporation which would have been liable if death had not ensued shall be liable to an action on the case for the damages notwithstanding the death of the person so injured, and although the death shall have been caused under such circumstances as amount in law to felony.

Sec. 6390. Every such action shall be brought by and in the names of the personal representatives of such deceased person, and the amount recovered in any such action shall be distributed to the persons, and in the proportion provided by law in relation to the distribution of personal property left by persons dying intestate; and in every such action the jury may give such amount of damages as they shall deem fair and just to the persons who may be entitled to such damages when recovered.

Sec. 9728. The following actions shall be commenced within six years next after the cause of action shall accrue, and not afterwards, that is to say:

*   *.   *   *   *   *   *   *   *   *

7. All other actions on the case, except actions for slanderous words or for libels.

Sec. 10,117a. In addition to the actions which survive by the common law, the following shall also survive; that is to say, actions of replevin, and trover, actions of assault and battery, false imprisonment, for goods taken and carried away, for negligent injury to persons, for damage done to real and personal estate, and actions to recover real estate where persons have been induced to part with the same through fraudulent representations and deceit.

Pub. Acts 1905, No. 89

Section 1. In all actions for negligent injury to persons hereafter prosecuted by the executor or administrator of an injured person, under the statute which declares that said actions shall survive, the measure of damage in each case, shall be such a sum as the court or jury shall deem fair and just with reference to the pecuniary injury resulting from the death of the injured person, to those per-

---

[5] Union railroad station and depot company.

sons who may be entitled to such damages under the law providing for the distribution of personal property left by persons dying intestate, and the amount recovered or paid in settlement of such damages shall not be subject to the claims of creditors of the deceased, but shall otherwise be distributed to the persons and in the proportions provided by law in relation to the distribution of personal property left by persons dying intestate.

Sec. 2. All acts or parts of acts in anywise contravening the provisions of this act are hereby repealed.

This act is ordered to take immediate effect.

Approved May 3, 1905.

MINNESOTA

Rev. Laws 1905

Sec. 4502. A cause of action arising out of an injury to the person dies with the person of either party, except as provided in § 4503. All the causes of action by one against another, whether arising on contract or not, survive to the personal representatives of the former and against those of the latter.

Sec. 4503. When death is caused by the wrongful act or omission of any person or corporation, the personal representative of the decedent may maintain an action therefor if he might have maintained an action, had he lived, for an injury caused by the same act or omission. The action may be commenced within two years after the act or omission. The damages therein cannot exceed seven thousand five hundred dollars, and shall be for the exclusive benefit of the surviving spouse and next of kin, to be distributed to them in the same proportion as personal property of persons dying intestate; but funeral expenses, and any demand for the support of the decedent, duly allowed by the probate court, shall first be deducted and paid: Provided, that if an action for such injury shall have been commenced by such decedent, and not finally determined during his life, it may be continued by his personal representative for the benefit of the same persons and for recovery of the same damages as herein provided, and the court on motion may make an order, allowing such continuance, and directing pleadings to be made and issues framed conformably to the practice in action begun under this section. (As amended Laws 1911, c. 281.)

MISSISSIPPI

Constitution 1890

Sec. 193. Every employé of any railroad corporation shall have the same right and remedies for any injury suffered by him from the act or omission of said corporation or its employés, as are allowed by law to other persons not employés, where the injury results from the negligence of a superior agent or officer, or of a person having the right to control or direct the services of the party injured, and also when the injury results from the negligence of a fellow-servant engaged in another department of labor from that of the party injured, or of a fellow-servant on another train of cars, or one engaged about a different piece of work. Knowledge by any employé injured, of the defective or unsafe character or condition of any machinery, ways, or appliances, shall be no defense to an action for injury caused thereby, except as to conductors or engineers in charge of dangerous or unsafe cars, or engines voluntarily operated by them. Where death ensues from any injury to employés, the legal or personal representatives of the person injured shall have the same right and remedies as are allowed by law to such representatives of other persons. Any contract or agreement, express or implied, made by any employé to waive the benefit of this section shall be null and void; and this section shall not be construed to deprive any employé of a corporation or his legal or personal representative, of any right or remedy that he now has by the law of the land. The legislature may extend the remedies herein provided for to any other class of employés.

Code 1906, § 721, as amended Laws 1908, c. 167

Sec. 721. Whenever the death of any person shall be caused by any real wrongful or negligent act, or omission, or by such unsafe machinery, way or appliances as would, if death had not ensued, have entitled the party injured, or damaged thereby to maintain an action and recover damages in respect thereof, and such deceased person shall have left a widow or children, or both, or husband, or father, or mother, or sister, or brother, the person or corporation, or both, that would have been liable if death had not ensued, and the representative of such person shall be liable for damages, not withstanding the death, and the fact that death is instantaneous shall, in no case, affect the right of recovery. The action for such damages may be brought in the name of the widow, for the death of her husband, or by the husband for the death of the wife, or by the parent for the death of a child, or in the name of a child for the death of a parent, or by a brother for the death of a sister, or by a sister for the death of a brother, or by a sister for the death of a sister, or by a brother for the death of a brother, or all parties interested may join in the suit, and there shall be but one suit for the same death which shall ensue for the benefit of all parties concerned, but the determination of such suit shall not bar another action unless it be decided on its merits. In such action the party or parties suing shall recover such damages as the jury may determine to be just, taking into consideration all the damages of every kind to the decedent and all damages of every kind to any and all parties interested in the suit. Executors or administrators shall not sue for damages or injury causing death except as below provided. This section shall apply to all personal injuries of servants or employés received in the service or business of the master or employer, where such injuries result in death. Damages recovered under the provisions of this section shall not be subject to the payment of the debts or liabilities of the deceased, and such damages shall be distributed as follows: Damages for the injury and death of a married man shall be equally distributed to his wife and children, and if he has no children all shall go to his wife; damages for the injury and death of a married woman shall be equally distributed to the husband and children, and if she has no children all shall go to the husband; if the deceased has no husband or wife, the damages shall be equally distributed to the children; if the deceased has no husband, nor wife nor children, the damages shall be distributed equally to the father, mother, brothers and sisters, or such of them as the deceased may have living at his or her death. If the deceased have neither husband, or wife, or children, or father, or mother, or sister, or brother, then the damages shall go to the legal representatives, subject to debts and general distribution, and the executor may sue for and recover such damages on the same terms as are prescribed for recovery by the next of kin in this section, and the fact that deceased was instantly killed shall not affect the right of the legal representatives to recover. The provisions of this section shall apply to illegitimate children on account of the death of the mother and to the mothers on account of the death of an illegitimate child or children, and they shall have all the benefits, rights and remedies conferred by this section on legitimates.

MISSOURI

Rev. St. 1909

Sec. 5425. Whenever any person, including an employé of the corporation, individual or individuals hereinafter referred to whose death is caused by the negligence of a co-employé thereof, shall die from any injury resulting or occasioned by the negligence, unskillfulness or criminal intent of any officer, agent, servant or employé, whilst running, conducting or managing any locomotive, car or train of cars, or any street, electric or terminal car or train of cars, or of any master, pilot, engineer, agent or employé whilst running, conducting or managing any steamboat, or any of the machinery thereof, or of any driver of any stage coach, automobile, motor car or other public conveyance whilst in charge of the same as a driver; and when any passenger shall die from any injury resulting from or occasioned by any defect or insufficiency in any railroad, whether the same be a steam, street, electric or terminal railroad or any part thereof, or in any locomotive, car, street car, electric car or terminal car, or in any steamboat, or the machinery thereof, or in any stage coach, automobile, motor car. or other public conveyance, the corporation, individual or individuals in whose employ any such officer, agent, servant, employé, master, pilot, engineer or driver shall be at the time such injury is committed, or who owns, operates or conducts any such railroad, locomotive, car, street car, electric car, terminal car, automobile, motor car, stage coach or other public conveyance at the time any injury is received resulting from or occasioned by any defect or insufficiency, unskillfulness, negligence or criminal intent above declared, shall forfeit and pay as a penalty, for every such person, employé or passenger so dying, the sum of not less than two thousand dollars and not exceeding ten thousand dollars, in the discretion of the jury, which may be sued for and recovered: First, by the husband or wife of the deceased; or, second, if there be no husband or wife, or he or she fails to sue within six months after such death, then by the minor child or children of the deceased, whether such minor child or children of the deceased be the natural born or adopted child or children of the deceased: Provided, that if adopted, such minor child or children shall have been duly adopted according to the laws of adoption of the state where the person executing the deed of adoption resided at the time of such adoption; or, third, if such deceased be a minor and unmarried, whether such deceased unmarried minor be a natural born or adopted child, if such deceased unmarried minor shall have been duly adopted according to the laws of adoption of the state where the person executing the deed of adoption resided at the time of such adoption, then by the father and mother, who may join in the suit, and each shall have an equal interest in the judgment; or if either of them be dead, then by the survivor; or, fourth, if there be no husband, wife, minor child or minor children, natural born or adopted as hereinbefore indicated, or if the deceased be an unmarried minor and there be no father or mother, then in such case suit may be instituted and recovery had by the administrator or executor of the deceased and the amount recovered shall be distributed according to the laws of descent, and such corporation, individual or individuals may show as a defense that such death was caused by the negligence of the deceased. In suits instituted under this section, it shall be competent for the defendant, for his defense, to show that the defect or insufficiency named in this section was not of a negligent defect or insufficiency, and that the injury received was not the result of unskillfulness, negligence or criminal intent.

Sec. 5426. Whenever the death of a person shall be caused by a wrongful act, neglect or default of another, and the act, neglect or default is such as would, if death had not ensued, have entitled the party injured to maintain an action and recover damages in respect thereof, then, and in every such case, the person who or the corporation which would have been liable if death had not ensued shall be liable to an action for damages notwithstanding the death of the person injured.

Sec. 5427. Damages accruing under the last preceding section shall be sued for and recovered by the same parties and in the same manner as provided in section 5425; and in every such action the jury may give such damages, not exceeding ten thousand dollars, as they may deem fair and just, with reference to the necessary injury resulting from such death, to the surviving parties who may be entitled to sue, and also having regard to the mitigating and aggravating circumstances attending such wrongful act, neglect or default.

Sec. 5429. Every action instituted by virtue of the preceding sections of this article shall be commenced within one year after the cause of action shall accrue: Provided, that if any defendant, whether a resident or nonresident of the state at the time any such cause of action accrues, shall then or thereafter be absent or depart from the state, so that personal service cannot be had upon such defendant in the state in any such action heretofore or hereafter accruing, the time during which such defendant is so absent from the state shall not be deemed or taken as any part of the time limited for the commencement of such action against him; and provided, that if any such action shall have been commenced within the time prescribed in this section, and the plaintiff therein take or suffer a nonsuit, or after a verdict for him the judgment be arrested, or after a judgment for him the same be reversed on appeal or error, such plaintiff may commence a new action from time to time within one year after such nonsuit suffered or such judgment arrested or reversed; and in determining whether such new action has been begun within the period so limited, the time during which such nonresident or absent defendant is so absent from the state shall not be deemed or taken as any part of such period of limitation.

Sec. 8471. For any injury to persons or property occasioned by any violation of this article [6] or failure to comply with any of its provisions, a right of action shall accrue to the party injured for any direct damages sustained thereby; and in case of loss of life by reason of such violation or failure as aforesaid, a right of action shall accrue to the widow of the person so killed, his lineal heirs or adopted children, or to any person, or persons who were, before such loss of life, dependent for support on the person or persons so killed, for a like recovery of damages sustained by reason of such loss of life or lives: Provided, that all suits brought under this article shall be commenced within one year after any cause of action shall have accrued under this article and not afterward; and provided further, that any person entitled to sue under this section for loss of life or lives may recover any sum not exceeding ten thousand dollars.

MONTANA

Rev. Codes 1907

Sec. 6485. A father, or in case of his death, or desertion of his family, the mother may maintain an action for the injury or death of a minor, child, and a guardian for the injury or death of his ward, when such injury or death is caused by the wrongful act or neglect of another. Such action may be maintained against the person causing the injury or death, or if such person be employed by another person who is responsible for his conduct, also against such other person.

Sec. 6486. When the death of a person, not being a minor, is caused by the wrongful act or neglect of another, his heirs or personal representatives may maintain an action for damages against the person causing the death; or if such person be employed by another person who is responsible for his conduct then also against

---

[6] Providing for the safety and inspection of mines.

such other person. In every action under this and the preceding section such damages may be given as under all the circumstances of the case may be just.

Sec. 5248. That every company, corporation, or individual operating any mine, smelter, or mill for the refining of ores shall be liable for any damages sustained by any employés thereof within this state, without contributing negligence on his part, when such damage is caused by the negligence of any superintendent, foreman, shift-boss, hoisting, or other engineer, or crane men.

Sec. 5249. No contract of insurance, relief, benefit, or indemnity in case of injury or death, nor any other contract entered into before the injury, between the person injured and any of the employers named in this act shall constitute any bar or defense to any cause of action brought under the provision of this act.

Sec. 5250. In case of the death of any such employés in consequence of any injury or damages so sustained, the right of action shall survive and may be prosecuted and maintained by its heirs, or personal representatives.

Sec. 5251. Every person or corporation operating a railway or railroad in this state shall be liable for all damages sustained by any employé of such person or corporation in consequence of the neglect of any other employé or employés thereof, or by the mismanagement of any other employé or employés thereof, and in consequence of the wilful wrongs, whether of commission or omission, of any other employé or employés thereof, when such neglect, mismanagement or wrongs are in any manner connected with the use and operation of any railway or railroad on or about which they shall be employed, and no contract which restricts such liability shall be legal or binding.

Sec. 5252. In case of the death of any such employé in consequence of any injury or damage so sustained, the right of action shall survive and may be prosecuted and maintained by his heirs or personal representatives.

NEBRASKA

Cobbey's Ann. St. 1911

Sec. 5199. That whenever the death of a person shall be caused by the wrongful act, neglect, or default of any person, company or corporation, and the act, neglect, or default is such as would, if death had not ensued, have entitled the party injured to maintain an action and recover damages, in respect thereof, then, and in every such case, the person who, or company or corporation which, would have been liable if death had not ensued, shall be liable to an action for damages notwithstanding the death of the person injured, and although the death shall have been caused under such circumstances as amount in law to felony.

Sec. 5200. That every such action shall be brought by and in the names of the personal representatives of such deceased person, and the amount recovered in every such action shall be for the exclusive benefit of the widow or widower and the next of kin of such deceased person shall be distributed to such widow and the next of kin in the proportion provided by law in relation to the distribution of personal property left by persons dying intestate, and in every such action the jury may give such damages as they shall deem a fair and just compensation with reference to the pecuniary injuries resulting from such death, to the widow or widower and next of kin of such deceased person: Provided, that every such action shall be commenced within two years after the death of such person.

NEVADA

Rev. Laws 1912

Sec. 4996. A father, or in case of his death or desertion of his family, the mother, may maintain an action for the death or injury of a minor child, when such injury or death is caused by the wrongful act or neglect of another; and a guardian may maintain an action for the injury or death of his ward, if the ward be of lawful age, when such injury or death is caused by the wrongful act or neglect of another, the action by the guardian to be prosecuted for the benefit of the heirs of the ward. Any such action may be maintained against the person causing the injury or death, or, if such person be employed by another person who is responsible for his conduct, also against such other person.

Sec. 4997. When the death of a person not a minor is caused by the wrongful act or neglect of another, his heirs, or his personal representatives for the benefit of his heirs, may maintain an action for damages against the person causing the death, or, if such person be employed by another person who is responsible for his conduct, then also against such other person. If such adult person have a guardian at the time of his death, only one action can be maintained for the injury to or death of such person, and such action may be brought by either the personal representatives of such adult person deceased for the benefit of his heirs, or by such guardian for the benefit of his heirs as provided in section 54 [4996]. In every action under this and the preceding section such damages may be given as under all the circumstances of the case may be just.

Sec. 5647. Whenever the death of a person shall be caused by wrongful act, neglect, or default, and the act, neglect, or default is such as would, if death had not ensued, have entitled the party injured to maintain an action and recover damages in respect thereof, then, and in every such case, the persons who, or the corporation which, would have been liable if death had not ensued, shall be liable to an action for damages notwithstanding the death of the person injured, and although the death shall have been caused under such circumstances as amount in law to a felony.

Sec. 5648. The proceeds of any judgment obtained in any action brought under the provisions of this act shall not be liable for any debt of the deceased: Provided, he or she shall have left a husband, wife, child, father, mother, brother, sister, or child or children of a deceased child; but shall be distributed as follows: 1. If there be a surviving husband or wife, and no child, then to such husband or wife; if there be a surviving husband or wife, and a child or children or grandchildren, then equally to each, the grandchild or children taking by right of representation; if there be no husband or wife, but a child or children, or grandchild or children, then to such child or children, and grandchild or children, by right of representation; if there be no child or grandchild, then to a surviving father or mother; if there be no father or mother, then to a surviving brother or sister, or brothers or sisters, if there be any; if there be none of the kindred hereinbefore named, then the proceeds of such judgment shall be disposed of in the manner authorized by law for the disposition of the personal property of deceased persons: Provided, every such action shall be brought by and in the name of the personal representative or representatives of such deceased person; and, provided, further, the jury in every such action may give such damages, pecuniary and exemplary, as they shall deem fair and just, and may take into consideration the pecuniary injury resulting from such death to the kindred as herein named.

Sec. 5649. Whenever any person shall suffer personal injury by wrongful act, neglect or default of another, the person causing the injury shall be liable to the person injured for damages; and where the person causing such injury is employed by another person or corporation responsible for his conduct, such person or corporation so responsible shall be liable to the person injured for damages.

Sec. 5650. That every common carrier engaged in trade or commerce in the state of Nevada, and every mine and mill owner and operator actually engaged in mining, or in milling or reduction of ores, in the state of Nevada, shall be liable to any of its employés, or, in case of the death of such employé, to his personal representative for the benefit of his widow and children, if any, and if none, then for his next of kin, for all damages which may result from the negligence of the officers, agents, or employés of said common carrier or mine or mill operator, or by reason of any defect or insufficiency due to their negligence in its cars, engines, appliances, machinery, track, roadbed, ways or works, or to their negligent handling or storing of explosives.

Sec. 5651. That in all actions hereinafter brought against any common carrier or mine or mill owner and operator to recover damages for personal injuries to or death of any employé, the fact that the employé may have been guilty of contributory negligence shall not bar a recovery where his contributory negligence was slight and the negligence of the employer, or its officers, agents, or employés was gross in comparison. All questions of negligence and contributory negligence shall be for the jury.

Sec. 5652. That no contract of employment, insurance, relief benefit, or indemnity for injury or death, entered into by or on behalf of any employé, nor the acceptance of any insurance, relief benefit or indemnity by the person entitled thereto, shall constitute any bar or defense to any action brought to recover damages for personal injuries to, or death of such employé: Provided, however, that upon the trial of such action the defendant may set off therein any sum it has contributed toward any such insurance, relief benefit, or indemnity that may have been paid to the person entitled thereto.

NEW HAMPSHIRE

Pub. St. 1901, c. 191

Sec. 8. Actions of tort for physical injuries to the person, although inflicted by a person while committing a felony and the causes of such actions, shall survive, to the extent, and subject to the limitations, set forth in the five following sections, and not otherwise:

Sec. 9. If such an action is pending at the time of the decease of one of the parties, it shall abate, and be forever barred, unless the administrator of the deceased party, if the deceased was plaintiff, shall appear and assume the prosecution of the action before the end of the second term after the decease of such party; or, if the deceased party was defendant, unless the plaintiff shall procure a scire facias to be issued to the administrator of the deceased party before the end of the second term after the original grant of admin- istration upon his estate.

Sec. 10. If an action is not then pending and has not already become barred by the statute of limitations, one may be brought for such cause at any time within two years after the death of the deceased party, and not afterwards.

Sec. 11. The damages recoverable in any such action shall not exceed seven thousand dollars.

Sec. 12. If the administrator of the deceased party is plaintiff, and the death of such party was caused by the injury complained of in the action, the mental and physical pain suffered by him in consequence of the injury, the reasonable expenses occasioned to his estate by the injury, the probable duration of his life but for the injury, and his capacity to earn money, may be considered as elements of damage, in connection with other elements allowed by law.

Sec. 13. In such case the damages recovered, less the expenses of recovery, shall belong and be distributed as follows:

1. To the widow or widower of the deceased, one half thereof; and to the children of the deceased the other half, in equal shares.

2. If there be no child, to the widow or widower, the whole thereof.

3. If there be no child and no widow or widower, to the heirs at law of the deceased, according to the laws of distribution.

4. If there be a child and children and no widow or widower, to the children of the deceased in equal shares the whole thereof.

Sec. 14. All other actions and causes of action existing in favor of or against a deceased person, except those for the recovery of penalties and forfeitures of money under penal statutes, shall survive, and may be prosecuted or defended by his administrator.

NEW JERSEY

Comp. St. 1910, p. 1907

Sec. 7. That whenever the death of a person shall be caused by wrongful act, neglect, or default, and the act, neglect, or default is such as would, if death had not ensued, have entitled the party injured to maintain an action and recover damages in respect thereof, then and in every such case the person who, or the corporation which, would have been liable if death had not ensued, shall be liable to an action for damages, notwithstanding the death of the person injured, and although the death shall have been caused under such circumstances as amount in law to felony.

Sec. 8. Every such person shall be brought by and in the names of the personal representatives of such deceased person, and the amount recovered in every such action shall be for the exclusive benefit of the widow and next of kin of such deceased person, and shall be distributed to such widow and next of kin in proportion provided by law in relation to the distribution of personal property left by persons dying intestate; and in every such action the jury may give such damages as they shall deem fair and just with reference to the pecuniary injury resulting from such death to the wife and next of kin of such deceased person: Provided, that where such deceased person has left or shall leave him surviving a widow, but no children or descendants of any children, the widow shall be entitled to the whole of the damages which she shall sustain and which shall be hereafter recovered in any such action and the same shall be paid to her; and provided further, that every such action shall be commenced within twenty-four calendar months after the death of such deceased person.

Sec. 9. That on request by the defendant, or the defendant's attorney, the plaintiff on the record shall be required to deliver to the defendant, or to the defendant's attorney a ~particular account in writing of the nature of the claim in respect to which damages shall be sought to be recovered.

NEW MEXICO

Comp. Laws 1897

Sec. 3213. Whenever any person shall die from any injury resulting from, or occasioned by the negligence, unskillfulness or criminal intent of any officer, agent, servant or employé whilst running, conducting or managing any locomotive, car, or train of cars, or of any driver of any stagecoach or other public conveyance while in charge of the same as driver; and when any passenger shall die from any injury resulting from, or occasioned by any defect or insufficiency in any railroad, or any part thereof, or in any locomotive or car, or in any stagecoach or other public conveyance, the corporation, individual or individuals, in whose employ any such officer, agent, servant, employé, engineer or driver shall be at the time such injury was committed, or who owns any such railroad, locomotive, car, stagecoach, or other public conveyance at the time any injury is received, resulting from, or occasioned by any defect or insufficiency above declared, shall forfeit and pay for every person or passenger so dying the sum of five thousand dollars, which may be sued and recovered: First, by the husband or wife of the deceased; or second, if there be no husband or wife, or if he or she fails to sue within six months after such death, then by the minor child or children of the deceased; or third, if such deceased be a minor and unmarried, then by the father and mother, who may join in the suit, and each shall have an equal interest in the judgment; or, if either of them be dead, then by the survivor. In suits instituted under this section it shall be competent for the defendant for his defense, to show that the defect or insufficiency named in this section was not of a negligent defect or insufficiency.

Sec. 3214. Whenever the death of a person shall be caused by the wrongful act, neglect or default of another, although such death shall have been caused under such circumstances as amount in law to a felony, and the act, or neglect, or default, is such as would, if death had not ensued, have entitled the party injured to maintain an action and recover damages in respect thereof, then, and in every such case, the person who, or the corporation which, would have been liable, if death had not ensued, shall be liable to an action for damages notwithstanding the death of the person injured.

Sec. 3215. Every such action as mentioned in the next preceding section, shall be brought by and in the name or names of the personal representative or representatives of such deceased person, and the jury in every such action may give such damages, compensatory and exemplary, as they shall deem fair and just, taking into consideration the pecuniary injury or injuries resulting from such death to the surviving party or parties entitled to the judgment, or any interest therein, recovered in such action, and also having regard to the mitigating or aggravating circumstances attending such wrongful act, neglect or default. The proceeds of any judgment obtained in any such action shall not be liable for any debt of the deceased: Provided, he or she shall have left a husband, wife, child, father, mother, brother, sister, or child or children of the deceased child, but shall be distributed as follows: First. If there be a surviving husband or wife, and no child, then to such husband or wife; if there be a surviving husband or wife and a child or children or grandchildren, then equally to each, the grandchild or grandchildren taking by right of representation; if there be no husband or wife, but a child or children, or grandchild or grandchildren, then to such child or children and grandchild or grandchildren by right of representation; if there be no child or grandchild, then to a surviving brother or sister, or brothers or sisters, if there be any; if there be none of the kindred hereinbefore named, then the proceeds of such judgment shall be disposed of in the manner authorized by law for the disposition of the personal property of deceased persons.

Sec. 3216. Every corporation operating a railway in this territory shall be liable in a sum sufficient to compensate such employé for all damages sustained by any employé of such corporation, the person injured or damaged being without fault on his or her part, occurring or sustained in consequence of any mismanagement, carelessness, neglect, default or wrongful act of any agent or employé of such corporation while in the exercise of their several duties, when such mismanagement, carelessness; neglect, default or wrongful act of such employé or agent could have been avoided by such corporation through the exercise of reasonable care or diligence in the selection of competent employés or agents, or by not over working said employés, or requiring or allowing them to work an unusual or unreasonable number of hours; and any contract restricting such liability shall be deemed to be contrary to the public policy of this territory and therefore void.

Sec. 3217. It shall be unlawful for any such corporation knowingly and willfully to use or operate any car or locomotive that is defective, or any car or locomotive upon which the machinery or attachments thereto belonging are in any manner defective, or shops, or machinery and attachments thereof which are in any manner defective, which defects might have been previously ascertained by ordinary care and diligence by said corporation.

If the employé of any such corporation shall receive any injury by reason of such defect in any car or locomotive or machinery or attachments thereto belonging, or shops or machinery and attachments thereof, owned and operated, or being run and operated by such corporation, through no fault of his own, such corporation shall be liable for such injury, and upon proof of the same in an action brought by such employé or his legal representatives, in any court of proper jurisdiction, against such railroad corporation for damages on account of such injury so received, shall be entitled to recover against such corporation any sum commensurate with the injuries sustained: Provided, that it shall be the duty of all the employés of railroad corporations to promptly report all defects coming to their knowledge in any such car or locomotive or shops or machinery and attachments thereof to the proper officer or agent of such corporation and after such report the doctrine of contributory negligence shall not apply to such employé.

Sec. 3218. Whenever the death of an employé shall be caused under circumstances from which a cause of action would have accrued under the provisions of the two preceding sections, if death had not ensued, an action therefor shall be brought in the manner provided by section three thousand two hundred and fifteen, and any sum recovered therein shall be subject to all of the provisions of said section three thousand two hundred and fifteen.

Sec. 2913. The following suits or actions may be brought within the time hereinafter limited, respectively, after their causes accrue, and not afterwards, except when otherwise specially provided.

Sec. 2916. Those founded upon accounts and unwritten contracts; those brought for injuries to property or for the conversion of personal property or for relief upon the ground of fraud, and all other actions not herein otherwise provided for and specified, within four years.

NEW YORK

Const. art. 1

Sec. 18. The right of action now existing to recover damages for injuries resulting in death, shall never be abrogated; and the amount recoverable shall not be subject to any statutory limitation.

Code Civil Proc. 1909

Sec. 1902. [Am'd, 1909.] The executor or administrator of a decedent who has left him or her surviving a husband, or wife, or next of kin, may maintain an action to recover damages for a wrongful act, neglect or default, by which the decedent's death was caused, against a natural person who, or a corporation which, would have been liable to an action in favor of the decedent by reason thereof if death had not ensued. Such an action must be commenced within two years after the decedent's death. When the husband, wife or next of kin do not participate in the estate of the decedent, under a will appointing an executor, other than such husband, wife or next of kin, who refuses to bring such action, then such husband, wife or next of kin shall be entitled to have an administrator appointed for the purpose of prosecuting such action for their benefit.

Sec. 1903. The damages recovered in an action, brought as prescribed in the last section, are exclusively for the benefit of the decedent's husband or wife, and next of kin; and when they are collected, they must be distributed by the plaintiff, as if they were unbequeathed assets, left in his hands, after payment of all debts, and expenses of administration; subject, however, to the following provision, to wit: In case the decedent shall have left him surviving a wife, or a husband, but no children, the damages recovered shall be for the sole benefit of such wife or husband. The plaintiff may deduct from the recovery the reasonable expenses of the action, the reasonable funeral expenses of the decedent, and his commissions upon the residue; which must be allowed by the surrogate, upon notice, given in such a manner and to such persons, as the surrogate deems proper. (As amended Laws 1911, c. 122.)

Sec. 1904. [Am'd, 1895.] The damages awarded to the plaintiff may be such a sum as the jury upon a writ of inquiry, or upon a trial, or where issues of fact are tried without a jury, the court or the referee, deems to be a fair and just compensation for the pecuniary injuries, resulting from the decedent's death, to the person or persons, for whose benefit the action is brought. When final judgment for the plaintiff is rendered, the clerk must add to the sum so awarded, interest thereupon from the decedent's death, and include it in the judgment. The inquisition, verdict, report or decision, may specify the day from which interest is to be computed; if it omits so to do, the day may be determined by the clerk, upon affidavits.

Sec. 1905. The term "next of kin," as used in the foregoing sections, has the meaning specified in section 1870 of this act.

Sec. 1870. The term "next of kin," as used in this title, includes all those entitled, under the provisions of law relating to the distribution of personal property, to share in the unbequeathed assets of a decedent, after payment of debts and expenses, other than a surviving husband or wife.

Sec. 1899. Where the violation of a right admits of a civil and also of a criminal prosecution, the one is not merged in the other.

NORTH CAROLINA

Revisal 1905

Sec. 59. Whenever the death of a person is caused by a wrongful act, neglect or default of another, such as would, if the injured party had lived, have entitled him to an action for damages therefor, the person or corporation that would have been so liable, and his or their executors, administrators, collectors or successors, shall be liable to an action for damages, to be brought within one year after such death, by the executor, administrator or collector of the decedent; and this notwithstanding the death, and although the wrongful act, neglect or default, causing the death, amount in law to a felony. The amount recovered in such action is not liable to be applied as assets, in the payment of debts or legacies, but shall be disposed of as provided in this chapter for the distribution of personal property in case of intestacy.

Sec. 60. The plaintiff in such action may recover such damages as are a fair and just compensation for the pecuniary injury resulting from such death.

Sec. 153. All sums of money, or other estate of whatever kind, which shall remain in the hands of any executor, administrator or collector for five years after his qualification, unrecovered or un-reclaimed by suit, by creditors, next of kin, or others entitled thereto, shall be paid by the executor, administrator or collector to the trustees of the University of North Carolina; and the said trustees are authorized to demand, sue for, recover, and collect such moneys or other estate of whatever kind, and hold the same without liability for profit or interest, until a just claim therefor shall be preferred by creditors, next of kin, or others entitled thereto; and, if no such claim shall be preferred within ten years after such money or other estate be received by the said trustees, then the same shall be held by them absolutely.

NORTH DAKOTA

Rev. Codes 1905

Sec. 7686. Whenever the death of a person shall be caused by a wrongful act, neglect or default and the act, neglect or default is such as would, if death had not ensued, have entitled the party injured to maintain an action and recover damages in respect thereof, then and in every such case the person who, or the corporation or company which, would have been liable if death had not ensued, shall be liable to an action for damages, notwithstanding the death of the person injured, and although the death shall have been caused under such circumstances as amount in law to felony.

Sec. 7687. In such actions the jury shall give such damages as they think proportionate to the injury resulting from the death to the persons entitled to the recovery.

Sec. 7688. The action shall be brought by the following persons in the order named:

1. The surviving husband or wife, if any.
2. The surviving children, if any.
3. The personal representative.

If any person entitled to bring the action refuses or neglects so to do for a period of thirty days after demand of the person next in order, such person may bring the same.

Sec. 7689. The amount recovered shall not be liable for the debts of the decedent, but shall inure to the exclusive benefit of his heirs at law in such shares as the judge before whom the case is tried shall fix in the order for judgment, and for the purpose of determining such shares the judge may after the trial make any investigation which he deems necessary.

Sec. 7690. The action shall not abate by the death of either party to the record. If the plaintiff dies pending the action the person next in order, entitled to bring the action, shall by order of the court be made plaintiff therein.

Sec. 7691. The person entitled to bring the action may compromise the same, or the right thereto, and such compromise shall be binding upon all persons authorized to bring the action or to share in the recovery.

OHIO

Gen. Code 1912

Sec. 10,770. When the death of a person is caused by wrongful act, neglect or default such as would have entitled the party injured to maintain an action and recover damages in respect thereof, if death had not ensued the corporation which, or the person who would have been liable if death had not ensued, or the administrator or executor of the estate of such person, as such administrator or executor shall be liable to an action for damages, notwithstanding the death of the person injured, and although the death was caused under circumstances which make it in law murder in the first or second degree, or manslaughter. When the action is against such administrator or executor the damages recovered shall be a valid claim against the estate of such deceased person.

When death is caused by a wrongful act, neglect or default in another state, territory or foreign country, for which a right to maintain an action and recover damages in respect thereof is given by a statute of such other state, territory, or foreign country, such right of action may be enforced in this state, in all cases where such other state, territory or foreign country allows the enforcement in its courts of the statute of this state of a like character; but in no case shall the damages exceed the amount authorized to be recovered for a wrongful neglect or default in this state, causing death. Every such action brought under this act shall be commenced within the time prescribed for the commencement of such action by the statute of such other state, territory or foreign country.

Sec. 10,772. Such action shall be for the exclusive benefit of the wife, or husband, and children, or if there be neither of them, then of the parents and next of kin of the person whose death was so caused: It must be brought in the name of the personal representative of the deceased person; and where it shall appear that any such action is for the benefit of children, widow, widower, mother, father, brother or sister, the jury may give such damages, not exceeding in any case ten thousand dollars, and where it shall appear that any such action is for the benefit of a widow and one or more minor children, the jury may give such damages, not exceeding in any case twelve thousand dollars, as the jury may think proportioned to the pecuniary injury resulting from such death, to the persons, respectively for whose benefit the action was brought. Every such action must be commenced within two years after the death of such deceased person, except as provided in section 10,-773—1. Such personal representative, if he was appointed in this state, with the consent of the court making such appointment may at any time, before or after the commencement of a suit, settle with the defendant the amount to be paid. The amount received by such personal representative, whether by settlement, or otherwise, shall be apportioned among the beneficiaries unless adjusted between themselves, by the court making the appointment, in such manner as shall be fair and equitable, having reference to the age and condition of such beneficiaries and the laws of descent and distribution of personal estates left by persons dying in the state.

Sec. 10,773—1. That in every such action for wrongful death commenced or attempted to be commenced within the time herein specified, if a judgment for the plaintiff be reversed, or if the plaintiff fail, otherwise than upon the merits, and the time limited herein for the commencement of such action has at the date of such reversal, or failure, expired, the plaintiff, or if he die and the cause of action survive, his representative may commence a new action within one year after such date.

Sec. 11,235. In addition to the causes which survive at common law, causes of action for mesne profits, or injuries to the person or property, or for deceit or fraud, also shall survive; and the action may be brought notwithstanding the death of the person entitled or liable thereto.

Sec. 11,397. Unless otherwise provided, no action or proceeding pending in any court shall abate by the death of either or both of the parties thereto, except actions for libel, slander, malicious prosecution, for a nuisance, or against a justice of the peace for misconduct in office, which shall abate by the death of either party.

Sec. 6242. That in all actions brought to recover from an employer for personal injuries suffered by his employé or for death resulting to such employé from such personal injuries, while in the employ of such employer, arising from the negligence of such employer or any of such employer's officers, agents, or employés, it shall be held in addition to the liability now existing by law that any person in the employ of such employer, in any way having power or authority in directing or controlling any other employé of such employer, is not the fellow servant, but superior to such other employé; any person in the employ of such employer in any way hav-

ing charge or control of employés, in any separate branch or department, shall be held to be the superior and not fellow servant of all
employés in any other branch or department in which they are employed; any person in the employ of such employer whose duty it
is to repair or inspect the ways, works, boats, wharves, plant, machinery, appliances or tools, in any way connected with or in any
way used in the business of the employer or to receive, give or trans-
mit any signal, instruction, or warning to or for such employés shall
be held to be the superior and not fellow servant to such other employés of such employer.

Sec. 6243. That if the employé of any such employer shall receive any personal injury by reason of any defect or unsafe condition in any ways, works, boats, wharves, plant, machinery, appliances or tools, except simple tools, in any way connected with or
in any way used in the business of the employer, such employer shall
be deemed to have had knowledge of such defect, before and at the
time such injury was so sustained, and when the fact of such defect
shall be made to appear upon trial of an action brought by such employé or his personal or legal representatives, against any such employer for damages, on account of such injuries so received, the
same shall be prima facie evidence of neglect on the part of such
employer; but the employer may show by way of defense that such
defect was not discoverable in the exercise of ordinary care.

Sec. 6244. That in all such actions the negligence of a fellow
servant of the employé shall not be a defense where the injury or
death was in any way caused or contributed to by any of the following causes, to-wit: Any defect or unsafe condition in the ways,
works, boats, wharves, plant, machinery, appliances or tools, except
simple tools, in any way connected with or in any way used in the
business of the employer; the negligence of any person engaged as
superintendent, manager, foreman, inspector, repairman, signal man,
or any person in any way having charge, care or control of such ways,
works, boats, wharves, plant, machinery, appliances or tools; the negligence of any person in charge of or directing the particular work
in which the employé was engaged at the time of the injury or
death; the negligence of any person to whose orders the employé
was bound to conform and·by reason of his having conformed thereto the injuries or death resulted; the negligent act of any fellow
servant done in obedience to the immediate or peremptory instructions or orders given by the employer, or any person who has authority to direct the doing of said act; the want of necessary and
sufficient rules and regulations for the government of such employés
and the operation and maintenance of such ways, works, boats,
wharves, plant, machinery, appliances or tools.

Sec. 6245. That in any such action when it shall appear that the injury or death was caused in whole or in part by any of the following, to-wit: The neglect of such employer in failing to properly furnish, maintain, construct, guard, repair, inspect, or protect any of the ways, works, boats, wharves, plant, machinery, appliances or tools, in any way connected with or in any way used in the business of the employer, in any manner required by statute or law of the state or United States; any defective or unsafe condition in the ways, works, boats, wharves, plant, machinery, appliances or tools, except simple tools, in any way connected with or in any way used in the business, of the employer, the fact that such employé continued in said employment with knowledge of such negligent omission or want of care or such defective or unsafe condition shall not be a defense unless by the terms of his employment it was expressly made the duty of such employé to report such neglect or such defective or unsafe condition to the employer and the evidence discloses that such employé failed so to report, and that the employer was not otherwise possessed of knowledge of such negligent, unsafe or defective condition. Such employé shall not be held to have assumed the risk of the negligent act of any fellow servant or employé of such employer, done in obedience to the immediate or peremptory instructions or orders given by the employer, or any other person who has authority to direct the doing of said act; the want of necessary and sufficient rules and regulations or the lack of enforcement of same for the government of such employés in the construction, operation and maintenance of such ways, works, boats, wharves, machinery, plant, appliances or tools, or the employing or retention of any incompetent servant.

Sec. 6245—1. That in all such actions hereafter brought, the fact that the employé may have been guilty of contributory negligence shall not bar a recovery where his contributory negligence is slight and the negligence of the employer is gross in comparison. But the damages shall be diminished by the jury in proportion to the amount of negligence attributable to such employé. Provided that no such employé who may be injured or killed shall be held in any degree to have been guilty of contributory negligence in any case where the violation of such employer of any statute or law of the state, or United States enacted for the safety of employés in any way contributed to the injury or death of such employé unless by the terms of his employment it was expressly made the duty of such employé to report such violation to the employer and the evidence shows that such employé failed so to report and that the employer was not possessed of knowledge of such violation. All questions of negligence, contributory negligence, and assumption of risk, shall be for the jury, under the instruction of the court.

Sec. 6245—2. That in all such actions where a minor employé has been employed or retained in employment contrary to any statute or law of the state or United States, such employé shall not be deemed or held to have been guilty of contributory negligence nor to have assumed any of the risks of such employment; but the employer may show by way of defense any fraud or misrepresentation made by such employé.

Sec. 6245—3. That in all such actions any contract, rule, regulation or device whatsoever, the purpose or intent of which shall be to enable any employer to exempt himself or itself from any liability created by this act, shall to that extent be void; provided, that in any action brought against any employer under or by virtue of any other provisions of this act, such employer may set off therein, any sum he or it has contributed or paid to any insurance, relief, benefit, or indemnity that may have been paid to the injured employé or the person entitled thereto on account of the injury or death for which said action was brought.

OKLAHOMA

Const. art. 23

Sec. 7. The right of action to recover damages for injuries resulting in death shall never be abrogated, and the amount recoverable shall not be subject to any statutory limitation.

Const. art. 9

Sec. 36. The common law doctrine of the fellow-servant, so far as it affects the liability of the master for injuries to his servant, resulting from the acts or omissions of any other servant or servants of the common master, is abrogated as to every employé of every railroad company and every street railway company or interurban railway company, and of every person, firm, or corporation engaged in mining in this state; and every such employé shall have the same right to recover for every injury suffered by him for the acts or omissions of any other employé or employés of the common master that a servant would have if such acts or omissions were those of the master himself in the performance of a non-assignable duty; and when death, whether instantaneous or not, results to such employé from any injury for which he could have recovered under the above provisions, had not death occurred, then his legal or personal representative, surviving consort or relatives, or any trustee, curator, committee or guardian of such consort, or relatives, shall have the same rights and remedies with respect thereto, as if death had been caused by the negligence of the master. And every railroad company and every street railway company or interurban railway company, and every person, firm, or corporation engaged in underground mining in this state shall be liable under this section, for the acts of his or its receivers.

Nothing contained in this section shall restrict the power of the Legislature to extend to the employés of any person, firm, or corporation, the rights and remedies herein provided for.

Comp. Laws 1909

Sec. 5943. In addition to the causes of action which survive at common law, causes of action for mesne profits, or for an injury to the person, or to real or personal estate, or for any deceit or fraud, shall also survive; and the action may be brought, notwithstanding the death of the person entitled or liable to the same.

Sec. 5944. No action pending in any court shall abate by the death of either or both the parties thereto, except an action for libel, slander, malicious prosecution, for a nuisance, or against a justice of the peace for misconduct in office, which shall abate by the death of the defendant.

Sec. 5945. When the death of one is caused by the wrongful act or omission of another, the personal representatives of the former may maintain an action therefor against the latter, if the former might have maintained an action had he lived, against the latter for an injury for the same act or omission. The action must be commenced within two years. The damages cannot exceed ten thousand dollars, and must inure to the exclusive benefit of the widow and children, if any, or next of kin, to be distributed in the same manner as personal property of the deceased.

Sec. 5946. That in all cases where the residence of the party whose death has been or hereafter shall be caused as set forth in section 5945 of this article, is or has been at the time of his death in any other state or territory, or when, being a resident of this state, no personal representative is or has been appointed, the action provided in said section 5945 may be brought by the widow, or where there is no widow, by the next of kin of such deceased.

TIFF.DEATH W.A.(2D ED.)—35

OREGON

Lord's Or. Laws 1910

Sec. 378. A cause of action arising out of an injury to the person dies with the person of either party, except as provided in section 380; but the provisions of this chapter shall not be construed so as to abate the action mentioned in section 39, or to defeat or prejudice the right of action given by section 34.

Sec. 379. All other causes of action by one person against another, whether arising on contract or otherwise, survive to the personal representatives of the former, and against the personal representatives of the latter. When the cause of action survives as herein provided, the executors or administrators may maintain an action at law thereon against the party against whom the cause of action accrued, or, after his death, against his personal representatives.

Sec. 380. When the death of a person is caused by the wrongful act or omission of another, the personal representatives of the former may maintain an action at law therefor against the latter, if the former might have maintained an action, had he lived, against the latter, for an injury done by the same act or omission. Such action shall be commenced within two years after the death, and the damages therein shall not exceed $7,500, and the amount recovered, if any, shall be administered as other personal property of the deceased person.

Sec. 34. A father, or in case of the death or desertion of his family, the mother, may maintain an action as plaintiff for the injury or death of a child, and a guardian for the injury or death of his ward.

Sec. 38. No action shall abate by the death, marriage, or other disability of a party, or by the transfer of any interest therein, if the cause of action survive or continue. In case of the death, marriage, or other disability of a party, the court may, at any time within one year thereafter, on motion, allow the action to be continued by or against his personal representatives or successors in interest.

Sec. 39. An action for a wrong shall not abate by the death of any party, after a verdict has been given therein, but the action shall proceed thereafter in the same manner as in cases where the cause of action survives.

Lord's Or. Laws 1910, p. xxxvi

Section 1. All owners, contractors, subcontractors, corporations, or persons whatsoever, engaged in the construction, repairing, alteration, removal, or painting of any building, bridge, viaduct, or other structure, or in the erection or operation of any machinery, or in the manufacture, transmission, and use of electricity, or in the manufacture or use of any dangerous appliance or substance, shall see that all metal, wood, rope, glass, rubber, gutta percha, or other material whatever, shall be carefully selected and inspected and tested, so as to detect any defects, and all scaffolding, staging, false work, or other temporary structure shall be constructed to bear four times the maximum weight to be sustained by said structure, and such structure shall not at any time be overloaded or overcrowded; and all scaffolding, staging, or other structure more than twenty feet from the ground or floor shall be secured from swaying and provided with a strong and efficient safety rail or other contrivance, so as to prevent any person from falling therefrom, and all dangerous machinery shall be securely covered and protected to the fullest extent that the proper operation of the machinery permits, and all shafts, wells, floor openings, and similar places of danger shall be enclosed, and all machinery other than that operated by hand power shall, whenever necessary for the safety of persons employed in or about the same, or for the safety of the general public, be provided with a system of communication by means of signals, so that at all times there may be prompt and efficient communication between the employés or other persons and the operator of the motive power, and in the transmission and use of electricity of a dangerous voltage full and complete insulation shall be provided at all points where the public or the employés of the owner, contractor, or subcontractor transmitting or using said electricity are liable to come in contact with the wire, and dead wires shall not be mingled with live wires, nor strung upon the same support, and the arms or supports bearing live wires shall be especially designated by a color or other designation which is instantly apparent and live electrical wires carrying a dangerous voltage shall be strung at such distance from the poles or supports as to permit repairmen to freely engage in their work without danger of shock; and generally, all owners, contractors, or subcontractors, and other persons having charge of, or responsible for, any work involving a risk or danger to the employés or the public, shall use every device, care, and precaution which it is practicable to use for the protection and safety of life and limb, limited only by the necessity for preserving the efficiency of the structure, machine, or other apparatus or device, and without regard to the additional cost of suitable material or safety appliance and devices.

Sec. 2. The manager, superintendent, foreman, or other person in charge or control of the construction or works or operation, or any part thereof, shall be held to be the agent of the employer in all suits for damages for death or injury suffered by an employé.

Sec. 3. It shall be the duty of owners, contractors, subcontractors, foremen, architects, or other persons having charge of the particular work, to see that the requirements of this act are complied with, and for any failure in this respect the person or persons delinquent shall, upon conviction of violating any of the provisions of this act, be fined not less than $10, nor more than $1,000, or imprisoned not less than ten days, nor more than one year, or both, in the discretion of the court, and this shall not effect or lessen the civil liability of such persons as the case may be.

Sec. 4. If there shall be any loss of life by reason of the neglects or failures or violations of the provisions of this act by any owner, contractor, subcontractor, or any person liable under the provisions of this act, the widow of the person so killed, his lineal heirs or adopted children, or the husband, mother, or father, as the case may be, shall have a right of action without any limit as to the amount of damages which may be awarded.

Sec. 5. In all actions brought to recover from an employer for injuries suffered by an employé the negligence of a fellow servant shall not be a defense where the injury was caused or contributed to by any of the following causes, namely: Any defect in the structure, materials, works, plant, or machinery of which the employer or his agent could have had knowledge by the exercise of ordinary care; the neglect of any person engaged as superintendent, manager, fore-man, or other person in charge or control of the works, plant, ma-chinery, or appliances; the incompetence or negligence of any per-son in charge of, or directing the particular work in which the em-ployé was engaged at the time of the injury or death; the incom-petence or negligence of any person to whose orders the employé was bound to conform and did conform and by reason of his having conformed thereto the injury or death resulted; the act of any fel-low servant done in obedience to the rules, instructions, or orders given by the employer or any other person who has authority to di-rect the doing of said act.

Sec. 6. The contributory negligence of the person injured shall not be a defense, but may be taken into account by the jury in fixing the amount of the damages.

Sec. 7. All acts or parts of acts inconsistent herewith are hereby repealed.

PENNSYLVANIA

Const. 1874, art 3

Sec. 21. No act of the general assembly shall limit the amount to be recovered for injuries resulting in death, or for injuries to persons or property; and, in case of death from such injuries, the right of action shall survive, and the general assembly shall prescribe for whose benefit such actions shall be prosecuted. No act shall prescribe any limitations of time within which suits may be brought against corporations for injuries to persons or property, or for other causes, different from those fixed by general laws regulating actions against natural persons; and such acts now existing are avoided.

Pepper & Lewis' Dig. pp. 5331–5340

Sec. 1. No action hereafter brought to recover damages for injuries to the person by negligence or default shall abate by reason of the death of the plaintiff; but the personal representatives of the deceased may be substituted as plaintiff, and prosecute the suit to final judgment and satisfaction.

Sec. 2. Whenever death shall be occasioned by unlawful violence or negligence, and no suit for damages be brought by the party injured during his or her life, the widow of any such deceased, or if there be no widow, the personal representatives, may maintain an action for and recover damages for the death thus occasioned.

Sec. 3. That the persons entitled to recover damages for any injuries causing death shall be the husband, widow, children, or parents of the deceased, and no other relatives; and that such husband, widow, children, or parents of the deceased shall be entitled to recover, whether he, she, or they be citizens or residents of the commonwealth of Pennsylvania, or citizens or residents of any other state or place subject to the jurisdiction of the United States, or of any foreign country, or subjects of any foreign potentate; and the sum recovered shall go to them in the proportion they would take his or her personal estate in case of intestacy, and that without liability to creditors under the laws of this commonwealth. (As amended Act June 7, 1911 [P. L. 678].)

Sec. 4. The declaration shall state who are the parties entitled in such action; the action shall be brought within one year after the death, and not thereafter.

Sec. 5. Any right of action which may hereafter come into being by reason of injury wrongfully done to the person of another shall survive the death of the wrong-doer, and may be enforced against his executor or administrator either by continuing against such personal representative a suit which may have been brought against the wrong-doer himself in his lifetime, or by bringing an original suit against his representative after his death. 1895, June 24; P. L. 236, § 1.

Sec. 6. When any person shall sustain personal injury or loss of life while lawfully engaged or employed on or about the roads, works, depots and premises of a railroad company, or in or about any train or car therein or thereon, of which company such person is not an employé, the right of action and recovery in all such cases against the company shall be such only as would exist if such person were an employé: Provided, that this section shall not apply to passengers. 1868, April 4; P. L. 58, § 1.

Sec. 7. In all actions brought to recover from an employer for injury suffered by his employé, the negligence of a fellow-servant of the employé shall not be a defense, where the injury was caused or contributed to by any of the following causes; namely,—

Any defect in the works, plant, or machinery, of which the employer could have had knowledge by the exercise of ordinary care; the neglect of any person engaged as superintendent, manager, foreman, or any other person in charge or control of the works, plant, or machinery; the negligence of any person in charge of or directing the particular work in which the employé was engaged at the time of the injury or death; the negligence of any person to whose orders the employé was bound to conform, and did conform, and, by reason of his having conformed thereto, the injury or death resulted; the act of any fellow-servant, done in obedience to the rules, instructions, or orders given by the employer, or any other person who has authority to direct the doing of said act. 1907, June 10; P. L. 523, § 1.

Sec. 8. The manager, superintendent, foreman, or other person in charge or control of the works, or any part of the works, shall, under this act, be held as the agent of the employer, in all suits for damages for death or injury suffered by employés. 1907, June 10, P. L. 523, § 2.

Sec. 9. All acts or parts of acts inconsistent herewith be and the same are hereby repealed. 1907, June 10; P. L. 523, § 3.

Pepper & Lewis' Dig. p. 5131

Sec. 265. For any injury to person or property occasioned by any violation of this act,[7] or any failure to comply with its provisions, by any owner, operator, superintendent, mine foreman or fire boss of

---

[7] Act providing for safety of persons employed in mines.

any coal mine or colliery, a right of action shall accrue to the party injured against said owner or operator for any direct damages he may have sustained thereby; and in case of loss of life by reason of such neglect or failure aforesaid, a right of action shall accrue to the widow and lineal heirs of the person whose life shall be lost, for like recovery of damages for the injury they shall have sustained. 1891, June 2; P. L. 176, art. xvii, § 8.

RHODE ISLAND

Gen. Laws 1909, c. 283

Sec. 7. In addition to the causes of action and actions which at common law survive the death of the plaintiff or defendant therein, the following causes of action or actions shall also survive:

* * * * * * * * * * * *

Third. Causes of action and actions of trespass and trespass on the case for damages to the person or to real and personal estate.

Sec. 8. All the causes of action and actions in the preceding section mentioned may be originally brought and prosecuted by and against executors and administrators; and if brought or prosecuted by or against any person in his lifetime, may be prosecuted or defended by his executor or administrator.

Sec. 9. Whenever any of said causes of action or actions are, originally or by survival, brought or prosecuted by or against the executor or administrator of the party originally liable, the plaintiff shall be entitled to recover only the value of the goods taken, or the damage actually sustained, without any vindictive or exemplary damages, or damages for any alleged outrage to the feelings of the injured party.

Sec. 14. Whenever the death of a person shall be caused by the wrongful act, neglect, or default of another, and the act, neglect, or default is such as would, if death had not ensued, have entitled the party injured to maintain an action and recover damages in respect thereof, the person who, or the corporation which, would have been liable if death had not ensued shall be liable to an action for damages, notwithstanding the death of the person injured, and although the death shall have been caused under such circumstances as amount in law to a felony. Every such action shall be brought by and in the name of the executor or administrator of such deceased person, whether appointed or qualified within or without the state, and the amount recovered in every such action shall one-half thereof go to the husband or widow, and one-half thereof to the children of the deceased, and if there be no children the whole shall go to the husband or widow, and, if there be no husband or widow, to the next of kin, in the proportion provided by law in relation to the distribution of personal property left by persons dying intestate: Provided, that every such action shall be commenced within two years after the death of such person. If there is no executor or administrator, or if, there being one, no action is brought in his name within six months after the death, one action may be brought in the names of all the beneficiaries, either by all, or by part stating that they sue for the benefit of all, and stating their respective relations to the deceased: Provided, that if all do not bring suit, only those bringing it shall be responsible for costs; but judgment shall be for the benefit of all, and shall be entered as several judgments for each in his proportion as aforesaid, and executions thereon shall issue in favor of each respectively: Provided, further, that if action be brought by the beneficiaries, no action shall thereafter be brought by the executor or administrator. There shall be but one bill of costs in favor of the plaintiffs, which shall enure equally for the benefit of those bringing the suit, and of them only.

Sec. 15. In order to maintain any action given in and by the preceding section, it shall not be necessary to first institute criminal proceedings against the defendant.

SOUTH CAROLINA

Civ. Code 1902

Sec. 2851. Whenever the death of a person shall be caused by the wrongful act, neglect, or default of another, and the act, neglect, or default is such as would, if death had not ensued, have entitled the party injured to maintain an action and recover damages in respect thereof, then, and in every such case, the person or corporation who would have been liable, if death had not ensued, shall be liable to an action for damages notwithstanding the death of the person injured, although the death shall have been caused under such circumstances as make the killing in law a felony.

Sec. 2852. Every such action shall be for the benefit of the wife or husband and child, or children, of the person whose death shall have been so caused; and if there be no such wife, or husband, or child, or children, then for the benefit of the parent or parents; and if there be none such, then for the benefit of the heirs at law or the distributees of the person whose death shall have been caused as may be dependent on him for support, and shall be brought by or in the name of the executor or administrator of such person; and in every such action the jury may give such damages, including exemplary damages where such wrongful act, neglect or default was the result of recklessness, willfulness or malice, as they may think proportioned to the injury resulting from such death to the parties respectively, for whom and for whose benefit such action shall be brought. And the amount so recovered shall be divided among the before mentioned parties, in such shares as they would have been entitled to if the deceased had died intestate and the amount recovered had been personal assets of his or her estate.

Sec. 2853. All such actions must be brought within six years from the death of such person, and the executor or administrator, plaintiff in action, shall be liable to costs in case there be a verdict for the defendant, or nonsuit or discontinuance, out of the goods, chattels and lands of the testator or intestate, if any. (As amended Laws 1903, p. 96, No. 60.)

Sec. 2854. The provisions of the three preceding sections of this chapter shall not apply to any case where the person injured has, for such injury, brought action, which has proceeded to trial and final judgment before his or her death.

SOUTH DAKOTA

2 Comp. Laws 1910, p. 444a, c. 301

Sec. 1. Whenever the death of a person shall be caused by wrongful act, neglect or default, and the act, neglect or default is such as would (if death had not ensued), have entitled the party injured to maintain an action and recover damages in respect thereof, then and in every such case, the corporation which, or the person who, would have been liable if death had not ensued, or the administrator or executor of the estate of such person as such administrator or executor, shall be liable to an action for damages, notwithstanding the death of the person injured, and although the death shall have been caused under such circumstances as amount in law to a felony; and when the action is against such administrator or executor, the damages recovered shall be a valid claim against the estate of such deceased person.

Sec. 2. Whenever the death of a citizen of this state has been caused by a wrongful act, neglect or default in another state, territory or foreign country for which a right to maintain an action and recover damages in respect thereof is given by a statute of such other state, territory or foreign country, such right of action may be enforced in this state within the time prescribed for the commencement of such action, by the statute of such other state, territory or foreign country.

Sec. 3. Every such action shall be for the exclusive benefit of the wife or husband and children, or if there be neither of them, then of the parents and next of kin of the person whose death shall be so caused; and it shall be brought in the name of the personal representative of the deceased person; and in e‾ery action the jury may give such damages, not exceeding in any case ten thousand dollars ($10,000.00), as they may think proportionate to the pecuniary injury resulting from such death to the persons respectively for whose benefit such action shall be brought. Every such action shall be commenced within three years after the death of such deceased person. Such personal representative, if he was appointed in this state, may, with the consent of the court making such appointment, at any time before or after the commencement of a suit, settle with the defendant the amount to be paid to him, and the amount received by such personal representative, whether by settlement or otherwise, shall be apportioned among the beneficiaries, unless adjusted between themselves, by the court making the appointment, in such manner as shall be fair and equitable having reference to the age and condition of such beneficiaries and the laws of descent and distribution of personal estates left by persons dying intestate.

TENNESSEE

Shannon's Code 1896

Sec. 4025. The right of action which a person who dies from injuries received from another, or whose death is caused by the wrongful act, omission, or killing by another, would have had against the wrongdoer in case death had not ensued, shall not abate or be extinguished by his death, but shall pass to his widow, and, in case there is no widow, to his children, or to his personal representative, for the benefit of his widow or next of kin, free from the claims of creditors.

Sec. 4026. The action may be instituted by the personal representative of the deceased; but if he decline it, the widow and children of the deceased may, without the consent of the representative, use his name in bringing and prosecuting the suit, on giving bond and security for costs, or in the form prescribed for paupers. The personal representative shall not, in such case, be responsible for costs, unless he sign his name to the prosecution bond.

Sec. 4027. The action may also be instituted by the widow in her own name, or, if there be no widow, by the children.

Sec. 4028. If the deceased had commenced an action before his death, it shall proceed without a revivor. The damages shall go to the widow and next of kin, free from the claims of the creditors of the deceased, to be distributed as personal property.

Sec. 4029. Where a person's death is caused by the wrongful act, fault, or omission of another, and suit is brought for damages, as provided for by sections 4025 to 4027, inclusive, the party suing shall, if entitled to damages, have the right to recover for the mental and physical suffering, loss of time, and necessary expenses resulting [to the deceased from the personal injuries, and also the damages resulting] to the parties for whose use and benefit the right of action survives from the death consequent upon the injuries received.

Sec. 4466. All civil actions, other than those for causes embraced in the foregoing article, shall be commenced after the cause of action has accrued, within the periods prescribed in this chapter, unless otherwise expressly provided.

Sec. 4469. Actions for libel, for injuries to the person, false imprisonment, malicious prosecution, criminal conversation, seduction, breach of marriage promise, and statute penalties, within one year after cause of action accrued.

Acts 1903, c. 317

Section 1. That no suit now pending or hereafter brought for personal injuries or death from wrongful act in any of the courts of this State, whether by appeal or otherwise, and whether in an inferior or superior court, shall abate or be abated, because or on account of the death of the beneficiary or beneficiaries for whose use and benefit said suit was brought, and that such suit shall be proceeded with to final judgment, as though such beneficiary or beneficiaries had not died, for the use and benefit of the heirs at law of such deceased beneficiary.

Acts 1897, c. 86

Section 1. The damages which may be recovered for the wrongful killing of any married woman shall go to the surviving husband and children of the deceased equally, the husband taking a child's share, and if any child be dead having descendants such descendants shall take the deceased child's part. If there are no children nor descendants of children, then the damages shall go exclusively to the husband. If the husband shall die after the cause of action accrued and before recovery is collected, then his share will go to his next of kin.

Sec. 2. A suit for the wrongful killing of the wife may be brought in the name of the husband for the benefit of himself and the children of the wife, or in the name of administrator of the deceased wife.

TEXAS

Const. art. 16

Sec. 26. Every person, corporation, or company that may commit a homicide, through willful act or omission or gross neglect, shall be responsible in exemplary damages, to the surviving husband, wife, heirs of his or her body, or such of them as there may be, without regard to any criminal proceeding that may or may not be had in relation to the homicide.

Rev. St. 1895

Art. 3017. An action for actual damages on account of injuries causing the death of any person may be brought in the following cases:

1. When the death of any person is caused by the negligence or carelessness of the proprietor, owner, charterer, hirer of any railroad, steamboat, stage coach, or other vehicle for the conveyance of goods or passengers, or by the unfitness, negligence or carelessness of their servants or agents; when the death of any person is caused by the negligence or carelessness of the receiver or receivers or other person or persons in charge or control of any railroad, their servants or agents, and the liability of receivers shall extend to cases in which the death may be caused by reason of the bad or unsafe condition of the railroad or machinery or other reason or cause by which an action may be brought for damages on account of injuries, the same as if said railroad were being operated by the railroad company.

2. When the death of any person is caused by the wrongful act, negligence, unskillfulness or default of another.   `

Art. 3018. The wrongful act, negligence, carelessness, unskillfulness, or default mentioned in the preceding article must be of such a character as would, if death had not ensued, have entitled the party injured to maintain an action for such injury.

Art. 3019. When the death is caused by the willful act or omission or gross negligence of the defendant, exemplary as well as actual damages may be recovered.

Art. 3020. The action may be commenced and prosecuted, although the death shall have been caused under such circumstances as amount in law to a felony, and without regard to any criminal proceeding that may or may not be had in relation to the homicide.

Art. 3021. The action shall be for the sole and exclusive benefit of the surviving husband, wife, children and parents of the person whose death shall have been so caused, and the amount recovered therein shall not be liable for the debts of the deceased.

Art. 3022. The action may be brought by all of the parties entitled thereto, or by any one or more of them for the benefit of all.

Art. 3023. If the parties entitled to the benefit of the action shall fail to commence the same within three calendar months after the death of the deceased, it shall be the duty of the executor or administrator of the deceased to commence and prosecute the action, unless requested by all of the parties entitled thereto not to prosecute the same.

Art. 3024. The action shall not abate by the death of either party to the record if any person entitled to the benefit of the action survives. If the plaintiff die pending the suit, when there is only one plaintiff, some one or more of the parties entitled to the money recovered may, by order of the court, be made plaintiff, and the suit be prosecuted to judgment in the name of such plaintiff, for the benefit of the persons entitled.

Art. 3025. If the sole plaintiff die pending the suit, and he is the only party entitled to the money recovered, the suit shall abate.

Art. 3026. If the defendant die pending the suit, his executor or administrator may be made a party and the suit be prosecuted to judgment, as though such defendant had continued alive. The judgment in such case, if rendered in favor of the plaintiff, shall be, to be paid in due course of administration.

Art. 3027. The jury may give such damages as they may think proportioned to the injury resulting from such death; and the amount so recovered shall be divided among the persons entitled to the benefit of the action, or such of them as shall then be alive, in such shares as the jury shall find by their verdict.

Art. 3353. There shall be commenced and prosecuted within one year after the cause of the action shall have accrued, and not afterwards, all actions or suits in court of the following description:

*   *   *   *   *   *   *   *   *

4. Actions for injuries done to the person of another where death ensued from such injuries; and the cause of action shall be considered as having accrued at the death of the party injured.

UTAH

Const. art. 16

Sec. 5. The right of action to recover damages for injuries resulting in death, shall never be abrogated, and the amount recoverable shall not be subject to any statutory limitation.

Comp. Laws 1907

Sec. 2911. A father, or, in case of his death or desertion of his family, the mother, may maintain an action for the death or injury of a minor child, when such injury or death is caused by the wrongful act or neglect of another; and a guardian may maintain an action for the injury or death of his ward, if the ward be of lawful age, when such injury or death is caused by the wrongful act or neglect of another, the action by the guardian to be prosecuted for the benefit of the heirs of the ward. Any such action may be maintained against the person causing the injury or death, or, if such person be employed by another person who is responsible for his conduct, also against such other person.

Sec. 2912. When the death of a person not a minor is caused by the wrongful act or neglect of another, his heirs, or his personal representatives for the benefit of his heirs, may maintain an action for damages against the person causing the death, or, if such person be employed by another person who is responsible for his conduct, then also against such other person. If such adult person have a guardian at the time of his death, only one action can be maintained for the injury to or death of such person, and such action may be brought by either the personal representatives of such adult person deceased for the benefit of his heirs, or by such guardian for the benefit of his heirs as provided in § 2911. In every action under this and the preceding section such damages may be given as under all the circumstances of the case may be just.

Sec. 2873. The periods prescribed for the commencement of actions other than for the recovery of real property are as hereinafter provided.

Sec. 2878. Within two years:

*   *   *   *   *   *   *   *   *

2. An action to recover damages for the death of one caused by the wrongful act or neglect of another.

VERMONT

Public St. 1906

Sec. 2834. Actions of ejectment or other proper actions to recover the seisin or possession of lands, tenements or hereditaments, actions of replevin and trover, and actions of trespass and trespass on the case for damages done to real or personal estate, shall survive, in addition to the actions which survive by the common law, and may be commenced and prosecuted by the executor or administrator.

Sec. 2835. If, in an action for the recovery of damages for a bodily hurt or injury, occasioned to the plaintiff by the act or default of the defendant or defendants, either party dies during the pendency of such action, the action shall survive, and may be prosecuted to final judgment by or against the executors or administrators of such deceased party; but when there are several defendants in such action, and one or more, but not all, die, it shall be prosecuted against the surviving defendant or defendants only.

Sec. 2836. The causes of action mentioned in the two preceding sections shall survive; and the actions may be commenced and prosecuted, or, when commenced in the lifetime of the deceased, may be prosecuted by or against the executor or administrator, where by law that mode of prosecution is authorized; and, when commissioners are appointed, claims on which such actions might be founded may be presented and prosecuted before the commissioners, except actions of ejectment or other actions for the recovery of the seisin or possession of lands, and actions of replevin.

Sec. 2839. When the death of a person is caused by the wrongful act, neglect or default of a person or corporation, and the act, neglect or default is such as would, if death had not ensued, have entitled the party injured to maintain an action and recover damages in respect thereof, the person or corporation liable to such action, if death had not ensued, shall be liable to an action for damages, notwithstanding the death of the person injured, and although the death is caused under such circumstances as amount in law to a felony.

Sec. 2840. Such action shall be brought in the name of the personal representative of such deceased person, and commenced within two years from his decease, and the court or jury before whom the issue is tried may give such damages as are just, with reference to the pecuniary injury resulting from such death, to the wife and next of kin, and the amount recovered shall be for the benefit of such wife and next of kin, who shall receive the same proportions as in the distribution of the personal estate of persons dying intestate.

VIRGINIA

Code 1904

Sec. 2902. Whenever the death of a person shall be caused by the wrongful act, neglect, or default of any person or corporation, or of any ship or vessel, and the act, neglect, or default is such as would (if death had not ensued) have entitled the party injured to maintain an action, or to proceed in rem against said ship or vessel, or in personam against the owners thereof or those having control of her, and to recover damages in respect thereof, then, and in every such case, the person who, or corporation or ship or vessel which, would have been liable, if death had not ensued, shall be liable to an action for damages, or, if a ship or vessel, to a libel in rem, and her owners or those responsible for her acts or defaults or negligence, to a libel in personam, notwithstanding the death of the person injured, and although the death shall have been caused under such circumstances as amount in law to a felony.

Sec. 2903. Every such action shall be brought by and in the name of the personal representative of such deceased person and within twelve months after his or her death, but if any such action is brought within said period of twelve months after said party's death, and for any cause abates or is dismissed without determining the merits of said action, the time said action is pending shall not be counted as any part of said period of twelve months, and another suit may be brought within the remaining period of said twelve months as if such former suit had not been instituted. The jury in any such action may award such damages as to it may seem fair and just, not exceeding ten thousand dollars, and may direct in what proportion they shall be distributed to the wife, husband, or child, or, if there be no wife, husband, or child, then to the parents, brothers, and sisters of the deceased. But nothing in this section shall be construed to deprive the court of the power to grant new trials as in other cases.

Sec. 2904. The amount recovered in any such action shall be paid to the personal representative, and after the payment of costs and reasonable attorney's fees, shall be distributed by such personal representative to the wife, husband, and child, or if there be no wife, husband, or child, then to the parents, brothers, and sisters of the deceased in such proportions as the jury may have directed, or, if they have not directed, according to the statute of distributions, and shall be free from all debts and liabilities of the deceased; but if there be no wife, husband, child, parent, brother, or sister, the amount so received shall be assets in the hands of the personal representative to be disposed of according to law. This and the preceding section are subject to this proviso: Where there is a widowed mother of the deceased and a widow but no children of the deceased, the amount recovered shall be divided between the mother and the widow in such portions as the jury or the court may direct.

Sec. 2905. The personal representative of the deceased may compromise any claim to damages arising under section twenty-nine hundred and two, with the consent of the persons who would be entitled to the damages recovered in an action therefor brought by such representative under section twenty-nine hundred and three; or, if any such persons are incapable, from any cause, of giving consent, the personal representative may make the compromise, with the approval of the judge of the circuit court of the county, or the circuit or corporation court of the corporation, wherein such an action is allowed by law to be brought. Such approval may be applied for by the personal representative on petition to the said judge, in term or vacation, stating the compromise, the terms thereof, and reasons therefor, and convening the parties in interest. If the judge approve the compromise, and the parties in interest do not agree upon the distribution to be made of what has been or may be received by the personal representative under the said compromise, or if any of them are incapable of making a valid agreement, the judge may direct such distribution as a jury might direct under section twenty-nine hundred and three, as to damages awarded by them. In other respects, what is received by the personal representative under the compromise shall be treated as if recovered by him in an action under the section last mentioned. When the judge acts in vacation, he shall return all the papers in the case, and orders made therein, to the clerk's office of his said court. The clerk shall file the papers in his office as soon as received, and forthwith enter the orders in the order book on the law side of the court. Such orders, and all the proceedings in vacation, shall have the same force and effect as if made or had in term.

Sec. 2906. The right of action under sections twenty-nine hundred and two and twenty-nine hundred and three shall not determine nor the action when brought abate by the death of the defendant or the dissolution of the corporation when a corporation is the defendant; and where an action is brought by a party injured for damage caused by the wrongful act, neglect, or default of any person or corporation and the party injured dies pending the action the action shall not abate by reason of his death, but his death being suggested it may be revived in the name of his personal representative.

WASHINGTON

Rem. & Ball. Code 1909

Sec. 183. The widow, or widow and her children, or child or children if no widow, of a man killed in a duel, shall have a right of action against the person killing him, and against the seconds and all aiders and abettors. When the death of a person is caused by the wrongful act or neglect of another, his heirs or personal representatives may maintain an action for damages against the person causing the death. If the deceased leave no widow or issue, then his parents, sisters or minor brothers who may be dependent upon him for support and who are resident within the United States at the time of his death, may maintain said action. When the death of a person is caused by an injury received in falling through any opening or defective place in any sidewalk, street, alley, square or wharf, his heirs or personal representatives, or if deceased leaves no widow or issue, then his parents, sisters or minor brothers who may be dependent upon him for support, and who are resident within the United States at the time of his death, may maintain an action for damages against the person whose duty it was, at the time of the injury, to have kept in repair such sidewalk or other place. In every such action the jury may give such damages, as under all circumstances of the case may to them seem just.

Sec. 184. A father or in case of the death or desertion of his family the mother may maintain an action as plaintiff for the injury or death of a child, and a guardian for the injury or death of his ward.

Sec. 194. No action for a personal injury to any person occasioning his death shall abate, nor shall such right of action determine, by reason of such death, if he have a wife or child living, or leaving no wife or issue, if he have dependent upon him for support and resident within the United States at the time of his death, parents, sisters, or minor brothers; but such action may be prosecuted, or commenced and prosecuted, in favor of such wife or in favor of the wife and children, or if no wife, in favor of such child or children, or if no wife, or child or children, then in favor of his parents, sisters or minor brothers who may be dependent upon him for support, and resident in the United States at the time of his death.

WEST VIRGINIA
Code 1906

Sec. 3488. Whenever the death of a person shall be caused by wrongful act, neglect, or default, and the act, neglect, or default is such as would, if death had not ensued, have entitled the party injured to maintain an action to recover damages in respect thereof; then, and in every such case, the person who, or the corporation which, would have been liable if death had not ensued, shall be liable to an action for damages notwithstanding the death of the person injured, and although the death shall have been caused under such circumstances as amount in law to murder in the first or second degree, or manslaughter.

Sec. 3489. Every such action shall be brought by and in the name of the personal representative of such deceased person; and the amount recovered in every such action shall be distributed to the parties and in the proportion provided by law in relation to the distribution of personal estate left by persons dying intestate. In every such action the jury may give such damages as they shall deem fair and just, not exceeding ten thousand dollars, and the amount so recovered shall not be subject to any debts or liabilities of the deceased: Provided, that every such action shall be commenced within two years after the death of such deceased person.

WISCONSIN
Rev. St. 1898

Sec. 4253. In addition to the actions which survive at common law, the following shall also survive: Actions for the recovery of personal property or the unlawful withholding or conversion thereof, for assault and battery, false imprisonment, or other damage to the person, for all damage done to the property rights or interests of another, for goods taken and carried away, for damages done to real or personal estate, equitable actions to set aside conveyances of real estate, to compel a reconveyance thereof, or to quiet the title thereto, and for a specific performance of contracts relating to real estate. (As amended Laws 1907, c. 353.)

Sec. 4255. Whenever the death of a person shall be caused by a wrongful act, neglect or default, and the act, neglect or default is such as would, if death had not ensued, have entitled the party injured to maintain an action and recover damages in respect thereof, then and in every such case the person who, or the corporation which, would have been liable, if death had not ensued, shall be liable to an action for damages notwithstanding the death of the person injured: Provided, that such action shall be brought for a death caused in this state.

Sec. 4256. Every such action shall be brought by and in the name of the personal representative of such deceased person, and the amount recovered shall belong and be paid over to the husband or widow of such deceased person, if such relative survive him or her; but if no husband or widow survive the deceased the amount recovered shall be paid over to his or her lineal descendants and to his or her lineal ancestors in default of such descendants, but if no husband, or widow, or lineal descendant, or ancestor survive the deceased, the amount recovered shall be paid over to the brothers and sisters; and in every such action the jury may give such damages, not exceeding ten thousand dollars, as they may deem fair and just in reference to the pecuniary injury, resulting from such death to the relatives of the deceased specified in this section; and nonresident alien surviving relatives shall be entitled to the benefits of this section. (As amended Laws 1911, c. 226.)

Sec. 4219. The following actions must be commenced within the periods, respectively, hereinafter prescribed, after the cause of action has accrued:

*   *   *   *   *   *   *   *   *

Sec. 4224. Within two years:

*   *   *   *   *   *   *   *   *

3. An action brought by the personal representatives of a deceased person to recover damages, when the death of such person was caused by the wrongful act, neglect or default of another.

WYOMING

Const. art. 9

Sec. 4. For any injury to person or property caused by wilful failure to comply with the provisions of this article, or laws passed in pursuance hereof, a right of action shall accrue to the party injured, for the damage sustained thereby, and in all cases in this state, whenever the death of a person shall be caused by wrongful act, neglect or default, such as would, if death had not ensued, have entitled the party injured to maintain an action to recover damages in respect thereof, the person who, or the corporation which would have been liable, if death had not ensued, shall be liable to an action for damages notwithstanding the death of the person injured, and the legislature shall provide by law at its first session for the manner in which the right of action in respect thereto shall be enforced.

Comp. St. 1910

Sec. 4291. Whenever the death of a person shall be caused by wrongful act, neglect or default, and the act, neglect or default is such as would (if death had not ensued) have entitled the party injured to maintain an action to recover damages in respect thereof, then, and in every such case, the person who, or the corporation which, would have been liable if death had not ensued, shall be liable to an action for damages notwithstanding the death of the person injured, and although the death shall have been caused under such circumstances as amount in law to murder in the first or second degree, or manslaughter.

Sec. 4292. Every such action shall be brought by, and in the name of, the personal representative of such deceased person; and the amount recovered in every such action shall be distributed to the parties and in the proportions provided by law in relation to the distribution of personal estates left by persons dying intestate. In every such case the jury shall give such damages as they shall deem fair and just, and the amount so recovered shall not be subject to any debts or liabilities of the deceased: Provided, that every such action shall be commenced within two years after the death of such deceased person.

UNITED STATES

U. S. Comp. St. Supp. 1911, p. 1316

Act June 11, 1906, c. 3073. [H. R. 239.]

[An act relating to liability of common carriers in the District of Columbia and territories and common carriers engaged in commerce between the states and between the states and foreign nations to their employees. (34 Stat. 232.)]

Be it enacted, &c., that every common carrier engaged in trade or commerce in the District of Columbia, or in any territory of the United States, or between the several states, or between any territory and another, or between any territory or territories and any state or states, or the District of Columbia, or with foreign nations, or between the District of Columbia and any state or states or foreign nations, shall be liable to any of its employees, or, in the case of his death, to his personal representative for the benefit of his widow and children, if any, if none, then for his parents, if none, then for his next of kin dependent upon him, for all damages which may result from the negligence of any of its officers, agents, or employees, or by reason of any defect or insufficiency due to its negligence in its cars, engines, appliances, machinery, track, roadbed, ways, or works.

Sec. 2. That in all actions hereafter brought against any common carriers to recover damages for personal injuries to an employee, or where such injuries have resulted in his death, the fact that the employee may have been guilty of contributory negligence shall not bar a recovery where his contributory negligence was slight and that of the employer was gross in comparison, but the damages shall be diminished by the jury in proportion to the amount of negligence attributable to such employee. All questions of negligence and contributory negligence shall be for the jury.

Sec. 3. That no contract of employment, insurance, relief benefit, or indemnity for injury or death entered into by or on behalf of any employee, nor the acceptance of any such insurance, relief benefit, or indemnity by the person entitled thereto, shall constitute any bar or defense to any action brought to recover damages for personal injuries to or death of such employee: Provided, however, that upon the trial of such action against any common carrier the defendant may set off therein any sum it has contributed toward any such insurance, relief benefit, or indemnity that may have been paid to the injured employee, or, in case of his death, to his personal representative.

Sec. 4. That no action shall be maintained under this act, unless commenced within one year from the time the cause of action accrued.

Sec. 5. That nothing in this act shall be held to limit the duty of common carriers by railroads or impair the rights of their employés under the safety-appliance act of March second, eighteen hundred and ninety-three, as amended April first, eighteen hundred and ninety-six, and March second, nineteen hundred and three.

U. S. Comp. St. Supp. 1911, p. 1322

Act April 22, 1908, c. 149. [H. R. 20310.]

[An act relating to the liability of common carriers by railroad to their employés in certain cases. (35 Stat. 65.)]

Be it enacted, &c., that every common carrier by railroad while engaging in commerce between any of the several states or territories, or between any of the states and territories, or between the District of Columbia and any of the states or territories, or between the District of Columbia or any of the states or territories and any foreign nation or nations, shall be liable in damages to any person suffering injury while he is employed by such carrier in such commerce, or, in case of the death of such employé, to his or her personal representative, for the benefit of the surviving widow or husband and children of such employee; and, if none, then of such employee's parents; and, if none, then of the next of kin dependent upon such employee, for such injury or death resulting in whole or in part from the negligence of any of the officers, agents, or employees of such carrier, or by reason of any defect or insufficiency, due to its negligence, in its cars, engines, appliances, machinery, track, roadbed, works, boats, wharves, or other equipment.

Sec. 2. That every common carrier by railroad in the territories, the District of Columbia, the Panama Canal Zone, or other possessions of the United States, shall be liable in damages to any person suffering injury while he is employed by such carrier in any of said jurisdictions, or, in case of the death of such employé, to his or her personal representative, for the benefit of the surviving widow or husband and children of such employé; and, if none, then of such employé's parents; and, if none, then of the next of kin dependent upon such employé, for such injury or death resulting in whole or in part from the negligence of any of the officers, agents, or employés of such carrier, or by reason of any defect or insufficiency, due to its negligence, in its cars, engines, appliances, machinery, track, roadbed, works, boats, wharves, or other equipment.

Sec. 3. That in all actions hereafter brought against any such common carrier by railroad under or by virtue of any of the provisions of this act, to recover damages for personal injuries to an employé, or where such injuries have resulted in his death, the fact that the employé may have been guilty of contributory negligence shall not bar a recovery, but the damages shall be diminished by the jury in proportion to the amount of negligence attributable to such employé: Provided, that no such employé who may be injured or killed shall be held to have been guilty of contributory negligence in any case where the violation by such common carrier of any statute enacted for the safety of employés contributed to the injury or death of such employé.

Sec. 4. That in any action brought against any common carrier under or by virtue of any of the provisions of this act to recover damages for injuries to, or the death of, any of its employés, such employé shall not be held to have assumed the risks of his employment in any case where the violation by such common carrier of any statute enacted for the safety of employés contributed to the injury or death of such employé.

Sec. 5.   That any contract, rule, regulation, or device whatsoever, the purpose or intent of which shall be to enable any common carrier to exempt itself from any liability created by this act, shall to that extent be void: Provided, that in any action brought against any such common carrier under or by virtue of any of the provisions of this act, such common carrier may set off therein any sum it has contributed or paid to any insurance, relief benefit, or indemnity that may have been paid to the injured employé or the person entitled thereto on account of the injury or death for which said action was brought.

Sec. 6.   That no action shall be maintained under this act unless commenced within two years from the day the cause of action accrued.

Sec. 7.   That the term "common carrier" as used in this act shall include the receiver or receivers or other persons or corporations charged with the duty of the management and operation of the business of a common carrier.

Sec. 8.   That nothing in this act shall be held to limit the duty or liability of common carriers, or to impair the rights of their employés under any other act or acts of congress, or to affect the prosecution of any pending proceeding or right of action under the act of congress entitled, "An Act Relating to Liability of Common Carriers in the District of Columbia and Territories, and to Common Carriers Engaged in Commerce between the States and Foreign Nations to their Employés," approved June eleventh, nineteen hundred and six. [34 Stat. at L. 232, chap. 3073, U. S. Comp. Stat. Supp. 1909, p. 1148.]

Approved April 22, 1908.

Act Cong. April 5, 1910, c. 143, 36 Stat. 291 (U. S. Comp. St. Supp. 1911, pp. 1324, 1325)

[An act to amend an act entitled "An act relating to the liability of common carriers by railroad to their employés in certain cases," approved April twenty-second, nineteen hundred and eight.]

Be it enacted by the senate and house of representatives of the United States of America in congress assembled, that an act entitled "An act relating to the liability of common carriers by railroad to their employés in certain cases," approved April twenty-second, nineteen hundred and eight, be amended in section six so that said section shall read:

"Sec. 6. That no action shall be maintained under this act unless commenced within two years from the day the cause of action accrued.

"Under this act an action may be brought in a circuit court of the United States, in the district of the residence of the defendant, or in which the cause of action arose, or in which the defendant shall be doing business at the time of commencing such action. The jurisdiction of the courts of the United States under this act shall be concurrent with that of the courts of the several states, and no case arising under this act and brought in any state court of competent jurisdiction shall be removed to any court of the United States."

Sec. 2. That said act be further amended by adding the following section as section nine of said act:

"Sec. 9. That any right of action given by this act to a person suffering injury shall survive to his or her personal representative, for the benefit of the surviving widow or husband and children of such employé, and, if none, then of such employé's parents; and, if none, then of the next of kin dependent upon such employé, but in such cases there shall be only one recovery for the same injury."

Approved April 5, 1910.

TABLE OF CASES CITED

Baltimore & O. R. Co. v. Ray, 39.

Baltimore & O. R. Co. v. Ryan, 200—1.

Baltimore & O. R. Co. v. Sherman's Adm'x, 56, 65.

Baltimore & O. R. Co. v. State, 62, 65, 68, 70, 100, 160, 169, 185.

Baltimore & O. R. Co. v. Taylor, 151.

Baltimore & O. R. Co. v. Wightman's Adm'r, 56, 160, 162, 176.

Baltimore & O. S. W. R. Co. v. Bradford, 39.

Baltimore & O. S. W. R. Co. v. Gillard, 116.

Baltimore & O. S. W. R. Co. v. Pletz, 68.

Baltimore & O. S. W. R. Co. v. Then, 177.

Baltimore & P. R. Co. v. Mackey, 160, 161.

Baltimore & P. R. Co. v. State, 65.

Baltimore & R. Turnpike Road v. State, 160.

Bamberger v. Citizens' St. R. Co., 71.

Bammel v. Kirby, 55.

Bancroft v. Boston & W. R. Corp., 74.

Barker v. Hannibal & St. J. R. Co., 103, 182.

Barksdale v. Seaboard Air Line Ry., 145—2.

Barley v. Chicago & A. R. Co., 124, 154.

Barnes v. Brooklyn, 122.

Barnes v. Columbia Lead Co., 139.

Barnes v. Ward, 182.

Barnett v. Lucas, 18, 127.

Barnum v. Chicago, M. & St. P. R. Co., 80, 182, 184.

Baron v. Illinois Cent. R. Co., 154, 184.

Barrett v. Dolan, 78.

Barretto v. Mouquin-Offerman-Wells Coal Co., 164.

Barth v. Kansas City El. R. Co., 139.

Bartlett v. Chicago, R. I. & P. R. Co., 182.

Bartley v. Boston & N. St. R. Co., 182.

Barton v. Brown, 206.

Bates v. Sylvester, 87, 119.

Batton v. Public Service Corp. of New Jersey, 76.

Bauer v. Richter, 160.

Baxter v. Auburn & S. Electric R. Co., 65.

Bayley v. Eastern R. Co., 44.

Beach v. Bay State Co., 32.

Beach v. Bay State Steamboat Co., 11, 195.

Beaman v. Martha Washington Min. Co., 165.

Beard v. Skeldon, 59—1, 173.

Beauchamp v. Saginaw Min. Co., 76.

Beavers' Adm'x v. Putnam's Curator, 23, 119.

Beck v. Firmenich Mfg. Co., 66.

Beck v. Johnson, 77.

Becke v. Missouri Pac. R. Co., 45, 77.

Becker v. Crow, 41.

Beckett v. Grand Trunk R. Co., 176.

Beckman v. Georgia Pac. R. Co., 74.

Beecher v. Long Island R. Co., 172.

Beeler v. Butte & London Copper Development Co., 45—1, 139—1.

Beems v. Chicago, R. I. & P. R. Co., 184, 174.

Beeson v. Green Mountain Gold Min. Co., 154.

Behen v. St. Louis Transit Co., 87.

Belding v. Black Hills & Ft. P. R. Co., 53.

Belding v. Johnson, 78.

Belgenland, The, 206.

Belgenland, The, v. Jenson, 206.

Bell v. Central R. R., 38, 187.

Bell v. Hannibal & St. J. R. Co., 191.

Bell v. Wooten, 38.

Bellamy v. Whitsell, 23, 103.

Bellison v. Apland, 78.

Benjamin v. Eldridge, 121.

Bennett's Claim, In re, 78.

Benton v. Chicago, R. I. & P. R. Co., 40, 173.

Benton v. North Carolina R. Co., 142.

Berg v. Berg's Adm'r, 41.

Bernina, The, 67, 208.

Berry v. Kansas City, Ft. S. & M. R. Co., 97—1.

Cavanagh v. Ocean Steam Nav. Co., 121, 200.

Caven v. City of Troy, 76.

Central Branch U. P. R. Co. v. Henigh, 68.

Central Foundry Co. v. Bennett, 130.

Central of Georgia R. Co. v. Alexander, 130, 180.

Central of Georgia R. Co. v. Bond, 133.

Central of Georgia R. Co. v. Foshee, 187.

Central of Georgia R. Co. v. Henson, 38, 187.

Central of Georgia R. Co. v. Minor, 133, 174.

Central R. Co. v. Crosby, 133, 174, 178.

Central R. Co. v. Hubbard, 181.

Central R. Co. v. Moore, 173, 193.

Central R. Co. v. Roach, 38.

Central R. Co. v. Rouse, 133, 173, 189.

Central R. Co. v. Sears, 175.

Central R. Co. v. Swint, 110, 196, 197.

Central R. Co. v. Thompson, 66, 133, 174.

Central Railroad & Banking Co. v. Kitchens, 66.

Cephalonia, The, 204.

Cerrillos Coal R. Co. v. Deserant, 139.

Cetofonte v. Camden Coke Co., 86.

Chaloux v. International Paper Co., 47.

Chambers v. Baltimore & O. R. Co., 198.

Chambers v. Kupper-Benson Hotel Co., 174.

Chambers v. Porter, 107.

Chandler v. New York, N. H. & H. R. Co., 198.

Chant v. South Eastern R. Co., 163.

Chapman v. Rothwell, 164, 180.

Charlebois v. Gogebic & M. R. R. Co., 180.

Charles Morgan, The, 204.

Charlton v. St. Louis & S. F. R. Co., 97—1.

Chase v. American Steamboat Co., 52, 118, 199.

Chattanooga Cotton-Oil Co. v. Shamblin, 181.

Chattanooga Electric R. Co. v. Johnson, 107.

Cheatam v. Red River Line, 75.

Cherokee & P. Coal & Min. Co. v. Limb, 168.

Cherry v. Louisiana & A. R. Co., 136.

Chesapeake O. & S. W. R. Co. v. Hendricks, 147.

Chesapeake & O. R. Co. v. Banks' Adm'r, 41.

Chesapeake & O. R. Co. v. Dixon's Adm'x, 41.

Chesapeake & O. R. Co. v. Dupee's Adm'r, 41.

Chesapeake & O. R. Co. v. Hawkins, 151.

Chesapeake & O. R. Co. v. Higgins, 86.

Chesapeake & O. R. Co. v. Judd's Adm'r, 41.

Chesapeake & O. R. Co. v. Kelley's Adm'r, 122.

Chesapeake & O. R. Co. v. Lang's Adm'r, 41.

Chesapeake & O. R. Co. v. Rodgers' Adm'x, 149.

Chester v. Cape May Real Estate Co., 189.

Chicago v. Keefe, 164.

Chicago Bridge & Iron Co. v. La Mantia, 32, 170, 180.

Chicago, B. & Q. R. Co. v. Bond, 182, 184.

Chicago, B. & Q. R. Co. v. Gould, 111.

Chicago, B. & Q. R. Co. v. Gregory, 189.

Chicago, B. & Q. R. Co. v. Harwood, 177.

Chicago, B. & Q. R. Co. v. Healy, 124.

Chicago, B. & Q. R. Co. v. Oyster, 182.

Chicago, B. & Q. R. Co. v. Payne, 66.

Chicago, B. & Q. R. Co. v. Sykes, 177.

Chicago, B. & Q. R. Co. v. Triplett, 65, 66.

Clatsop Chief, The, 204, 205.
Clay v. Central R. & B. Co., 38.
Cleary v. City R. Co., 154.
Cleveland, A. & C. R. Co. v. Workman, 71, 72.
Cleveland, C., C. & St. L. R. Co. v. Drumm, 170, 177.
Cleveland, C., C. & St. L. R. Co. v. Dukeman, 167.
Cleveland, C., C. & St. L. R. Co. v. Henry, 18, 65, 184.
Cleveland, C., C. & St. L. R. Co. v. Miles, 164.
Cleveland, C., C. & St. L. R. Co. v. Miller, 65.
Cleveland, C., C. & St. L. R. Co. v. Osgood, 86, 125.
Cleveland, C., C. & St. L. R. Co. v. Starks, 162, 184.
Cleveland, C. & C. R. Co. v. Crawford, 71, 72.
Cleveland & P. R. Co. v. Rowan, 145, 154, 157.
Cline v. Crescent City R. Co., 76, 136.
Clore v. McIntire, 80, 183.
Clune v. Ristine, 176.
Clyde S. S. Co., In re, 174.
Coal Run Coal Co. v. Jones, 59.
Coates v. Burlington, C. R. & N. R. Co., 134, 174.
Cochran's Adm'r v. Krause, 189.
Coe's Estate, In re, 200—1.
Coffeyville Mining & Gas Co. v. Carter, 173, 174.
Cogdell v. Wilmington & W. R. Co., 65, 189.
Coggins v. Helmsley, 204.
Coldrick v. Patridge, Jones & Co., 65.
Cole v. Mayne, 59.
Cole v. Parker, 55.
Coleman v. Himmelberger-Harrison Land & Lumber Co., 139.
Coleman v. Hyer, 38.
Coley v. Statesville, 76.
Collier v. Arrington's Ex'rs, 142.
Collins v. Davidson, 154.
Collins v. East Tennessee, V. & G. R. Co., 107, 147.
Collins Coal Co. v. Hadley, 59.
Collison v. Illinois Cent. R. Co., 189.

Colorado Coal & Iron Co. v. Lamb, 168.
Colorado Milling & Elevator Co. v. Mitchell, 123.
Columbia, The, 204.
Columbus & W. R. Co. v. Bradford, 92, 182.
Columbus & W. R. Co. v. Bridges, 130.
Comitez v. Parkerson, 76.
Commercial Club of Indianapolis v. Hilliker, 154, 168, 184.
Com. v. Boston & A. R. Co., 44, 80, 182.
Com. v. Boston & L. R. Corp., 44.
Com. v. Boston & M. R. R., 44.
Com. v. Boston & W. R. Corp., 44, 121, 182.
Com. v. Brockton St. R. Co., 44.
Com. v. Coburn, 44.
Com. v. East Boston Ferry Co., 44, 110, 121.
Com. v. Eastern R. Co., 44, 80, 182.
Com. v. Fitchburg R. Co., 44.
Com. v. Metropolitan R. Co., 44, 73.
Com. v. Sanford, 44, 110.
Com. v. Vermont & M. R. Co., 44, 124.
Com. v. Wilmington, 44.
Conant v. Griffin, 80, 154, 177, 182.
Condliff v. Condliff, 89.
Condon v. Great Southern & W. R. Co., 164.
Congrave v. Southern Pac. R. Co., 65.
Conklin v. Central New York Telephone & Telegraph Co., 170.
Conley v. Maine Cent. R. Co., 137, 160.
Conley v. Portland Gaslight Co., 43.
Conlin v. City Council of Charleston, 80.
Connaughton v. Sun Printing & Publishing Ass'n, 164, 165.
Connecticut Mut. Life Ins. Co. v. New York & N. H. R. Co., 11, 16.
Conner's Adm'x v. Paul, 41, 110.

Conners v. Burlington, C. R. & N. R. Co., 40, 75.

Connor v. Chicago, R. I. & P. R. Co., 45.

Connor v. New York, N. H. & H. R. Co., 110.

Connors v. Holden, 65.

Conover v. Pennsylvania R. Co., 105.

Conrad v. New York Cent. & H. R. R. Co., 172, 173.

Conroy v. Pennsylvania R. Co., 51.

Consolidated Coal Co. v. Maehl, 59—1.

Consolidated Gas, Electric Light & Power Co. v. State, 173.

Consolidated Ice Mach. Co. v. Keifer, 76, 190.

Consolidated Stone Co. v. Morgan, 160, 176.

Consolidated Stone Co. v. Staggs, 177.

Consolidated Traction Co. v. Hone, 71, 157.

Conway v. New York, 122.

Cook v. American E. C. & Schulte Gunpowder Co., 164.

Cook v. Big Muddy Carterville Min. Co., 161.

Cook v. Chicago, R. I. & P. R. Co., 189.

Cook v. Clay St. Hill R. Co., 154.

Cook v. Houston Direct Nav. Co., 70.

Cook v. New York Cent. R. Co., 192.

Cook v. New York Cent. & H. R. R. Co., 175.

Cook's Estate, In re, 40.

Coolidge v. New York, 173.

Cooper v. Lake Shore & M. S. R. Co., 165, 173, 174.

Cooper v. New York, O. & W. R. Co., 172.

Cooper v. Shore Electric Co., 87.

Coover v. Moore, 103, 139.

Copeland v. Seattle, 57.

Corbett v. Oregon Short Line R. Co., 70, 148—1.

Corcoran v. Boston & A. R. Co., 74.

Corliss v. Worcester, N. & C. R. Co., 47.

Cornwall v. Mills, 175.

Corsair, The, 75, 205, 206.

Cottingham v. Weeks, 193.

Coulter v. Pine Tp., 176.

Countryman v. Fonda, J. & G. R. Co., 172.

Covington St. R. Co. v. Packer, 11, 17, 116.

Cowen v. Ray, 124, 200—1.

Cox v. Kansas City, 97—1.

Cox v. Wilkeson Coal & Coke Co., 150.

Cox v. Wilmington City R. Co., 160.

Cox's Adm'r v. Louisville & A. R. Co., 41.

Coy v. Indianapolis Gas Co., 181.

Crabtree v. Missouri Pac. R. Co., 165, 173.

Crane v. Chicago & W. I. R. Co., 196.

Crane v. Little, 44.

Crapo v. Kelly, 200.

Crapo v. Syracuse, 122, 123.

Crawford v. Southern R. Co., 38.

Cregin v. Brooklyn Crosstown R. Co., 18.

Crockett v. St. Louis Transfer Co., 103, 112.

Crohn v. Kansas City Home Tel. Co., 45, 103.

Crosby v. Leng, 13.

Cross v. Guthery, 6, 11.

Crowley v. Panama R. Co., 11, 18, 195.

Crumpley v. Hannibal & St. J. R. Co., 45, 77.

Culbertson v. Metropolitan St. R. Co., 45.

Cumberland Telephone & Telegraph Co. v. Anderson, 138—2.

Cumberland Telephone & Telegraph Co. v. Pitchford, 138—2.

Cunningham v. Mutual Reserve Life Ins. Co., 173.

Curley v. Illinois Cent. R. Co., 42.

Curran v. Percival, 78.

Curran v. Warren Chemical & Mfg. Co., 65.

Cutting v. Seabury, 6, 11, 204.

Czezewzka v. Benton-Bellefontaine R. Co., 70, 103.

D

East Tennessee, V. & G. R. Co. v. Lilly, 80, 83.

East Tennessee, V. & G. R. Co. v. Maloy, 38, 194.

East Tennessee, V. & G. R. Co. v. Mitchell, 147.

East Tennessee, V. & G. R. Co. v. Toppins, 147.

E. B. Ward, Jr., The, 200, 204, 205.

Economy Light & Power Co. v. Stephen, 173.

Eden v. Lexington & F. R. Co., 5, 8.

Edgar v. Castello, 11, 116.

Edmonson v. Kentucky Cent. R. Co., 41.

Edwards v. Elliott, 206.

Edwards v. Gimbel, 51.

Eginoire v. Union County, 134, 164.

Eichorn v. New Orleans & C. R., Light & Power Co., 42, 136.

Ellerbe v. Carolina Cent. R. Co., 49.

Elliott v. Brazil Block Coal Co., 122.

Elliott v. St. Louis & I. M. R. Co., 45, 65.

Ellis v. Metropolitan St. R. Co., 139.

Ellis v. Republic Oil Co., 164.

Ellison v. Georgia R. Co., 38.

Ellyson v. International & G. N. R. Co., 76.

El Paso & N. E. R. Co. of Texas v. Whatley, 108.

El Paso & N. R. Co. v. Gutierrez, 59—1.

Elwood Electric St. R. Co. v. Ross, 68, 184.

Ely v. Detroit United Ry., 44—1.

Emery v. Philadelphia, 174.

Emory v. Addis, 78.

Engvall v. Des Moines City R. Co., 160.

Entwhistle v. Feighner, 190, 194.

Epsilon, The, 204, 209.

Erb v. Morasch, 184.

Erdner v. Chicago & N. W. R. Co., 164.

Erickson v. Pacific Coast S. S. Co., 196.

Ervin v. St. Louis, I. M. & S. R. Co., 181.

Erwin v. Neversink Steamboat Co., 172, 175, 192.

Escambia County Electric Light & Power Co. v. Sutherland, 161.

Eskridge's Ex'rs v. Cincinnati, N. O. & T. P. R. Co., 41.

Eustace v. Jahns, 32.

Evans v. Newland, 62, 188.

Evans v. Oregon Short Line R. Co., 148—1, 173.

Evans' Adm'r v. Cumberland Telephone & Telegraph Co., 76.

Evansville & C. R. Co. v. Lowdermilk, 65.

Evansville & C. R. Co. v. Wolf, 68.

Evarts v. Santa Barbara Consol. R. Co., 173.

Evensen v. Lexington & B. St. R. Co., 44.

Ewell v. Chicago & N. W. R. Co., 121, 122.

Ewen v. Chicago & N. W. R. Co., 68, 159, 164, 173, 183, 184.

Explorer, The, 208.

F

Fabel v. Cleveland, C., C. & St. L. R. Co., 201.

Falkenau v. Rowland, 180.

Farmer v. Sellers, 64.

Farmers' & Mechanics' Nat. Bank v. Hanks, 32, 55.

Farrara v. Auric Min. Co., 86.

Farrell v. Chicago, R. I. & P. R. Co., 164, 174.

Fegan v. Boston, 44.

Fejdowski v. President, etc., of Delaware & H. Canal Co., 189.

Felt v. Puget Sound Electric Ry., 150, 178.

Felton v. Spiro, 107, 161.

Fidelity Land & Improvement Co. v. Buzzard, 165.

Findlay v. Chicago & G. T. R. Co., 111.

Fink v. Garman, 73, 78.

Fish v. Illinois Cent. R. Co., 134, 194.

Fisher v. Boutelle Transportation & Towing Co., 206.

Fisher v. Central Lead Co., 161.

Fisher v. Newbern, 65.

Fisher v. Waupaca Electric Light & R. Co., 163.

Green v. Chicago & W. M. R. Co., 68.

Green v. Hudson River R. Co., 11, 15, 16, 109, 154.

Green v. Smith, 44.

Green v. Southern Pac. Co., 154, 173.

Green v. Thompson, 119.

Greenlaw v. Louisville & N. R. Co., 65.

Greenlee v. East Tennessee, V. & G. R. Co., 107, 125.

Greenwood v. King, 159, 168, 184.

Gregory v. Illinois Cent. R. Co., 11.

Gretschmann v. Fix, 207.

Griffin's Estate, In re, 89.

Griffith v. Griffith, 38.

Griffiths v. Earl of Dudley, 124.

Grimsley v. Hankins, 35, 205.

Grogan v. Broadway Foundry Co., 164.

Gross v. Electric Traction Co., 112.

Grosso v. Delaware, L. & W. R. Co., 11, 14.

Grotenkemper v. Harris, 170, 171.

Gruber v. La Salle County Carbon Coal Co., 121.

Gubbitosi v. Rothschild, 164.

Guldager v. Rockwell, 125.

Guldfaxe, The, 208.

Gulf, C. & S. F. R. Co. v. Beall, 11.

Gulf, C. & S. F. R. Co. v. Brown, 168.

Gulf, C. & S. F. R. Co. v. Compton, 108, 165, 174.

Gulf, C. & S. F. R. Co. v. Farmer, 154.

Gulf, C. & S. F. R. Co. v. McGinnis, 59—1.

Gulf, C. & S. F. R. Co. v. Southwick, 157.

Gulf, C. & S. F. R. Co. v. Younger, 173, 176, 184.

Gulledge v. Seaboard Air Line R. Co., 121.

Gunderson v. Northwestern Elevator Co., 164.

Gundy v. Nye-Schneider-Fowler Co., 173.

Gunn v. Ohio River R. Co., 71.

Gurney v. Grand Trunk R. Co., 110, 196, 202.

Gurofsky v. Lehigh Valley R. Co., 86, 200—1.

Gustafson v. Washburn & Moen Mfg. Co., 44.

Guthrie v. Southern Pac. Co., 193.

Gutierrez v. El Paso & N. E. R. Co., 123.

H

Hach v. St. Louis, I. M. & S. R. Co., 139.

Hackett v. Louisville, St. L. & T. P. R. Co., 41.

Hackett v. McIlwain, 88.

Hackett v. Smelsley, 78.

Hackett v. Wisconsin Cent. R. Co., 169.

Hackney v. Delaware & A. Telegraph & Telephone Co., 160.

Hagen v. Kean, 116.

Hagerty v. Hughes, 183.

Haggerty v. Central R. Co., 32, 82.

Haigh v. Royal Mail S. P. Co., 124.

Haines v. Pearson, 139.

Halbert v. Texas Tie & Lumber Preserving Co., 55.

Hale v. Kearly, 190.

Hale v. San Bernadino Val. Traction Co., 154, 160.

Haley v. Chicago & N. W. R. Co., 76.

Haley v. Mobile & O. R. Co., 75, 147.

Hall v. Galveston, H. & S. A. R. Co., 168.

Hall v. Louisville & N. R. Co., 187.

Hall v. Southern R. Co., 89, 110, 187.

Halvorson v. Seattle Electric Co., 160.

Hamann v. Milwaukee Bridge Co., 161, 173.

Hamilton, The, 174, 206, 209.

Hamilton v. Bordentown Electric Light & Motor Co., 182.

Hamilton v. Delaware, L. & W. R. Co., 65.

Hamilton v. Hannibal & St. J. R. Co., 198.

Hamilton v. Jones, 23, 32, 119.

Hamilton v. Morgan's L. & T. R. & S. S. Co., 75, 136.

[The figures refer to sections]

Houston & T. C. R. Co. v. Nixon, 165.

Houston & T. C. R. Co. v. Roberts, 55.

Houston & T. C. R. Co. v. Wells Fargo & Co., 55.

Hover v. Pennsylvania Co., 195, 198.

Howard v. Delaware & H. Canal Co., 171, 180, 182.

Howard v. Fall River Iron Works, 44.

Howard v. Illinois Cent. R. Co., 59—1.

Howard's Adm'r v. Hunter, 41.

Howell v. Board of Com'rs of Yancey County, 116.

Howell v. Rochester R. Co., 164.

Howey v. New England Nav. Co., 154.

Howlan v. New York & N. J. Tel. Co., 197.

Hoxie v. New York, N. H. & H. R. Co., 59—1.

Hubbard v. Chicago & N. W. R. Co., 58—1.

Huberwald v. Orleans R. Co., 42.

Hubgh v. New Orleans & C. R. Co., 1, 11, 42.

Hudson v. Houser, 65, 160, 190.

Hudson v. Lynn & B. R. Co., 44.

Huerzeler v. Central Cross-Town R. Co., 68, 164.

Huff v. Peoria & E. R. Co., 168.

Hughes v. Auburn, 65, 118.

Hughes v. President, etc., of Delaware & H. Canal Co., 194.

Hughes v. Richter, 183.

Hulbert v. Topeka, 23, 73, 110, 126.

Hull v. Great Northern R. Co., 169.

Humboldt Lumber Manufacturers' Ass'n, In re, 205.

Hund v. Geier, 68.

Hunn v. Michigan Cent. R. Co., 173, 174.

Hunt v. Conner, 32, 158, 162, 173.

Hunt v. Kile, 177.

Hunter v. Southern R. Co., 49.

Huntington & B. T. M. R. & Coal Co. v. Decker, 105, 161.

Hupfer v. National Distilling Co., 123, 180.

Hurst v. Detroit City R. Co., 68, 127, 165, 180, 184.

Hutchins v. St. Paul, M. & M. R. Co., 111, 154, 168, 178.

Hutchinson v. York, N. C. & B. R. Co., 65.

Hutchinson v. West Jersey & S. R. Co., 157.

Hyatt v. Adams, 11, 13, 14, 16, 17, 79.

Hyde v. Southern R. Co., 59—1.

Hyde v. Union Pac. R. Co., 148—1, 154.

Hyde v. Wabash, St. L. & P. R. Co., 18, 195.

I

Ihl v. Forty-Second St. & G. St. Ferry R. Co., 68, 164, 180.

Illinois Cent. R. Co. v. Baches, 173.

Illinois Cent. R. Co. v. Bandy, 68.

Illinois Cent. R. Co. v. Barron, 154, 156, 171, 177.

Illinois Cent. R. Co. v. Bentz, 147.

Illinois Cent. R. Co. v. Cozby, 124, 189.

Illinois Cent. R. Co. v. Cragin, 111.

Illinois Cent. R. Co. v. Crudup, 110, 173, 174, 196, 201.

Illinois Cent. R. Co. v. Davis, 107.

Illinois Cent. R. Co. v. Harris, 76.

Illinois Cent. R. Co. v. Hicks, 177.

Illinois Cent. R. Co. v. Hunter, 44—2.

Illinois Cent. R. Co. v. Johnson, 44—2, 85, 164, 177.

Illinois Cent. R. Co. v. Josey's Adm'x, 41.

Illinois Cent. R. Co. v. Kief, 189.

Illinois Cent. R. Co. v. O'Neill, 41.

Illinois Cent. R. Co. v. Pendergrass, 44—2, 74.

Illinois Cent. R. Co. v. Prickett, 176.

Illinois Cent. R. Co. v. Sheegog's Adm'r, 41.

Illinois Cent. R. Co. v. Slater, 68, 164, 173.

Illinois Cent. R. Co. v. Spence, 147, 177.

Illinois Cent. R. Co. v. Warriner, 72, 165.

Leahy v. Davis, 139.

Le Bar v. New York & S. W. R. Co., 187.

Le Blanc v. Sweet, 136.

Le Blanc v. United Irrigation & Rice Mill. Co., 42.

Lee v. Missouri Pac. R. Co., 195, 201.

Lee v. Publishers: Knapp & Co., 103, 139.

Lee v. Reliance Mills Co., 189.

Legg v. Britton, 126, 127.

Leggott v. Great Northern R. Co., 18, 23, 80, 127.

Lehigh Iron Co. v. Rupp, 105, 157, 165, 168.

Lehman v. Brooklyn, 65, 164, 180.

Lehmann v. Farwell, 58—1, 74.

Leman v. Baltimore & O. R. Co., 187, 196.

Lemasters v. Southern Pac. Co., 65.

Le May v. Missouri Pac. R. Co., 45, 139.

Lemon's Adm'r v. Louisville & N. R. Co., 195.

Lenahan v. Crescent Coal Min. Co., 77.

Lennan v. Hamburg-American S. S. Co., 199.

Leonard v. Columbia Steam Nav. Co., 110, 196, 197.

Leque v. Madison Gas & Electric Co., 169.

Lett v. St. Lawrence & O. R. Co., 158, 163.

Levey v. Dry Dock, E. B. & B. R. Co., 68.

Levin v. Metropolitan St. R. Co., 70.

Lewin v. Lehigh Val. R. Co., 68, 71, 72.

Lewis v. Hollahan, 145.

Lewis v. Hunlock's Creek & M. Turnpike Co., 89.

Lewis' Adm'r v. Taylor Coal Co., 41.

Lexington & Carter County Min. Co. v. Huffman's Adm'r, 41.

Lexington & Carter County Min. Co. v. Stephens' Adm'r, 41.

Leyhan v. Leyhan, 39.

Liermann v. Chicago, M. & St. P. R. Co., 161.

Lilly v. Charlotte, C. & A. R. Co., 80, 187.

Limekiller v. Hannibal & St. J. R. Co., 110.

Linck's Adm'r v. Louisville & N. R. Co., 41.

Lindsay v. Canadian Pac. R. Co., 71.

Lindstrom v. International Nav. Co., 169, 200.

Linss v. Chesapeake & O. R. Co., 41.

Lintz v. Holy Terror Min. Co., 53.

Lipp v. Otis Bros. & Co., 172.

Lipscomb v. Houston & T. C. R. Co., 55, 176.

Litchfield Coal Co. v. Taylor, 59.

Little v. Bousfield & Co., 31—1, 174, 178.

Little v. Dusenberry, 118.

Littlejohn v. Fitchburg R. Co., 44.

Little Rock, M. R. & T. R. Co. v. Leverett, 173, 194.

Little Rock & Ft. S. R. Co. v. Barker, 11, 154, 157, 164, 165, 178.

Little Rock & Ft. S. R. Co. v. Caveness, 65.

Little Rock & Ft. S. R. Co. v. Townsend, 80.

Little Rock & Ft. S. R. Co. v. Voss, 168.

Littlewood v. New York, 23, 124.

Livermore v. Fitchburg R. Co., 44.

Loague v. Memphis & C. R. Co., 80, 87, 107, 147.

Locher v. Kluga, 64, 170.

Lockhart v. Lichtenthaler, 67.

Lockwood v. New York, L. E. & W. R. Co., 172.

Lofton v. Vogles, 79.

Lomoe v. Superior Water, Light & Power Co., 164.

Londriggan v. New York, N. H. & H. R. Co., 121.

Long v. Morrison, 109, 154.

Long Island, N. S., P. & F. Transp. Co., In re, 204, 205, 209.

Looram v. Third Ave. R. Co., 76.

Lord v. Pueblo Smelting & Refining Co., 65, 194.

Lothrop v. Fitchburg R. Co., 44.

Lotta, The, 206, 209.

Louisville & N. R. Co. v. Sullivan's Adm'x, 41.

Louisville & N. R. Co. v. Taafe's Adm'r, 41.

Louisville & N. R. Co. v. Tegner, 130.

Louisville & N. R. Co. v. Trammell, 130, 160, 183.

Louisville & N. R. Co. v. Tucker's Adm'r, 41.

Louisville & N. R. Co. v. Ueltschi's Ex'rs, 41.

Louisville & N. R. Co. v. Ward's Adm'r, 41.

Louisville & N. R. Co. v. Whitlow's Adm'r, 200—1.

Louisville & N. R. Co. v. Williams, 195, 196.

Louisville & N. R. Co. v. Young, 130.

Louisville & P. Canal Co. v. Murphy, 41.

Lounsbury v. Davis, 184.

Lovell v. De Bardelaben, C. & I. Co., 35, 92.

Lowe v. Chicago, St. P., M. & O. R. Co., 134.

Lower v. Segal, 187, 201.

Lowham's Estate, In re, 110, 111, 196.

Low Moor Iron Co. v. La Bianca's Adm'r, 86.

L. T. Dickason Coal Co. v. Liddil, 32, 39, 85.

L. T. Dickason Coal Co. v. Unverferth, 59.

Lubrano v. Atlantic Mills, 52, 73, 126.

Lucas v. New York Cent. R. Co., 11, 80.

Luessen v. Oshkosh Electric Light & Power Co., 164, 184.

Luke v. Calhoun County, 86.

Lundin v. Kansas Pac. R. Co., 31—1.

Lung Chung v. Northern Pac. R. Co., 208.

Lustig v. New York, L. E. & W. R. Co., 172, 187, 196, 202.

Lutterell v. Reynell, 13.

Lutz v. Atlantic & P. R. Co., 45.

Lykiardopoulo v. New Orleans & C. R. Light & Power Co., 86.

Lyman v. Boston & A. R. Co., 198—1.

Lynch v. Davis, 11, 109.

Lynch v. Knoop, 85.

Lynch v. Metropolitan St. R. Co., 45.

Lynch v. Southwestern Tel. & T. Co., 118.

Lyon v. Boston & M. R. Co., 47, 198.

Lyons v. Woodward, 11.

M

McAdory v. Louisville & N. R. Co., 130.

McBride v. Berman, 93.

McCabe v. Guinness, 185.

McCabe v. Narragansett Electric Lighting Co., 145—1, 162.

McCafferty v. Pennsylvania R. Co., 51, 76.

McCahill v. Detroit City R. Co., 164.

McCahill v. New York Transp. Co., 76.

McCarthy v. Chicago, R. I. & P. R. Co., 73, 97—1, 126, 198.

McCarthy v. Claflin, 160.

McCarty v. Clinton Gaslight Co., 44.

McCarty v. New York, L. E. & W. R. Co., 196.

McCarty v. St. Louis Transit Co., 139.

McCarty v. State ex rel. Boone, 78.

McCarty v. Wells, 78.

McCaughey v. Tripp, 52.

McClellan v. Ft. Wayne & B. I. R. Co., 65.

McClure v. Alexander, 41.

McClurg v. Ingleheart, 64.

McCray v. Moweaqua Coal Mining & Mfg. Co., 59.

McCubbin v. Hastings, 42.

McCue v. Klein, 78.

McDermott v. Iowa Falls & S. C. R. Co., 134, 189.

McDonald v. Champion Iron & Steel Co., 178.

McDonald v. Eagle & P. Mfg. Co., 38.

Meyer v. Hart, 179.

Meyer v. Southern R. Co., 77.

Meyer's Adm'r v. Zoll, 41.

Michigan Cent. R. Co. v. Campau, 65.

Middle Georgia & A. R. Co. v. Barnett, 38.

Middleton v. Holmes, 79.

Midland Val. R. Co. v. Le Moyne, 59—1.

Miles v. St. Louis, I. M. & S. R. Co., 71.

Millar v. St. Louis Transit Co., 87.

Miller v. Meade Tp., 68.

Miller v. Missouri Pac. R. Co., 45.

Miller v. Sadowsky, 138—1.

Miller v. Southern Pac. R. Co., 193.

Miller v. Southwestern R. Co., 95. 116.

Mills' Adm'r v. Cavanaugh, 68, 187.

Mississippi Oil Co. v. Smith, 138—2, 174.

Mississippi & T. R. Co. v. Ayres, 174, 196, 197.

Missouri Furnace Co. v. Abend, 189.

Missouri, K. & T. R. Co. v. Elliott, 73, 93.

Missouri, K. & T. R. Co. v. Foreman, 93.

Missouri, K. & T. R. Co. v. McLaughlin, 170, 171.

Missouri, K. & T. R. Co. of Texas v. Freeman, 55.

Missouri, K. & T. R. Co. of Texas v. Smith, 76.

Missouri, K. & T. R. Co. of Texas v. Wall, 89.

Missouri Pac. R. Co. v. Barber, 80.

Missouri Pac. R. Co. v. Bennett's Estate, 97—1.

Missouri Pac. R. Co. v. Bradley, 111.

Missouri Pac. R. Co. v. Brown, 55.

Missouri Pac. R. Co. v. Henry, 89, 108, 169.

Missouri Pac. R. Co. v. Lee, 168, 177.

Missouri Pac. R. Co. v. Lehmberg, 160.

Missouri Pac. R. Co. v. Lewis, 110, 111, 196, 197.

Missouri Pac. R. Co. v. Moffatt, 160.

Missouri Pac. R. Co. v. Peregoy, 165, 173.

Mitchell v. Colorado Milling & Elevator Co., 123.

Mitchell v. New York Cent. & H. R. R. Co., 163, 172.

Mitchell v. Worcester, 44.

Mize v. Rocky Mountain Bell Tel. Co., 139—1.

Mobile Electric Co. v. Sanges, 130.

Mobile, J. & K. C. R. Co. v. Bromberg, 35, 77.

Mobile, J. & K. C. R. Co. v. Hicks, 44—2.

Mobile Life Ins. Co. v. Brame, 11.

Mobile & O. R. Co. v. Stroud, 181.

Moe v. Smiley, 119.

Moers v. Michigan United Rys. Co., 165.

Moffatt v. Tenney, 139.

Mollie Gibson Consol. Min. & Mill. Co. v. Sharp, 139.

Monaghan v. Horn, 208.

Mondou v. New York, N. H. & H. R. Co., 59—1.

Monongahela River Consol. Coal & Coke Co. v. Schinnerer, 206.

Moody v. Pacific R. Co., 187.

Mooney v. Carter, 65.

Moore v. Logan Iron & Steel Co., 65.

Moran v. Hollings, 74.

Moran v. Milford & U. St. R. Co., 44.

Morehead's Adm'x v. Bittner, 41, 119.

Moren v. New Orleans Ry. & Light Co., 136.

Morena v. Winston, 44.

Morgan v. Barnhill, 55, 64.

Morgan v. Durfee, 64, 139.

Morgan v. Southern Pac. Co., 154.

Morgan v. Thompson, 41.

Morhard v. Richmond Light & R. Co., 172, 189.

Morhart v. North Jersey St. R. Co., 165.

Oliver v. Houghton County St. R. Co., 44—1, 138—1, 161.

Olsen v. Montana Ore Purchasing Co., 139—1.

Olston v. Oregon Water Power & R. Co., 81.

Omaha & R. V. R. Co. v. Crow, 184.

Omaha Water Co. v. Schamel, 162, 169.

O'Malley v. St. Paul, M. & M. R. Co., 68, 164.

O'Malley's Adm'r v. McLean, 41.

O'Mara v. Hudson River R. Co., 164.

O'Mellia v. Kansas City, St. J. & C. B. R. Co., 174.

Onoko, The. 76, 205.

Opsahl v. Judd, 168, 199.

Oregon, The, 206.

O'Reilly v. New York & N. E. R. Co., 198—1.

O'Reilly v. Utah, N. & C. Stage Co., 31.

Orendorf v. New York Cent. & H. R. R. Co., 160.

Orgall v. Chicago, B. & Q. R. Co., 184.

Orman v. Mannix, 139.

Orth v. Belgrade, 123.

Osborn v. Gillett, 4, 5, 7, 13, 15, 18.

Osborne v. McMasters, 77.

O'Shea v. Lehigh Val. R. Co., 71, 72.

O. S. Richardson Fueling Co. v. Peters, 176.

Osteen v. Southern Ry., 23, 145 —1.

Ostrander v. Orange County Traction Co., 76.

Ott v. Johnson, 55.

Otto Kuehne Preserving Co. v. Allen, 139.

Oulighan v. Butler, 44, 118, 182.

Overby v. Mears Min. Co., 139.

Overholt v. Vieths, 173.

Owen v. Brockschmidt, 125, 139, 157, 191.

Owensboro & N. R. Co. v. Barclay's Adm'r, 41.

Oyster v. Burlington Relief Department of Chicago, B. & Q. R. Co., 124, 182.

P

Pack v. New York, 11.

Packard v. Hannibal & St. J. R. Co., 103, 118.

Paducah City Ry. v. Alexander's Adm'r, 41.

Palfrey v. Portland, S. & P. R. Co., 7.

Palmer v. New York Cent. & H. R. R. Co., 77.

Palmer v. Philadelphia, B. & W. R. Co., 155.

Palmer v. Schurz, 78.

Palmer v. Utah & N. R. Co., 118.

Parish v. Eden, 68, 121, 123.

Parker v. Crowell & Spencer Lumber Co., 136.

Parker v. Dupree, 118.

Parker v. Hannibal & St. J. R. Co., 45.

Parker v. Providence & S. Steamboat Co., 181.

Parks v. Miller, 173.

Parsons v. Missouri Pac. R. Co., 45, 139, 164, 177.

Paschal v. Owen, 108, 121, 160.

Passamaneck v. Louisville R. Co., 41.

Patch v. Wabash R. Co., 110.

Patek v. American Smelting & Refining Co., 86.

Patterson v. Wallace, 1, 154.

Patton v. Pittsburgh, C. & St. L. R. Co., 196, 201.

Paulmier v. Erie R. Co., 168.

Payne v. Chicago, R. I. & P. R. Co., 67.

Payne v. Illinois Cent. R. Co., 65.

Peake v. Baltimore & O. R. Co., 127.

Pearlstein v. New York, N. H. & H. R. Co., 44.

Pearson v. Wilcox, 189.

Peden v. American Bridge Co., 184.

Peebles v. Charleston & W. C. R. Co., 87.

Peers v. Nevada Power, Light & Water Co., 182, 184.

Pegram v. Seaboard Air Line R. Co., 65.

Pegram v. Storts, 78.

Pickett v. Wilmington & W. R. Co., 142.

Pierce v. Conners, 103, 139, 165.

Pierce v. Cunard S. S. Co., 74.

Pierce v. Seaboard Air Line Ry., 181.

Pietraroia v. New Jersey & H. R. R. & Ferry Co., 111, 197.

Pineo v. New York Cent. & H. R. R. Co., 172.

Pinson v. Southern Ry., 145—2.

Piper v. Boston & M. R., 31—1, 47, 189.

Pisano v. B. M. & J. F. Shanley Co., 111, 125.

Pitkin v. New York Cent. & H. R. R. Co., 174.

Pittsburg, A. & M. R. Co. v. Pearson, 70.

Pittsburgh, C., C. & St. L. R. Co. v. Hosea, 39, 124.

Pittsburgh, C., C. & St. L. R. Co. v. Kinnare, 173.

Pittsburgh, C., C. & St. L. R. Co. v. Moore, 124.

Pittsburg, C., C. & St. L. R. Co. v. Naylor, 86.

Pittsburg, C., C. & St. L. R. Co. v. Reed, 39, 80, 170.

Pittsburgh, C., C. & St. L. R. Co. v. Rogers, 65, 174.

Pittsburgh, C., C. & St. L. R. Co. v. Sudhoff, 177.

Pittsburgh, C. & St. L. R. Co. v. Hine, 32, 121.

Pittsburgh, Ft. W. & C. R. Co. v. Vining's Adm'r, 39, 68.

Pittsburg Vitrified Pav. & Bldg. Brick Co. v. Fisher, 168.

Pizzi v. Reid, 182, 184.

Ploof v. Burlington Traction Co., 71.

Plummer v. Webb, 6, 204.

Pocahontas Collieries Co. v. Rukas' Adm'r, 86.

Poe v. Raleigh & A. Air Line R. Co., 142.

Poff v. New England Telephone & Telegraph Co., 47, 121.

Pool v. Southern Pac. Co., 148—1, 160.

Poole v. East Tennessee, V. & G. R. Co., 194.

Poor v. Watson, 59.

Pope v. Kansas City C. R. Co., 181.

Popp v. Cincinnati, H. & D. R. Co., 110.

Portsmouth St. R. Co. v. Peed's Adm'r, 149.

Post v. Olmsted, 164.

Potter v. Chicago & N. W. R. Co., 154, 156, 164, 165, 173, 178.

Potter v. Metropolitan Dist. R. Co., 18.

Potter v. New York Cent. & H. R. R. Co., 189.

Potter v. St. Louis & S. F. R. Co., 45, 139.

Powell v. St. Louis & S. F. R. Co., 65.

Powell's Adm'x v. Powell, 89.

Powers v. Pere Marquette R. Co., 189.

Prater v. Tennessee Producers' Marble Co., 125.

Pratt v. Missouri Pac. R. Co., 103, 139.

Preble v. Wabash R. Co., 84, 173.

Predmore v. Consumers' Light & Power Co., 172.

Premier, The, 206.

Prendergast v. Chicago City R. Co., 167.

Pressman v. Mooney, 164.

Price v. Richmond & D. R. Co., 124.

Pries v. Ashland Home Tel. Co., 86, 182.

Prince v. Lowell Electric Light Corp., 189.

Proctor v. Hannibal & St. J. R. Co., 45.

Proctor v. San Antonio St. R. Co., 169.

Prosser v. West Jersey & Seashore R. Co., 65.

Prouty v. Chicago, 123.

Pugmire v. Diamond Coal & Coke Co., 187.

Pulaski Gaslight Co. v. McClintock, 130—1.

Pulling v. Great Eastern R. Co., 18.

Pulom v. Jacob Dold Packing Co., 11, 55.

Purcell v. Laurer, 120.

Putman v. Southern Pac. Co., 128.

[The figures refer to sections]

Pym v. Great Northern R. Co., 63, 162, 167, 171, 176, 178.

Q

Quill v. New York Cent. & H. R. R. Co., 76.

Quill v. Southern Pac. Co., 154.

Quin v. Moore, 80, 82, 88, 164, 180, 191.

Quincy Coal Co. v. Hood, 80, 180, 182.

Quinn v. Chicago, M. & St. P. R. Co., 23, 31—1.

Quinn v. New York, N. H. & H. R. Co., 66.

Quinn v. Power, 65, 172.

Quinn's Adm'r v. Newport News & M. V. Co., 41.

R

Racho v. Detroit, 77.

Rader v. Galveston, H. & S. A. R. Co., 169, 180.

Radezky v. Sargent & Co., 121, 122.

Rafferty v. Buckman, 78.

Rafferty v. Erie R. Co., 170.

Rahe v. Cuyahoga County Com'rs, 118.

Railway Co. v. Valleley, 76.

Rains v. St. Louis, I♦ M. & S. R. Co., 139, 157, 164.

Raisor v. Chicago & A. R. Co., 198—1.

Rajnowski v. Detroit, B. C. & A. R. Co., 164, 174.

Ramsdell v. Grady, 137.

Ramsdell v. New York & N. E. R. Co., 44.

Randall v. New Orleans & N. E. R. Co., 76.

Randle v. Birmingham Ry., Light & Power Co., 35, 130.

Randolph's Adm'r v. Snyder, 41, 187.

Rankin v. Central R. Co. of New Jersey, 187, 195.

Rankin v. Merchants' & M. T. Co., 38.

Rapp v. St. Joseph & I. R. Co., 45.

Rautman v. Chicago Consol. Traction Co., 83, 167.

Ravary v. Grand Trunk R. Co., 1.

Read v. Great Eastern R. Co., 124.

Receivers of Kirby Lumber Co. v. Owens, 55.

Redfield v. Oakland Consol. St. R. Co., 93—1, 162.

Reed v. Northeastern R. Co., 73, 187.

Regan v. Chicago, M. & St. P. R. Co., 180, 184.

Reilly v. Hannibal & St. J. R. Co., 70, 191.

Reiter-Connolly Mfg. Co. v. Hamlin, 130.

Renlund v. Commodore Min. Co., 86.

Reynolds v. Narragansett Electric Lighting Co., 145—1.

Rhoads v. Chicago & A. R. Co., 170, 171.

Rice v. Crescent City R. Co., 136.

Rice v. Interurban St. R. Co., 173.

Rich v. Chicago, M. & St. P. R. Co., 189.

Rich v. St. Louis & S. F. R. Co., 59—1.

Richards v. Burgin, 64.

Richardson v. New York Cent. R. Co., 89, 198.

Richmond v. Chicago & W. M. R. Co., 89, 168.

Richmond, F. & P. R. Co. v. Martin's Adm'r, 56, 71.

Richmond & D. R. Co. v. Freeman, 130.

Richmond & D. R. Co. v. Hammond, 130, 194.

Richmond & D. R. Co. v. Johnston, 38.

Rietveld v. Wabash R. Co., 86.

Riggs v. Northern Pac. R. Co., 57.

Riley v. Connecticut River R. Co., 74.

Riley v. Salt Lake Rapid Transit Co., 164.

Rinard v. Omaha & K. C. & E. R. Co., 45.

Rine v. Chicago & A. R. Co., 45.

Ritz v. Austin, 118.

Roach v. Imperial Min. Co., 46, 73, 182.

Roach v. Kelly, 78.

Robel v. Chicago, M. & St. P. R. Co., 164.

St. Louis, I. M. & S. R. Co. v. Haist, 196, 202.

St. Louis, I. M. & S. R. Co. v. Hesterly, 50.

St. Louis, I. M. & S. R. Co. v. Hitt, 130—1, 174.

St. Louis, I. M. & S. R. Co. v. McCain, 130—1.

St. Louis, I. M. & S. R. Co. v. McCormick, 198.

St. Louis, I. M. & S. R. Co. v. McNamara, 23.

St. Louis, I. M. & S. R. Co. v. Maddry, 162, 176.

St. Louis, I. M. & S. R. Co. v. Needham, 89, 93, 128. 171. 174.

St. Louis, I. M. & S. R. Co. v. Pate, 130—1.

St. Louis, I. M. & S. R. Co. v. Robbins, 130—1.

St. Louis, I. M. & S. R. Co. v. Stamps, 74, 130—1.

St. Louis, I. M. & S. R. Co. v. Standifer, 162.

St. Louis, I. M. & S. R. Co. v. Sweet, 35—3, 157. 160.

St. Louis, I. M. & S. R. Co. v. Watson, 93.

St. Louis, I. M. & S. R. Co. v. Yocum, 182.

St. Louis, M. & S. E. R. Co. v. Garner, 93, 168.

St. Louis Southwestern R. Co. v. Cochran, 70.

St. Louis Southwestern R. Co. v. Graham, 110.

St. Louis Southwestern R. Co. v. Henson, 93.

St. Louis Southwestern R.· Co. v. Mahoney, 130—1.

St. Louis Southwestern R. Co. v. Shiflet, 165.

St. Louis Southwestern R. Co. of Texas v. Bishop, 169.

St. Louis Southwestern R. Co. of Texas v. Huey, 168.

St. Louis & N. A. R. Co. v. Mathis, 130—1, 162.

St. Louis & S. F. R. Co. v. French, 169.

St. Louis & S. F. R. Co. v. Hicks, 156.

St. Louis & S. F. R. Co. v. Townsend, 162, 189.

St. Luke's Hospital v. Foster, 182.

Salem Bedford Stone Co. v. Hobbs, 184.

Salmon v. Rathjens, 93—1, 116, 157.

Salter v. Utica & B. R. R. Co., 175.

S. A. McCaulley, The, 209.

Sample v. Consolidated Light & Ry. Co., 151.

San Antonio Gas & Electric Co. v. Badders, 55.

San Antonio St. R. Co. v. Cailloutte, 55, 70, 108, 181.

San Antonio St. R. Co. v. Mechler, 89.

San Antonio St. R. Co. v. Renken, 108.

San Antonio Traction Co. v. White, 165.

San Antonio & A. P. R. Co. v. Bennett, 174.

San Antonio & A. P. R. Co. v. Long, 169, 176.

San Antonio & A. P. R. Co. v. Mertink, 108.

San Antonio & A. P. R. Co. v. Wallace, 65.

Sanbo v. Union Pac. Coal Co., 110, 201.

Sanders' Adm'x v. Louisville & N. R. Co., 87.

Sanderson v. Sanderson, 89.

San Rafael, The, 179.

Satterberg v. Minneapolis, St. P. & S. S. M. R. Co., 104—1.

Sauter v. New York Cent. & H. R. R. Co., 76, 174.

Savage v. Hayes Bros. Co., 164.

Savannah Electric Co. v. Bell, 38, 133.

Savannah, F. & W. R. Co. v. Flannagan, 133.

Savannah, F. & W. R. Co. v. Stewart, 133.

Savannah & M. R. Co. v. Shearer, 130.

Saveljich v. Lytle Logging & Mercantile Co., 86.

Sawtell v. Western & A. R. Co., 79.

Sawyer v. Perry, 43, 187.

[The figures refer to sections]

[The figures refer to sections]

Wheelan v. Chicago, M. & St. P. R. Co., 134, 174.

Wheeler v. St. Joseph & W. R. Co., 111.

Whelan v. Rio Grande Western R. Co., 45—1.

White v. Conly, 76.

White v. Fort, 79.

White v. Maxcy, 64, 181.

White v. Spettigue, 13.

White v. Ward, 11.

Whitford v. Panama R. Co., 11, 23, 124, 156, 195.

Whitlow v. Nashville, C. & St. L. R. Co., 197.

Whitmore v. Alabama Consol. Coal & Iron Co., 35.

Whiton v. Chicago & N. W. R. Co., 109, 154, 163.

Wiese v. Remme, 70.

Wiest v. Electric Traction Co., 171.

Wigmore v. Jay, 65.

Wilcox v. Wilmington City R. Co., 157.

Wilds v. Hudson River R. Co., 65.

Willamette, The, 206.

Willetts v. Buffalo & R. R. Co., 65.

Willey v. Boston Electric Light Co., 44.

Wm. Camerson & Co. v. McSween, 55.

Williams v. Alabama Great Southern R. Co., 35.

Williams v. Camden Interstate R. Co., 201.

Williams v. Fambro, 79.

Williams v. Gardiner, 68.

Williams v. Metropolitan St. R. Co., 139.

Williams v. Nona Mills Co., 42.

Williams v. Northern Texas Traction Co., 55.

Williams v. Quebec S. S. Co., 122, 204.

Williams v. South & N. A. R. Co., 35, 92.

Williams v. Texas & P. R. Co., 70.

Williams' Estate, In re, 200—1.

Willis v. Missouri Pac. R. Co., 195.

Willis Coal & Mining Co. v. Grizzell, 59, 59—1.

Willsen v. Metropolitan St. Ry., 179.

Wilmot v. McPadden, 132.

Wilson v. Banner Lumber Co., 42.

Wilson v. Bumstead, 116.

Wilson v. Illinois Cent. R. Co., 189.

Wilson v. Jackson Hill Coal & Coke Co., 122.

Wilson v. New York, N. H. & H. R. Co., 145—1.

Wilson v. Tootle, 198, 201.

Wiltse v. Tilden, 80, 173.

Winfree v. Northern Pac. R. Co., 57, 122.

Winnegar's Adm'r v. Central Pass R. Co., 18.

Winnt v. International & G. N. R. Co., 55, 108, 168.

Winston's Adm'r v. Illinois Cent. R. Co., 41.

Wintuska's Adm'r v. Louisville & N. R. Co., 196.

Wise v. Teerpenning, 154.

Witherley v. Regent's Canal Co., 65.

Wolf v. Lake Erie & W. R. Co., 71, 72.

Wolfe v. Great Northern R. Co., 164.

Wolford v. Lyon Gravel Gold Min. Co., 179.

Womack v. Central R. & B. Co., 38.

Wood v. Omaha, 154.

Wood v. Philadelphia, B. & W. R. Co., 189.

Wood v. Philadelphia, W. & B. R. Co., 160.

Woodard v. Michigan, S. & N. I. R. Co., 198.

Wooden v. Western N. Y. & P. R. Co., 196, 197, 201.

Woodstock Iron Works v. Kline, 92, 130, 182.

Woodward v. Chicago & N. W. R. Co., 80, 87, 202.

Wooten v. United Irrigation & Rice Milling Co., 136.

Worden v. Humeston & S. R. Co., 40, 75, 174.

Workman v. New York, 206.

Worley v. Cincinnati, H. & D. R. Co., 11, 116.

Wright v. Malden & M. R. Co., 68.

Wright v. Woods' Adm'r, 41.

Wyatt v. Williams, 11.

[The figures refer to sections]

INDEX

[In this Index the section numbers refer to the body of the treatise, (pages 1 to 484;) the Roman page numbers refer to the Analytical Table preceding the body of the treatise; and the Arabic page numbers refer to the Appendix of Statutes following the treatise.]

A

ABATEMENT,
Of right of action for death, § 119.
See Survival.

ACCUMULATIONS,
See Damages.
Loss of probable accumulations to estate of deceased as affecting damages, §§ 159, 171.

ACQUITTAL,
Former, see Evidence.

ACT,
See Wrongful Act, Neglect, or Default.

ACTION,
See Injuries Causing Death.
Abatement, § 119.

ACTIO PERSONALIS,
Moritur cum persona, §§ 1, 15.

ADMINISTRATOR,
See Executors and Administrators.

ADMIRALTY,
See Jurisdiction.

ADMISSIONS,
Of deceased, as evidence, § 194.

AIDOR AND ABETTOR,
Of wrongful act liable, § 76.

ALABAMA,
Statute of, Appendix, p. 487.
Analysis, p. xx.
Similar to Lord Campbell's Act, § 24.

ALABAMA—Continued,
   When action lies, § 35.
   Who may sue, § 92.
   Measure of damages, § 130.
   Exemplary damages, § 155.

ALASKA,
   Statute of, Appendix, p. 490.
      Analysis, p. xxii.
      Dissimilar to Lord Campbell's Act, § 25.
   When action lies, §§ 35—1, 81.
   Existence of beneficiaries not necessary, § 81.

ALIEN,
   May be beneficiary, § 86.

AMENDMENT,
   Of statute, effect on existing right of action, § 31—1.
   Of pleading, when allowable, § 187.
      Under foreign statute, § 202.

ARIZONA,
   Statute of, Appendix, p. 490.
      Analysis, p. xxii.
      Dissimilar to Lord Campbell's Act, § 25.
   When action lies, § 35—2.
   Existence of beneficiaries not necessary, § 81.
   Distribution of damages recovered, § 89.

ARKANSAS,
   Statute of, Appendix, p. 491.
      Analysis, p. xxii.
      Similar to Lord Campbell's Act, § 24.
   When action lies, § 35—3.
   Survival of right of action of party injured, §§ 35—3, 126.
   Who may sue, § 93.
   Measure of damages, § 130—1.

ASSETS,
   Whether right of action for death is, § 111.

ASSIGNMENT,
   Of right of beneficiary, § 88.

ASSUMPTION OF RISKS OF EMPLOYMENT,
   Death resulting from injury within risks of employment, § 65.

B

BASTARD,
   See Illegitimate Child.

BENEFICIARIES,
   Contributory negligence of, §§ 69-72.
      See Contributory Negligence.

C

D

E

HEIR,
    When may sue, § 114.

HIGH SEAS,
    Death on, §§ 195, 200.
        See Jurisdiction.

HOMICIDE,
    What is, in Georgia, § 38.
        See Felonious Killing.

HUSBAND,
    Whether included in next of kin, § 83.
    Damages for death of, § 159.
        Loss of support, §§ 160, 161.
        See Damages; Widow; Widower; Wife.

I

IDAHO,
    Statute of, Appendix, p. 501.
        Analysis, p. xxviii.
        Similar to Lord Campbell's Act, § 24.
    Damages for loss of society and support, § 154.

ILLEGITIMATE CHILD,
    Whether may be beneficiary, § 85.

ILLINOIS,
    Statute of, Appendix, p. 502.
        Analysis, p. xxx.
        Similar to Lord Campbell's Act, § 24.
    When action lies, § 38—1.
        Under miners act, § 59.
    Survival of right of action of party injured, §§ 38—1, 126.

IMPUTED NEGLIGENCE,
    In action for death, § 67.
    In action for death of child, § 68.
        See Negligence.

INDIANA,
    Statute of, Appendix, p. 505.
        Analysis, p. xxxii.
        Similar to Lord Campbell's Act, § 24.
    When action lies, § 39.
    Survival of right of action for death, § 87.
    Who may sue, § 96.
    No damages for solatium, § 154.

IOWA,

    Statute of, Appendix, p. 509.

        Analysis, p. xxxii.

        Dissimilar to Lord Campbell's Act, §§ 25, 26.

    When action lies, § 40.

    Contributory negligence of beneficiaries, § 71.

    Action lies, though death is instantaneous, § 75.

    Who may sue, § 97.

    Statute of limitation, § 122.

    Measure of damages, § 134.

    No damages for solatium, § 154.

J

JOINDER,

    Of parties, § 117.

        See Parties.

JURISDICTION,

    Of probate court to appoint administrator, § 111.

    Of state courts, in actions for death, §§ 195–202.

        Statute has no extraterritorial force, § 195.

    Action based on foreign statute, §§ 196–198.

        Jurisdiction sustained, §§ 196, 197.

            State where act or neglect occurred determines which law, § 196.

        Jurisdiction denied, § 198.

        Whether similar statute must exist in state of tribunal, § 197.

        Action under foreign penal statute, § 198—1.

    In case of death on navigable waters of United States, within state, § 199.

    In case of death on high seas on vessel owned in state, § 200.

    Action under foreign statute, substantive rights, § 200—1.

    Who may sue under foreign statute, § 201.

    Pleading foreign statute, § 201.

    Of federal courts, §§ 203–209.

        In general, § 203.

        Removal to, § 203.

        Suit in admiralty for death not maintainable independently of statute, § 204.

        Jurisdiction, in admiralty under state statute gives no lien, § 205.

            In rem where statute creates no lien, § 205.

            In personam, § 206.

            In rem where statute creates lien, § 206.

            Contributory negligence in admiralty, § 207.

    Of admiralty, in England, under Lord Campbell's Act, § 208.

    Of federal courts, in admiralty under limited liability act, § 209.

JURY,

Discretion of, in respect to damages, § 177.

K

KANSAS,

Statute of, Appendix, p. 510.

Analysis, p. xxxii.

Similar to Lord Campbell's Act, § 24.

When action lies, § 40—1.

Survival of right of action of party injured, §§ 40—1, 97, 126.

Who may sue, § 97—1.

KENTUCKY,

Statute of, §§ 27, 29.

Appendix, p. 511.

Analysis, p. xxxiv.

When action lies, § 41.

General death act, § 41, p. 58.

Measure of damages, § 41, p. 62.

Who may sue, § 41, p. 65.

Distribution, § 41, p. 66.

Killing by deadly weapon, or in duel, § 41, p. 66.

Survival act, § 41, p. 68.

Survival of right of action by party injured, § 41, p. 68, § 74.

Statute of limitation, §§ 120–123.

Exemplary damages, § 155.

L

LESSOR,

Cannot be sued, § 118.

LIBEL,

In admiralty, see Jurisdiction.

LIEN,

Jurisdiction in admiralty in rem, where statute creates no lien, § 205.

Where state creates lien, § 206.

LIFE,

Tables, as evidence, § 174.

LIMITATION,

Statutes of, §§ 120–123.

Varying provisions, § 120.

Nature of limitation, § 121.

Limitation need not be pleaded, § 121.

When time begins to run, § 122.

Notice of claim and special limitation, § 123.

Amendment of complaint after time has run, § 187.

Foreign statute governs, §§ 200—1, 202.

M

N

PUNITIVE DAMAGES,
See Damages.

R

RAILROAD COMPANY,
Laws giving right of action for death against, not unconstitu-
.tional, § 31.

RECEIVER,
Liability of, in Texas, § 55.
May be sued, § 118.

RECOVERY,
See Former Recovery; Limit of Recovery.

RELATIVE,
See Collateral Relative.

RELEASE,
By party injured, a bar, § 124.
Contract abridging right of beneficiary in case of death, §
124.
Contract exempting railroad company for injury of pas-
senger, § 124.
By plaintiff, or beneficiary a bar, § 125.
By sole beneficiary, a bar, § 125.
By one of several beneficiaries, § 125.

REMITTITUR,
Of part of verdict, § 178.

REMOVAL,
Of action into federal court, § 203.

REPEAL OF STATUTE,
Effect on existing right of action, § 31—1.

RES GESTÆ,
Declarations when admissible as part of, § 194.

RHODE ISLAND,
Statute of, Appendix, p. 551.
Analysis, p. lviii.
Similar to Lord Campbell's Act, § 24.
When action lies, § 52.
Who may sue, § 106.
Measure of damages, § 145—1.

RISKS OF EMPLOYMENT,
Death resulting from injury within, § 65.

S

SCOTCH LAW,
Action maintainable by, for causing death, § 1.
Damages for solatium, § 154.
Lord Campbell's Act does not apply to Scotland, Appendix, p.
486.

T

WISCONSIN,
 Statute of, Appendix, p. 563.
  Analysis, p. lxvi.
  Similar to Lord Campbell's Act, § 24.
 When action lies, § 58—1.
 Evidence of number of children, § 161.

WITNESS,
 See Evidence.

WRONGFUL ACT, NEGLECT, OR DEFAULT,
 Nature of, §§ 60–72, 77–79.
 In general, § 61.
 Meaning of "wrongful," § 62.
 Act or neglect must be such that party injured might have main-
   tained action, § 63.
 Intentional killing, § 64.
 Death caused by negligence, § 65.
  Contributory negligence of party injured, § 65.
  Risks of employment, § 65.
 Contributory negligence of deceased, § 66.
 Deceased's violation of law as contributory cause, § 66—1.
 Imputed negligence, § 67.
  In action for death of child, § 68.
 Contributory negligence of beneficiaries, in general, § 69.
  In action by beneficiaries, § 70.
  In action by personal representative, § 71.
  Where some, but not all, beneficiaries are negligent, § 72.
 Instantaneous death, § 73.
  Under statutes providing for survival of action, § 74.
  In Connecticut, Iowa, Louisiana, and Tennessee, § 75.
 Proximate cause of death, § 76.
 Death resulting from neglect of statutory duty, § 77.
  From liquor sold by defendant, § 78.
 Felonious killing, § 79.
 How pleaded, § 181.
  See Former Recovery; Neglect; Negligence; Release.

WYOMING,
 Statute of, Appendix, p. 564.
  Analysis, p. lxvi.
  Similar to Lord Campbell's Act, § 24.

[END OF VOLUME]

Lightning Source UK Ltd.
Milton Keynes UK
UKHW011558120219
337178UK00008B/530/P